Numerical Computing with Python

Harness the power of Python to analyze and find hidden patterns in the data

Pratap Dangeti
Allen Yu
Claire Chung
Aldrin Yim
Theodore Petrou

BIRMINGHAM - MUMBAI

Numerical Computing with Python

First Published: December 2018
Production Reference: 1191218

Published by Packt Publishing Ltd.
Livery Place, 35 Livery Street
Birmingham, B3 2PB, U.K.

ISBN 978-1-78995-363-3

www.packtpub.com

Contributors

About the authors

Pratap Dangeti is currently working as a Senior Data Scientist at Bidgely Technologies, Bangalore. He has a vast experience in analytics and data science. He received his master's degree from IIT Bombay in its industrial engineering and operations research program. Pratap is an artificial intelligence enthusiast. When not working, he likes to read about next-gen technologies and innovative methodologies.

First and foremost, I would like to thank my mom, Lakshmi, for her support throughout my career and in writing this book. She has been my inspiration and motivation for continuing to improve my knowledge and helping me move ahead in my career. She is my strongest supporter, and I dedicate this book to her. I also thank my family and friends for their encouragement, without which it would not be possible to write this book.

I would like to thank my acquisition editor, Aman Singh, and content development editor, Mayur Pawanikar, who chose me to write this book and encouraged me constantly throughout the period of writing with their invaluable feedback and input.

Allen Yu, Ph.D., is a Chevening Scholar, 2017-18, and an MSC student in computer science at the University of Oxford. He holds a Ph.D. degree in Biochemistry from the Chinese University of Hong Kong, and he has used Python and Matplotlib extensively during his 10 years of bioinformatics experience.

Apart from academic research, Allen is the co-founder of Codex Genetics Limited, which aims to provide a personalized medicine service in Asia through the use of the latest genomics technology.

I wish to thank my fiancée, Dorothy, for her constant love and support, especially during the difficult time in balancing family, work, and life. On behalf of the authors, I would like to thank the wonderful team at Packt Publishing—Mayur, Tushar, Vikrant, Vivek, and the whole editorial team who helped in the creation of this book. Thanks to Tushar's introduction, the authors feel greatly honored to take part in this amazing project. Special thanks and much appreciation to Mayur for guiding the production of this book from the ground up. The authors truly appreciate the comprehensive reviews from Nikhil Borkar. We cannot be thankful enough to the entire Matplotlib and Python community for their hard work in creating open and incredibly useful tools. Last but not least, I would like to express my sincere gratitude to Prof. Ting-Fung Chan, my parents, friends, and colleagues for their guidance in my life and work.

Chevening Scholarships, the UK government's global scholarship programme, are funded by the Foreign and Commonwealth Office (FCO) and partner organizations.

Claire Chung is pursuing her Ph.D. degree as a Bioinformatician at the Chinese University of Hong Kong. She enjoys using Python daily for work and lifehack. While passionate in science, her challenge-loving character motivates her to go beyond data analytics. She has participated in web development projects, as well as developed skills in graphic design and multilingual translation. She led the Campus Network Support Team in college and shared her experience in data visualization in PyCon HK 2017.

I would like to thank Allen for getting me on board in this exciting authorship journey, and for being a helpful senior, always generous in sharing his experience and insights. It has been a great pleasure to work closely with Allen, Aldrin and the whole editorial team at Packt. I am grateful to everyone along the way that brought my interest in computer to daily practice. I wish to extend my sincere gratitude to my supervisor, Prof. Ting-Fung Chan, my parents, teachers, colleagues, and friends. I would like to make a special mention to my dearest group of high school friends for their unfailing support and source of cheer. I would also like to thank my childhood friend, Eugene, for introducing and provoking me into technological areas. With all the support, I will continue to prove that girls are capable of achieving in the STEM field.

Aldrin Yim is a Ph.D. candidate and Markey Scholar in the Computation and System Biology program at Washington University, School of Medicine. His research focuses on applying big data analytics and machine learning approaches in studying neurological diseases and cancer. He is also the founding CEO of Codex Genetics Limited, which provides precision medicine solutions to patients and hospitals in Asia.

It is not a one-man task to write a book, and I would like to thank Allen and Claire for their invaluable input and effort during the time; the authors also owe a great debt of gratitude to all the editors and reviewers that made this book happened. I also wish to thank my parents for their love and understanding over the years, as well as my best friends, Charles and Angus, for accompanying me through my ups and downs over the past two decades. Last but not least, I also wish to extend my heartfelt thanks to Kimmy for all the love and support in life and moving all the way to Chicago to keep our love alive.

Theodore Petrou is a data scientist and the founder of Dunder Data, a professional educational company focusing on exploratory data analysis. He is also the head of Houston Data Science, a meetup group with more than 2,000 members that has the primary goal of getting local data enthusiasts together in the same room to practice data science. Before founding Dunder Data, Ted was a data scientist at Schlumberger, a large oil services company, where he spent the vast majority of his time exploring data.

Some of his projects included using targeted sentiment analysis to discover the root cause of past failures from engineer text, developing customized client/server dashboarding applications, and real-time web services to avoid mispricing sales items. Ted received his Master's degree in statistics from Rice University and used his analytical skills to play poker professionally and teach math before becoming a data scientist. Ted is a strong supporter of learning through practice and can often be found answering questions about pandas on Stack Overflow.

About the reviewers

Manuel Amunategui is vice president of data science at SpringML, a startup offering Google Cloud TensorFlow and Salesforce enterprise solutions. Prior to that, he worked as a quantitative developer on Wall Street for a large equity-options market-making firm and as a software developer at Microsoft. He holds master degrees in predictive analytics and international administration.

He is a data science advocate, blogger/vlogger (`amunategui.github.io`) and a trainer on Udemy and O'Reilly Media, and technical reviewer at Packt Publishing.

Nikhil Borkar holds a CQF designation and a postgraduate degree in quantitative finance. He also holds certified financial crime examiner and certified anti-money laundering professional qualifications. He is a registered research analyst with the Securities and Exchange Board of India (SEBI) and has a keen grasp of laws and regulations pertaining to securities and investment. He is currently working as an independent FinTech and legal consultant. Prior to this, he worked with Morgan Stanley Capital International as a Global RFP project manager. He is self-motivated, intellectually curious, and hardworking. He loves to approach problems using a multi-disciplinary, holistic approach. Currently, he is actively working on machine learning, artificial intelligence, and deep learning projects. He has expertise in the following areas:

- Quantitative investing: equities, futures and options, and derivatives engineering
- Econometrics: time series analysis, statistical modeling
- Algorithms: parametric, non-parametric, and ensemble machine learning algorithms
- Code: R programming, Python, Scala, Excel VBA, SQL, and big data ecosystems.
- Data analysis: Quandl and Quantopian
- Strategies: trend following, mean reversion, cointegration, Monte-Carlo srimulations, Value at Risk, Credit Risk Modeling and Credit Rating
- Data visualization: Tableau and Matplotlib

Sonali Dayal is a masters candidate in biostatistics at the University of California, Berkeley. Previously, she has worked as a freelance software and data science engineer for early stage start-ups, where she built supervised and unsupervised machine learning models as well as data pipelines and interactive data analytics dashboards. She received her bachelor of science (B.S.) in biochemistry from Virginia Tech in 2011.

Kuntal Ganguly is a big data machine learning engineer focused on building large-scale data-driven systems using big data frameworks and machine learning. He has around 7 years of experience building several big data and machine learning applications.

Kuntal provides solutions to AWS customers in building real-time analytics systems using managed cloud services and open source Hadoop ecosystem technologies such as Spark, Kafka, Storm, Solr, and so on, along with machine learning and deep learning frameworks such as scikit-learn, TensorFlow, Keras, and BigDL. He enjoys hands-on software development, and has single-handedly conceived, architectured, developed, and deployed several large scale distributed applications. He is a machine learning and deep learning practitioner and very passionate about building intelligent applications.

Kuntal is the author of the books: *Learning Generative Adversarial Network* and *R Data Analysis Cookbook - Second Edition*, Packt Publishing.

Shilpi Saxena is a seasoned professional who leads in management with an edge of being a technology evangelist--she is an engineer who has exposure to a variety of domains (machine-to-machine space, healthcare, telecom, hiring, and manufacturing). She has experience in all aspects of the conception and execution of enterprise solutions. She has been architecting, managing, and delivering solutions in the big data space for the last 3 years, handling high performance geographically distributed teams of elite engineers. Shilpi has around 12+ years (3 years in the big data space) experience in the development and execution of various facets of enterprise solutions, both in the product/services dimensions of the software industry. An engineer by degree and profession who has worn various hats--developer, technical leader, product owner, tech manager--and has seen all the flavors that the industry has to offer. She has architectured and worked through some of the pioneer production implementation in big data on Storm and Impala with auto scaling in AWS. LinkedIn: http://in.linkedin.com/pub/shilpi-saxena/4/552/a30

Packt is searching for authors like you

If you're interested in becoming an author for Packt, please visit `authors.packtpub.com` and apply today. We have worked with thousands of developers and tech professionals, just like you, to help them share their insight with the global tech community. You can make a general application, apply for a specific hot topic that we are recruiting an author for, or submit your own idea.

`mapt.io`

Mapt is an online digital library that gives you full access to over 5,000 books and videos, as well as industry leading tools to help you plan your personal development and advance your career. For more information, please visit our website.

Why subscribe?

- Spend less time learning and more time coding with practical eBooks and Videos from over 4,000 industry professionals

- Improve your learning with Skill Plans built especially for you

- Get a free eBook or video every month

- Mapt is fully searchable

- Copy and paste, print, and bookmark content

Packt.com

Did you know that Packt offers eBook versions of every book published, with PDF and ePub files available? You can upgrade to the eBook version at `www.packt.com` and as a print book customer, you are entitled to a discount on the eBook copy. Get in touch with us at `customercare@packtpub.com` for more details.

At `www.packt.com`, you can also read a collection of free technical articles, sign up for a range of free newsletters, and receive exclusive discounts and offers on Packt books and eBooks.

Table of Contents

Preface

Data mining, or parsing the data to extract useful insights, is a niche skill that can transform your career as a data scientist Python is a flexible programming language that is equipped with a strong suite of libraries and toolkits, and gives you the perfect platform to sift through your data and mine the insights you seek. This Learning Path is designed to familiarize you with the Python libraries and the underlying statistics that you need to get comfortable with data mining.

You will learn how to use Pandas, Python's popular library to analyze different kinds of data, and leverage the power of Matplotlib to generate appealing and impressive visualizations for the insights you have derived. You will also explore different machine learning techniques and statistics that enable you to build powerful predictive models.

By the end of this Learning Path, you will have the perfect foundation to take your data mining skills to the next level and set yourself on the path to become a sought-after data science professional.

This Learning Path includes content from the following Packt products:

- Statistics for Machine Learning by Pratap Dangeti
- Matplotlib 2.x By Example by Allen Yu, Claire Chung, Aldrin Yim
- Pandas Cookbook by Theodore Petrou

Who this book is for

If you want to learn how to use the many libraries of Python to extract impactful information from your data and present it as engaging visuals, then this is the ideal Learning Path for you. Some basic knowledge of Python is enough to get started with this Learning Path.

What this book covers

Chapter 1, *Journey from Statistics to Machine Learning*, introduces you to all the necessary fundamentals and basic building blocks of both statistics and machine learning. All fundamentals are explained with the support of both Python and R code examples across the chapter.

Chapter 2, *Tree-Based Machine Learning Models*, focuses on the various tree-based machine learning models used by industry practitioners, including decision trees, bagging, random forest, AdaBoost, gradient boosting, and XGBoost with the HR attrition example in both languages.

Chapter 3, *K-Nearest Neighbors and Naive Bayes*, illustrates simple methods of machine learning. K-nearest neighbors is explained using breast cancer data. The Naive Bayes model is explained with a message classification example using various NLP preprocessing techniques.

Chapter 4, *Unsupervised Learning*, presents various techniques such as k-means clustering, principal component analysis, singular value decomposition, and deep learning based deep auto encoders. At the end is an explanation of why deep auto encoders are much more powerful than the conventional PCA techniques.

Chapter 5, *Reinforcement Learning*, provides exhaustive techniques that learn the optimal path to reach a goal over the episodic states, such as the Markov decision process, dynamic programming, Monte Carlo methods, and temporal difference learning. Finally, some use cases are provided for superb applications using machine learning and reinforcement learning.

Chapter 6, *Hello Plotting World!*, covers the basic constituents of a Matplotlib figure, as well as the latest features of Matplotlib version 2.

Chapter 7, *Visualizing Online Data*, teaches you how to design intuitive infographics for effective storytelling through the use of real-world datasets.

Chapter 8, *Visualizing Multivariate Data*, gives you an overview of the plot types that are suitable for visualizing datasets with multiple features or dimensions.

Chapter 9, *Adding Interactivity and Animating Plots*, shows you that Matplotlib is not limited to creating static plots. You will learn how to create interactive charts and animations.

Chapter 10, *Selecting Subsets of Data*, covers the many varied and potentially confusing ways of selecting different subsets of data.

Chapter 11, *Boolean Indexing*, covers the process of querying your data to select subsets of it based on Boolean conditions.

Chapter 12, *Index Alignment*, targets the very important and often misunderstood `index` object. Misuse of the Index is responsible for lots of erroneous results, and these recipes show you how to use it correctly to deliver powerful results.

Chapter 13, *Grouping for Aggregation, Filtration, and Transformation*, covers the powerful grouping capabilities that are almost always necessary during a data analysis. You will build customized functions to apply to your groups.

Chapter 14, *Restructuring Data into a Tidy Form*, explains what tidy data is and why it's so important, and then it shows you how to transform many different forms of messy datasets into tidy ones.

Chapter 15, *Combining Pandas Objects*, covers the many available methods to combine DataFrames and Series vertically or horizontally. We will also do some web-scraping to compare President Trump's and Obama's approval rating and connect to an SQL relational database.

To get the most out of this book

This book assumes that you know the basics of Python and R and how to install the libraries. It does not assume that you are already equipped with the knowledge of advanced statistics and mathematics, like linear algebra and so on.

The following versions of software are used throughout this book, but it should run fine with any more recent ones as well:

- Anaconda 3–4.3.1 (all Python and its relevant packages are included in Anaconda, Python 3.6.1, NumPy 1.12.1, Pandas 0.19.2, and scikit-learn 0.18.1)
- R 3.4.0 and RStudio 1.0.143
- Theano 0.9.0
- Keras 2.0.2
- A Windows 7+, macOS 10.10+, or Linux-based computer with 4 GB RAM or above is recommended.

Download the example code files

You can download the example code files for this book from your account at www.packt.com. If you purchased this book elsewhere, you can visit www.packt.com/support and register to have the files emailed directly to you.

You can download the code files by following these steps:

1. Log in or register at www.packt.com.
2. Select the **SUPPORT** tab.
3. Click on **Code Downloads & Errata**.
4. Enter the name of the book in the **Search** box and follow the onscreen instructions.

Once the file is downloaded, please make sure that you unzip or extract the folder using the latest version of:

- WinRAR/7-Zip for Windows
- Zipeg/iZip/UnRarX for Mac
- 7-Zip/PeaZip for Linux

The code bundle for the book is also hosted on GitHub at https://github.com/PacktPublishing/Numerical-Computing-with-Python. In case there's an update to the code, it will be updated on the existing GitHub repository.

We also have other code bundles from our rich catalog of books and videos available at https://github.com/PacktPublishing/. Check them out!

Conventions used

Code words in text, database table names, folder names, filenames, file extensions, pathnames, dummy URLs, user input, and Twitter handles are shown as follows: "The mode function was not implemented in the numpy package.". Any command-line input or output is written as follows:

```
>>> import numpy as np
>>> from scipy import stats
>>> data = np.array([4,5,1,2,7,2,6,9,3])
# Calculate Mean
>>> dt_mean = np.mean(data) ;
print ("Mean :",round(dt_mean,2))
```

New terms and **important words** are shown in bold.

 Warnings or important notes appear like this.

 Tips and tricks appear like this.

Get in touch

Feedback from our readers is always welcome.

General feedback: If you have questions about any aspect of this book, mention the book title in the subject of your message and email us at customercare@packtpub.com.

Errata: Although we have taken every care to ensure the accuracy of our content, mistakes do happen. If you have found a mistake in this book, we would be grateful if you would report this to us. Please visit www.packt.com/submit-errata, selecting your book, clicking on the Errata Submission Form link, and entering the details.

Piracy: If you come across any illegal copies of our works in any form on the Internet, we would be grateful if you would provide us with the location address or website name. Please contact us at copyright@packt.com with a link to the material.

If you are interested in becoming an author: If there is a topic that you have expertise in and you are interested in either writing or contributing to a book, please visit authors.packtpub.com.

Reviews

Please leave a review. Once you have read and used this book, why not leave a review on the site that you purchased it from? Potential readers can then see and use your unbiased opinion to make purchase decisions, we at Packt can understand what you think about our products, and our authors can see your feedback on their book. Thank you!

For more information about Packt, please visit packt.com.

Journey from Statistics to Machine Learning

In recent times, **machine learning** (**ML**) and data science have gained popularity like never before. This field is expected to grow exponentially in the coming years. First of all, what is machine learning? And why does someone need to take pains to understand the principles? Well, we have the answers for you. One simple example could be book recommendations in e-commerce websites when someone went to search for a particular book or any other product recommendations which were bought together to provide an idea to users which they might like. Sounds magic, right? In fact, utilizing machine learning can achieve much more than this.

Machine learning is a branch of study in which a model can learn automatically from the experiences based on data without exclusively being modeled like in statistical models. Over a period and with more data, model predictions will become better.

In this first chapter, we will introduce the basic concepts which are necessary to understand statistical learning and create a foundation for full-time statisticians or software engineers who would like to understand the statistical workings behind the ML methods.

Statistical terminology for model building and validation

Statistics is the branch of mathematics dealing with the collection, analysis, interpretation, presentation, and organization of numerical data.

Statistics are mainly classified into two subbranches:

- **Descriptive statistics**: These are used to summarize data, such as the mean, standard deviation for continuous data types (such as age), whereas frequency and percentage are useful for categorical data (such as gender).
- **Inferential statistics**: Many times, a collection of the entire data (also known as population in statistical methodology) is impossible, hence a subset of the data points is collected, also called a sample, and conclusions about the entire population will be drawn, which is known as inferential statistics. Inferences are drawn using hypothesis testing, the estimation of numerical characteristics, the correlation of relationships within data, and so on.

Statistical modeling is applying statistics on data to find underlying hidden relationships by analyzing the significance of the variables.

Machine learning

Machine learning is the branch of computer science that utilizes past experience to learn from and use its knowledge to make future decisions. Machine learning is at the intersection of computer science, engineering, and statistics. The goal of machine learning is to generalize a detectable pattern or to create an unknown rule from given examples. An overview of machine learning landscape is as follows:

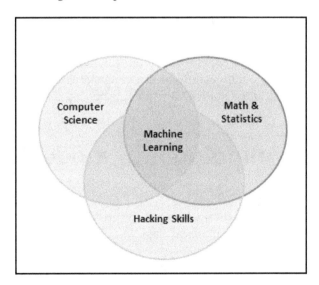

Machine learning is broadly classified into three categories but nonetheless, based on the situation, these categories can be combined to achieve the desired results for particular applications:

- **Supervised learning**: This is teaching machines to learn the relationship between other variables and a target variable, similar to the way in which a teacher provides feedback to students on their performance. The major segments within supervised learning are as follows:
  - Classification problem
  - Regression problem
- **Unsupervised learning**: In unsupervised learning, algorithms learn by themselves without any supervision or without any target variable provided. It is a question of finding hidden patterns and relations in the given data. The categories in unsupervised learning are as follows:
  - Dimensionality reduction
  - Clustering
- **Reinforcement learning**: This allows the machine or agent to learn its behavior based on feedback from the environment. In reinforcement learning, the agent takes a series of decisive actions without supervision and, in the end, a reward will be given, either +1 or -1. Based on the final payoff/reward, the agent reevaluates its paths. Reinforcement learning problems are closer to the artificial intelligence methodology rather than frequently used machine learning algorithms.

In some cases, we initially perform unsupervised learning to reduce the dimensions followed by supervised learning when the number of variables is very high. Similarly, in some artificial intelligence applications, supervised learning combined with reinforcement learning could be utilized for solving a problem; an example is self-driving cars in which, initially, images are converted to some numeric format using supervised learning and combined with driving actions (left, forward, right, and backward).

Statistical fundamentals and terminology for model building and validation

Statistics itself is a vast subject on which a complete book could be written; however, here the attempt is to focus on key concepts that are very much necessary with respect to the machine learning perspective. In this section, a few fundamentals are covered and the remaining concepts will be covered in later chapters wherever it is necessary to understand the statistical equivalents of machine learning.

Predictive analytics depends on one major assumption: that history repeats itself!

By fitting a predictive model on historical data after validating key measures, the same model will be utilized for predicting future events based on the same explanatory variables that were significant on past data.

The first movers of statistical model implementers were the banking and pharmaceutical industries; over a period, analytics expanded to other industries as well.

Statistical models are a class of mathematical models that are usually specified by mathematical equations that relate one or more variables to approximate reality. Assumptions embodied by statistical models describe a set of probability distributions, which distinguishes it from non-statistical, mathematical, or machine learning models

Statistical models always start with some underlying assumptions for which all the variables should hold, then the performance provided by the model is statistically significant. Hence, knowing the various bits and pieces involved in all building blocks provides a strong foundation for being a successful statistician.

In the following section, we have described various fundamentals with relevant codes:

- **Population**: This is the totality, the complete list of observations, or all the data points about the subject under study.

- **Sample**: A sample is a subset of a population, usually a small portion of the population that is being analyzed.

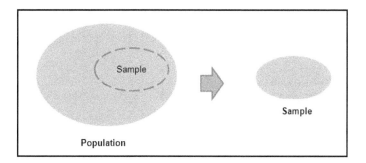

 Usually, it is expensive to perform an analysis of an entire population; hence, most statistical methods are about drawing conclusions about a population by analyzing a sample.

- **Parameter versus statistic**: Any measure that is calculated on the population is a parameter, whereas on a sample it is called a **statistic**.
- **Mean**: This is a simple arithmetic average, which is computed by taking the aggregated sum of values divided by a count of those values. The mean is sensitive to outliers in the data. An outlier is the value of a set or column that is highly deviant from the many other values in the same data; it usually has very high or low values.
- **Median**: This is the midpoint of the data, and is calculated by either arranging it in ascending or descending order. If there are N observations.
- **Mode**: This is the most repetitive data point in the data:

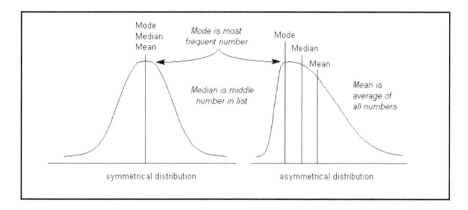

The Python code for the calculation of mean, median, and mode using a
numpy array and the stats package is as follows:

```
>>> import numpy as np
>>> from scipy import stats

>>> data = np.array([4,5,1,2,7,2,6,9,3])

# Calculate Mean
>>> dt_mean = np.mean(data) ; print ("Mean :",round(dt_mean,2))

# Calculate Median
>>> dt_median = np.median(data) ; print ("Median :",dt_median)

# Calculate Mode
>>> dt_mode =  stats.mode(data); print ("Mode :",dt_mode[0][0])
```

The output of the preceding code is as follows:

```
Mean : 4.33333333333
Median : 4.0
Mode : 2
[Finished in 0.3s]
```

We have used a NumPy array instead of a basic list as the data structure;
the reason behind using this is the scikit-learn package built on top of
NumPy array in which all statistical models and machine learning
algorithms have been built on NumPy array itself. The mode function is
not implemented in the numpy package, hence we have used SciPy's
stats package. SciPy is also built on top of NumPy arrays.

The R code for descriptive statistics (mean, median, and mode) is given as
follows:

```
data <- c(4,5,1,2,7,2,6,9,3)
dt_mean = mean(data) ; print(round(dt_mean,2))
dt_median = median (data); print (dt_median)

func_mode <- function (input_dt) {
  unq <- unique(input_dt)
unq[which.max(tabulate(match(input_dt,unq)))]
}

dt_mode = func_mode (data); print (dt_mode)
```

We have used the default `stats` package for R; however, the `mode` function was not built-in, hence we have written custom code for calculating the mode.

- **Measure of variation**: Dispersion is the variation in the data, and measures the inconsistencies in the value of variables in the data. Dispersion actually provides an idea about the spread rather than central values.
- **Range**: This is the difference between the maximum and minimum of the value.
- **Variance**: This is the mean of squared deviations from the mean (xi = data points, μ = mean of the data, N = number of data points). The dimension of variance is the square of the actual values. The reason to use denominator *N-1* for a sample instead of N in the population is due the degree of freedom. *1* degree of freedom lost in a sample by the time of calculating variance is due to extraction of substitution of sample:

$$population\ variance = \frac{1}{N}\sum_{i=1}^{N}(x_i - \mu)^2 \quad sample\ variance = \frac{1}{N-1}\sum_{i=1}^{N}(x_i - \mu)^2$$

- **Standard deviation**: This is the square root of variance. By applying the square root on variance, we measure the dispersion with respect to the original variable rather than square of the dimension:

$$population\ standard\ deviation\ (\sigma) = \sqrt{\frac{1}{N}\sum_{i=1}^{N}(x_i - \mu)^2} \quad sample\ standard\ deviation\ (s) = \sqrt{\frac{1}{N-1}\sum_{i=1}^{N}(x_i - \mu)^2}$$

- **Quantiles**: These are simply identical fragments of the data. Quantiles cover percentiles, deciles, quartiles, and so on. These measures are calculated after arranging the data in ascending order:
  - **Percentile**: This is nothing but the percentage of data points below the value of the original whole data. The median is the 50th percentile, as the number of data points below the median is about 50 percent of the data.
  - **Decile**: This is 10th percentile, which means the number of data points below the decile is 10 percent of the whole data.
  - **Quartile**: This is one-fourth of the data, and also is the 25th percentile. The first quartile is 25 percent of the data, the second quartile is 50 percent of the data, the third quartile is 75 percent of the data. The second quartile is also known as the median or 50th percentile or 5th decile.
  - **Interquartile range**: This is the difference between the third quartile and first quartile. It is effective in identifying outliers in data. The interquartile range describes the middle 50 percent of the data points.

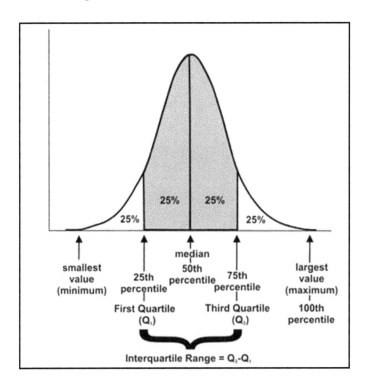

The Python code is as follows:

```
>>> from statistics import variance, stdev
>>> game_points =
np.array([35,56,43,59,63,79,35,41,64,43,93,60,77,24,82])

# Calculate Variance
>>> dt_var = variance(game_points) ; print ("Sample variance:",
round(dt_var,2))

# Calculate Standard Deviation
>>> dt_std = stdev(game_points) ; print ("Sample std.dev:",
round(dt_std,2))
# Calculate Range
>>> dt_rng = np.max(game_points,axis=0) -
np.min(game_points,axis=0) ; print ("Range:",dt_rng)

#Calculate percentiles
>>> print ("Quantiles:")
>>> for val in [20,80,100]:
>>>       dt_qntls = np.percentile(game_points,val)
>>>       print (str(val)+"%" ,dt_qntls)
# Calculate IQR
>>> q75, q25 = np.percentile(game_points, [75 ,25]); print ("Inter
quartile range:",q75-q25)
```

The output of the preceding code is as follows:

```
Sample variance: 400.64
Sample std.dev: 20.02
Range: 69
Quantiles:
20% 39.8
80% 77.4
100% 93.0
Inter quartile range: 28.5
[Finished in 0.2s]
```

The R code for dispersion (variance, standard deviation, range, quantiles, and IQR) is as follows:

```
game_points <- c(35,56,43,59,63,79,35,41,64,43,93,60,77,24,82)
dt_var = var(game_points); print(round(dt_var,2))
dt_std = sd(game_points); print(round(dt_std,2))
range_val<-function(x) return(diff(range(x)))
```

```
dt_range = range_val(game_points); print(dt_range)
dt_quantile = quantile(game_points,probs = c(0.2,0.8,1.0));
print(dt_quantile)
dt_iqr = IQR(game_points); print(dt_iqr)
```

- **Hypothesis testing**: This is the process of making inferences about the overall population by conducting some statistical tests on a sample. Null and alternate hypotheses are ways to validate whether an assumption is statistically significant or not.

- **P-value**: The probability of obtaining a test statistic result is at least as extreme as the one that was actually observed, assuming that the null hypothesis is true (usually in modeling, against each independent variable, a p-value less than 0.05 is considered significant and greater than 0.05 is considered insignificant; nonetheless, these values and definitions may change with respect to context).

  The steps involved in hypothesis testing are as follows:

  1. Assume a null hypothesis (usually no difference, no significance, and so on; a null hypothesis always tries to assume that there is no anomaly pattern and is always homogeneous, and so on).
  2. Collect the sample.
  3. Calculate test statistics from the sample in order to verify whether the hypothesis is statistically significant or not.
  4. Decide either to accept or reject the null hypothesis based on the test statistic.

- **Example of hypothesis testing**: A chocolate manufacturer who is also your friend claims that all chocolates produced from his factory weigh at least 1,000 g and you have got a funny feeling that it might not be true; you both collected a sample of 30 chocolates and found that the average chocolate weight as 990 g with sample standard deviation as 12.5 g. Given the 0.05 significance level, can we reject the claim made by your friend?

  The null hypothesis is that $\mu0 \geq 1000$ (all chocolates weigh more than 1,000 g).

  Collected sample:

  $$\bar{x} = 990, s = 12.5, n = 30$$

Calculate test statistic:

$$t = \frac{(\bar{x} - \mu_0)}{(\frac{s}{\sqrt{n}})}$$

t = (990 - 1000) / (12.5/sqrt(30)) = - 4.3818

Critical t value from t tables = t0.05, 30 = 1.699 => - t0.05, 30 = -1.699

P-value = 7.03 e-05

Test statistic is -4.3818, which is less than the critical value of -1.699. Hence, we can reject the null hypothesis (your friend's claim) that the mean weight of a chocolate is above 1,000 g.

Also, another way of deciding the claim is by using the p-value. A p-value less than *0.05* means both claimed values and distribution mean values are significantly different, hence we can reject the null hypothesis:

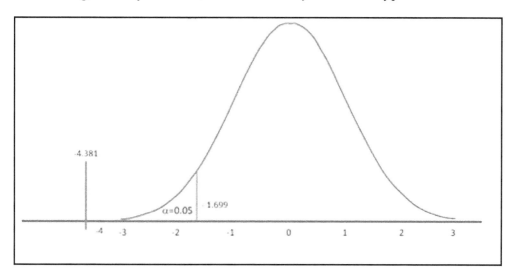

The Python code is as follows:

```
>>> from scipy import stats
>>> xbar = 990; mu0 = 1000; s = 12.5; n = 30

# Test Statistic
>>> t_smple  = (xbar-mu0)/(s/np.sqrt(float(n))); print ("Test
Statistic:",round(t_smple,2))

# Critical value from t-table
>>> alpha = 0.05
>>> t_alpha = stats.t.ppf(alpha,n-1); print ("Critical value
from t-table:",round(t_alpha,3))

#Lower tail p-value from t-table
>>> p_val = stats.t.sf(np.abs(t_smple), n-1); print ("Lower
tail p-value from t-table", p_val)
```

```
Test Statistic: -4.38
Critical value from t-table: -1.699
Lower tail p-value from t-table 7.03502572901e-05
[Finished in 0.3s]
```

The R code for T-distribution is as follows:

```
xbar = 990; mu0 = 1000; s = 12.5 ; n = 30
t_smple = (xbar - mu0)/(s/sqrt(n));print (round(t_smple,2))

alpha = 0.05
t_alpha = qt(alpha,df= n-1);print (round(t_alpha,3))

p_val = pt(t_smple,df = n-1);print (p_val)
```

- **Type I and II error**: Hypothesis testing is usually done on the samples rather than the entire population, due to the practical constraints of available resources to collect all the available data. However, performing inferences about the population from samples comes with its own costs, such as rejecting good results or accepting false results, not to mention separately, when increases in sample size lead to minimizing type I and II errors:
    - **Type I error**: Rejecting a null hypothesis when it is true
    - **Type II error**: Accepting a null hypothesis when it is false

- **Normal distribution**: This is very important in statistics because of the central limit theorem, which states that the population of all possible samples of size n from a population with mean μ and variance $\sigma 2$ approaches a normal distribution:

$$f(x) = \frac{1}{\sigma\sqrt{2\Pi}} e^{-\frac{(x-\mu)^2}{2\sigma^2}} \qquad X \sim N(\mu,\, \sigma^2)$$

Example: Assume that the test scores of an entrance exam fit a normal distribution. Furthermore, the mean test score is *52* and the standard deviation is *16.3*. What is the percentage of students scoring *67* or more in the exam?

$$pr(X \geq 67) = pr\left(Z \geq \frac{(67-\mu)}{\sigma}\right) = 1 - pr\left(Z \leq \frac{(67-\mu)}{\sigma}\right)$$

$$= 1 - pr\left(Z \leq \frac{(67-52)}{16.3}\right) = 1 - 0.8212 = 0.1788$$

probability of students scoring more than 67 marks is $= 17.88\,\%$

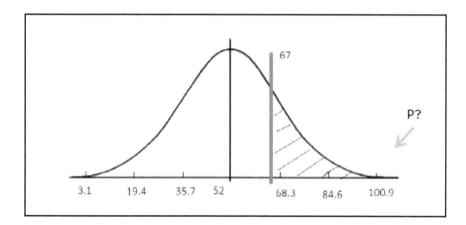

The Python code is as follows:

```
>>> from scipy import stats
>>> xbar = 67; mu0 = 52; s = 16.3

# Calculating z-score
>>> z = (67-52)/16.3

# Calculating probability under the curve
>>> p_val = 1- stats.norm.cdf(z)
>>> print ("Prob. to score more than 67 is
",round(p_val*100,2),"%")
```

```
Prob. to score more than 67 is  17.87 %
[Finished in 0.4s]
```

The R code for normal distribution is as follows:

```
xbar = 67; mu0 = 52; s = 16.3
pr = 1- pnorm(67, mean=52, sd=16.3)
print (paste("Prob. to score more than 67 is
",round(pr*100,2),"%"))
```

- **Chi-square**: This test of independence is one of the most basic and common hypothesis tests in the statistical analysis of categorical data. Given two categorical random variables X and Y, the chi-square test of independence determines whether or not there exists a statistical dependence between them.

  The test is usually performed by calculating $\chi2$ from the data and $\chi2$ with ($m-1$, $n-1$) degrees from the table. A decision is made as to whether both variables are independent based on the actual value and table value, whichever is higher:

  $$\chi^2 = \sum_i \frac{(o_i - e_i)^2}{e_i} \qquad o_i = observed\,, e_i = expected$$

Example: In the following table, calculate whether the smoking habit has an impact on exercise behavior:

	Exercise: Frequent	Exercise: None	Exercise: Sometimes
Smoke: Heavy	7	1	3
Smoke: Never	87	18	84
Smoke: Occasional	12	3	4
Smoke: Regularly	9	1	7

The Python code is as follows:

```
>>> import pandas as pd
>>> from scipy import stats

>>> survey = pd.read_csv("survey.csv")

# Tabulating 2 variables with row & column variables
respectively
>>> survey_tab = pd.crosstab(survey.Smoke, survey.Exer, margins
= True)
```

While creating a table using the `crosstab` function, we will obtain both row and column totals field extra. However, in order to create the observed table, we need to extract the variables part and ignore the totals:

```
# Creating observed table for analysis
>>> observed = survey_tab.ix[0:4,0:3]
```

The `chi2_contingency` function in the stats package uses the observed table and subsequently calculates its expected table, followed by calculating the p-value in order to check whether two variables are dependent or not. If *p-value < 0.05*, there is a strong dependency between two variables, whereas if *p-value > 0.05*, there is no dependency between the variables:

```
>>> contg = stats.chi2_contingency(observed= observed)
>>> p_value = round(contg[1],3)
>>> print ("P-value is: ",p_value)
```

```
P-value is:  0.483
[Finished in 0.6s]
```

The p-value is `0.483`, which means there is no dependency between the smoking habit and exercise behavior.

The R code for chi-square is as follows:

```
survey = read.csv("survey.csv",header=TRUE)
tbl = table(survey$Smoke, survey$Exer)
p_val = chisq.test(tbl)
```

- **ANOVA**: Analyzing variance tests the hypothesis that the means of two or more populations are equal. ANOVAs assess the importance of one or more factors by comparing the response variable means at the different factor levels. The null hypothesis states that all population means are equal while the alternative hypothesis states that at least one is different.

  Example: A fertilizer company developed three new types of universal fertilizers after research that can be utilized to grow any type of crop. In order to find out whether all three have a similar crop yield, they randomly chose six crop types in the study. In accordance with the randomized block design, each crop type will be tested with all three types of fertilizer separately. The following table represents the yield in g/m^2. At the 0.05 level of significance, test whether the mean yields for the three new types of fertilizers are all equal:

Fertilizer 1	Fertilizer 2	Fertilizer 3
62	54	48
62	56	62
90	58	92

42	36	96
84	72	92
64	34	80

The Python code is as follows:

```
>>> import pandas as pd
>>> from scipy import stats
>>> fetilizers = pd.read_csv("fetilizers.csv")
```

Calculating one-way ANOVA using the `stats` package:

```
>>> one_way_anova = stats.f_oneway(fetilizers["fertilizer1"],
fetilizers["fertilizer2"], fetilizers["fertilizer3"])

>>> print ("Statistic :", round(one_way_anova[0],2),", p-value
:",round(one_way_anova[1],3))
```

```
Statistic : 4.13 , p-value : 0.037
[Finished in 0.6s]
```

Result: The p-value did come as less than 0.05, hence we can reject the null hypothesis that the mean crop yields of the fertilizers are equal. Fertilizers make a significant difference to crops.

The R code for ANOVA is as follows:

```
fetilizers = read.csv("fetilizers.csv",header=TRUE)
r = c(t(as.matrix(fetilizers)))
f = c("fertilizer1","fertilizer2","fertilizer3")
k = 3; n = 6
tm = gl(k,1,n*k,factor(f))
blk = gl(n,k,k*n)
av = aov(r ~ tm + blk)
smry = summary(av)
```

- **Confusion matrix**: This is the matrix of the actual versus the predicted. This concept is better explained with the example of cancer prediction using the model:

	Predicted: Yes	Predicted: No
Actual: Yes	TP	FN
Actual: No	FP	TN

Some terms used in a confusion matrix are:

- **True positives (TPs)**: True positives are cases when we predict the disease as yes when the patient actually does have the disease.
- **True negatives (TNs)**: Cases when we predict the disease as no when the patient actually does not have the disease.
- **False positives (FPs)**: When we predict the disease as yes when the patient actually does not have the disease. FPs are also considered to be type I errors.
- **False negatives (FNs)**: When we predict the disease as no when the patient actually does have the disease. FNs are also considered to be type II errors.
- **Precision (P)**: When yes is predicted, how often is it correct?

(TP/TP+FP)

- **Recall (R)/sensitivity/true positive rate**: Among the actual yeses, what fraction was predicted as yes?

(TP/TP+FN)

- **F1 score (F1)**: This is the harmonic mean of the precision and recall. Multiplying the constant of *2* scales the score to *1* when both precision and recall are *1*:

$$F_1 = \frac{2}{\frac{1}{P} + \frac{1}{R}} \quad \gg \quad F_1 = \frac{2 * P * R}{P + R}$$

- **Specificity**: Among the actual nos, what fraction was predicted as no? Also equivalent to *1- false positive rate*:

(TN/TN+FP)

- **Area under curve (ROC)**: Receiver operating characteristic curve is used to plot between **true positive rate** (**TPR**) and **false positive rate** (**FPR**), also known as a sensitivity and *1- specificity* graph:

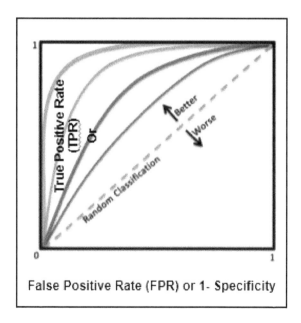

Area under curve is utilized for setting the threshold of cut-off probability to classify the predicted probability into various classes.

- **Observation and performance window**: In statistical modeling, the model tries to predict the event in advance rather than at the moment, so that some buffer time will exist to work on corrective actions. For example, a question from a credit card company would be, for example, what is the probability that a particular customer will default in the coming 12-month period? So that I can call him and offer any discounts or develop my collection strategies accordingly.

  In order to answer this question, a probability of default model (or behavioral scorecard in technical terms) needs to be developed by using independent variables from the past 24 months and a dependent variable from the next 12 months. After preparing data with X and Y variables, it will be split into 70 percent - 30 percent as train and test data randomly; this method is called **in-time validation** as both train and test samples are from the same time period:

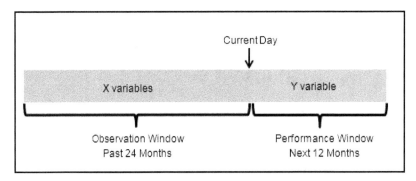

- **In-time and out-of-time validation**: In-time validation implies obtaining both a training and testing dataset from the same period of time, whereas out-of-time validation implies training and testing datasets drawn from different time periods. Usually, the model performs worse in out-of-time validation rather than in-time due to the obvious reason that the characteristics of the train and test datasets might differ.

- **R-squared (coefficient of determination)**: This is the measure of the percentage of the response variable variation that is explained by a model. It also a measure of how well the model minimizes error compared with just utilizing the mean as an estimate. In some extreme cases, R-squared can have a value less than zero also, which means the predicted values from the model perform worse than just taking the simple mean as a prediction for all the observations.

$$\bar{y} = \frac{1}{n}\sum_{i=1}^{n} y_i \;\; ; \;\; SS_{tot} = \sum_i (y_i - \bar{y})^2 \;\; ; \;\; SS_{reg} = \sum_i (f_i - \bar{y})^2 \;\; ; \;\; SS_{res} = \sum_i (y_i - f_i)^2 = \sum_i e_i^2$$

$$R^2 \equiv 1 - \frac{SS_{res}}{SS_{tot}}$$

- **Adjusted R-squared**: The explanation of the adjusted R-squared statistic is almost the same as R-squared but it penalizes the R-squared value if extra variables without a strong correlation are included in the model:

$$R^2_{adjusted} = 1 - \frac{(1 - R^2)(n - 1)}{n - k - 1}$$

Here, $R2$ = sample R-squared value, n = sample size, k = number of predictors (or) variables.

Adjusted R-squared value is the key metric in evaluating the quality of linear regressions. Any linear regression model having the value of $R2$ *adjusted* >= *0.7* is considered as a good enough model to implement.

Example: The R-squared value of a sample is *0.5,* with a sample size of *50* and the independent variables are *10* in number. Calculated adjusted R-squared:

$$R^2_{adjusted} = 1 - \frac{(1 - 0.5)(50 - 1)}{50 - 10 - 1} = 0.402$$

- **Maximum likelihood estimate (MLE)**: This is estimating the parameter values of a statistical model (logistic regression, to be precise) by finding the parameter values that maximize the likelihood of making the observations.

- **Akaike information criteria (AIC)**: This is used in logistic regression, which is similar to the principle of adjusted R-square for linear regression. It measures the relative quality of a model for a given set of data:

$$AIC = -2 * \ln(L) + 2 * k$$

Here, k = number of predictors or variables

The idea of AIC is to penalize the objective function if extra variables without strong predictive abilities are included in the model. This is a kind of regularization in logistic regression.

- **Entropy**: This comes from information theory and is the measure of impurity in the data. If the sample is completely homogeneous, the entropy is zero and if the sample is equally divided, it has an entropy of *1*. In decision trees, the predictor with the most heterogeneousness will be considered nearest to the root node to classify given data into classes in a greedy mode. We will cover this topic in more depth in Chapter 2, *Tree-Based Machine Learning Models*:

$$Entropy = -p_1 * log_2\, p_1 - \ldots - -p_n * log_2\, p_n$$

Here, n = number of classes. Entropy is maximal at the middle, with the value of *1* and minimal at the extremes as *0*. A low value of entropy is desirable as it will segregate classes better:

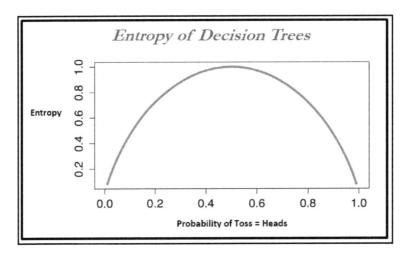

Example: Given two types of coin in which the first one is a fair one (*1/2* head and *1/2* tail probabilities) and the other is a biased one (*1/3* head and *2/3* tail probabilities), calculate the entropy for both and justify which one is better with respect to modeling:

$$Entropy\ of\ a\ Fair\ Coin\ =\ -\frac{1}{2}*log_2\frac{1}{2}\ -\ \frac{1}{2}*log_2\frac{1}{2}\ =\ 1\ bits$$

$$Entropy\ of\ a\ Biased\ Coin\ =\ -\frac{1}{3}*log_2\frac{1}{3}\ -\ \frac{2}{3}*log_2\frac{2}{3}\ =\ 0.9183\ bits$$

From both values, the decision tree algorithm chooses the biased coin rather than the fair coin as an observation splitter due to the fact the value of entropy is less.

- **Information gain**: This is the expected reduction in entropy caused by partitioning the examples according to a given attribute. The idea is to start with mixed classes and to keep partitioning until each node reaches its observations of the purest class. At every stage, the variable with maximum information gain is chosen in greedy fashion:

*Information gain = Entropy of parent - sum (weighted % * Entropy of child)*

Weighted % = Number of observations in particular child / sum (observations in all child nodes)

- **Gini**: Gini impurity is a measure of misclassification, which applies in a multiclass classifier context. Gini works almost the same as entropy, except Gini is faster to calculate:

$$Gini\ =\ 1\ -\ \sum_i p_i^2$$

Here, i = number of classes. The similarity between Gini and entropy is shown as follows:

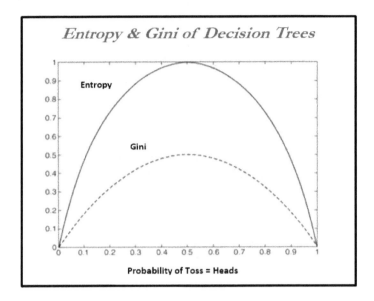

Bias versus variance trade-off

Every model has both bias and variance error components in addition to white noise. Bias and variance are inversely related to each other; while trying to reduce one component, the other component of the model will increase. The true art lies in creating a good fit by balancing both. The ideal model will have both low bias and low variance.

Errors from the bias component come from erroneous assumptions in the underlying learning algorithm. High bias can cause an algorithm to miss the relevant relations between features and target outputs; this phenomenon causes an underfitting problem.

On the other hand, errors from the variance component come from sensitivity to change in the fit of the model, even a small change in training data; high variance can cause an overfitting problem:

$$E\left(y_0 - \hat{f}(x_0)\right)^2 = Var\left(\hat{f}(x_0)\right) + \left[Bias(\hat{f}(x_0))\right]^2 + Var(\varepsilon)$$

An example of a high bias model is logistic or linear regression, in which the fit of the model is merely a straight line and may have a high error component due to the fact that a linear model could not approximate underlying data well.

An example of a high variance model is a decision tree, in which the model may create a wiggly curve as a fit, in which even a small change in training data will cause a drastic change in the fit of the curve.

At the moment, state-of-the-art models are utilizing high variance models such as decision trees and performing ensemble on top of them to reduce the errors caused by high variance and at the same time not compromising on increases in errors due to the bias component. The best example of this category is random forest, in which many decision trees will be grown independently and ensemble in order to come up with the best fit; we will cover this in upcoming chapters:

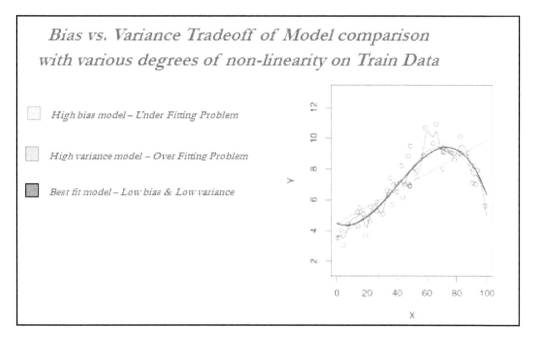

Train and test data

In practice, data usually will be split randomly 70-30 or 80-20 into train and test datasets respectively in statistical modeling, in which training data utilized for building the model and its effectiveness will be checked on test data:

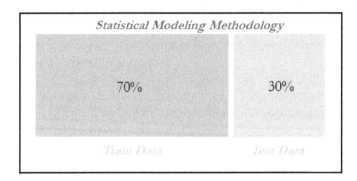

In the following code, we split the original data into train and test data by 70 percent - 30 percent. An important point to consider here is that we set the seed values for random numbers in order to repeat the random sampling every time we create the same observations in training and testing data. Repeatability is very much needed in order to reproduce the results:

```
# Train & Test split
>>> import pandas as pd
>>> from sklearn.model_selection import train_test_split

>>> original_data = pd.read_csv("mtcars.csv")
```

In the following code, `train size` is `0.7`, which means 70 percent of the data should be split into the training dataset and the remaining 30% should be in the testing dataset. Random state is seed in this process of generating pseudo-random numbers, which makes the results reproducible by splitting the exact same observations while running every time:

```
>>> train_data,test_data = train_test_split(original_data,train_size =
0.7,random_state=42)
```

The R code for the train and test split for statistical modeling is as follows:

```
full_data = read.csv("mtcars.csv",header=TRUE)
set.seed(123)
numrow = nrow(full_data)
trnind = sample(1:numrow,size = as.integer(0.7*numrow))
train_data = full_data[trnind,]
test_data = full_data[-trnind,]
```

Summary

In this chapter, we have gained a high-level view of various basic building blocks and subcomponents involved in statistical modeling and machine learning, such as mean, variance, interquartile range, p-value, bias versus variance trade-off, AIC, Gini, the area under the curve, and so on with respect to the statistics context.

In the next chapter, we will be covering complete tree-based models such as decision trees, random forest, boosted trees, ensemble of models, and so on to improve accuracy!

Tree-Based Machine Learning Models

2

The goal of tree-based methods is to segment the feature space into a number of simple rectangular regions, to subsequently make a prediction for a given observation based on either mean or mode (mean for regression and mode for classification, to be precise) of the training observations in the region to which it belongs. Unlike most other classifiers, models produced by decision trees are easy to interpret. In this chapter, we will be covering the following decision tree-based models on HR data examples for predicting whether a given employee will leave the organization in the near future or not. In this chapter, we will learn the following topics:

- Decision trees - simple model and model with class weight tuning
- Bagging (bootstrap aggregation)
- Random Forest - basic random forest and application of grid search on hyperparameter tuning
- Boosting (AdaBoost, gradient boost, extreme gradient boost - XGBoost)
- Ensemble of ensembles (with heterogeneous and homogeneous models)

Introducing decision tree classifiers

Decision tree classifiers produce rules in simple English sentences, which can easily be interpreted and presented to senior management without any editing. Decision trees can be applied to either classification or regression problems. Based on features in data, decision tree models learn a series of questions to infer the class labels of samples.

In the following figure, simple recursive decision rules have been asked by a programmer himself to do relevant actions. The actions would be based on the provided answers for each question, whether yes or no.

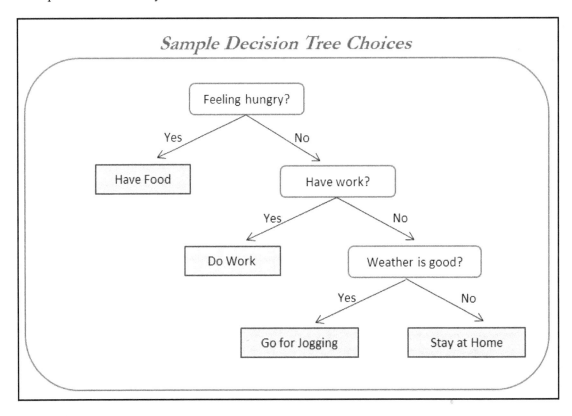

Terminology used in decision trees

Decision Trees do not have much machinery as compared with logistic regression. Here we have a few metrics to study. We will majorly focus on impurity measures; decision trees split variables recursively based on set impurity criteria until they reach some stopping criteria (minimum observations per terminal node, minimum observations for split at any node, and so on):

- **Entropy:** Entropy came from information theory and is the measure of impurity in data. If the sample is completely homogeneous, the entropy is zero, and if the sample is equally divided, it has entropy of one. In decision trees, the predictor with most heterogeneousness will be considered nearest to the root node to classify the given data into classes in a greedy mode. We will cover this topic in more depth in this chapter:

$$Entropy = -p_1 * log_2 \, p_1 - \; ... \; - -p_n * log_2 \, p_n$$

  Where n = number of classes. Entropy is maximum in the middle, with a value of *1* and minimum at the extremes with a value of *0*. The low value of entropy is desirable, as it will segregate classes better.

- **Information Gain:** Information gain is the expected reduction in entropy caused by partitioning the examples according to a given attribute. The idea is to start with mixed classes and to continue partitioning until each node reaches its observations of purest class. At every stage, the variable with maximum information gain is chosen in a greedy fashion.

  *Information Gain = Entropy of Parent - sum (weighted % * Entropy of Child)*

  Weighted % = Number of observations in particular child/sum (observations in all child nodes)

- **Gini:** Gini impurity is a measure of misclassification, which applies in a multi-class classifier context. Gini works similar to entropy, except Gini is quicker to calculate:

$$Gini = 1 - \sum_i p_i^2$$

Where *i = Number of classes*. The similarity between Gini and entropy is shown in the following figure:

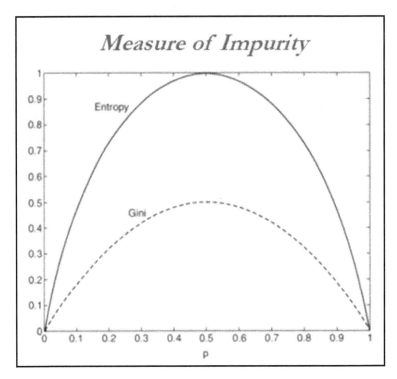

Decision tree working methodology from first principles

In the following example, the response variable has only two classes: whether to play tennis or not. But the following table has been compiled based on various conditions recorded on various days. Now, our task is to find out which output the variables are resulting in most significantly: YES or NO.

1. This example comes under the Classification tree:

Day	Outlook	Temperature	Humidity	Wind	Play tennis
D1	Sunny	Hot	High	Weak	No
D2	Sunny	Hot	High	Strong	No
D3	Overcast	Hot	High	Weak	Yes
D4	Rain	Mild	High	Weak	Yes
D5	Rain	Cool	Normal	Weak	Yes
D6	Rain	Cool	Normal	Strong	No
D7	Overcast	Cool	Normal	Strong	Yes
D8	Sunny	Mild	High	Weak	No
D9	Sunny	Cool	Normal	Weak	Yes
D10	Rain	Mild	Normal	Weak	Yes
D11	Sunny	Mild	Normal	Strong	Yes
D12	Overcast	Mild	High	Strong	Yes
D13	Overcast	Hot	Normal	Weak	Yes
D14	Rain	Mild	High	Strong	No

2. Taking the Humidity variable as an example to classify the Play Tennis field:
    - **CHAID:** Humidity has two categories and our expected values should be evenly distributed in order to calculate how distinguishing the variable is:

Humidity category	Play tennis		Expected		Difference	
	No	Yes	No	Yes	No	Yes
High	4	3	2.5	4.5	1.5	-1.5
Normal	1	6	2.5	4.5	-1.5	1.5
	5	9	5	9		

Calculating x^2 (Chi-square) value:

$$= \Sigma \frac{(O-E)^2}{E} = \frac{(1.5)^2}{2.5} + \frac{(-1.5)^2}{4.5} + \frac{(-1.5)^2}{2.5} + \frac{(1.5)^2}{4.5} = 2.8$$

Calculating degrees of freedom = (r-1) * (c-1)

Where r = number of row components/number of variable categories, C = number of response variables.

Here, there are two row categories (High and Normal) and two column categories (No and Yes).

Hence = *(2-1) * (2-1) = 1*

p-value for Chi-square 2.8 with 1 d.f = 0.0942

p-value can be obtained with the following Excel formulae: = *CHIDIST (2.8, 1) = 0.0942*

In a similar way, we will calculate the *p-value* for all variables and select the best variable with a low p-value.

- **ENTROPY:**

Entropy $= - \Sigma \, p * \log_2 p$

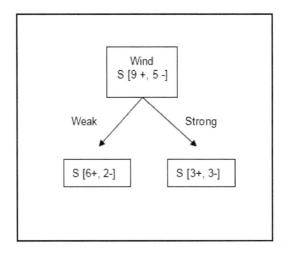

$$\text{Entropy} = -\left(\frac{9}{14}\right) * Log_2\left(\frac{9}{14}\right) - \left(\frac{5}{14}\right) * Log_2\left(\frac{5}{14}\right)$$

$$= 0.4097 + 0.5305 = 0.9402$$

$$Log_2\left(\frac{9}{14}\right) = Log\,(9/14)\,/\,Log\,2 = -0.6374$$

$$\text{Entropy}_{High} = -\left(\frac{3}{7}\right) * Log_2\left(\frac{3}{7}\right) - \left(\frac{4}{7}\right) * Log_2\left(\frac{4}{7}\right)$$
$$= 0.523 + 0.4613 = 0.9851$$

$$\text{Entropy}_{Normal} = -\left(\frac{1}{7}\right) * Log_2\left(\frac{1}{7}\right) - \left(\frac{6}{7}\right) * Log_2\left(\frac{6}{7}\right)$$
$$= 0.4010 + 0.1906 = 0.5916$$

$$\text{Information gain} = Total\ Entropy - \left(\frac{7}{14}\right) * Entropy_{High} - \left(\frac{7}{14}\right) * Entropy_{Normal}$$

$$= 0.9402 - \left(\frac{7}{14}\right) * 0.9851 - \left(\frac{7}{14}\right) * 0.5916 = 0.1518$$

In a similar way, we will calculate *information gain* for all variables and select the best variable with the *highest information gain*.

- **GINI**:

$$Gini = 1 - \Sigma p^2$$

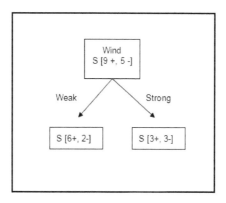

$$\text{Gini} = 1 - \left(\frac{9}{14}\right)^2 - \left(\frac{5}{14}\right)^2 = 0.459$$

$$\text{Gini}_{\text{Normal}} = 1 - \left(\frac{1}{7}\right)^2 - \left(\frac{6}{7}\right)^2 = 0.2448$$

$$\text{Expected Gini} = \left(\frac{7}{14}\right) * 0.489 + \left(\frac{7}{14}\right) * 0.2448 = 0.3669$$

In a similar way, we will calculate *Expected Gini* for all variables and select the best with the *lowest expected value*.

For the purpose of a better understanding, we will also do similar calculations for the Wind variable:

- **CHAID:** Wind has two categories and our expected values should be evenly distributed in order to calculate how distinguishing the variable is:

	Play tennis		Expected		Difference	
	No	Yes	No	Yes	No	Yes
Weak	2	6	2.5	4.5	-0.5	1.5
Strong	3	3	2.5	4.5	0.5	-1.5
	5	9	5	9		

$$= \frac{(-0.5)^2}{2.5} + \frac{(1.5)^2}{4.5} + \frac{(0.5)^2}{2.5} + \frac{(-1.5)^2}{4.5} = 1.2$$

$$\text{p-value} = 0.2733$$

- **ENTROPY:**

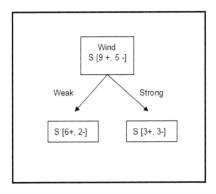

$$\text{Entropy}_{\text{Weak}} = -\left(\frac{6}{8}\right) * Log_2\left(\frac{6}{8}\right) - \left(\frac{2}{8}\right) * Log_2\left(\frac{2}{8}\right)$$
$$= 0.3112 + 0.5 = 0.8112$$

$$\text{Entropy}_{\text{Strong}} = -\left(\frac{3}{6}\right) * Log_2\left(\frac{3}{6}\right) - \left(\frac{3}{6}\right) * Log_2\left(\frac{3}{6}\right) = 0.5 + 0.5 = 1$$

$$\text{Information gain} = Total\ Entropy - \left(\frac{8}{14}\right) * Entropy_{Weak} - \left(\frac{6}{14}\right) * Entropy_{Strong}$$
$$= 0.9402 - \left(\frac{8}{14}\right) * 0.8112 - \left(\frac{6}{14}\right) * 1 = 0.0482$$

- **GINI**:

$$\text{Gini}_{\text{Weak}} = 1 - \left(\frac{6}{8}\right)^2 - \left(\frac{2}{8}\right)^2 = 0.375$$

$$\text{Gini}_{\text{Strong}} = 1 - \left(\frac{3}{6}\right)^2 - \left(\frac{3}{6}\right)^2 = 0.5$$

$$\text{Expected Gini} = \left(\frac{8}{14}\right) * 0.375 + \left(\frac{6}{14}\right) * 0.5 = 0.4285$$

Now we will compare both variables for all three metrics so that we can understand them better.

Variables	CHAID (p-value)	Entropy information gain	Gini expected value
Humidity	0.0942	0.1518	0.3669
Wind	0.2733	0.0482	0.4285
Better	Low value	High value	Low value

For all three calculations, Humidity is proven to be a better classifier than Wind. Hence, we can confirm that all methods convey a similar story.

Comparison between logistic regression and decision trees

Before we dive into the coding details of decision trees, here, we will quickly compare the differences between logistic regression and decision trees, so that we will know which model is better and in what way.

Logistic regression	Decision trees
Logistic regression model looks like an equation between independent variables with respect to its dependent variable.	Tree classifiers produce rules in simple English sentences, which can be easily explained to senior management.
Logistic regression is a parametric model, in which the model is defined by having parameters multiplied by independent variables to predict the dependent variable.	Decision Trees are a non-parametric model, in which no pre-assumed parameter exists. Implicitly performs variable screening or feature selection.
Assumptions are made on response (or dependent) variable, with binomial or Bernoulli distribution.	No assumptions are made on the underlying distribution of the data.
Shape of the model is predefined (logistic curve).	Shape of the model is not predefined; model fits in best possible classification based on the data instead.
Provides very good results when independent variables are continuous in nature, and also linearity holds true.	Provides best results when most of the variables are categorical in nature.
Difficult to find complex interactions among variables (non-linear relationships between variables).	Non-linear relationships between parameters do not affect tree performance. Often uncover complex interactions. Trees can handle numerical data with highly skewed or multi-modal, as well as categorical predictors with either ordinal or non-ordinal structure.
Outliers and missing values deteriorate the performance of logistic regression.	Outliners and missing values are dealt with grace in decision trees.

Comparison of error components across various styles of models

Errors need to be evaluated in order to measure the effectiveness of the model in order to improve the model's performance further by tuning various knobs. Error components consist of a bias component, variance component, and pure white noise:

$$E(y_0 - \hat{f}(x_0))^2 = Var\left(\hat{f}(x_0)\right) + [Bias\left(\hat{f}(x_0)\right)]^2 + Var(\varepsilon)$$

Out of the following three regions:

- The first region has high bias and low variance error components. In this region, models are very robust in nature, such as linear regression or logistic regression.
- Whereas the third region has high variance and low bias error components, in this region models are very wiggly and vary greatly in nature, similar to decision trees, but due to the great amount of variability in the nature of their shape, these models tend to overfit on training data and produce less accuracy on test data.
- Last but not least, the middle region, also called the second region, is the ideal sweet spot, in which both bias and variance components are moderate, causing it to create the lowest total errors.

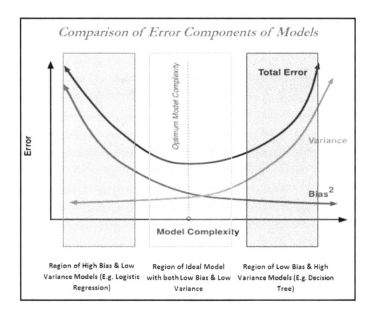

Remedial actions to push the model towards the ideal region

Models with either high bias or high variance error components do not produce the ideal fit. Hence, some makeovers are required to do so. In the following diagram, the various methods applied are shown in detail. In the case of linear regression, there would be a high bias component, meaning the model is not flexible enough to fit some non-linearities in data. One turnaround is to break the single line into small linear pieces and fit them into the region by constraining them at knots, also called **Linear Spline**. Whereas decision trees have a high variance problem, meaning even a slight change in X values leads to large changes in its corresponding Y values, this issue can be resolved by performing an ensemble of the decision trees:

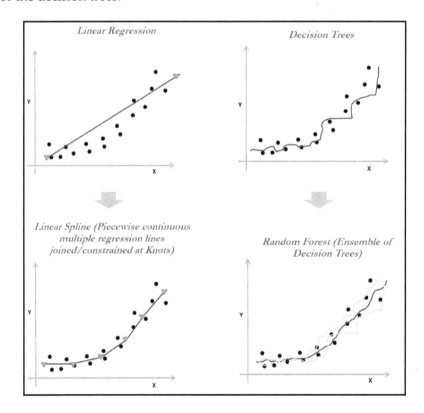

In practice, implementing splines would be a difficult and not so popular method, due to the involvement of the many equations a practitioner has to keep tabs on, in addition to checking the linearity assumption and other diagnostic KPIs (p-values, AIC, multi-collinearity, and so on) of each separate equation. Instead, performing ensemble on decision trees is most popular in the data science community, similar to bagging, random forest, and boosting, which we will be covering in depth in later parts of this chapter. Ensemble techniques tackle variance problems by aggregating the results from highly variable individual classifiers such as decision trees.

HR attrition data example

In this section, we will be using IBM Watson's HR Attrition data (the data has been utilized in the book after taking prior permission from the data administrator) shared in Kaggle datasets under open source license agreement https://www.kaggle.com/pavansubhasht/ ibm-hr-analytics-attrition-dataset to predict whether employees would attrite or not based on independent explanatory variables:

```
>>> import pandas as pd
>>> hrattr_data = pd.read_csv("WA_Fn-UseC_-HR-Employee-Attrition.csv")

>>> print (hrattr_data.head())
```

There are about 1470 observations and 35 variables in this data, the top five rows are shown here for a quick glance of the variables:

RelationshipSatisfaction	StandardHours	StockOptionLevel	TotalWorkingYears	TrainingTimesLastYear	WorkLifeBalance	YearsAtCompany	YearsInCurrentRole	YearsSinceLastPromotion	YearsWithCurrManager
1	80	0	8	0	1	6	4	0	5
4	80	1	10	3	3	10	7	1	7
2	80	0	7	3	3	0	0	0	0
3	80	0	8	3	3	8	7	3	0
4	80	1	6	3	3	2	2	2	2

HourlyRate	JobInvolvement	JobLevel	JobRole	JobSatisfaction	MaritalStatus	MonthlyIncome	MonthlyRate	NumCompaniesWorked	Over18	OverTime	PercentSalaryHike	PerformanceRating
94	3	2	Sales Executive	4	Single	5993	19479	8	Y	Yes	11	3
61	2	2	Research Scientist	2	Married	5130	24907	1	Y	No	23	4
92	2	1	Laboratory Technician	3	Single	2090	2396	6	Y	Yes	15	3
56	3	1	Research Scientist	3	Married	2909	23159	1	Y	Yes	11	3
40	3	1	Laboratory Technician	2	Married	3468	16632	9	Y	No	12	3

Age	Attrition	BusinessTravel	DailyRate	Department	DistanceFromHome	Education	EducationField	EmployeeCount	EmployeeNumber	EnvironmentSatisfaction	Gender
41	Yes	Travel_Rarely	1102	Sales	1	2	Life Sciences	1	1	2	Female
49	No	Travel_Frequently	279	Research & Development	8	1	Life Sciences	1	2	3	Male
37	Yes	Travel_Rarely	1373	Research & Development	2	2	Other	1	4	4	Male
33	No	Travel_Frequently	1392	Research & Development	3	4	Life Sciences	1	5	4	Female
27	No	Travel_Rarely	591	Research & Development	2	1	Medical	1	7	1	Male

The following code is used to convert Yes or No categories into 1 and 0 for modeling purposes, as scikit-learn does not fit the model on character/categorical variables directly, hence dummy coding is required to be performed for utilizing the variables in models:

```
>>> hrattr_data['Attrition_ind'] = 0
>>> hrattr_data.loc[hrattr_data['Attrition'] =='Yes', 'Attrition_ind'] = 1
```

Dummy variables are created for all seven categorical variables (shown here in alphabetical order), which are `Business Travel`, `Department`, `Education Field`, `Gender`, `Job Role`, `Marital Status`, and `Overtime`. We have ignored four variables from the analysis, as they do not change across the observations, which are `Employee count`, `Employee number`, `Over18`, and `Standard Hours`:

```
>>> dummy_busnstrvl = pd.get_dummies(hrattr_data['BusinessTravel'],
prefix='busns_trvl')
>>> dummy_dept = pd.get_dummies(hrattr_data['Department'], prefix='dept')
>>> dummy_edufield = pd.get_dummies(hrattr_data['EducationField'],
prefix='edufield')
>>> dummy_gender = pd.get_dummies(hrattr_data['Gender'], prefix='gend')
>>> dummy_jobrole = pd.get_dummies(hrattr_data['JobRole'],
prefix='jobrole')
>>> dummy_maritstat = pd.get_dummies(hrattr_data['MaritalStatus'],
prefix='maritalstat')
>>> dummy_overtime = pd.get_dummies(hrattr_data['OverTime'],
prefix='overtime')
```

Continuous variables are separated and will be combined with the created dummy variables later:

```
>>> continuous_columns = ['Age','DailyRate','DistanceFromHome',
'Education',
'EnvironmentSatisfaction','HourlyRate','JobInvolvement','JobLevel','JobSati
sfaction', 'MonthlyIncome', 'MonthlyRate',
'NumCompaniesWorked','PercentSalaryHike',  'PerformanceRating',
'RelationshipSatisfaction','StockOptionLevel', 'TotalWorkingYears',
'TrainingTimesLastYear','WorkLifeBalance', 'YearsAtCompany',
'YearsInCurrentRole', 'YearsSinceLastPromotion','YearsWithCurrManager']

>>> hrattr_continuous = hrattr_data[continuous_columns]
```

In the following step, both derived dummy variables from categorical variables and straight continuous variables are combined:

```
>>> hrattr_data_new = pd.concat([dummy_busnstrvl, dummy_dept,
dummy_edufield, dummy_gender, dummy_jobrole, dummy_maritstat,
dummy_overtime, hrattr_continuous, hrattr_data['Attrition_ind']],axis=1)
```

Here, we have not removed one extra derived dummy variable for each categorical variable due to the reason that multi-collinearity does not create a problem in decision trees as it does in either logistic or linear regression, hence we can simply utilize all the derived variables in the rest of the chapter, as all the models utilize decision trees as an underlying model, even after performing ensembles of it.

Once basic data has been prepared, it needs to be split by 70-30 for training and testing purposes:

```
# Train and Test split
>>> from sklearn.model_selection import train_test_split
>>> x_train,x_test,y_train,y_test = train_test_split( hrattr_data_new.drop
(['Attrition_ind'], axis=1),hrattr_data_new['Attrition_ind',    train_size
= 0.7, random_state=42)
```

R Code for Data Preprocessing on HR Attrition Data:

```
hrattr_data = read.csv("WA_Fn-UseC_-HR-Employee-Attrition.csv")
str(hrattr_data);summary(hrattr_data)
hrattr_data$Attrition_ind = 0;
hrattr_data$Attrition_ind[   hrattr_data$Attrition=="Yes"]=1
hrattr_data$Attrition_ind=   as.factor(hrattr_data$Attrition_ind)
remove_cols = c("EmployeeCount","EmployeeNumber","Over18",
"StandardHours","Attrition")
hrattr_data_new =   hrattr_data[,!(names(hrattr_data) %in% remove_cols)]
set.seed(123)
numrow = nrow(hrattr_data_new)
trnind = sample(1:numrow,size =   as.integer(0.7*numrow))
train_data =   hrattr_data_new[trnind,]
test_data = hrattr_data_new[-trnind,]
# Code for calculating   precision, recall for 0 and 1 categories and # at
overall level which   will be used in all the classifiers in # later
sections
frac_trzero =    (table(train_data$Attrition_ind)[[1]])/nrow(train_data)
frac_trone =    (table(train_data$Attrition_ind)[[2]])/nrow(train_data)
frac_tszero =    (table(test_data$Attrition_ind)[[1]])/nrow(test_data)
frac_tsone = (table(test_data$Attrition_ind)[[2]])/nrow(test_data)
prec_zero <-    function(act,pred){   tble = table(act,pred)
return( round(    tble[1,1]/(tble[1,1]+tble[2,1]),4))}
```

```
prec_one <-    function(act,pred){ tble = table(act,pred)
return( round(    tble[2,2]/(tble[2,2]+tble[1,2]),4))}
recl_zero <-    function(act,pred){tble = table(act,pred)
return( round(    tble[1,1]/(tble[1,1]+tble[1,2]),4))}
recl_one <-    function(act,pred){ tble = table(act,pred)
return( round(    tble[2,2]/(tble[2,2]+tble[2,1]),4))}
accrcy <-    function(act,pred){ tble = table(act,pred)
return(    round((tble[1,1]+tble[2,2])/sum(tble),4))}
```

Decision tree classifier

The `DecisionTtreeClassifier` from scikit-learn has been utilized for modeling purposes, which is available in the `tree` submodule:

```
# Decision Tree Classifier
>>> from sklearn.tree import DecisionTreeClassifier
```

The parameters selected for the DT classifier are in the following code with splitting criterion as Gini, Maximum depth as 5, the minimum number of observations required for qualifying split is 2, and the minimum samples that should be present in the terminal node is 1:

```
>>> dt_fit = DecisionTreeClassifier(criterion="gini",
max_depth=5,min_samples_split=2,  min_samples_leaf=1,random_state=42)
>>> dt_fit.fit(x_train,y_train)

>>> print ("\nDecision Tree - Train Confusion  Matrix\n\n",
pd.crosstab(y_train, dt_fit.predict(x_train),rownames =
["Actuall"],colnames = ["Predicted"]))
>>> from sklearn.metrics import accuracy_score, classification_report
>>> print ("\nDecision Tree - Train accuracy\n\n",round(accuracy_score
(y_train, dt_fit.predict(x_train)),3))
>>> print ("\nDecision Tree - Train Classification Report\n",
classification_report(y_train, dt_fit.predict(x_train)))

>>> print ("\n\nDecision Tree - Test Confusion
Matrix\n\n",pd.crosstab(y_test, dt_fit.predict(x_test),rownames =
["Actuall"],colnames = ["Predicted"]))
>>> print ("\nDecision Tree - Test accuracy",round(accuracy_score(y_test,
dt_fit.predict(x_test)),3))
>>> print ("\nDecision Tree - Test Classification Report\n",
classification_report( y_test, dt_fit.predict(x_test)))
```

```
Decision Tree - Train Confusion Matrix

Predicted    0   1
Actuall
0          844   9
1           98  78

Decision Tree - Train accuracy: 0.896

Decision Tree - Train Classification Report
              precision    recall  f1-score   support

           0       0.90      0.99      0.94       853
           1       0.90      0.44      0.59       176

avg / total        0.90      0.90      0.88      1029



Decision Tree - Test Confusion Matrix

Predicted    0   1
Actuall
0          361  19
1           49  12

Decision Tree - Test accuracy: 0.846

Decision Tree - Test Classification Report
              precision    recall  f1-score   support

           0       0.88      0.95      0.91       380
           1       0.39      0.20      0.26        61

avg / total        0.81      0.85      0.82       441
```

By carefully observing the results, we can infer that, even though the test accuracy is high (84.6%), the precision and recall of one category (*Attrition = Yes*) is low (*precision = 0.39* and *recall = 0.20*). This could be a serious issue when management tries to use this model to provide some extra benefits proactively to the employees with a high chance of attrition prior to actual attrition, as this model is unable to identify the real employees who will be leaving. Hence, we need to look for other modifications; one way is to control the model by using class weights. By utilizing class weights, we can increase the importance of a particular class at the cost of an increase in other errors.

For example, by increasing class weight to category *1*, we can identify more employees with the characteristics of actual attrition, but by doing so, we will mark some of the non-potential churner employees as potential attriters (which should be acceptable).

Another classic example of the important use of class weights is, in banking scenarios. When giving loans, it is better to reject some good applications than accepting bad loans. Hence, even in this case, it is a better idea to use higher weight to defaulters over non-defaulters:

R Code for Decision Tree Classifier Applied on HR Attrition Data:

```
# Decision Trees using C5.0    package
library(C50)
dtree_fit = C5.0(train_data[-31],train_data$Attrition_ind,costs    =
NULL,control = C5.0Control(minCases = 1))
summary(dtree_fit)
tr_y_pred = predict(dtree_fit,    train_data,type = "class")
ts_y_pred =    predict(dtree_fit,test_data,type = "class")
tr_y_act =    train_data$Attrition_ind;ts_y_act = test_data$Attrition_ind
tr_tble =    table(tr_y_act,tr_y_pred)
print(paste("Train    Confusion Matrix"))
print(tr_tble)
tr_acc =    accrcy(tr_y_act,tr_y_pred)
trprec_zero =    prec_zero(tr_y_act,tr_y_pred);
trrecl_zero =    recl_zero(tr_y_act,tr_y_pred)
trprec_one =    prec_one(tr_y_act,tr_y_pred);
trrecl_one =    recl_one(tr_y_act,tr_y_pred)
trprec_ovll = trprec_zero *frac_trzero    + trprec_one*frac_trone
trrecl_ovll = trrecl_zero    *frac_trzero + trrecl_one*frac_trone
print(paste("Decision Tree    Train accuracy:",tr_acc))
print(paste("Decision Tree    - Train Classification Report"))
print(paste("Zero_Precision",trprec_zero,"Zero_Recall",trrecl_zero))
print(paste("One_Precision",trprec_one,"One_Recall",trrecl_one))
print(paste("Overall_Precision",round(trprec_ovll,4),"Overall_Recall",
round(trrecl_ovll,4)))
ts_tble =    table(ts_y_act,ts_y_pred)
print(paste("Test    Confusion Matrix"))
print(ts_tble)
ts_acc =    accrcy(ts_y_act,ts_y_pred)
tsprec_zero =    prec_zero(ts_y_act,ts_y_pred); tsrecl_zero =
recl_zero(ts_y_act,ts_y_pred)
tsprec_one =    prec_one(ts_y_act,ts_y_pred); tsrecl_one =
recl_one(ts_y_act,ts_y_pred)
tsprec_ovll = tsprec_zero *frac_tszero    + tsprec_one*frac_tsone
tsrecl_ovll = tsrecl_zero    *frac_tszero + tsrecl_one*frac_tsone
print(paste("Decision Tree    Test accuracy:",ts_acc))
print(paste("Decision Tree    - Test Classification Report"))
print(paste("Zero_Precision",tsprec_zero,"Zero_Recall",tsrecl_zero))
print(paste("One_Precision",tsprec_one,"One_Recall",tsrecl_one))
print(paste("Overall_Precision",round(tsprec_ovll,4),
"Overall_Recall",round(tsrecl_ovll,4)))
```

Tuning class weights in decision tree classifier

In the following code, class weights are tuned to see the performance change in decision trees with the same parameters. A dummy DataFrame is created to save all the results of various precision-recall details of combinations:

```
>>> dummyarray = np.empty((6,10))
>>> dt_wttune = pd.DataFrame(dummyarray)
```

Metrics to be considered for capture are weight for zero and one category (for example, if the weight for zero category given is 0.2, then automatically, weight for the one should be 0.8, as total weight should be equal to 1), training and testing accuracy, precision for zero category, one category, and overall. Similarly, recall for zero category, one category, and overall are also calculated:

```
>>> dt_wttune.columns = ["zero_wght","one_wght","tr_accuracy",
"tst_accuracy", "prec_zero","prec_one", "prec_ovll",
"recl_zero","recl_one","recl_ovll"]
```

Weights for the zero category are verified from 0.01 to 0.5, as we know we do not want to explore cases where the zero category will be given higher weightage than one category:

```
>>> zero_clwghts = [0.01,0.1,0.2,0.3,0.4,0.5]

>>> for i in range(len(zero_clwghts)):
...     clwght = {0:zero_clwghts[i],1:1.0-zero_clwghts[i]}
...     dt_fit = DecisionTreeClassifier(criterion="gini",  max_depth=5,
... min_samples_split=2, min_samples_leaf=1,random_state=42,class_weight =
clwght)
...     dt_fit.fit(x_train,y_train)
...     dt_wttune.loc[i, 'zero_wght'] = clwght[0]
...     dt_wttune.loc[i, 'one_wght'] = clwght[1]
...     dt_wttune.loc[i, 'tr_accuracy'] = round(accuracy_score(y_train,
dt_fit.predict( x_train)),3)
...     dt_wttune.loc[i, 'tst_accuracy'] =
round(accuracy_score(y_test,dt_fit.predict( x_test)),3)
...     clf_sp =
classification_report(y_test,dt_fit.predict(x_test)).split()
...     dt_wttune.loc[i, 'prec_zero'] = float(clf_sp[5])
...     dt_wttune.loc[i, 'prec_one'] = float(clf_sp[10])
...     dt_wttune.loc[i, 'prec_ovll'] = float(clf_sp[17])
...     dt_wttune.loc[i, 'recl_zero'] = float(clf_sp[6])
...     dt_wttune.loc[i, 'recl_one'] = float(clf_sp[11])
...     dt_wttune.loc[i, 'recl_ovll'] = float(clf_sp[18])
```

```
...      print ("\nClass Weights",clwght,"Train
accuracy:",round(accuracy_score( y_train,dt_fit.predict(x_train)),3),"Test
accuracy:",round(accuracy_score(y_test, dt_fit.predict(x_test)),3))
...      print ("Test Confusion
Matrix\n\n",pd.crosstab(y_test,dt_fit.predict( x_test),rownames =
["Actuall"],colnames = ["Predicted"]))
```

```
Class Weights {0: 0.01, 1: 0.99} Train accuracy: 0.342 Test accuracy: 0.272
Test Confusion Matrix

Predicted   0   1
Actuall
0          65  315
1           6   55

Class Weights {0: 0.1, 1: 0.9} Train accuracy: 0.806 Test accuracy: 0.732
Test Confusion Matrix

Predicted   0   1
Actuall
0          282  98
1           20  41

Class Weights {0: 0.2, 1: 0.8} Train accuracy: 0.871 Test accuracy: 0.83
Test Confusion Matrix

Predicted   0   1
Actuall
0          341  39
1           36  25

Class Weights {0: 0.3, 1: 0.7} Train accuracy: 0.881 Test accuracy: 0.839
Test Confusion Matrix

Predicted   0   1
Actuall
0          345  35
1           36  25

Class Weights {0: 0.4, 1: 0.6} Train accuracy: 0.894 Test accuracy: 0.832
Test Confusion Matrix

Predicted   0   1
Actuall
0          346  34
1           40  21

Class Weights {0: 0.5, 1: 0.5} Train accuracy: 0.896 Test accuracy: 0.846
Test Confusion Matrix

Predicted   0   1
Actuall
0          361  19
1           49  12
```

From the preceding screenshot, we can see that at class weight values of 0.3 (for zero) and 0.7 (for one) it is identifying a higher number of attriters (25 out of 61) without compromising test accuracy 83.9% using decision trees methodology:

R Code for Decision Tree Classifier with class weights Applied on HR Attrition Data:

```
#Decision Trees using C5.0   package - Error Costs
library(C50)
class_zero_wgt =   c(0.01,0.1,0.2,0.3,0.4,0.5)
for (cwt in class_zero_wgt){
  cwtz = cwt
  cwto = 1-cwtz
  cstvr = cwto/cwtz
  error_cost <- matrix(c(0,   1, cstvr, 0), nrow = 2)
  dtree_fit = C5.0(train_data[-31],train_data$Attrition_ind,
  costs = error_cost,control = C5.0Control(  minCases =   1))
  summary(dtree_fit)
  tr_y_pred =   predict(dtree_fit, train_data,type = "class")
  ts_y_pred =   predict(dtree_fit,test_data,type = "class")
  tr_y_act =   train_data$Attrition_ind;
  ts_y_act =   test_data$Attrition_ind
  tr_acc =   accrcy(tr_y_act,tr_y_pred)
  ts_acc =   accrcy(ts_y_act,ts_y_pred)
  print(paste("Class   weights","{0:",cwtz,"1:",cwto,"}",
              "Decision   Tree Train accuracy:",tr_acc,
              "Decision   Tree Test accuracy:",ts_acc))
  ts_tble =   table(ts_y_act,ts_y_pred)
  print(paste("Test   Confusion Matrix"))
  print(ts_tble)
}
```

Bagging classifier

As we have discussed already, decision trees suffer from high variance, which means if we split the training data into two random parts separately and fit two decision trees for each sample, the rules obtained would be very different. Whereas low variance and high bias models, such as linear or logistic regression, will produce similar results across both samples. Bagging refers to bootstrap aggregation (repeated sampling with replacement and perform aggregation of results to be precise), which is a general purpose methodology to reduce the variance of models. In this case, they are decision trees.

Aggregation reduces the variance, for example, when we have n independent observations $x_1, x_2, ..., x_n$ each with variance σ^2 and the variance of the mean $\bar{x}$ of the observations is given by σ^2/n, which illustrates by averaging a set of observations that it reduces variance. Here, we are reducing variance by taking many samples from training data (also known as bootstrapping), building a separate decision tree on each sample separately, averaging the predictions for regression, and calculating mode for classification problems in order to obtain a single low-variance model that will have both low bias and low variance:

$$Predictions\ from\ each\ decision\ tree\ classifier \quad \hat{f}_1(x), \hat{f}_2(x), ... \hat{f}_B(x)$$

$$\widehat{f_{avg}}(x) = \frac{1}{B} \sum_{b=1}^{B} \hat{f}_b(x)$$

In a bagging procedure, rows are sampled while selecting all the columns/variables (whereas, in a random forest, both rows and columns would be sampled, which we will cover in the next section) and fitting individual trees for each sample. In the following diagram, two colors (pink and blue) represent two samples, and for each sample, a few rows are sampled, but all the columns (variables) are selected every time. One issue that exists due to the selection of all columns is that most of the trees will describe the same story, in which the most important variable will appear initially in the split, and this repeats in all the trees, which will not produce de-correlated trees, so we may not get better performance when applying variance reduction. This issue will be avoided in random forest (we will cover this in the next section of the chapter), in which we will sample both rows and columns as well:

Bootstrap Aggregation (Bagging)

In the following code, the same HR data has been used to fit the bagging classifier in order to compare the results apple to apple with respect to decision trees:

```
# Bagging Classifier
>>> from sklearn.tree import DecisionTreeClassifier
>>> from sklearn.ensemble import BaggingClassifier
```

The base classifier used here is Decision Trees with the same parameter setting that we used in the decision tree example:

```
>>> dt_fit = DecisionTreeClassifier(criterion="gini",
max_depth=5,min_samples_split=2,
min_samples_leaf=1,random_state=42,class_weight = {0:0.3,1:0.7})
```

Parameters used in bagging are, n_estimators to represent the number of individual decision trees used as 5,000, maximum samples and features selected are 0.67 and 1.0 respectively, which means it will select 2/3rd of observations for each tree and all the features. For further details, please refer to the scikit-learn manual http://scikit-learn. org/stable/modules/generated/sklearn.ensemble.BaggingClassifier.html:

```
>>> bag_fit = BaggingClassifier(base_estimator= dt_fit,n_estimators=5000,
max_samples=0.67,
...                   max_features=1.0,bootstrap=True,
...                   bootstrap_features=False, n_jobs=-1,random_state=42)

>>> bag_fit.fit(x_train, y_train)

>>> print ("\nBagging - Train Confusion Matrix\n\n",pd.crosstab(y_train,
bag_fit.predict(x_train),rownames = ["Actuall"],colnames = ["Predicted"]))
>>> print ("\nBagging- Train accuracy",round(accuracy_score(y_train,
bag_fit.predict(x_train)),3))
>>> print ("\nBagging   - Train Classification
Report\n",classification_report(y_train, bag_fit.predict(x_train)))

>>> print ("\n\nBagging - Test Confusion Matrix\n\n",pd.crosstab(y_test,
bag_fit.predict(x_test),rownames = ["Actuall"],colnames = ["Predicted"]))
>>> print ("\nBagging - Test accuracy",round(accuracy_score(y_test,
bag_fit.predict(x_test)),3))
>>> print ("\nBagging - Test Classification
Report\n",classification_report(y_test, bag_fit.predict(x_test)))
```

```
Bagging - Train Confusion Matrix

Predicted    0    1
Actuall
0          846    7
1           72  104

Bagging- Train accuracy 0.923

Bagging  - Train Classification Report
             precision    recall  f1-score    support

         0       0.92      0.99      0.96        853
         1       0.94      0.59      0.72        176

avg / total      0.92      0.92      0.92       1029




Bagging - Test Confusion Matrix

Predicted    0    1
Actuall
0          372    8
1           48   13

Bagging - Test accuracy 0.873

Bagging - Test Classification Report
             precision    recall  f1-score    support

         0       0.89      0.98      0.93        380
         1       0.62      0.21      0.32         61

avg / total      0.85      0.87      0.85        441
```

After analyzing the results from bagging, the test accuracy obtained was 87.3%, whereas for decision tree it was 84.6%. Comparing the number of actual attrited employees identified, there were 13 in bagging, whereas in decision tree there were 12, but the number of 0 classified as 1 significantly reduced to 8 compared with 19 in DT. Overall, bagging improves performance over the single tree:

R Code for Bagging Classifier Applied on HR Attrition Data:

```
# Bagging Classifier - using   Random forest package but all variables
selected
library(randomForest)
set.seed(43)
rf_fit = randomForest(Attrition_ind~.,data   = train_data,mtry=30,maxnodes=
64,classwt = c(0.3,0.7), ntree=5000,nodesize =   1)
tr_y_pred = predict(rf_fit,data   = train_data,type = "response")
```

```
ts_y_pred =    predict(rf_fit,newdata = test_data,type = "response")
tr_y_act = train_data$Attrition_ind;ts_y_act    = test_data$Attrition_ind
tr_tble =    table(tr_y_act,tr_y_pred)
print(paste("Train   Confusion Matrix"))
print(tr_tble)
tr_acc =    accrcy(tr_y_act,tr_y_pred)
trprec_zero =    prec_zero(tr_y_act,tr_y_pred); trrecl_zero =
recl_zero(tr_y_act,tr_y_pred)
trprec_one =    prec_one(tr_y_act,tr_y_pred);
trrecl_one =    recl_one(tr_y_act,tr_y_pred)
trprec_ovll = trprec_zero   *frac_trzero + trprec_one*frac_trone
trrecl_ovll = trrecl_zero   *frac_trzero + trrecl_one*frac_trone
print(paste("Random Forest   Train accuracy:",tr_acc))
print(paste("Random Forest   - Train Classification Report"))
print(paste("Zero_Precision",trprec_zero,"Zero_Recall",trrecl_zero))
print(paste("One_Precision",trprec_one,"One_Recall",trrecl_one))
print(paste("Overall_Precision",round(trprec_ovll,4),"Overall_Recall",
round(trrecl_ovll,4)))
ts_tble =    table(ts_y_act,ts_y_pred)
print(paste("Test   Confusion Matrix"))
print(ts_tble)
ts_acc =    accrcy(ts_y_act,ts_y_pred)
tsprec_zero =    prec_zero(ts_y_act,ts_y_pred); tsrecl_zero =
recl_zero(ts_y_act,ts_y_pred)
tsprec_one =    prec_one(ts_y_act,ts_y_pred);
tsrecl_one =    recl_one(ts_y_act,ts_y_pred)
tsprec_ovll = tsprec_zero   *frac_tszero + tsprec_one*frac_tsone
tsrecl_ovll = tsrecl_zero   *frac_tszero + tsrecl_one*frac_tsone
print(paste("Random Forest   Test accuracy:",ts_acc))
print(paste("Random Forest   - Test Classification Report"))
print(paste("Zero_Precision",tsprec_zero,"Zero_Recall",tsrecl_zero))
print(paste("One_Precision",tsprec_one,"One_Recall",tsrecl_one))
print(paste("Overall_Precision",round(tsprec_ovll,4),"Overall_Recall",
round(tsrecl_ovll,4)))
```

Random forest classifier

Random forests provide an improvement over bagging by doing a small tweak that utilizes de-correlated trees. In bagging, we build a number of decision trees on bootstrapped samples from training data, but the one big drawback with the bagging technique is that it selects all the variables. By doing so, in each decision tree, the order of candidate/variable chosen to split remains more or less the same for all the individual trees, which look correlated with each other. Variance reduction on correlated individual entities does not work effectively while aggregating them.

In random forest, during bootstrapping (repeated sampling with replacement), samples were drawn from training data; not just simply the second and third observations randomly selected, similar to bagging, but it also selects the few predictors/columns out of all predictors (m predictors out of total p predictors).

The thumb rule for variable selection of m variables out of total variables p is $m = sqrt(p)$ for classification and $m = p/3$ for regression problems randomly to avoid correlation among the individual trees. By doing so, significant improvement in the accuracy can be achieved. This ability of RF makes it one of the favorite algorithms used by the data science community, as a winning recipe across various competitions or even for solving practical problems in various industries.

In the following diagram, different colors represent different bootstrap samples. In the first sample, the 1st, 3rd, 4th and 7th columns are selected, whereas, in the second bootstrap sample, the 2nd, 3rd, 4th and 5th columns are selected respectively. In this way, any columns can be selected at random, whether they are adjacent to each other or not. Though the thumb rules of $sqrt(p)$ or $p/3$ are given, readers are encouraged to tune the number of predictors to be selected:

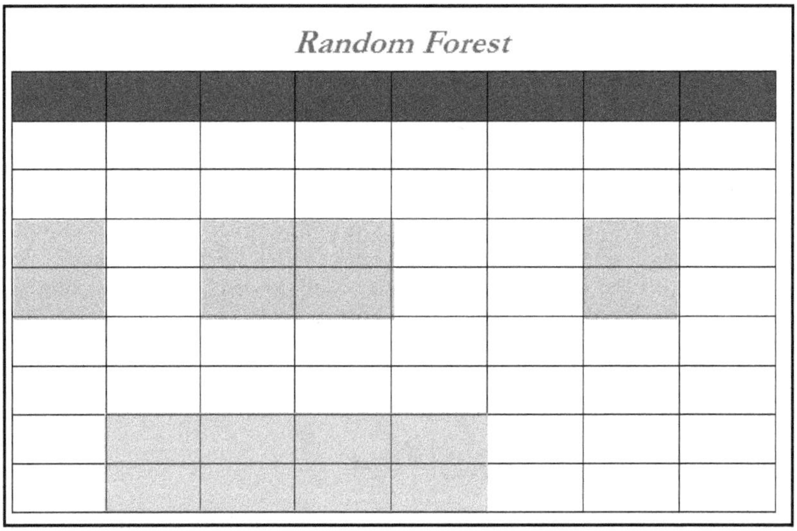

The sample plot shows the impact of a test error change while changing the parameters selected, and it is apparent that a *m = sqrt(p)* scenario gives better performance on test data compared with *m =p* (we can call this scenario bagging):

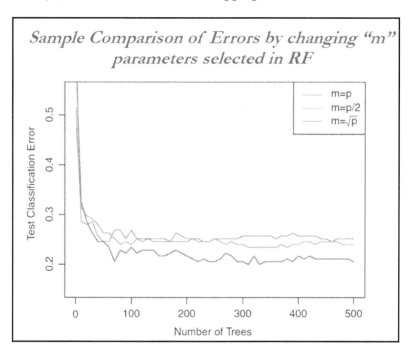

Random forest classifier has been utilized from the `scikit-learn` package here for illustration purposes:

```
# Random Forest Classifier
>>> from sklearn.ensemble import RandomForestClassifier
```

The parameters used in random forest are: `n_estimators` representing the number of individual decision trees used is 5000, maximum features selected are *auto*, which means it will select *sqrt(p)* for classification and *p/3* for regression automatically. Here is the straightforward classification problem though. Minimum samples per leaf provide the minimum number of observations required in the terminal node:

```
>>> rf_fit = RandomForestClassifier(n_estimators=5000,criterion="gini",
max_depth=5,
min_samples_split=2,bootstrap=True,max_features='auto',random_state=42,
min_samples_leaf=1,class_weight = {0:0.3,1:0.7})
>>> rf_fit.fit(x_train,y_train)

>>> print ("\nRandom Forest - Train Confusion
```

```
Matrix\n\n",pd.crosstab(y_train, rf_fit.predict(x_train),rownames =
["Actuall"],colnames = ["Predicted"]))
>>> print ("\nRandom Forest - Train accuracy",round(accuracy_score(y_train,
rf_fit.predict(x_train)),3))
>>> print ("\nRandom Forest  - Train Classification
Report\n",classification_report( y_train, rf_fit.predict(x_train)))

>>> print ("\n\nRandom Forest - Test Confusion
Matrix\n\n",pd.crosstab(y_test, rf_fit.predict(x_test),rownames =
["Actuall"],colnames = ["Predicted"]))
>>> print ("\nRandom Forest - Test accuracy",round(accuracy_score(y_test,
rf_fit.predict(x_test)),3))
>>> print ("\nRandom Forest - Test Classification
Report\n",classification_report( y_test, rf_fit.predict(x_test)))
```

```
Random Forest - Train Confusion Matrix

Predicted     0    1
Actuall
0           841   12
1            76  100

Random Forest - Train accuracy 0.914

Random Forest  - Train Classification Report
              precision    recall  f1-score   support

           0       0.92      0.99      0.95       853
           1       0.89      0.57      0.69       176

avg / total        0.91      0.91      0.91      1029



Random Forest - Test Confusion Matrix

Predicted     0    1
Actuall
0           373    7
1            47   14

Random Forest - Test accuracy 0.878

Random Forest - Test Classification Report
              precision    recall  f1-score   support

           0       0.89      0.98      0.93       380
           1       0.67      0.23      0.34        61

avg / total        0.86      0.88      0.85       441
```

Random forest classifier produced 87.8% test accuracy compared with bagging 87.3%, and also identifies 14 actually attrited employees in contrast with bagging, for which 13 attrited employees have been identified:

```
# Plot of Variable importance by mean decrease in gini
>>> model_ranks =
pd.Series(rf_fit.feature_importances_,index=x_train.columns,
name='Importance').sort_values(ascending=False, inplace=False)
>>> model_ranks.index.name = 'Variables'
>>> top_features =
model_ranks.iloc[:31].sort_values(ascending=True,inplace=False)
>>> import matplotlib.pyplot as plt
>>> plt.figure(figsize=(20,10))
>>> ax = top_features.plot(kind='barh')
>>> _ = ax.set_title("Variable Importance Plot")
>>> _ = ax.set_xlabel('Mean decrease in Variance')
>>> _ = ax.set_yticklabels(top_features.index, fontsize=13)
```

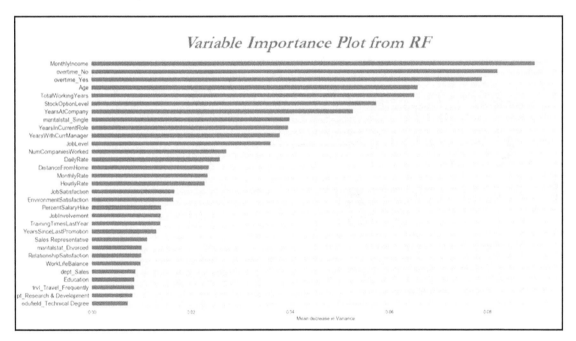

From the variable importance plot, it seems that the monthly income variable seems to be most significant, followed by overtime, total working years, stock option levels, years at company, and so on. This provides us with some insight into what are major contributing factors that determine whether the employee will remain with the company or leave the organization:

R Code for Random Forest Classifier Applied on HR Attrition Data:

```r
# Random Forest
library(randomForest)
set.seed(43)
rf_fit =   randomForest(Attrition_ind~.,data = train_data,mtry=6, maxnodes=
64,classwt =   c(0.3,0.7),ntree=5000,nodesize = 1)
tr_y_pred = predict(rf_fit,data   = train_data,type = "response")
ts_y_pred =   predict(rf_fit,newdata = test_data,type = "response")
tr_y_act =   train_data$Attrition_ind;ts_y_act = test_data$Attrition_ind
tr_tble =   table(tr_y_act,tr_y_pred)
print(paste("Train   Confusion Matrix"))
print(tr_tble)
tr_acc =   accrcy(tr_y_act,tr_y_pred)
trprec_zero = prec_zero(tr_y_act,tr_y_pred);   trrecl_zero =
recl_zero(tr_y_act,tr_y_pred)
trprec_one =   prec_one(tr_y_act,tr_y_pred); trrecl_one =
recl_one(tr_y_act,tr_y_pred)
trprec_ovll = trprec_zero   *frac_trzero + trprec_one*frac_trone
trrecl_ovll = trrecl_zero   *frac_trzero + trrecl_one*frac_trone
print(paste("Random Forest   Train accuracy:",tr_acc))
print(paste("Random Forest   - Train Classification Report"))
print(paste("Zero_Precision",trprec_zero,"Zero_Recall",trrecl_zero))
print(paste("One_Precision",trprec_one,"One_Recall",trrecl_one))
print(paste("Overall_Precision",round(trprec_ovll,4),"Overall_Recall",round
(trrecl_ovll,4)))
ts_tble =   table(ts_y_act,ts_y_pred)
print(paste("Test   Confusion Matrix"))
print(ts_tble)
ts_acc =   accrcy(ts_y_act,ts_y_pred)
tsprec_zero = prec_zero(ts_y_act,ts_y_pred);   tsrecl_zero =
recl_zero(ts_y_act,ts_y_pred)
tsprec_one =   prec_one(ts_y_act,ts_y_pred); tsrecl_one =
recl_one(ts_y_act,ts_y_pred)
tsprec_ovll = tsprec_zero   *frac_tszero + tsprec_one*frac_tsone
tsrecl_ovll = tsrecl_zero   *frac_tszero + tsrecl_one*frac_tsone
print(paste("Random Forest   Test accuracy:",ts_acc))
print(paste("Random Forest   - Test Classification Report"))
print(paste("Zero_Precision",tsprec_zero,"Zero_Recall",tsrecl_zero))
print(paste("One_Precision",tsprec_one,"One_Recall",tsrecl_one))
print(paste("Overall_Precision",round(tsprec_ovll,4),"Overall_Recall",round
(tsrecl_ovll,4)))
```

Random forest classifier - grid search

Tuning parameters in a machine learning model play a critical role. Here, we are showing a grid search example on how to tune a random forest model:

```
# Random Forest Classifier - Grid Search
>>> from sklearn.pipeline import Pipeline
>>> from sklearn.model_selection import train_test_split,GridSearchCV

>>> pipeline = Pipeline([
('clf',RandomForestClassifier(criterion='gini',class_weight =
{0:0.3,1:0.7}))])
```

Tuning parameters are similar to random forest parameters apart from verifying all the combinations using the pipeline function. The number of combinations to be evaluated will be *(3 x 3 x 2 x 2) *5 =36*5 = 180* combinations. Here 5 is used in the end, due to the cross-validation of five-fold:

```
>>> parameters = {
...             'clf__n_estimators':(2000,3000,5000),
...             'clf__max_depth':(5,15,30),
...             'clf__min_samples_split':(2,3),
...             'clf__min_samples_leaf':(1,2)   }

>>> grid_search =
GridSearchCV(pipeline,parameters,n_jobs=-1,cv=5,verbose=1,
scoring='accuracy')
>>> grid_search.fit(x_train,y_train)

>>> print ('Best Training score: %0.3f' % grid_search.best_score_)
>>> print ('Best parameters set:')
>>> best_parameters = grid_search.best_estimator_.get_params()
>>> for param_name in sorted(parameters.keys()):
...     print ('\t%s: %r' % (param_name, best_parameters[param_name]))

>>> predictions = grid_search.predict(x_test)

>>> print ("Testing accuracy:",round(accuracy_score(y_test,
predictions),4))
>>> print ("\nComplete report of Testing
data\n",classification_report(y_test, predictions))
```

```
>>> print ("\n\nRandom Forest Grid Search- Test Confusion
Matrix\n\n",pd.crosstab( y_test, predictions,rownames =
["Actuall"],colnames = ["Predicted"]))
```

```
Fitting 5 folds for each of 36 candidates, totalling 180 fits
[Parallel(n_jobs=-1)]: Done  34 tasks     | elapsed:  1.3min
[Parallel(n_jobs=-1)]: Done 180 out of 180 | elapsed:  7.1min finished
Best Training score: 0.867
Best parameters set:
        clf__max_depth: 5
        clf__min_samples_leaf: 2
        clf__min_samples_split: 2
        clf__n_estimators: 3000
Testing accuracy: 0.8753


Complete report of Testing data
                precision   recall  f1-score   support

            0        0.89     0.98      0.93       380
            1        0.64     0.23      0.34        61

avg / total          0.85     0.88      0.85       441



Random Forest Grid Search- Test Confusion Matrix

Predicted    0   1
Actuall
0          372   8
1           47  14
```

In the preceding results, grid search seems to not provide many advantages compared with the already explored random forest result. But, practically, most of the times, it will provide better and more robust results compared with a simple exploration of models. However, by carefully evaluating many different combinations, it will eventually discover the best parameters combination:

R Code for random forest classifier with grid search applied on HR attrition data:

```
# Grid Search - Random Forest
library(e1071)
library(randomForest)
rf_grid =   tune(randomForest,Attrition_ind~.,data = train_data,classwt =
c(0.3,0.7),ranges = list( mtry = c(5,6),
    maxnodes = c(32,64), ntree =   c(3000,5000), nodesize = c(1,2)
```

```
),
tunecontrol =    tune.control(cross = 5) )
print(paste("Best   parameter from Grid Search"))
print(summary(rf_grid))
best_model = rf_grid$best.model
tr_y_pred=predict(best_model,data   = train_data,type ="response")
ts_y_pred=predict(best_model,newdata   = test_data,type= "response")
tr_y_act =   train_data$Attrition_ind;
ts_y_act= test_data$Attrition_ind
tr_tble =   table(tr_y_act,tr_y_pred)
print(paste("Random Forest   Grid search Train Confusion Matrix"))
print(tr_tble)
tr_acc =   accrcy(tr_y_act,tr_y_pred)
trprec_zero =   prec_zero(tr_y_act,tr_y_pred); trrecl_zero =
recl_zero(tr_y_act,tr_y_pred)
trprec_one =   prec_one(tr_y_act,tr_y_pred); trrecl_one =
recl_one(tr_y_act,tr_y_pred)
trprec_ovll = trprec_zero   *frac_trzero + trprec_one*frac_trone
trrecl_ovll = trrecl_zero   *frac_trzero + trrecl_one*frac_trone
print(paste("Random Forest   Grid Search Train accuracy:",tr_acc))
print(paste("Random Forest   Grid Search - Train Classification Report"))
print(paste("Zero_Precision",trprec_zero,"Zero_Recall",trrecl_zero))
print(paste("One_Precision",trprec_one,"One_Recall",trrecl_one))
print(paste("Overall_Precision",round(trprec_ovll,4),"Overall_Recall",round
(trrecl_ovll,4)))
ts_tble =   table(ts_y_act,ts_y_pred)
print(paste("Random Forest   Grid search Test Confusion Matrix"))
print(ts_tble)
ts_acc =   accrcy(ts_y_act,ts_y_pred)
tsprec_zero =   prec_zero(ts_y_act,ts_y_pred); tsrecl_zero =
recl_zero(ts_y_act,ts_y_pred)
tsprec_one =   prec_one(ts_y_act,ts_y_pred); tsrecl_one =
recl_one(ts_y_act,ts_y_pred)
tsprec_ovll = tsprec_zero   *frac_tszero + tsprec_one*frac_tsone
tsrecl_ovll = tsrecl_zero   *frac_tszero + tsrecl_one*frac_tsone
print(paste("Random Forest   Grid Search Test accuracy:",ts_acc))
print(paste("Random Forest   Grid Search - Test Classification Report"))
print(paste("Zero_Precision",tsprec_zero,"Zero_Recall",tsrecl_zero))
print(paste("One_Precision",tsprec_one,"One_Recall",tsrecl_one))
print(paste("Overall_Precision",round(tsprec_ovll,4),"Overall_Recall",round
(tsrecl_ovll,4)))
```

AdaBoost classifier

Boosting is another state-of-the-art model that is being used by many data scientists to win so many competitions. In this section, we will be covering the **AdaBoost** algorithm, followed by **gradient boost** and **extreme gradient boost** (**XGBoost**). Boosting is a general approach that can be applied to many statistical models. However, in this book, we will be discussing the application of boosting in the context of decision trees. In bagging, we have taken multiple samples from the training data and then combined the results of individual trees to create a single predictive model; this method runs in parallel, as each bootstrap sample does not depend on others. Boosting works in a sequential manner and does not involve bootstrap sampling; instead, each tree is fitted on a modified version of an original dataset and finally added up to create a strong classifier:

$$H(x) = \sum_t \rho_t h_t(x)$$

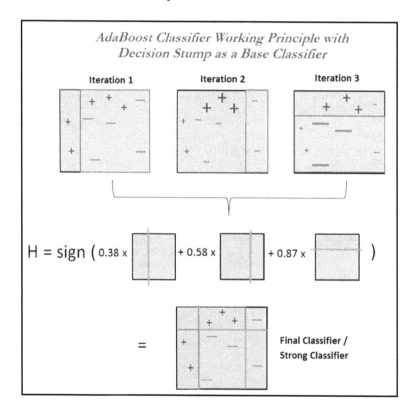

The preceding figure is the sample methodology on how AdaBoost works. We will cover step-by-step procedures in detail in the following algorithm description. Initially, a simple classifier has been fitted on the data (also called a decision stump, which splits the data into just two regions) and whatever the classes correctly classified will be given less weightage in the next iteration (iteration 2) and higher weightage for misclassified classes (observer + blue icons), and again another decision stump/weak classifier will be fitted on the data and will change the weights again for the next iteration (iteration 3, here check the - symbols for which weight has been increased). Once it finishes the iterations, these are combined with weights (weights automatically calculated for each classifier at each iteration based on error rate) to come up with a strong classifier, which predicts the classes with surprising accuracy.

Algorithm for AdaBoost consists of the following steps:

1. Initialize the observation weights w_i = 1/N, i=1, 2, ..., N. Where N = *Number of observations.*

2. For m = 1 to M:
   - Fit a classifier $Gm(x)$ to the training data using weights w_i
   - Compute:

$$err_m = \frac{\sum_{i=1}^{N} w_i I(y_i \neq G_m(x_i))}{\sum_{i=1}^{N} w_i}$$

   - Compute:

$$\alpha_m = \log\left(\frac{1-err_m}{err_m}\right)$$

   - Set:

$$w_i < - w_i * \exp\left[\alpha_m * I\left(y_i \neq G_m(x_i)\right)\right], i = 1,2,...,N$$

3. Output:

$$G(x) = sign[\sum_{m=1}^{M} \alpha_m G_m(x)]$$

All the observations are given equal weight.

In bagging and random forest algorithms, we deal with the columns of the data; whereas, in boosting, we adjust the weights of each observation and don't elect a few columns.

We fit a classifier on the data and evaluate overall errors. The error used for calculating weight should be given for that classifier in the final additive model (α) evaluation. The intuitive sense is that the higher weight will be given for the model with fewer errors. Finally, weights for each observation will be updated. Here, weight will be increased for incorrectly classified observations in order to give more focus to the next iterations, and weights will be reduced for correctly classified observations.

All the weak classifiers are combined with their respective weights to form a strong classifier. In the following figure, a quick idea is shared on how weights changed in the last iteration compared with the initial iteration:

```
# Adaboost Classifier
>>> from sklearn.tree import DecisionTreeClassifier
>>> from sklearn.ensemble import AdaBoostClassifier
```

Decision stump is used as a base classifier for AdaBoost. If we observe the following code, the depth of the tree remains as 1, which has decision taking ability only once (also considered a weak classifier):

```
>>> dtree = DecisionTreeClassifier(criterion='gini',max_depth=1)
```

In AdaBoost, decision stump has been used as a base estimator to fit on whole datasets and then fits additional copies of the classifier on the same dataset up to 5000 times. The learning rate shrinks the contribution of each classifier by 0.05. There is a trade-off between the learning rate and number of estimators. By carefully choosing a low learning rate and a long number of estimators, one can converge optimum very much, however at the expense of computing power:

```
>>>adabst_fit = AdaBoostClassifier(base_estimator=
dtree,n_estimators=5000,learning_rate=0.05,random_state=42)

>>>adabst_fit.fit(x_train, y_train)
>>>print ("\nAdaBoost - Train Confusion Matrix\n\n", pd.crosstab(y_train,
adabst_fit.predict(x_train), rownames = ["Actuall"],colnames =
["Predicted"]))
>>>print ("\nAdaBoost - Train
accuracy",round(accuracy_score(y_train,adabst_fit.predict(x_train)), 3))
>>>print ("\nAdaBoost  - Train Classification
Report\n",classification_report(y_train,adabst_fit.predict(x_train)))
```

```
AdaBoost - Train Confusion Matrix

Predicted   0    1
Actuall
0          844    9
1           55  121

AdaBoost  - Train accuracy 0.938

AdaBoost  - Train Classification Report
              precision    recall  f1-score   support

          0       0.94      0.99      0.96       853
          1       0.93      0.69      0.79       176

avg / total       0.94      0.94      0.93      1029



AdaBoost   - Test Confusion Matrix

Predicted   0   1
Actuall
0          360  20
1           38  23

AdaBoost  - Test accuracy 0.868

AdaBoost - Test Classification Report
              precision    recall  f1-score   support

          0       0.90      0.95      0.93       380
          1       0.53      0.38      0.44        61

avg / total       0.85      0.87      0.86       441
```

The result of the AdaBoost seems to be much better than the known best random forest classifiers in terms of the recall of 1 value. Though there is a slight decrease in accuracy to 86.8% compared with the best accuracy of 87.8%, the number of 1's predicted is 23 from the RF, which is 14 with some expense of an increase in 0's, but it really made good progress in terms of identifying actual attriters:

R Code for AdaBoost classifier applied on HR attrition data:

```
# Adaboost classifier using  C5.0 with trails included for boosting
library(C50)
class_zero_wgt = 0.3
class_one_wgt = 1-class_zero_wgt
cstvr =  class_one_wgt/class_zero_wgt
error_cost <- matrix(c(0, 1,  cstvr, 0), nrow = 2)
# Fitting Adaboost model
ada_fit = C5.0(train_data[-31],train_data$Attrition_ind,costs  =
error_cost, trails = 5000,control = C5.0Control(minCases = 1))
summary(ada_fit)
tr_y_pred = predict(ada_fit,  train_data,type = "class")
ts_y_pred =  predict(ada_fit,test_data,type = "class")
tr_y_act =  train_data$Attrition_ind;ts_y_act = test_data$Attrition_ind
tr_tble = table(tr_y_act,tr_y_pred)
print(paste("AdaBoost -  Train Confusion Matrix"))
print(tr_tble)
tr_acc =  accrcy(tr_y_act,tr_y_pred)
trprec_zero =  prec_zero(tr_y_act,tr_y_pred); trrecl_zero =
recl_zero(tr_y_act,tr_y_pred)
trprec_one =  prec_one(tr_y_act,tr_y_pred); trrecl_one =
recl_one(tr_y_act,tr_y_pred)
trprec_ovll = trprec_zero  *frac_trzero + trprec_one*frac_trone
trrecl_ovll = trrecl_zero  *frac_trzero + trrecl_one*frac_trone
print(paste("AdaBoost  Train accuracy:",tr_acc))
print(paste("AdaBoost -  Train Classification Report"))
print(paste("Zero_Precision",trprec_zero,"Zero_Recall",trrecl_zero))
print(paste("One_Precision",trprec_one,"One_Recall",trrecl_one))
print(paste("Overall_Precision",round(trprec_ovll,4),"Overall_Recall",round
(trrecl_ovll,4)))
ts_tble =  table(ts_y_act,ts_y_pred)
print(paste("AdaBoost -  Test Confusion Matrix"))
print(ts_tble)
ts_acc =  accrcy(ts_y_act,ts_y_pred)
tsprec_zero =  prec_zero(ts_y_act,ts_y_pred); tsrecl_zero =
recl_zero(ts_y_act,ts_y_pred)
tsprec_one =  prec_one(ts_y_act,ts_y_pred); tsrecl_one =
recl_one(ts_y_act,ts_y_pred)
tsprec_ovll = tsprec_zero  *frac_tszero + tsprec_one*frac_tsone
tsrecl_ovll = tsrecl_zero  *frac_tszero + tsrecl_one*frac_tsone
```

```
print(paste("AdaBoost Test   accuracy:",ts_acc))
print(paste("AdaBoost -   Test Classification Report"))
print(paste("Zero_Precision",tsprec_zero,"Zero_Recall",tsrecl_zero))
print(paste("One_Precision",tsprec_one,"One_Recall",tsrecl_one))
print(paste("Overall_Precision",round(tsprec_ovll,4),"Overall_Recall",round
(tsrecl_ovll,4)))
```

Gradient boosting classifier

Gradient boosting is one of the competition-winning algorithms that work on the principle of boosting weak learners iteratively by shifting focus towards problematic observations that were difficult to predict in previous iterations and performing an ensemble of weak learners, typically decision trees. It builds the model in a stage-wise fashion as other boosting methods do, but it generalizes them by allowing optimization of an arbitrary differentiable loss function.

Let's start understanding Gradient Boosting with a simple example, as GB challenges many data scientists in terms of understanding the working principle:

1. Initially, we fit the model on observations producing 75% accuracy and the remaining unexplained variance is captured in the *error* term:

$$Y = F(x) + error$$

2. Then we will fit another model on the error term to pull the extra explanatory component and add it to the original model, which should improve the overall accuracy:

$$error = G(x) + error2$$

3. Now, the model is providing 80% accuracy and the equation looks as follows:

$$Y = F(x) + G(x) + error2$$

4. We continue this method one more time to fit a model on the **error2** component to extract a further explanatory component:

$$error2 = H(x) + error3$$

5. Now, model accuracy is further improved to 85% and the final model equation looks as follows:

$$Y = F(x) + G(x) + H(x) + error3$$

6. Here, if we use weighted average (higher importance given to better models that predict results with greater accuracy than others) rather than simple addition, it will improve the results further. In fact, this is what the gradient boosting algorithm does!

$$Y = \alpha * F(x) + \beta * G(x) + \gamma * H(x) + error4$$

 After incorporating weights, the name of the error changed from **error3** to **error4**, as both errors may not be exactly the same. If we find better weights, we will probably get an accuracy of 90% instead of simple addition, where we have only got 85%.

Gradient boosting involves three elements:

- **Loss function to be optimized:** Loss function depends on the type of problem being solved. In the case of regression problems, mean squared error is used, and in classification problems, the logarithmic loss will be used. In boosting, at each stage, unexplained loss from prior iterations will be optimized rather than starting from scratch.

- **Weak learner to make predictions:** Decision trees are used as a weak learner in gradient boosting.

- **Additive model to add weak learners to minimize the loss function:** Trees are added one at a time and existing trees in the model are not changed. The gradient descent procedure is used to minimize the loss when adding trees.

The algorithm for Gradient boosting consists of the following steps:

1. Initialize:

$$f_0(x) = argmin_\gamma \sum_{i=1}^{N} L(y_i, \gamma)$$

2. For $m = 1$ to M:

- a) For $i = 1, 2, ..., N$ compute:

$$r_{im} = -[\frac{\partial L(y_i, f(x_i))}{\partial f(x_i)}]_{f=f_{m-1}}$$

- b) Fit a regression tree to the targets r_{im} giving terminal regions R_{jm}, $j = 1, 2, ..., J_m$,
- c) For $j = 1, 2, ..., J_m$, compute:

$$\gamma_{jm} = \arg\min_\gamma \sum_{x_i \in R_{jm}} L(y_i, f_{m-1}(x_i) + \gamma)$$

- d) Update:

$$f_m(x) = f_{m-1}(x) + \sum_{j=1}^{J_m} \gamma_{jm} I(x \in R_{jm})$$

3. Output:

$$\hat{f}(x) = f_M(x)$$

Initializes the constant optimal constant model, which is just a single terminal node that will be utilized as a starting point to tune it further in the next steps. *(2a)*, calculates the residuals/errors by comparing actual outcome with predicted results, followed by *(2b and 2c)* in which the next decision tree will be fitted on error terms to bring in more explanatory power to the model, and in *(2d)* add the extra component to the model at last iteration. Finally, ensemble all weak learners to create a strong learner.

Comparison between AdaBoosting versus gradient boosting

After understanding both AdaBoost and gradient boost, readers may be curious to see the differences in detail. Here, we are presenting exactly that to quench your thirst!

AdaBoost	GradientBoost
Both AdaBoost and Gradient Boost use a base weak learner and they try to boost the performance of a weak learner by iteratively shifting the focus towards problematic observations that were difficult to predict. At the end, a strong learner is formed by addition (or weighted addition) of the weak learners.	
In AdaBoost, shift is done by up-weighting observations that were misclassified before.	Gradient boost identifies difficult observations by large residuals computed in the previous iterations.
In AdaBoost "shortcomings" are identified by high-weight data points.	In Gradientboost "shortcomings" are identified by gradients.
Exponential loss of AdaBoost gives more weights for those samples fitted worse.	Gradient boost further dissect error components to bring in more explanation.
AdaBoost is considered as a special case of Gradient boost in terms of loss function, in which exponential losses.	Concepts of gradients are more general in nature.

The gradient boosting classifier from the scikit-learn package has been used for computation here:

```
# Gradientboost Classifier
>>> from sklearn.ensemble import GradientBoostingClassifier
```

Parameters used in the gradient boosting algorithms are as follows. Deviance has been used for loss, as the problem we are trying to solve is 0/1 binary classification. The learning rate has been chosen as 0.05, number of trees to build is 5000 trees, minimum sample per leaf/terminal node is 1, and minimum samples needed in a bucket for qualification for splitting is 2:

```
>>> gbc_fit = GradientBoostingClassifier (loss='deviance',
learning_rate=0.05, n_estimators=5000, min_samples_split=2,
min_samples_leaf=1, max_depth=1, random_state=42 )
```

```
>>> gbc_fit.fit(x_train,y_train)
>>> print ("\nGradient Boost - Train Confusion
Matrix\n\n",pd.crosstab(y_train, gbc_fit.predict(x_train),rownames =
["Actuall"],colnames = ["Predicted"]))
>>> print ("\nGradient Boost - Train
accuracy",round(accuracy_score(y_train, gbc_fit.predict(x_train)),3))
>>> print ("\nGradient Boost - Train Classification
Report\n",classification_report( y_train, gbc_fit.predict(x_train)))

>>> print ("\n\nGradient Boost - Test Confusion
Matrix\n\n",pd.crosstab(y_test, gbc_fit.predict(x_test),rownames =
["Actuall"],colnames = ["Predicted"]))
>>> print ("\nGradient Boost - Test accuracy",round(accuracy_score(y_test,
gbc_fit.predict(x_test)),3)) >>> print ("\nGradient Boost - Test
Classification Report\n",classification_report( y_test,
gbc_fit.predict(x_test)))
```

```
Ensemble of Models - Test Confusion Matrix

Predicted    0    1
Actuall
0          367   13
1           42   19

Ensemble of Models - Test accuracy 0.875

Ensemble of Models - Test Classification Report
              precision   recall  f1-score   support

         0       0.90     0.97      0.93       380
         1       0.59     0.31      0.41        61

avg / total      0.86     0.88      0.86       441
```

If we analyze the results, Gradient boosting has given better results than AdaBoost with the highest possible test accuracy of 87.5% with most 1's captured as 24, compared with AdaBoost with which the test accuracy obtained was 86.8%. Hence, it has been proven that it is no wonder why every data scientist tries to use this algorithm to win competitions!

The R code for gradient boosting classifier applied on HR attrition data:

```
# Gradient boosting
library(gbm)

library(caret)
set.seed(43)
# Giving weights to all the observations in a way that total #weights will
be euqal 1
model_weights <- ifelse(train_data$Attrition_ind == "0",
        (1/table(train_data$Attrition_ind)[1]) * 0.3,
          (1/table(train_data$Attrition_ind)[2]) * 0.7)
# Setting parameters for GBM
grid <- expand.grid(n.trees = 5000, interaction.depth = 1, shrinkage = .04,
n.minobsinnode = 1)
# Fitting the GBM model
gbm_fit <- train(Attrition_ind ~ ., data = train_data, method = "gbm",
weights = model_weights,
                   tuneGrid=grid,verbose = FALSE)
# To print variable importance plot
summary(gbm_fit)

tr_y_pred = predict(gbm_fit, train_data,type = "raw")
ts_y_pred = predict(gbm_fit,test_data,type = "raw")
tr_y_act = train_data$Attrition_ind;ts_y_act = test_data$Attrition_ind

tr_tble = table(tr_y_act,tr_y_pred)
print(paste("Gradient Boosting - Train Confusion Matrix"))
print(tr_tble)

tr_acc = accrcy(tr_y_act,tr_y_pred)
trprec_zero = prec_zero(tr_y_act,tr_y_pred); trrecl_zero =
recl_zero(tr_y_act,tr_y_pred)
trprec_one = prec_one(tr_y_act,tr_y_pred); trrecl_one =
recl_one(tr_y_act,tr_y_pred)

trprec_ovll = trprec_zero *frac_trzero + trprec_one*frac_trone
trrecl_ovll = trrecl_zero *frac_trzero + trrecl_one*frac_trone

print(paste("Gradient Boosting Train accuracy:",tr_acc))
print(paste("Gradient Boosting - Train Classification Report"))
print(paste("Zero_Precision",trprec_zero,"Zero_Recall",trrecl_zero))
print(paste("One_Precision",trprec_one,"One_Recall",trrecl_one))
print(paste("Overall_Precision",round(trprec_ovll,4),"Overall_Recall",round
(trrecl_ovll,4)))


ts_tble = table(ts_y_act,ts_y_pred)
```

```
print(paste("Gradient Boosting - Test Confusion Matrix"))
print(ts_tble)
ts_acc = accrcy(ts_y_act,ts_y_pred)
tsprec_zero = prec_zero(ts_y_act,ts_y_pred); tsrecl_zero =
recl_zero(ts_y_act,ts_y_pred)
tsprec_one = prec_one(ts_y_act,ts_y_pred); tsrecl_one =
recl_one(ts_y_act,ts_y_pred)
tsprec_ovll = tsprec_zero *frac_tszero + tsprec_one*frac_tsone
tsrecl_ovll = tsrecl_zero *frac_tszero + tsrecl_one*frac_tsone
print(paste("Gradient Boosting Test accuracy:",ts_acc))
print(paste("Gradient Boosting - Test Classification Report"))
print(paste("Zero_Precision",tsprec_zero,"Zero_Recall",tsrecl_zero))
print(paste("One_Precision",tsprec_one,"One_Recall",tsrecl_one))
print(paste("Overall_Precision",round(tsprec_ovll,4),"Overall_Recall",round
(tsrecl_ovll,4)))

# Use the following code for performing cross validation on data - At the
moment commented though
#fitControl <- trainControl(method = "repeatedcv", number = 4, repeats = 4)
# gbmFit1 <- train(Attrition_ind ~ ., data = train_data,
method = # "gbm", trControl = fitControl,tuneGrid=grid,verbose = FALSE)
```

Extreme gradient boosting - XGBoost classifier

XGBoost is the new algorithm developed in 2014 by *Tianqi Chen* based on the Gradient boosting principles. It has created a storm in the data science community since its inception. XGBoost has been developed with both deep consideration in terms of system optimization and principles in machine learning. The goal of the library is to push the extremes of the computation limits of machines to provide scalable, portable, and accurate results:

```
# Xgboost Classifier
>>> import xgboost as xgb
>>> xgb_fit = xgb.XGBClassifier(max_depth=2, n_estimators=5000,
learning_rate=0.05)
>>> xgb_fit.fit(x_train, y_train)

>>> print ("\nXGBoost - Train Confusion Matrix\n\n",pd.crosstab(y_train,
xgb_fit.predict(x_train),rownames = ["Actuall"],colnames = ["Predicted"]))
>>> print ("\nXGBoost - Train accuracy",round(accuracy_score(y_train,
xgb_fit.predict(x_train)),3))
>>> print ("\nXGBoost  - Train Classification
Report\n",classification_report(y_train, xgb_fit.predict(x_train)))
>>> print ("\n\nXGBoost - Test Confusion Matrix\n\n",pd.crosstab(y_test,
```

```
xgb_fit.predict(x_test),rownames = ["Actuall"],colnames = ["Predicted"]))
>>> print ("\nXGBoost - Test accuracy",round(accuracy_score(y_test,
xgb_fit.predict(x_test)),3))
>>> print ("\nXGBoost - Test Classification
Report\n",classification_report(y_test, xgb_fit.predict(x_test)))
```

```
XGBoost - Train Confusion Matrix

Predicted    0    1
Actuall
0          853    0
1            0  176

XGBoost - Train accuracy 1.0

XGBoost  - Train Classification Report
              precision    recall  f1-score   support

          0       1.00      1.00      1.00       853
          1       1.00      1.00      1.00       176

avg / total       1.00      1.00      1.00      1029



XGBoost - Test Confusion Matrix

Predicted    0    1
Actuall
0          361   19
1           38   23

XGBoost - Test accuracy 0.871

XGBoost - Test Classification Report
              precision    recall  f1-score   support

          0       0.90      0.95      0.93       380
          1       0.55      0.38      0.45        61

avg / total       0.86      0.87      0.86       441
```

The results obtained from **XGBoost** are almost similar to gradient boosting. The test accuracy obtained was 87.1%, whereas boosting got 87.5%, and also the number of 1's identified is 23 compared with 24 in gradient boosting. The greatest advantage of XGBoost over Gradient boost is in terms of performance and the options available to control model tune. By changing a few of them, makes XGBoost even beat gradient boost as well!

The R code for xtreme gradient boosting (XGBoost) classifier applied on HR attrition data:

```
# Xgboost Classifier
library(xgboost); library(caret)

hrattr_data = read.csv("WA_Fn-UseC_-HR-Employee-Attrition.csv")
str(hrattr_data); summary(hrattr_data)
# Target variable creation
hrattr_data$Attrition_ind = 0;
hrattr_data$Attrition_ind[hrattr_data$Attrition=="Yes"]=1

# Columns to be removed due to no change in its value across observations
remove_cols =
c("EmployeeCount","EmployeeNumber","Over18","StandardHours","Attrition")
hrattr_data_new = hrattr_data[,!(names(hrattr_data) %in% remove_cols)]

# List of  variables with continuous values
continuous_columns = c('Age','DailyRate', 'DistanceFromHome', 'Education',
'EnvironmentSatisfaction', 'HourlyRate', 'JobInvolvement', 'JobLevel',
'JobSatisfaction','MonthlyIncome', 'MonthlyRate', 'NumCompaniesWorked',
'PercentSalaryHike', 'PerformanceRating', 'RelationshipSatisfaction',
'StockOptionLevel', 'TotalWorkingYears',  'TrainingTimesLastYear',
'WorkLifeBalance', 'YearsAtCompany', 'YearsInCurrentRole',
'YearsSinceLastPromotion', 'YearsWithCurrManager')

# list of categorical variables
ohe_feats = c('BusinessTravel', 'Department',
'EducationField','Gender','JobRole', 'MaritalStatus', 'OverTime')

# one-hot-encoding categorical features
dummies <- dummyVars(~ BusinessTravel+Department+
EducationField+Gender+JobRole+MaritalStatus+OverTime, data =
hrattr_data_new)
df_all_ohe <- as.data.frame(predict(dummies, newdata = hrattr_data_new))

# Cleaning column names and replace . with _

colClean <- function(x){ colnames(x) <- gsub("\\.", "_", colnames(x)); x }
df_all_ohe = colClean(df_all_ohe)

hrattr_data_new$Attrition_ind = as.integer(hrattr_data_new$Attrition_ind)
```

```
# Combining both continuous and dummy variables from categories
hrattr_data_v3 = cbind(df_all_ohe,hrattr_data_new [, (names(hrattr_data_new)
%in% continuous_columns)], hrattr_data_new$Attrition_ind)

names(hrattr_data_v3)[52] = "Attrition_ind"

# Train and Test split based on 70% and 30%
set.seed(123)
numrow = nrow(hrattr_data_v3)
trnind = sample(1:numrow,size = as.integer(0.7*numrow))
train_data = hrattr_data_v3[trnind,]
test_data = hrattr_data_v3[-trnind,]

# Custom functions for calculation of Precision and Recall
frac_trzero = (table(train_data$Attrition_ind)[[1]])/nrow(train_data)
frac_trone = (table(train_data$Attrition_ind)[[2]])/nrow(train_data)

frac_tszero = (table(test_data$Attrition_ind)[[1]])/nrow(test_data)
frac_tsone = (table(test_data$Attrition_ind)[[2]])/nrow(test_data)
prec_zero <- function(act,pred){  tble = table(act,pred)
return( round( tble[1,1]/(tble[1,1]+tble[2,1]),4)   ) }

prec_one <- function(act,pred){ tble = table(act,pred)
return( round( tble[2,2]/(tble[2,2]+tble[1,2]),4)   ) }

recl_zero <- function(act,pred){tble = table(act,pred)
return( round( tble[1,1]/(tble[1,1]+tble[1,2]),4)   ) }

recl_one <- function(act,pred){ tble = table(act,pred)
return( round( tble[2,2]/(tble[2,2]+tble[2,1]),4)   ) }

accrcy <- function(act,pred){ tble = table(act,pred)
return( round((tble[1,1]+tble[2,2])/sum(tble),4)) }

y = train_data$Attrition_ind

# XGBoost Classifier Training
xgb <- xgboost(data = data.matrix(train_data[,-52]),label = y,eta =
0.04,max_depth = 2, nround=5000, subsample = 0.5, colsample_bytree = 0.5,
seed = 1, eval_metric = "logloss", objective = "binary:logistic",nthread =
3)

# XGBoost value prediction on train and test data
tr_y_pred_prob <- predict(xgb, data.matrix(train_data[,-52]))
tr_y_pred <- as.numeric(tr_y_pred_prob > 0.5)
ts_y_pred_prob <- predict(xgb, data.matrix(test_data[,-52]))
ts_y_pred <- as.numeric(ts_y_pred_prob > 0.5)
tr_y_act = train_data$Attrition_ind;ts_y_act = test_data$Attrition_ind
```

```
tr_tble = table(tr_y_act,tr_y_pred)

# XGBoost Metric predictions on Train Data
print(paste("Xgboost - Train Confusion Matrix"))
print(tr_tble)
tr_acc = accrcy(tr_y_act,tr_y_pred)
trprec_zero = prec_zero(tr_y_act,tr_y_pred); trrecl_zero =
recl_zero(tr_y_act,tr_y_pred)
trprec_one = prec_one(tr_y_act,tr_y_pred); trrecl_one =
recl_one(tr_y_act,tr_y_pred)
trprec_ovll = trprec_zero *frac_trzero + trprec_one*frac_trone
trrecl_ovll = trrecl_zero *frac_trzero + trrecl_one*frac_trone

print(paste("Xgboost Train accuracy:",tr_acc))
print(paste("Xgboost - Train Classification Report"))
print(paste("Zero_Precision",trprec_zero,"Zero_Recall",trrecl_zero))
print(paste("One_Precision",trprec_one,"One_Recall",trrecl_one))
print(paste("Overall_Precision",round(trprec_ovll,4),"Overall_Recall",round
(trrecl_ovll,4)))

# XGBoost Metric predictions on Test Data
ts_tble = table(ts_y_act,ts_y_pred)
print(paste("Xgboost - Test Confusion Matrix"))
print(ts_tble)
ts_acc = accrcy(ts_y_act,ts_y_pred)
tsprec_zero = prec_zero(ts_y_act,ts_y_pred); tsrecl_zero =
recl_zero(ts_y_act,ts_y_pred)
tsprec_one = prec_one(ts_y_act,ts_y_pred); tsrecl_one =
recl_one(ts_y_act,ts_y_pred)
tsprec_ovll = tsprec_zero *frac_tszero + tsprec_one*frac_tsone
tsrecl_ovll = tsrecl_zero *frac_tszero + tsrecl_one*frac_tsone

print(paste("Xgboost Test accuracy:",ts_acc))
print(paste("Xgboost - Test Classification Report"))
print(paste("Zero_Precision",tsprec_zero,"Zero_Recall",tsrecl_zero))
print(paste("One_Precision",tsprec_one,"One_Recall",tsrecl_one))
print(paste("Overall_Precision",round(tsprec_ovll,4),"Overall_Recall",round
(tsrecl_ovll,4)))
```

Ensemble of ensembles - model stacking

Ensemble of ensembles or model stacking is a method to combine different classifiers into a meta-classifier that has a better generalization performance than each individual classifier in isolation. It is always advisable to take opinions from many people when you are in doubt, when dealing with problems in your personal life too! There are two ways to perform ensembles on models:

- **Ensemble with different types of classifiers:** In this methodology, different types of classifiers (for example, logistic regression, decision trees, random forest, and so on) are fitted on the same training data and results are combined based on either majority voting or average, based on if it is classification or regression problems.

- **Ensemble with a single type of classifiers, but built separately on various bootstrap samples:** In this methodology, bootstrap samples are drawn from training data and, each time, separate models will be fitted (individual models could be decision trees, random forest, and so on) on the drawn sample, and all these results are combined at the end to create an ensemble. This method suits dealing with highly flexible models where variance reduction still improves performance.

Ensemble of ensembles with different types of classifiers

As briefly mentioned in the preceding section, different classifiers will be applied on the same training data and the results ensembled either taking majority voting or applying another classifier (also known as a meta-classifier) fitted on results obtained from individual classifiers. This means, for meta-classifier X, variables would be model outputs and Y variable would be an actual 0/1 result. By doing this, we will obtain the weightage that should be given for each classifier and those weights will be applied accordingly to classify unseen observations. All three methods of application of ensemble of ensembles are shown here:

- **Majority voting or average:** In this method, a simple mode function (classification problem) is applied to select the category with the major number of appearances out of individual classifiers. Whereas, for regression problems, an average will be calculated to compare against actual values.

- **Method of application of meta-classifiers on outcomes:** Predict actual outcome either 0 or 1 from individual classifiers and apply a meta-classifier on top of 0's and 1's. A small problem with this type of approach is that the meta-classifier will be a bit brittle and rigid. I mean 0's and 1's just gives the result, rather than providing exact sensibility (such as probability).
- **Method of application of meta-classifiers on probabilities:** In this method, probabilities are obtained from individual classifiers instead of 0's and 1's. Applying meta-classifier on probabilities makes this method a bit more flexible than the first method. Though users can experiment with both methods to see which one performs better. After all, machine learning is all about exploration and trial and error methodologies.

In the following diagram, the complete flow of model stacking has been described with various stages:

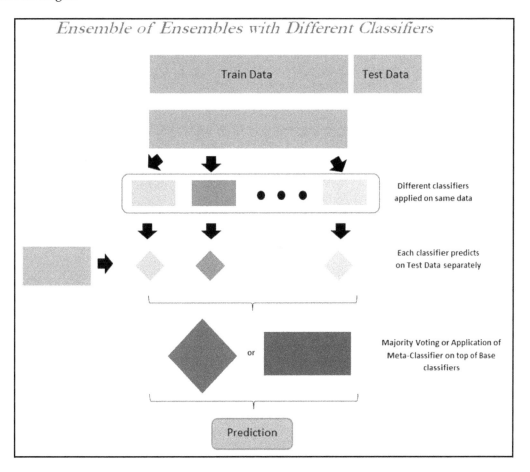

Steps in the following ensemble with multiple classifiers example:

- Four classifiers have been used separately on training data (logistic regression, decision tree, random forest, and AdaBoost)
- Probabilities have been determined for all four classifiers, however, only the probability for category 1 has been utilized in meta-classifier due to the reason that the probability of class 0 + probability of class 1 = 1, hence only one probability is good enough to represent, or else multi-collinearity issues appearing
- Logistic regression has been used as a meta-classifier to model the relationship between four probabilities (obtained from each individual classifier) with respect to a final 0/1 outcome
- Coefficients have been calculated for all four variables used in meta-classifier and applied on new data for calculating the final aggregated probability for classifying observations into the respective categories:

```
#Ensemble of Ensembles - by fitting various classifiers
>>> clwght = {0:0.3,1:0.7}

# Classifier 1 - Logistic Regression
>>> from sklearn.linear_model import LogisticRegression
>>> clf1_logreg_fit =
LogisticRegression(fit_intercept=True,class_weight=clwght)
>>> clf1_logreg_fit.fit(x_train,y_train)

>>> print ("\nLogistic Regression for Ensemble - Train Confusion
Matrix\n\n",pd.crosstab( y_train, clf1_logreg_fit.predict(x_train),rownames
= ["Actuall"],colnames = ["Predicted"]))
>>> print ("\nLogistic Regression for Ensemble - Train accuracy",round(
accuracy_score(y_train,clf1_logreg_fit.predict(x_train)),3))
>>> print ("\nLogistic Regression for Ensemble - Train Classification
Report\n", classification_report(y_train,clf1_logreg_fit.predict(x_train)))
>>> print ("\n\nLogistic Regression for Ensemble - Test Confusion
Matrix\n\n",pd.crosstab( y_test,clf1_logreg_fit.predict(x_test),rownames =
["Actuall"],colnames = ["Predicted"]))       >
>> print ("\nLogistic Regression for Ensemble - Test accuracy",round(
accuracy_score(y_test,clf1_logreg_fit.predict(x_test)),3))
>>> print ("\nLogistic Regression for Ensemble - Test Classification
Report\n", classification_report( y_test,clf1_logreg_fit.predict(x_test)))

# Classifier 2 - Decision Tree
>>> from sklearn.tree import DecisionTreeClassifier
>>> clf2_dt_fit = DecisionTreeClassifier(criterion="gini", max_depth=5,
min_samples_split=2, min_samples_leaf=1, random_state=42,
class_weight=clwght)
```

```
>>> clf2_dt_fit.fit(x_train,y_train)

>>> print ("\nDecision Tree for Ensemble - Train Confusion
Matrix\n\n",pd.crosstab( y_train, clf2_dt_fit.predict(x_train),rownames =
["Actuall"],colnames = ["Predicted"]))
>>> print ("\nDecision Tree for Ensemble - Train accuracy",
round(accuracy_score( y_train,clf2_dt_fit.predict(x_train)),3))
>>> print ("\nDecision Tree for Ensemble - Train Classification Report\n",
classification_report(y_train,clf2_dt_fit.predict(x_train)))
>>> print ("\n\nDecision Tree for Ensemble - Test Confusion Matrix\n\n",
pd.crosstab(y_test, clf2_dt_fit.predict(x_test),rownames =
["Actuall"],colnames = ["Predicted"]))
>>> print ("\nDecision Tree for Ensemble - Test
accuracy",round(accuracy_score(y_test, clf2_dt_fit.predict(x_test)),3))

>>> print ("\nDecision Tree for Ensemble - Test Classification Report\n",
classification_report(y_test, clf2_dt_fit.predict(x_test)))

# Classifier 3 - Random Forest
>>> from sklearn.ensemble import RandomForestClassifier
>>> clf3_rf_fit = RandomForestClassifier(n_estimators=10000,
criterion="gini", max_depth=6,
min_samples_split=2,min_samples_leaf=1,class_weight = clwght)
>>> clf3_rf_fit.fit(x_train,y_train)

>>> print ("\nRandom Forest for Ensemble - Train Confusion Matrix\n\n",
pd.crosstab(y_train, clf3_rf_fit.predict(x_train),rownames =
["Actuall"],colnames = ["Predicted"]))
>>> print ("\nRandom Forest for Ensemble - Train
accuracy",round(accuracy_score( y_train,clf3_rf_fit.predict(x_train)),3))
>>> print ("\nRandom Forest for Ensemble - Train Classification Report\n",
classification_report(y_train,clf3_rf_fit.predict(x_train)))

>>> print ("\n\nRandom Forest for Ensemble - Test Confusion
Matrix\n\n",pd.crosstab( y_test, clf3_rf_fit.predict(x_test),rownames =
["Actuall"],colnames = ["Predicted"]))
>>> print ("\nRandom Forest for Ensemble - Test
accuracy",round(accuracy_score( y_test,clf3_rf_fit.predict(x_test)),3))
>>> print ("\nRandom Forest for Ensemble - Test Classification Report\n",
classification_report(y_test,clf3_rf_fit.predict(x_test)))

# Classifier 4 - Adaboost classifier
>>> from sklearn.ensemble import AdaBoostClassifier
>>> clf4_dtree =
DecisionTreeClassifier(criterion='gini',max_depth=1,class_weight = clwght)
>>> clf4_adabst_fit = AdaBoostClassifier(base_estimator= clf4_dtree,
                n_estimators=5000,learning_rate=0.05,random_state=42)
>>> clf4_adabst_fit.fit(x_train, y_train)
```

```
>>> print ("\nAdaBoost for Ensemble  - Train Confusion
Matrix\n\n",pd.crosstab(y_train, clf4_adabst_fit.predict(x_train),rownames
= ["Actuall"],colnames = ["Predicted"]))
>>> print ("\nAdaBoost for Ensemble  - Train
accuracy",round(accuracy_score(y_train,
clf4_adabst_fit.predict(x_train)),3))
>>> print ("\nAdaBoost for Ensemble  - Train Classification Report\n",
classification_report(y_train,clf4_adabst_fit.predict(x_train)))
>>> print ("\n\nAdaBoost for Ensemble  - Test Confusion Matrix\n\n",
pd.crosstab(y_test, clf4_adabst_fit.predict(x_test),rownames =
["Actuall"],colnames = ["Predicted"]))
>>> print ("\nAdaBoost for Ensemble  - Test
accuracy",round(accuracy_score(y_test, clf4_adabst_fit.predict(x_test)),3))
>>> print ("\nAdaBoost for Ensemble  - Test Classification Report\n",
classification_report(y_test, clf4_adabst_fit.predict(x_test)))
```

In the following step, we perform an ensemble of classifiers:

```
>> ensemble = pd.DataFrame()
```

In the following step, we take probabilities only for category 1, as it gives intuitive sense for high probability and indicates the value towards higher class 1. But this should not stop someone if they really want to fit probabilities on a 0 class instead. In that case, low probability values are preferred for category 1, which gives us a little bit of a headache!

```
>>> ensemble["log_output_one"] =
pd.DataFrame(clf1_logreg_fit.predict_proba( x_train))[1]
>>> ensemble["dtr_output_one"] =
pd.DataFrame(clf2_dt_fit.predict_proba(x_train))[1]
>>> ensemble["rf_output_one"] =
pd.DataFrame(clf3_rf_fit.predict_proba(x_train))[1]
>>> ensemble["adb_output_one"] =
pd.DataFrame(clf4_adabst_fit.predict_proba( x_train))[1]
>>> ensemble = pd.concat([ensemble,pd.DataFrame(y_train).reset_index(drop =
True )],axis=1)

# Fitting meta-classifier
>>> meta_logit_fit =  LogisticRegression(fit_intercept=False)
>>> meta_logit_fit.fit(ensemble[['log_output_one', 'dtr_output_one',
'rf_output_one', 'adb_output_one']],ensemble['Attrition_ind'])
>>> coefs =  meta_logit_fit.coef_
>>> ensemble_test = pd.DataFrame()
>>> ensemble_test["log_output_one"] =
pd.DataFrame(clf1_logreg_fit.predict_proba( x_test))[1]
>>> ensemble_test["dtr_output_one"] =
pd.DataFrame(clf2_dt_fit.predict_proba( x_test))[1]
>>> ensemble_test["rf_output_one"] =
pd.DataFrame(clf3_rf_fit.predict_proba( x_test))[1]
```

```
>>> ensemble_test["adb_output_one"] =
pd.DataFrame(clf4_adabst_fit.predict_proba( x_test))[1]
>>> coefs =  meta_logit_fit.coef_
>>> ensemble_test = pd.DataFrame()
>>> ensemble_test["log_output_one"] =
pd.DataFrame(clf1_logreg_fit.predict_proba( x_test))[1]
>>> ensemble_test["dtr_output_one"] =
pd.DataFrame(clf2_dt_fit.predict_proba( x_test))[1]
>>> ensemble_test["rf_output_one"] =
pd.DataFrame(clf3_rf_fit.predict_proba( x_test))[1]
>>> ensemble_test["adb_output_one"] =
pd.DataFrame(clf4_adabst_fit.predict_proba( x_test))[1]
>>> print ("\n\nEnsemble of Models - Test Confusion
Matrix\n\n",pd.crosstab(
ensemble_test['Attrition_ind'],ensemble_test['all_one'],rownames =
["Actuall"], colnames = ["Predicted"]))
>>> print ("\nEnsemble of Models - Test accuracy",round(accuracy_score
(ensemble_test['Attrition_ind'],ensemble_test['all_one']),3))
>>> print ("\nEnsemble of Models - Test Classification Report\n",
classification_report( ensemble_test['Attrition_ind'],
ensemble_test['all_one']))
```

```
Ensemble of Models - Test Confusion Matrix

Predicted    0   1
Actuall
0          367  13
1           42  19

Ensemble of Models - Test accuracy 0.875

Ensemble of Models - Test Classification Report
            precision    recall  f1-score   support

         0       0.90      0.97      0.93       380
         1       0.59      0.31      0.41        61

avg / total       0.86      0.88      0.86       441
```

Though code prints **Train**, **Test accuracies**, **Confusion Matrix**, and **Classification Reports**, we have not shown them here due to space constraints. Users are advised to run and check the results on their computers. Test accuracy came as *87.5%*, which is the highest value (the same as gradient boosting results). However, by careful tuning, ensembles do give much better results based on adding better models and removing models with low weights:

```
>>> coefs = meta_logit_fit.coef_
>>> print ("Co-efficients for LR, DT, RF and AB are:",coefs)
```

```
Co-efficients for LR, DT, RF & AB are: [[ 0.89396453  1.10803139  6.58847747 -8.25118547]]
```

It seems that, surprisingly, AdaBoost is dragging down performance of the ensemble. A tip is to either change the parameters used in AdaBoost and rerun the entire exercise, or remove the AdaBoost classifier from the ensemble and rerun the ensemble step to see if there is any improvement in ensemble test accuracy, precision, and recall values:

R Code for Ensemble of Ensembles with different Classifiers Applied on HR Attrition Data:

```
# Ensemble of Ensembles with different type of Classifiers setwd
("D:\\Book writing\\Codes\\Chapter 4")

hrattr_data = read.csv("WA_Fn-UseC_-HR-Employee-Attrition.csv")
str(hrattr_data)
summary(hrattr_data)

hrattr_data$Attrition_ind = 0;
hrattr_data$Attrition_ind[hrattr_data$Attrition=="Yes"]=1
hrattr_data$Attrition_ind = as.factor(hrattr_data$Attrition_ind)

remove_cols = c ("EmployeeCount","EmployeeNumber","Over18",
"StandardHours","Attrition")
hrattr_data_new = hrattr_data[,!(names(hrattr_data) %in% remove_cols)]

set.seed(123)
numrow = nrow(hrattr_data_new)
trnind = sample(1:numrow,size = as.integer(0.7*numrow))
train_data = hrattr_data_new[trnind,]
test_data = hrattr_data_new[-trnind,]

# Ensemble of Ensembles with different type of Classifiers
train_data$Attrition_ind = as.factor(train_data$Attrition_ind)

# Classifier 1 - Logistic Regression
glm_fit = glm(Attrition_ind ~.,family = "binomial",data = train_data)
glm_probs = predict(glm_fit,newdata = train_data,type = "response")

# Classifier 2 - Decision Tree classifier
library(C50)
dtree_fit = C5.0(train_data[-31],train_data$Attrition_ind,
          control = C5.0Control(minCases = 1))
dtree_probs = predict(dtree_fit,newdata = train_data,type = "prob")[,2]

# Classifier 3 - Random Forest
library(randomForest)
rf_fit = randomForest(Attrition_ind~., data = train_data,mtry=6,maxnodes=
64,ntree=5000,nodesize = 1)
rf_probs = predict(rf_fit,newdata = train_data,type = "prob")[,2]

# Classifier 4 - Adaboost
```

```
ada_fit = C5.0(train_data[-31],train_data$Attrition_ind,trails =
5000,control = C5.0Control(minCases = 1))
ada_probs = predict(ada_fit,newdata = train_data,type = "prob")[,2]

# Ensemble of Models
ensemble = data.frame(glm_probs,dtree_probs,rf_probs,ada_probs)
ensemble = cbind(ensemble,train_data$Attrition_ind)
names(ensemble)[5] = "Attrition_ind"
rownames(ensemble) <- 1:nrow(ensemble)

# Meta-classifier on top of individual classifiers
meta_clf = glm(Attrition_ind~.,data = ensemble,family = "binomial")
meta_probs = predict(meta_clf, ensemble,type = "response")

ensemble$pred_class = 0
ensemble$pred_class[meta_probs>0.5]=1

# Train confusion and accuracy metrics
tr_y_pred = ensemble$pred_class
tr_y_act = train_data$Attrition_ind;ts_y_act = test_data$Attrition_ind
tr_tble = table(tr_y_act,tr_y_pred)
print(paste("Ensemble - Train Confusion Matrix"))
print(tr_tble)

tr_acc = accrcy(tr_y_act,tr_y_pred)
print(paste("Ensemble Train accuracy:",tr_acc))

# Now verifing on test data
glm_probs = predict(glm_fit,newdata = test_data,type = "response")
dtree_probs = predict(dtree_fit,newdata = test_data,type = "prob")[,2]
rf_probs = predict(rf_fit,newdata = test_data,type = "prob")[,2]
ada_probs = predict(ada_fit,newdata = test_data,type = "prob")[,2]

ensemble_test = data.frame(glm_probs,dtree_probs,rf_probs,ada_probs)
ensemble_test = cbind(ensemble_test,test_data$Attrition_ind)
names(ensemble_test)[5] = "Attrition_ind"

rownames(ensemble_test) <- 1:nrow(ensemble_test)
meta_test_probs = predict(meta_clf,newdata = ensemble_test,type =
"response")
ensemble_test$pred_class = 0
ensemble_test$pred_class[meta_test_probs>0.5]=1

# Test confusion and accuracy metrics
ts_y_pred = ensemble_test$pred_class
ts_tble = table(ts_y_act,ts_y_pred)
print(paste("Ensemble - Test Confusion Matrix"))
print(ts_tble)
```

```
ts_acc = accrcy(ts_y_act,ts_y_pred)
print(paste("Ensemble Test accuracy:",ts_acc))
```

Ensemble of ensembles with bootstrap samples using a single type of classifier

In this methodology, bootstrap samples are drawn from training data and, each time, separate models will be fitted (individual models could be decision trees, random forest, and so on) on the drawn sample, and all these results are combined at the end to create an ensemble. This method suits dealing with highly flexible models where variance reduction will still improve performance:

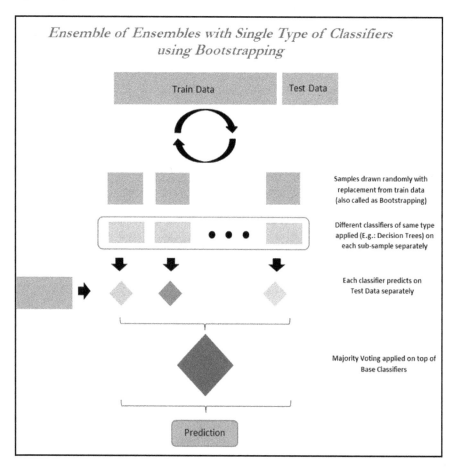

In the following example, AdaBoost is used as a base classifier and the results of individual AdaBoost models are combined using the bagging classifier to generate final outcomes. Nonetheless, each AdaBoost is made up of decision trees with a depth of 1 (decision stumps). Here, we would like to show that classifier inside classifier inside classifier is possible (sounds like the Inception movie though!):

```
# Ensemble of Ensembles - by applying bagging on simple classifier
>>> from sklearn.tree import DecisionTreeClassifier
>>> from sklearn.ensemble import BaggingClassifier
>>> from sklearn.ensemble import AdaBoostClassifier
>>> clwght = {0:0.3,1:0.7}
```

The following is the base classifier (decision stump) used in the AdaBoost classifier:

```
>>> eoe_dtree =
DecisionTreeClassifier(criterion='gini',max_depth=1,class_weight = clwght)
```

Each AdaBoost classifier consists of 500 decision trees with a learning rate of 0.05:

```
>>> eoe_adabst_fit = AdaBoostClassifier(base_estimator= eoe_dtree,
n_estimators=500,learning_rate=0.05,random_state=42)
>>> eoe_adabst_fit.fit(x_train, y_train)

>>> print ("\nAdaBoost - Train Confusion Matrix\n\n",pd.crosstab(y_train,
eoe_adabst_fit.predict(x_train),rownames = ["Actuall"],colnames =
["Predicted"]))
>>> print ("\nAdaBoost - Train accuracy",round(accuracy_score(y_train,
eoe_adabst_fit.predict(x_train)),3))
>>> print ("\nAdaBoost - Train Classification
Report\n",classification_report(y_train, eoe_adabst_fit.predict(x_train)))

>>> print ("\n\nAdaBoost - Test Confusion Matrix\n\n",pd.crosstab(y_test,
eoe_adabst_fit.predict(x_test),rownames = ["Actuall"],colnames =
["Predicted"]))
>>> print ("\nAdaBoost - Test accuracy",round(accuracy_score(y_test,
eoe_adabst_fit.predict(x_test)),3))
>>> print ("\nAdaBoost - Test Classification
Report\n",classification_report(y_test, eoe_adabst_fit.predict(x_test)))
```

The bagging classifier consists of 50 AdaBoost classifiers to ensemble the ensembles:

```
>>> bag_fit = BaggingClassifier(base_estimator=
eoe_adabst_fit,n_estimators=50,
max_samples=1.0,max_features=1.0, bootstrap=True,
bootstrap_features=False,n_jobs=-1,random_state=42)
>>> bag_fit.fit(x_train, y_train)
>>> print ("\nEnsemble of AdaBoost - Train Confusion
Matrix\n\n",pd.crosstab( y_train,bag_fit.predict(x_train),rownames =
```

```
["Actuall"],colnames = ["Predicted"]))
>>> print ("\nEnsemble of AdaBoost - Train
accuracy",round(accuracy_score(y_train, bag_fit.predict(x_train)),3))
>>> print ("\nEnsemble of AdaBoost - Train Classification Report\n",
classification_report( y_train,bag_fit.predict(x_train)))

>>> print ("\n\nEnsemble of AdaBoost - Test Confusion
Matrix\n\n",pd.crosstab(y_test, bag_fit.predict(x_test),rownames =
["Actuall"],colnames = ["Predicted"]))
>>> print ("\nEnsemble of AdaBoost - Test
accuracy",round(accuracy_score(y_test,bag_fit.predict(x_test)),3))
>>> print ("\nEnsemble of AdaBoost - Test Classification Report\n",
classification_report(y_test,bag_fit.predict(x_test)))
```

```
Ensemble of AdaBoost - Train Confusion Matrix

Predicted     0    1
Actuall
0           824   29
1            69  107

Ensemble of AdaBoost - Train accuracy 0.905

Ensemble of AdaBoost  - Train Classification Report
             precision    recall  f1-score   support

          0       0.92      0.97      0.94       853
          1       0.79      0.61      0.69       176

avg / total        0.90      0.90      0.90      1029




Ensemble of AdaBoost - Test Confusion Matrix

Predicted     0   1
Actuall
0           359  21
1            36  25

Ensemble of AdaBoost - Test accuracy 0.871

Ensemble of AdaBoost - Test Classification Report
             precision    recall  f1-score   support

          0       0.91      0.94      0.93       380
          1       0.54      0.41      0.47        61

avg / total        0.86      0.87      0.86       441
```

The results of the ensemble on AdaBoost have shown some improvements, in which the test accuracy obtained is 87.1%, which is almost to that of gradient boosting at 87.5%, which is the best value we have seen so far. However, the number of 1's identified is 25 here, which is greater than Gradient Boosting. Hence, it has been proven that an ensemble of ensembles does work! Unfortunately, these types of functions are not available in R software, hence we are not writing the equivalent R-code here.

Summary

In this chapter, you have learned the complete details about tree-based models, which are currently the most used in the industry, including individual decision trees with grid search and an ensemble of trees such as bagging, random forest, boosting (including AdaBoost, gradient boost and XGBoost), and finally, ensemble of ensembles, also known as model stacking, for further improving accuracy by reducing variance errors by aggregating results further. In model stacking, you have learned how to determine the weights for each model, so that decisions can be made as to which model to keep in the final results to obtain the best possible accuracy.

In the next chapter, you will be learning k-nearest neighbors and Naive Bayes, which are less computationally intensive than tree-based models. The Naive Bayes model will be explained with an NLP use case. In fact, Naive Bayes and SVM are often used where variables (number of dimensions) are very high in number to classify.

K-Nearest Neighbors and Naive Bayes

3

In the previous chapter, we have learned about computationally intensive methods. In contrast, this chapter discusses the simple methods to balance it out! We will be covering the two techniques, called **k-nearest neighbors** (**KNN**)and Naive Bayes here. Before touching on KNN, we explained the issue with the curse of dimensionality with a simulated example. Subsequently, breast cancer medical examples have been utilized to predict whether the cancer is malignant or benign using KNN. In the final section of the chapter, Naive Bayes has been explained with spam/ham classification, which also involves the application of the **natural language processing** (**NLP**) techniques consisting of the following basic preprocessing and modeling steps:

- Punctuation removal
- Word tokenization and lowercase conversion
- Stopwords removal
- Stemming
- Lemmatization with POS tagging
- Conversion of words into TF-IDF to create numerical representation of words
- Application of the Naive Bayes model on TF-IDF vectors to predict if the message is either spam or ham on both train and test data

K-nearest neighbors

K-nearest neighbors is a non-parametric machine learning model in which the model memorizes the training observation for classifying the unseen test data. It can also be called instance-based learning. This model is often termed as lazy learning, as it does not learn anything during the training phase like regression, random forest, and so on. Instead, it starts working only during the testing/evaluation phase to compare the given test observations with the nearest training observations, which will take significant time in comparing each test data point. Hence, this technique is not efficient on big data; also, performance does deteriorate when the number of variables is high due to the **curse of dimensionality**.

KNN voter example

KNN is explained better with the following short example. The objective is to predict the party for which voter will vote based on their neighborhood, precisely geolocation (latitude and longitude). Here we assume that we can identify the potential voter to which political party they would be voting based on majority voters did vote for that particular party in that vicinity so that they have a high probability to vote for the majority party. However, tuning the k-value (number to consider, among which majority should be counted) is the million-dollar question (as same as any machine learning algorithm):

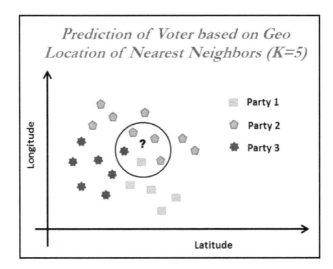

In the preceding diagram, we can see that the voter of the study will vote for **Party 2**. As within the vicinity, one neighbor has voted for **Party 1** and the other voter voted for **Party 3**. But three voters voted for **Party 2**. In fact, by this way, KNN solves any given classification problem. Regression problems are solved by taking mean of its neighbors within the given circle or vicinity or k-value.

Curse of dimensionality

KNN completely depends on distance. Hence, it is worth studying about the curse of dimensionality to understand when KNN deteriorates its predictive power with the increase in the number of variables required for prediction. This is an obvious fact that high-dimensional spaces are vast. Points in high-dimensional spaces tend to be dispersing from each other more compared with the points in low-dimensional space. Though there are many ways to check the curve of dimensionality, here we are using uniform random values between zero and one generated for 1D, 2D, and 3D space to validate this hypothesis.

In the following lines of codes, the mean distance between 1,000 observations has been calculated with the change in dimensions. It is apparent that with the increase in dimensions, distance between points increases logarithmically, which gives us the hint that we need to have an exponential increase in data points with increase in dimensions in order to make machine learning algorithms work correctly:

```
>>> import numpy as np
>>> import pandas as pd

# KNN Curse of Dimensionality
>>> import random,math
```

The following code generates random numbers between zero and one from uniform distribution with the given dimension, which is equivalent of length of array or list:

```
>>> def random_point_gen(dimension):
...     return [random.random() for _ in range(dimension)]
```

The following function calculates root mean sum of squares of Euclidean distances (2-norm) between points by taking the difference between points and sum the squares and finally takes the square root of total distance:

```
>>> def distance(v,w):
...     vec_sub = [v_i-w_i for v_i,w_i in zip(v,w)]
...     sum_of_sqrs = sum(v_i*v_i for v_i in vec_sub)
...     return math.sqrt(sum_of_sqrs)
```

Both dimension and number of pairs are utilized for calculating the distances with the following code:

```
>>> def random_distances_comparison(dimension, number_pairs):
...         return
[distance(random_point_gen(dimension), random_point_gen(dimension))
            for _ in range(number_pairs)]

>>> def mean(x):
...         return sum(x) / len(x)
```

The experiment has been done by changing dimensions from 1 to 201 with an increase of 5 dimensions to check the increase in distance:

```
>>> dimensions = range(1, 201, 5)
```

Both minimum and average distances have been calculated to check, however, both illustrate the similar story:

```
>>> avg_distances = []
>>> min_distances = []

>>> dummyarray = np.empty((20,4))
>>> dist_vals = pd.DataFrame(dummyarray)
>>> dist_vals.columns =
["Dimension","Min_Distance","Avg_Distance","Min/Avg_Distance"]

>>> random.seed(34)
>>> i = 0
>>> for dims in dimensions:
...         distances = random_distances_comparison(dims, 1000)
...         avg_distances.append(mean(distances))
...         min_distances.append(min(distances))
...         dist_vals.loc[i,"Dimension"] = dims
...         dist_vals.loc[i,"Min_Distance"] = min(distances)
...         dist_vals.loc[i,"Avg_Distance"] = mean(distances)
...         dist_vals.loc[i,"Min/Avg_Distance"] =
min(distances)/mean(distances)
...         print(dims, min(distances), mean(distances), min(distances)*1.0 /
mean( distances))
...         i = i+1

# Plotting Average distances for Various Dimensions
>>> import matplotlib.pyplot as plt
>>> plt.figure()
>>> plt.xlabel('Dimensions')
>>> plt.ylabel('Avg. Distance')
>>> plt.plot(dist_vals["Dimension"],dist_vals["Avg_Distance"])
```

```
>>> plt.legend(loc='best')

>>> plt.show()
```

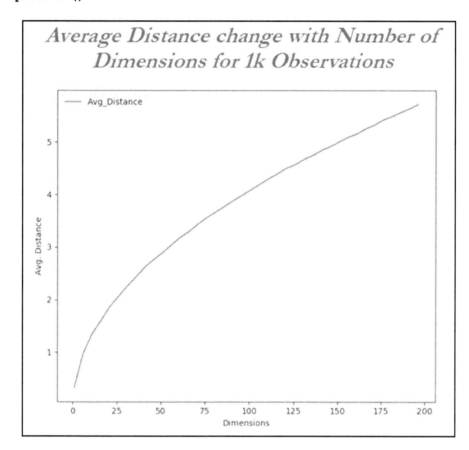

From the preceding graph, it is proved that with the increase in dimensions, mean distance increases logarithmically. Hence the higher the dimensions, the more data is needed to overcome the curse of dimensionality!

Curse of dimensionality with 1D, 2D, and 3D example

A quick analysis has been done to see how distance 60 random points are expanding with the increase in dimensionality. Initially, random points are drawn for one-dimension:

```
# 1-Dimension Plot
>>> import numpy as np
```

```
>>> import pandas as pd
>>> import matplotlib.pyplot as plt

>>> one_d_data = np.random.rand(60,1)
>>> one_d_data_df = pd.DataFrame(one_d_data)
>>> one_d_data_df.columns = ["1D_Data"]
>>> one_d_data_df["height"] = 1

>>> plt.figure()
>>> plt.scatter(one_d_data_df['1D_Data'],one_d_data_df["height"])
>>> plt.yticks([])
>>> plt.xlabel("1-D points")
>>> plt.show()
```

If we observe the following graph, all 60 data points are very nearby in one-dimension:

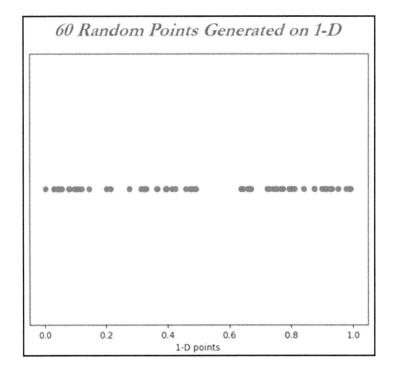

Here we are repeating the same experiment in a 2D space, by taking 60 random numbers with x and y coordinate space and plotted them visually:

```
# 2- Dimensions Plot
>>> two_d_data = np.random.rand(60,2)
>>> two_d_data_df = pd.DataFrame(two_d_data)
>>> two_d_data_df.columns = ["x_axis","y_axis"]

>>> plt.figure()
>>> plt.scatter(two_d_data_df['x_axis'],two_d_data_df["y_axis"])
>>> plt.xlabel("x_axis");plt.ylabel("y_axis")
>>> plt.show()
```

By observing the 2D graph we can see that more gaps have been appearing for the same 60 data points:

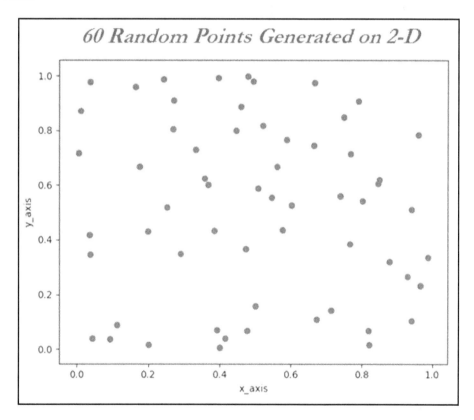

Finally, 60 data points are drawn for 3D space. We can see a further increase in spaces, which is very apparent. This has proven to us visually by now that with the increase in dimensions, it creates a lot of space, which makes a classifier weak to detect the signal:

```
# 3- Dimensions Plot
>>> three_d_data = np.random.rand(60,3)
>>> three_d_data_df = pd.DataFrame(three_d_data)
>>> three_d_data_df.columns = ["x_axis","y_axis","z_axis"]

>>> from mpl_toolkits.mplot3d import Axes3D
>>> fig = plt.figure()
>>> ax = fig.add_subplot(111, projection='3d')
>>>
ax.scatter(three_d_data_df['x_axis'],three_d_data_df["y_axis"],three_d_data
_df ["z_axis"])
>>> plt.show()
```

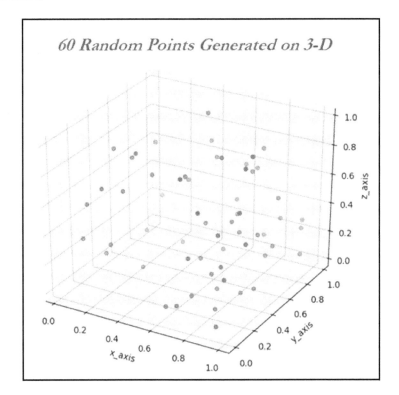

60 Random Points Generated on 3-D

KNN classifier with breast cancer Wisconsin data example

Breast cancer data has been utilized from the UCI machine learning repository http://archive.ics.uci.edu/ml/datasets/Breast+Cancer+Wisconsin+%28Diagnostic%29 for illustration purposes. Here the task is to find whether the cancer is malignant or benign based on various collected features such as clump thickness and so on using the KNN classifier:

```
# KNN Classifier - Breast Cancer
>>> import numpy as np
>>> import pandas as pd
>>> from sklearn.metrics import accuracy_score,classification_report
>>> breast_cancer = pd.read_csv("Breast_Cancer_Wisconsin.csv")
```

The following are the first few rows to show how the data looks like. The Class value has class 2 and 4. Value 2 and 4 represent benign and malignant class, respectively. Whereas all the other variables do vary between value 1 and 10, which are very much categorical in nature:

ID_Number	Clump_Thickness	Unif_Cell_Size	Unif_Cell_Shape	Marg_Adhesion	Single_Epith_Cell_Size	Bare_Nuclei	Bland_Chromatin	Normal_Nucleoli	Mitoses	Class
1000025	5	1	1	1	2	1	3	1	1	2
1002945	5	4	4	5	7	10	3	2	1	2
1015425	3	1	1	1	2	2	3	1	1	2
1016277	6	8	8	1	3	4	3	7	1	2
1017023	4	1	1	3	2	1	3	1	1	2

Only the Bare_Nuclei variable has some missing values, here we are replacing them with the most frequent value (category value 1) in the following code:

```
>>> breast_cancer['Bare_Nuclei'] =
breast_cancer['Bare_Nuclei'].replace('?', np.NAN)
>>> breast_cancer['Bare_Nuclei'] =
breast_cancer['Bare_Nuclei'].fillna(breast_cancer[
'Bare_Nuclei'].value_counts().index[0])
```

Use the following code to convert the classes to a 0 and 1 indicator for using in the classifier:

```
>>> breast_cancer['Cancer_Ind'] = 0
>>> breast_cancer.loc[breast_cancer['Class']==4,'Cancer_Ind'] = 1
```

In the following code, we are dropping non-value added variables from analysis:

```
>>> x_vars = breast_cancer.drop(['ID_Number','Class','Cancer_Ind'],axis=1)
>>> y_var = breast_cancer['Cancer_Ind']
>>> from sklearn.preprocessing import StandardScaler
>>> x_vars_stdscle = StandardScaler().fit_transform(x_vars.values)
>>> from sklearn.model_selection import train_test_split
```

As KNN is very sensitive to distances, here we are standardizing all the columns before applying algorithms:

```
>>> x_vars_stdscle_df = pd.DataFrame(x_vars_stdscle, index=x_vars.index,
columns=x_vars.columns)
>>> x_train,x_test,y_train,y_test =
train_test_split(x_vars_stdscle_df,y_var, train_size = 0.7,random_state=42)
```

KNN classifier is being applied with neighbor value of 3 and p value indicates it is 2-norm, also known as Euclidean distance for computing classes:

```
>>> from sklearn.neighbors import KNeighborsClassifier
>>> knn_fit = KNeighborsClassifier(n_neighbors=3,p=2,metric='minkowski')
>>> knn_fit.fit(x_train,y_train)

>>> print ("\nK-Nearest Neighbors - Train Confusion
Matrix\n\n",pd.crosstab(y_train, knn_fit.predict(x_train),rownames =
["Actuall"],colnames = ["Predicted"]) )
>>> print ("\nK-Nearest Neighbors - Train
accuracy:",round(accuracy_score(y_train, knn_fit.predict(x_train)),3))
>>> print ("\nK-Nearest Neighbors - Train Classification Report\n",
classification_report( y_train,knn_fit.predict(x_train)))

>>> print ("\n\nK-Nearest Neighbors - Test Confusion
Matrix\n\n",pd.crosstab(y_test, knn_fit.predict(x_test),rownames =
["Actuall"],colnames = ["Predicted"]))
>>> print ("\nK-Nearest Neighbors - Test accuracy:",round(accuracy_score(
y_test,knn_fit.predict(x_test)),3))
>>> print ("\nK-Nearest Neighbors - Test Classification Report\n",
classification_report(y_test,knn_fit.predict(x_test)))
```

```
K-Nearest Neighbors - Train Confusion Matrix

 Predicted    0    1
Actuall
0          309    6
1            4  170

K-Nearest Neighbors - Train accuracy: 0.98

K-Nearest Neighbors - Train Classification Report
             precision    recall  f1-score   support

          0       0.99      0.98      0.98       315
          1       0.97      0.98      0.97       174

avg / total       0.98      0.98      0.98       489



K-Nearest Neighbors - Test Confusion Matrix

 Predicted    0    1
Actuall
0          141    2
1            3   64

K-Nearest Neighbors - Test accuracy: 0.976

K-Nearest Neighbors - Test Classification Report
             precision    recall  f1-score   support

          0       0.98      0.99      0.98       143
          1       0.97      0.96      0.96        67

avg / total       0.98      0.98      0.98       210
```

From the results, it is appearing that KNN is working very well in classifying malignant and benign classes well, obtaining test accuracy of 97.6 percent with 96 percent of recall on malignant class. The only deficiency of KNN classifier would be, it is computationally intensive during test phase, as each test observation will be compared with all the available observations in train data, which practically KNN does not learn a thing from training data. Hence, we are also calling it a lazy classifier!

The R code for KNN classifier is as follows:

```
# KNN Classifier
setwd("D:\\Book writing\\Codes\\Chapter 5")
breast_cancer = read.csv("Breast_Cancer_Wisconsin.csv")

# Column Bare_Nuclei have some missing values with "?" in place, we are
replacing with median values
# As Bare_Nuclei is discrete variable
breast_cancer$Bare_Nuclei = as.character(breast_cancer$Bare_Nuclei)
breast_cancer$Bare_Nuclei[breast_cancer$Bare_Nuclei=="?"] =
median(breast_cancer$Bare_Nuclei,na.rm = TRUE)
breast_cancer$Bare_Nuclei = as.integer(breast_cancer$Bare_Nuclei)
# Classes are 2 & 4 for benign & malignant respectively, we # have
converted #
to zero-one problem, as it is easy to convert to work # around with models
breast_cancer$Cancer_Ind = 0
breast_cancer$Cancer_Ind[breast_cancer$Class==4]=1
breast_cancer$Cancer_Ind = as.factor( breast_cancer$Cancer_Ind)

# We have removed unique id number from modeling as unique # numbers does
not provide value in modeling
# In addition, original class variable also will be removed # as the same
has been replaced with derived variable

remove_cols = c("ID_Number","Class")
breast_cancer_new = breast_cancer[,!(names(breast_cancer) %in%
remove_cols)]

# Setting seed value for producing repetitive results
# 70-30 split has been made on the data

set.seed(123)
numrow = nrow(breast_cancer_new)
trnind = sample(1:numrow,size = as.integer(0.7*numrow))
train_data = breast_cancer_new[trnind,]
test_data = breast_cancer_new[-trnind,]

# Following is classical code for computing accuracy, # precision & recall

frac_trzero = (table(train_data$Cancer_Ind)[[1]])/nrow(train_data)
frac_trone = (table(train_data$Cancer_Ind)[[2]])/nrow(train_data)

frac_tszero = (table(test_data$Cancer_Ind)[[1]])/nrow(test_data)
frac_tsone = (table(test_data$Cancer_Ind)[[2]])/nrow(test_data)

prec_zero <- function(act,pred){ tble = table(act,pred)
return( round( tble[1,1]/(tble[1,1]+tble[2,1]),4) ) }
```

```
prec_one <- function(act,pred){ tble = table(act,pred)
return( round( tble[2,2]/(tble[2,2]+tble[1,2]),4) ) }

recl_zero <- function(act,pred){tble = table(act,pred)
return( round( tble[1,1]/(tble[1,1]+tble[1,2]),4) ) }

recl_one <- function(act,pred){ tble = table(act,pred)
return( round( tble[2,2]/(tble[2,2]+tble[2,1]),4) ) }

accrcy <- function(act,pred){ tble = table(act,pred)
return( round((tble[1,1]+tble[2,2])/sum(tble),4)) }

# Importing Class package in which KNN function do present library(class)

# Choosing sample k-value as 3 & apply on train & test data # respectively

k_value = 3
tr_y_pred = knn(train_data,train_data,train_data$Cancer_Ind,k=k_value)
ts_y_pred = knn(train_data,test_data,train_data$Cancer_Ind,k=k_value)

# Calculating confusion matrix, accuracy, precision & # recall on train
data

tr_y_act = train_data$Cancer_Ind;ts_y_act = test_data$Cancer_Ind
tr_tble = table(tr_y_act,tr_y_pred)
print(paste("Train Confusion Matrix"))
print(tr_tble)

tr_acc = accrcy(tr_y_act,tr_y_pred)
trprec_zero = prec_zero(tr_y_act,tr_y_pred); trrecl_zero =
recl_zero(tr_y_act,tr_y_pred)
trprec_one = prec_one(tr_y_act,tr_y_pred); trrecl_one =
recl_one(tr_y_act,tr_y_pred)
trprec_ovll = trprec_zero *frac_trzero + trprec_one*frac_trone
trrecl_ovll = trrecl_zero *frac_trzero + trrecl_one*frac_trone

print(paste("KNN Train accuracy:",tr_acc))
print(paste("KNN - Train Classification Report"))
print(paste("Zero_Precision",trprec_zero,"Zero_Recall",trrecl_zero))
print(paste("One_Precision",trprec_one,"One_Recall",trrecl_one))
print(paste("Overall_Precision",round(trprec_ovll,4),"Overall_Recall",round
(trrecl_ovll,4)))

# Calculating confusion matrix, accuracy, precision & # recall on test data

ts_tble = table(ts_y_act, ts_y_pred)
print(paste("Test Confusion Matrix"))
print(ts_tble)
```

```
ts_acc = accrcy(ts_y_act,ts_y_pred)
tsprec_zero = prec_zero(ts_y_act,ts_y_pred); tsrecl_zero =
recl_zero(ts_y_act,ts_y_pred)
tsprec_one = prec_one(ts_y_act,ts_y_pred); tsrecl_one =
recl_one(ts_y_act,ts_y_pred)

tsprec_ovll = tsprec_zero *frac_tszero + tsprec_one*frac_tsone
tsrecl_ovll = tsrecl_zero *frac_tszero + tsrecl_one*frac_tsone

print(paste("KNN Test accuracy:",ts_acc))
print(paste("KNN - Test Classification Report"))
print(paste("Zero_Precision",tsprec_zero,"Zero_Recall",tsrecl_zero))
print(paste("One_Precision",tsprec_one,"One_Recall",tsrecl_one))
print(paste("Overall_Precision",round(tsprec_ovll,4),"Overall_Recall",round
(tsrecl_ovll,4)))
```

Tuning of k-value in KNN classifier

In the previous section, we just checked with only the k-value of three. Actually, in any machine learning algorithm, we need to tune the knobs to check where the better performance can be obtained. In the case of KNN, the only tuning parameter is k-value. Hence, in the following code, we are determining the best k-value with grid search:

```
# Tuning of K- value for Train & Test data
>>> dummyarray = np.empty((5,3))
>>> k_valchart = pd.DataFrame(dummyarray)
>>> k_valchart.columns = ["K_value","Train_acc","Test_acc"]

>>> k_vals = [1,2,3,4,5]

>>> for i in range(len(k_vals)):
...      knn_fit =
KNeighborsClassifier(n_neighbors=k_vals[i],p=2,metric='minkowski')
...      knn_fit.fit(x_train,y_train)

...      print ("\nK-value",k_vals[i])
...      tr_accscore =
round(accuracy_score(y_train,knn_fit.predict(x_train)),3)
...      print ("\nK-Nearest Neighbors - Train Confusion
Matrix\n\n",pd.crosstab( y_train, knn_fit.predict(x_train),rownames =
["Actuall"],colnames = ["Predicted"]) )
...      print ("\nK-Nearest Neighbors - Train accuracy:",tr_accscore)
...      print ("\nK-Nearest Neighbors - Train Classification Report\n",
classification_report(y_train,knn_fit.predict(x_train)))

...      ts_accscore =
```

```
round(accuracy_score(y_test,knn_fit.predict(x_test)),3)
...     print ("\n\nK-Nearest Neighbors - Test Confusion
Matrix\n\n",pd.crosstab( y_test,knn_fit.predict(x_test),rownames =
["Actuall"],colnames = ["Predicted"]))
...     print ("\nK-Nearest Neighbors - Test accuracy:",ts_accscore)
...     print ("\nK-Nearest Neighbors - Test Classification
Report\n",classification_report(y_test,knn_fit.predict(x_test)))
...     k_valchart.loc[i, 'K_value'] = k_vals[i]
...     k_valchart.loc[i, 'Train_acc'] = tr_accscore
...     k_valchart.loc[i, 'Test_acc'] = ts_accscore

# Ploting accuracies over varied K-values
>>> import matplotlib.pyplot as plt
>>> plt.figure()
>>> plt.xlabel('K-value')
>>> plt.ylabel('Accuracy')
>>> plt.plot(k_valchart["K_value"],k_valchart["Train_acc"])
>>> plt.plot(k_valchart["K_value"],k_valchart["Test_acc"])

>>> plt.axis([0.9,5, 0.92, 1.005])
>>> plt.xticks([1,2,3,4,5])

>>> for a,b in zip(k_valchart["K_value"],k_valchart["Train_acc"]):
...     plt.text(a, b, str(b),fontsize=10)

>>> for a,b in zip(k_valchart["K_value"],k_valchart["Test_acc"]):
...     plt.text(a, b, str(b),fontsize=10)
>>> plt.legend(loc='upper right')
>>> plt.show()
```

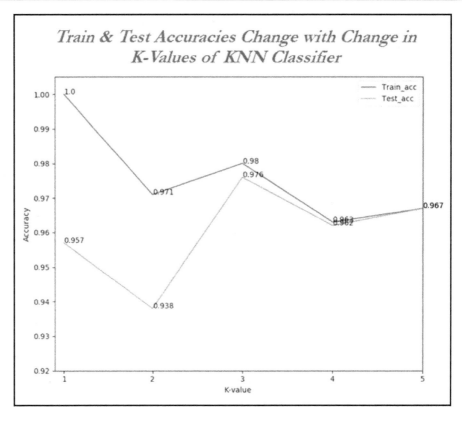

It appears that with less value of k-value, it has more overfitting problems due to the very high value of accuracy on train data and less on test data, with the increase in k-value more the train and test accuracies are converging and becoming more robust. This phenomenon illustrates the typical machine learning phenomenon. As for further analysis, readers are encouraged to try k-values higher than five and see how train and test accuracies are changing. The R code for tuning of k-value in KNN classifier is as follows:

```
# Tuning of K-value on Train & Test Data
k_valchart = data.frame(matrix( nrow=5, ncol=3))
colnames(k_valchart) = c("K_value","Train_acc","Test_acc")
k_vals = c(1,2,3,4,5)

i = 1
for (kv in k_vals) {
  tr_y_pred = knn(train_data,train_data,train_data$Cancer_Ind,k=kv)
  ts_y_pred = knn(train_data,test_data,train_data$Cancer_Ind,k=kv)
  tr_y_act = train_data$Cancer_Ind;ts_y_act = test_data$Cancer_Ind
  tr_tble = table(tr_y_act,tr_y_pred)
  print(paste("Train Confusion Matrix"))
```

```
  print(tr_tble)
  tr_acc = accrcy(tr_y_act,tr_y_pred)
  trprec_zero = prec_zero(tr_y_act,tr_y_pred); trrecl_zero =
recl_zero(tr_y_act, tr_y_pred)
  trprec_one = prec_one(tr_y_act,tr_y_pred); trrecl_one =
recl_one(tr_y_act,tr_y_pred)
  trprec_ovll = trprec_zero *frac_trzero + trprec_one*frac_trone
  trrecl_ovll = trrecl_zero *frac_trzero + trrecl_one*frac_trone
  print(paste("KNN Train accuracy:",tr_acc))
  print(paste("KNN - Train Classification Report"))

print(paste("Zero_Precision",trprec_zero,"Zero_Recall",trrecl_zero))
print(paste("One_Precision",trprec_one,"One_Recall",trrecl_one))
print(paste("Overall_Precision",round(trprec_ovll,4),"Overall_Recall",round
(trrecl_ovll,4)))
  ts_tble = table(ts_y_act,ts_y_pred)
  print(paste("Test Confusion Matrix"))
  print(ts_tble)
  ts_acc = accrcy(ts_y_act,ts_y_pred)
  tsprec_zero = prec_zero(ts_y_act,ts_y_pred); tsrecl_zero =
recl_zero(ts_y_act,ts_y_pred)
  tsprec_one = prec_one(ts_y_act,ts_y_pred); tsrecl_one =
recl_one(ts_y_act,ts_y_pred)
  tsprec_ovll = tsprec_zero *frac_tszero + tsprec_one*frac_tsone
  tsrecl_ovll = tsrecl_zero *frac_tszero + tsrecl_one*frac_tsone

  print(paste("KNN Test accuracy:",ts_acc))
  print(paste("KNN - Test Classification Report"))

print(paste("Zero_Precision",tsprec_zero,"Zero_Recall",tsrecl_zero))
print(paste("One_Precision",tsprec_one,"One_Recall",tsrecl_one))
print(paste("Overall_Precision",round(tsprec_ovll,4),"Overall_Recall",round
(tsrecl_ovll,4)))

  k_valchart[i,1] =kv
  k_valchart[i,2] =tr_acc
  k_valchart[i,3] =ts_acc i = i+1 }
# Plotting the graph
library(ggplot2)
library(grid)
ggplot(k_valchart, aes(K_value))
+ geom_line(aes(y = Train_acc, colour = "Train_Acc")) +
geom_line(aes(y = Test_acc, colour = "Test_Acc"))+
labs(x="K_value",y="Accuracy") +
geom_text(aes(label = Train_acc, y = Train_acc), size = 3)+
geom_text(aes(label = Test_acc, y = Test_acc), size = 3)
```

Naive Bayes

Bayes algorithm concept is quite old and exists from the 18th century. Thomas Bayes developed the foundational mathematical principles for determining the probability of unknown events from the known events. For example, if all apples are red in color and average diameter would be about 4 inches then, if at random one fruit is selected from the basket with red color and diameter of 3.7 inches, what is the probability that the particular fruit would be an apple? Naive term does assume independence of particular features in a class with respect to others. In this case, there would be no dependency between color and diameter. This independence assumption makes the Naive Bayes classifier most effective in terms of computational ease for particular tasks such as email classification based on words in which high dimensions of vocab do exist, even after assuming independence between features. Naive Bayes classifier performs surprisingly really well in practical applications.

Bayesian classifiers are best applied to problems in which information from a very high number of attributes should be considered simultaneously to estimate the probability of final outcome. Bayesian methods utilize all available evidence to consider for prediction even features have weak effects on the final outcome to predict. However, we should not ignore the fact that a large number of features with relatively minor effects, taken together its combined impact would form strong classifiers.

Probability fundamentals

Before diving into Naive Bayes, it would be good to reiterate the fundamentals. Probability of an event can be estimated from observed data by dividing the number of trails in which an event occurred with the total number of trails. For instance, if a bag contains red and blue balls and randomly picked *10* balls one by one with replacement and out of *10, 3* red balls appeared in trails we can say that probability of red is *0.3*, $p_{red} = 3/10 = 0.3$. Total probability of all possible outcomes must be 100 percent.

If a trail has two outcomes such as email classification either it is spam or ham and both cannot occur simultaneously, these events are considered as mutually exclusive with each other. In addition, if those outcomes cover all possible events, it would be called as **exhaustive events**. For example, in email classification if *P (spam) = 0.1*, we will be able to calculate *P (ham) = 1- 0.1 = 0.9*, these two events are mutually exclusive. In the following Venn diagram, all the email possible classes are represented (the entire universe) with the type of outcomes:

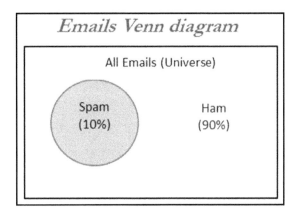

Joint probability

Though mutually exclusive cases are simple to work upon, most of the actual problems do fall under the category of non-mutually exclusive events. By using the joint appearance, we can predict the event outcome. For example, if emails messages present the word like *lottery*, which is very highly likely of being spam rather than ham. The following Venn diagram indicates the joint probability of spam with *lottery*. However, if you notice in detail, lottery circle is not contained completely within the spam circle. This implies that not all spam messages contain the word *lottery* and not every email with the word *lottery* is spam.

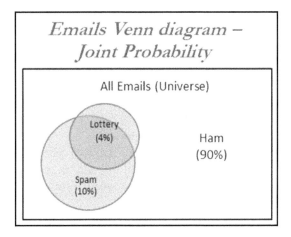

In the following diagram, we have expanded the spam and ham category in addition to the *lottery* word in Venn diagram representation:

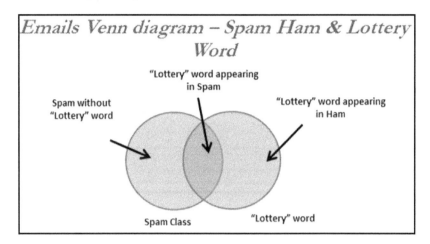

We have seen that 10 percent of all the emails are spam and 4 percent of emails have the word *lottery* and our task is to quantify the degree of overlap between these two proportions. In other words, we need to identify the joint probability of both *p(spam)* and *p(lottery)* occurring, which can be written as *p(spam ∩ lottery)*. In case if both the events are totally unrelated, they are called **independent events** and their respective value is *p(spam ∩ lottery) = p(spam) * p(lottery) = 0.1 * 0.04 = 0.004*, which is 0.4 percent of all messages are spam containing the word Lottery. In general, for independent events *P(A∩ B) = P(A) * P(B)*.

Understanding Bayes theorem with conditional probability

Conditional probability provides a way of calculating relationships between dependent events using Bayes theorem. For example, *A* and *B* are two events and we would like to calculate *P(A\B)* can be read as the probability of an event occurring *A* given the fact that event *B* already occurred, in fact, this is known as **conditional probability**, the equation can be written as follows:

$$P(A\backslash B) = \frac{P(B\backslash A) * P(A)}{P(B)} = \frac{P(A \cap B)}{P(B)}$$

To understand better, we will now talk about the email classification example. Our objective is to predict whether an email is a spam given the word lottery and some other clues. In this case, we already knew the overall probability of spam, which is 10 percent also known as **prior probability**. Now suppose you have obtained an additional piece of information that probability of word lottery in all messages, which is 4 percent, also known as **marginal likelihood**. Now, we know the probability that *lottery* was used in previous spam messages and is called the **likelihood**.

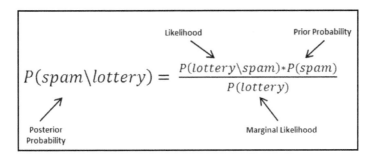

By applying the Bayes theorem to the evidence, we can calculate the posterior probability that calculates the probability that the message is how likely a spam; given the fact that lottery was appearing in the message. On average if the probability is greater than 50 percent it indicates that the message is spam rather than ham.

	Word Frequency & Likelihood of Lottery with Spam & Ham							
		Lottery					Lottery	
Frequency	yes	no	Total		Likelihood	yes	no	Total
spam	3	19	22		spam	3/22	19/22	22
ham	2	76	78		ham	2/78	76/78	78
Total	5	95	100		Total	5/100	95/100	100

In the previous table, the sample frequency table that records the number of times *Lottery* appeared in spam and ham messages and its respective likelihood has been shown. Likelihood table reveals that *P(Lottery \ Spam)*= 3/22 = 0.13, indicating that probability is 13 percent that a spam message contains the term *Lottery*. Subsequently we can calculate the *P(Spam ∩ Lottery) = P(Lottery \ Spam) * P(Spam) =* (3/22) * (22/100) = 0.03. In order to calculate the posterior probability, we divide *P(Spam ∩ Lottery)* with *P(Lottery)*, which means (3/22)*(22/100) / (4/100) = 0.75. Therefore, the probability is 75 percent that a message is spam, given that message contains the word *Lottery*. Hence, don't believe in quick fortune guys!

Naive Bayes classification

In the past example, we have seen with a single word called *lottery*, however, in this case, we will be discussing with a few more additional words such as *Million* and *Unsubscribe* to show how actual classifiers do work. Let us construct the likelihood table for the appearance of the three words (*W1*, *W2*, and *W3*), as shown in the following table for *100* emails:

Likelihood	Lottery (W1)		Million (W2)		Unsubscribe (W3)		Total
	yes	no	yes	no	yes	no	
spam	3/22	19/22	11/22	11/22	13/22	9/22	22
ham	2/78	76/78	15/78	63/78	21/78	57/78	78
Total	5/100	95/100	26/100	74/100	34/100	66/100	100

When a new message is received, the posterior probability will be calculated to determine that email message is spam or ham. Let us assume that we have an email with terms *Lottery* and *Unsubscribe*, but it does not have word *Million* in it, with this details, what is the probability of spam?

By using Bayes theorem, we can define the problem as *Lottery = Yes*, *Million = No* and *Unsubscribe = Yes*:

$$P(Spam|W_1 \cap \neg W_2 \cap W_3) = \frac{P(W_1 \cap \neg W_2 \cap W_3 \mid Spam) * P(Spam)}{P(W_1 \cap \neg W_2 \cap W_3)}$$

Solving the preceding equations will have high computational complexity due to the dependency of words with each other. As a number of words are added, this will even explode and also huge memory will be needed for processing all possible intersecting events. This finally leads to intuitive turnaround with independence of words (**cross-conditional independence**) for which it got name of the Naive prefix for Bayes classifier. When both events are independent we can write *P(A ∩ B) = P(A) * P(B)*. In fact, this equivalence is much easier to compute with less memory requirement:

$$P(Spam \mid W_1 \cap \neg W_2 \cap W_3) = \frac{P(W_1 \mid Spam) * P(\neg W_2 \mid Spam) * P(W_3 \mid Spam) * P(Spam)}{P(W_1) * P(\neg W_2) * P(W_3)}$$

In a similar way, we will calculate the probability for ham messages as well, as follows:

$$P(Ham \mid W_1 \cap \neg W_2 \cap W_3) = \frac{P(W_1 \mid Ham) * P(\neg W_2 \mid Ham) * P(W_3 \mid Ham) * P(Ham)}{P(W_1) * P(\neg W_2) * P(W_3)}$$

By substituting the preceding likelihood table in the equations, due to the ratio of spam/ham we can just simply ignore the denominator terms in both the equations. Overall likelihood of spam is:

$$P(Spam \mid W_1 \cap \neg W_2 \cap W_3) = \left(\frac{3}{22}\right) * \left(\frac{11}{22}\right) * \left(\frac{13}{22}\right) * \left(\frac{22}{100}\right) = 0.008864$$

$$P(Ham \mid W_1 \cap \neg W_2 \cap W_3) = \left(\frac{2}{78}\right) * \left(\frac{63}{78}\right) * \left(\frac{21}{78}\right) * \left(\frac{78}{100}\right) = 0.004349$$

After calculating the ratio, *0.008864/0.004349 = 2.03*, which means that this message is two times more likely to be spam than ham. But we can calculate the probabilities as follows:

$$P(Spam) = 0.008864/(0.008864+0.004349) = 0.67$$

$$P(Ham) = 0.004349/(0.008864+0.004349) = 0.33$$

By converting likelihood values into probabilities, we can show in a presentable way for either to set-off some thresholds, and so on.

Laplace estimator

In the previous calculation, all the values are nonzeros, which makes calculations well. Whereas in practice some words never appear in past for specific category and suddenly appear at later stages, which makes entire calculations as zeros.

For example, in the previous equation W_3 did have a *0* value instead of *13*, and it will convert entire equations to *0* altogether:

$$P(Spam \mid W_1 \cap \neg W_2 \cap W_3) = \left(\frac{3}{22}\right) * \left(\frac{11}{22}\right) * \left(\frac{0}{22}\right) * \left(\frac{22}{100}\right) = 0$$

In order to avoid this situation, Laplace estimator essentially adds a small number to each of the counts in the frequency table, which ensures that each feature has a nonzero probability of occurring with each class. Usually, Laplace estimator is set to *1*, which ensures that each class-feature combination is found in the data at least once:

$$P(Spam|W_1 \cap \neg W_2 \cap W_3) = \left(\frac{4}{25}\right) * \left(\frac{12}{25}\right) * \left(\frac{1}{25}\right) * \left(\frac{22}{100}\right) = 0$$

 If you observe the equation carefully, value *1* is added to all three words in the numerator and at the same time, three has been added to all denominators to provide equivalence.

Naive Bayes SMS spam classification example

Naive Bayes classifier has been developed using the SMS spam collection data available at `http://www.dt.fee.unicamp.br/~tiago/smsspamcollection/`. In this chapter, various techniques available in NLP techniques have been discussed to preprocess prior to build the Naive Bayes model:

```
>>> import csv

>>> smsdata = open('SMSSpamCollection.txt','r')
>>> csv_reader = csv.reader(smsdata,delimiter='\t')
```

The following `sys` package lines code can be used in case of any `utf-8` errors encountered while using older versions of Python, or else does not necessary with the latest version of Python 3.6:

```
>>> import sys
>>> reload (sys)
>>> sys.setdefaultendocing('utf-8')
```

Normal coding starts from here as usual:

```
>>> smsdata_data = []
>>> smsdata_labels = []

>>> for line in csv_reader:
...        smsdata_labels.append(line[0])
...        smsdata_data.append(line[1])

>>> smsdata.close()
```

The following code prints the top 5 lines:

```
>>> for i in range(5):
...        print (smsdata_data[i],smsdata_labels[i])
```

```
Go until jurong point, crazy.. Available only in bugis n great world la e buffet... Cine there got amore
wat... ham
Ok lar... Joking wif u oni... ham
Free entry in 2 a wkly comp to win FA Cup final tkts 21st May 2005. Text FA to 87121 to receive entry
question(std txt rate)T&C's apply 08452810075over18's spam
U dun say so early hor... U c already then say... ham
Nah I don't think he goes to usf, he lives around here though ham
```

After getting preceding output run following code:

```
>>> from collections import Counter
>>> c = Counter( smsdata_labels )
>>> print(c)
```

```
Counter({'ham': 4825, 'spam': 747})
```

Out of 5,572 observations, 4,825 are ham messages, which are about 86.5 percent and 747 spam messages are about remaining 13.4 percent.

Using NLP techniques, we have preprocessed the data for obtaining finalized word vectors to map with final outcomes spam or ham. Major preprocessing stages involved are:

- **Removal of punctuations**: Punctuations needs to be removed before applying any further processing. Punctuations from the `string` library are `!"#$%&\'()*+,-./:;<=>?@[\\]^_`{|}~`, which are removed from all the messages.
- **Word tokenization**: Words are chunked from sentences based on white space for further processing.

- **Converting words into lowercase**: Converting to all lower case provides removal of duplicates, such as *Run* and *run*, where the first one comes at start of the sentence and the later one comes in the middle of the sentence, and so on, which all needs to be unified to remove duplicates as we are working on bag of words technique.

- **Stop word removal**: Stop words are the words that repeat so many times in literature and yet are not a differentiator in the explanatory power of sentences. For example: *I, me, you, this, that,* and so on, which needs to be removed before further processing.

- **of length at least three**: Here we have removed words with length less than three.

- **Stemming of words**: Stemming process stems the words to its respective root words. Example of stemming is bringing down running to run or runs to run. By doing stemming we reduce duplicates and improve the accuracy of the model.

- **Part-of-speech (POS) tagging**: This applies the speech tags to words, such as noun, verb, adjective, and so on. For example, POS tagging for *running* is verb, whereas for *run* is noun. In some situation *running* is noun and lemmatization will not bring down the word to root word *run*, instead, it just keeps the *running* as it is. Hence, POS tagging is a very crucial step necessary for performing prior to applying the lemmatization operation to bring down the word to its root word.

- **Lemmatization of words**: Lemmatization is another different process to reduce the dimensionality. In lemmatization process, it brings down the word to root word rather than just truncating the words. For example, bring *ate* to its root word as *eat* when we pass the *ate* word into lemmatizer with the POS tag as verb.

The `nltk` package has been utilized for all the preprocessing steps, as it consists of all the necessary NLP functionality in one single roof:

```
>>> import nltk
>>> from nltk.corpus import stopwords
>>> from nltk.stem import WordNetLemmatizer
>>> import string
>>> import pandas as pd
>>> from nltk import pos_tag
>>> from nltk.stem import PorterStemmer
```

Function has been written (preprocessing) consists of all the steps for convenience. However, we will be explaining all the steps in each section:

```
>>> def preprocessing(text):
```

The following line of the code splits the word and checks each character if it is in standard punctuations if so it will be replaced with blank and or else it just does not replace with blanks:

```
...     text2 = " ".join("".join([" " if ch in string.punctuation else ch
for ch in text]).split())
```

The following code tokenizes the sentences into words based on white spaces and put them together as a list for applying further steps:

```
...     tokens = [word for sent in nltk.sent_tokenize(text2) for word in
                nltk.word_tokenize(sent)]
```

Converting all the cases (upper, lower, and proper) into lowercase reduces duplicates in corpus:

```
...     tokens = [word.lower() for word in tokens]
```

As mentioned earlier, stop words are the words that do not carry much weight in understanding the sentence; they are used for connecting words, and so on. We have removed them with the following line of code:

```
...     stopwds = stopwords.words('english')
...     tokens = [token for token in tokens if token not in stopwds]
```

Keeping only the words with length greater than 3 in the following code for removing small words, which hardly consists of much of a meaning to carry:

```
...     tokens = [word for word in tokens if len(word)>=3]
```

Stemming is applied on the words using `PorterStemmer` function, which stems the extra suffixes from the words:

```
...     stemmer = PorterStemmer()
...     tokens = [stemmer.stem(word) for word in tokens]
```

POS tagging is a prerequisite for lemmatization, based on whether the word is noun or verb, and so on, it will reduce it to the root word:

```
...     tagged_corpus = pos_tag(tokens)
```

The `pos_tag` function returns the part of speed in four formats for noun and six formats for verb. NN (noun, common, singular), NNP (noun, proper, singular), NNPS (noun, proper, plural), NNS (noun, common, plural), VB (verb, base form), VBD (verb, past tense), VBG (verb, present participle), VBN (verb, past participle), VBP (verb, present tense, not third person singular), VBZ (verb, present tense, third person singular):

```
...       Noun_tags = ['NN','NNP','NNPS','NNS']
...       Verb_tags = ['VB','VBD','VBG','VBN','VBP','VBZ']
...       lemmatizer = WordNetLemmatizer()
```

The `prat_lemmatize` function has been created only for the reasons of mismatch between the `pos_tag` function and intake values of the lemmatize function. If the tag for any word falls under the respective noun or verb tags category, n or v will be applied accordingly in the lemmatize function:

```
...       def prat_lemmatize(token,tag):
...           if tag in Noun_tags:
...               return lemmatizer.lemmatize(token,'n')
...           elif tag in Verb_tags:
...               return lemmatizer.lemmatize(token,'v')
...           else:
...               return lemmatizer.lemmatize(token,'n')
```

After performing tokenization and applied all the various operations, we need to join it back to form stings and the following function performs the same:

```
...       pre_proc_text =  " ".join([prat_lemmatize(token,tag) for token,tag
in tagged_corpus])
...       return pre_proc_text
```

The following step applies the preprocessing function to the data and generates new corpus:

```
>>> smsdata_data_2 = []
>>> for i in smsdata_data:
...       smsdata_data_2.append(preprocessing(i))
```

Data will be split into train and test based on 70-30 split and converted to the NumPy array for applying machine learning algorithms:

```
>>> import numpy as np
>>> trainset_size = int(round(len(smsdata_data_2)*0.70))
>>> print ('The training set size for this classifier is ' +
str(trainset_size) + '\n')
>>> x_train = np.array([''.join(rec) for rec in
smsdata_data_2[0:trainset_size]])
>>> y_train = np.array([rec for rec in smsdata_labels[0:trainset_size]])
>>> x_test = np.array([''.join(rec) for rec in
smsdata_data_2[trainset_size+1:len( smsdata_data_2)]])
>>> y_test = np.array([rec for rec in smsdata_labels[trainset_size+1:len(
smsdata_labels)]])
```

The following code converts the words into a vectorizer format and applies **term frequency-inverse document frequency (TF-IDF)** weights, which is a way to increase weights to words with high frequency and at the same time penalize the general terms such as *the*, *him*, *at*, and so on. In the following code, we have restricted to most frequent 4,000 words in the vocabulary, none the less we can tune this parameter as well for checking where the better accuracies are obtained:

```
# building TFIDF vectorizer
>>> from sklearn.feature_extraction.text import TfidfVectorizer
>>> vectorizer = TfidfVectorizer(min_df=2, ngram_range=(1, 2),
stop_words='english',
    max_features= 4000, strip_accents='unicode',  norm='12')
```

The TF-IDF transformation has been shown as follows on both train and test data. The `todense` function is used to create the data to visualize the content:

```
>>> x_train_2 = vectorizer.fit_transform(x_train).todense()
>>> x_test_2 = vectorizer.transform(x_test).todense()
```

Multinomial Naive Bayes classifier is suitable for classification with discrete features (example word counts), which normally requires large feature counts. However, in practice, fractional counts such as TF-IDF will also work well. If we do not mention any Laplace estimator, it does take the value of *1.0* means and it will add *1.0* against each term in numerator and total for denominator:

```
>>> from sklearn.naive_bayes import MultinomialNB
>>> clf = MultinomialNB().fit(x_train_2, y_train)

>>> ytrain_nb_predicted = clf.predict(x_train_2)
>>> ytest_nb_predicted = clf.predict(x_test_2)

>>> from sklearn.metrics import classification_report, accuracy_score
```

```
>>> print ("\nNaive Bayes - Train Confusion
Matrix\n\n",pd.crosstab(y_train, ytrain_nb_predicted,rownames =
["Actuall"],colnames = ["Predicted"]))
>>> print ("\nNaive Bayes- Train accuracy",round(accuracy_score(y_train,
ytrain_nb_predicted),3))
>>> print ("\nNaive Bayes  - Train Classification
Report\n",classification_report(y_train, ytrain_nb_predicted))

>>> print ("\nNaive Bayes - Test Confusion Matrix\n\n",pd.crosstab(y_test,
ytest_nb_predicted,rownames = ["Actuall"],colnames = ["Predicted"]))
>>> print ("\nNaive Bayes- Test accuracy",round(accuracy_score(y_test,
ytest_nb_predicted),3))
>>> print ("\nNaive Bayes  - Test Classification
Report\n",classification_report( y_test, ytest_nb_predicted))
```

```
Naive Bayes - Train Confusion Matrix

 Predicted   ham  spam
Actuall
ham          3381    0
spam           78   441

Naive Bayes- Train accuracy 0.98

Naive Bayes  - Train Classification Report
             precision    recall  f1-score   support

        ham       0.98      1.00      0.99      3381
       spam       1.00      0.85      0.92       519

avg / total       0.98      0.98      0.98      3900


Naive Bayes - Test Confusion Matrix

 Predicted   ham  spam
Actuall
ham          1440    3
spam           54  174

Naive Bayes- Test accuracy 0.966

Naive Bayes  - Test Classification Report
             precision    recall  f1-score   support

        ham       0.96      1.00      0.98      1443
       spam       0.98      0.76      0.86       228

avg / total       0.97      0.97      0.96      1671
```

From the previous results, it is appearing that Naive Bayes has produced excellent results of 96.6 percent test accuracy with significant recall value of 76 percent for spam and almost 100 percent for ham.

However, if we would like to check what are the top 10 features based on their coefficients from Naive Bayes, the following code will be handy for this:

```
# printing top features
>>> feature_names = vectorizer.get_feature_names()
>>> coefs = clf.coef_
>>> intercept = clf.intercept_
>>> coefs_with_fns = sorted(zip(clf.coef_[0], feature_names))

>>> print ("\n\nTop 10 features - both first & last\n")
>>> n=10
>>> top_n_coefs = zip(coefs_with_fns[:n], coefs_with_fns[:-(n + 1):-1])
>>> for (coef_1, fn_1), (coef_2, fn_2) in top_n_coefs:
...         print('\t%.4f\t%-15s\t\t%.4f\t%-15s' % (coef_1, fn_1, coef_2,
fn_2))
```

```
Top 10 features - both first & last

        -8.7128 1hr                     -5.5773 free
        -8.7128 1st love                -5.7141 txt
        -8.7128 2go                     -5.8715 text
        -8.7128 2morrow                 -6.0127 claim
        -8.7128 2mrw                    -6.0740 stop
        -8.7128 2nd inning              -6.0809 mobil
        -8.7128 2nd sm                  -6.1059 repli
        -8.7128 30ish                   -6.1593 prize
        -8.7128 3rd                     -6.1994 servic
        -8.7128 3rd natur               -6.2101 tone
```

Though the R language is not a popular choice for NLP processing, here we have presented the code. Readers are encouraged to change the code and see how accuracies are changing for a better understanding of concepts. The R code for Naive Bayes classifier on SMS spam/ham data is as follows:

```
# Naive Bayes
smsdata = read.csv("SMSSpamCollection.csv",stringsAsFactors = FALSE)
# Try the following code for reading in case if you have
#issues while reading regularly with above code
#smsdata = read.csv("SMSSpamCollection.csv",
#stringsAsFactors = FALSE,fileEncoding="latin1")
str(smsdata)
```

```
smsdata$Type = as.factor(smsdata$Type)
table(smsdata$Type)

library(tm)
library(SnowballC)
# NLP Processing
sms_corpus <- Corpus(VectorSource(smsdata$SMS_Details))
corpus_clean_v1 <- tm_map(sms_corpus, removePunctuation)
corpus_clean_v2 <- tm_map(corpus_clean_v1, tolower)
corpus_clean_v3 <- tm_map(corpus_clean_v2, stripWhitespace)
corpus_clean_v4 <- tm_map(corpus_clean_v3, removeWords, stopwords())
corpus_clean_v5 <- tm_map(corpus_clean_v4, removeNumbers)
corpus_clean_v6 <- tm_map(corpus_clean_v5, stemDocument)

# Check the change in corpus
inspect(sms_corpus[1:3])
inspect(corpus_clean_v6[1:3])

sms_dtm <- DocumentTermMatrix(corpus_clean_v6)

smsdata_train <- smsdata[1:4169, ]
smsdata_test <- smsdata[4170:5572, ]

sms_dtm_train <- sms_dtm[1:4169, ]
sms_dtm_test <- sms_dtm[4170:5572, ]

sms_corpus_train <- corpus_clean_v6[1:4169]
sms_corpus_test <- corpus_clean_v6[4170:5572]

prop.table(table(smsdata_train$Type))
prop.table(table(smsdata_test$Type))
frac_trzero = (table(smsdata_train$Type)[[1]])/nrow(smsdata_train)
frac_trone = (table(smsdata_train$Type)[[2]])/nrow(smsdata_train)
frac_tszero = (table(smsdata_test$Type)[[1]])/nrow(smsdata_test)
frac_tsone = (table(smsdata_test$Type)[[2]])/nrow(smsdata_test)

Dictionary <- function(x) {
  if( is.character(x) ) {
    return (x)
  }
  stop('x is not a character vector')
}
# Create the dictionary with at least word appears 1 time
sms_dict <- Dictionary(findFreqTerms(sms_dtm_train, 1))
sms_train <- DocumentTermMatrix(sms_corpus_train,list(dictionary =
sms_dict))
sms_test <- DocumentTermMatrix(sms_corpus_test,list(dictionary = sms_dict))
convert_tofactrs <- function(x) {
```

```
  x <- ifelse(x > 0, 1, 0)
  x <- factor(x, levels = c(0, 1), labels = c("No", "Yes"))
  return(x)
}
sms_train <- apply(sms_train, MARGIN = 2, convert_tofactrs)
sms_test <- apply(sms_test, MARGIN = 2, convert_tofactrs)

# Application of Naïve Bayes Classifier with laplace Estimator
library(e1071)
nb_fit <- naiveBayes(sms_train, smsdata_train$Type,laplace = 1.0)

tr_y_pred = predict(nb_fit, sms_train)
ts_y_pred = predict(nb_fit,sms_test)
tr_y_act = smsdata_train$Type;ts_y_act = smsdata_test$Type

tr_tble = table(tr_y_act,tr_y_pred)
print(paste("Train Confusion Matrix"))
print(tr_tble)

tr_acc = accrcy(tr_y_act,tr_y_pred)
trprec_zero = prec_zero(tr_y_act,tr_y_pred);  trrecl_zero =
recl_zero(tr_y_act,tr_y_pred)
trprec_one = prec_one(tr_y_act,tr_y_pred); trrecl_one =
recl_one(tr_y_act,tr_y_pred)
trprec_ovll = trprec_zero *frac_trzero + trprec_one*frac_trone
trrecl_ovll = trrecl_zero *frac_trzero + trrecl_one*frac_trone

print(paste("Naive Bayes Train accuracy:",tr_acc))
print(paste("Naive Bayes - Train Classification Report"))
print(paste("Zero_Precision",trprec_zero,"Zero_Recall",trrecl_zero))
print(paste("One_Precision",trprec_one,"One_Recall",trrecl_one))
print(paste("Overall_Precision",round(trprec_ovll,4),"Overall_Recall",round
(trrecl_ovll,4)))

ts_tble = table(ts_y_act,ts_y_pred)
print(paste("Test Confusion Matrix"))
print(ts_tble)

ts_acc = accrcy(ts_y_act,ts_y_pred)
tsprec_zero = prec_zero(ts_y_act,ts_y_pred); tsrecl_zero =
recl_zero(ts_y_act,ts_y_pred)
tsprec_one = prec_one(ts_y_act,ts_y_pred); tsrecl_one =
recl_one(ts_y_act,ts_y_pred)
tsprec_ovll = tsprec_zero *frac_tszero + tsprec_one*frac_tsone
tsrecl_ovll = tsrecl_zero *frac_tszero + tsrecl_one*frac_tsone

print(paste("Naive Bayes Test accuracy:",ts_acc))
print(paste("Naive Bayes - Test Classification Report"))
```

```
print(paste("Zero_Precision",tsprec_zero,"Zero_Recall",tsrecl_zero))
print(paste("One_Precision",tsprec_one,"One_Recall",tsrecl_one))
print(paste("Overall_Precision",round(tsprec_ovll,4),"Overall_Recall",round
(tsrecl_ovll,4)))
```

Summary

In this chapter, you have learned about KNN and Naive Bayes techniques, which require somewhat a little less computational power. KNN, in fact, is called a lazy learner, as it does not learn anything apart from comparing with training data points to classify them into class. Also, you have seen how to tune the k-value using grid search technique. Whereas explanation has been provided for Naive Bayes classifier, NLP examples have been provided with all the famous NLP processing techniques to give you a flavor of this field in a very crisp manner. Though in text processing, either Naive Bayes or SVM techniques could be used as these two techniques can handle data with high dimensionality, which is very relevant in NLP, as the number of word vectors is relatively high in dimensions and sparse at the same time.

In the next chapter, we will be covering the details of unsupervised learning, more precisely, clustering and principal component analysis models.

4
Unsupervised Learning

The goal of unsupervised learning is to discover the hidden patterns or structures of the data in which no target variable exists to perform either classification or regression methods. Unsupervised learning methods are often more challenging, as the outcomes are subjective and there is no simple goal for the analysis, such as predicting the class or continuous variable. These methods are performed as part of exploratory data analysis. On top of that, it can be hard to assess the results obtained from unsupervised learning methods, since there is no universally accepted mechanism for performing the validation of results.

Nonetheless, unsupervised learning methods have growing importance in various fields as a trending topic nowadays, and many researchers are actively working on them at the moment to explore this new horizon. A few good applications are:

- **Genomics**: Unsupervised learning applied to understanding genomic-wide biological insights from DNA to better understand diseases and peoples. These types of tasks are more exploratory in nature.
- **Search engine**: Search engines might choose which search results to display to a particular individual based on the click histories of other similar users.
- **Knowledge extraction**: To extract the taxonomies of concepts from raw text to generate the knowledge graph to create the semantic structures in the field of NLP.
- **Segmentation of customers**: In the banking industry, unsupervised learning like clustering is applied to group similar customers, and based on those segments, marketing departments design their contact strategies. For example, older, low-risk customers will be targeted with fixed deposit products and high-risk, younger customers will be targeted with credit cards or mutual funds, and so on.
- **Social network analysis**: To identify the cohesive groups of people in networks who are more connected with each other and have similar characteristics in common.

In this chapter, we will be covering the following techniques to perform unsupervised learning with data which is openly available:

- K-means clustering
- Principal component analysis
- Singular value decomposition
- Deep auto encoders

K-means clustering

Clustering is the task of grouping observations in such a way that members of the same cluster are more similar to each other and members of different clusters are very different from each other.

Clustering is commonly used to explore a dataset to either identify the underlying patterns in it or to create a group of characteristics. In the case of social networks, they can be clustered to identify communities and to suggest missing connections between people. Here are a few examples:

- In anti-money laundering measures, suspicious activities and individuals can be identified using anomaly detection
- In biology, clustering is used to find groups of genes with similar expression patterns
- In marketing analytics, clustering is used to find segments of similar customers so that different marketing strategies can be applied to different customer segments accordingly

The k-means clustering algorithm is an iterative process of moving the centers of clusters or centroids to the mean position of their constituent points, and reassigning instances to their closest clusters iteratively until there is no significant change in the number of cluster centers possible or number of iterations reached.

The cost function of k-means is determined by the Euclidean distance (square-norm) between the observations belonging to that cluster with its respective centroid value. An intuitive way to understand the equation is, if there is only one cluster (*k=1*), then the distances between all the observations are compared with its single mean. Whereas, if, number of clusters increases to 2 (*k= 2*), then two-means are calculated and a few of the observations are assigned to cluster *1* and other observations are assigned to cluster two-based on proximity. Subsequently, distances are calculated in cost functions by applying the same distance measure, but separately to their cluster centers:

$$J = \sum_{k=1}^{K} \sum_{i \in C_k} \| x_i - \mu_k \|^2$$

K-means working methodology from first principles

The k-means working methodology is illustrated in the following example in which 12 instances are considered with their *X* and *Y* values. The task is to determine the optimal clusters out of the data.

Instance	X	Y
1	7	8
2	2	4
3	6	4
4	3	2
5	6	5
6	5	7
7	3	3
8	1	4
9	5	4
10	7	7
11	7	6
12	2	1

After plotting the data points on a 2D chart, we can see that roughly two clusters are possible, where below-left is the first cluster and the top-right is another cluster, but in many practical cases, there would be so many variables (or dimensions) that, we cannot simply visualize them. Hence, we need a mathematical and algorithmic way to solve these types of problems.

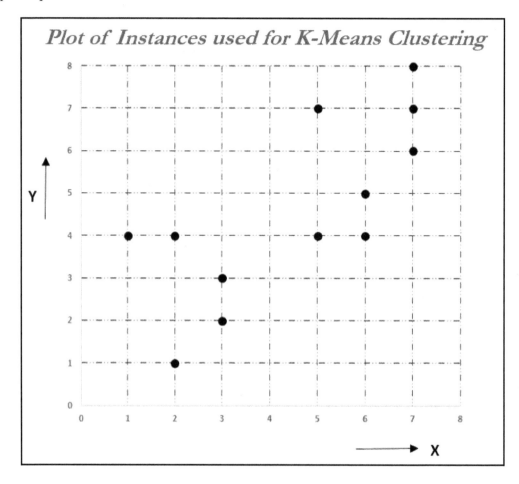

Iteration 1: Let us assume two centers from two instances out of all the *12* instances. Here, we have chosen instance *1* (*X* = *7*, *Y* = *8*) and instance *8* (*X* = *1*, *Y* = *4*), as they seem to be at both extremes. For each instance, we will calculate its Euclidean distances with respect to both centroids and assign it to the nearest cluster center.

Instance	X	Y	Centroid 1 distance	Centroid 2 distance	Assigned cluster
1	7	8	7.21	0.00	C2
2	2	4	1.00	6.40	C1
3	6	4	5.00	4.12	C2
4	3	2	2.83	7.21	C1
5	6	5	5.10	3.16	C2
6	5	7	5.00	2.24	C2
7	3	3	2.24	6.40	C1
8	1	4	0.00	7.21	C1
9	5	4	4.00	4.47	C1
10	7	7	6.71	1.00	C2
11	7	6	6.32	2.00	C2
12	2	1	3.16	8.60	C1
Centroid 1	1	4			
Centroid 2	7	8			

The Euclidean distance between two points *A* (*X1, Y1*) and *B* (*X2, Y2*) is shown as follows:

$$Euclidean\ Distance\ between\ A\ \&\ B = \sqrt{(X2 - X1)^2 + (Y2 - Y1)^2}$$

Centroid distance calculations are performed by taking Euclidean distances. A sample calculation has been shown as follows. For instance, six with respect to both centroids (centroid 1 and centroid 2).

$$Distance\ w.r.to\ Centroid\ 1\ for\ Instance\ 6 = \sqrt{(5-1)^2 + (7-4)^2} = 5.00$$

$$Distance\ w.r.to\ Centroid\ 2\ for\ Instance\ 6 = \sqrt{(5-7)^2 + (7-8)^2} = 2.24$$

The following chart describes the assignment of instances to both centroids, which was shown in the preceding table format:

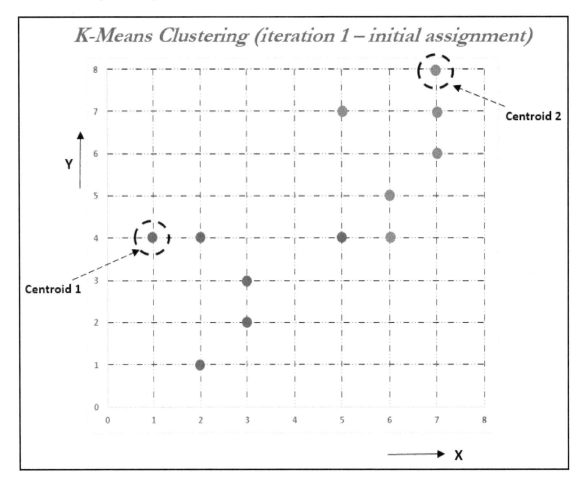

If we carefully observe the preceding chart, we realize that all the instances seem to be assigned appropriately apart from instance 9 (X =5, Y = 4). However, in later stages, it should be assigned appropriately. Let us see in the below steps how the assignments evolve.

Iteration 2: In this iteration, new centroids are calculated from the assigned instances for that cluster or centroid. New centroids are calculated based on the simple average of the assigned points.

Instance	X	Y	Assigned cluster
1	7	8	C2
2	2	4	C1
3	6	4	C2
4	3	2	C1
5	6	5	C2
6	5	7	C2
7	3	3	C1
8	1	4	C1
9	5	4	C1
10	7	7	C2
11	7	6	C2
12	2	1	C1
Centroid 1	2.67	3	
Centroid 2	6.33	6.17	

Sample calculations for centroids 1 and 2 are shown as follows. A similar methodology will be applied on all subsequent iterations as well:

$$Centroid\ 1\ coordinates = Average\ coordinates\ (Instance\ 2,4,7,8,9,\&12)$$

$$Centroid\ 2\ coordinates = Average\ coordinates\ (Instance\ 1,3,5,6,10\ \&11)$$

$$Centroid\ 1\ X = \frac{(2 + 3 + 3 + 1 + 5 + 2)}{6} = 2.67$$

$$Centroid\ 1\ Y = \frac{(4 + 2 + 3 + 4 + 4 + 1)}{6} = 3.0$$

$$Centroid\ 2\ X = \frac{(7 + 6 + 6 + 5 + 7 + 7)}{6} = 6.33$$

$$Centroid\ 2\ Y = \frac{(8 + 4 + 5 + 7 + 7 + 6)}{6} = 6.17$$

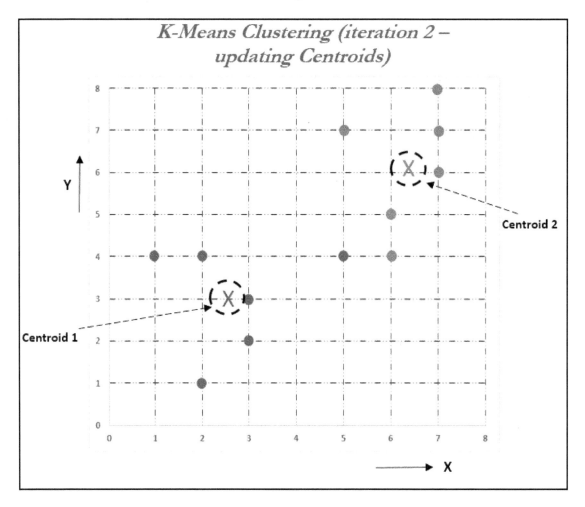

After updating the centroids, we need to reassign the instances to the nearest centroids, which we will be performing in iteration 3.

Iteration 3: In this iteration, new assignments are calculated based on the Euclidean distance between instances and new centroids. In the event of any changes, new centroids will be calculated iteratively until no changes in assignments are possible or the number of iterations is reached. The following table describes the distance measures between new centroids and all the instances:

Instance	X	Y	Centroid 1 distance	Centroid 2 distance	Previously assigned cluster	Newly assigned cluster	Changed?
1	7	8	6.61	1.95	C2	C2	No
2	2	4	1.20	4.84	C1	C1	No
3	6	4	3.48	2.19	C2	C2	No
4	3	2	1.05	5.34	C1	C1	No
5	6	5	3.88	1.22	C2	C2	No
6	5	7	4.63	1.57	C2	C2	No
7	3	3	0.33	4.60	C1	C1	No
8	1	4	1.95	5.75	C1	C1	No
9	5	4	2.54	2.55	C1	C1	No
10	7	7	5.89	1.07	C2	C2	No
11	7	6	5.27	0.69	C2	C2	No
12	2	1	2.11	6.74	C1	C1	No
Centroid 1	2.67	3					
Centroid 2	6.33	6.17					

It seems that there are no changes registered. Hence, we can say that the solution is converged. One important thing to note here is that all the instances are very clearly classified well, apart from instance *9 (X = 5, Y = 4)*. Based on instinct, it seems like it should be assigned to centroid 2, but after careful calculation, that instance is more proximate to cluster 1 than cluster 2. However, the difference in distance is low (2.54 with centroid 1 and 2.55 with centroid 2).

Optimal number of clusters and cluster evaluation

Though selecting number of clusters is more of an art than science, optimal number of clusters are chosen where there will not be a much marginal increase in explanation ability by increasing number of clusters are possible. In practical applications, usually business should be able to provide what would be approximate number of clusters they are looking for.

The elbow method

The elbow method is used to determine the optimal number of clusters in k-means clustering. The elbow method plots the value of the cost function produced by different values of k. As you know, if k increases, average distortion will decrease, each cluster will have fewer constituent instances, and the instances will be closer to their respective centroids. However, the improvements in average distortion will decline as k increases. The value of k at which improvement in distortion declines the most is called the elbow, at which we should stop dividing the data into further clusters.

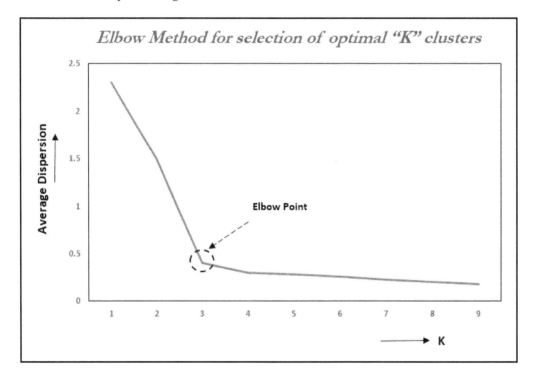

Evaluation of clusters with silhouette coefficient: the silhouette coefficient is a measure of the compactness and separation of the clusters. Higher values represent a better quality of cluster. The silhouette coefficient is higher for compact clusters that are well separated and lower for overlapping clusters. Silhouette coefficient values do change from -1 to +1, and the higher the value is, the better.

The silhouette coefficient is calculated per instance. For a set of instances, it is calculated as the mean of the individual sample's scores.

$$s = \frac{ba}{\max(a, b)}$$

a is the mean distance between the instances in the cluster, *b* is the mean distance between the instance and the instances in the next closest cluster.

K-means clustering with the iris data example

The famous iris data has been used from the UCI machine learning repository for illustration purposes using k-means clustering. The link for downloading the data is here: `http://archive.ics.uci.edu/ml/datasets/Iris`. The iris data has three types of flowers: setosa, versicolor, and virginica and their respective measurements of sepal length, sepal width, petal length, and petal width. Our task is to group the flowers based on their measurements. The code is as follows:

```
>>> import os
""" First change the following directory link to where all input files do
exist """
>>> os.chdir("D:\\Book writing\\Codes\\Chapter 8")

K-means algorithm from scikit-learn has been utilized in the following
example

# K-means clustering
>>> import numpy as np
>>> import pandas as pd
>>> import matplotlib.pyplot as plt
>>> from scipy.spatial.distance import cdist, pdist

>>> from sklearn.cluster import KMeans
>>> from sklearn.metrics import silhouette_score
```

```
>>> iris = pd.read_csv("iris.csv")
>>> print (iris.head())
```

sepal_length	sepal_width	petal_length	petal_width	class
5.1	3.5	1.4	0.2	Iris-setosa
4.9	3	1.4	0.2	Iris-setosa
4.7	3.2	1.3	0.2	Iris-setosa
4.6	3.1	1.5	0.2	Iris-setosa
5	3.6	1.4	0.2	Iris-setosa

Following code is used to separate class variable as dependent variable for creating colors in plot and unsupervised learning algorithm applied on given x variables without any target variable does present:

```
>>> x_iris = iris.drop(['class'],axis=1)
>>> y_iris = iris["class"]
```

As sample metrics, three clusters have been used, but in real life, we do not know how many clusters data will fall under in advance, hence we need to test the results by trial and error. The maximum number of iterations chosen here is 300 in the following, however, this value can also be changed and the results checked accordingly:

```
>>> k_means_fit = KMeans(n_clusters=3,max_iter=300)
>>> k_means_fit.fit(x_iris)

>>> print ("\nK-Means Clustering - Confusion
Matrix\n\n",pd.crosstab(y_iris, k_means_fit.labels_,rownames =
["Actuall"],colnames = ["Predicted"]) )
>>> print ("\nSilhouette-score: %0.3f" % silhouette_score(x_iris,
k_means_fit.labels_, metric='euclidean'))
```

```
K-Means Clustering - Confusion Matrix

 Predicted           0    1    2
Actuall
Iris-setosa         50    0    0
Iris-versicolor      0   48    2
Iris-virginica       0   14   36

Silhouette-score: 0.553
```

From the previous confusion matrix, we can see that all the setosa flowers are clustered correctly, whereas 2 out of 50 versicolor, and 14 out of 50 virginica flowers are incorrectly classified.

> Again, to reiterate, in real-life examples we do not have the category names in advance, so we cannot measure accuracy, and so on.

Following code is used to perform sensitivity analysis to check how many number of clusters does actually provide better explanation of segments:

```
>>> for k in range(2,10):
...      k_means_fitk = KMeans(n_clusters=k,max_iter=300)
...      k_means_fitk.fit(x_iris)
...      print ("For K value",k,",Silhouette-score: %0.3f" %
silhouette_score(x_iris, k_means_fitk.labels_, metric='euclidean'))
```

```
For K value 2 ,Silhouette-score: 0.681
For K value 3 ,Silhouette-score: 0.553
For K value 4 ,Silhouette-score: 0.498
For K value 5 ,Silhouette-score: 0.489
For K value 6 ,Silhouette-score: 0.368
For K value 7 ,Silhouette-score: 0.360
For K value 8 ,Silhouette-score: 0.363
For K value 9 ,Silhouette-score: 0.339
```

The silhouette coefficient values in the preceding results shows that K value 2 and K value 3 have better scores than all the other values. As a thumb rule, we need to take the next K value of the highest silhouette coefficient. Here, we can say that K value 3 is better. In addition, we also need to see the average within cluster variation value and elbow plot before concluding the optimal K value.

```
# Avg. within-cluster sum of squares
>>> K = range(1,10)

>>> KM = [KMeans(n_clusters=k).fit(x_iris) for k in K]
>>> centroids = [k.cluster_centers_ for k in KM]

>>> D_k = [cdist(x_iris, centrds, 'euclidean') for centrds in centroids]

>>> cIdx = [np.argmin(D,axis=1) for D in D_k]
>>> dist = [np.min(D,axis=1) for D in D_k]
>>> avgWithinSS = [sum(d)/x_iris.shape[0] for d in dist]
```

```
# Total with-in sum of square
>>> wcss = [sum(d**2) for d in dist]
>>> tss = sum(pdist(x_iris)**2)/x_iris.shape[0]
>>> bss = tss-wcss

# elbow curve - Avg. within-cluster sum of squares
>>> fig = plt.figure()
>>> ax = fig.add_subplot(111)
>>> ax.plot(K, avgWithinSS, 'b*-')
>>> plt.grid(True)
>>> plt.xlabel('Number of clusters')
>>> plt.ylabel('Average within-cluster sum of squares')
```

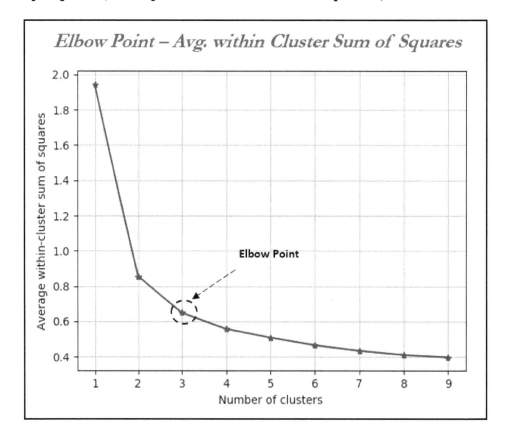

From the elbow plot, it seems that at the value of three, the slope changes drastically. Here, we can select the optimal k-value as three.

```
# elbow curve - percentage of variance explained
>>> fig = plt.figure()
>>> ax = fig.add_subplot(111)
>>> ax.plot(K, bss/tss*100, 'b*-')
>>> plt.grid(True)
>>> plt.xlabel('Number of clusters')
>>> plt.ylabel('Percentage of variance explained')
>>> plt.show()
```

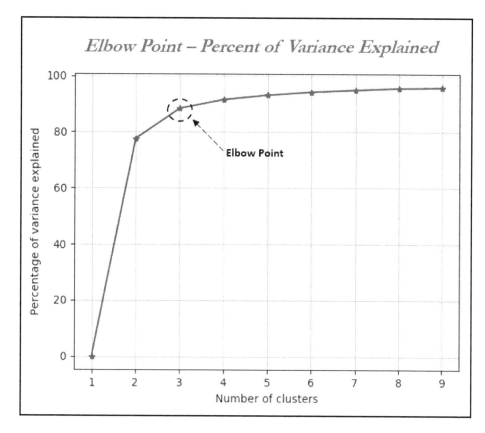

Last but not least, the total percentage of variance explained value should be greater than 80 percent to decide the optimal number of clusters. Even here, a k-value of three seems to give a decent value of total variance explained. Hence, we can conclude from all the preceding metrics (silhouette, average within cluster variance, and total variance explained), that three clusters are ideal.

The R code for k-means clustering using iris data is as follows:

```
setwd("D:\\Book writing\\Codes\\Chapter 8")
iris_data = read.csv("iris.csv")
x_iris =   iris_data[,!names(iris_data) %in% c("class")]
y_iris = iris_data$class
km_fit = kmeans(x_iris,centers   = 3,iter.max = 300 )
print(paste("K-Means   Clustering- Confusion matrix"))
table(y_iris,km_fit$cluster)
mat_avgss = matrix(nrow = 10,   ncol = 2)
# Average within the cluster   sum of square
print(paste("Avg. Within   sum of squares"))
for (i in (1:10)){
  km_fit =   kmeans(x_iris,centers = i,iter.max = 300 )
  mean_km =   mean(km_fit$withinss)
  print(paste("K-Value",i,",Avg.within   sum of squares",round(mean_km,
2)))
  mat_avgss[i,1] = i
  mat_avgss[i,2] = mean_km
}
plot(mat_avgss[,1],mat_avgss[,2],type   = 'o',xlab = "K_Value",ylab = "Avg.
within sum of square")
title("Avg. within sum of   squares vs. K-value")
mat_varexp = matrix(nrow = 10,   ncol = 2)
# Percentage of Variance   explained
print(paste("Percent.   variance explained"))
for (i in (1:10)){
  km_fit =   kmeans(x_iris,centers = i,iter.max = 300 )
  var_exp =   km_fit$betweenss/km_fit$totss
  print(paste("K-Value",i,",Percent   var explained",round(var_exp,4)))
  mat_varexp[i,1]=i
  mat_varexp[i,2]=var_exp
}
plot(mat_varexp[,1],mat_varexp[,2],type   = 'o',xlab = "K_Value",ylab =
"Percent Var explained")
title("Avg. within sum of   squares vs. K-value")
```

Principal Component Analysis - PCA

Principal Component Analysis (PCA) is the dimensionality reduction technique which has so many utilities. PCA reduces the dimensions of a dataset by projecting the data onto a lower-dimensional subspace. For example, a 2D dataset could be reduced by projecting the points onto a line. Each instance in the dataset would then be represented by a single value, rather than a pair of values. In a similar way, a 3D dataset could be reduced to two dimensions by projecting variables onto a plane. PCA has the following utilities:

- Mitigate the course of dimensionality
- Compress the data while minimizing the information lost at the same time
- Principal components will be further utilized in the next stage of supervised learning, in random forest, boosting, and so on
- Understanding the structure of data with hundreds of dimensions can be difficult, hence, by reducing the dimensions to 2D or 3D, observations can be visualized easily

PCA can easily be explained with the following diagram of a mechanical bracket which has been drawn in the machine drawing module of a mechanical engineering course. The left-hand side of the diagram depicts the top view, front view, and side view of the component. However, on the right-hand side, an isometric view has been drawn, in which one single image has been used to visualize how the component looks. So, one can imagine that the left-hand images are the actual variables and the right-hand side is the first principal component, in which most variance has been captured.

Finally, three images have been replaced by a single image by rotating the axis of direction. In fact, we replicate the same technique in PCA analysis.

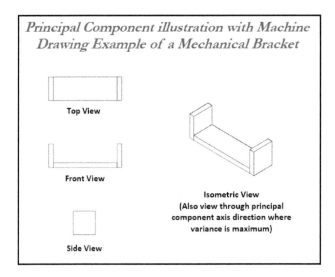

Principal component working methodology is explained in the following sample example, in which actual data has been shown in a 2D space, in which X and Y axis are used to plot the data. Principal components are the ones in which maximum variation of the data is captured.

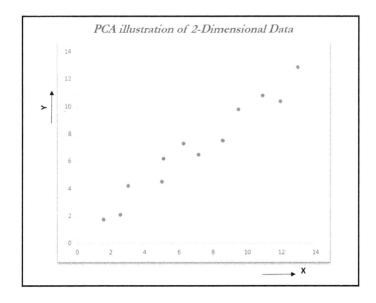

The following diagram illustrates how it looks after fitting the principal components. The first principal component covers the maximum variance in the data and the second principal component is orthogonal to the first principal component, as we know all principal components are orthogonal to each other. We can represent whole data with the first principal component itself. In fact, that is how it is advantageous to represent the data with fewer dimensions, to save space and also to grab maximum variance in the data, which can be utilized for supervised learning in the next stage. This is the core advantage of computing principal components.

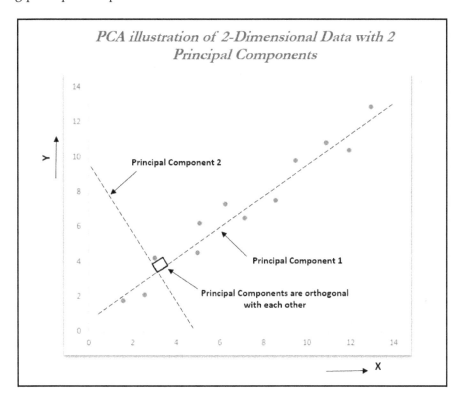

Eigenvectors and eigenvalues have significant importance in the field of linear algebra, physics, mechanics, and so on. Refreshing, basics on eigenvectors and eigenvalues is necessary when studying PCAs. Eigenvectors are the axes (directions) along which a linear transformation acts simply by *stretching/compressing* and/or *flipping*; whereas, eigenvalues give you the factors by which the compression occurs. In another way, an eigenvector of a linear transformation is a nonzero vector whose direction does not change when that linear transformation is applied to it.

More formally, A is a linear transformation from a vector space and $\vec{v}$ is a nonzero vector, then eigen vector of A if $A\vec{v}$ is a scalar multiple of $\vec{v}$. The condition can be written as the following equation:

$$A\vec{v} = \lambda\vec{v}$$

In the preceding equation, $\vec{v}$ is an eigenvector, A is a square matrix, and λ is a scalar called an eigenvalue. The direction of an eigenvector remains the same after it has been transformed by A; only its magnitude has changed, as indicated by the eigenvalue, That is, multiplying a matrix by one of its eigenvectors is equal to scaling the eigenvector, which is a compact representation of the original matrix. The following graph describes eigenvectors and eigenvalues in a graphical representation in a 2D space:

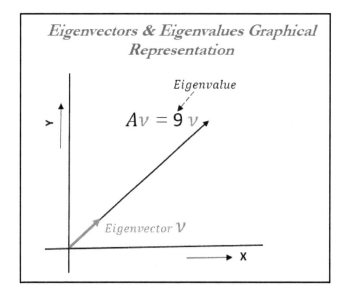

The following example describes how to calculate eigenvectors and eigenvalues from the square matrix and its understanding. Note that eigenvectors and eigenvalues can be calculated only for square matrices (those with the same dimensions of rows and columns).

$$A = \begin{bmatrix} 2 & -4 \\ 4 & -6 \end{bmatrix}$$

Recall the equation that the product of A and any eigenvector of A must be equal to the eigenvector multiplied by the magnitude of eigenvalue:

$$(A - \lambda I)\vec{v} = 0$$

$$|A - \lambda * I| = \left| \begin{bmatrix} 2 & -4 \\ 4 & -6 \end{bmatrix} - \begin{bmatrix} \lambda & 0 \\ 0 & \lambda \end{bmatrix} \right| = 0$$

A characteristic equation states that the determinant of the matrix, that is the difference between the data matrix and the product of the identity matrix and an eigenvalue is 0.

$$\left| \begin{bmatrix} 2 - \lambda & -4 \\ 4 & -6 - \lambda \end{bmatrix} \right| = (\lambda + 2)(\lambda + 2) = 0$$

Both eigenvalues for the preceding matrix are equal to -2. We can use eigenvalues to substitute for eigenvectors in an equation:

$$A\vec{v} = \lambda \vec{v}$$

$$(A - \lambda I)\vec{v} = 0$$

$$\left(\begin{bmatrix} 2 & -4 \\ 4 & -6 \end{bmatrix} - \begin{bmatrix} \lambda & 0 \\ 0 & \lambda \end{bmatrix} \right) \vec{v} = \begin{bmatrix} 2 - \lambda & -4 \\ 4 & -6 - \lambda \end{bmatrix} \vec{v} =$$

$$\begin{bmatrix} 2 - \lambda & -4 \\ 4 & -6 - \lambda \end{bmatrix} \begin{bmatrix} v_{1,1} \\ v_{1,2} \end{bmatrix} = 0$$

Substituting the value of eigenvalue in the preceding equation, we will obtain the following formula:

$$\begin{bmatrix} 2 - (-2) & -4 \\ 4 & -6 - (-2) \end{bmatrix} \begin{bmatrix} v_{1,1} \\ v_{1,2} \end{bmatrix} = \begin{bmatrix} 4 & -4 \\ 4 & -4 \end{bmatrix} \begin{bmatrix} v_{1,1} \\ v_{1,2} \end{bmatrix} = 0$$

The preceding equation can be rewritten as a system of equations, as follows:

$$4 * v_{1,1} - 4 * v_{1,2} = 0$$

$$4 * v_{1,1} - 4 * v_{1,2} = 0$$

This equation indicates it can have multiple solutions of eigenvectors we can substitute with any values which hold the preceding equation for verification of equation. Here, we have used the vector *[1 1]* for verification, which seems to be proved.

$$\begin{bmatrix} 2 & -4 \\ 4 & -6 \end{bmatrix} \begin{bmatrix} 1 \\ 1 \end{bmatrix} = -2 \begin{bmatrix} 1 \\ 1 \end{bmatrix} = \begin{bmatrix} -2 \\ -2 \end{bmatrix}$$

PCA needs unit eigenvectors to be used in calculations, hence we need to divide the same with the norm or we need to normalize the eigenvector. The 2-norm equation is shown as follows:

$$\|x\| = \sqrt{x_1^2 + x_2^2 + \cdots + x_n^2}$$

The norm of the output vector is calculated as follows:

$$\left\| \begin{bmatrix} 1 \\ 1 \end{bmatrix} \right\| = \sqrt{1^2 + 1^2} = \sqrt{2}$$

The unit eigenvector is shown as follows:

$$\begin{bmatrix} 1 \\ 1 \end{bmatrix} / \sqrt{2} = \begin{bmatrix} 0.7071 \\ 0.7071 \end{bmatrix}$$

PCA working methodology from first principles

PCA working methodology is described in the following sample data, which has two dimensions for each instance or data point. The objective here is to reduce the 2D data into one dimension (also known as the **principal component**):

Instance	X	Y
1	0.72	0.13
2	0.18	0.23
3	2.50	2.30
4	0.45	0.16
5	0.04	0.44
6	0.13	0.24
7	0.30	0.03

8	2.65	2.10
9	0.91	0.91
10	0.46	0.32
Column mean	0.83	0.69

The first step, prior to proceeding with any analysis, is to subtract the mean from all the observations, which removes the scale factor of variables and makes them more uniform across dimensions.

X	Y
0.72 - 0.83 = -0.12	0.13 - 0.69 = - 0.55
0.18 - 0.83 = -0.65	0.23 - 0.69 = - 0.46
2.50 - 0.83 = 1.67	2.30 - 0.69 = 1.61
0.45 - 0.83 = -0.38	0.16 - 0.69 = - 0.52
0.04 - 0.83 = -0.80	0.44 - 0.69 = - 0.25
0.13 - 0.83 = -0.71	0.24 - 0.69 = - 0.45
0.30 - 0.83 = -0.53	0.03 - 0.69 = - 0.66
2.65 - 0.83 = 1.82	2.10 - 0.69 = 1.41
0.91 - 0.83 = 0.07	0.91 - 0.69 = 0.23
0.46 - 0.83 = -0.37	0.32 - 0.69 = -0.36

Principal components are calculated using two different techniques:

- Covariance matrix of the data
- Singular value decomposition

We will be covering the singular value decomposition technique in the next section. In this section, we will solve eigenvectors and eigenvalues using covariance matrix methodology.

Covariance is a measure of how much two variables change together and it is a measure of the strength of the correlation between two sets of variables. If the covariance of two variables is zero, we can conclude that there will not be any correlation between two sets of the variables. The formula for covariance is as follows:

$$cov\,(x,y) = \frac{\sum_{i=1}^{n}(X_i - \bar{X})(Y_i - \bar{Y})}{n-1}$$

A sample covariance calculation is shown for X and Y variables in the following formulas. However, it is a 2 x 2 matrix of an entire covariance matrix (also, it is a square matrix).

$$cov\,(Y,Y) =$$
$$\frac{((-0.55)^2 + (-0.46)^2 + (1.61)^2 + (-0.52)^2 + (-0.25)^2 + (-0.45)^2 + (-0.66)^2 + (1.41)^2 + (0.23)^2 + (-0.36)^2)}{10-1}$$

$$cov\,(Y,Y) = 0.697029$$

$$Covariance\ matrix = C = \begin{bmatrix} 0.91335 & 0.75969 \\ 0.75969 & 0.69702 \end{bmatrix}$$

Since the covariance matrix is square, we can calculate eigenvectors and eigenvalues from it. You can refer to the methodology explained in an earlier section.

$$|A - \lambda * I| = \left| \begin{bmatrix} 0.91335 & 0.75969 \\ 0.75969 & 0.69702 \end{bmatrix} - \begin{bmatrix} \lambda & 0 \\ 0 & \lambda \end{bmatrix} \right| = 0$$

By solving the preceding equation, we can obtain eigenvectors and eigenvalues, as follows:

$$Eigenvalues = [1.5725 \quad 0.0378]$$

$$Unit\ Eigenvectors = \begin{bmatrix} 0.7553 & -0.6553 \\ 0.6553 & 0.7553 \end{bmatrix}$$

The preceding mentioned results can be obtained with the following Python syntax:

```
>>> import numpy as np
>>> w, v = np.linalg.eig(np.array([[ 0.91335 ,0.75969 ],[
0.75969,0.69702]]))
\>>> print ("\nEigen Values\n", w)
>>> print ("\nEigen Vectors\n", v)
```

```
Eigen Values
 [ 1.57253666  0.03783334]

Eigen Vectors
 [[ 0.75530088 -0.6553782 ]
 [ 0.6553782   0.75530088]]
```

Once we obtain the eigenvectors and eigenvalues, we can project data into principal components. The first eigenvector has the greatest eigenvalue and is the first principal component, as we would like to reduce the original 2D data into 1D data.

$$
\begin{bmatrix}
-0.12 & -0.55 \\
-0.65 & -0.46 \\
1.67 & 1.61 \\
-0.38 & -0.52 \\
-0.80 & -0.25 \\
-0.71 & -0.45 \\
-0.53 & -0.66 \\
1.82 & 1.41 \\
0.07 & 0.23 \\
-0.37 & -0.36
\end{bmatrix}
\begin{bmatrix}
0.7553 \\
0.6553
\end{bmatrix}
=
\begin{bmatrix}
-0.45 \\
-0.79 \\
2.31 \\
-0.63 \\
-0.76 \\
-0.82 \\
-0.83 \\
2.29 \\
0.20 \\
-0.51
\end{bmatrix}
$$

From the preceding result, we can see the 1D projection of the first principal component from the original 2D data. Also, the eigenvalue of 1.5725 explains the fact that the principal component explains variance of 57 percent more than the original variables. In the case of multi-dimensional data, the thumb rule is to select the eigenvalues or principal components with a value greater than what should be considered for projection.

PCA applied on handwritten digits using scikit-learn

The PCA example has been illustrated with the handwritten digits example from scikit-learn datasets, in which handwritten digits are created from 0-9 and its respective 64 features (8 x 8 matrix) of pixel intensities. Here, the idea is to represent the original features of 64 dimensions into as few as possible:

```
# PCA - Principal Component Analysis
>>> import matplotlib.pyplot as plt
```

```
>>> from sklearn.decomposition import PCA
>>> from sklearn.datasets import load_digits

>>> digits = load_digits()
>>> X = digits.data
>>> y = digits.target


>>> print (digits.data[0].reshape(8,8))
```

```
[[  0.   0.   5.  13.   9.   1.   0.   0.]
 [  0.   0.  13.  15.  10.  15.   5.   0.]
 [  0.   3.  15.   2.   0.  11.   8.   0.]
 [  0.   4.  12.   0.   0.   8.   8.   0.]
 [  0.   5.   8.   0.   0.   9.   8.   0.]
 [  0.   4.  11.   0.   1.  12.   7.   0.]
 [  0.   2.  14.   5.  10.  12.   0.   0.]
 [  0.   0.   6.  13.  10.   0.   0.   0.]]
```

Plot the graph using the `plt.show` function:

```
>>> plt.matshow(digits.images[0])
>>> plt.show()
```

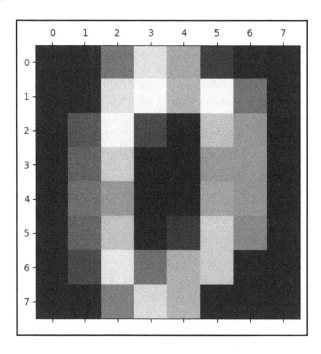

Before performing PCA, it is advisable to perform scaling of input data to eliminate any issues due to different dimensions of the data. For example, while applying PCA on customer data, their salary has larger dimensions than the customer's age. Hence, if we do not put all the variables in a similar dimension, one variable will explain the entire variation rather than its actual impact. In the following code, we have applied scaling on all the columns separately:

```
>>> from sklearn.preprocessing import scale
>>> X_scale = scale(X,axis=0)
```

In the following, we have used two principal components, so that we can represent the performance on a 2D graph. In later sections, we have applied 3D as well.

```
>>> pca = PCA(n_components=2)
>>> reduced_X = pca.fit_transform(X_scale)

>>> zero_x, zero_y = [],[] ; one_x, one_y = [],[]
>>> two_x,two_y = [],[]; three_x, three_y = [],[]
>>> four_x,four_y = [],[]; five_x,five_y = [],[]
>>> six_x,six_y = [],[]; seven_x,seven_y = [],[]
>>> eight_x,eight_y = [],[]; nine_x,nine_y = [],[]
```

In the following section of code, we are appending the relevant principal components to each digit separately so that we can create a scatter plot of all 10 digits:

```
>>> for i in range(len(reduced_X)):
...     if y[i] == 0:
...         zero_x.append(reduced_X[i][0])
...         zero_y.append(reduced_X[i][1])
...     elif y[i] == 1:
...         one_x.append(reduced_X[i][0])
...         one_y.append(reduced_X[i][1])

...     elif y[i] == 2:
...         two_x.append(reduced_X[i][0])
...         two_y.append(reduced_X[i][1])

...     elif y[i] == 3:
...         three_x.append(reduced_X[i][0])
...         three_y.append(reduced_X[i][1])

...     elif y[i] == 4:
...         four_x.append(reduced_X[i][0])
...         four_y.append(reduced_X[i][1])

...     elif y[i] == 5:
...         five_x.append(reduced_X[i][0])
```

```
...            five_y.append(reduced_X[i][1])

...        elif y[i] == 6:
...            six_x.append(reduced_X[i][0])
...            six_y.append(reduced_X[i][1])

...        elif y[i] == 7:
...            seven_x.append(reduced_X[i][0])
...            seven_y.append(reduced_X[i][1])

...        elif y[i] == 8:
...            eight_x.append(reduced_X[i][0])
...            eight_y.append(reduced_X[i][1])
...        elif y[i] == 9:
...            nine_x.append(reduced_X[i][0])
...            nine_y.append(reduced_X[i][1])

>>> zero = plt.scatter(zero_x, zero_y, c='r', marker='x',label='zero')
>>> one = plt.scatter(one_x, one_y, c='g', marker='+')
>>> two = plt.scatter(two_x, two_y, c='b', marker='s')

>>> three = plt.scatter(three_x, three_y, c='m', marker='*')
>>> four = plt.scatter(four_x, four_y, c='c', marker='h')
>>> five = plt.scatter(five_x, five_y, c='r', marker='D')

>>> six = plt.scatter(six_x, six_y, c='y', marker='8')
>>> seven = plt.scatter(seven_x, seven_y, c='k', marker='*')
>>> eight = plt.scatter(eight_x, eight_y, c='r', marker='x')

>>> nine = plt.scatter(nine_x, nine_y, c='b', marker='D')


>>> plt.legend((zero,one,two,three,four,five,six,seven,eight,nine),
...            ('zero','one','two','three','four','five','six',
'seven','eight','nine'),
...            scatterpoints=1,
...            loc='lower left',
...            ncol=3,
...            fontsize=10)

>>> plt.xlabel('PC 1')
>>> plt.ylabel('PC 2')

>>> plt.show()
```

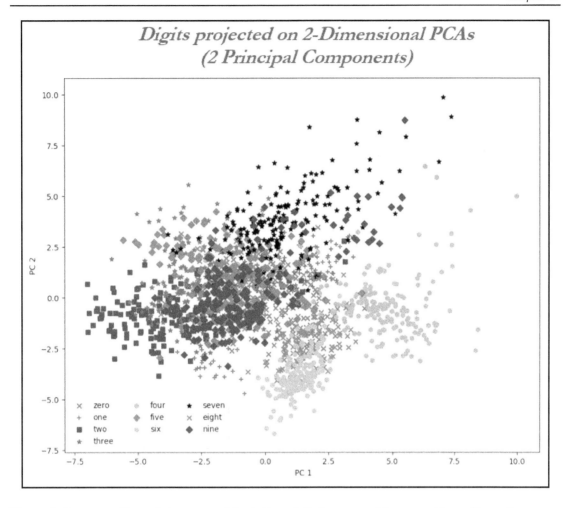

Digits projected on 2-Dimensional PCAs
(2 Principal Components)

Though the preceding plot seems a bit cluttered, it does provide some idea of how the digits are close to and distant from each other. We get the idea that digits *6* and *8* are very similar and digits *4* and *7* are very distant from the center group, and so on. However, we should also try with a higher number of PCAs, as, sometimes, we might not be able to represent every variation in two dimensions itself.

In the following code, we have applied three PCAs so that we can get a better view of the data in a 3D space. The procedure is very much similar as with two PCAs, except for creating one extra dimension for each digit (*X*, *Y*, and *Z*).

```python
# 3-Dimensional data
>>> pca_3d = PCA(n_components=3)
>>> reduced_X3D = pca_3d.fit_transform(X_scale)

>>> zero_x, zero_y, zero_z = [],[],[] ; one_x, one_y, one_z = [],[],[]
>>> two_x, two_y, two_z = [],[],[]; three_x, three_y, three_z = [],[],[]
>>> four_x, four_y, four_z = [],[],[]; five_x, five_y, five_z = [],[],[]
>>> six_x, six_y, six_z = [],[],[]; seven_x, seven_y, seven_z = [],[],[]
>>> eight_x, eight_y, eight_z = [],[],[]; nine_x, nine_y, nine_z = [],[],[]


>>> for i in range(len(reduced_X3D)):
...         if y[i]==10:
...             continue
...         elif y[i] == 0:
...             zero_x.append(reduced_X3D[i][0])
...             zero_y.append(reduced_X3D[i][1])
...             zero_z.append(reduced_X3D[i][2])
...         elif y[i] == 1:
...             one_x.append(reduced_X3D[i][0])
...             one_y.append(reduced_X3D[i][1])
...             one_z.append(reduced_X3D[i][2])

...         elif y[i] == 2:
...             two_x.append(reduced_X3D[i][0])
...             two_y.append(reduced_X3D[i][1])
...             two_z.append(reduced_X3D[i][2])

...         elif y[i] == 3:
...             three_x.append(reduced_X3D[i][0])
...             three_y.append(reduced_X3D[i][1])
...             three_z.append(reduced_X3D[i][2])

...         elif y[i] == 4:
...             four_x.append(reduced_X3D[i][0])
...             four_y.append(reduced_X3D[i][1])
...             four_z.append(reduced_X3D[i][2])

...         elif y[i] == 5:
...             five_x.append(reduced_X3D[i][0])
...             five_y.append(reduced_X3D[i][1])
...             five_z.append(reduced_X3D[i][2])

...         elif y[i] == 6:
```

```
...             six_x.append(reduced_X3D[i][0])
...             six_y.append(reduced_X3D[i][1])
...             six_z.append(reduced_X3D[i][2])

...         elif y[i] == 7:
...             seven_x.append(reduced_X3D[i][0])
...             seven_y.append(reduced_X3D[i][1])
...             seven_z.append(reduced_X3D[i][2])

...         elif y[i] == 8:
...             eight_x.append(reduced_X3D[i][0])
...             eight_y.append(reduced_X3D[i][1])
...             eight_z.append(reduced_X3D[i][2])
...         elif y[i] == 9:
...             nine_x.append(reduced_X3D[i][0])
...             nine_y.append(reduced_X3D[i][1])
...             nine_z.append(reduced_X3D[i][2])


# 3- Dimensional plot
>>> from mpl_toolkits.mplot3d import Axes3D
>>> fig = plt.figure()
>>> ax = fig.add_subplot(111, projection='3d')

>>> ax.scatter(zero_x, zero_y,zero_z, c='r', marker='x',label='zero')
>>> ax.scatter(one_x, one_y,one_z, c='g', marker='+',label='one')
>>> ax.scatter(two_x, two_y,two_z, c='b', marker='s',label='two')

>>> ax.scatter(three_x, three_y,three_z, c='m', marker='*',label='three')
>>> ax.scatter(four_x, four_y,four_z, c='c', marker='h',label='four')
>>> ax.scatter(five_x, five_y,five_z, c='r', marker='D',label='five')

>>> ax.scatter(six_x, six_y,six_z, c='y', marker='8',label='six')
>>> ax.scatter(seven_x, seven_y,seven_z, c='k', marker='*',label='seven')
>>> ax.scatter(eight_x, eight_y,eight_z, c='r', marker='x',label='eight')

>>> ax.scatter(nine_x, nine_y,nine_z, c='b', marker='D',label='nine')

>>> ax.set_xlabel('PC 1')
>>> ax.set_ylabel('PC 2')
>>> ax.set_zlabel('PC 3')
```

```
>>> plt.legend(loc='upper left', numpoints=1, ncol=3, fontsize=10,
bbox_to_anchor=(0, 0))

>>> plt.show()
```

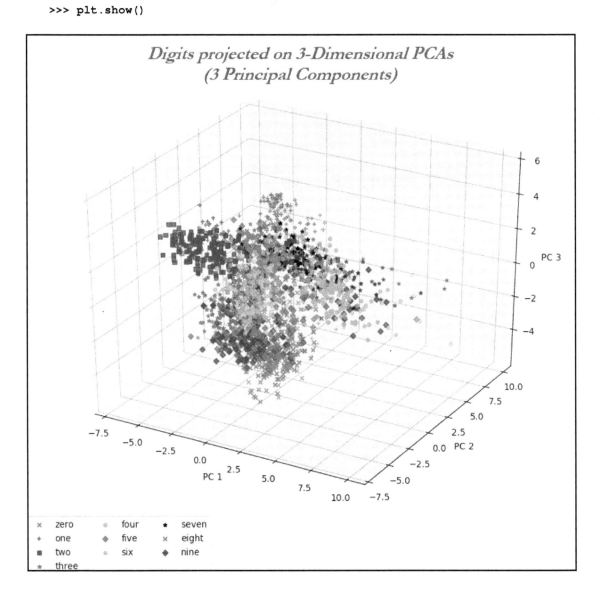

matplotlib plots have one great advantage over other software plots such as R plot, and so on. They are interactive, which means that we can rotate them and see how they look from various directions. We encourage the reader to observe the plot by rotating and exploring. In a 3D plot, we can see a similar story with more explanation. Digit 2 is at the extreme left and digit 0 is at the lower part of the plot. Whereas digit 4 is at the top-right end, digit 6 seems to be more towards the *PC 1* axis. In this way, we can visualize and see how digits are distributed. In the case of 4 PCAs, we need to go for subplots and visualize them separately.

Choosing the number of PCAs to be extracted is an open-ended question in unsupervised learning, but there are some turnarounds to get an approximated view. There are two ways we can determine the number of clusters:

- Check where the total variance explained is diminishing marginally
- Total variance explained greater than 80 percent

The following code does provide the total variance explained with the change in number of principal components. With the more number of PCs, more variance will be explained. But however, the challenge is to restrict it as fewer PCs possible, this will be achieved by restricting where the marginal increase in variance explained start diminishes.

```
# Choosing number of Principal Components
>>> max_pc = 30

>>> pcs = []
>>> totexp_var = []

>>> for i in range(max_pc):
...     pca = PCA(n_components=i+1)
...     reduced_X = pca.fit_transform(X_scale)
...     tot_var = pca.explained_variance_ratio_.sum()
...     pcs.append(i+1)
...     totexp_var.append(tot_var)

>>> plt.plot(pcs,totexp_var,'r')
>>> plt.plot(pcs,totexp_var,'bs')
>>> plt.xlabel('No. of PCs',fontsize = 13)
>>> plt.ylabel('Total variance explained',fontsize = 13)
```

```
>>> plt.xticks(pcs,fontsize=13)
>>> plt.yticks(fontsize=13)
>>> plt.show()
```

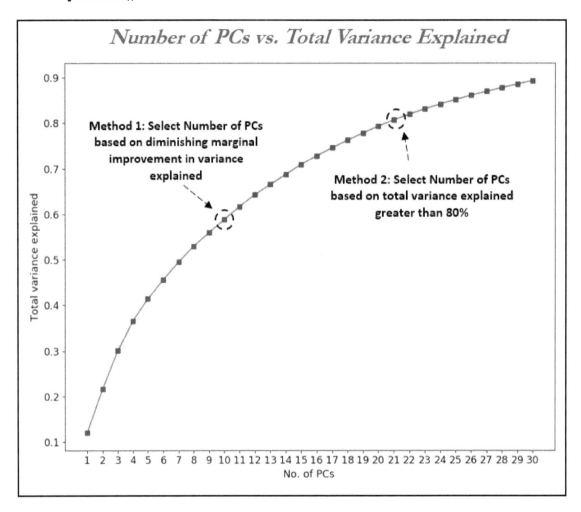

From the previous plot, we can see that total variance explained diminishes marginally at 10 PCAs; whereas, total variance explained greater than 80 percent is given at 21 PCAs. It is up to the business and user which value to choose.

The R code for PCA applied on handwritten digits data is as follows:

```
# PCA
digits_data = read.csv("digitsdata.csv")
remove_cols = c("target")
```

```
x_data =   digits_data[,!(names(digits_data) %in% remove_cols)]
y_data = digits_data[,c("target")]
# Normalizing the data
normalize <- function(x)   {return((x - min(x)) / (max(x) - min(x)))}
data_norm <-   as.data.frame(lapply(x_data, normalize))
data_norm <-   replace(data_norm, is.na(data_norm), 0.0)
# Extracting Principal   Components
pr_out =prcomp(data_norm)
pr_components_all = pr_out$x
# 2- Dimensional PCA
K_prcomps = 2
pr_components =   pr_components_all[,1:K_prcomps]
pr_components_df =   data.frame(pr_components)
pr_components_df =   cbind(pr_components_df,digits_data$target)
names(pr_components_df)[K_prcomps+1]   = "target"
out <- split(   pr_components_df , f = pr_components_df$target )
zero_df = out$`0`;one_df =   out$`1`;two_df = out$`2`; three_df = out$`3`;
four_df = out$`4`
five_df = out$`5`;six_df =   out$`6`;seven_df = out$`7`;eight_df =
out$`8`;nine_df = out$`9`
library(ggplot2)
# Plotting 2-dimensional PCA
ggplot(pr_components_df, aes(x   = PC1, y = PC2, color =
factor(target,labels = c("zero","one","two",   "three","four",
"five","six","seven","eight","nine"))))   +
geom_point()+ggtitle("2-D   PCA on Digits Data") +
labs(color = "Digtis")
# 3- Dimensional PCA
# Plotting 3-dimensional PCA
K_prcomps = 3
pr_components =   pr_components_all[,1:K_prcomps]
pr_components_df =   data.frame(pr_components)
pr_components_df =   cbind(pr_components_df,digits_data$target)
names(pr_components_df)[K_prcomps+1]   = "target"
pr_components_df$target =   as.factor(pr_components_df$target)
out <- split(   pr_components_df , f = pr_components_df$target )
zero_df = out$`0`;one_df =   out$`1`;two_df = out$`2`; three_df = out$`3`;
four_df = out$`4`
five_df = out$`5`;six_df =   out$`6`;seven_df = out$`7`;eight_df =
out$`8`;nine_df = out$`9`
library(scatterplot3d)
colors <- c("darkred",   "darkseagreen4", "deeppink4", "greenyellow",
"orange",   "navyblue", "red", "tan3", "steelblue1",   "slateblue")
colors <- colors[as.numeric(pr_components_df$target)]
s3d =   scatterplot3d(pr_components_df[,1:3], pch = 16, color=colors,
xlab = "PC1",ylab = "PC2",zlab   = "PC3",col.grid="lightblue",main = "3-D
PCA on   Digits Data")
legend(s3d$xyz.convert(3.1,   0.1, -3.5), pch = 16, yjust=0,
```

```
      legend =    levels(pr_components_df$target),col =colors,cex =
1.1,xjust = 0)
# Choosing number of Principal    Components
pr_var =pr_out$sdev ^2
pr_totvar = pr_var/sum(pr_var)
plot(cumsum(pr_totvar), xlab="Principal    Component", ylab ="Cumilative
Prop. of Var.",    ylim=c(0,1),type="b",main = "PCAs vs. Cum prop of Var
Explained")
```

Singular value decomposition - SVD

Many implementations of PCA use singular value decomposition to calculate eigenvectors and eigenvalues. SVD is given by the following equation:

$$X = U \: \Sigma \: V^T$$

Operations performed on data = (rotate) (stretch) (rotate)

Columns of U are called left singular vectors of the data matrix, the columns of V are its right singular vectors, and the diagonal entries of Σ are its singular values. Left singular vectors are the eigenvectors of the covariance matrix and the diagonal element of Σ are the square roots of the eigenvalues of the covariance matrix.

Before proceeding with SVD, it would be advisable to understand a few advantages and important points about SVD:

- SVD can be applied even on rectangular matrices; whereas, eigenvalues are defined only for square matrices. The equivalent of eigenvalues obtained through the SVD method are called singular values, and vectors obtained equivalent to eigenvectors are known as singular vectors. However, as they are rectangular in nature, we need to have left singular vectors and right singular vectors respectively for their dimensions.
- If a matrix A has a matrix of eigenvectors P that is not invertible, then A does not have an eigen decomposition. However, if A is m x n real matrix with $m > n$, then A can be written using a singular value decomposition.
- Both U and V are orthogonal matrices, which means $U^T U = I$ (I with m x m dimension) or $V^T V = I$ (here I with n x n dimension), where two identity matrices may have different dimensions.
- Σ is a non-negative diagonal matrix with m x n dimensions.

Then computation of singular values and singular vectors is done with the following set of equations:

$$X^T X = V \Sigma^T \Sigma V^T$$

In the first stage, singular values/eigenvalues are calculated with the equation. Once we obtain the singular/eigenvalues, we will substitute to determine the V or right singular/eigen vectors:

$$\det(X^T X - \lambda * I) = 0$$

Once we obtain the right singular vectors and diagonal values, we will substitute to obtain the left singular vectors U using the equation mentioned as follows:

$$X V = U \Sigma$$

In this way, we will calculate the singular value decompositions of the original system of equations matrix.

SVD applied on handwritten digits using scikit-learn

SVD can be applied on the same handwritten digits data to perform an apple-to-apple comparison of techniques.

```
# SVD
>>> import matplotlib.pyplot as plt
>>> from sklearn.datasets import load_digits

>>> digits = load_digits()
>>> X = digits.data
>>> y = digits.target
```

In the following code, 15 singular vectors with 300 iterations are used, but we encourage the reader to change the values and check the performance of SVD. We have used two types of SVD functions, as a function `randomized_svd` provide the decomposition of the original matrix and a `TruncatedSVD` can provide total variance explained ratio. In practice, uses may not need to view all the decompositions and they can just use the `TruncatedSVD` function for their practical purposes.

```
>>> from sklearn.utils.extmath import randomized_svd
>>> U, Sigma, VT =
randomized_svd(X, n_components=15, n_iter=300, random_state=42)

>>> import pandas as pd
>>> VT_df = pd.DataFrame(VT)

>>> print ("\nShape of Original Matrix:", X.shape)
>>> print ("\nShape of Left Singular vector:", U.shape)
>>> print ("Shape of Singular value:", Sigma.shape)
>>> print ("Shape of Right Singular vector", VT.shape)
```

```
Shape of Original Matrix: (1797, 64)

Shape of Left Singular vector: (1797, 15)
Shape of Singular value: (15,)
Shape of Right Singular vector (15, 64)
```

By looking at the previous screenshot, we can see that the original matrix of dimension (1797 x 64) has been decomposed into a left singular vector (1797 x 15), singular value (diagonal matrix of 15), and right singular vector (15 x 64). We can obtain the original matrix by multiplying all three matrices in order.

```
>>> n_comps = 15
>>> from sklearn.decomposition import TruncatedSVD
>>> svd = TruncatedSVD(n_components=n_comps, n_iter=300, random_state=42)
>>> reduced_X = svd.fit_transform(X)

>>> print("\nTotal Variance explained for %d singular features are
%0.3f"%(n_comps, svd.explained_variance_ratio_.sum()))
```

```
Total Variance explained for 15 singular features is 0.834
```

The total variance explained for 15 singular value features is 83.4 percent. But the reader needs to change the different values to decide the optimum value.

The following code illustrates the change in total variance explained with respective to change in number of singular values:

```
# Choosing number of Singular Values
>>> max_singfeat = 30
>>> singfeats = []
>>> totexp_var = []

>>> for i in range(max_singfeat):
...        svd = TruncatedSVD(n_components=i+1, n_iter=300, random_state=42)
...        reduced_X = svd.fit_transform(X)
...        tot_var = svd.explained_variance_ratio_.sum()
...        singfeats.append(i+1)
...        totexp_var.append(tot_var)

>>> plt.plot(singfeats,totexp_var,'r')
>>> plt.plot(singfeats,totexp_var,'bs')
>>> plt.xlabel('No. of Features',fontsize = 13)
>>> plt.ylabel('Total variance explained',fontsize = 13)

>>> plt.xticks(pcs,fontsize=13)
>>> plt.yticks(fontsize=13)
>>> plt.show()
```

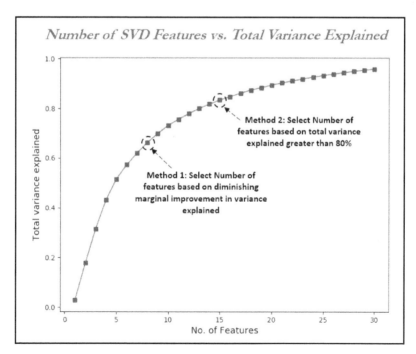

From the previous plot, we can choose either 8 or 15 singular vectors based on the requirement.

The R code for SVD applied on handwritten digits data is as follows:

```
#SVD
library(svd)
digits_data = read.csv("digitsdata.csv")
remove_cols = c("target")
x_data =   digits_data[,!(names(digits_data) %in% remove_cols)]
y_data = digits_data[,c("target")]
sv2 <- svd(x_data,nu=15)
# Computing the square of the   singular values, which can be thought of as
the vector of matrix energy
# in order to pick top singular   values which preserve at least 80% of
variance explained
energy <- sv2$d ^ 2
tot_varexp = data.frame(cumsum(energy)    / sum(energy))
names(tot_varexp) = "cum_var_explained"
tot_varexp$K_value =    1:nrow(tot_varexp)
plot(tot_varexp[,2],tot_varexp[,1],type    = 'o',xlab = "K_Value",ylab =
"Prop. of Var Explained")
title("SVD - Prop. of Var    explained with K-value")
```

Deep auto encoders

The auto encoder neural network is an unsupervised learning algorithm that applies backpropagation setting the target values to be equal to the inputs $y^{(i)} = x^{(i)}$. Auto encoder tries to learn a function $h_{w,b}(x) \approx x$, means it tries to learn an approximation to the identity function, so that output $\hat{x}$ that is similar to x.

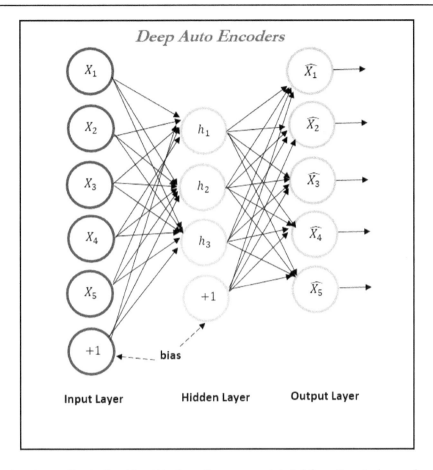

Though trying to replicate the identity function seems trivial function to learn, by placing the constraints on the network, such as by limiting number of hidden units, we can discover interesting structures about the data. Let's say input picture of size 10 x 10 pixels has intensity values which have, altogether, 100 input values, the number of neurons in the second layer (hidden layer) is 50 units, and the output layer, finally, has 100 units of neurons as we need to pass the image to map it to itself and while achieving this representation in the process we would force the network to learn a compressed representation of the input, which is hidden unit activations $a^{(2)} \varepsilon R^{100}$, with which we must try to reconstruct the 100 pixel input x. If the input data is completely random without any correlations, and so on. it would be very difficult to compress, whereas if the underlying data have some correlations or detectable structures, then this algorithm will be able to discover the correlations and represent them compactly. In fact, auto encoder often ends up learning a low-dimensional representation very similar to PCAs.

Model building technique using encoder-decoder architecture

Training the auto encoder model is a bit tricky, hence a detailed illustration has been provided for better understanding. During the training phase, the whole encoder-decoder section is trained against the same input as an output of decoder. In order to achieve the desired output, features will be compressed during the middle layer, as we are passing through the convergent and divergent layers. Once enough training has been done by reducing the error values over the number of iterations, we will use the trained encoder section to create the latent features for next stage of modeling, or for visualization, and so on.

In the following diagram, a sample has been shown. The input and output layers have five neurons, whereas the number of neurons has been gradually decreased in the middle sections. The compressed layer has only two neurons, which is the number of latent dimensions we would like to extract from the data.

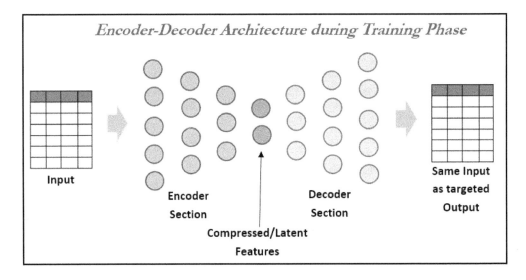

The following diagram depicts using the trained encoder section to create latent features from the new input data, which will be utilized for visualization or for utilizing in the next stage of the model:

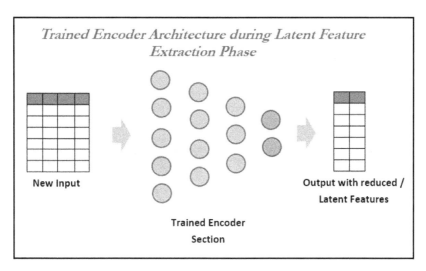

Deep auto encoders applied on handwritten digits using Keras

Deep auto encoders are explained with same handwritten digits data to show the comparison of how this non-linear method differs to linear methods like PCA and SVD. Non-linear methods generally perform much better, but these methods are kind of black-box models and we cannot determine the explanation behind that. Keras software has been utilized to build the deep auto encoders here, as they work like Lego blocks, which makes it easy for users to play around with different architectures and parameters of the model for better understanding:

```
# Deep Auto Encoders
>>> import matplotlib.pyplot as plt
>>> from sklearn.preprocessing import StandardScaler
>>> from sklearn.datasets import load_digits

>>> digits = load_digits()
>>> X = digits.data
>>> y = digits.target

>>> print (X.shape)
```

```
>>> print (y.shape)
>>> x_vars_stdscle = StandardScaler().fit_transform(X)
>>> print (x_vars_stdscle.shape)
```

```
(1797L, 64L)
(1797L,)
(1797L, 64L)
```

Dense neuron modules from Keras used for constructing encoder-decoder architecture:

```
>>> from keras.layers import Input,Dense
>>> from keras.models import Model
```

```
Using Theano backend.
WARNING (theano.sandbox.cuda): The cuda backend is deprecated and will be removed in the next release (v0.10).
Please switch to the gpuarray backend. You can get more information about how to switch at this URL:
 https://github.com/Theano/Theano/wiki/Converting-to-the-new-gpu-back-end%28gpuarray%29

Using gpu device 0: GeForce GTX 1060 6GB (CNMeM is enabled with initial size: 80.0% of memory, cuDNN 5105)
```

GPU of NVIDIA GTX 1060 has been used here, also cuDNN and CNMeM libraries are installed for further enhancement of speed up to 4x-5x on the top of regular GPU performance. These libraries utilize 20 percent of GPU memory, which left the 80 percent of memory for working on the data. The user needs to be careful, if they have low memory GPUs like 3 GB to 4 GB, they may not be able to utilize these libraries.

 The reader needs to consider one important point that, syntax of Keras code, will remain same in both CPU and GPU mode.

The following few lines of codes are the heart of the model. Input data have 64 columns. We need to take those columns into the input of the layers, hence we have given the shape of 64. Also, names have been assigned to each layer of the neural network, which we will explain the reason for in an upcoming section of the code. In the first hidden layer, 32 dense neurons are utilized, which means all the 64 inputs from the input layer are connected to 32 neurons in first hidden layer. The entire flow of dimensions are like *64, 32, 16, 2, 16, 32, 64*. We have compressed input to two neurons, in order to plot the components on a 2D plot, whereas, if we need to plot a 3D data (which we will be covering in the next section), we need to change the hidden three-layer number to three instead of two. After training is complete, we need to use encoder section and predict the output.

```
# 2-Dimensional Architecture

>>> input_layer = Input(shape=(64,),name="input")

>>> encoded = Dense(32, activation='relu',name="h1encode")(input_layer)
>>> encoded = Dense(16, activation='relu',name="h2encode")(encoded)
>>> encoded = Dense(2, activation='relu',name="h3latent_layer")(encoded)

>>> decoded = Dense(16, activation='relu',name="h4decode")(encoded)
>>> decoded = Dense(32, activation='relu',name="h5decode")(decoded)
>>> decoded = Dense(64, activation='sigmoid',name="h6decode")(decoded)
```

To train the model, we need to pass the starting and ending point of the architecture. In the following code, we have provided input as `input_layer` and output as `decoded`, which is the last layer (the name is `h6decode`):

```
>>> autoencoder = Model(input_layer, decoded)
```

Adam optimization has been used to optimize the mean square error, as we wanted to reproduce the original input at the end of the output layer of the network:

```
>>> autoencoder.compile(optimizer="adam", loss="mse")
```

The network is trained with 100 epochs and a batch size of 256 observations per each batch. Validation split of 20 percent is used to check the accuracy on randomly selected validation data in order to ensure robustness, as if we just train only on the train data may create the overfitting problem, which is very common with highly non-linear models:

```
# Fitting Encoder-Decoder model
>>> autoencoder.fit(x_vars_stdscle, x_vars_stdscle,
epochs=100,batch_size=256, shuffle=True,validation_split= 0.2 )
```

```
Train on 1437 samples, validate on 360 samples
Epoch 1/100
1437/1437 [==============================] - 0s - loss: 1.2314 - val_loss: 1.0451
Epoch 2/100
1437/1437 [==============================] - 0s - loss: 1.2164 - val_loss: 1.0279
Epoch 3/100
1437/1437 [==============================] - 0s - loss: 1.1970 - val_loss: 1.0047
Epoch 4/100
1437/1437 [==============================] - 0s - loss: 1.1722 - val_loss: 0.9756
Epoch 5/100
1437/1437 [==============================] - 0s - loss: 1.1430 - val_loss: 0.9419
Epoch 95/100
1437/1437 [==============================] - 0s - loss: 0.9084 - val_loss: 0.7339
Epoch 96/100
1437/1437 [==============================] - 0s - loss: 0.9079 - val_loss: 0.7341
Epoch 97/100
1437/1437 [==============================] - 0s - loss: 0.9075 - val_loss: 0.7334
Epoch 98/100
1437/1437 [==============================] - 0s - loss: 0.9073 - val_loss: 0.7331
Epoch 99/100
1437/1437 [==============================] - 0s - loss: 0.9067 - val_loss: 0.7330
Epoch 100/100
1437/1437 [==============================] - 0s - loss: 0.9061 - val_loss: 0.7326
Out[6]: <keras.callbacks.History at 0x6985c978>
```

From the previous results, we can see that the model has been trained on 1,437 train examples and validation on 360 examples. By looking into the loss value, both train and validation losses have decreased from 1.2314 to 0.9361 and 1.0451 to 0.7326 respectively. Hence, we are moving in the right direction. However, readers are encouraged to try various architectures and number of iterations, batch sizes, and so on to see how much the accuracies can be further improved.

Once the encoder-decoder section has been trained, we need to take only the encoder section to compress the input features in order to obtain the compressed latent features, which is the core idea of dimensionality reduction altogether! In the following code, we have constructed another model with a trained input layer and a middle hidden layer (`h3latent_layer`). This is the reason behind assigning names for each layer of the network.

```
# Extracting Encoder section of the Model for prediction of latent
variables
>>> encoder =
Model(autoencoder.input,autoencoder.get_layer("h3latent_layer").output)

Extracted encoder section of the whole model used for prediction of input
variables to generate sparse 2-dimensional representation, which is being
performed with the following code
# Predicting latent variables with extracted Encoder model
>>> reduced_X = encoder.predict(x_vars_stdscle)
```

Just to check the dimensions of the reduced input variables and we can see that for all observations, we can see two dimensions or two column vector:

```
>>> print (reduced_X.shape)
```

```
(1797L, 2L)
```

The following section of the code is very much similar to 2D PCA:

```
>>> zero_x, zero_y = [],[] ; one_x, one_y = [],[]
>>> two_x,two_y = [],[]; three_x, three_y = [],[]
>>> four_x,four_y = [],[]; five_x,five_y = [],[]
>>> six_x,six_y = [],[]; seven_x,seven_y = [],[]
>>> eight_x,eight_y = [],[]; nine_x,nine_y = [],[]

# For 2-Dimensional data
>>> for i in range(len(reduced_X)):
...         if y[i] == 0:
...             zero_x.append(reduced_X[i][0])
...             zero_y.append(reduced_X[i][1])
...         elif y[i] == 1:
...             one_x.append(reduced_X[i][0])
...             one_y.append(reduced_X[i][1])

...         elif y[i] == 2:
...             two_x.append(reduced_X[i][0])
...             two_y.append(reduced_X[i][1])
```

```
...        elif y[i] == 3:
...            three_x.append(reduced_X[i][0])
...            three_y.append(reduced_X[i][1])

...        elif y[i] == 4:
...            four_x.append(reduced_X[i][0])
...            four_y.append(reduced_X[i][1])

...        elif y[i] == 5:
...            five_x.append(reduced_X[i][0])
...            five_y.append(reduced_X[i][1])

...        elif y[i] == 6:
...            six_x.append(reduced_X[i][0])
...            six_y.append(reduced_X[i][1])

...        elif y[i] == 7:
...            seven_x.append(reduced_X[i][0])
...            seven_y.append(reduced_X[i][1])

...        elif y[i] == 8:
...            eight_x.append(reduced_X[i][0])
...            eight_y.append(reduced_X[i][1])
...        elif y[i] == 9:
...            nine_x.append(reduced_X[i][0])
...            nine_y.append(reduced_X[i][1])


>>> zero = plt.scatter(zero_x, zero_y, c='r', marker='x',label='zero')
>>> one = plt.scatter(one_x, one_y, c='g', marker='+')
>>> two = plt.scatter(two_x, two_y, c='b', marker='s')

>>> three = plt.scatter(three_x, three_y, c='m', marker='*')
>>> four = plt.scatter(four_x, four_y, c='c', marker='h')
>>> five = plt.scatter(five_x, five_y, c='r', marker='D')

>>> six = plt.scatter(six_x, six_y, c='y', marker='8')
>>> seven = plt.scatter(seven_x, seven_y, c='k', marker='*')
>>> eight = plt.scatter(eight_x, eight_y, c='r', marker='x')

>>> nine = plt.scatter(nine_x, nine_y, c='b', marker='D')


>>> plt.legend((zero,one,two,three,four,five,six,seven,eight,nine),
...
('zero','one','two','three','four','five','six','seven','eight','nine'),
...            scatterpoints=1,loc='lower right',ncol=3,fontsize=10)
```

```
>>> plt.xlabel('Latent Feature 1',fontsize = 13)
>>> plt.ylabel('Latent Feature 2',fontsize = 13)

>>> plt.show()
```

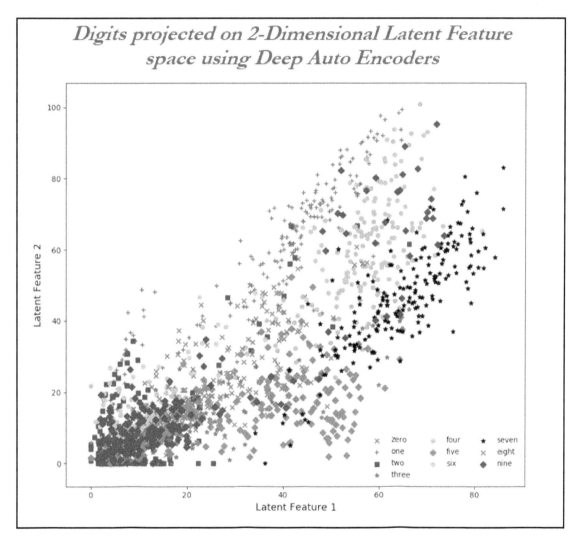

From the previous plot we can see that data points are well separated, but the issue is the direction of view, as these features do not vary as per the dimensions perpendicular to each other, similar to principal components, which are orthogonal to each other. In the case of deep auto encoders, we need to change the view of direction from the *(0, 0)* to visualize this non-linear classification, which we will see in detail in the following 3D case.

The following is the code for 3D latent features. All the code remains the same apart from the `h3latent_layer`, in which we have to replace the value from 2 to 3, as this is the end of encoder section and we will utilize it in creating the latent features and, eventually, it will be used for plotting purposes.

```
# 3-Dimensional architecture
>>> input_layer = Input(shape=(64,),name="input")

>>> encoded = Dense(32, activation='relu',name="h1encode")(input_layer)
>>> encoded = Dense(16, activation='relu',name="h2encode")(encoded)
>>> encoded = Dense(3, activation='relu',name="h3latent_layer")(encoded)

>>> decoded = Dense(16, activation='relu',name="h4decode")(encoded)
>>> decoded = Dense(32, activation='relu',name="h5decode")(decoded)
>>> decoded = Dense(64, activation='sigmoid',name="h6decode")(decoded)

>>> autoencoder = Model(input_layer, decoded)
autoencoder.compile(optimizer="adam", loss="mse")

# Fitting Encoder-Decoder model
>>> autoencoder.fit(x_vars_stdscle, x_vars_stdscle,
epochs=100,batch_size=256, shuffle=True,validation_split= 0.2)
```

```
Train on 1437 samples, validate on 360 samples
Epoch 1/100
1437/1437 [==============================] - 0s - loss: 1.2355 - val_loss: 1.0553
Epoch 2/100
1437/1437 [==============================] - 0s - loss: 1.2274 - val_loss: 1.0466
Epoch 3/100
1437/1437 [==============================] - 0s - loss: 1.2167 - val_loss: 1.0340
Epoch 4/100
1437/1437 [==============================] - 0s - loss: 1.2010 - val_loss: 1.0156
Epoch 5/100
1437/1437 [==============================] - 0s - loss: 1.1786 - val_loss: 0.9891
Epoch 95/100
1437/1437 [==============================] - 0s - loss: 0.8047 - val_loss: 0.6486
Epoch 96/100
1437/1437 [==============================] - 0s - loss: 0.8044 - val_loss: 0.6477
Epoch 97/100
1437/1437 [==============================] - 0s - loss: 0.8041 - val_loss: 0.6472
Epoch 98/100
1437/1437 [==============================] - 0s - loss: 0.8037 - val_loss: 0.6467
Epoch 99/100
1437/1437 [==============================] - 0s - loss: 0.8033 - val_loss: 0.6466
Epoch 100/100
1437/1437 [==============================] - 0s - loss: 0.8032 - val_loss: 0.6464
```

From the previous results we can see that, with the inclusion of three dimensions instead of two, loss values obtained are less than in the 2D use case. Train and validation losses for two latent factors after 100 epochs are 0.9061 and 0.7326, and for three latent factors after 100 epochs, are 0.8032 and 0.6464. This signifies that, with the inclusion of one more dimension, we can reduce the errors significantly. This way, the reader can change various parameters to determine the ideal architecture for dimensionality reduction:

```
# Extracting Encoder section of the Model for prediction of latent
variables
>>> encoder =
Model(autoencoder.input,autoencoder.get_layer("h3latent_layer").output)

# Predicting latent variables with extracted Encoder model
>>> reduced_X3D = encoder.predict(x_vars_stdscle)

>>> zero_x, zero_y,zero_z = [],[],[] ; one_x, one_y,one_z = [],[],[]
>>> two_x,two_y,two_z = [],[],[]; three_x, three_y,three_z = [],[],[]
>>> four_x,four_y,four_z = [],[],[]; five_x,five_y,five_z = [],[],[]
>>> six_x,six_y,six_z = [],[],[]; seven_x,seven_y,seven_z = [],[],[]
>>> eight_x,eight_y,eight_z = [],[],[]; nine_x,nine_y,nine_z = [],[],[]

>>> for i in range(len(reduced_X3D)):
...         if y[i]==10:
...             continue
...         elif y[i] == 0:
...             zero_x.append(reduced_X3D[i][0])
...             zero_y.append(reduced_X3D[i][1])
...             zero_z.append(reduced_X3D[i][2])
...         elif y[i] == 1:
...             one_x.append(reduced_X3D[i][0])
...             one_y.append(reduced_X3D[i][1])
...             one_z.append(reduced_X3D[i][2])

...         elif y[i] == 2:
...             two_x.append(reduced_X3D[i][0])
...             two_y.append(reduced_X3D[i][1])
...             two_z.append(reduced_X3D[i][2])

...         elif y[i] == 3:
...             three_x.append(reduced_X3D[i][0])
...             three_y.append(reduced_X3D[i][1])
...             three_z.append(reduced_X3D[i][2])

...         elif y[i] == 4:
...             four_x.append(reduced_X3D[i][0])
...             four_y.append(reduced_X3D[i][1])
...             four_z.append(reduced_X3D[i][2])
```

```
...         elif y[i] == 5:
...             five_x.append(reduced_X3D[i][0])
...             five_y.append(reduced_X3D[i][1])
...             five_z.append(reduced_X3D[i][2])

...         elif y[i] == 6:
...             six_x.append(reduced_X3D[i][0])
...             six_y.append(reduced_X3D[i][1])
...             six_z.append(reduced_X3D[i][2])

...         elif y[i] == 7:
...             seven_x.append(reduced_X3D[i][0])
...             seven_y.append(reduced_X3D[i][1])
...             seven_z.append(reduced_X3D[i][2])

...         elif y[i] == 8:
...             eight_x.append(reduced_X3D[i][0])
...             eight_y.append(reduced_X3D[i][1])
...             eight_z.append(reduced_X3D[i][2])
...         elif y[i] == 9:
...             nine_x.append(reduced_X3D[i][0])
...             nine_y.append(reduced_X3D[i][1])
...             nine_z.append(reduced_X3D[i][2])


# 3- Dimensional plot
>>> from mpl_toolkits.mplot3d import Axes3D
>>> fig = plt.figure()
>>> ax = fig.add_subplot(111, projection='3d')

>>> ax.scatter(zero_x, zero_y,zero_z, c='r', marker='x',label='zero')
>>> ax.scatter(one_x, one_y,one_z, c='g', marker='+',label='one')
>>> ax.scatter(two_x, two_y,two_z, c='b', marker='s',label='two')

>>> ax.scatter(three_x, three_y,three_z, c='m', marker='*',label='three')
>>> ax.scatter(four_x, four_y,four_z, c='c', marker='h',label='four')
>>> ax.scatter(five_x, five_y,five_z, c='r', marker='D',label='five')

>>> ax.scatter(six_x, six_y,six_z, c='y', marker='8',label='six')
>>> ax.scatter(seven_x, seven_y,seven_z, c='k', marker='*',label='seven')
>>> ax.scatter(eight_x, eight_y,eight_z, c='r', marker='x',label='eight')

>>> ax.scatter(nine_x, nine_y,nine_z, c='b', marker='D',label='nine')

>>> ax.set_xlabel('Latent Feature 1',fontsize = 13)
>>> ax.set_ylabel('Latent Feature 2',fontsize = 13)
>>> ax.set_zlabel('Latent Feature 3',fontsize = 13)
```

```
>>> ax.set_xlim3d(0,60)

>>> plt.legend(loc='upper left', numpoints=1, ncol=3, fontsize=10,
bbox_to_anchor=(0, 0))

>>> plt.show()
```

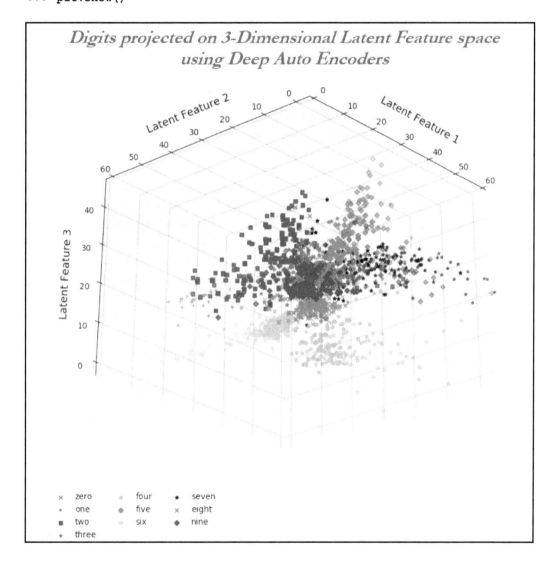

3D plots from deep auto encoders do provide well separated classification compared with three PCAs. Here we have got better separation of the digits. One important point the reader should consider here is that the above plot is the rotated view from *(0, 0, 0)*, as data separation does not happen across orthogonal planes (like PCAs), hence we need to see the view from origin in order to see this non-linear classification.

Summary

In this chapter, you have learned about various unsupervised learning methods to identify the structures and patterns within the data using k-mean clustering, PCA, SVD and deep auto encoders. Also, the k-means clustering algorithm explained with iris data. Methods were shown on how to choose the optimal k-value based on various performance metrics. Handwritten data from scikit-learn was been utilized to compare the differences between linear methods like PCA and SVD with non-linear techniques and deep auto encoders. The differences between PCA and SVD were given in detail so that the reader can understand SVD, which can be applied even on rectangular matrices where the number of users and number of products is not necessarily equal. In the end, through visualization, it has been proven that deep auto encoders are better at separating digits than linear unsupervised learning methods like PCA and SVD.

In the next chapter, we will be discussing various reinforcement learning methods and their utilities in artificial intelligence and so on.

5
Reinforcement Learning

Reinforcement learning (**RL**) is the third major section of machine learning after supervised and unsupervised learning. These techniques have gained a lot of traction in recent years in the application of artificial intelligence. In reinforcement learning, sequential decisions are to be made rather than one shot decision making, which makes it difficult to train the models in a few cases. In this chapter, we would be covering various techniques used in reinforcement learning with practical examples to support with. Though covering all topics are beyond the scope of this book, but we did cover the most important fundamentals here for a reader to create enough enthusiasm on this subject. Topics discussed in this chapter are:

- Markov decision process
- Bellman equations
- Dynamic programming
- Monte Carlo methods
- Temporal difference learning

Reinforcement learning basics

Before we deep dive into the details of reinforcement learning, I would like to cover some of the basics necessary for understanding the various nuts and bolts of RL methodologies. These basics appear across various sections of this chapter, which we will explain in detail whenever required:

- **Environment:** This is any system that has states, and mechanisms to transition between states. For example, the environment for a robot is the landscape or facility it operates.
- **Agent:** This is an automated system that interacts with the environment.
- **State:** The state of the environment or system is the set of variables or features that fully describe the environment.
- **Goal or absorbing state or terminal state:** This is the state that provides a higher discounted cumulative reward than any other state. A high cumulative reward prevents the best policy from being dependent on the initial state during training. Whenever an agent reaches its goal, we will finish one episode.
- **Action:** This defines the transition between states. The agent is responsible for performing, or at least recommending an action. Upon execution of the action, the agent collects a reward (or punishment) from the environment.
- **Policy:** This defines the action to be selected and executed for any state of the environment. In other words, policy is the agent's behavior; it is a map from state to action. Policies could be either deterministic or stochastic.
- **Best policy:** This is the policy generated through training. It defines the model in Q-learning and is constantly updated with any new episode.
- **Rewards**: This quantifies the positive or negative interaction of the agent with the environment. Rewards are usually immediate earnings made by the agent reaching each state.

- **Returns or value function**: A value function (also called returns) is a prediction of future rewards of each state. These are used to evaluate the goodness/badness of the states, based on which, the agent will choose/act on for selecting the next best state:

$$V_\pi(S) = E_\pi[\, R_t + \gamma\, R_{t+1} + \gamma^2\, R_{t+2} + \cdots \setminus S_t = s\,]$$

- **Episode:** This defines the number of steps necessary to reach the goal state from an initial state. Episodes are also known as trials.
- **Horizon:** This is the number of future steps or actions used in the maximization of the reward. The horizon can be infinite, in which case, the future rewards are discounted in order for the value of the policy to converge.
- **Exploration versus Exploitation:** RL is a type of trial and error learning. The goal is to find the best policy; and at the same time, remain alert to explore some unknown policies. A classic example would be treasure hunting: if we just go to the locations greedily (exploitation), we fail to look for other places where hidden treasure might also exist (exploration). By exploring the unknown states, and by taking chances, even when the immediate rewards are low and without losing the maximum rewards, we might achieve greater goals. In other words, we are escaping the local optimum in order to achieve a global optimum (which is exploration), rather than just a short-term focus purely on the immediate rewards (which is exploitation). Here are a couple of examples to explain the difference:
    - **Restaurant selection**: By exploring unknown restaurants once in a while, we might find a much better one than our regular favorite restaurant:
        - **Exploitation**: Going to your favorite restaurant
        - **Exploration**: Trying a new restaurant
    - **Oil drilling example:** By exploring new untapped locations, we may get newer insights that are more beneficial that just exploring the same place:
        - **Exploitation**: Drill for oil at best known location
        - **Exploration**: Drill at a new location

- **State-Value versus State-Action Function:** In action-value, Q represents the expected return (cumulative discounted reward) an agent is to receive when taking Action *A* in State *S*, and behaving according to a certain policy π(a|s) afterwards (which is the probability of taking an action in a given state).

  In state-value, the value is the expected return an agent is to receive from being in state *s* behaving under a policy *π(a|s)*. More specifically, the state-value is an expectation over the action-values under a policy:

$$V(S) = \sum_a \pi(a \backslash s)\, Q(s, a)$$

- **On-policy versus off-policy TD control:** An off-policy learner learns the value of the optimal policy independently of the agent's actions. Q-learning is an off-policy learner. An on-policy learner learns the value of the policy being carried out by the agent, including the exploration steps.
- **Prediction and control problems:** Prediction talks about how well I do, based on the given policy: meaning, if someone has given me a policy and I implement it, how much reward I will get for that. Whereas, in control, the problem is to find the best policy so that I can maximize the reward.
- **Prediction:** Evaluation of the values of states for a given policy.

  For the uniform random policy, what is the value function for all states?

- **Control:** Optimize the future by finding the best policy.

  What is the optimal value function over all possible policies, and what is the optimal policy?

  Usually, in reinforcement learning, we need to solve the prediction problem first, in order to solve the control problem after, as we need to figure out all the policies to figure out the best or optimal one.

- **RL Agent Taxonomy:** An RL agent includes one or more of the following components:
    - **Policy:** Agent's behavior function (map from state to action); Policies can be either deterministic or stochastic
    - **Value function:** How good is each state (or) prediction of expected future reward for each state

- **Model:** Agent's representation of the environment. A model predicts what the environment will do next:
  - **Transitions:** p predicts the next state (that is, dynamics):

$$P_{s,a}(S') = \mathbb{P}[S' = s' \mid S = s, A = a]$$

  - **Rewards:** R predicts the next (immediate) reward

$$R_a(S) = \mathbb{E}[R \mid S = s, A = a]$$

Let us explain the various categories possible in RL agent taxonomy, based on combinations of policy and value, and model individual components with the following maze example. In the following maze, you have both the start and the goal; the agent needs to reach the goal as quickly as possible, taking a path to gain the total maximum reward and the minimum total negative reward. Majorly five categorical way this problem can be solved:

- Value based
- Policy based
- Actor critic
- Model free
- Model based

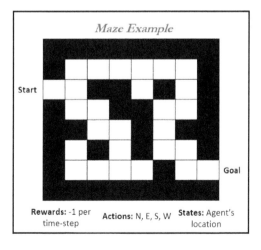

Category 1 - value based

Value function does look like the right-hand side of the image (the sum of discounted future rewards) where every state has some value. Let's say, the state one step away from the goal has a value of -1; and two steps away from the goal has a value of -2. In a similar way, the starting point has a value of -16. If the agent gets stuck in the wrong place, the value could be as much as -24. In fact, the agent does move across the grid based on the best possible values to reach its goal. For example, the agent is at a state with a value of -15. Here, it can choose to move either north or south, so it chooses to move north due to the high reward, which is -14 rather, than moving south, which has a value of -16. In this way, the agent chooses its path across the grid until it reaches the goal.

- **Value Function**: Only values are defined at all states
- **No Policy (Implicit)**: No exclusive policy is present; policies are chosen based on the values at each state

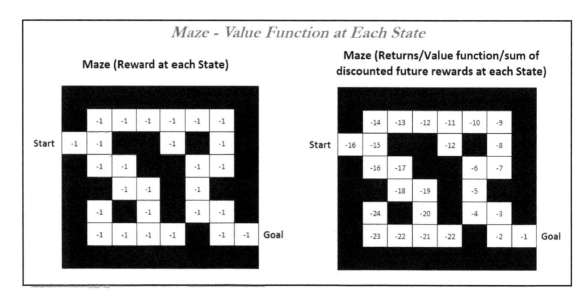

Category 2 - policy based

The arrows in the following image represent what an agent chooses as the direction of the next move while in any of these states. For example, the agent first moves east and then north, following all the arrows until the goal has been reached. This is also known as mapping from states to actions. Once we have this mapping, an agent just needs to read it and behave accordingly.

- **Policy**: Policies or arrows that get adjusted to reach the maximum possible future rewards. As the name suggests, only policies are stored and optimized to maximize rewards.
- **No value function**: No values exist for the states.

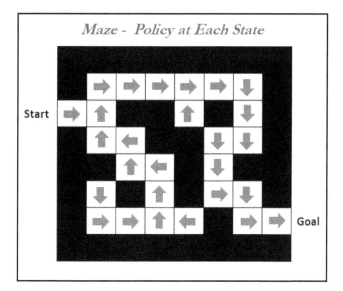

Category 3 - actor-critic

In Actor-Critic, we have both policy and value functions (or a combination of value-based and policy-based). This method is the best of both worlds:

- Policy
- Value Function

Category 4 - model-free

In RL, a fundamental distinction is if it is model-based or model-free. In model-free, we do not explicitly model the environment, or we do not know the entire dynamics of a complete environment. Instead, we just go directly to the policy or value function to gain the experience and figure out how the policy affects the reward:

- Policy and/or value function
  - No model

Category 5 - model-based

In model-based RL, we first build the entire dynamics of the environment:

- Policy and/or value function
- Model

After going through all the above categories, the following Venn diagram shows the entire landscape of the taxonomy of an RL agent at one single place. If you pick up any paper related to reinforcement learning, those methods can fit in within any section of this landscape.

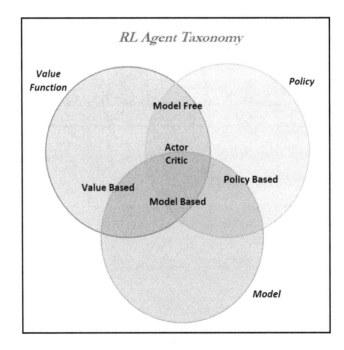

Fundamental categories in sequential decision making

There are two fundamental types of problems in sequential decision making:

- **Reinforcement learning** (for example, autonomous helicopter, and so on):
    - Environment is initially unknown
    - Agent interacts with the environment and obtain policies, rewards, values from the environment
    - Agent improves its policy
- **Planning** (for example, chess, Atari games, and so on):
    - Model of environment or complete dynamics of environment is known
    - Agent performs computation with its model (without any external interaction)
    - Agent improves its policy
    - These are the type of problems also known as reasoning, searching, introspection, and so on

Though the preceding two categories can be linked together as per the given problem, but this is basically a broad view of the two types of setups.

Markov decision processes and Bellman equations

Markov decision process (**MDP**) formally describes an environment for reinforcement learning. Where:

- Environment is fully observable
- Current state completely characterizes the process (which means the future state is entirely dependent on the current state rather than historic states or values)
- Almost all RL problems can be formalized as MDPs (for example, optimal control primarily deals with continuous MDPs)

Central idea of MDP: MDP works on the simple Markovian property of a state; for example, S_{t+1} is entirely dependent on latest state S_t rather than any historic dependencies. In the following equation, the current state captures all the relevant information from the history, which means the current state is a sufficient statistic of the future:

$$\mathbb{P}\left[S_{t+1} \mid S_t\right] = \mathbb{P}\left[S_{t+1} \mid S_1, S_2, \ldots\ldots, S_t\right]$$

An intuitive sense of this property can be explained with the autonomous helicopter example: the next step is for the helicopter to move either to the right, left, to pitch, or to roll, and so on, entirely dependent on the current position of the helicopter, rather than where it was five minutes before.

Modeling of MDP: RL problems models the world using MDP formulation as a five tuple $(S, A, \{P_{sa}\}, y, R)$

- S - Set of States (set of possible orientations of the helicopter)
- A - Set of Actions (set of all possible positions that can pull the control stick)
- P_{sa} - State transition distributions (or state transition probability distributions) provide transitions from one state to another and the respective probabilities needed for the Markov process:

$$\sum_{s'} P_{s,a}(s') = 1 \ ; \ P_{s,a}(s') \geq 0$$

$$State\ Transition\ Probabilities = from\ state(s) \begin{array}{c} to\ state(s') \\ \begin{bmatrix} p_{11} & \cdots & p_{1n} \\ \vdots & \ddots & \vdots \\ p_{m1} & \cdots & p_{mn} \end{bmatrix} \end{array}$$

- γ - Discount factor:

$$0 \leq \gamma < 1$$

- R - Reward function (maps set of states to real numbers, either positive or negative):

$$R : S \rightarrow \mathbb{R}$$

Returns are calculated by discounting the future rewards until terminal state is reached.

Bellman Equations for MDP: Bellman equations are utilized for the mathematical formulation of MDP, which will be solved to obtain the optimal policies of the environment. Bellman equations are also known as **dynamic programming equations** and are a necessary condition for the optimality associated with the mathematical optimization method that is known as dynamic programming. Bellman equations are linear equations which can be solvable for the entire environment. However, the time complexity for solving these equations is $O\ (n^3)$, which becomes computationally very expensive when the number of states in an environment is large; and sometimes, it is not feasible to explore all the states because the environment itself is very large. In those scenarios, we need to look at other ways of solving problems.

In Bellman equations, value function can be decomposed into two parts:

- Immediate reward R_{t+1}, from the successor state you will end up with
- Discounted value of successor states $\gamma v(S_{t+1})$ you will get from that timestep onwards:

$$v(s) = \mathbb{E}\left[G_t \mid S_t = s\right]$$

$$= \mathbb{E}\left[R_{t+1} + \gamma R_{t+2} + \gamma^2 R_{t+3} + \cdots \mid S_t = s\right]$$

$$= \mathbb{E}\left[R_{t+1} + \gamma(R_{t+2} + \gamma R_{t+3} + \cdots) \mid S_t = s\right]$$

$$= \mathbb{E}\left[R_{t+1} + \gamma(G_{t+1}) \mid S_t = s\right]$$

$$= \mathbb{E}\left[R_{t+1} + \gamma(G_{t+1}) \mid S_t = s\right]$$

$$= \mathbb{E}\left[R_{t+1} + \gamma v(S_{t+1}) \mid S_t = s\right]$$

Grid world example of MDP: Robot navigation tasks live in the following type of grid world. An obstacle is shown the cell (2,2), through which the robot can't navigate. We would like the robot to move to the upper-right cell (4,3) and when it reaches that position, the robot will get a reward of +1. The robot should avoid the cell (4,2), as, if it moved into that cell, it would receive a-1 reward.

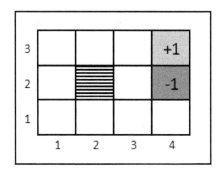

Robot can be in any of the following positions:

- *11 States* - (except cell (2,2), in which we have got an obstacle for the robot)
- A = {N-north, S-south, E-east, W-west}

In the real world, robot movements are noisy, and a robot may not be able to move exactly where it has been asked to. Examples might include that some of its wheels slipped, its parts were loosely connected, it had incorrect actuators, and so on. When asked to move by 1 meter, it may not be able to move exactly 1 meter; instead, it may move 90-105 centimeters, and so on.

In a simplified grid world, stochastic dynamics of a robot can be modeled as follows. If we command the robot to go north, there is a 10% chance that the robot could drag towards the left and a 10 % chance that it could drag towards the right. Only 80 percent of the time it may actually go north. When a robot bounces off the wall (including obstacles) and just stays at the same position, nothing happens:

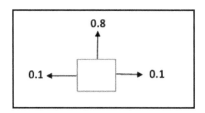

Every state in this grid world example is represented by (x, y) coordinates. Let's say it is at state (3,1) and we asked the robot to move north, then the state transition probability matrices are as follows:

$$State\ transisition\ probabilites\ =\ P_{s,a}(s')$$

$$P_{(3,1),N}((3,2)) = 0.8$$

$$P_{(3,1),N}((4,1)) = 0.1$$

$$P_{(3,1),N}((4,1)) = 0.1$$

$$P_{(3,1),N}((3,3)) = 0$$

The probability of staying in the same position is 0 for the robot.

As we know, that sum of all the state transition probabilities sums up to 1:

$$\sum_{s'} P_{s,a}(s') = 1$$

Reward function:

$$R((4,3)) = +1$$

$$R((4,2)) = -1$$

$$For\ all\ other\ states, R(S) = -0.02$$

For all the other states, there are small negative reward values, which means it charges the robot for battery or fuel consumption when running around the grid, which creates solutions that do not waste moves or time while reaching the goal of reward +1, which encourages the robot to reach the goal as quickly as possible with as little fuel used as possible.

The world ends when the robot reaches either +1 or -1 states. No more rewards are possible after reaching any of these states; these can be called absorbing states. These are zero-cost absorbing states and the robot stays there forever.

MDP working model:

- At state S_0
- Choose a_0
- Get to $S_1 \sim P_{s0, a0}$
- Choose a_1
- Get to $S_2 \sim P_{s1, a1}$
- and so on ....

After a while, it takes all the rewards and sums up to obtain:

$$Total\ Payoff = R(S_0) + \gamma\ R(S_1) + \gamma^2 R(S_2) + \cdots$$

$$where\ 0 \leq \gamma < 1$$

Discount factor models an economic application, in which one dollar earned today is more valuable than one dollar earned tomorrow.

The robot needs to choose actions over time (a_0, a_1, a_2, ...) to maximize the expected payoff:

$$E\ [\ R(S_0) + \gamma\ R(S_1) + \gamma^2 R(S_2) + \cdots\ ]$$

Over the period, a reinforcement learning algorithm learns a policy which is a mapping of actions for each state, which means it is a recommended action, which the robot needs to take based on the state in which it exists:

$$Policy\ \Pi : S \rightarrow A$$

Optimal Policy for Grid World: Policy maps from states to actions, which means that, if you are in a particular state, you need to take this particular action. The following policy is the optimal policy which maximizes the expected value of the total payoff or sum of discounted rewards. Policy always looks into the current state rather than previous states, which is the Markovian property:

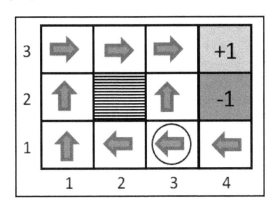

One tricky thing to look at is at the position (3,1): optimal policy shows to go left (West) rather than going (north), which may have a fewer number of states; however, we have an even riskier state that we may step into. So, going left may take longer, but it safely arrives at the destination without getting into negative traps. These types of things can be obtained from computing, which do not look obvious to humans, but a computer is very good at coming up with these policies:

Define: V^π, V^*, π^*

V^π = For any given policy π, value function is $V^\pi : S \rightarrow R$ such that $V^\pi(S)$ is expected total payoff starting in state S, and execute π

$$V^\Pi(S) = E\left[R(S_0) + \gamma R(S_1) + \gamma^2 R(S_2) + \cdots \setminus \pi, S_0 = s\right]$$

Random policy for grid world: The following is an example of a random policy and its value functions. This policy is a rather bad policy with negative values. For any policy, we can write down the value function for that particular policy:

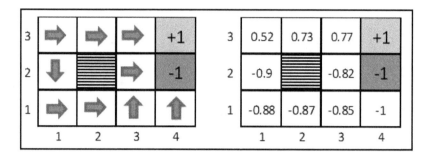

$$V^{\Pi}(S) = E\,[\,R(S_0) + \gamma\,(\,R(S_1) + \gamma\,R(S_2) + \cdots\,)\setminus \pi, S_0 = s\,]$$

$$V^{\Pi}(S) = E\,[\,R(S_0) + V^{\Pi}(S_1)\setminus \pi, S_0 = s\,]$$

$$S_0 \rightarrow s\,;\ \ S_1 \rightarrow\ s\,'$$

$$P_{S\,\pi(S)} = probability\ of\ taking\ action\ from\ state\ s$$

$$Bellman\ Equations:\quad V^{\Pi}(S) = R(S) + \gamma \sum_{S'} P_{S\,\pi(S)}\,(S')\,V^{\pi}(S')$$

In simple English, Bellman equations illustrate that the value of the current state is equal to the immediate reward and discount factor applied to the expected total payoff of new states (S') multiplied by their probability to take action (policy) into those states.

Bellman equations are used to solve value functions for a policy in close form, given fixed policy, how to solve the value function equations.

Bellman equations impose a set of linear constraints on value functions. It turns out that we solve the value function at any state S by solving a set of linear equations.

Example of Bellman equations with a grid world problem:

The chosen policy for cell *(3,1)* is to move north. However, we have stochasticity in the system that about 80 percent of the time it moves in the said direction, and *20%* of the time it drifts sideways, either left (10 percent) or right (10 percent).

$$\pi\left((3,1)\right) \doteq North$$

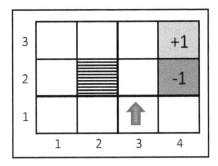

$$V^{\Pi}\left((3,1)\right) = R\left((3,1)\right) + \gamma \left[0.8 * V^{\Pi}\left((3,2)\right) + 0.1 * V^{\Pi}\left((4,1)\right) + 0.1 * V^{\Pi}\left((2,1)\right)\right]$$

Similar equations can be written for all the 11 states of the MDPs within the grid. We can obtain the following metrics, from which we will solve all the unknown values, using a system of linear equation methods:

- 11 equations
- 11 unknown value function variables
- 11 constraints

This is solving an n variables with n equations problem, for which we can find the exact form of a solution using a system of equations easily to get an exact solution for V (π) for the entire closed form of the grid, which consists of all the states.

Dynamic programming

Dynamic programming is a sequential way of solving complex problems by breaking them down into sub-problems and solving each of them. Once it solves the sub-problems, then it puts those subproblem solutions together to solve the original complex problem. In the reinforcement learning world, Dynamic Programming is a solution methodology to compute optimal policies given a perfect model of the environment as a Markov Decision Process (MDP).

Dynamic programming holds good for problems which have the following two properties. MDPs, in fact, satisfy both properties, which makes DP a good fit for solving them by solving Bellman Equations:

- Optimal substructure
    - Principle of optimality applies
    - Optimal solution can be decomposed into sub-problems
- Overlapping sub-problems
    - Sub-problems recur many times
    - Solutions can be cached and reused
- MDP satisfies both the properties - luckily!
    - Bellman equations have recursive decomposition of state-values
    - Value function stores and reuses solutions

Though, classical DP algorithms are of limited utility in reinforcement learning, both because of their assumptions of a perfect model and high computational expense. However, it is still important, as they provide an essential foundation for understanding all the methods in the RL domain.

Algorithms to compute optimal policy using dynamic programming

Standard algorithms to compute optimal policies for MDP utilizing Dynamic Programming are as follows, and we will be covering both in detail in later sections of this chapter:

- **Value Iteration algorithm:** An iterative algorithm, in which state values are iterated until it reaches optimal values; and, subsequently, optimum values are utilized to determine the optimal policy
- **Policy Iteration algorithm:** An iterative algorithm, in which policy evaluation and policy improvements are utilized alternatively to reach optimal policy

Value Iteration algorithm: Value Iteration algorithms are easy to compute for the very reason of applying iteratively on only state values. First, we will compute the optimal value function V^*, then plug those values into the optimal policy equation to determine the optimal policy. Just to give the size of the problem, for 11 possible states, each state can have four policies (N-north, S-south, E-east, W-west), which gives an overall 11^4 possible policies. The value iteration algorithm consists of the following steps:

1. Initialize $V(S) = 0$ for all states S
2. For every S, update:

$$V(S) = R(S) + \max_a \gamma \sum_{s'} P_{s,a}(S') V(S')$$

3. By repeatedly computing step 2, we will eventually converge to optimal values for all the states:

$$\boxed{V(S) \to V^*(S)}$$

There are two ways of updating the values in step 2 of the algorithm

- **Synchronous update** - By performing synchronous update (or Bellman backup operator) we will perform RHS computing and substitute LHS of the equation represented as follows:

    Synchronous update or Bellman backup operator => $V := B(V)$

- **Asynchronous update** - Update the values of the states one at a time rather than updating all the states at the same time, in which states will be updated in a fixed order (update state number 1, followed by 2, and so on.). During convergence, asynchronous updates are a little faster than synchronous updates.

Illustration of value iteration on grid world example: The application of the Value iteration on a grid world is explained in the following image, and the complete code for solving a real problem is provided at the end of this section. After applying the previous value iteration algorithm on MDP using Bellman equations, we've obtained the following optimal values V* for all the states (Gamma value chosen as *0.99*):

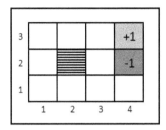

When we plug these values in to our policy equation, we obtain the following policy grid:

$$Optimal\ Policy\ Equation = \ \Pi^*(S) = \underset{a}{\text{argmax}} \sum_{s'} P_{s,a}(S')\,V^*(S')$$

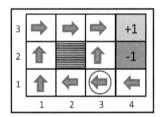

Here, at position (3,1) we would like to prove mathematically why an optimal policy suggests taking going left (west) rather than moving up (north):

$$West\ Direction = \sum_{s'} P_{s,a}(S')\,V^*(S')$$

$$= 0.8 * 0.75 + 0.1 * 0.69 + 0.1 * 0.71\ = 0.740$$

Due to the wall, whenever the robot tries to move towards South (downwards side), it will remain in the same place, hence we assigned the value of the current position 0.71 for a probability of 0.1.

Similarly, for north, we calculated the total payoff as follows:

$$North\ Direction = \sum_{S'} P_{s,a}(S')\, V^*(S')$$

$$= 0.8 * 0.69 + 0.1 * 0.75 + 0.1 * 0.49 \quad = 0.676$$

So, it would be optimal to move towards the west rather than north, and therefore the optimal policy is chosen to do so.

Policy Iteration Algorithm: Policy iterations are another way of obtaining optimal policies for MDP in which policy evaluation and policy improvement algorithms are applied iteratively until the solution converges to the optimal policy. Policy Iteration Algorithm consists of the following steps:

1. Initialize random policy π
2. Repeatedly do the following until convergence happens
   - Solve Bellman equations for the current policy for obtaining V^π for using system of linear equations:

$$Solve\ Bellman\ Equations\ for\ a\ given\ policy => \quad V := V^\Pi$$

   - Update the policy as per the new value function to improve the policy by pretending the new value is an optimal value using argmax formulae:

$$Calculate\ optimal\ policy\ for\ a\ given\ value\ function => \quad \Pi(S)$$
$$= \underset{a}{argmax} \sum_{S'} P_{s,a}(S')\, V(S')$$

3. By repeating these steps, both value and policy will converge to optimal values:

$$V \rightarrow V^*$$

$$\Pi \rightarrow \Pi^*$$

Policy iterations tend to do well with smaller problems. If an MDP has an enormous number of states, policy iterations will be computationally expensive. As a result, large MDPs tend to use value iterations rather than policy iterations.

What if we don't know exact state transition probabilities in real life examples $P_{s,a}$?

We need to estimate the probabilities from the data by using the following simple formulae:

$$P_{s,a}(S') = \frac{Number\ of\ times\ took\ action\ "a"\ in\ state\ "s"\ got\ to\ "s'\ "}{Number\ of\ times\ took\ action\ "a"\ in\ "s"}$$

$$or = \frac{1}{|S|}\ if\ we\ do\ not\ have\ data\ for\ some\ states$$

If for some states no data is available, which leads to 0/0 problem, we can take a default probability from uniform distributions.

Grid world example using value and policy iteration algorithms with basic Python

The classic grid world example has been used to illustrate value and policy iterations with Dynamic Programming to solve MDP's Bellman equations. In the following grid, the agent will start at the south-west corner of the grid in (1,1) position and the goal is to move towards the north-east corner, to position (4,3). Once it reaches the goal, the agent will get a reward of +1. During the journey, it should avoid the danger zone (4,2), because this will give out a negative penalty of reward -1. The agent cannot get into the position where the obstacle (2,2) is present from any direction. Goal and danger zones are the terminal states, which means the agent continues to move around until it reaches one of these two states. The reward for all the other states would be -0.02. Here, the task is to determine the optimal policy (direction to move) for the agent at every state (11 states altogether), so that the agent's total reward is the maximum, or so that the agent can reach the goal as quickly as possible. The agent can move in 4 directions: north, south, east and west.

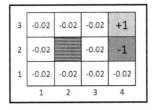

The complete code was written in the Python programming language with class implementation. For further reading, please refer to object oriented programming in Python to understand class, objects, constructors, and so on.

Import the `random` package for generating moves in any of the N, E, S, W directions:

```
>>> import random, operator
```

The following `argmax` function calculated the maximum state among the given states, based on the value for each state:

```
>>> def argmax(seq, fn):
...     best = seq[0]; best_score = fn(best)
...     for x in seq:
...         x_score = fn(x)
...     if x_score > best_score:
...         best, best_score = x, x_score
...     return best
```

To add two vectors at component level, the following code has been utilized for:

```
>>> def vector_add(a, b):
...     return tuple(map(operator.add, a, b))
```

Orientations provide what the increment value would be, which needs to be added to the existing position of the agent; orientations can be applied on the *x*-axis or *y*-axis:

```
>>> orientations = [(1,0), (0, 1), (-1, 0), (0, -1)]
```

The following function is used to turn the agent in the right direction, as we know at every command the agent moves in that direction about 80% of the time, whilst 10% of the time it would move right, and 10% it would move left.:

```
>>> def turn_right(orientation):
...     return orientations[orientations.index(orientation)-1]
>>> def turn_left(orientation):
...     return orientations[(orientations.index(orientation)+1) %
len(orientations)]
>>> def isnumber(x):
...     return hasattr(x, '__int__')
```

The Markov decision process is defined as a class here. Every MDP is defined by an initial position, state, transition model, reward function, and gamma values.

```
>>> class MDP:
... def __init__(self, init_pos, actlist, terminals, transitions={},
states=None, gamma=0.99):
...        if not (0 < gamma <= 1):
...            raise ValueError("MDP should have 0 < gamma <= 1 values")
...        if states:
...            self.states = states
...        else:
...            self.states = set()
...            self.init_pos = init_pos
...            self.actlist = actlist
...            self.terminals = terminals
...            self.transitions = transitions
...            self.gamma = gamma
...            self.reward = {}
```

Returns a numeric reward for the state:

```
... def R(self, state):
...        return self.reward[state]
```

Transition model with from a state and an action returns a list of (probability, result-state) pairs for each state:

```
... def T(self, state, action):
...        if(self.transitions == {}):
...            raise ValueError("Transition model is missing")
...        else:
...            return self.transitions[state][action]
```

Set of actions that can be performed at a particular state:

```
... def actions(self, state):
...        if state in self.terminals:
...            return [None]
...        else:
...            return self.actlist
```

Class `GridMDP` is created for modeling a 2D grid world with grid values at each state, terminal positions, initial position, and gamma value (discount):

```
>>> class GridMDP(MDP):
... def __init__(self, grid, terminals, init_pos=(0, 0), gamma=0.99):
```

The following code is used for reversing the grid, as we would like to see *row 0* at the bottom instead of at the top:

```
... grid.reverse()
```

The following __init__ command is a constructor used within the grid class for initializing parameters:

```
... MDP.__init__(self, init_pos, actlist=orientations,
terminals=terminals, gamma=gamma)
... self.grid = grid
... self.rows = len(grid)
... self.cols = len(grid[0])
... for x in range(self.cols):
...     for y in range(self.rows):
...         self.reward[x, y] = grid[y][x]
...         if grid[y][x] is not None:
...             self.states.add((x, y))
```

State transitions provide randomly 80% toward the desired direction and 10% for left and right. This is to model the randomness in a robot which might slip on the floor, and so on:

```
... def T(self, state, action):
...     if action is None:
...         return [(0.0, state)]
...     else:
...         return [(0.8, self.go(state, action)),
...                 (0.1, self.go(state, turn_right(action))),
...                 (0.1, self.go(state, turn_left(action)))]
```

Returns the state that results from going in the direction, subject to where that state is in the list of valid states. If the next state is not in the list, like hitting the wall, then the agent should remain in the same state:

```
... def go(self, state, direction):
...     state1 = vector_add(state, direction)
...     return state1 if state1 in self.states else state
```

Convert a mapping from (x, y) to v into [[..., v, ...]] grid:

```
... def to_grid(self, mapping):
...     return list(reversed([[mapping.get((x, y), None)
...                            for x in range(self.cols)]
...                            for y in range(self.rows)]))
```

Convert orientations into arrows for better graphical representations:

```
... def to_arrows(self, policy):
...     chars = {(1, 0): '>', (0, 1): '^', (-1, 0): '<', (0, -1):
        'v', None: '.'}
...     return self.to_grid({s: chars[a] for (s, a) in policy.items()})
```

The following code is used for solving an MDP, using value iterations, and returns optimum state values:

```
>>> def value_iteration(mdp, epsilon=0.001):
...     STSN = {s: 0 for s in mdp.states}
...     R, T, gamma = mdp.R, mdp.T, mdp.gamma
...     while True:
...         STS = STSN.copy()
...         delta = 0
...         for s in mdp.states:
...             STSN[s] = R(s) + gamma * max([sum([p * STS[s1] for
...             (p, s1) in T(s,a)]) for a in mdp.actions(s)])
...             delta = max(delta, abs(STSN[s] - STS[s]))
...         if delta < epsilon * (1 - gamma) / gamma:
...             return STS
```

Given an MDP and a utility function `STS`, determine the best policy, as a mapping from state to action:

```
>>> def best_policy(mdp, STS):
...     pi = {}
...     for s in mdp.states:
...         pi[s] = argmax(mdp.actions(s), lambda a: expected_utility(a, s,
STS, mdp))
...     return pi
```

The expected utility of doing `a` in state `s`, according to the MDP and STS:

```
>>> def expected_utility(a, s, STS, mdp):
...     return sum([p * STS[s1] for (p, s1) in mdp.T(s, a)])
```

The following code is used to solve an MDP using policy iterations by alternatively performing policy evaluation and policy improvement steps:

```
>>> def policy_iteration(mdp):
...     STS = {s: 0 for s in mdp.states}
...     pi = {s: random.choice(mdp.actions(s)) for s in mdp.states}
...     while True:
...         STS = policy_evaluation(pi, STS, mdp)
...         unchanged = True
...         for s in mdp.states:
```

```
...                    a = argmax(mdp.actions(s),lambda a: expected_utility(a, s,
STS, mdp))
...                    if a != pi[s]:
...                        pi[s] = a
...                        unchanged = False
...            if unchanged:
...                return pi
```

The following code is used to return an updated utility mapping U from each state in the MDP to its utility, using an approximation (modified policy iteration):

```
>>> def policy_evaluation(pi, STS, mdp, k=20):
...        R, T, gamma = mdp.R, mdp.T, mdp.gamma
 ..        for i in range(k):
...        for s in mdp.states:
...            STS[s] = R(s) + gamma * sum([p * STS[s1] for (p, s1) in T(s,
pi[s])])
...        return STS

>>> def print_table(table, header=None, sep=' ', numfmt='{}'):
...        justs = ['rjust' if isnumber(x) else 'ljust' for x in table[0]]
...        if header:
...            table.insert(0, header)
...        table = [[numfmt.format(x) if isnumber(x) else x for x in row]
...                for row in table]
...        sizes = list(map(lambda seq: max(map(len, seq)),
...                    list(zip(*[map(str, row) for row in table]))))
...        for row in table:
...            print(sep.join(getattr(str(x), j)(size) for (j, size, x)
...                in zip(justs, sizes, row)))
```

The following is the input grid of a 4 x 3 grid environment that presents the agent with a sequential decision-making problem:

```
>>> sequential_decision_environment = GridMDP([[-0.02, -0.02, -0.02, +1],
...                                             [-0.02, None, -0.02, -1],
...                                             [-0.02, -0.02, -0.02,
-0.02]],
...                                             terminals=[(3, 2), (3, 1)])
```

The following code is for performing a value iteration on the given sequential decision-making environment:

```
>>> value_iter =
best_policy(sequential_decision_environment,value_iteration
(sequential_decision_environment, .01))
```

```
>>> print("\n Optimal Policy based on Value Iteration\n")
>>> print_table(sequential_decision_environment.to_arrows(value_iter))
```

```
Optimal Policy based on Value Iteration

 >   >        >    .
 ^      None    ^    .
 ^     <        <    <
```

The code for policy iteration is:

```
>>> policy_iter = policy_iteration(sequential_decision_environment)
>>> print("\n Optimal Policy based on Policy Iteration & Evaluation\n")
>>> print_table(sequential_decision_environment.to_arrows(policy_iter))
```

```
Optimal Policy based on Policy Iteration & Evaluation

 >   >       >   .
 ^     None    ^   .
 ^    <       <   <
```

From the preceding output with two results, we can conclude that both value and policy iterations provide the same optimal policy for an agent to move across the grid to reach the goal state in the quickest way possible. When the problem size is large enough, it is computationally advisable to go for value iteration rather than policy iteration, as in policy iterations, we need to perform two steps at every iteration of the policy evaluation and policy improvement.

Monte Carlo methods

Using **Monte Carlo** (**MC**) methods, we will compute the value functions first and determine the optimal policies. In this method, we do not assume complete knowledge of the environment. MC require only experience, which consists of sample sequences of states, actions, and rewards from actual or simulated interactions with the environment. Learning from actual experiences is striking because it requires no prior knowledge of the environment's dynamics, but still attains optimal behavior. This is very similar to how humans or animals learn from actual experience rather than any mathematical model. Surprisingly, in many cases, it is easy to generate experience sampled according to the desired probability distributions, but infeasible to obtain the distributions in explicit form.

Monte Carlo methods solve the reinforcement learning problem based on averaging the sample returns over each episode. This means that we assume experience is divided into episodes, and that all episodes eventually terminate, no matter what actions are selected. Values are estimated and policies are changed only after the completion of each episode. MC methods are incremental in an episode-by-episode sense, but not in a step-by-step (which is an online learning, and which we will cover the same in Temporal Difference learning section) sense.

Monte Carlo methods sample and average returns for each state-action pair over the episode. However, within the same episode, the return after taking an action in one stage depends on the actions taken in later states. Because all the action selections are undergoing learning, the problem becomes non-stationary from the point of view of the earlier state. In order to handle this non-stationarity, we adapt the idea of policy iteration from dynamic programming, in which, first, we compute the value function for a fixed arbitrary policy; and, later, we improve the policy.

Monte Carlo prediction

As we know, Monte Carlo methods predict the state-value function for a given policy. The value of any state is the expected return or expected cumulative future discounted rewards starting from that state. These values are estimated in MC methods simply to average the returns observed after visits to that state. As more and more values are observed, the average should converge to the expected value based on the law of large numbers. In fact, this is the principle applicable in all Monte Carlo methods. The Monte Carlo Policy Evaluation Algorithm consist of the following steps:

1. Initialize:

   $\pi \leftarrow policy\ to\ be\ evaluated$
   $V \leftarrow arbitrary\ state - value\ function$
   $Returns(s) \leftarrow an\ empty\ list, for\ all\ s \in S$

2. Repeat forever:
   - Generate an episode using π
   - For each state s appearing in the episode:
     - G return following the first occurrence of s
     - Append G to Returns(s)
     - V(s) average(Returns(s))

The suitability of Monte Carlo prediction on grid-world problems

The following diagram has been plotted for illustration purposes. However, practically, Monte Carlo methods cannot be easily used for solving grid-world type problems, due to the fact that termination is not guaranteed for all the policies. If a policy was ever found that caused the agent to stay in the same state, then the next episode would never end. Step-by-step learning methods like (**State-Action-Reward-State-Action** (**SARSA**), which we will be covering in a later part of this chapter in TD Learning Control) do not have this problem because they quickly learn during the episode that such policies are poor, and switch to something else.

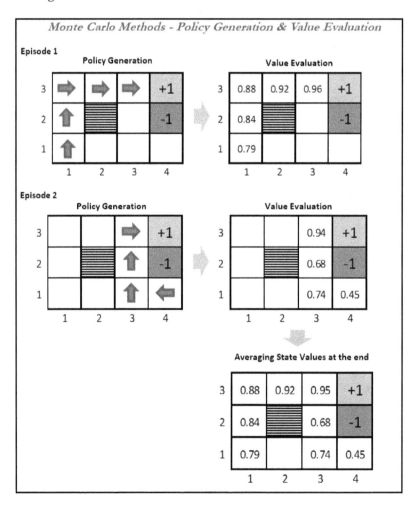

Modeling Blackjack example of Monte Carlo methods using Python

The objective of the popular casino card game Blackjack is to obtain cards, the sum of whose numerical values is as great as possible, without exceeding the value of 21. All face cards (king, queen, and jack) count as 10, and an ace can count as either 1 or as 11, depending upon the way the player wants to use it. Only the ace has this flexibility option. All the other cards are valued at face value. The game begins with two cards dealt with both dealer and players. One of the dealer's cards is face up and the other is face down. If the player has a 'Natural 21' from these first two cards (an ace and a 10-card), the player wins unless the dealer also has a Natural, in which case the game is a draw. If the player does not have a natural, then he can ask for additional cards, one by one (hits), until he either stops (sticks) or exceeds 21 (goes bust). If the player goes bust, he loses; if the player sticks, then it's the dealer's turn. The dealer hits or sticks according to a fixed strategy without choice: the dealer usually sticks on any sum of 17 or greater, and hits otherwise. If the dealer goes bust, then the player automatically wins. If he sticks, the outcome would be either win, lose, or draw, determined by whether the dealer or the player's sum total is closer to 21.

The Blackjack problem can be formulated as an episodic finite MDP, in which each game of Blackjack is an episode. Rewards of +1, -1, and 0 are given for winning, losing, and drawing for each episode respectively at the terminal state and the remaining rewards within the state of game are given the value as 0 with no discount (gamma = 1). Therefore, the terminal rewards are also the returns for this game. We draw the cards from an infinite deck so that no traceable pattern exists. The entire game is modeled in Python in the following code.

The following snippets of code have taken inspiration from *Shangtong Zhang*'s Python codes for RL, and are published in this book with permission from the student of *Richard S. Sutton*, the famous author of *Reinforcement : Learning: An Introduction* (details provided in the *Further reading* section).

The following package is imported for array manipulation and visualization:

```
>>> from __future__ import print_function
>>> import numpy as np
>>> import matplotlib.pyplot as plt
>>> from mpl_toolkits.mplot3d import Axes3D
```

At each turn, the player or dealer can take one of the actions possible: either to hit or to stand. These are the only two states possible :

```
>>> ACTION_HIT = 0
>>> ACTION_STAND = 1
>>> actions = [ACTION_HIT, ACTION_STAND]
```

The policy for player is modeled with 21 arrays of values, as the player will get bust after going over the value of 21:

```
>>> policyPlayer = np.zeros(22)

>>> for i in range(12, 20):
...         policyPlayer[i] = ACTION_HIT
```

The player has taken the policy of stick if he gets a value of either 20 or 21, or else he will keep hitting the deck to draw a new card:

```
>>> policyPlayer[20] = ACTION_STAND
>>> policyPlayer[21] = ACTION_STAND
```

Function form of target policy of a player:

```
>>> def targetPolicyPlayer(usableAcePlayer, playerSum, dealerCard):
...         return policyPlayer[playerSum]
```

Function form of behavior policy of a player:

```
>>> def behaviorPolicyPlayer(usableAcePlayer, playerSum, dealerCard):
...         if np.random.binomial(1, 0.5) == 1:
...             return ACTION_STAND
...         return ACTION_HIT
```

Fixed policy for the dealer is to keep hitting the deck until value is 17 and then stick between 17 to 21:

```
>>> policyDealer = np.zeros(22)
>>> for i in range(12, 17):
...         policyDealer[i] = ACTION_HIT
>>> for i in range(17, 22):
...         policyDealer[i] = ACTION_STAND
```

The following function is used for drawing a new card from the deck with replacement:

```
>>> def getCard():
...     card = np.random.randint(1, 14)
...     card = min(card, 10)
...     return card
```

Let's play the game!

```
>>> def play(policyPlayerFn, initialState=None, initialAction=None):
```

1. Sum of the player, player's trajectory and whether player uses ace as 11:

```
...         playerSum = 0
...         playerTrajectory = []
...         usableAcePlayer = False
```

2. Dealer status of drawing cards:

```
...         dealerCard1 = 0
...         dealerCard2 = 0
...         usableAceDealer = False

...         if initialState is None:
```

3. Generate a random initial state:

```
...             numOfAce = 0
```

4. Initializing the player's cards:

```
...             while playerSum < 12:
```

5. If the sum of a player's cards is less than 12, always hit the deck for drawing card:

```
...                 card = getCard()
...                 if card == 1:
...                     numOfAce += 1
...                     card = 11
...                     usableAcePlayer = True
...                 playerSum += card
```

6. If the player's sum is larger than 21, he must hold at least one ace, but two aces are also possible. In that case, he will use ace as 1 rather than 11. If the player has only one ace, then he does not have a usable ace any more:

```
...             if playerSum > 21:
...                 playerSum -= 10
...                 if numOfAce == 1:
...                     usableAcePlayer = False
```

7. Initializing the dealer cards:

```
...             dealerCard1 = getCard()
...             dealerCard2 = getCard()

...         else:
...             usableAcePlayer = initialState[0]
...             playerSum = initialState[1]
...             dealerCard1 = initialState[2]
...             dealerCard2 = getCard()
```

8. Initialize the game state:

```
...         state = [usableAcePlayer, playerSum, dealerCard1]
```

9. Initializing the dealer's sum:

```
...         dealerSum = 0
...         if dealerCard1 == 1 and dealerCard2 != 1:
...             dealerSum += 11 + dealerCard2
...             usableAceDealer = True
...         elif dealerCard1 != 1 and dealerCard2 == 1:
...             dealerSum += dealerCard1 + 11
...             usableAceDealer = True
...         elif dealerCard1 == 1 and dealerCard2 == 1:
...             dealerSum += 1 + 11
...             usableAceDealer = True
...         else:
...             dealerSum += dealerCard1 + dealerCard2
```

10. The game starts from here, as the player needs to draw extra cards from here onwards:

```
...        while True:
...            if initialAction is not None:
...                action = initialAction
...                initialAction = None
...            else:
```

11. Get action based on the current sum of a player:

```
...                action = policyPlayerFn(usableAcePlayer, playerSum,
dealerCard1)
```

12. Tracking the player's trajectory for importance sampling:

```
...                playerTrajectory.append([action, (usableAcePlayer,
playerSum, dealerCard1)])

...            if action == ACTION_STAND:
...                break
```

13. Get new a card if the action is to hit the deck:

```
...            playerSum += getCard()
```

14. Player busts here if the total sum is greater than 21, the game ends, and he gets a reward of -1. However, if he has an ace at his disposal, he can use it to save the game, or else he will lose.

```
...            if playerSum > 21:
...                if usableAcePlayer == True:
...                    playerSum -= 10
...                    usableAcePlayer = False
...                else:
...                    return state, -1, playerTrajectory
```

15. Now it's the dealer's turn. He will draw cards based on a sum: if he reaches 17, he will stop, otherwise keep on drawing cards. If the dealer also has ace, he can use it to achieve the bust situation, otherwise, he goes bust:

```
...        while True:
...            action = policyDealer[dealerSum]
...            if action == ACTION_STAND:
...                break
...            dealerSum += getCard()
...            if dealerSum > 21:
...                if usableAceDealer == True:
```

```
        ...              dealerSum -= 10
        ...              usableAceDealer = False
        ...          else:
        ...              return state, 1, playerTrajectory
```

16. Now we compare the player's sum with the dealer's sum to decide who wins without going bust:

```
        ...      if playerSum > dealerSum:
        ...          return state, 1, playerTrajectory
        ...      elif playerSum == dealerSum:
        ...          return state, 0, playerTrajectory
        ...      else:
        ...          return state, -1, playerTrajectory
```

The following code illustrates the Monte Carlo sample with *On-Policy*:

```
>>> def monteCarloOnPolicy(nEpisodes):
...      statesUsableAce = np.zeros((10, 10))
...      statesUsableAceCount = np.ones((10, 10))
...      statesNoUsableAce = np.zeros((10, 10))
...      statesNoUsableAceCount = np.ones((10, 10))
...      for i in range(0, nEpisodes):
...          state, reward, _ = play(targetPolicyPlayer)
...          state[1] -= 12
...          state[2] -= 1
...          if state[0]:
...              statesUsableAceCount[state[1], state[2]] += 1
...              statesUsableAce[state[1], state[2]] += reward
...          else:
...              statesNoUsableAceCount[state[1], state[2]] += 1
...              statesNoUsableAce[state[1], state[2]] += reward
...      return statesUsableAce / statesUsableAceCount, statesNoUsableAce /
statesNoUsableAceCount
```

The following code discusses Monte Carlo with Exploring Starts, in which all the returns for each state-action pair are accumulated and averaged, irrespective of what policy was in force when they were observed:

```
>>> def monteCarloES(nEpisodes):
...      stateActionValues = np.zeros((10, 10, 2, 2))
...      stateActionPairCount = np.ones((10, 10, 2, 2))
```

Behavior policy is greedy, which gets `argmax` of the average returns (s, a):

```
...         def behaviorPolicy(usableAce, playerSum, dealerCard):
...             usableAce = int(usableAce)
...             playerSum -= 12
...             dealerCard -= 1
...             return np.argmax(stateActionValues[playerSum, dealerCard,
usableAce, :]
                        / stateActionPairCount[playerSum, dealerCard,
usableAce, :])
```

Play continues for several episodes and, at each episode, randomly initialized state, action, and update values of state-action pairs:

```
...         for episode in range(nEpisodes):
...             if episode % 1000 == 0:
...                 print('episode:', episode)
...             initialState = [bool(np.random.choice([0, 1])),
...                             np.random.choice(range(12, 22)),
...                             np.random.choice(range(1, 11))]
...             initialAction = np.random.choice(actions)
...             _, reward, trajectory = play(behaviorPolicy, initialState,
initialAction)
...             for action, (usableAce, playerSum, dealerCard) in trajectory:
...                 usableAce = int(usableAce)
...                 playerSum -= 12
...                 dealerCard -= 1
```

Update values of state-action pairs:

```
...                 stateActionValues[playerSum, dealerCard, usableAce, action]
+= reward
...                 stateActionPairCount[playerSum, dealerCard, usableAce,
action] += 1
...         return stateActionValues / stateActionPairCount
```

Print the state value:

```
>>> figureIndex = 0
>>> def prettyPrint(data, tile, zlabel='reward'):
...     global figureIndex
...     fig = plt.figure(figureIndex)
...     figureIndex += 1
...     fig.suptitle(tile)
...     ax = fig.add_subplot(111, projection='3d')
...     x_axis = []
...     y_axis = []
...     z_axis = []
```

```
...            for i in range(12, 22):
...                for j in range(1, 11):
...                    x_axis.append(i)
...                    y_axis.append(j)
...                    z_axis.append(data[i - 12, j - 1])
...            ax.scatter(x_axis, y_axis, z_axis,c='red')
...            ax.set_xlabel('player sum')
...            ax.set_ylabel('dealer showing')
...            ax.set_zlabel(zlabel)
```

On-Policy results with or without a usable ace for 10,000 and 500,000 iterations:

```
>>> def onPolicy():
...        statesUsableAce1, statesNoUsableAce1 = monteCarloOnPolicy(10000)
...        statesUsableAce2, statesNoUsableAce2 = monteCarloOnPolicy(500000)
...        prettyPrint(statesUsableAce1, 'Usable Ace & 10000 Episodes')
...        prettyPrint(statesNoUsableAce1, 'No Usable Ace & 10000 Episodes')
...        prettyPrint(statesUsableAce2, 'Usable Ace & 500000 Episodes')
...        prettyPrint(statesNoUsableAce2, 'No Usable Ace & 500000 Episodes')
...        plt.show()
```

Optimized or Monte Carlo control of policy iterations:

```
>>> def MC_ES_optimalPolicy():
...        stateActionValues = monteCarloES(500000)
...        stateValueUsableAce = np.zeros((10, 10))
...        stateValueNoUsableAce = np.zeros((10, 10))
      # get the optimal policy
...        actionUsableAce = np.zeros((10, 10), dtype='int')
...        actionNoUsableAce = np.zeros((10, 10), dtype='int')
...        for i in range(10):
...            for j in range(10):
...                stateValueNoUsableAce[i, j] = np.max(stateActionValues[i,
j, 0, :])
...                stateValueUsableAce[i, j] = np.max(stateActionValues[i, j,
1, :])
...                actionNoUsableAce[i, j] = np.argmax(stateActionValues[i, j,
0, :])
...                actionUsableAce[i, j] = np.argmax(stateActionValues[i, j,
1, :])
...        prettyPrint(stateValueUsableAce, 'Optimal state value with usable
Ace')
...        prettyPrint(stateValueNoUsableAce, 'Optimal state value with no
usable Ace')
...        prettyPrint(actionUsableAce, 'Optimal policy with usable Ace',
'Action (0 Hit, 1 Stick)')
...        prettyPrint(actionNoUsableAce, 'Optimal policy with no usable Ace',
'Action (0 Hit, 1 Stick)')
```

```
...        plt.show()

# Run on-policy function
>>> onPolicy()
```

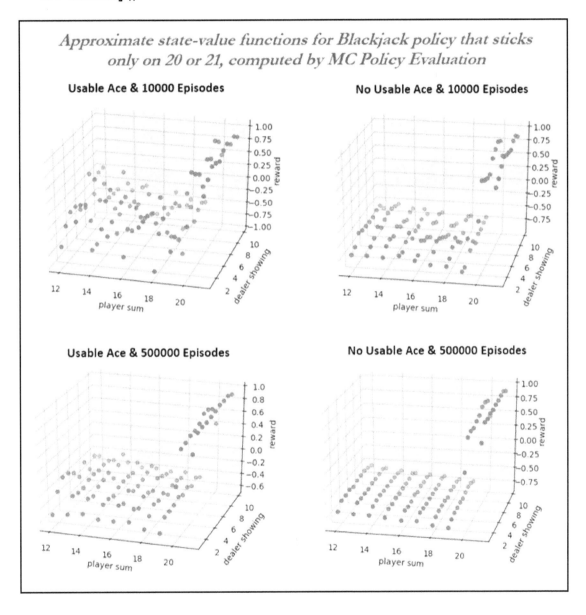

Approximate state-value functions for Blackjack policy that sticks only on 20 or 21, computed by MC Policy Evaluation

From the previous diagram, we can conclude that a usable ace in a hand gives much higher rewards even at the low player sum combinations, whereas for a player without a usable ace, values are pretty distinguished in terms of earned reward if those values are less than 20.

```
# Run Monte Carlo Control or Explored starts
>>> MC_ES_optimalPolicy()
```

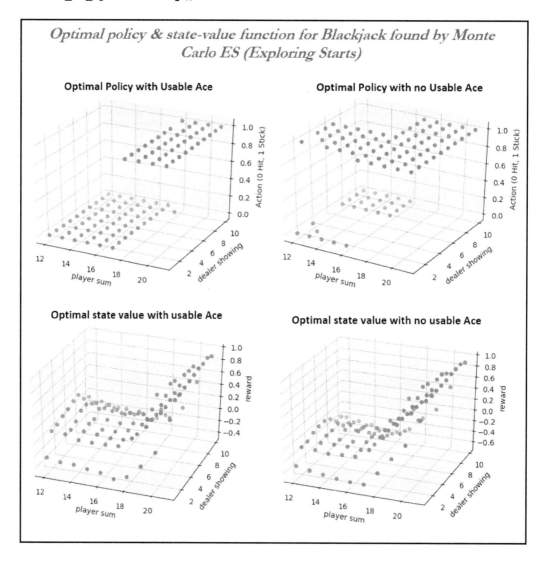

From the optimum policies and state values, we can conclude that, with a usable ace at our disposal, we can hit more than stick, and also that the state values for rewards are much higher compared with when there is no ace in a hand. Though the results we are talking about are obvious, we can see the magnitude of the impact of holding an ace in a hand.

Temporal difference learning

Temporal Difference (**TD**) learning is the central and novel theme of reinforcement learning. TD learning is the combination of both **Monte Carlo** (**MC**) and **Dynamic Programming** (**DP**) ideas. Like Monte Carlo methods, TD methods can learn directly from the experiences without the model of the environment. Similar to Dynamic Programming, TD methods update estimates based in part on other learned estimates, without waiting for a final outcome, unlike MC methods, in which estimates are updated after reaching the final outcome only.

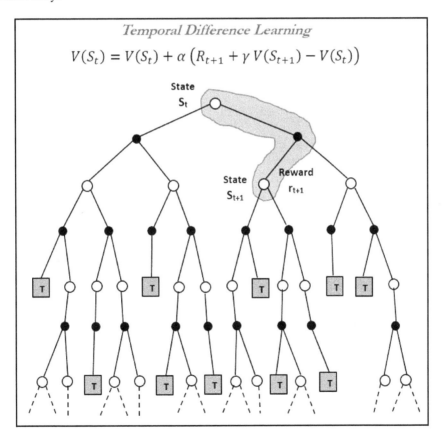

TD prediction

Both TD and MC use experience to solve z prediction problem. Given some policy π, both methods update their estimate v of v_π for the non-terminal states S_t occurring in that experience. Monte Carlo methods wait until the return following the visit is known, then use that return as a target for $V(S_t)$.

$$V(S_t) \leftarrow V(S_t) + \alpha\,[G_t - V(S_t)\,]$$

$$G_t - actual\ return\ following\ time\ t\ ;\ \alpha - constant\ step\ size\ parameter$$

The preceding method can be called as a constant - α MC, where MC must wait until the end of the episode to determine the increment to $V(S_t)$ (only then is G_t known).

TD methods need to wait only until the next timestep. At time $t+1$, they immediately form a target and make a useful update using the observed reward R_{t+1} and the estimate $V(S_{t+1})$. The simplest TD method, known as *TD(0)*, is:

$$V(S_t) \leftarrow V(S_t) + \alpha\,[R_{t+1} + \gamma\,V(S_{t+1}) - V(S_t)\,]$$

Target for MC update is G_t, whereas the target for the TD update is $R_{t+1} + y\,V(S_{t+1})$.

In the following diagram, a comparison has been made between TD with MC methods. As we've written in equation TD(0), we use one step of real data and then use the estimated value of the value function of next state. In a similar way, we can also use two steps of real data to get a better picture of the reality and estimate value function of the third stage. However, as we increase the steps, which eventually need more and more data to perform parameter updates, the more time it will cost.

When we take infinite steps until it touches the terminal point for updating parameters in each episode, TD becomes the Monte Carlo method.

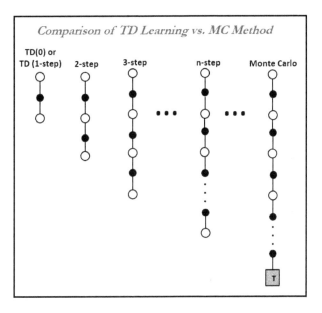

TD (0) for estimating v algorithm consists of the following steps:

1. Initialize:

    Input policy to be evaluated $\rightarrow \pi$
    Initialize arbitrary state $-$ *value function* $\rightarrow V(s)$ $(e.g: V(s) = 0, \forall s \in S^+)$

2. Repeat (for each episode):
    - Initialize S
    - Repeat (for each step of episode):
        - A <- action given by π for S
        - Take action A, observe R,S'
        - $V(S) \leftarrow V(S) + \alpha [R + \gamma V(S') - V(S)]$
        - $S \leftarrow S'$

3. Until S is terminal.

Driving office example for TD learning

In this simple example, you travel from home to the office every day and you try to predict how long it will take to get to the office in the morning. When you leave your home, you note that time, the day of the week, the weather (whether it is rainy, windy, and so on) any other parameter which you feel is relevant. For example, on Monday morning you leave at exactly 8 a.m. and you estimate it takes 40 minutes to reach the office. At 8:10 a.m., and you notice that a VIP is passing, and you need to wait until the complete convoy has moved out, so you re-estimate that it will take 45 minutes from then, or a total of 55 minutes. Fifteen minutes later you have completed the highway portion of your journey in good time. Now you enter a bypass road and you now reduce your estimate of total travel time to 50 minutes. Unfortunately, at this point, you get stuck behind a bunch of bullock carts and the road is too narrow to pass. You end up having to follow those bullock carts until you turn onto the side street where your office is located at 8:50. Seven minutes later, you reach your office parking. The sequence of states, times, and predictions are as follows:

State	Elapsed Time (minutes)	Predicted Time to Go	Predicted Total Time
leaving home, Monday at 8 a.m.	0	40	40
reaching car, minister convoy passes by	10	45	55
exiting highway	25	25	50
by pass road, behind bullockcarts	30	20	50
entering office street	50	7	57
arrive office parking space	57	0	57

Rewards in this example are the elapsed time at each leg of the journey and we are using a discount factor (gamma, $v = 1$), so the return for each state is the actual time to go from that state to the destination (office). The value of each state is the predicted time to go, which is the second column in the preceding table, also known the current estimated value for each state encountered.

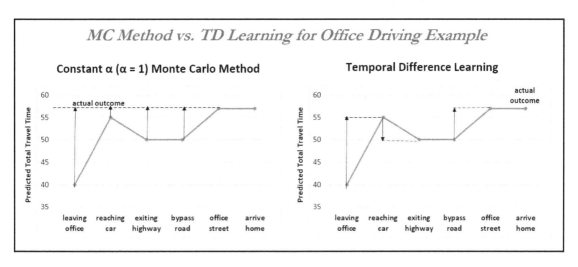

In the previous diagram, Monte Carlo is used to plot the predicted total time over the sequence of events. Arrows always show the change in predictions recommended by the constant-α MC method. These are errors between the estimated value in each stage and the actual return (57 minutes). In the MC method, learning happens only after finishing, for which it needs to wait until 57 minutes passed. However, in reality, you can estimate before reaching the final outcome and correct your estimates accordingly. TD works on the same principle, at every stage it tries to predict and correct the estimates accordingly. So, TD methods learn immediately and do not need to wait until the final outcome. In fact, that is how humans predict in real life. Because of these many positive properties, TD learning is considered as novel in reinforcement learning.

SARSA on-policy TD control

State-action-reward-state-action (**SARSA**) is an on-policy TD control problem, in which policy will be optimized using policy iteration (GPI), only time TD methods used for evaluation of predicted policy. In the first step, the algorithm learns a SARSA function. In particular, for an on-policy method we estimate $q_\pi (s, a)$ for the current behavior policy π and for all states (s) and actions (a), using the TD method for learning v_π.

Now, we consider transitions from state-action pair to state-action pair, and learn the values of state-action pairs:

$$Q(S,A) \leftarrow Q(S,A) + \alpha \left[R + \gamma\, Q(S',A) - Q(S,A) \right]$$

This update is done after every transition from a non-terminal state S_t. If S_{t+1} is terminal, then $Q(S_{t+1},\, A_{t+1})$ is defined as zero. This rule uses every element of the quintuple of events $(S_t, A_t, Rt, St_{+1}, A_{t+1})$, which make up a transition from one state-action pair to the next. This quintuple gives rise to the name SARSA for the algorithm.

As in all on-policy methods, we continually estimate q_π for the behavior policy π, and at the same time change π toward greediness with respect to q_π. The algorithm for computation of SARSA is given as follows:

1. Initialize:

$$Q(s,a), \forall\, s \in S, a \in A(s),\ arbitrarily, and\ Q(terminal - state,.) = 0$$

2. Repeat (for each episode):
   - Initialize S
   - Choose A from S using policy derived from Q (for example, ε- greedy)
   - Repeat (for each step of episode):
     - Take action A, observe R,S'
     - Choose A' from using S' policy derived from Q (for example, ε - greedy)
     - $Q(S,A) \leftarrow Q(S,A) + \alpha \left[R + \gamma\, Q(S',A) - Q(S,A) \right]$
     - $S \leftarrow S'; A \leftarrow A'$

3. Until S is terminal

Q-learning - off-policy TD control

Q-learning is the most popular method used in practical applications for many reinforcement learning problems. The off-policy TD control algorithm is known as Q-learning. In this case, the learned action-value function, Q directly approximates q_*, the optimal action-value function, independent of the policy being followed. This approximation simplifies the analysis of the algorithm and enables early convergence proofs. The policy still has an effect, in that it determines which state-action pairs are visited and updated. However, all that is required for correct convergence is that all pairs continue to be updated. As we know, this is a minimal requirement in the sense that any method guaranteed to find optimal behavior in the general case must require it. An algorithm of convergence is shown in the following steps:

1. Initialize:

$$Q(s,a), \forall\, s \in S, a \in A(s),\ arbitrarily, and\ Q(terminal - state,.) = 0$$

2. Repeat (for each episode):
    - Initialize S
    - Repeat (for each step of episode):
        - Choose A from S using policy derived from Q (for example, ε - greedy)
        - Take action A, observe R,S'
        - $Q(S,A) \leftarrow Q(S,A) + \alpha\, [R + \gamma\, Q(S',A) - Q(S,A)]$
        - $S \leftarrow S'; A \leftarrow A'$

3. Until S is terminal

Cliff walking example of on-policy and off-policy of TD control

A cliff walking grid-world example is used to compare SARSA and Q-learning, to highlight the differences between on-policy (SARSA) and off-policy (Q-learning) methods. This is a standard undiscounted, episodic task with start and end goal states, and with permitted movements in four directions (north, west, east and south). The reward of -1 is used for all transitions except the regions marked *The Cliff*, stepping on this region will penalize the agent with reward of -100 and sends the agent instantly back to the start position.

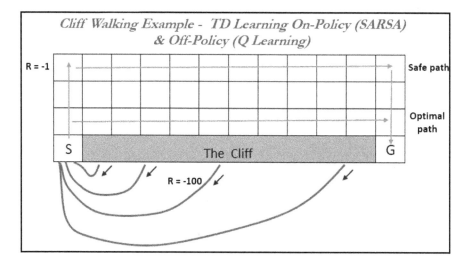

The following snippets of code have taken inspiration from Shangtong Zhang's Python codes for RL and are published in this book with permission from the student of *Richard S. Sutton*, the famous author of *Reinforcement Learning: An Introduction* (details provided in the *Further reading* section):

```
# Cliff-Walking - TD learning - SARSA & Q-learning
>>> from __future__ import print_function
>>> import numpy as np
>>> import matplotlib.pyplot as plt

# Grid dimensions
>>> GRID_HEIGHT = 4
>>> GRID_WIDTH = 12

# probability for exploration, step size,gamma
>>> EPSILON = 0.1
>>> ALPHA = 0.5
```

```
>>> GAMMA = 1

# all possible actions
>>> ACTION_UP = 0; ACTION_DOWN = 1;ACTION_LEFT = 2;ACTION_RIGHT = 3
>>> actions = [ACTION_UP, ACTION_DOWN, ACTION_LEFT, ACTION_RIGHT]

# initial state action pair values
>>> stateActionValues = np.zeros((GRID_HEIGHT, GRID_WIDTH, 4))
>>> startState = [3, 0]
>>> goalState = [3, 11]

# reward for each action in each state
>>> actionRewards = np.zeros((GRID_HEIGHT, GRID_WIDTH, 4))
>>> actionRewards[:, :, :] = -1.0
>>> actionRewards[2, 1:11, ACTION_DOWN] = -100.0
>>> actionRewards[3, 0, ACTION_RIGHT] = -100.0

# set up destinations for each action in each state
>>> actionDestination = []
>>> for i in range(0, GRID_HEIGHT):
...     actionDestination.append([])
...     for j in range(0, GRID_WIDTH):
...         destinaion = dict()
...         destinaion[ACTION_UP] = [max(i - 1, 0), j]
...         destinaion[ACTION_LEFT] = [i, max(j - 1, 0)]
...         destinaion[ACTION_RIGHT] = [i, min(j + 1, GRID_WIDTH - 1)]
...         if i == 2 and 1 <= j <= 10:
...             destinaion[ACTION_DOWN] = startState
...         else:
...             destinaion[ACTION_DOWN] = [min(i + 1, GRID_HEIGHT - 1), j]
...         actionDestination[-1].append(destinaion)
>>> actionDestination[3][0][ACTION_RIGHT] = startState

# choose an action based on epsilon greedy algorithm
>>> def chooseAction(state, stateActionValues):
...     if np.random.binomial(1, EPSILON) == 1:
...         return np.random.choice(actions)
...     else:
...         return np.argmax(stateActionValues[state[0], state[1], :])


# SARSA update

>>> def sarsa(stateActionValues, expected=False, stepSize=ALPHA):
...     currentState = startState
...     currentAction = chooseAction(currentState, stateActionValues)
...     rewards = 0.0
...     while currentState != goalState:
```

```
...             newState = actionDestination[currentState[0]][currentState[1]]
[currentAction]

...             newAction = chooseAction(newState, stateActionValues)
...             reward = actionRewards[currentState[0], currentState[1],
currentAction]
...             rewards += reward
...             if not expected:
...                 valueTarget = stateActionValues[newState[0], newState[1],
newAction]
...             else:
...                 valueTarget = 0.0
...                 actionValues = stateActionValues[newState[0], newState[1],
:]
...                 bestActions = np.argwhere(actionValues ==
np.max(actionValues))
...                 for action in actions:
...                     if action in bestActions:

...                         valueTarget += ((1.0 - EPSILON) / len(bestActions)
+ EPSILON / len(actions)) * stateActionValues[newState[0], newState[1],
action]

...                     else:
...                         valueTarget += EPSILON / len(actions) *
stateActionValues[newState[0], newState[1], action]
...             valueTarget *= GAMMA
...             stateActionValues[currentState[0], currentState[1],
currentAction] += stepSize * (reward+ valueTarget -
stateActionValues[currentState[0], currentState[1], currentAction])
...             currentState = newState
...             currentAction = newAction
...         return rewards

# Q-learning update
>>> def qlearning(stateActionValues, stepSize=ALPHA):
...     currentState = startState
...     rewards = 0.0
...     while currentState != goalState:
...         currentAction = chooseAction(currentState, stateActionValues)
...         reward = actionRewards[currentState[0], currentState[1],
currentAction]
...         rewards += reward
...         newState = actionDestination[currentState[0]][currentState[1]]
[currentAction]
...         stateActionValues[currentState[0], currentState[1],
currentAction] += stepSize * (reward + GAMMA *
np.max(stateActionValues[newState[0], newState[1], :]) -
```

```
...                  stateActionValues[currentState[0], currentState[1],
currentAction])
...            currentState = newState
...        return rewards


# print optimal policy
>>> def printOptimalPolicy(stateActionValues):
...        optimalPolicy = []
...        for i in range(0, GRID_HEIGHT):
...            optimalPolicy.append([])
...            for j in range(0, GRID_WIDTH):
...                if [i, j] == goalState:
...                    optimalPolicy[-1].append('G')
...                    continue
...                bestAction = np.argmax(stateActionValues[i, j, :])
...                if bestAction == ACTION_UP:
...                    optimalPolicy[-1].append('U')
...                elif bestAction == ACTION_DOWN:
...                    optimalPolicy[-1].append('D')
...                elif bestAction == ACTION_LEFT:
...                    optimalPolicy[-1].append('L')
...                elif bestAction == ACTION_RIGHT:
...                    optimalPolicy[-1].append('R')
...        for row in optimalPolicy:
...            print(row)

>>> def SARSAnQLPlot():
    # averaging the reward sums from 10 successive episodes
...        averageRange = 10

    # episodes of each run
...        nEpisodes = 500

    # perform 20 independent runs
...        runs = 20

...        rewardsSarsa = np.zeros(nEpisodes)
...        rewardsQlearning = np.zeros(nEpisodes)
...        for run in range(0, runs):
...            stateActionValuesSarsa = np.copy(stateActionValues)
...            stateActionValuesQlearning = np.copy(stateActionValues)
...            for i in range(0, nEpisodes):
                # cut off the value by -100 to draw the figure more elegantly
...                rewardsSarsa[i] += max(sarsa(stateActionValuesSarsa), -100)
...                rewardsQlearning[i] +=
max(qlearning(stateActionValuesQlearning), -100)
```

```
      # averaging over independent runs
...       rewardsSarsa /= runs
...       rewardsQlearning /= runs

      # averaging over successive episodes
...       smoothedRewardsSarsa = np.copy(rewardsSarsa)
...       smoothedRewardsQlearning = np.copy(rewardsQlearning)
...       for i in range(averageRange, nEpisodes):
...           smoothedRewardsSarsa[i] = np.mean(rewardsSarsa[i -
averageRange: i + 1])
...           smoothedRewardsQlearning[i] = np.mean(rewardsQlearning[i -
averageRange: i + 1])

      # display optimal policy
...       print('Sarsa Optimal Policy:')
...       printOptimalPolicy(stateActionValuesSarsa)
...       print('Q-learning Optimal Policy:')
...       printOptimalPolicy(stateActionValuesQlearning)

      # draw reward curves
...       plt.figure(1)
...       plt.plot(smoothedRewardsSarsa, label='Sarsa')
...       plt.plot(smoothedRewardsQlearning, label='Q-learning')
...       plt.xlabel('Episodes')
...       plt.ylabel('Sum of rewards during episode')
...       plt.legend()


# Sum of Rewards for SARSA versus Qlearning
>>> SARSAnQLPlot()
```

```
Sarsa Optimal Policy:
['R', 'R', 'R', 'R', 'R', 'R', 'R', 'R', 'D', 'R', 'R', 'D']
['U', 'U', 'U', 'U', 'R', 'U', 'U', 'R', 'D', 'R', 'U', 'D']
['R', 'R', 'R', 'U', 'U', 'R', 'U', 'U', 'R', 'R', 'R', 'D']
['U', 'U', 'U', 'U', 'U', 'U', 'U', 'U', 'U', 'U', 'U', 'G']
Q-Learning Optimal Policy:
['D', 'R', 'D', 'R', 'R', 'D', 'R', 'D', 'D', 'D', 'D', 'D']
['R', 'R', 'R', 'R', 'R', 'D', 'D', 'D', 'R', 'D', 'D', 'D']
['R', 'R', 'R', 'R', 'R', 'R', 'R', 'R', 'R', 'R', 'R', 'D']
['U', 'U', 'U', 'U', 'U', 'U', 'U', 'U', 'U', 'U', 'U', 'G']
```

After an initial transient, Q-learning learns the value of optimal policy to walk along the optimal path, in which the agent travels right along the edge of the cliff. Unfortunately, this will result in occasionally falling off the cliff because of ε-greedy action selection. Whereas SARSA, on the other hand, takes the action selection into account and learns the longer and safer path through the upper part of the grid. Although Q-learning learns the value of the optimal policy, its online performance is worse than that of the SARSA, which learns the roundabout and safest policy. Even if we observe the following sum of rewards displayed in the following diagram, SARSA has a less negative sum of rewards during the episode than Q-learning.

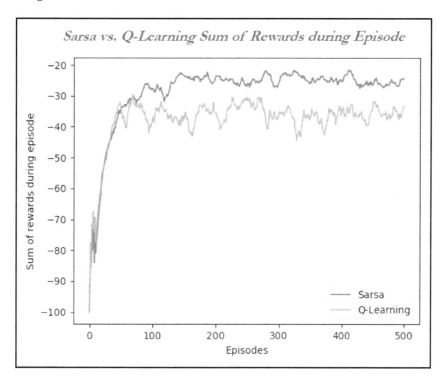

Further reading

There are many classic resources available for reinforcement learning, and we encourage the reader to go through them:

- R.S. Sutton and A.G. Barto, *Reinforcement Learning: An Introduction. MIT Press, Cambridge, MA, USA,* 1998
- *RL Course* by *David Silver* from YouTube: `https://www.youtube.com/watch?v=2pWv7GOvuf0list=PL7-jPKtc4r78-wCZcQn5IqyuWhBZ8fOxT`
- *Machine Learning* (Stanford) by *Andrew NG* form YouTube (Lectures 16-20): `https://www.youtube.com/watch?v=UzxYlbK2c7Elist=PLA89DCFA6ADACE599`
- *Algorithms for reinforcement learning* by *Csaba* from *Morgan & Claypool* Publishers
- *Artificial Intelligence: A Modern Approach* 3rd Edition, by *Stuart Russell* and *Peter Norvig, Prentice Hall*

Summary

In this chapter, you've learned various reinforcement learning techniques, like Markov decision process, Bellman equations, dynamic programming, Monte Carlo methods, Temporal Difference learning, including both on-policy (SARSA) and off-policy (Q-learning), with Python examples to understand its implementation in a practical way. You also learned how Q-learning is being used in many practical applications nowadays, as this method learns from trial and error by interacting with environments.

Finally, *Further reading* has been provided for you if you would like to pursue reinforcement learning full-time. We wish you all the best!

6
Hello Plotting World!

To learn programming, we often start with printing the "Hello world!" message. For graphical plots that contain all the elements from data, axes, labels, lines and ticks, how should we begin?

This chapter gives an overview of Matplotlib's functionalities and latest features. We will guide you through the setup of the Matplotlib plotting environment. You will learn to create a simple line graph, view, and save your figures. By the end of this chapter, you will be confident enough to start building your own plots and be ready to learn about customization and more advanced techniques in the coming sections.

Come and say "Hello!" to the world of plots!

Here is a list of topics covered in this chapter:

- What is Matplotlib?
- Plotting the first simple line graph
- Loading data into Matplotlib
- Exporting the figure

Hello Matplotlib!

Welcome to the world of Matplotlib 2.0! Follow our simple example in the chapter and draw your first "Hello world" plot.

What is Matplotlib?

Matplotlib is a versatile Python library that generates plots for data visualization. With the numerous plot types and refined styling options available, it works well for creating professional figures for presentations and scientific publications. Matplotlib provides a simple way to produce figures to suit different purposes, from slideshows, high-quality poster printing, and animations to web-based interactive plots. Besides typical 2D plots, basic 3D plotting is also supported.

On the development side, the hierarchical class structure and object-oriented plotting interface of Matplotlib make the plotting process intuitive and systematic. While Matplotlib provides a native graphical user interface for real-time interaction, it can also be easily integrated into popular IPython-based interactive development environments, such as Jupyter notebook and PyCharm.

What's new in Matplotlib 2.0?

Matplotlib 2.0 features many improvements, including the appearance of default styles, image support, and text rendering speed. We have selected a number of important changes to highlight later. The details of all new changes can be found on the documentation site at `http://matplotlib.org/devdocs/users/whats_new.html`.

If you are already using previous versions of Matplotlib, you may want to pay more attention to this section to update your coding habits. If you are totally new to Matplotlib or even Python, you may jump ahead to start using Matplotlib first and revisit here later.

Changes to the default style

The most prominent change to Matplotlib in version 2.0 is to the default style. You can find the list of changes here: `http://matplotlib.org/devdocs/users/dflt_style_changes.html`.

Color cycle

For quick plotting without having to set colors for each data series, Matplotlib uses a list of colors called the default property cycle, whereby each series is assigned one of the default colors in the cycle. In Matplotlib 2.0, the list has been changed from the original red, green, blue, cyan, magenta, yellow, and black, noted as `['b', 'g', 'r', 'c', 'm', 'y', 'k']`, to the current category10 color palette introduced by the Tableau software. As implied by the name, the new palette has 10 distinct colors suitable for categorical display. The list can be accessed by importing Matplotlib and calling `matplotlib.rcParams['axes.prop_cycle']` in Python.

Colormap

Colormaps are useful in showing gradient. The yellow to blue "viridis" colormap is now the default one in Matplotlib 2.0. This perceptually uniform colormap better represents the transition of numerical values visually than the classic "jet" scheme. This is a comparison between two colormaps:

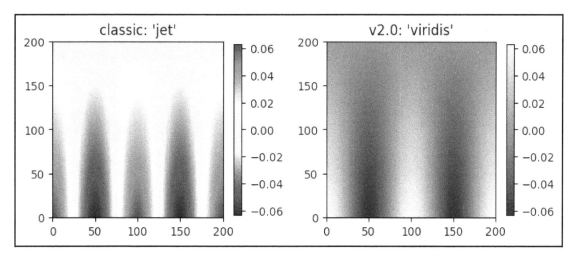

Besides defaulting to a perceptually continuous colormap, qualitative colormaps are now available for grouping values into categories:

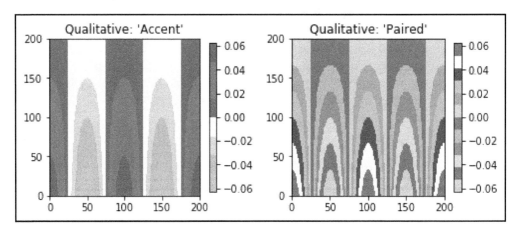

Scatter plot

Points in a scatter plot have a larger default size and no longer have a black edge, giving clearer visuals. Different colors in the default color cycle will be used for each data series if the color is not specified:

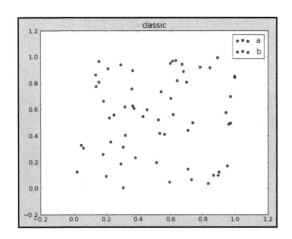 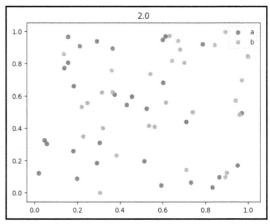

Legend

While previous versions set the legend in the upper-right corner, Matplotlib 2.0 sets the legend location as "best" by default. It automatically avoids overlapping of the legend with the data. The legend box also has rounded corners, lighter edges, and a partially transparent background to keep the focus of the readers on the data. The curve of square numbers in the classic and current default styles demonstrates the case:

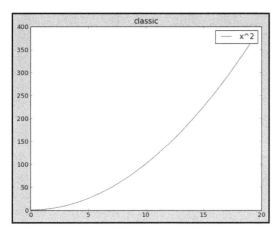 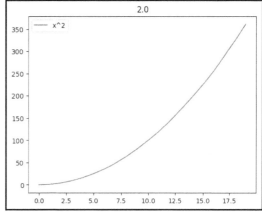

Line style

Dash patterns in line styles can now scale with the line width to display bolder dashes for clarity:

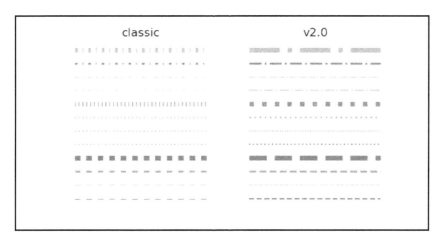

From the documentation (https://matplotlib.org/users/dflt_style_changes.html#plot)

Patch edges and color

Just like the dots in the scatter plot shown before, most filled elements no longer have a black edge by default, making the graphics less cluttered:

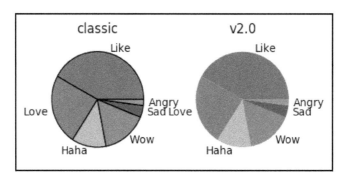

Fonts

The default font is now changed from "Bitstream Vera Sans" to "DejaVu Sans". The current font supports additional international, math, and symbol characters, including emojis.

Improved functionality or performance

Matplotlib 2.0 presents new features that improve the user experience, including speed and output quality as well as resource usage.

Improved color conversion API and RGBA support

The alpha channel, which specifies the degree of transparency, is now fully supported in Matplotlib 2.0.

Improved image support

Matplotlib 2.0 now resamples images with less memory and less data type conversion.

Faster text rendering

It is claimed that the speed of text rendering by the Agg backend is increased by 20%. We will discuss more on backends in Chapter 9, *Adding Interactivity and Animating Plots*.

Change in the default animation codec

To generate a video output of animated plots, a more efficient codec, H.264, is now used by default in place of MPEG-4. As H.264 has a higher compression rate, the smaller output file size permits longer video record time and reduces the time and network data needed to load them. Real-time playback of H.264 videos is generally more fluent and in better quality than those encoded in MPEG-4.

Changes in settings

Some of the settings are changed in Matplotlib v2.0 for convenience or consistency, or to avoid unexpected results.

New configuration parameters (rcParams)

New parameters are added, such as `date.autoformatter.year` for date time string formatting.

Style parameter blacklist

Style files are no longer allowed to configure settings unrelated to the style to prevent unexpected consequences. These parameters include the following:

```
'interactive', 'backend', 'backend.qt4', 'webagg.port',
'webagg.port_retries', 'webagg.open_in_browser', 'backend_fallback',
'toolbar', 'timezone', 'datapath', 'figure.max_open_warning',
'savefig.directory', tk.window_focus', 'docstring.hardcopy'
```

Change in Axes property keywords

The Axes properties `axisbg` and `axis_bgcolor` are replaced by `facecolor` to keep the keywords consistent.

Plotting our first graph

We will start with a simple line graph of a curve of squares, that is, $y = x^2$.

Loading data for plotting

To visualize data, we should start with "having" some data. While we assume you have some nice data on hand to show, we will briefly show you how to load it in Python for plotting.

Data structures

There are several common data structures we will keep coming across.

List

List is a basic Python data type for storing a collection of values. A list is created by putting element values inside a square bracket. To reuse our list, we can give it a name and store it like this:

```
evens = [2,4,6,8,10]
```

When we want to get a series in a greater range, for instance, to get more data points for our curve of squares to make it smoother, we may use the Python `range()` function:

```
evens = range(2,102,2)
```

This command will give us all even numbers from 2 to 100 (both inclusive) and store it in a list named `evens`.

Numpy array

Very often, we deal with more complex data. If you need a matrix with multiple columns or want to perform mathematical operations over all elements in a collection, then numpy is for you:

```
import numpy as np
```

We abbreviated `numpy` to `np` by convention, keeping our code succinct.

`np.array()` converts a supported data type, a list in this case, into a Numpy array. To produce a numpy array from our `evens` list, we do the following:

```
np.array(evens)
```

pandas dataframe

A pandas dataframe is useful when we have some non-numerical labels or values in our matrix. It does not require homogeneous data, unlike Numpy. Columns can be named. There are also functions such as `melt()` and `pivot_table()` that add convenience in reshaping the table to facilitate analysis and plotting.

To convert a list into a pandas dataframe, we do the following:

```
import pandas as pd
pd.DataFrame(evens)
```

You can also convert a numpy array into a pandas dataframe.

Loading data from files

While all this gives you a refresher of the data structures we will be working on, in real life, instead of inventing data, we read it from data sources. A tab-delimited plaintext file is the simplest and most common type of data input. Imagine we have a file called `evens.txt` containing the aforementioned even numbers. There are two columns. The first column only records unnecessary information. We want to load the data in the second column.

Here is what the dummy text file looks like:

```
 1  abc  2
 2  abc  4
 3  abc  6
 4  abc  8
 5  abc  10
 6  abc  12
 7  abc  14
 8  abc  16
 9  abc  18
10  abc  20
11  abc  22
12  abc  24
13  abc  26
14  abc  28
15  abc  30
16  abc  32
17  abc  34
```

The basic Python way

We can initialize an empty list, read the file line by line, split each line, and append the second element to our list:

```
evens = []
with open as f:
    for line in f.readlines():
        evens.append(line.split()[1])
```

Of course, you can also do this in a one-liner:

```
evens = [int(x.split()[1]) for x in
open('evens.txt').readlines()]
```

We are just trying to go step by step, following the Zen of Python: simple is better than complex.

The Numpy way

It is simple when we have a file with only two columns, and only one column to read, but it can get more tedious when we have an extended table containing thousands of columns and rows and we want to convert them into a Numpy matrix later.

Numpy provides a standard one-liner solution:

```
import numpy as np
np.loadtxt('evens.txt',delimiter='\t',usecols=1,dtype=np.int32)
```

The first parameter is the path of the data file. The `delimiter` parameter specifies the string used to separate values, which is a tab here. Because `numpy.loadtxt()` by default separate values separated by any whitespace into columns by default, this argument can be omitted here. We have set it for demonstration.

For `usecols` and `dtype` that specify which columns to read and what data type each column corresponds to, you may pass a single value to each, or a sequence (such as list) for reading multiple columns.

Numpy also by default skips lines starting with #, which typically marks comment or header lines. You may change this behavior by setting the `comment` parameter.

The pandas way

Similar to Numpy, pandas offers an easy way to load text files into a pandas dataframe:

```
import pandas as pd
pd.read_csv(usecols=1)
```

Here the separation can be denoted by either `sep` or `delimiter`, which is set as comma , by default (**CSV** stands for **comma-separated values**).

There is a long list of less commonly used options available as to determine how different data formats, data types, and errors should be handled. You may refer to the documentation at `http://pandas.pydata.org/pandas-docs/stable/generated/pandas.read_csv.html`. Besides flat CSV files, Pandas also has other built-in functions for reading other common data formats, such as Excel, JSON, HTML, HDF5, SQL, and Google BigQuery.

To stay focused on data visualization, we will not dig deep into the methods of data cleaning in this book, but this is a survival skill set very helpful in data science. If interested, you can check out resources on data handling with Python.

Importing the Matplotlib pyplot module

The Matplotlib package includes many modules, including artist that controls the aesthetics, and rcParams for setting default values. The Pyplot module is the plotting interface we will mostly deal with, which creates plots of data in an object-oriented manner.

By convention, we use the `plt` abbreviation when importing:

```
import matplotlib.pylot as plt
```

Don't forget to run the Jupyter Notebook cell magic `%matplotlib inline` to embed your figure in the output.

Don't use the pylab module!

The use of the pylab module is now discouraged, and generally replaced by the **object-oriented** (**OO**) interface. While pylab provides some convenience by importing `matplotlib.pyplot` and `numpy` under a single namespace. Many pylab examples are still found online today, but it is much better to call the `Matplotlib.pyplot` and `numpy` modules separately.

Plotting a curve

Plotting a line graph of the list can be as simple as:

```
plt.plot(evens)
```

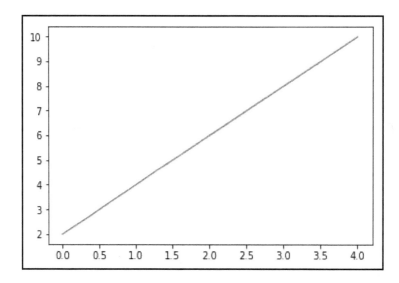

When only one parameter is specified, Pyplot assumes the data we input is on the y-axis and chooses a scale for the x-axis automatically.

To plot a graph, call `plt.plot(x,y)` where x and y are the x coordinates and y coordinates of data points:

```
plt.plot(evens,evens**2)
```

To label the curve with a legend, we add the label information in the `plot` function:

```
plt.plot(evens,evens**2,label = 'x^2')
plt.legend()
```

Viewing the figure

Now, don't forget to call `plt.show()` to display the figure!

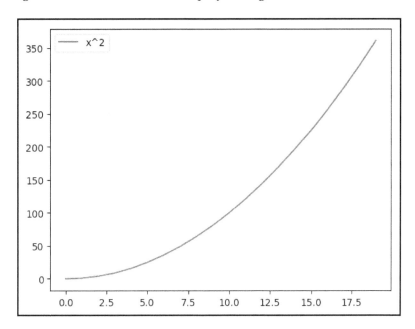

Saving the figure

Now we have drawn our first figure. Let's save our work! Surely we don't want to resort to screen capture. Here is a simple way to do it by calling `pyplot.savefig()`.

If you want to both view the image on screen and save it in file, remember to call `pyplot.savefig()` before `pyplot.show()` to make sure you don't save a blank canvas.

Setting the output format

The pyplot.savefig() function takes the path of the output file and automatically outputs it in the specified extension. For example, pyplot.savefig('output.png') will generate a PNG image. If no extension is specified, an SVG image will be generated by default. If the specified format is unsupported, let's say .doc, a ValueError Python exception will be thrown:

```
In [3]:  plt.savefig('test.doc')

---------------------------------------------------------------------------
ValueError                                Traceback (most recent call last)
<ipython-input-3-dfc7fc198e20> in <module>()
----> 1 plt.savefig('test.doc')

c:¥users¥claire¥appdata¥local¥programs¥python¥python36¥lib¥site-packages¥matplotlib¥pyplot.py in savefig(*args, **kwargs)
    695     def savefig(*args, **kwargs):
    696         fig = gcf()
--> 697         res = fig.savefig(*args, **kwargs)
    698         fig.canvas.draw_idle()   # need this if 'transparent=True' to reset colors
    699         return res

c:¥users¥claire¥appdata¥local¥programs¥python¥python36¥lib¥site-packages¥matplotlib¥figure.py in savefig(self, *args, **kwargs)
   1570                 self.set_frameon(frameon)
   1571
-> 1572                 self.canvas.print_figure(*args, **kwargs)
   1573
   1574                 if frameon:

c:¥users¥claire¥appdata¥local¥programs¥python¥python36¥lib¥site-packages¥matplotlib¥backend_bases.py in print_figure(self, filename, dpi, facecolor, edgecolor, orientation, format, **kwargs)
   2143
   2144             # get canvas object and print method for format
-> 2145             canvas = self._get_output_canvas(format)
   2146             print_method = getattr(canvas, 'print_%s' % format)
   2147

c:¥users¥claire¥appdata¥local¥programs¥python¥python36¥lib¥site-packages¥matplotlib¥backend_bases.py in _get_output_canvas(self, format)
   2083             raise ValueError('Format "%s" is not supported.¥n'
   2084                              'Supported formats: '
-> 2085                              '%s.' % (format, ', '.join(formats)))
   2086
   2087     def print_figure(self, filename, dpi=None, facecolor=None, edgecolor=None,

ValueError: Format "doc" is not supported.
Supported formats: eps, pdf, pgf, png, ps, raw, rgba, svg, svgz.
```

PNG (Portable Network Graphics)

Compared to JPEG, another common image file format, PNG, has the advantage of allowing a transparent background. PNG is widely supported by most image viewers and handlers.

PDF (Portable Document Format)

A PDF is a standard document format, which you don't have to worry about the availability of readers. However, most Office software do not support the import of PDF as image.

SVG (Scalable Vector Graphics)

SVG is a vector graphics format that can be scaled without losing details. Hence, better quality can be achieved with a smaller file size. It goes well on the web with HTML5. It may not be supported by some primitive image viewers.

Post (Postscript)

Postscript is a page description language for electronic publishing. It is useful for batch processing images to publish.

The **Gimp Drawing Kit** (**GDK**) raster graphics rendering is deprecated in 2.0, which means image formats such as JPG and TIFF are no longer supported with the default backend. We will discuss the backends later in more detail.

Adjusting the resolution

Resolution measures the details recorded in an image. It determines how much you can enlarge your image without losing details. An image with higher resolution retains high quality at larger dimensions but also has a bigger file size.

Depending on the purpose, you may want to output your figures at different resolutions. Resolution is measured as the number of color pixel **dot per inch** (**dpi**). You may adjust the resolution of a figure output by specifying the `dpi` parameter in the `pyplot.savefig()` function, for example, by:

```
plt.savefig('output.png',dpi=300)
```

While a higher resolution delivers better image quality, it also means a larger file size and demands more computer resources. Here are some references for how high should you set your image resolution:

- Slideshow presentations: 96 dpi+

Here are some suggestions by Microsoft for graphics resolution for Powerpoint presentations for different screen sizes: `https://support.microsoft.com/en-us/help/` `827745/how-to-change-the-export-resolution-of-a-powerpoint-slide`:

Screen height (pixel)	Resolution (dpi)
720	96 (default)
750	100
1125	150
1500	200
1875	250
2250	300

- Poster presentation: 300 dpi+
- Web: 72 dpi+ (SVG that can scale responsively is recommended)

Summary

In this chapter, you learned to use Matplotlib to draw a simple line graph. We set up the environment, imported data, and output the figure as an image in different formats. In the next chapter, you will learn how to visualize online data.

7
Visualizing Online Data

At this point, we have already covered the basics of creating and customizing plots using Matplotlib. In this chapter, we begin the journey of understanding more advanced Matplotlib usage through examples in specialized topics.

When considering the visualization of a concept, the following important factors have to be considered carefully:

- Source of the data
- Filtering and data processing
- Choosing the right plot type for the data:
    - Visualizing the trend of data:
        - Line chart, area chart, and stacked area chart
    - Visualizing univariate distribution:
        - Bar chart, histogram, and kernel density estimation
    - Visualizing bivariate distribution:
        - Scatter plot, KDE density chart, and hexbin chart
    - Visualizing categorical data:
        - Categorical scatter plot, box plot, swarm plot, violin plot
- Adjusting figure aesthetics for effective storytelling

We will cover these topics via the use of demographic and financial data. First, we will discuss typical data formats when we fetch data from the **Application Programming Interface (API)**. Next, we will explore how we can integrate Matplotlib 2.0 with other Python packages such as Pandas, Scipy, and Seaborn for the visualization of different data types.

Typical API data formats

Many websites offer their data via an API, which bridges applications via standardized architecture. While we are not going to cover the details of using APIs here as site-specific documentation is usually available online; we will show you the three most common data formats as used in many APIs.

CSV

CSV (Comma-Separated Values) is one of the oldest file formats, which was introduced long before the internet even existed. However, it is now becoming deprecated as other advanced formats, such as JSON and XML, are gaining popularity. As the name suggests, data values are separated by commas. The preinstalled `csv` package and the `pandas` package contain classes to read and write data in CSV format. This CSV example defines a population table with two countries:

```
Country,Time,Sex,Age,Value
United Kingdom,1950,Male,0-4,2238.735
United States of America,1950,Male,0-4,8812.309
```

JSON

JSON (JavaScript Object Notation) is gaining popularity these days due to its efficiency and simplicity. JSON allows the specification of number, string, Boolean, array, and object. Python provides the default `json` package for parsing JSON. Alternatively, the `pandas.read_json` class can be used to import JSON as a Pandas dataframe. The preceding population table can be represented as JSON in the following example:

```
{
  "population": [
  {
  "Country": "United Kingdom",
  "Time": 1950,
  "Sex", "Male",
```

```
"Age", "0-4",
"Value",2238.735
},{
"Country": "United States of America",
"Time": 1950,
"Sex", "Male",
"Age", "0-4",
"Value",8812.309
},
]
}
```

XML

XML (**eXtensible Markup Language**) is the Swiss Army knife of data formats, and it has become the default container for Microsoft Office, Apple iWork, XHTML, SVG, and more. XML's versatility comes with a price, as it makes XML verbose and slower. There are several ways to parse XML in Python, but `xml.etree.ElementTree` is recommended due to its Pythonic interface, backed by an efficient C backend. We are not going to cover XML parsing in this book, but good tutorials exist elsewhere (such as `http://eli.thegreenplace.net/2012/03/15/processing-xml-in-python-with-elementtree`).

As an example, the same population table can be transformed into XML:

```
<?xml version='1.0' encoding='utf-8'?>
<populations>
 <population>
 <Country>United Kingdom</Country>
 <Time>1950</Time>
 <Sex>Male</Sex>
 <Age>0-4</Age>
 <Value>2238.735</Value>
 </population>
 <population>
 <Country>United States of America</Country>
 <Time>1950</Time>
 <Sex>Male</Sex>
 <Age>0-4</Age>
 <Value>8812.309</Value>
 </population>
</populations>
```

Introducing pandas

Beside NumPy and SciPy, pandas is one of the most common scientific computing libraries for Python. Its authors aim to make pandas the most powerful and flexible open source data analysis and manipulation tool available in any language, and in fact, they are almost achieving that goal. Its powerful and efficient library is a perfect match for data scientists. Like other Python packages, Pandas can easily be installed via PyPI:

```
pip install pandas
```

First introduced in version 1.5, Matplotlib supports the use of pandas DataFrame as the input in various plotting classes. Pandas DataFrame is a powerful two-dimensional labeled data structure that supports indexing, querying, grouping, merging, and some other common relational database operations. DataFrame is similar to spreadsheets in the sense that each row of the DataFrame contains different variables of an instance, while each column contains a vector of a specific variable across all instances.

 pandas DataFrame supports heterogeneous data types, such as string, integer, and float. By default, rows are indexed sequentially and columns are composed of pandas Series. Optional row labels or column labels can be specified through the index and columns attributes.

Importing online population data in the CSV format

Let's begin by looking at the steps to import an online CSV file as a pandas DataFrame. In this example, we are going to use the annual population summary published by the Department of Economic and Social Affairs, United Nations, in 2015. Projected population figures towards 2100 were also included in the dataset:

```
import numpy as np # Python scientific computing package
import pandas as pd # Python data analysis package

# URL for Annual Population by Age and Sex - Department of Economic
# and Social Affairs, United Nations
source =
"https://github.com/PacktPublishing/Matplotlib-2.x-By-Example/blob/master/W
PP2015_DB04_Population_Annual.zip"

# Pandas support both local or online files
data = pd.read_csv(source, header=0, compression='zip', encoding='latin_1')
```

```
# Show the first five rows of the DataFrame
data.head()
```

The expected output of the code is shown here:

LocID	Location	VarID	Variant	Time	MidPeriod	SexID	Sex	AgeGrp	AgeGrpStart	AgeGrpSpan	Value
0	4	Afghanistan	2	Medium	1950	1950.5	1	Male	0-4	0	5	630.044
1	4	Afghanistan	2	Medium	1950	1950.5	1	Male	5-9	5	5	516.205
2	4	Afghanistan	2	Medium	1950	1950.5	1	Male	10-14	10	5	461.378
3	4	Afghanistan	2	Medium	1950	1950.5	1	Male	15-19	15	5	414.368
4	4	Afghanistan	2	Medium	1950	1950.5	1	Male	20-24	20	5	374.110

> **TIP**
> The `pandas.read_csv` class is extremely versatile, supporting column headers, custom delimiters, various compressed formats (for example, `.gzip`, `.bz2`, `.zip`, and `.xz`), different text encodings, and much more. Readers can consult the documentation page (`http://pandas.pydata.org/pandas-docs/stable/generated/pandas.read_csv.html`) for more information.

By calling the `.head()` function of the Pandas DataFrame object, we can quickly observe the first five rows of the data.

As we progress through this chapter, we are going to integrate this population dataset with other datasets in Quandl. However, Quandl uses three-letter country codes (ISO 3166 alpha-3) to denote geographical locations; therefore we need to reformat the location names accordingly.

The `pycountry` package is an excellent choice for conversion of country names according to ISO 3166 standards. Similarly, `pycountry` can be installed through PyPI:

```
pip install pycountry
```

Continuing the previous code example, we are going to add a new `country` column to the dataframe:

```
from pycountry import countries


def get_alpha_3(location):
    """Convert full country name to three letter code (ISO 3166 alpha-3)

    Args:
        location: Full location name
    Returns:
        three letter code or None if not found"""
```

```
try:
    return countries.get(name=location).alpha_3
except:
    return None

# Add a new country column to the dataframe
population_df['country'] = population_df['Location'].apply(lambda x:
get_alpha_3(x))
population_df.head()
```

The expected output of the code is shown here:

-	LocID	Location	VarID	Variant	Time	MidPeriod	SexID	Sex	AgeGrp	AgeGrpStart	AgeGrpSpan	Value	country
0	4	Afghanistan	2	Medium	1950	1950.5	1	Male	0-4	0	5	630.044	AFG
1	4	Afghanistan	2	Medium	1950	1950.5	1	Male	5-9	5	5	516.205	AFG
2	4	Afghanistan	2	Medium	1950	1950.5	1	Male	10-14	10	5	461.378	AFG
3	4	Afghanistan	2	Medium	1950	1950.5	1	Male	15-19	15	5	414.368	AFG
4	4	Afghanistan	2	Medium	1950	1950.5	1	Male	20-24	20	5	374.110	AFG

Importing online financial data in the JSON format

In this chapter, we will also draw upon financial data from Quandl's API to create insightful visualizations. If you are not familiar with Quandl, it is a financial and economic data warehouse that stores millions of datasets from hundreds of publishers. The best thing about Quandl is that these datasets are delivered via the unified API, without worrying about the procedures to parse the data correctly. Anonymous users can get up to 50 API calls per day, and you get up to 500 free API calls if you are a registered user. Readers can sign up for a free API key at https://www.quandl.com/?modal=register.

At Quandl, every dataset is identified by a unique ID, as defined by the Quandl Code on each search result webpage. For example, the Quandl code GOOG/NASDAQ_SWTX defines the historical NASDAQ index data published by Google Finance. Every dataset is available in three formats--CSV, JSON, and XML.

Although an official Python client library is available from Quandl, we are not going to use that for the sake of demonstrating the general procedures of importing JSON data. According to Quandl's documentation, we can fetch JSON formatted data tables through the following API call:

```
GET https://www.quandl.com/api/v3/datasets/{Quandl code}/data.json
```

Let's try to get the Big Mac index data from Quandl.

```python
from urllib.request import urlopen
import json
import time
import pandas as pd


def get_bigmac_codes():
    """Get a Pandas DataFrame of all codes in the Big Mac index dataset

    The first column contains the code, while the second header
    contains the description of the code.
    for example,
    ECONOMIST/BIGMAC_ARG,Big Mac Index - Argentina
    ECONOMIST/BIGMAC_AUS,Big Mac Index - Australia
    ECONOMIST/BIGMAC_BRA,Big Mac Index - Brazil
    Returns:
        codes: Pandas DataFrame of Quandl dataset codes"""
    codes_url = "https://www.quandl.com/api/v3/databases/ECONOMIST/codes"
    codes = pd.read_csv(codes_url, header=None, names=['Code',
'Description'],
                        compression='zip', encoding='latin_1')
    return codes

def get_quandl_dataset(api_key, code):
    """Obtain and parse a quandl dataset in Pandas DataFrame format

    Quandl returns dataset in JSON format, where data is stored as a
    list of lists in response['dataset']['data'], and column headers
    stored in response['dataset']['column_names'].
    for example, {'dataset': {...,
            'column_names': ['Date',
                             'local_price',
                             'dollar_ex',
                             'dollar_price',
                             'dollar_ppp',
                             'dollar_valuation',
                             'dollar_adj_valuation',
                             'euro_adj_valuation',
                             'sterling_adj_valuation',
```

```
                                'yen_adj_valuation',
                                'yuan_adj_valuation'],
                 'data': [['2017-01-31',
                           55.0,
                           15.8575,
                           3.4683903515687,
                           10.869565217391,
                           -31.454736135007,
                           6.2671477203176,
                           8.2697553162259,
                           29.626894343348,
                           32.714616745128,
                           13.625825886047],
                          ['2016-07-31',
                           50.0,
                           14.935,
                           3.3478406427854,
                           9.9206349206349,
                           -33.574590420925,
                           2.0726096168216,
                           0.40224795003514,
                           17.56448458418,
                           19.76377270142,
                           11.643103380531]
                          ],
                 'database_code': 'ECONOMIST',
                 'dataset_code': 'BIGMAC_ARG',
                 ... }}
    A custom column--country is added to denote the 3-letter country code.
    Args:
        api_key: Quandl API key
        code: Quandl dataset code

    Returns:
        df: Pandas DataFrame of a Quandl dataset

    """
    base_url = "https://www.quandl.com/api/v3/datasets/"
    url_suffix = ".json?api_key="

    # Fetch the JSON response
    u = urlopen(base_url + code + url_suffix + api_key)
    response = json.loads(u.read().decode('utf-8'))
    # Format the response as Pandas Dataframe
    df = pd.DataFrame(response['dataset']['data'],
columns=response['dataset']['column_names'])
    # Label the country code
    df['country'] = code[-3:]
```

```
        return df


quandl_dfs = []
codes = get_bigmac_codes()

# Replace this with your own API key
api_key = "INSERT YOUR KEY HERE"

for code in codes.Code:
    # Get the DataFrame of a Quandl dataset
    df = get_quandl_dataset(api_key, code)
    # Store in a list
    quandl_dfs.append(df)
    # Prevents exceeding the API speed limit
    time.sleep(2)
# Concatenate the list of dataframes into a single one
bigmac_df = pd.concat(quandl_dfs)
bigmac_df.head()
```

The expected output is as follows:

	Date	local_price	dollar_ex	dollar_price	dollar_ppp	dollar_valuation	dollar_adj_valuation	euro_adj_valuation	sterling_adj_valuation	yen_adj_valuation	yuan_adj_valuation	country
0	2017-01-31	55.0	15.85750	3.468390	10.869565	-31.454736	6.26715	8.26976	29.6269	32.7146	13.6258	ARG
1	2016-07-31	50.0	14.93500	3.347841	9.920635	-33.574590	2.07261	0.402248	17.5645	19.7638	11.6431	ARG
2	2016-01-31	33.0	13.80925	2.389703	6.693712	-51.527332	-24.8619	-18.714	-18.7209	0.40859	-17.029	ARG
3	2015-07-31	28.0	9.13500	3.065134	5.845511	-36.009727	-4.7585	-0.357918	-6.01091	30.8609	5.02868	ARG
4	2015-01-31	28.0	8.61000	3.252033	5.845511	-32.107881	0.540242	-0.804495	-2.49468	34.3905	6.01183	ARG

The Big Mac index was invented by The Economist in 1986 as a lighthearted guide to check whether currencies are at their correct level. It is based on the theory of **purchasing power parity** (**PPP**) and is considered an informal measure of currency exchange rates at PPP. It measures their value against a similar basket of goods and services, in this case, a Big Mac. Differing prices at market exchange rates would imply that one currency is undervalued or overvalued.

The code for parsing JSON from the Quandl API is a bit more complicated, and thus extra explanations might help you to understand it. The first function, get_bigmac_codes(), parses the list of all available dataset codes in the Quandl Economist database as a pandas DataFrame. Meanwhile, the second function, get_quandl_dataset(api_key, code), converts the JSON response of a Quandl dataset API query to a pandas DataFrame. All datasets obtained are concatenated using pandas.concat().

Visualizing the trend of data

Once we have imported the two datasets, we can set out on a further visualization journey. Let's begin by plotting the world population trends from 1950 to 2017. To select rows based on the value of a column, we can use the following syntax: `df[df.variable_name == "target"]` or `df[df['variable_name'] == "target"]`, where `df` is the dataframe object. Other conditional operators, such as larger than > or smaller than <, are also supported. Multiple conditional statements can be chained together using the "and" operator &, or the "or" operator |.

To aggregate the population across all age groups within a year, we are going to rely on `df.groupby().sum()`, as shown in the following example:

```
import matplotlib.pyplot as plt


# Select the aggregated population data from the world for both genders,
# during 1950 to 2017.
selected_data = data[(data.Location == 'WORLD') & (data.Sex == 'Both') &
(data.Time <= 2017) ]

# Calculate aggregated population data across all age groups for each year
# Set as_index=False to avoid the Time variable to be used as index
grouped_data = selected_data.groupby('Time', as_index=False).sum()

# Generate a simple line plot of population vs time
fig = plt.figure()
plt.plot(grouped_data.Time, grouped_data.Value)

# Label the axis
plt.xlabel('Year')
plt.ylabel('Population (thousands)')

plt.show()
```

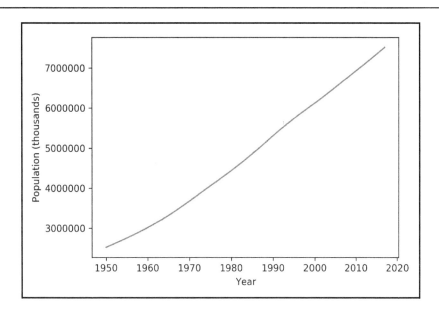

Area chart and stacked area chart

Sometimes, we may want to shade the area under the line plot with color for a greater visual impact. This can be achieved via the `fill_between` class:

```
fill_between(x, y1, y2=0, where=None, interpolate=False, step=None)
```

By default, `fill_between` shades the region between `y=0` and the line when `y2` is not specified. More complex shading behavior can be specified using the where, interpolate, and step keyword arguments. Readers can refer to the following link for more information: `https://matplotlib.org/examples/pylab_examples/fill_between_demo.html`.

Let's try to plot a more detailed chart by separating the two genders. We are going to explore the relative contribution of males and females towards the population growth. To do that, we can prepare a stacked area chart using the `stackplot` class:

```
# Select the aggregated population data from the world for each gender,
# during 1950 to 2017.
male_data = data[(data.Location == 'WORLD') & (data.Sex == 'Male') &
(data.Time <= 2017) ]
female_data = data[(data.Location == 'WORLD') & (data.Sex == 'Female') &
(data.Time <= 2017) ]

# Calculate aggregated population data across all age groups for each year
```

```
# Set as_index=False to avoid the Time variable to be used as index
grouped_male_data = male_data.groupby('Time', as_index=False).sum()
grouped_female_data = female_data.groupby('Time', as_index=False).sum()

# Create two subplots with shared y-axis (sharey=True)
fig, (ax1, ax2) = plt.subplots(nrows=1, ncols=2, figsize=(12,4),
sharey=True)

# Generate a simple line plot of population vs time,
# then shade the area under the line in sky blue.
ax1.plot(grouped_data.Time, grouped_data.Value)
ax1.fill_between(grouped_data.Time, grouped_data.Value, color='skyblue')

# Use set_xlabel() or set_ylabel() instead to set the axis label of an
# axes object
ax1.set_xlabel('Year')
ax1.set_ylabel('Population (thousands)')

# Generate a stacked area plot of population vs time
ax2.stackplot(grouped_male_data.Time, grouped_male_data.Value,
grouped_female_data.Value)

# Add a figure legend
ax2.legend(['Male', 'Female'], loc='upper left')

# Set the x-axis label only this time
ax2.set_xlabel('Year')
plt.show()
```

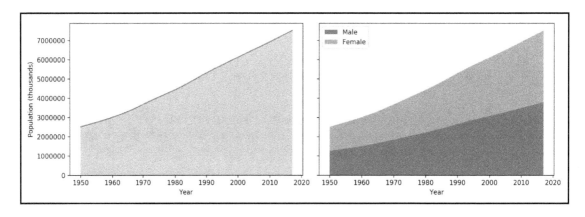

Introducing Seaborn

Seaborn by Michael Waskom is a statistical visualization library that is built on top of Matplotlib. It comes with handy functions for visualizing categorical variables, univariate distributions, and bivariate distributions. For more complex plots, various statistical methods such as linear regression models and clustering algorithms are available. Like Matplotlib, Seaborn also supports Pandas dataframes as input, plus automatically performing the necessary slicing, grouping, aggregation, and statistical model fitting to produce informative figures.

These Seaborn functions aim to bring publication-quality figures through an API with a minimal set of arguments, while maintaining the full customization capabilities of Matplotlib. In fact, many functions in Seaborn return a Matplotlib axis or grid object when invoked. Therefore, Seaborn is a great companion of Matplotlib. To install Seaborn through PyPI, you can issue the following command in the terminal:

```
pip install pandas
```

Seaborn will be imported as `sns` throughout this book. This section will not be a documentation of Seaborn. Rather our goal is to give a high-level overview of Seaborn's capabilities from the perspective of Matplotlib users. Readers can refer to the official Seaborn site (`http://seaborn.pydata.org/index.html`) for more information.

Visualizing univariate distribution

Seaborn makes the task of visualizing the distribution of a dataset much easier. Starting with the population data as discussed before, let's see how it distributes among different countries in 2017 by plotting a bar plot:

```
import seaborn as sns
import matplotlib.pyplot as plt


# Extract USA population data in 2017
current_population = population_df[(population_df.Location
                                   == 'United States of America') &
                                  (population_df.Time == 2017) &
                                  (population_df.Sex != 'Both')]

# Population Bar chart
sns.barplot(x="AgeGrp",y="Value", hue="Sex", data = current_population)

# Use Matplotlib functions to label axes rotate tick labels
```

```
ax = plt.gca()
ax.set(xlabel="Age Group", ylabel="Population (thousands)")
ax.set_xticklabels(ax.xaxis.get_majorticklabels(), rotation=45)
plt.title("Population Barchart (USA)")

# Show the figure
plt.show()
```

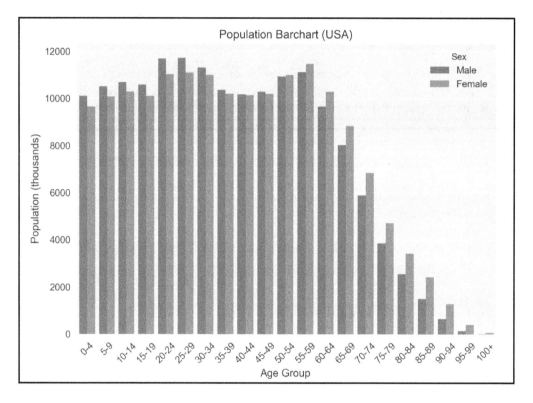

Bar chart in Seaborn

The seaborn.barplot() function shows a series of data points as rectangular bars. If multiple points per group are available, confidence intervals will be shown on top of the bars to indicate the uncertainty of the point estimates. Like most other Seaborn functions, various input data formats are supported, such as Python lists, Numpy arrays, pandas Series, and pandas DataFrame.

A more traditional way to show the population structure is through the use of a population pyramid.

So what is a population pyramid? As its name suggests, it is a pyramid-shaped plot that shows the age distribution of a population. It can be roughly classified into three classes, namely constrictive, stationary, and expansive for populations that are undergoing negative, stable, and rapid growth respectively. For instance, constrictive populations have a lower proportion of young people, so the pyramid base appears to be constricted. Stable populations have a more or less similar number of young and middle-aged groups. Expansive populations, on the other hand, have a large proportion of youngsters, thus resulting in pyramids with enlarged bases.

We can build a population pyramid by plotting two bar charts on two subplots with a shared y-axis:

```
import seaborn as sns
import matplotlib.pyplot as plt

# Extract USA population data in 2017
current_population = population_df[(population_df.Location
                                == 'United States of America') &
                             (population_df.Time == 2017) &
                             (population_df.Sex != 'Both')]

# Change the age group to descending order
current_population = current_population.iloc[::-1]

# Create two subplots with shared y-axis
fig, axes = plt.subplots(ncols=2, sharey=True)

# Bar chart for male
sns.barplot(x="Value",y="AgeGrp", color="darkblue", ax=axes[0],
            data = current_population[(current_population.Sex == 'Male')])
# Bar chart for female
sns.barplot(x="Value",y="AgeGrp", color="darkred", ax=axes[1],
            data = current_population[(current_population.Sex ==
'Female')])

# Use Matplotlib function to invert the first chart
axes[0].invert_xaxis()

# Use Matplotlib function to show tick labels in the middle
axes[0].yaxis.tick_right()

# Use Matplotlib functions to label the axes and titles
axes[0].set_title("Male")
axes[1].set_title("Female")
```

```
axes[0].set(xlabel="Population (thousands)", ylabel="Age Group")
axes[1].set(xlabel="Population (thousands)", ylabel="")
fig.suptitle("Population Pyramid (USA)")

# Show the figure
plt.show()
```

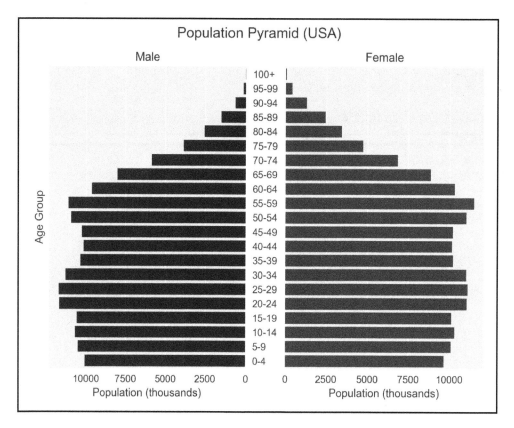

Since Seaborn is built on top of the solid foundations of Matplotlib, we can customize the plot easily using built-in functions of Matplotlib. In the preceding example, we used `matplotlib.axes.Axes.invert_xaxis()` to flip the male population plot horizontally, followed by changing the location of the tick labels to the right-hand side using `matplotlib.axis.YAxis.tick_right()`. We further customized the titles and axis labels for the plot using a combination of `matplotlib.axes.Axes.set_title()`, `matplotlib.axes.Axes.set()`, and `matplotlib.figure.Figure.suptitle()`.

Let's try to plot the population pyramids for Cambodia and Japan as well by changing the line `population_df.Location == 'United States of America'` to `population_df.Location == 'Cambodia'` or `population_df.Location == 'Japan'`. Can you classify the pyramids into one of the three population pyramid classes?

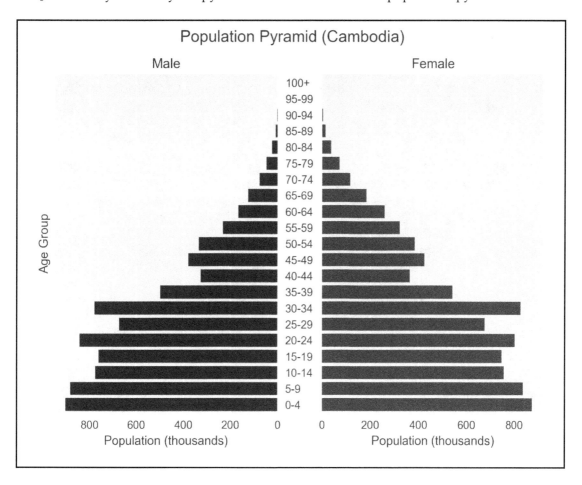

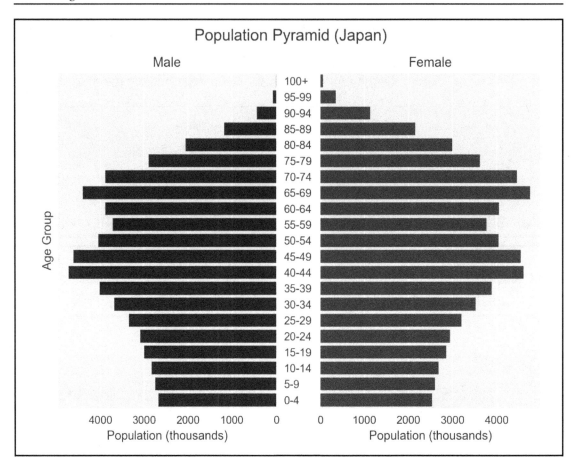

To see how Seaborn simplifies the code for relatively complex plots, let's see how a similar plot can be achieved using vanilla Matplotlib.

First, like the previous Seaborn-based example, we create two subplots with shared y-axis:

```
fig, axes = plt.subplots(ncols=2, sharey=True)
```

Next, we plot horizontal bar charts using `matplotlib.pyplot.barh()` and set the location and labels of ticks, followed by adjusting the subplot spacing:

```
# Get a list of tick positions according to the data bins
y_pos = range(len(current_population.AgeGrp.unique()))

# Horizontal barchart for male
axes[0].barh(y_pos, current_population[(current_population.Sex ==
             'Male')].Value, color="darkblue")

# Horizontal barchart for female
axes[1].barh(y_pos, current_population[(current_population.Sex ==
             'Female')].Value, color="darkred")

# Show tick for each data point, and label with the age group
axes[0].set_yticks(y_pos)
axes[0].set_yticklabels(current_population.AgeGrp.unique())

# Increase spacing between subplots to avoid clipping of ytick labels
plt.subplots_adjust(wspace=0.3)
```

Finally, we use the same code to further customize the look and feel of the figure:

```
# Invert the first chart
axes[0].invert_xaxis()

# Show tick labels in the middle
axes[0].yaxis.tick_right()

# Label the axes and titles
axes[0].set_title("Male")
axes[1].set_title("Female")
axes[0].set(xlabel="Population (thousands)", ylabel="Age Group")
axes[1].set(xlabel="Population (thousands)", ylabel="")
fig.suptitle("Population Pyramid (USA)")

# Show the figure
plt.show()
```

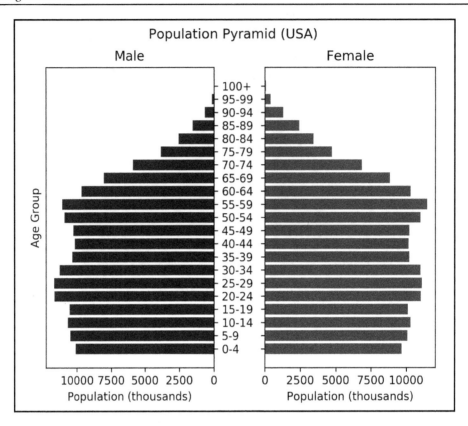

When compared to the Seaborn-based code, the pure Matplotlib implementation requires extra lines to define the tick positions, tick labels, and subplot spacing. For some other Seaborn plot types that include extra statistical calculations such as linear regression, and pearson correlation, the code reduction is even more dramatic. Therefore, Seaborn is a "batteries-included" statistical visualization package that allows users to write less verbose code.

Histogram and distribution fitting in Seaborn

In the population example, the raw data was already binned into different age groups. What if the data is not binned (for example, the BigMac Index data)? Turns out, `seaborn.distplot` can help us to process the data into bins and show us a histogram as a result. Let's look at this example:

```
import seaborn as sns
import matplotlib.pyplot as plt


# Get the BigMac index in 2017
current_bigmac = bigmac_df[(bigmac_df.Date == "2017-01-31")]

# Plot the histogram
ax = sns.distplot(current_bigmac.dollar_price)
plt.show()
```

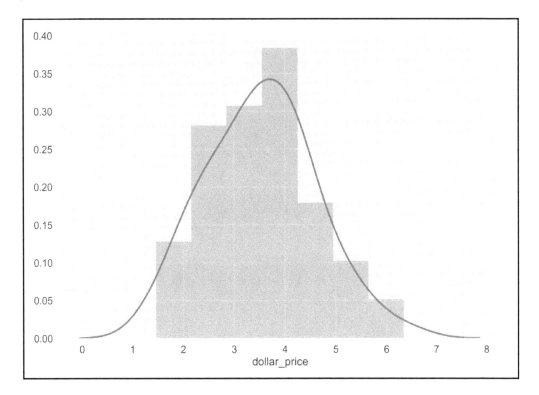

The `seaborn.distplot` function expects either pandas Series, single-dimensional numpy.array, or a Python list as input. Then, it determines the size of the bins according to the Freedman-Diaconis rule, and finally it fits a **kernel density estimate** (**KDE**) over the histogram.

KDE is a non-parametric method used to estimate the distribution of a variable. We can also supply a parametric distribution, such as beta, gamma, or normal distribution, to the `fit` argument.

In this example, we are going to fit the normal distribution from the `scipy.stats` package over the Big Mac Index dataset:

```
from scipy import stats

ax = sns.distplot(current_bigmac.dollar_price, kde=False, fit=stats.norm)
plt.show()
```

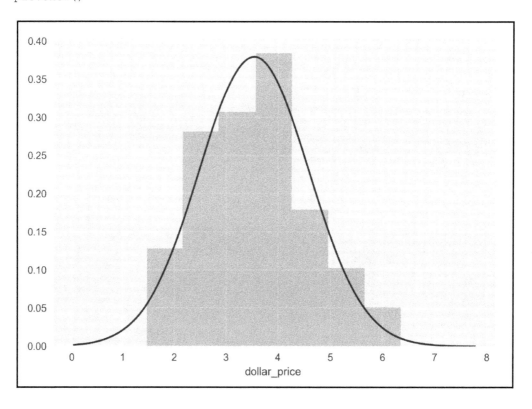

Visualizing a bivariate distribution

We should bear in mind that the Big Mac index is not directly comparable between countries. Normally, we would expect commodities in poor countries to be cheaper than those in rich ones. To represent a fairer picture of the index, it would be better to show the relationship between Big Mac pricing and **Gross Domestic Product** (**GDP**) per capita.

We are going to acquire GDP per capita from Quandl's **World Bank World Development Indicators** (**WWDI**) dataset. Based on the previous code example of acquiring JSON data from Quandl, can you try to adapt it to download the GDP per capita dataset?

For those who are impatient, here is the full code:

```python
import urllib
import json
import pandas as pd
import time
from urllib.request import urlopen


def get_gdp_dataset(api_key, country_code):
    """Obtain and parse a quandl GDP dataset in Pandas DataFrame format
    Quandl returns dataset in JSON format, where data is stored as a
    list of lists in response['dataset']['data'], and column headers
    stored in response['dataset']['column_names'].

    Args:
        api_key: Quandl API key
        country_code: Three letter code to represent country

    Returns:
        df: Pandas DataFrame of a Quandl dataset
    """
    base_url = "https://www.quandl.com/api/v3/datasets/"
    url_suffix = ".json?api_key="

    # Compose the Quandl API dataset code to get GDP per capita
    # (constant 2000 US$) dataset
    gdp_code = "WWDI/" + country_code + "_NY_GDP_PCAP_KD"

    # Parse the JSON response from Quandl API
    # Some countries might be missing, so we need error handling code
    try:
        u = urlopen(base_url + gdp_code + url_suffix + api_key)
    except urllib.error.URLError as e:
        print(gdp_code, e)
        return None
```

```
    response = json.loads(u.read().decode('utf-8'))

    # Format the response as Pandas Dataframe
    df = pd.DataFrame(response['dataset']['data'],
columns=response['dataset']['column_names'])

    # Add a new country code column
    df['country'] = country_code

    return df


api_key = "INSERT YOUR KEY HERE"
quandl_dfs = []

# Loop through all unique country code values in the BigMac index DataFrame
for country_code in bigmac_df.country.unique():
    # Fetch the GDP dataset for the corresponding country
    df = get_gdp_dataset(api_key, country_code)

    # Skip if the response is empty
    if df is None:
        continue

    # Store in a list DataFrames
    quandl_dfs.append(df)

    # Prevents exceeding the API speed limit
    time.sleep(2)

# Concatenate the list of DataFrames into a single one
gdp_df = pd.concat(quandl_dfs)
gdp_df.head()
```

The expected output:

```
WWDI/EUR_NY_GDP_PCAP_KD HTTP Error 404: Not Found
WWDI/SIN_NY_GDP_PCAP_KD HTTP Error 404: Not Found
WWDI/ROC_NY_GDP_PCAP_KD HTTP Error 404: Not Found
WWDI/UAE_NY_GDP_PCAP_KD HTTP Error 404: Not Found
```

	Date	Value	country
0	2015-12-31	10501.660269	ARG
1	2014-12-31	10334.780146	ARG
2	2013-12-31	10711.229530	ARG
3	2012-12-31	10558.265365	ARG
4	2011-12-31	10780.342508	ARG

We can see that the GDP per capita dataset is not available for four geographical locations, but we can ignore that for now.

Next, we will merge the two DataFrames that contain Big Mac Index and GDP per capita respectively using `pandas.merge()`. The most recent record in WWDI's GDP per capita dataset was collected at the end of 2015, so let's pair that up with the corresponding Big Mac index dataset in the same year.

For those who are familiar with the SQL language, `pandas.merge()` supports four modes, namely left, right, inner, and outer joins. Since we are interested in rows that have matching countries in both DataFrames only, we are going to choose inner join:

```
merged_df = pd.merge(bigmac_df[(bigmac_df.Date == "2015-01-31")],
gdp_df[(gdp_df.Date == "2015-12-31")], how='inner', on='country')
merged_df.head()
```

	Date_x	local_price	dollar_ex	dollar_price	dollar_ppp	dollar_valuation	dollar_adj_valuation	euro_adj_valuation	sterling_adj_valuation	yen_adj_valuation	yuan_adj_valuation	country	Date_y	Value
0	2015-01-31	28.00	8.610000	3.252033	5.845511	-32.107881	0.540242	-0.804495	-2.49468	34.3905	6.01183	ARG	2015-12-31	10501.660269
1	2015-01-31	5.30	1.227220	4.318705	1.106472	-9.839144	-17.8995	-18.9976	-20.3778	9.74234	-13.4315	AUS	2015-12-31	54688.445933
2	2015-01-31	13.50	2.592750	5.206827	2.818372	8.702019	68.4555	66.2024	63.3705	125.172	77.6231	BRA	2015-12-31	11211.891104
3	2015-01-31	2.89	0.661594	4.368235	0.603340	-8.805115	3.11257	1.73343	0	37.8289	8.72415	GBR	2015-12-31	41182.619517
4	2015-01-31	5.70	1.228550	4.639616	1.189979	-3.139545	-2.34134	-3.64753	-5.28928	30.5387	2.97343	CAN	2015-12-31	50108.065004

Scatter plot in Seaborn

A scatter plot is one of the most common plots in the scientific and business worlds. It is particularly useful for displaying the relationship between two variables. While we can simply use `matplotlib.pyplot.scatter` to draw a scatter plot, we can also use Seaborn to build similar plots with more advanced features.

The two functions `seaborn.regplot()` and `seaborn.lmplot()` display a linear relationship in the form of a scatter plot, a regression line, plus the 95% confidence interval around that regression line. The main difference between the two functions is that `lmplot()` combines `regplot()` with `FacetGrid` such that we can create color-coded or faceted scatter plots to show the interaction between three or more pairs of variables. We will demonstrate the use of `lmplot()` later in this chapter and the next chapter.

The simplest form of `seaborn.regplot()` supports numpy arrays, pandas Series, or pandas DataFrames as input. The regression line and the confidence interval can be removed by specifying `fit_reg=False`.

We are going to investigate the hypothesis that Big Macs are cheaper in poorer countries, and vice versa, checking whether there is any correlation between the Big Mac index and GDP per capita:

```
import seaborn as sns
import matplotlib.pyplot as plt

# seaborn.regplot() returns matplotlib.Axes object
ax = sns.regplot(x="Value", y="dollar_price", data=merged_df,
fit_reg=False)
ax.set_xlabel("GDP per capita (constant 2000 US$)")
ax.set_ylabel("BigMac index (US$)")

plt.show()
```

The expected output:

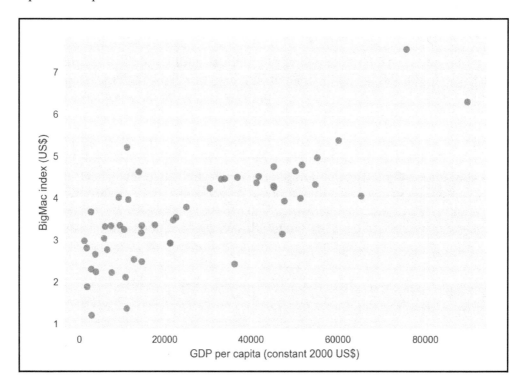

So far so good! It looks like the Big Mac index is positively correlated with GDP per capita. Let's turn the regression line back on and label a few countries that show extreme Big Mac index values:

```
ax = sns.regplot(x="Value", y="dollar_price", data=merged_df)
ax.set_xlabel("GDP per capita (constant 2000 US$)")
ax.set_ylabel("BigMac index (US$)")

# Label the country code for those who demonstrate extreme BigMac index
for row in merged_df.itertuples():
    if row.dollar_price >= 5 or row.dollar_price <= 2:
        ax.text(row.Value, row.dollar_price+0.1, row.country)

plt.show()
```

This is the expected output:

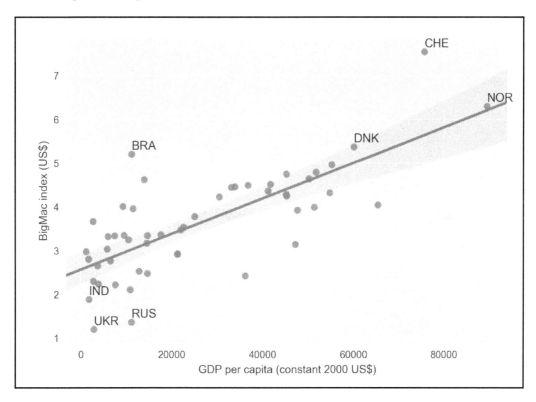

We can see that many countries fall within the confidence interval of the regression line. Given the GDP per capita level for each country, the linear regression model predicts the corresponding Big Mac index. The currency value shows signs of under- or over-valuation if the actual index deviates from the regression model.

By labeling the countries that show extremely high or low values, we can clearly see that the average price of a Big Mac in Brazil and Switzerland is overvalued, while it is undervalued in India, Russia, and Ukraine even if the differences in GDP are considered.

Since Seaborn is not a package for statistical analysis, we would need to rely on other packages, such as `scipy.stats` or `statsmodels`, to obtain the parameters of a regression model. In the next example, we are going to get the `slope` and `intercept` parameters from the regression model, and apply different colors for points that are above or below the regression line:

```python
from scipy.stats import linregress


ax = sns.regplot(x="Value", y="dollar_price", data=merged_df)
ax.set_xlabel("GDP per capita (constant 2000 US$)")
ax.set_ylabel("BigMac index (US$)")

# Calculate linear regression parameters
slope, intercept, r_value, p_value, std_err = linregress(merged_df.Value,
merged_df.dollar_price)

colors = []
for row in merged_df.itertuples():
    if row.dollar_price > row.Value * slope + intercept:
        # Color markers as darkred if they are above the regression line
        color = "darkred"
    else:
        # Color markers as darkblue if they are below the regression line
        color = "darkblue"

    # Label the country code for those who demonstrate extreme BigMac index
    if row.dollar_price >= 5 or row.dollar_price <= 2:
        ax.text(row.Value, row.dollar_price+0.1, row.country)

    # Highlight the marker that corresponds to China
    if row.country == "CHN":
        t = ax.text(row.Value, row.dollar_price+0.1, row.country)
        color = "yellow"

    colors.append(color)
```

```
# Overlay another scatter plot on top with marker-specific color
ax.scatter(merged_df.Value, merged_df.dollar_price, c=colors)

# Label the r squared value and p value of the linear regression model.
# transform=ax.transAxes indicates that the coordinates are given relative
# to the axes bounding box, with 0,0 being the lower left of the axes
# and 1,1 the upper right.
ax.text(0.1, 0.9, "$r^2={0:.3f}, p={1:.3e}$".format(r_value ** 2, p_value),
transform=ax.transAxes)

plt.show()
```

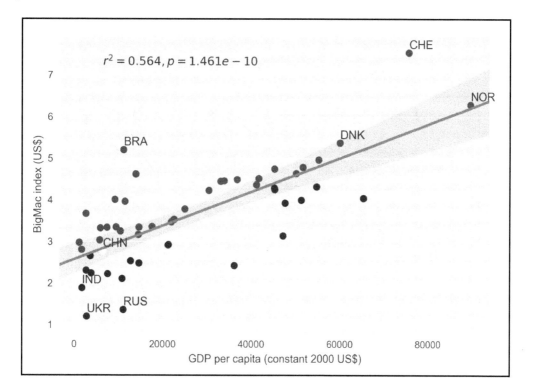

Contrary to popular belief, it looks like China's currency was not significantly under-valued in 2015 since its marker lies well within the 95% confidence interval of the regression line.

To better illustrate the distribution of values, we can combine histograms of x or y values with scatter plots using `seaborn.jointplot()`:

```
# seaborn.jointplot() returns a seaborn.JointGrid object
g = sns.jointplot(x="Value", y="dollar_price", data=merged_df)

# Provide custom axes labels through accessing the underlying axes object
# We can get matplotlib.axes.Axes of the scatter plot by calling g.ax_joint
g.ax_joint.set_xlabel("GDP per capita (constant 2000 US$)")
g.ax_joint.set_ylabel("BigMac index (US$)")

# Set the title and adjust the margin
g.fig.suptitle("Relationship between GDP per capita and BigMac Index")
g.fig.subplots_adjust(top=0.9)

plt.show()
```

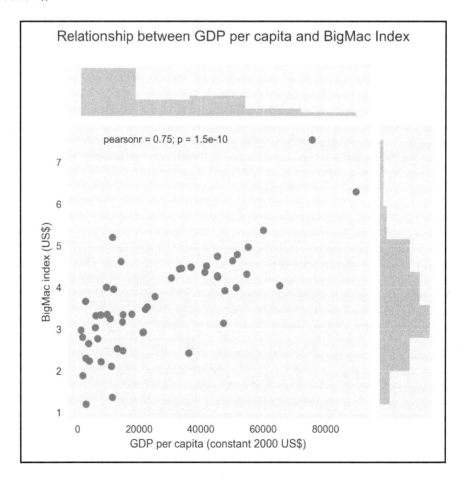

By additionally specifying the `kind` parameter in `jointplot` to `reg`, `resid`, `hex`, or `kde`, we can quickly change the plot type to regression, residual, hex bin, or KDE contour plot respectively.

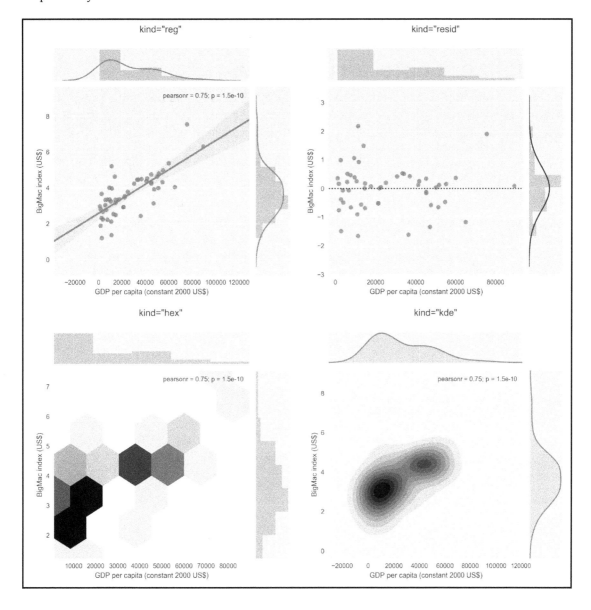

Here is a big disclaimer: with the data in our hands, it is still too early to make any conclusions about the valuation of currencies! Different business factors such as labor cost, rent, raw material costs, and taxation can all contribute to the pricing model of Big Mac, but this is beyond the scope of this book.

Visualizing categorical data

Towards the end of this chapter, let's try to integrate all datasets that we have processed so far. Remember that we briefly introduced the three categories of population structures (that is, constrictive, stable, and expansive) earlier in this chapter?

In this section, we are going to implement a naive algorithm for classifying populations into one of the three categories. After that, we will explore different techniques of visualizing categorical data.

Most references online discuss visual classification of population pyramids only (for example, `https://www.populationeducation.org/content/what-are-different-types-population-pyramids`). Clustering-based methods do exist (for example, Korenjak-Cˇ erne, Kejžar, Batagelj (2008). *Clustering of Population Pyramids*. Informatica. 32.), but to date, mathematical definitions of population categories are scarcely discussed. We will build a naive classifier based on the ratio of populations between "0-4" and "50-54" age groups in the next example:

```python
import pandas as pd
import seaborn as sns
import matplotlib.pyplot as plt


# Select total population for each country in 2015
current_population = population_df[(population_df.Time == 2015) &
                                  (population_df.Sex == 'Both')]

# A list for storing the population type for each country
pop_type_list = []

# Look through each country in the BigMac index dataset
for country in merged_df.country.unique():
    # Make sure the country also exist in the GDP per capita dataset
    if not country in current_population.country.values:
        continue

    # Calculate the ratio of population between "0-4" and "50-54"
    # age groups
    young = current_population[(current_population.country == country) &
```

```
                            (current_population.AgeGrp == "0-4")].Value

        midage = current_population[(current_population.country == country) &
                            (current_population.AgeGrp ==
"50-54")].Value

        ratio = float(young) / float(midage)

        # Classify the populations based on arbitrary ratio thresholds
        if ratio < 0.8:
            pop_type = "constrictive"
        elif ratio < 1.2 and ratio >= 0.8:
            pop_type = "stable"
        else:
            pop_type = "expansive"

        pop_type_list.append([country, ratio, pop_type])

# Convert the list to Pandas DataFrame
pop_type_df = pd.DataFrame(pop_type_list,
columns=['country','ratio','population type'])

# Merge the BigMac index DataFrame with population type DataFrame
merged_df2 = pd.merge(merged_df, pop_type_df, how='inner', on='country')
merged_df2.head()
```

The expected output is as follows:

	Date_x	local_price	dollar_ex	dollar_price	dollar_ppp	dollar_valuation	dollar_adj_valuation	euro_adj_valuation	sterling_adj_valuation	yen_adj_valuation	yuan_adj_valuation	country	Date_y	Value	ratio	population type
0	2015-01-31	28.00	8.610000	3.252033	5.845511	-32.107881	0.540242	-0.804495	-2.49468	34.3905	6.01183	ARG	2015-12-31	10501.660269	1.695835	expansive
1	2015-01-31	5.30	1.227220	4.318705	1.106472	-9.839144	-17.8995	-18.9976	-20.3778	9.74234	-13.4315	AUS	2015-12-31	54688.445933	0.961301	stable
2	2015-01-31	13.50	2.592750	5.206827	2.818372	8.702019	68.4555	66.2024	63.3705	125.172	77.6231	BRA	2015-12-31	11211.891104	1.217728	expansive
3	2015-01-31	2.89	0.661594	4.368235	0.603340	-8.805115	3.11257	1.73343	0	37.8289	8.72415	GBR	2015-12-31	41182.619517	0.872431	stable
4	2015-01-31	5.70	1.228550	4.639616	1.189979	-3.139545	-2.34134	-3.64753	-5.28928	30.5387	2.97343	CAN	2015-12-31	50108.065004	0.690253	constrictive

Categorical scatter plot

With the data classified into categories, we can check whether different population types exhibit different Big Mac index distributions.

We can use `seaborn.lmplot` to dissect the data and create a categorical scatter plot. As a recap, `lmplot()` combines `regplot()` with `FacetGrid` for visualization of three or more pairs of variables in faceted grids or color-coded scatter plots. In the upcoming examples, we are going to assign the population type variable to the `col`, `row`, or `hue` parameters of `lmplot()`. Let's see how the results look:

```
# Horizontal faceted grids (col="population type")
g = sns.lmplot(x="Value", y="dollar_price", col="population type",
data=merged_df2)
g.set_xlabels("GDP per capita (constant 2000 US$)")
g.set_ylabels("BigMac index (US$)")

plt.show()
```

The preceding code excerpt generates:

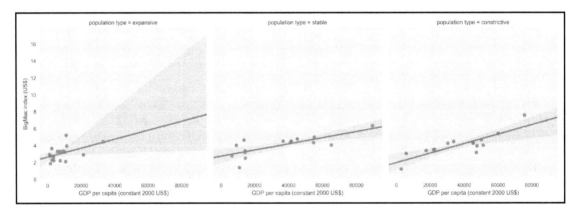

Alternatively, if we set `row="population type"` instead of `col="population type"` in the code excerpt, the following plot will be generated:

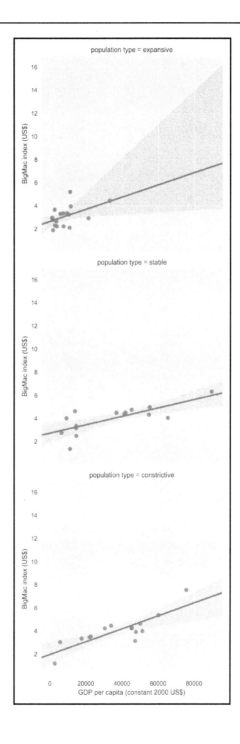

Finally, by changing `col="population type"` to `hue="population type"`, a color-coded categorical scatter plot will be generated:

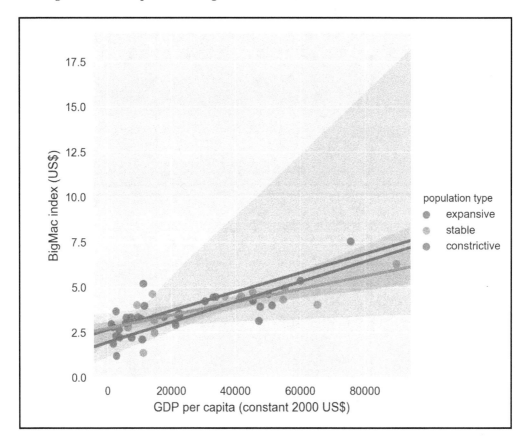

In fact, `col`, `row`, and `hue` can be mixed together to create a rich faceted grid. This is particularly useful when there are lots of dimensions in your data. Further discussion of facet grids will be available in the next chapter.

Strip plot and swarm plot

A strip is basically a scatter plot where the *x*-axis represents a categorical variable. Typical uses of a strip plot involve applying a small random jitter value to each data point such that the separation between points becomes clearer:

```
# Strip plot with jitter value
ax = sns.stripplot(x="population type", y="dollar_price", data=merged_df2,
jitter=True)
ax.set_xlabel("Population type")
ax.set_ylabel("BigMac index (US$)")

plt.show()
```

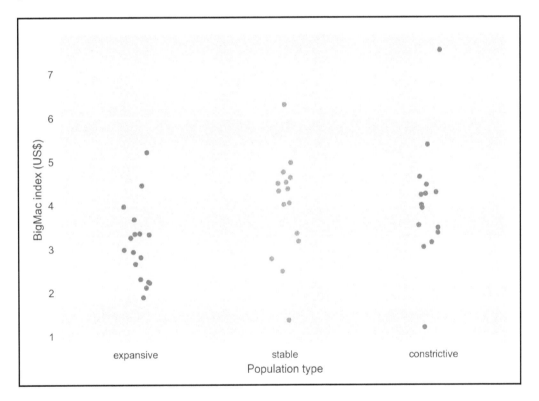

A swarm plot is very similar to a strip plot, yet the locations of points are adjusted automatically to avoid overlap even if the jitter value is not applied. These plots resemble bees swarming a position, and are likewise named.

If we change the Seaborn function call from `sns.stripplot` to `sns.swarmplot` in the preceding code excerpt, the result will be changed to this:

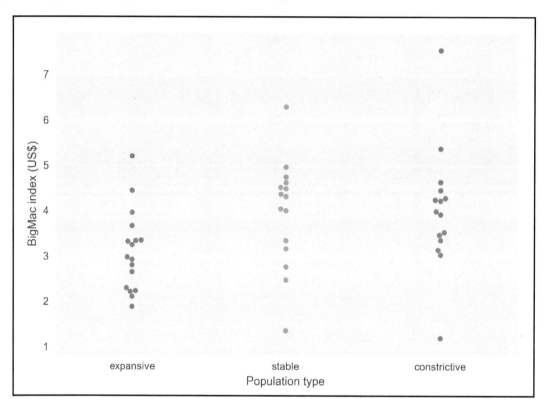

Box plot and violin plot

The way a strip plot and swarm plot represent data makes comparison difficult. Suppose you want to find out whether the stable or constrictive population type has a higher median BigMac index value. Can you do that based on the two previous example plots?

You might be tempted to think that the constrictive group has a higher median value because of the higher maximum data point, but in fact, the stable group has a higher median value.

Could there be a better plot type for comparing the distribution of categorical data? Here you go! Let's try a box plot:

```
# Box plot
ax = sns.boxplot(x="population type", y="dollar_price", data=merged_df2)
ax.set_xlabel("Population type")
ax.set_ylabel("BigMac index (US$)")

plt.show()
```

The expected output:

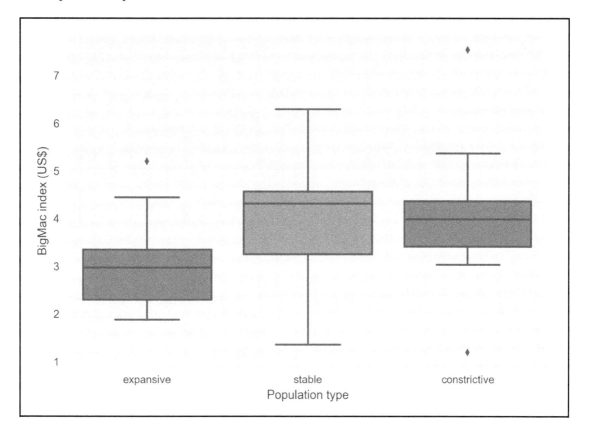

The box represents quartiles of the data, the center line denotes the median value, and the whiskers represent the full range of the data. Data points that deviate by more than 1.5 times the interquartile range from the upper or lower quartile are deemed to be outliers and show as fliers.

A violin plot combines the kernel density estimate of our data with the box plot. Both box plot and violin plot display the median and interquartile range, but a violin plot goes one step further by showing the full estimated probability distribution that is fit to the data. Therefore, we can tell whether there are peaks within the data and also compare their relative amplitude.

If we change the Seaborn function call from `sns.boxplot` to `sns.violinplot` in the code excerpt, the result would be like this:

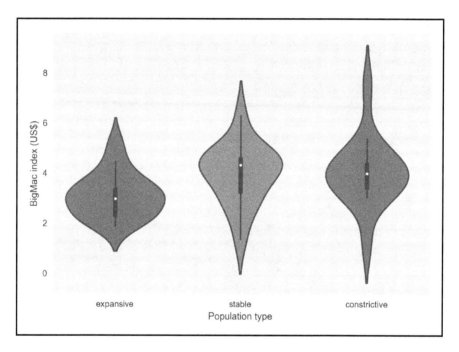

We can also overlay a strip plot or swarm plot on top of the box plot or swarm plot in order to get the best of both worlds. Here is an example code:

```
# Prepare a box plot
ax = sns.boxplot(x="population type", y="dollar_price", data=merged_df2)

# Overlay a swarm plot on top of the same axes
sns.swarmplot(x="population type", y="dollar_price", data=merged_df2,
color="w", ax=ax)
ax.set_xlabel("Population type")
ax.set_ylabel("BigMac index (US$)")

plt.show()
```

The expected output:

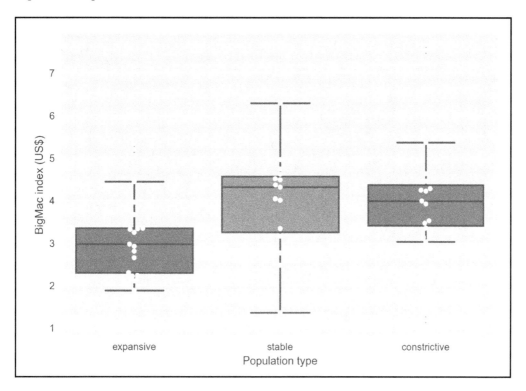

Controlling Seaborn figure aesthetics

While we can use Matplotlib to customize the figure aesthetics, Seaborn comes with several handy functions to make customization easier. If you are using Seaborn version 0.8 or later, `seaborn.set()` must be called explicitly after import if you would like to enable the beautiful Seaborn default theme. In earlier versions, `seaborn.set()` was called implicitly on import.

Preset themes

The five default themes in Seaborn, namely darkgrid, whitegrid, dark, white, and ticks, can be selected by calling the `seaborn.set_style()` function.

seaborn.set_style() must be called before issuing any plotting commands in order to display the theme properly.

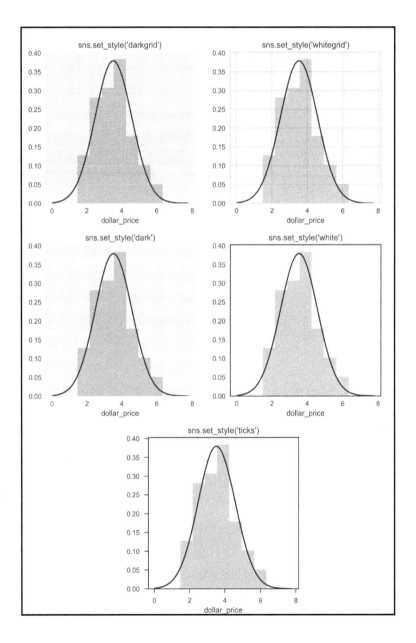

Removing spines from the figure

To remove or adjust the positions of spines, we can make use of the seaborn.despine function. By default, the spines on the top and right side of a figure are removed, and additional spines can be removed by setting left=True or bottom=True. Through the use of offset and trim parameters, the location of the spines can be adjusted as well.

 seaborn.despine has to be called after calling the Seaborn plotting functions.

Here are the results of different combinations of parameters in the seaborn.despine function:

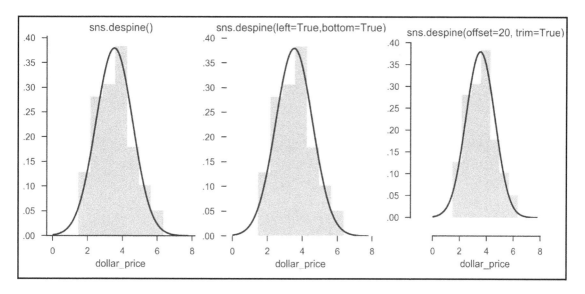

Changing the size of the figure

To control the height and width of the figure, we can rely on matplotlib.pyplot.figure(figsize=(WIDTH,HEIGHT)) as well.

In this example, we are going to change the size of the previous histogram example to 8 inches wide and 4 inches tall:

```
import seaborn as sns
import matplotlib.pyplot as plt
from scipy import stats

# Note: Codes related to data preparation are skipped for brevity
# Reset all previous theme settings to defaults
sns.set()

# Change the size to 8 inches wide and 4 inches tall
fig = plt.figure(figsize=(8,4))

# We are going to reuse current_bigmac that was generated earlier
# Plot the histogram
ax = sns.distplot(current_bigmac.dollar_price)
plt.show()
```

Here is the expected output from the preceding code:

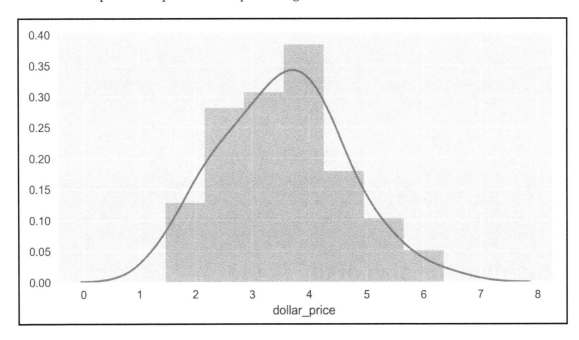

Seaborn also comes with the `seaborn.set_context()` function to control the scale of plot elements. There are four preset contexts, paper, notebook, talk, and poster, which are in ascending order of size. By default, the Notebook style is chosen. This is an example of setting the context to `poster`:

```
# Reset all previous theme settings to defaults
sns.set()

# Set Seaborn context to poster
sns.set_context("poster")

# We are going to reuse current_bigmac that was generated earlier
# Plot the histogram
ax = sns.distplot(current_bigmac.dollar_price)
plt.show()
```

Here is the expected output from the preceding code:

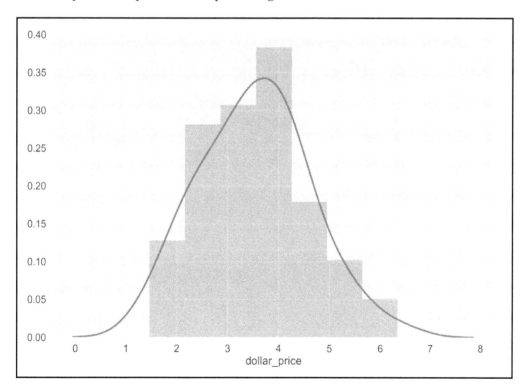

Fine-tuning the style of the figure

Almost every element in a Seaborn figure can be further customized via `seaborn.set`. Here is the list of parameters that are supported:

- `context`: One of the preset contexts--{paper, notebook, talk, poster}.
- `style`: One of the axes' styles--{darkgrid, whitegrid, dark, white, ticks}.
- `palette`: One of the color palettes as defined in `https://seaborn.pydata.org/generated/seaborn.color_palette.html#seaborn.color_palette`.
- `font`: A supported font or font family name, such as serif, sans-serif, cursive, fantasy, or monospace. For more information, visit `https://matplotlib.org/api/font_manager_api.html`.
- `font_scale`: An independent scaling factor of font elements.
- `rc`: A dictionary of extra `rc` parameters mappings. To obtain the full list of all `rc` parameters, we can run `seaborn.axes_style()`.

RC parameters that are not defined in the currently used preset context or axis style cannot be overridden. For more information on `seaborn.set()`, please visit `https://seaborn.pydata.org/generated/seaborn.set.html#seaborn.set`.

Let's try to increase the font scale, increase the line width of the KDE plot, and change the color of several plot elements:

```
# Get a dictionary of all parameters that can be changed
sns.axes_style()

"""
Returns
{'axes.axisbelow': True,
 'axes.edgecolor': '.8',
 'axes.facecolor': 'white',
 'axes.grid': True,
 'axes.labelcolor': '.15',
 'axes.linewidth': 1.0,
 'figure.facecolor': 'white',
 'font.family': [u'sans-serif'],
 'font.sans-serif': [u'Arial',
 u'DejaVu Sans',
 u'Liberation Sans',
 u'Bitstream Vera Sans',
 u'sans-serif'],
 'grid.color': '.8',
 'grid.linestyle': u'-',
```

```
'image.cmap': u'rocket',
'legend.frameon': False,
'legend.numpoints': 1,
'legend.scatterpoints': 1,
'lines.solid_capstyle': u'round',
'text.color': '.15',
'xtick.color': '.15',
'xtick.direction': u'out',
'xtick.major.size': 0.0,
'xtick.minor.size': 0.0,
'ytick.color': '.15',
'ytick.direction': u'out',
'ytick.major.size': 0.0,
'ytick.minor.size': 0.0}
"""

# Increase the font scale to 2, change the grid color to light grey,
# and axes label color to dark blue
sns.set(context="notebook",
 style="darkgrid",
 font_scale=2,
 rc={'grid.color': '0.6',
 'axes.labelcolor':'darkblue',
 "lines.linewidth": 2.5})

# Plot the histogram
ax = sns.distplot(current_bigmac.dollar_price)
plt.show()
```

The code generates the following histogram:

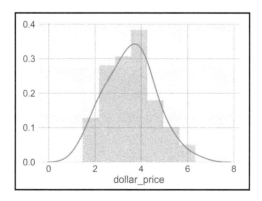

So far, only functions that control global aesthetics were introduced. What if we want to change the style of a specific plot only?

Luckily, most Seaborn plotting functions come with specific parameters for the customization of styles. This also means that there isn't a universal styling tutorial for all Seaborn plotting functions. However, we can take a closer look at this `seaborn.distplot()` code excerpt to get an idea:

```
# Note: Codes related to data preparation and imports are skipped for
# brevity
# Reset the style
sns.set(context="notebook", style="darkgrid")

# Plot the histogram with custom style
ax = sns.distplot(current_bigmac.dollar_price,
                  kde_kws={"color": "g",
                           "linewidth": 3,
                           "label": "KDE"},
                  hist_kws={"histtype": "step",
                            "alpha": 1,
                            "color": "k",
                            "label": "histogram"})

plt.show()
```

The expected result:

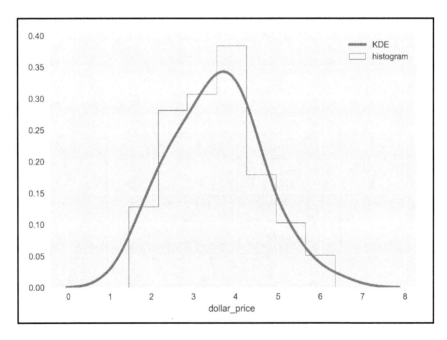

Some Seaborn functions support a more direct approach of customizing aesthetics. For example, `seaborn.barplot` can pass through keyword arguments such as `facecolor`, `edgecolor`, `ecolor`, and `linewidth` to the underlying `matplotlib.pyplot.bar` function:

```
# Note: Codes related to data preparation and imports are skipped
# for brevity
# Population Bar chart
sns.barplot(x="AgeGrp",y="Value", hue="Sex",
            linewidth=2, edgecolor="w",
            data = current_population)

# Use Matplotlib functions to label axes rotate tick labels
ax = plt.gca()
ax.set(xlabel="Age Group", ylabel="Population (thousands)")
ax.set_xticklabels(ax.xaxis.get_majorticklabels(), rotation=45)
plt.title("Population Barchart (USA)")

# Show the figure
plt.show()
```

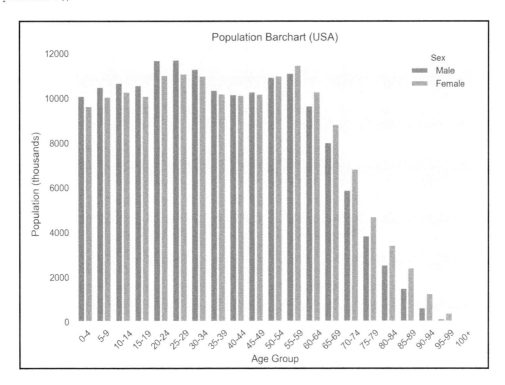

More about colors

Color is perhaps the most important aspect of figure style, and thus it deserves its own subsection. There are many great resources that discuss the principles of choosing colors in visualizations (for example, `https://betterfigures.org/2015/06/23/picking-a-colour-scale-for-scientific-graphics/` and `https://earthobservatory.nasa.gov/blogs/elegantfigures/2013/08/05/subtleties-of-color-part-1-of-6/`). The official Matplotlib documentation also contains a good overview of color maps (`http://matplotlib.org/users/colormaps.html`).

Effective use of color adds sufficient contrast to make something stand out and draw your audience's attention. Colors can also evoke emotions; for example, red is often associated with important or passionate, while green is often associated with natural or stable. If you are trying to deliver a story from your plots, do try to use an appropriate color scheme. It's estimated that 8% of men and 0.5% of women suffer from red-green color blindness, so we need to pick colors with these individuals in mind as well.

Color scheme and color palettes

There are three general kinds of color palettes available in seaborn--qualitative, diverging, and sequential:

- Qualitative palettes are best for data with discrete levels or nominal or categorical data. Custom qualitative palettes can be created by providing a list of Matplotlib colors to `seaborn.color_palette`.
- Diverging palettes are used for highlighting low and high values in a figure, with a neutrally colored midpoint. Custom diverging palettes can be created by passing two hue values plus the optional lightness and saturation values for the extremes to the `seaborn.diverging_palette` function.
- Sequential palettes are usually used for quantitative data that progresses continuously from low to high.
  Custom sequential palettes can be created by providing a single Matplotlib color to `seaborn.light_palette` or `seaborn.dark_palette`, which produces a palette that changes gradually from light or dark desaturated values to the seed color.

In the next example, we are going to plot the most commonly used qualitative, diverging, and sequential palettes, as well as a few custom palettes:

```python
import numpy as np
import matplotlib.pyplot as plt
from matplotlib.colors import ListedColormap


def palplot(pal, ax):
    """Plot the values in a color palette as a horizontal array.
    Adapted from seaborn.palplot
    Args:
        p : seaborn color palette
        ax : axes to plot the color palette
    """
    n = len(pal)
    ax.imshow(np.arange(n).reshape(1, n),
              cmap=ListedColormap(list(pal)),
              interpolation="nearest", aspect="auto")
    ax.set_xticks(np.arange(n) - .5)
    ax.set_yticks([-.5, .5])
    ax.set_xticklabels([])
    ax.set_yticklabels([])
palettes = {"qualitative": ["deep", "pastel", "bright", "dark",
                            "colorblind", "Accent", "Paired",
                            "Set1", "Set2", "Set3", "Pastel1",
                            "Pastel2", "Dark2"],
            "diverging": ["BrBG", "PiYG", "PRGn", "PuOr", "RdBu",
                          "RdBu_r", "RdGy", "RdGy_r", "RdYlGn",
                          "coolwarm"],
            "sequential": ["husl", "Greys", "Blues", "BuGn_r",
                           "GnBu_d", "plasma", "viridis","cubehelix"]}

#Reset to default Seaborn style
sns.set()

# Create one subplot per palette, the x-axis is shared
fig, axarr = plt.subplots(13, 3, sharex=True, figsize=(12,11))

# Plot 9 color blocks for each palette
for i, palette_type in enumerate(palettes.keys()):
    for j, palette in enumerate(palettes[palette_type]):
        pal = sns.color_palette(palettes[palette_type][j], 9)
        palplot(pal, axarr[j,i])
        axarr[j,i].set_xlabel(palettes[palette_type][j])

# Plot a few more custom diverging palette
custom_diverging_palette = [
```

```
    sns.diverging_palette(220, 20, n=9),
    sns.diverging_palette(10, 220, sep=80, n=9),
    sns.diverging_palette(145, 280, s=85, l=25, n=9)
]

for i, palette in enumerate(custom_diverging_palette):
    palplot(palette, axarr[len(palettes["diverging"])+i,1])
    axarr[len(palettes["diverging"])+i,1].set_xlabel("custom diverging
    {}".format(i+1))

# Plot a few more custom sequential palette
other_custom_palette = [
    sns.light_palette("green", 9),
    sns.light_palette("green", 9, reverse=True),
    sns.dark_palette("navy", 9),
    sns.dark_palette("navy", 9, reverse=True),
    sns.color_palette(["#49a17a","#4aae82","#4eb98a","#55c091","#c99b5f",
    "#cbb761","#c5cc62","#accd64","#94ce65"])
]

for i, palette in enumerate(other_custom_palette):
    palplot(palette, axarr[len(palettes["sequential"])+i,2])
    axarr[len(palettes["sequential"])+i,2].set_xlabel("custom sequential
    {}".format(i+1))

# Reduce unnecessary margin space
plt.tight_layout()

# Show the plot
plt.show()
```

The expected output is as follows:

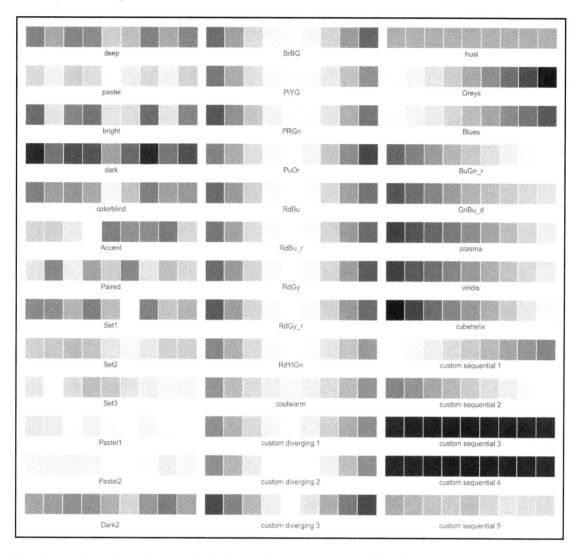

To change the color scheme of a Seaborn plot, we can use either the `color` or `palette` parameter available in most Seaborn functions. The `color` parameter supports a single color that will be applied to all of the elements. On the other hand, `palette` supports a range of colors to differentiate levels of the `hue` variable.

Some Seaborn functions support the `color` parameter only (for example, dist plot), while others can support both `color` and `palette` (for example, bar plot and box plot). Readers can refer to the official documentation to see which parameter is supported.

The following three code excerpts demonstrate the use of the `color` or `palette` parameter in a dist plot, bar plot, and box plot:

```
# Note: Codes related to data preparation and imports are skipped
# for brevity
# Change the color of histogram and KDE line to darkred
ax = sns.distplot(current_bigmac.dollar_price, color="darkred")
plt.show()
```

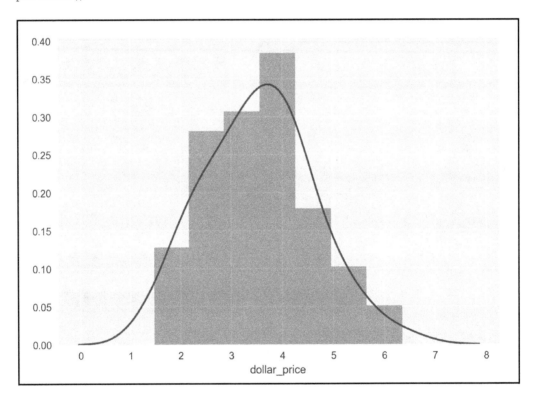

```
current_population = population_df[(population_df.Location == 'United
States of America') &
                                   (population_df.Time == 2017) &
                                   (population_df.Sex != 'Both')]
# Change the color palette of the bar chart to Paired
sns.barplot(x="AgeGrp",y="Value", hue="Sex", palette="Paired", data =
current_population)
# Rotate tick labels by 30 degree
plt.setp(plt.gca().get_xticklabels(), rotation=30,
horizontalalignment='right')
plt.show()
```

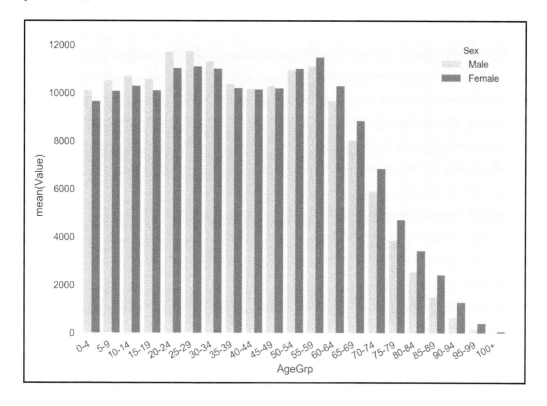

```
# Note: Codes related to data preparation and imports are skipped
# for brevity
# Change the color palette of the bar chart to Set2 from color
# brewer library
ax = sns.boxplot(x="population type", y="dollar_price", palette="Set2",
data=merged_df2)
plt.show()
```

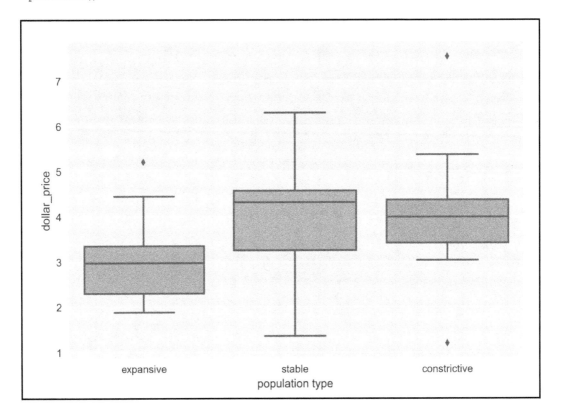

Summary

You just learned how we can parse online data in CSV or JSON formats using the versatile Pandas package. You further learned how to filter, subset, merge, and process data into insights. You have now equipped yourself with the knowledge to visualize time series, univariate, bivariate, and categorical data. The chapter concluded with a number of useful techniques to customize figure aesthetics for effective storytelling.

Phew! We have just completed a long chapter, so go grab a burger, have a break, and relax.

8
Visualizing Multivariate Data

When we have **big data** that contains many variables, the plot types in `Chapter 7`, *Visualizing Online Data* may no longer be an effective way of data visualization. We may try to cramp as many variables in a single plot as possible, but the overcrowded or cluttered details would quickly reach the boundary of a human's visual perception capabilities.

In this chapter, we aim to introduce multivariate data visualization techniques; they enable us to better understand the distribution of data and the relationships between variables. Here is the outline of this chapter:

- Getting End-of-Day (EOD) stock data from Quandl
- Two-dimensional faceted plots:
    - Factor plot in Seaborn
    - Faceted grid in Seaborn
    - Pair plot in Seaborn
- Other two-dimensional multivariate plots:
    - Heatmap in Seaborn
    - Candlestick plot in matplotlib.finance:
        - Visualizing various stock market indicators
    - Building a comprehensive stock chart
- Three-dimensional plots:
    - Scatter plot
    - Bar chart
    - Caveats of using Matplotlib 3D

First, we will discuss faceted plots, which is a divide-and-conquer approach to visualizing multivariate data. The gestalt of this approach is to slice input data into different facets such that only a handful of attributes will be represented in each visualization panel. This will reduce visual clutter by allowing inspection of variables in reduced subsets. Sometimes, finding a suitable way to represent multivariate data in a 2D graph is difficult. Therefore, we are going to introduce 3D plotting functions in Matplotlib as well.

The data used in this chapter was collected from Quandl's End-of-Day (EOD) stock database. Let's get the data from Quandl first.

Getting End-of-Day (EOD) stock data from Quandl

Since we are going to discuss stock data extensively, note that we do not guarantee the accuracy, completeness, or validity of the content presented; nor are we responsible for any errors or omissions that may have occurred. The data, visualizations, and analyses are provided on an "as is" basis for educational purposes only, without any representations, warranties, or conditions of any kind. Therefore, the publisher and the authors do not accept liability for your use of the content. It should be noted that past stock performance may not predict future performance. Readers should also be aware of the risks involved in stock investments and should not take any investment decisions based on the content in this chapter. In addition, readers are advised to conduct their own independent research into individual stocks before making an investment decision.

We are going to adapt the Quandl JSON API code in Chapter 7, *Visualizing Online Data* to get EOD stock data from Quandl. The historical stock data from January 1, 2017 to June 30, 2017 for six stock codes will be obtained: Apple Inc.(EOD/AAPL), The Procter & Gamble Company (EOD/PG), Johnson & Johnson (EOD/JNJ), Exxon Mobil Corporation (EOD/XOM), International Business Machines Corporation (EOD/IBM), and Microsoft Corporation (EOD/MSFT). Again, we will use the default `urllib` and `json` modules to handle Quandl API calls, followed by converting the data into a Pandas DataFrame:

```
from urllib.request import urlopen
import json
import pandas as pd
```

```python
def get_quandl_dataset(api_key, code, start_date, end_date):
    """Obtain and parse a quandl dataset in Pandas DataFrame format

    Quandl returns dataset in JSON format, where data is stored as a
    list of lists in response['dataset']['data'], and column headers
    stored in response['dataset']['column_names'].
    Args:
        api_key: Quandl API key
        code: Quandl dataset code

    Returns:
        df: Pandas DataFrame of a Quandl dataset

    """
    base_url = "https://www.quandl.com/api/v3/datasets/"
    url_suffix = ".json?api_key="
    date = "&start_date={}&end_date={}".format(start_date, end_date)

    # Fetch the JSON response
    u = urlopen(base_url + code + url_suffix + api_key + date)
    response = json.loads(u.read().decode('utf-8'))
    # Format the response as Pandas Dataframe
    df = pd.DataFrame(response['dataset']['data'],
columns=response['dataset']
    ['column_names'])
    return df


# Input your own API key here
api_key = "INSERT YOUR KEY HERE"

# Quandl code for six US companies
codes = ["EOD/AAPL", "EOD/PG", "EOD/JNJ", "EOD/XOM", "EOD/IBM", "EOD/MSFT"]
start_date = "2017-01-01"
end_date = "2017-06-30"

dfs = []
# Get the DataFrame that contains the EOD data for each company
for code in codes:
    df = get_quandl_dataset(api_key, code, start_date, end_date)
    df["Company"] = code[4:]
    dfs.append(df)

# Concatenate all dataframes into a single one
stock_df = pd.concat(dfs)

# Sort by ascending order of Company then Date
stock_df = stock_df.sort_values(["Company","Date"])
stock_df.head()
```

-	Date	Open	High	Low	Close	Volume	Dividend	Split	Adj_Open	Adj_High	Adj_Low	Adj_Close	Adj_Volume	Company
124	2017-01-03	115.80	116.3300	114.76	116.15	28781865.0	0.0	1.0	114.833750	115.359328	113.802428	115.180830	28781865.0	AAPL
123	2017-01-04	115.85	116.5100	115.75	116.02	21118116.0	0.0	1.0	114.883333	115.537826	114.784167	115.051914	21118116.0	AAPL
122	2017-01-05	115.92	116.8642	115.81	116.61	22193587.0	0.0	1.0	114.952749	115.889070	114.843667	115.636991	22193587.0	AAPL
121	2017-01-06	116.78	118.1600	116.47	117.91	31751900.0	0.0	1.0	115.805573	117.174058	115.498159	116.926144	31751900.0	AAPL
120	2017-01-09	117.95	119.4300	117.94	118.99	33561948.0	0.0	1.0	116.965810	118.433461	116.955894	117.997132	33561948.0	AAPL

The dataframe contains **Opening, High, Low, and Closing (OHLC)** prices for each stock. Extra information is also available; for example, the dividend column reflects the cash dividend value on that day. The split column shows the ratio of new shares to old shares if a split occurred on that day. The adjusted prices account for price fluctuations due to distributions or corporate actions by assuming that all these actions were reinvested into the current stock. For more information about these columns, consult the documentation pages on Quandl.

Grouping the companies by industry

As you may have noticed, three of the companies (AAPL, IBM, and MSFT) are tech companies, while the remaining three companies are not. Stock analysts often group companies by industry to gain deeper insights. Let's try to label the companies by industry:

```
# Classify companies by industry
tech_companies = set(["AAPL","IBM","MSFT"])
stock_df['Industry'] = ["Tech" if c in tech_companies else "Others" for c
in stock_df['Company']]
```

Converting the date to a supported format

The Date column in stock_df is recorded as a series of Python strings. Although Seaborn can use string-formatted dates in some functions, Matplotlib cannot. To make the dates malleable to data processing and visualizations, we need to convert the values to float numbers supported by Matplotlib:

```
from matplotlib.dates import date2num


# Convert Date column from string to Python datetime object,
# then to float number that is supported by Matplotlib.
stock_df["Datetime"] = date2num(pd.to_datetime(stock_df["Date"],
format="%Y-%m-%d").tolist())
```

Getting the percentage change of the closing price

Next, we want to calculate the change of the closing price with regard to the previous day's close. The `pct_change()` function in Pandas makes this task very easy:

```
import numpy as np


# Calculate percentage change versus the previous close
stock_df["Close_change"] = stock_df["Close"].pct_change()
# Since the DataFrame contain multiple companies' stock data,
# the first record in the "Close_change" should be changed to
# NaN in order to prevent referencing the price of incorrect company.
stock_df.loc[stock_df["Date"]=="2017-01-03", "Close_change"] = np.NaN
stock_df.head()
```

Two-dimensional faceted plots

We are going to introduce three major ways to create faceted plots: `seaborn.factorplot()`, `seaborn.FacetGrid()`, and `seaborn.pairplot()`. You might have seen some faceted plots in the previous chapter, when we talked about `seaborn.lmplot()`. Actually, the `seaborn.lmplot()` function combines `seaborn.regplot()` with `seaborn.FacetGrid()`, and the definitions of data subsets can be adjusted by the `hue`, `col`, and `row` parameters.

We are going to introduce three major ways to create faceted plots: `seaborn.factorplot()`, `seaborn.FacetGrid()`, and `seaborn.pairplot()`. These functions actually work similarly to `seaborn.lmplot()` in the way of defining facets.

Factor plot in Seaborn

With the help of `seaborn.factorplot()`, we can draw categorical point plots, box plots, violin plots, bar plots, or strip plots onto a `seaborn.FacetGrid()` by tuning the `kind` parameter. The default plot type for `factorplot` is point plot. Unlike other plotting functions in Seaborn, which support a wide variety of input data formats, `factorplot` supports pandas DataFrames as input only, while variable/column names can be supplied as string to x, y, hue, col, or row:

```
import seaborn as sns
import matplotlib.pyplot as plt


sns.set(style="ticks")

# Plot EOD stock closing price vs Date for each company.
# Color of plot elements is determined by company name (hue="Company"),
# plot panels are also arranged in columns accordingly (col="Company").
# The col_wrap parameter determines the number of panels per row
(col_wrap=3).
g = sns.factorplot(x="Date", y="Close",
                   hue="Company", col="Company",
                   data=stock_df, col_wrap=3)

plt.show()
```

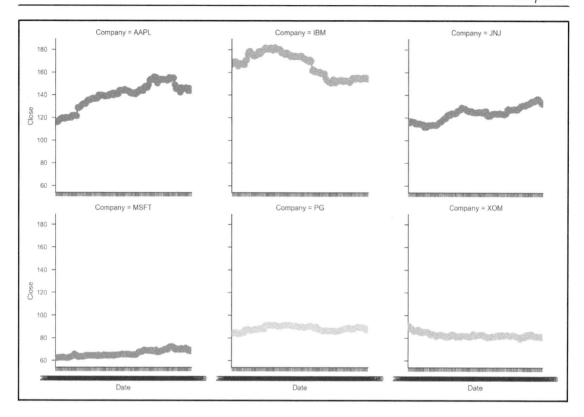

There are several issues in the preceding plot.

First, the aspect ratio (length divided by height) is slightly suboptimal for a time series chart. A wider plot would allow us to observe minute changes during the time period. We are going to adjust that using the `aspect` parameter.

Second, the lines and dots are too thick, thereby masking some details in the plot. We can reduce the size of these visual elements by tweaking the `scale` parameter.

Lastly, the ticks are too close to each other, and the tick labels are overlapping. After plotting, `sns.factorplot()` returns a FacetGrid, which was denoted as `g` in the code. We can further tweak the aesthetics of the plot, such as tick positions and labels, by calling the relevant functions in the `FacetGrid` object:

```
# Increase the aspect ratio and size of each panel
g = sns.factorplot(x="Date", y="Close",
                   hue="Company", col="Company",
                   data=stock_df,
                   col_wrap=3, size=3,
                   scale=0.5, aspect=1.5)

# Thinning of ticks (select 1 in 10)
locs, labels = plt.xticks()
g.set(xticks=locs[0::10], xticklabels=labels[0::10])

# Rotate the tick labels to prevent overlap
g.set_xticklabels(rotation=30)

# Reduce the white space between plots
g.fig.subplots_adjust(wspace=.1, hspace=.2)
plt.show()
```

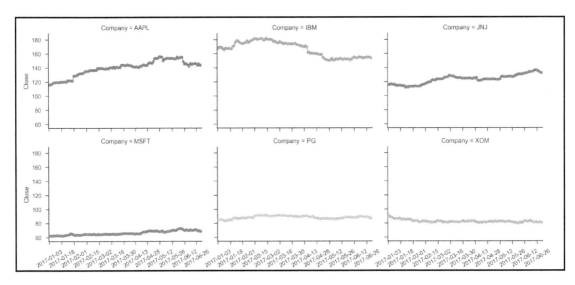

```
# Create faceted plot separated by industry
g = sns.factorplot(x="Date", y="Close",
                    hue="Company", col="Industry",
                    data=stock_df, size=4,
                    aspect=1.5, scale=0.5)

locs, labels = plt.xticks()
g.set(xticks=locs[0::10], xticklabels=labels[0::10])
g.set_xticklabels(rotation=30)
plt.show()
```

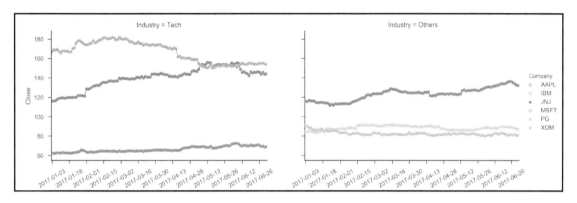

Faceted grid in Seaborn

Up until now, we have already mentioned FacetGrid a few times, but what exactly is it?

As you may know, FacetGrid is an engine for subsetting data and drawing plot panels determined by assigning variables to the rows and columns of hue parameters. While we can use wrapper functions such as lmplot and factorplot to scaffold plots on FacetGrid easily, it would be more flexible to build FacetGrid from scratch. To do that, we first supply a pandas DataFrame to the FacetGrid object and specify the way to lay out the grid via col, row, and hue parameters. Then we can assign a Seaborn or Matplotlib plotting function to each panel by calling the map() function of the FacetGrid object:

```
# Create a FacetGrid
g = sns.FacetGrid(stock_df, col="Company", hue="Company",
                  size=3, aspect=2, col_wrap=2)

# Map the seaborn.distplot function to the panels,
# which shows a histogram of closing prices.
g.map(sns.distplot, "Close")
```

```
# Label the axes
g.set_axis_labels("Closing price (US Dollars)", "Density")

plt.show()
```

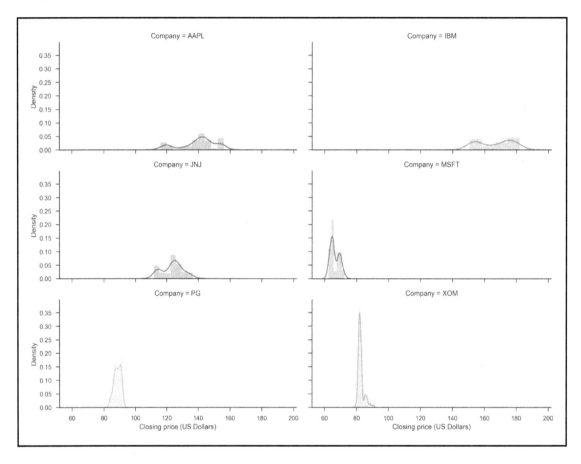

We can also supply keyword arguments to the plotting functions:

```
g = sns.FacetGrid(stock_df, col="Company", hue="Company",
                  size=3, aspect=2.2, col_wrap=2)

# We can supply extra kwargs to the plotting function.
# Let's turn off KDE line (kde=False), and plot raw
# frequency of bins only (norm_hist=False).
# By setting rug=True, tick marks that denotes the
# density of data points will be shown in the bottom.
g.map(sns.distplot, "Close", kde=False, norm_hist=False, rug=True)

g.set_axis_labels("Closing price (US Dollars)", "Density")

plt.show()
```

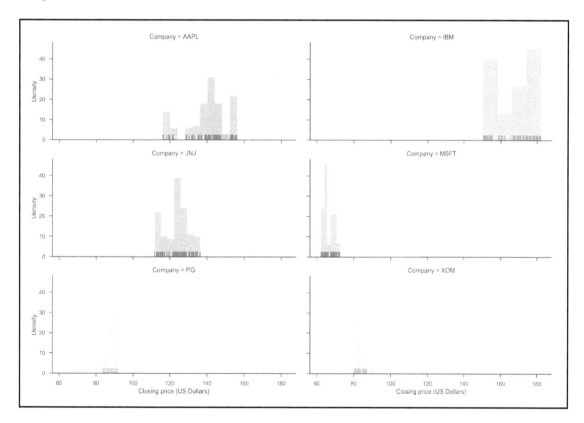

FacetGrid is not limited to the use of Seaborn plotting functions; let's try to map the good old Matplotlib.pyplot.plot() function to FacetGrid:

```
from matplotlib.dates import DateFormatter


g = sns.FacetGrid(stock_df, hue="Company", col="Industry",
                  size=4, aspect=1.5, col_wrap=2)

# plt.plot doesn't support string-formatted Date,
# so we need to use the Datetime column that we
# prepared earlier instead.
g.map(plt.plot, "Datetime", "Close", marker="o", markersize=3, linewidth=1)
g.add_legend()

# We can access individual axes through g.axes[column]
# or g.axes[row,column] if multiple rows are present.
# Let's adjust the tick formatter and rotate the tick labels
# in each axes.
for col in range(2):
    g.axes[col].xaxis.set_major_formatter(DateFormatter('%Y-%m-%d'))
    plt.setp(g.axes[col].get_xticklabels(), rotation=30)

g.set_axis_labels("", "Closing price (US Dollars)")
plt.show()
```

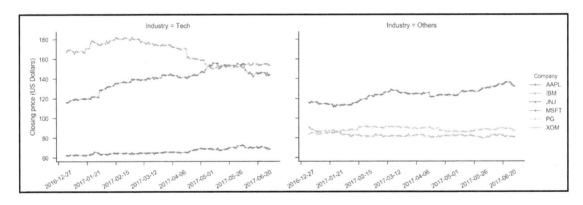

Pair plot in Seaborn

A pair plot is a special type of `FacetGrid`. Pairwise relationships between all variables in the input DataFrame will be visualized as scatter plots. In addition, a series of histograms will be displayed along the diagonal axes to show the distribution of the variable in that column:

```
# Show a pairplot of three selected variables (vars=["Open", "Volume",
"Close"])
g = sns.pairplot(stock_df, hue="Company",
                 vars=["Open", "Volume", "Close"])

plt.show()
```

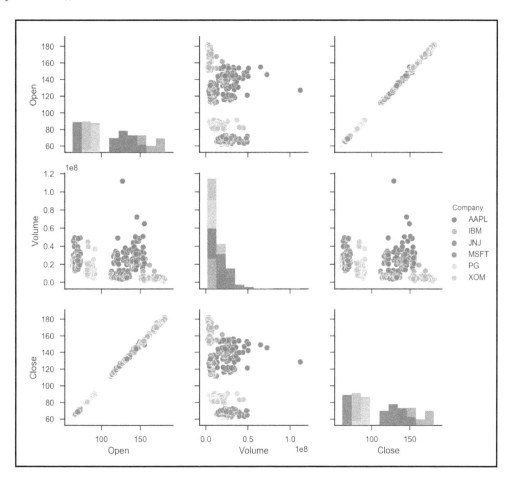

We can tweak many aspects of the plot. In the next example, we will increase the aspect ratio, change the plot type in the diagonal line to KDE plot, and adjust the aesthetics of the plots using keyword arguments:

```
# Adjust the aesthetics of the plot
g = sns.pairplot(stock_df, hue="Company",
                 aspect=1.5, diag_kind="kde",
                 diag_kws=dict(shade=True),
                 plot_kws=dict(s=15, marker="+"),
                 vars=["Open", "Volume", "Close"])

plt.show()
```

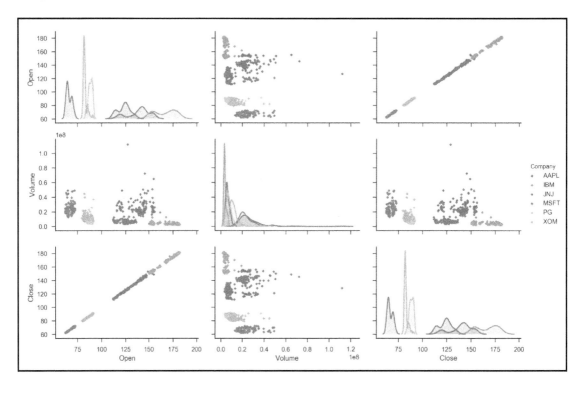

Similar to other plots based on FacetGrid, we can define the variables to be displayed in each panel. We can also manually define the comparisons that matter to us instead of an all-versus-all comparison by setting the x_vars and y_vars parameters. You may also use seaborn.PairGrid() directly if you require even higher flexibility for defining comparison groups:

```
# Manually defining the comparisons that we are interested.
g = sns.pairplot(stock_df, hue="Company", aspect=1.5,
                 x_vars=["Open", "Volume"],
                 y_vars=["Close", "Close_change"])

plt.show()
```

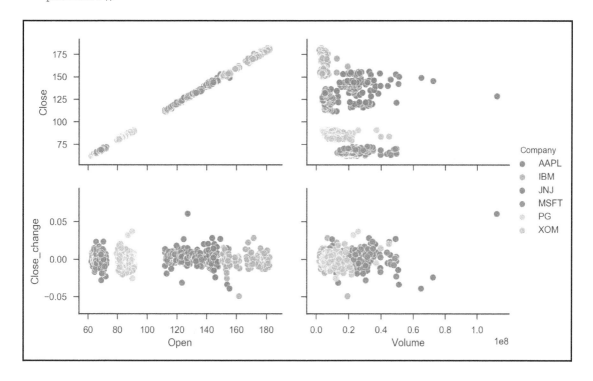

Other two-dimensional multivariate plots

FacetGrid, factor plot, and pair plot may take up a lot of space when we need to visualize more variables or samples. There are two special plot types that come in handy if you want the maximize space efficiency - Heatmaps and Candlestick plots.

Heatmap in Seaborn

A heatmap is an extremely compact way to display a large amount of data. In the finance world, color-coded blocks can give investors a quick glance at which stocks are up or down. In the scientific world, heatmaps allow researchers to visualize the expression level of thousands of genes.

The `seaborn.heatmap()` function expects a 2D list, 2D Numpy array, or pandas DataFrame as input. If a list or array is supplied, we can supply column and row labels via `xticklabels` and `yticklabels` respectively. On the other hand, if a DataFrame is supplied, the column labels and index values will be used to label the columns and rows respectively.

To get started, we will plot an overview of the performance of the six stocks using a heatmap. We define stock performance as the change of closing price when compared to the previous close. This piece of information was already calculated earlier in this chapter (that is, the `Close_change` column). Unfortunately, we can't supply the whole DataFrame to `seaborn.heatmap()` directly, since it expects company names as columns, date as index, and the change in closing price as values.

If you are familiar with Microsoft Excel, you might have experience in using pivot tables, a powerful technique to summarize the levels or values of a particular variable. pandas includes such functionality. The following code excerpt makes use of the wonderful `Pandas.DataFrame.pivot()` function to make a pivot table:

```
stock_change = stock_df.pivot(index='Date', columns='Company',
values='Close_change')
stock_change = stock_change.loc["2017-06-01":"2017-06-30"]
stock_change.head()
```

Company / Date	AAPL	IBM	JNJ	MSFT	PG	XOM
2017-06-01	0.002749	0.000262	0.004133	0.003723	0.000454	0.002484
2017-06-02	0.014819	-0.004061	0.010095	0.023680	0.005220	-0.014870
2017-06-05	-0.009778	0.002368	0.002153	0.007246	0.001693	0.007799
2017-06-06	0.003378	-0.000262	0.003605	0.003320	0.000676	0.013605

2017-06-07	0.005957	-0.009123	-0.000611	-0.001793	-0.000338	-0.003694

With the pivot table ready, we can proceed to plot our first heatmap:

```
ax = sns.heatmap(stock_change)
plt.show()
```

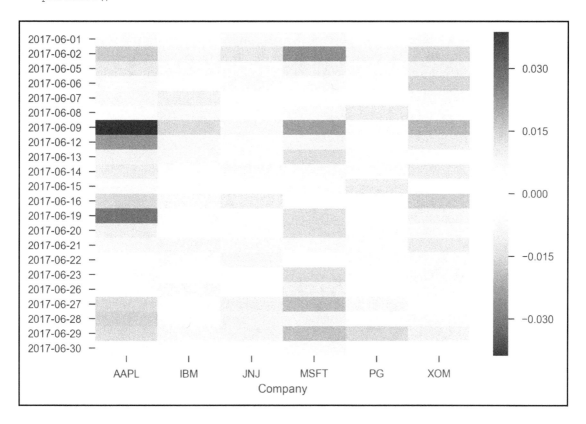

The default heatmap implementation is not really compact enough. Of course, we can resize the figure via `plt.figure(figsize=(width, height))`; we can also toggle the square parameter to create square-shaped blocks. To ease visual recognition, we can add a thin border around the blocks.

By US stock market convention, green denotes a rise and red denotes a fall in prices. Hence we can adjust the `cmap` parameter to adjust the color map. However, neither Matplotlib nor Seaborn includes a red-green color map, so we need to create our own:

At the end of `Chapter 7`, *Visualizing Online Data*, we briefly introduced functions for creating custom color maps. Here we will use `seaborn.diverging_palette()` to create the red-green color map, which requires us to specify the hues, saturation, and lightness (husl) for the negative and positive extents of the color map. You may also use this code to launch an interactive widget in Jupyter Notebook to help select the colors:

```
%matplotlib notebook
import seaborn as sns

sns.choose_diverging_palette(as_cmap=True)
```

```
# Create a new red-green color map using the husl color system
# h_neg and h_pos determines the hue of the extents of the color map.
# s determines the color saturation
# l determines the lightness
# sep determines the width of center point
# In addition, we need to set as_cmap=True as the cmap parameter of
# sns.heatmap expects matplotlib colormap object.
rdgn = sns.diverging_palette(h_neg=10, h_pos=140, s=80, l=50,
                             sep=10, as_cmap=True)

# Change to square blocks (square=True), add a thin
# border (linewidths=.5), and change the color map
# to follow US stocks market convention (cmap="RdGn").
ax = sns.heatmap(stock_change, cmap=rdgn,
                linewidths=.5, square=True)

# Prevent x axes label from being cropped
plt.tight_layout()
plt.show()
```

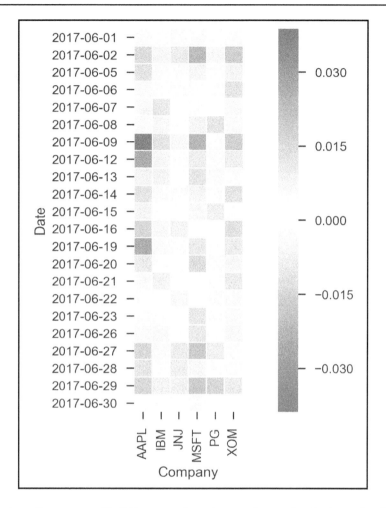

It could be hard to discern small differences in values when color is the only discriminative factor. Adding text annotations to each color block may help readers understand the magnitude of the difference:

```
fig = plt.figure(figsize=(6,8))

# Set annot=True to overlay the values.
# We can also assign python format string to fmt.
# For example ".2%" refers to percentage values with
# two decimal points.
```

```
ax = sns.heatmap(stock_change, cmap=rdgn,
                 annot=True, fmt=".2%",
                 linewidths=.5, cbar=False)
plt.show()
```

	AAPL	IBM	JNJ	MSFT	PG	XOM
17-06-01	0.27%	0.03%	0.41%	0.37%	0.05%	0.25%
17-06-02	1.48%	-0.41%	1.01%	2.37%	0.52%	-1.49%
17-06-05	-0.98%	0.24%	0.22%	0.72%	0.17%	0.78%
17-06-06	0.34%	-0.03%	0.36%	0.33%	0.07%	1.36%
17-06-07	0.60%	-0.91%	-0.06%	-0.18%	-0.03%	-0.37%
17-06-08	-0.24%	0.74%	-0.15%	-0.61%	-1.04%	-0.36%
17-06-09	-3.88%	1.31%	0.75%	-2.27%	0.35%	1.87%
17-06-12	-2.39%	0.70%	0.22%	-0.77%	0.09%	0.97%
17-06-13	0.80%	-0.60%	0.15%	1.25%	-0.20%	0.04%
17-06-14	-0.98%	-0.29%	0.57%	-0.54%	0.43%	-1.07%
17-06-15	-0.60%	0.27%	0.20%	-0.53%	1.06%	0.23%
17-06-16	-1.40%	0.75%	0.98%	0.14%	0.31%	1.50%
17-06-19	2.86%	-0.35%	-0.21%	1.24%	0.22%	-0.87%
17-06-20	-0.91%	0.07%	0.11%	-1.35%	-0.26%	-0.54%
17-06-21	0.59%	-0.75%	0.51%	0.51%	-0.26%	-1.06%
17-06-22	-0.16%	0.40%	0.85%	-0.01%	-0.41%	-0.44%
17-06-23	0.45%	-0.19%	0.28%	1.35%	0.44%	0.65%
17-06-26	-0.31%	0.73%	-0.07%	-0.95%	-0.07%	-0.45%
17-06-27	-1.43%	-0.31%	-0.98%	-1.87%	-0.84%	-0.16%
17-06-28	1.46%	0.37%	-0.88%	0.85%	-0.27%	0.52%
17-06-29	-1.47%	-0.77%	-0.88%	-1.88%	-1.56%	-1.02%
17-06-30	0.24%	-0.19%	-0.26%	0.64%	0.18%	0.04%

Company

Candlestick plot in matplotlib.finance

As you have seen in the first part of this chapter, our dataset contains the opening and closing prices as well as the highest and lowest price per trading day. None of the plots we have described thus far are able to describe the trend of all these variables in a single plot.

In the financial world, the candlestick plot is almost the default choice for describing price movements of stocks, currencies, and commodities over a time period. Each candlestick consists of the body, describing the opening and closing prices, and extended wicks illustrating the highest and lowest prices of a particular trading day. If the closing price is higher than the opening price, the candlestick is often colored black. Conversely, the candlestick is colored red if the closing price is lower. The trader can then infer the opening and closing prices based on the combination of color and the boundary of the candlestick body.

In the following example, we are going to prepare a candlestick chart of Apple Incorporation in the last 50 trading days of our DataFrame. We will also apply the tick formatter to label the ticks as dates:

```python
import matplotlib.pyplot as plt
from matplotlib.dates import date2num, WeekdayLocator, DayLocator,
DateFormatter, MONDAY
from matplotlib.finance import candlestick_ohlc


# Extract stocks data for AAPL.
# candlestick_ohlc expects Date (in floating point number), Open, High,
Low,
# Close columns only
# So we need to select the useful columns first using DataFrame.loc[].
Extra
# columns can exist,
# but they are ignored. Next we get the data for the last 50 trading only
for
# simplicity of plots.
candlestick_data = stock_df[stock_df["Company"]=="AAPL"]\
                    .loc[:, ["Datetime", "Open", "High", "Low", "Close",
                    "Volume"]]\
                    .iloc[-50:]

# Create a new Matplotlib figure
fig, ax = plt.subplots()

# Prepare a candlestick plot
candlestick_ohlc(ax, candlestick_data.values, width=0.6)
```

```
ax.xaxis.set_major_locator(WeekdayLocator(MONDAY)) # major ticks on the
mondays
ax.xaxis.set_minor_locator(DayLocator()) # minor ticks on the days
ax.xaxis.set_major_formatter(DateFormatter('%Y-%m-%d'))
ax.xaxis_date() # treat the x data as dates
# rotate all ticks to vertical
plt.setp(ax.get_xticklabels(), rotation=90, horizontalalignment='right')

ax.set_ylabel('Price (US $)') # Set y-axis label
plt.show()
```

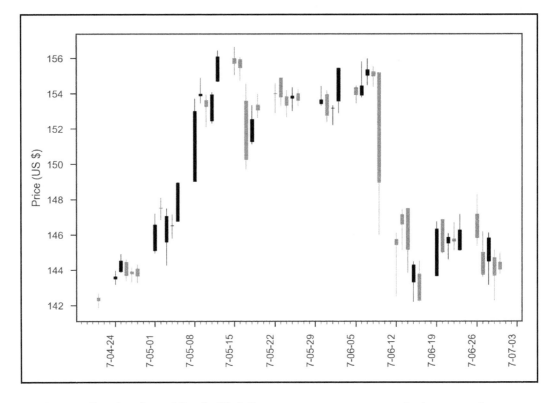

Starting from Matplotlib 2.0, `matplotlib.finance` is deprecated.
Readers should use `mpl_finance` (`https://github.com/matplotlib/`
`mpl_finance`) in the future instead. However, as of writing this chapter,
`mpl_finance` is not yet available on PyPI, so let's stick to
`matplotlib.finance` for the time being.

Visualizing various stock market indicators

The candlestick plot in the current form is a bit bland. Traders usually overlay stock indicators such as **Average True Range (ATR)**, Bollinger band, **Commodity Channel Index (CCI)**, **Exponential Moving Average (EMA)**, **Moving Average Convergence Divergence (MACD)**, **Relative Strength Index (RSI)**, and various other stats for technical analysis.

Stockstats (`https://github.com/jealous/stockstats`) is a great package for calculating these indicators/stats and many more. It wraps around pandas DataFrames and generate the stats on the fly when they are accessed. To use `stockstats`, we simply install it via PyPI: `pip install stockstats`.

Next, we can convert a pandas DataFrame to a stockstats DataFrame via `stockstats.StockDataFrame.retype()`. A plethora of stock indicators can then be accessed by following the pattern `StockDataFrame["variable_timeWindow_indicator"]`. For example, `StockDataFrame['open_2_sma']` would give us the 2-day simple moving average on the opening price. Shortcuts may be available for some indicators, so please consult the official documentation for more information:

```
from stockstats import StockDataFrame


# Convert to StockDataFrame
# Need to pass a copy of candlestick_data to StockDataFrame.retype
# Otherwise the original candlestick_data will be modified
stockstats = StockDataFrame.retype(candlestick_data.copy())

# 5-day exponential moving average on closing price
ema_5 = stockstats["close_5_ema"]
# 20-day exponential moving average on closing price
ema_20 = stockstats["close_20_ema"]
# 50-day exponential moving average on closing price
ema_50 = stockstats["close_50_ema"]
# Upper Bollinger band
boll_ub = stockstats["boll_ub"]
# Lower Bollinger band
boll_lb = stockstats["boll_lb"]
# 7-day Relative Strength Index
rsi_7 = stockstats['rsi_7']
# 14-day Relative Strength Index
rsi_14 = stockstats['rsi_14']
```

With the stock indicators ready, we can overlay them on the same candlestick chart:

```python
import datetime
import matplotlib.pyplot as plt
from matplotlib.dates import date2num, WeekdayLocator, DayLocator,
DateFormatter, MONDAY
from matplotlib.finance import candlestick_ohlc


# Create a new Matplotlib figure
fig, ax = plt.subplots()

# Prepare a candlestick plot
candlestick_ohlc(ax, candlestick_data.values, width=0.6)

# Plot stock indicators in the same plot
ax.plot(candlestick_data["Datetime"], ema_5, lw=1, label='EMA (5)')
ax.plot(candlestick_data["Datetime"], ema_20, lw=1, label='EMA (20)')
ax.plot(candlestick_data["Datetime"], ema_50, lw=1, label='EMA (50)')
ax.plot(candlestick_data["Datetime"], boll_ub, lw=2, linestyle="--",
label='Bollinger upper')
ax.plot(candlestick_data["Datetime"], boll_lb, lw=2, linestyle="--",
label='Bollinger lower')

ax.xaxis.set_major_locator(WeekdayLocator(MONDAY)) # major ticks on
# the mondays
ax.xaxis.set_minor_locator(DayLocator()) # minor ticks on the days
ax.xaxis.set_major_formatter(DateFormatter('%Y-%m-%d'))
ax.xaxis_date() # treat the x data as dates
# rotate all ticks to vertical
plt.setp(ax.get_xticklabels(), rotation=90, horizontalalignment='right')

ax.set_ylabel('Price (US $)') # Set y-axis label

# Limit the x-axis range from 2017-4-23 to 2017-7-1
datemin = datetime.date(2017, 4, 23)
datemax = datetime.date(2017, 7, 1)
ax.set_xlim(datemin, datemax)

plt.legend() # Show figure legend
plt.tight_layout()
plt.show()
```

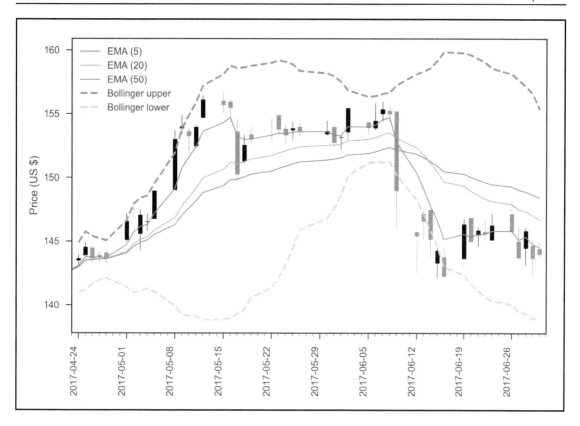

Building a comprehensive stock chart

In the following elaborate example, we are going to apply the many techniques that we have covered thus far to create a more comprehensive stock chart. In addition to the preceding plot, we will add a line chart to display the **Relative Strength Index** (**RSI**) and a bar chart to show trade volume. A special market event (`http://markets.` `businessinsider.com/news/stocks/apple-stock-price-falling-new-iphone-speed-` `2017-6-1002082799`) is going to be annotated on the chart as well:

If you look closely at the charts, you might notice some missing dates. These days are usually non-trading days or public holidays that were not present in our DataFrame.

```python
import datetime
import matplotlib.pyplot as plt
from matplotlib.dates import date2num, WeekdayLocator, DayLocator,
DateFormatter, MONDAY
from matplotlib.finance import candlestick_ohlc
from matplotlib.ticker import FuncFormatter


# FuncFormatter to convert tick values to Millions
def millions(x, pos):
    return '%dM' % (x/1e6)

# Create 3 subplots spread acrosee three rows, with shared x-axis.
# The height ratio is specified via gridspec_kw
fig, axarr = plt.subplots(nrows=3, ncols=1, sharex=True, figsize=(8,8),
                          gridspec_kw={'height_ratios':[3,1,1]})

# Prepare a candlestick plot in the first axes
candlestick_ohlc(axarr[0], candlestick_data.values, width=0.6)

# Overlay stock indicators in the first axes
axarr[0].plot(candlestick_data["Datetime"], ema_5, lw=1, label='EMA (5)')
axarr[0].plot(candlestick_data["Datetime"], ema_20, lw=1, label='EMA (20)')
axarr[0].plot(candlestick_data["Datetime"], ema_50, lw=1, label='EMA (50)')
axarr[0].plot(candlestick_data["Datetime"], boll_ub, lw=2, linestyle="--",
label='Bollinger upper')
axarr[0].plot(candlestick_data["Datetime"], boll_lb, lw=2, linestyle="--",
label='Bollinger lower')

# Display RSI in the second axes
axarr[1].axhline(y=30, lw=2, color = '0.7') # Line for oversold threshold
axarr[1].axhline(y=50, lw=2, linestyle="--", color = '0.8') # Neutral RSI
axarr[1].axhline(y=70, lw=2, color = '0.7') # Line for overbought threshold
axarr[1].plot(candlestick_data["Datetime"], rsi_7, lw=2, label='RSI (7)')
axarr[1].plot(candlestick_data["Datetime"], rsi_14, lw=2, label='RSI (14)')

# Display trade volume in the third axes
axarr[2].bar(candlestick_data["Datetime"], candlestick_data['Volume'])

# Mark the market reaction to the Bloomberg news
# https://www.bloomberg.com/news/articles/2017-06-09/apple-s-new
# -iphones-said-to-miss-out-on-higher-speed-data-links
# http://markets.businessinsider.com/news/stocks/apple-stock-price
```

```
# -falling-new-iphone-speed-2017-6-1002082799
axarr[0].annotate("Bloomberg News",
                  xy=(datetime.date(2017, 6, 9), 155), xycoords='data',
                  xytext=(25, 10), textcoords='offset points', size=12,
                  arrowprops=dict(arrowstyle="simple",
                  fc="green", ec="none"))

# Label the axes
axarr[0].set_ylabel('Price (US $)')
axarr[1].set_ylabel('RSI')
axarr[2].set_ylabel('Volume (US $)')

axarr[2].xaxis.set_major_locator(WeekdayLocator(MONDAY)) # major ticks on
the mondays
axarr[2].xaxis.set_minor_locator(DayLocator()) # minor ticks on the days
axarr[2].xaxis.set_major_formatter(DateFormatter('%Y-%m-%d'))
axarr[2].xaxis_date() # treat the x data as dates
axarr[2].yaxis.set_major_formatter(FuncFormatter(millions)) # Change the y-
axis ticks to millions
plt.setp(axarr[2].get_xticklabels(), rotation=90,
horizontalalignment='right') # Rotate x-tick labels by 90 degree

# Limit the x-axis range from 2017-4-23 to 2017-7-1
datemin = datetime.date(2017, 4, 23)
datemax = datetime.date(2017, 7, 1)
axarr[2].set_xlim(datemin, datemax)

# Show figure legend
axarr[0].legend()
axarr[1].legend()

# Show figure title
axarr[0].set_title("AAPL (Apple Inc.) NASDAQ", loc='left')

# Reduce unneccesary white space
plt.tight_layout()
plt.show()
```

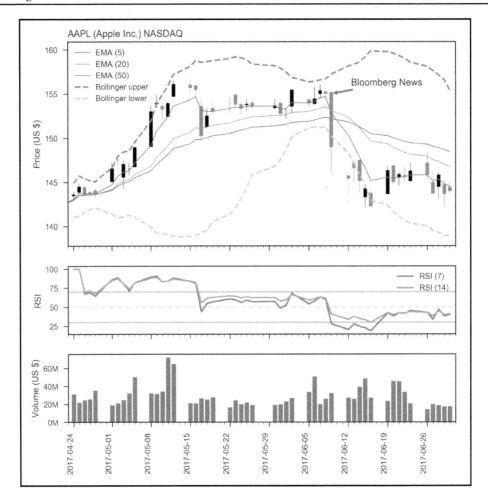

Three-dimensional (3D) plots

By transitioning to the three-dimensional space, you may enjoy greater creative freedom when creating visualizations. The extra dimension can also accommodate more information in a single plot. However, some may argue that 3D is nothing more than a visual gimmick when projected to a 2D surface (such as paper) as it would obfuscate the interpretation of data points.

In Matplotlib version 2, despite significant developments in the 3D API, annoying bugs or glitches still exist. We will discuss some workarounds toward the end of this chapter. More powerful Python 3D visualization packages do exist (such as MayaVi2, Plotly, and VisPy), but it's good to use Matplotlib's 3D plotting functions if you want to use the same package for both 2D and 3D plots, or you would like to maintain the aesthetics of its 2D plots.

For the most part, 3D plots in Matplotlib have similar structures to 2D plots. As such, we will not go through every 3D plot type in this section. We will put our focus on 3D scatter plots and bar charts.

3D scatter plot

In `Chapter 6`, *Hello Plotting World!*, we have already explored scatter plots in two dimensions. In this section, let's try to create a 3D scatter plot. Before doing that, we need some data points in three dimensions (x, y, z):

```
import pandas as pd

source =
"https://raw.githubusercontent.com/PointCloudLibrary/data/master/tutorials/
ism_train_cat.pcd"
cat_df = pd.read_csv(source, skiprows=11, delimiter=" ",
names=["x","y","z"], encoding='latin_1')
cat_df.head()
```

Point	x	y	z
0	-17.034178	18.972282	40.482403
1	-16.881481	21.815451	44.156799
2	-16.749582	18.154911	34.131474
3	-16.876919	20.598286	36.271809
4	-16.849340	17.403711	42.993984

To declare a 3D plot, we first need to import the `Axes3D` object from the `mplot3d` extension in `mpl_toolkits`, which is responsible for rendering 3D plots in a 2D plane. After that, we need to specify `projection='3d'` when we create subplots:

```
from mpl_toolkits.mplot3d import Axes3D
import matplotlib.pyplot as plt

fig = plt.figure()
ax = fig.add_subplot(111, projection='3d')
ax.scatter(cat_df.x, cat_df.y, cat_df.z)

plt.show()
```

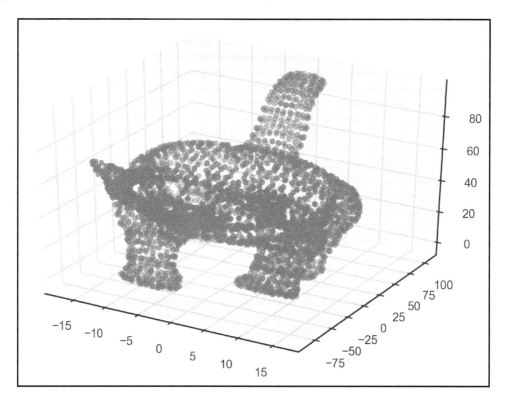

Behold, the mighty sCATter plot in 3D. Cats are currently taking over the internet. According to the New York Times, cats are "the essential building block of the Internet" (`https://www.nytimes.com/2014/07/23/upshot/what-the-internet-can-see-from-your-cat-pictures.html`). Undoubtedly, they deserve a place in this chapter as well.

Contrary to the 2D version of `scatter()`, we need to provide X, Y, and Z coordinates when we are creating a 3D scatter plot. Yet the parameters that are supported in 2D `scatter()` can be applied to 3D `scatter()` as well:

```
fig = plt.figure()
ax = fig.add_subplot(111, projection='3d')

# Change the size, shape and color of markers
ax.scatter(cat_df.x, cat_df.y, cat_df.z, s=4, c="g", marker="o")

plt.show()
```

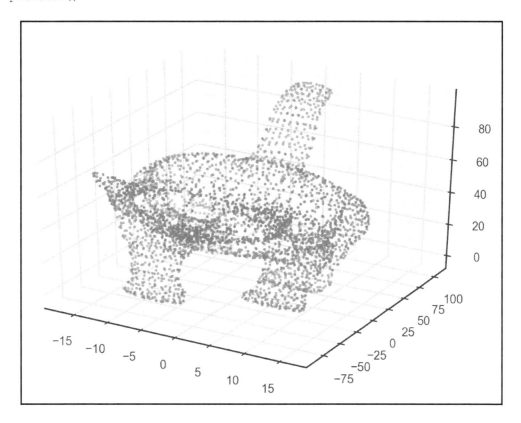

To change the viewing angle and elevation of the 3D plot, we can make use of `view_init()`. The `azim` parameter specifies the azimuth angle in the X-Y plane, while `elev` specifies the elevation angle. When the azimuth angle is 0, the X-Y plane would appear to the north from you. Meanwhile, an azimuth angle of 180 would show you the south side of the X-Y plane:

```
fig = plt.figure()
ax = fig.add_subplot(111, projection='3d')
ax.scatter(cat_df.x, cat_df.y, cat_df.z,s=4, c="g", marker="o")

# elev stores the elevation angle in the z plane azim stores the
# azimuth angle in the x,y plane
ax.view_init(azim=180, elev=10)

plt.show()
```

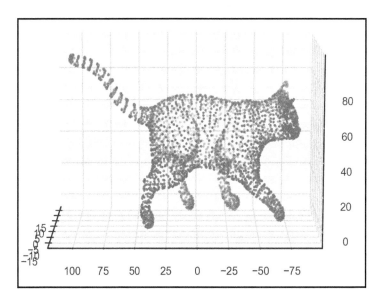

3D bar chart

We introduced candlestick plots for showing **Open-High-Low-Close (OHLC)** financial data. In addition, a 3D bar chart can be employed to show OHLC across time. The next figure shows a typical example of plotting a 5-day OHLC bar chart:

```
import matplotlib.pyplot as plt
import numpy as np
from mpl_toolkits.mplot3d import Axes3D
```

```
# Get 1 and every fifth row for the 5-day AAPL OHLC data
ohlc_5d = stock_df[stock_df["Company"]=="AAPL"].iloc[1::5, :]

fig = plt.figure()
ax = fig.add_subplot(111, projection='3d')

# Create one color-coded bar chart for Open, High, Low and Close prices.
for color, col, z in zip(['r', 'g', 'b', 'y'], ["Open", "High", "Low",
                          "Close"], [30, 20, 10, 0]):
    xs = np.arange(ohlc_5d.shape[0])
    ys = ohlc_5d[col]
    # Assign color to the bars
    colors = [color] * len(xs)
    ax.bar(xs, ys, zs=z, zdir='y', color=colors, alpha=0.8, width=5)

plt.show()
```

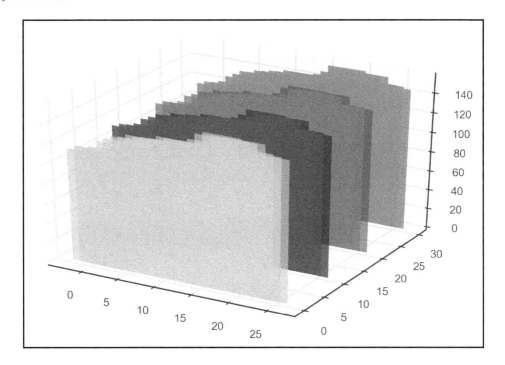

The method for setting ticks and labels is similar to other Matplotlib plotting functions:

```
fig = plt.figure(figsize=(9,7))
ax = fig.add_subplot(111, projection='3d')

# Create one color-coded bar chart for Open, High, Low and Close prices.
for color, col, z in zip(['r', 'g', 'b', 'y'], ["Open", "High", "Low",
                         "Close"], [30, 20, 10, 0]):
    xs = np.arange(ohlc_5d.shape[0])
    ys = ohlc_5d[col]
    # Assign color to the bars
    colors = [color] * len(xs)
    ax.bar(xs, ys, zs=z, zdir='y', color=colors, alpha=0.8)

# Manually assign the ticks and tick labels
ax.set_xticks(np.arange(ohlc_5d.shape[0]))
ax.set_xticklabels(ohlc_5d["Date"], rotation=20,
                   verticalalignment='baseline',
                   horizontalalignment='right',
                   fontsize='8')
ax.set_yticks([30, 20, 10, 0])
ax.set_yticklabels(["Open", "High", "Low", "Close"])

# Set the z-axis label
ax.set_zlabel('Price (US $)')

# Rotate the viewport
ax.view_init(azim=-42, elev=31)
plt.tight_layout()
plt.show()
```

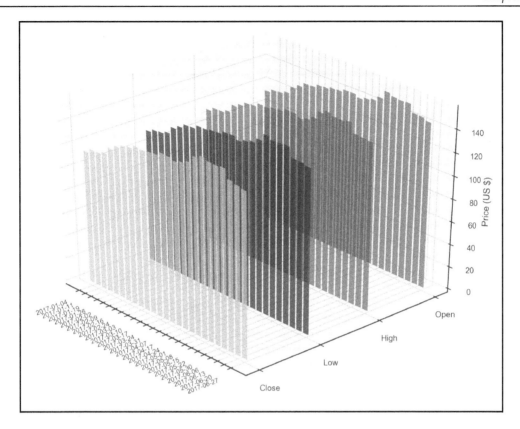

Caveats of Matplotlib 3D

Due to the lack of a true 3D graphical rendering backend (such as OpenGL) and proper algorithm for detecting 3D objects' intersections, the 3D plotting capabilities of Matplotlib are not great but just adequate for typical applications. In the official Matplotlib FAQ (`https://matplotlib.org/mpl_toolkits/mplot3d/faq.html`), the author noted that 3D plots may not look right at certain angles. Besides, we also reported that `mplot3d` would fail to clip bar charts if zlim is set (`https://github.com/matplotlib/matplotlib/issues/8902`; see also `https://github.com/matplotlib/matplotlib/issues/209`). Without improvements in the 3D rendering backend, these issues are hard to fix.

To better illustrate the latter issue, let's try to add `ax.set_zlim3d(bottom=110, top=150)` right above `plt.tight_layout()` in the previous 3D bar chart:

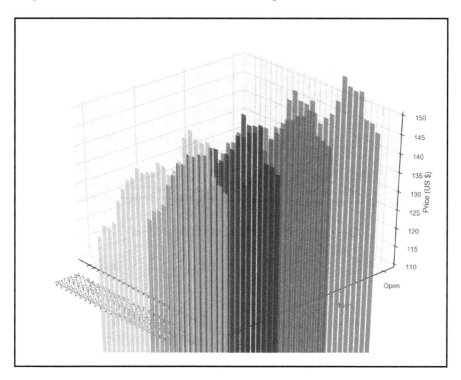

Clearly, something is going wrong, as the bars overshoot the lower boundary of the axes. We will try to address the latter issue through the following workaround:

```
# FuncFormatter to add 110 to the tick labels
def major_formatter(x, pos):
    return "{}".format(x+110)

fig = plt.figure(figsize=(9,7))
ax = fig.add_subplot(111, projection='3d')

# Create one color-coded bar chart for Open, High, Low and Close prices.
for color, col, z in zip(['r', 'g', 'b', 'y'], ["Open", "High", "Low",
                         "Close"], [30, 20, 10, 0]):
    xs = np.arange(ohlc_5d.shape[0])
    ys = ohlc_5d[col]

    # Assign color to the bars
    colors = [color] * len(xs)
```

```
    # Truncate the y-values by 110
    ax.bar(xs, ys-110, zs=z, zdir='y', color=colors, alpha=0.8)

# Manually assign the ticks and tick labels
ax.set_xticks(np.arange(ohlc_5d.shape[0]))
ax.set_xticklabels(ohlc_5d["Date"], rotation=20,
                verticalalignment='baseline',
                horizontalalignment='right',
                fontsize='8')

# Set the z-axis label
ax.set_yticks([30, 20, 10, 0])
ax.set_yticklabels(["Open", "High", "Low", "Close"])
ax.zaxis.set_major_formatter(FuncFormatter(major_formatter))
ax.set_zlabel('Price (US $)')

# Rotate the viewport
ax.view_init(azim=-42, elev=31)

plt.tight_layout()
plt.show()
```

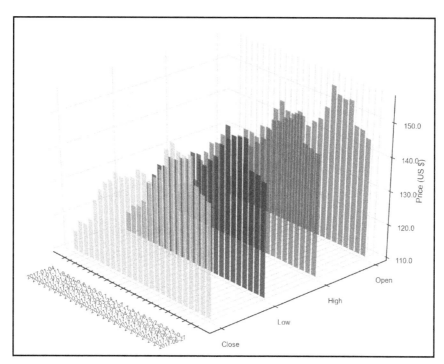

Basically, we truncated the y values by 110, and then we used a tick formatter (`major_formatter`) to shift the tick value back to the original. For 3D scatter plots, we can simply remove the data points that exceed the boundary of `set_zlim3d()` in order to generate a proper figure. However, these workarounds may not work for every 3D plot type.

Summary

You have successfully learned the techniques for visualizing multivariate data in 2D and 3D forms. Although most examples in this chapter revolved around the topic of stock trading, the data processing and visualization methods can be applied readily to other fields as well. In particular, the divide-and-conquer approach used to visualize multivariate data in facets is extremely useful in the scientific field.

We didn't go into too much detail of the 3D plotting capability of Matplotlib, as it is yet to be polished. For simple 3D plots, Matplotlib already suffices. The learning curve can be reduced if we use the same package for both 2D and 3D plots. You are advised to take a look at MayaVi2, Plotly, and VisPy if you require more powerful 3D plotting functions.

Adding Interactivity and Animating Plots

9

As a book focusing on the use of Matplotlib through elaborate examples, we opted to defer or simplify our discussion of the internals. For those of you who want to understand the nuts and bolts that make Matplotlib tick, you are advised to read *Mastering matplotlib* by Duncan M. McGreggor. At some point during our Matplotlib journey, it becomes inevitable for us to discuss more about backends, which turn plotting commands to graphics. These backends can be broadly classified as non-interactive or interactive. We will give examples that are pertinent to each backend class.

Matplotlib was not designed as an animation package from the get-go, thus it will appear sluggish in some advanced usages. For animation-centric applications, PyGame is a very good alternative (`https://www.pygame.org`); it supports OpenGL- and Direct3D-accelerated graphics for the ultimate speed in animating objects. Nevertheless, Matplotlib has acceptable performance most of the time, and we will guide you through the steps to create animations that are more engaging than static plots.

The examples in this chapter will be based on unemployment rates and earnings by educational attainment (2016), available from `data.gov` and curated by the Bureau of Labor Statistics, U.S. Department of Labor. Here is the outline of this chapter:

- Scraping information from websites
- Non-interactive backends
- Interactive backends: Tkinter, Jupyter, and Plot.ly
- Creating an animated plot
- Exporting an animation as a video

Scraping information from websites

Governments or jurisdictions around the world are increasingly embracing the importance of open data, which aims to increase citizen involvement and informs about decision making, making policies more open to public scrutiny. Some examples of open data initiatives around the world include `data.gov` (United States of America), `data.gov.uk` (United Kingdom), and `data.gov.hk` (Hong Kong).

These data portals often provide Application Programming Interfaces (APIs; see Chapter 7, *Visualizing Online Data*, for more details) for programmatic access to data. However, APIs are not available for some datasets; hence, we resort to good old web scraping techniques to extract information from websites.

BeautifulSoup (`https://www.crummy.com/software/BeautifulSoup/`) is an incredibly useful package used to scrape information from websites. Basically, everything marked with an HTML tag can be scraped with this wonderful package, from text, links, tables, and styles, to images. Scrapy is also a good package for web scraping, but it is more like a framework for writing powerful web crawlers. So, if you just need to fetch a table from a page, BeautifulSoup offers simpler procedures.

We are going to use BeautifulSoup version 4.6 throughout this chapter. To install BeautifulSoup 4, we can once again rely on PyPI:

```
pip install beautifulsoup4
```

The data on USA unemployment rates and earnings by educational attainment (2016) is available at `https://www.bls.gov/emp/ep_table_001.htm`. Currently, BeautifulSoup does not handle HTML requests. So we need to use the `urllib.request` or `requests` package to fetch a web page for us. Of the two options, the `requests` package is probably easier to use, due to its higher-level HTTP client interface. If `requests` is not available on your system, you can install it through PyPI:

```
pip install requests
```

Let's take a look at the web page before we write the web scraping code. If we use the Google Chrome browser to visit the Bureau of Labor Statistics website, we can inspect the HTML code corresponding to the table we need by right-clicking:

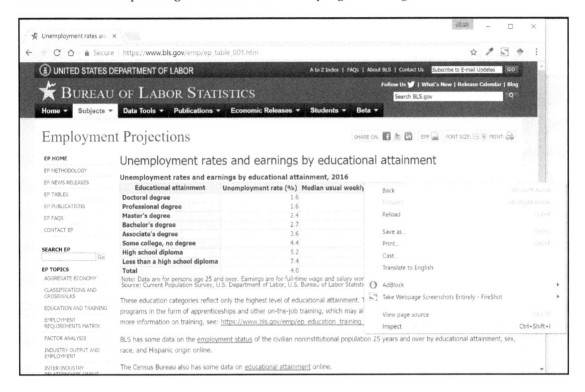

A pop-up window for code inspection will be shown, which allows us to read the code for each of the elements on the page.

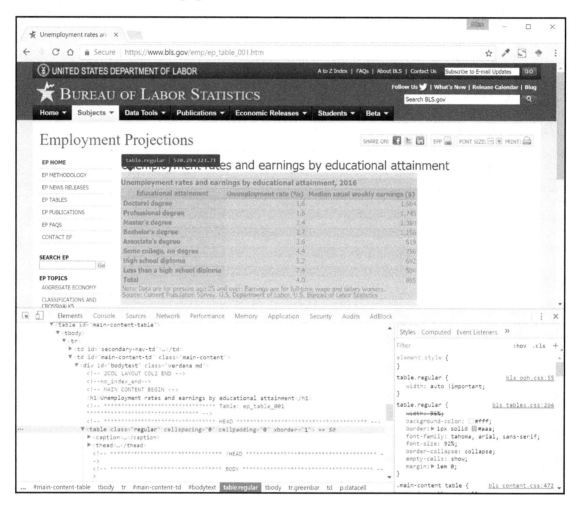

More specifically, we can see that the column names are defined in the `<thead>...</thead>` section, while the table content is defined in the `<tbody>...</tbody>` section.

In order to instruct BeautifulSoup to scrape the information we need, we need to give clear directions to it. We can right-click on the relevant section in the code inspection window and copy the unique identifier in the format of the CSS selector.

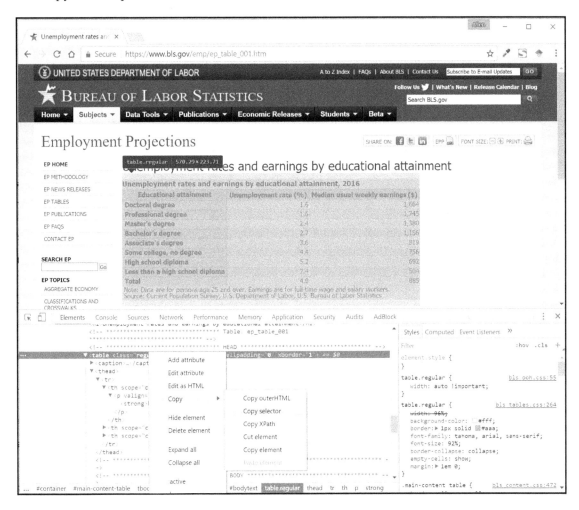

Cascading Style Sheets (**CSS**) selectors were originally designed for applying element-specific styles to a website. For more information, visit the following page: https://www.w3schools.com/cssref/css_selectors.asp.

Let's try to get the CSS selectors for `thead` and `tbody`, and use the `BeautifulSoup.select()` method to scrape the respective HTML code:

```
import requests
from bs4 import BeautifulSoup


# Specify the url
url = "https://www.bls.gov/emp/ep_table_001.htm"

# Query the website and get the html response
response = requests.get(url)

# Parse the returned html using BeautifulSoup
bs = BeautifulSoup(response.text)

# Select the table header by CSS selector
thead = bs.select("#bodytext > table > thead")[0]

# Select the table body by CSS selector
tbody = bs.select("#bodytext > table > tbody")[0]

# Make sure the code works
print(thead)
```

We see the following output from the previous code:

```
<thead> <tr> <th scope="col"><p align="center"
valign="top"><strong>Educational attainment</strong></p></th> <th
scope="col"><p align="center" valign="top">Unemployment rate (%)</p></th>
<th scope="col"><p align="center" valign="top">Median usual weekly earnings
($)</p></th> </tr> </thead>
```

Next, we are going to find all instances of `<th>...</th>` in `<thead>...</thead>`, which contains the name of each column. We will build a dictionary of lists with headers as keys to hold the data:

```
# Get the column names
headers = []

# Find all header columns in <thead> as specified by <th> html tags
for col in thead.find_all('th'):
    headers.append(col.text.strip())

# Dictionary of lists for storing parsed data
data = {header:[] for header in headers}
```

Finally, we parse the remaining rows (`<tr>...</tr>`) from the body
(`<tbody>...</tbody>`) of the table and convert the data into a pandas DataFrame:

```
import pandas as pd


# Parse the rows in table body
for row in tbody.find_all('tr'):
    # Find all columns in a row as specified by <th> or <td> html tags
    cols = row.find_all(['th','td'])

    # enumerate() allows us to loop over an iterable,
    # and return each item preceded by a counter
    for i, col in enumerate(cols):
        # Strip white space around the text
        value = col.text.strip()

        # Try to convert the columns to float, except the first column
        if i > 0:
            value = float(value.replace(',','')) # Remove all commas in
            # string

        # Append the float number to the dict of lists
        data[headers[i]].append(value)

# Create a dataframe from the parsed dictionary
df = pd.DataFrame(data)

# Show an excerpt of parsed data
df.head()
```

	Educational attainment	Median usual weekly earnings ($)	Unemployment rate (%)
0	Doctoral degree	1664.0	1.6
1	Professional degree	1745.0	1.6
2	Master's degree	1380.0	2.4
3	Bachelor's degree	1156.0	2.7
4	Associate's degree	819.0	3.6

We have now fetched the HTML table and formatted it as a structured pandas DataFrame.

Non-interactive backends

The code for plotting graphs is considered the frontend in Matplotlib terminology. We first mentioned backends in `Chapter 6`, *Hello Plotting World!*, when we were talking about output formats. In reality, Matplotlib backends differ much more than just in the support of graphical formats. Backends handle so many things behind the scenes! And that determines the support for plotting capabilities. For example, LaTeX text layout is only supported by AGG, PDF, PGF, and PS backends.

We have been using non-interactive backends so far, which include AGG, Cairo, GDK, PDF, PGF, PS, and SVG. Most of these backends work without extra dependencies, yet Cairo and GDK would require the Cairo graphics library or GIMP Drawing Kit, respectively, to work.

Non-interactive backends can be further classified into two groups--vector and raster. Vector graphics describe images in terms of points, paths, and shapes that are calculated using mathematical formulas. A vector graphic will always appear smooth, irrespective of scale and its size is usually much smaller than its raster counterpart. PDF, PGF, PS, and SVG backends belong to the "vector" group.

Raster graphics describe images in terms of a finite number of tiny color blocks (pixels). So, if we zoom in enough, we start to see a blurry image, or in other words, pixelation. By increasing the resolution or **Dots Per Inch** (**DPI**) of the image, we are less likely to observe pixelation. AGG, Cairo, and GDK belong to this group of backends. This table summarizes the key functionalities and differences among the non-interactive backends:

Backend	Vector/Raster	Output formats
Agg	Raster	PNG
Cairo	Vector/Raster	PDF, PNG, PS, or SVG
PDF	Vector	PDF
PGF	Vector	PDF or PGF
PS	Vector	PS
SVG	Vector	SVG
GDK (Deprecated in Matplotlib 2.0)	Raster	PNG, JPEG, or TIFF

Normally, we don't need to manually select a backend, as the default choice would work great for most tasks. On the other hand, we can specify a backend through the `matplotlib.use()` method before importing `matplotlib.pyplot`:

```
import matplotlib
matplotlib.use('SVG') # Change to SVG backend
import matplotlib.pyplot as plt
import textwrap # Standard library for text wraping


# Create a figure
fig, ax = plt.subplots(figsize=(6,7))

# Create a list of x ticks positions
ind = range(df.shape[0])

# Plot a bar chart of median usual weekly earnings by educational
# attainments
rects = ax.barh(ind, df["Median usual weekly earnings ($)"], height=0.5)

# Set the x-axis label
ax.set_xlabel('Median weekly earnings (USD)')

# Label the x ticks
# The tick labels are a bit too long, let's wrap them in 15-char lines
ylabels=[textwrap.fill(label,15) for label in df["Educational attainment"]]
ax.set_yticks(ind)
ax.set_yticklabels(ylabels)

# Give extra margin at the bottom to display the tick labels
fig.subplots_adjust(left=0.3)

# Save the figure in SVG format
plt.savefig("test.svg")
```

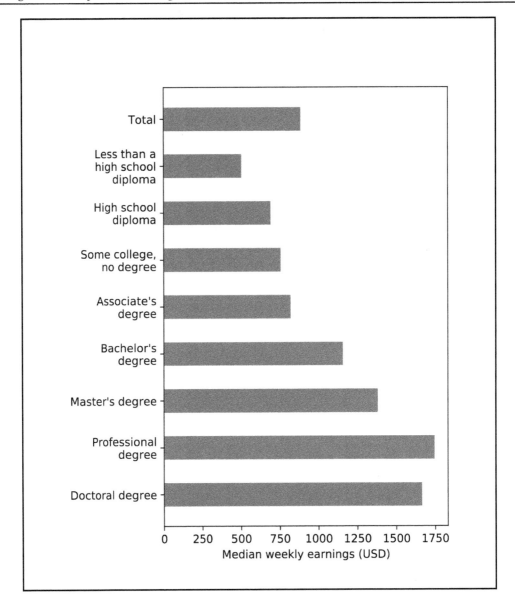

Interactive backends

Matplotlib can build interactive figures that are far more engaging for readers. Sometimes, a plot might be overwhelmed with graphical elements, making it hard to discern individual data points. On other occasions, some data points may appear so similar that it becomes hard to spot the differences with the naked eye. An interactive plot can address these two scenarios by allowing us to zoom in, zoom out, pan, and explore the plot in the way we want.

Through the use of interactive backends, plots in Matplotlib can be embedded in Graphical User Interface (GUI) applications. By default, Matplotlib supports the pairing of the Agg raster graphics renderer with a wide variety of GUI toolkits, including wxWidgets (Wx), GIMP Toolkit (GTK+), Qt, and Tkinter (Tk). As Tkinter is the de facto standard GUI for Python, which is built on top of Tcl/Tk, we can create an interactive plot just by calling `plt.show()` in a standalone Python script.

Tkinter-based backend

Let's try to copy the following code to a separate text file and name it `chapter6_gui.py`. After that, type `python chapter6_gui.py` in your terminal (Mac/Linux) or Command Prompt (Windows). If you are unsure about how to open a terminal or Command Prompt, refer to `Chapter 6`, *Hello Plotting World!*, for more details:

```python
import matplotlib
import matplotlib.pyplot as plt
import textwrap # Standard library for text wraping
import requests
import pandas as pd
from bs4 import BeautifulSoup


# Specify the url
url = "https://www.bls.gov/emp/ep_table_001.htm"

# Query the website and get the html response
response = requests.get(url)

# Parse the returned html using BeautifulSoup
bs = BeautifulSoup(response.text)

# Select the table header by CSS selector
thead = bs.select("#bodytext > table > thead")[0]
```

```python
# Select the table body by CSS selector
tbody = bs.select("#bodytext > table > tbody")[0]

# Get the column names
headers = []

# Find all header columns in <thead> as specified by <th> html tags
for col in thead.find_all('th'):
    headers.append(col.text.strip())

# Dictionary of lists for storing parsed data
data = {header:[] for header in headers}

# Parse the rows in table body
for row in tbody.find_all('tr'):
    # Find all columns in a row as specified by <th> or <td> html tags
    cols = row.find_all(['th','td'])

    # enumerate() allows us to loop over an iterable,
    # and return each item preceded by a counter
    for i, col in enumerate(cols):
        # Strip white space around the text
        value = col.text.strip()

        # Try to convert the columns to float, except the first column
        if i > 0:
            value = float(value.replace(',','')) # Remove all commas in
            # string

        # Append the float number to the dict of lists
        data[headers[i]].append(value)

# Create a dataframe from the parsed dictionary
df = pd.DataFrame(data)

# Create a figure
fig, ax = plt.subplots(figsize=(6,7))

# Create a list of x ticks positions
ind = range(df.shape[0])

# Plot a bar chart of median usual weekly earnings by educational
# attainments
rects = ax.barh(ind, df["Median usual weekly earnings ($)"], height=0.5)

# Set the x-axis label
ax.set_xlabel('Median weekly earnings (USD)')
```

```
# Label the x ticks
# The tick labels are a bit too long, let's wrap them in 15-char lines
ylabels=[textwrap.fill(label,15) for label in df["Educational attainment"]]
ax.set_yticks(ind)
ax.set_yticklabels(ylabels)

# Give extra margin at the bottom to display the tick labels
fig.subplots_adjust(left=0.3)

# Show the figure in a GUI
plt.show()
```

We see a pop-up window similar to the following. We can pan, zoom to selection, configure subplot margins, save, and go back and forth between different views by clicking on the buttons on the bottom toolbar. If we put our mouse over the plot, we can also observe the exact coordinates in the bottom-right corner. This feature is extremely useful for dissecting data points that are close to each other.

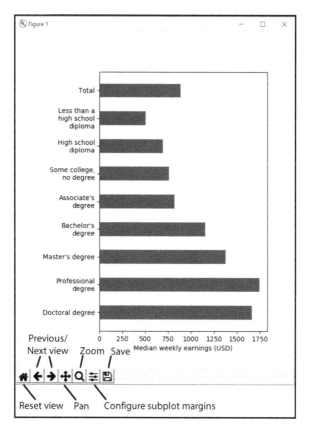

Next, we are going to extend the application by adding a radio button widget on top of the figure, such that we can switch between the display of weekly earnings or unemployment rates. The radio button can be found in `matplotlib.widgets`, and we are going to attach a data updating function to the `.on_clicked()` event of the button. You can paste the following code right before the `plt.show()` line in the previous code example (`chapter6_gui.py`). Let's see how it works:

```
# Import Matplotlib radio button widget
from matplotlib.widgets import RadioButtons

# Create axes for holding the radio selectors.
# supply [left, bottom, width, height] in normalized (0, 1) units
bax = plt.axes([0.3, 0.9, 0.4, 0.1])
radio = RadioButtons(bax, ('Weekly earnings', 'Unemployment rate'))

# Define the function for updating the displayed values
# when the radio button is clicked
def radiofunc(label):
    # Select columns from dataframe, and change axis label depending on
    # selection
    if label == 'Weekly earnings':
        data = df["Median usual weekly earnings ($)"]
        ax.set_xlabel('Median weekly earnings (USD)')
    elif label == 'Unemployment rate':
        data = df["Unemployment rate (%)"]
        ax.set_xlabel('Unemployment rate (%)')

    # Update the bar heights
    for i, rect in enumerate(rects):
        rect.set_width(data[i])

    # Rescale the x-axis range
    ax.set_xlim(xmin=0, xmax=data.max()*1.1)

    # Redraw the figure
    plt.draw()

# Attach radiofunc to the on_clicked event of the radio button
radio.on_clicked(radiofunc)
```

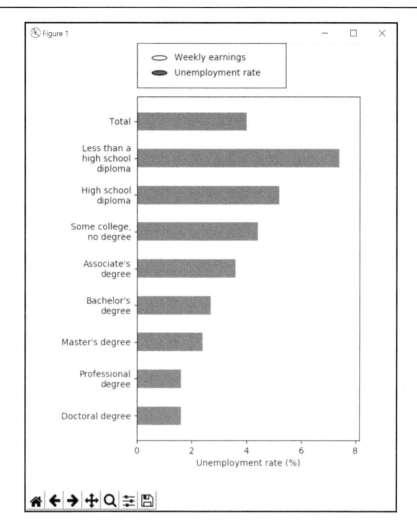

You will be welcomed by a new radio selector box at the top of the figure. Try switching between the two states and see if the figure is updated accordingly. The complete code is also available as `chapter6_tkinter.py` in our code repository.

Interactive backend for Jupyter Notebook

Before we conclude this section, we are going to introduce two more interactive backends that are rarely covered by books. Starting with Matplotlib 1.4, there is an interactive backend specifically designed for Jupyter Notebook. To invoke that, we simply need to paste `%matplotlib notebook` at the start of our notebook. We are going to adapt one of the earlier examples in this chapter to use this backend:

```python
# Import the interactive backend for Jupyter notebook
%matplotlib notebook
import matplotlib
import matplotlib.pyplot as plt
import textwrap


fig, ax = plt.subplots(figsize=(6,7))
ind = range(df.shape[0])
rects = ax.barh(ind, df["Median usual weekly earnings ($)"], height=0.5)
ax.set_xlabel('Median weekly earnings (USD)')
ylabels=[textwrap.fill(label,15) for label in df["Educational attainment"]]
ax.set_yticks(ind)
ax.set_yticklabels(ylabels)
fig.subplots_adjust(left=0.3)

# Show the figure using interactive notebook backend
plt.show()
```

You will see an interactive interface coming up, with buttons similar to a Tkinter-based application:

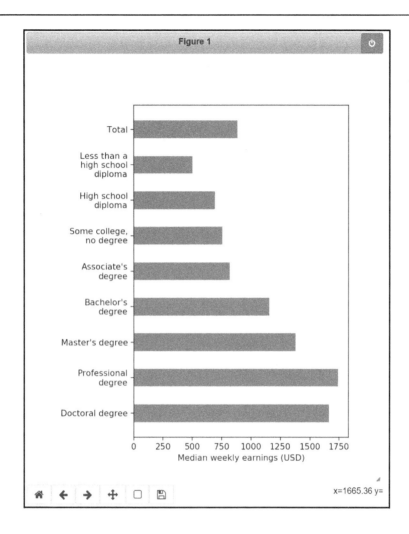

Plot.ly-based backend

Lastly, we will talk about Plot.ly, which is a D3.js-based interactive graphing library with many programming language bindings, including Python. Plot.ly has quickly gained traction in the area of online data analytics due to its powerful data dashboard, high performance, and detailed documentation. For more information, please visit Plot.ly's website (`https://plot.ly`).

Plot.ly offers easy transformation of Matplotlib figures into online interactive charts through its Python bindings. To install Plotly.py, we can use PyPI:

```
pip install plotly
```

Let us show you a quick example of integrating Matplotlib with Plot.ly:

```
import matplotlib.pyplot as plt
import numpy as np
import plotly.plotly as py
from plotly.offline import init_notebook_mode, enable_mpl_offline,
iplot_mpl


# Plot offline in Jupyter Notebooks, not required for standalone script
# Note: Must be called before any plotting actions
init_notebook_mode()

# Convert mpl plots to locally hosted HTML documents, not required if you
# are a registered plot.ly user and have a API key
enable_mpl_offline()

# Create two subplots with shared x-axis
fig, axarr = plt.subplots(2, sharex=True)

# The code for generating "df" is skipped for brevity, please refer to the
# "Tkinter-based backend" section for details of generating "df"
ind = np.arange(df.shape[0]) # the x locations for the groups
width = 0.35

# Plot a bar chart of the weekly earnings in the first axes
axarr[0].bar(ind, df["Median usual weekly earnings ($)"], width)

# Plot a bar chart of the unemployment rate in the second axes
axarr[1].bar(ind, df["Unemployment rate (%)"], width)

# Set the ticks and labels
axarr[1].set_xticks(ind)
# Reduce verbosity of labels by removing " degree"
axarr[1].set_xticklabels([value.replace(" degree","") for value in
df["Educational attainment"]])

# Offline Interactive plot using plot.ly
# Note: import and use plotly.offline.plot_mpl instead for standalone
# Python scripts
iplot_mpl(fig)
```

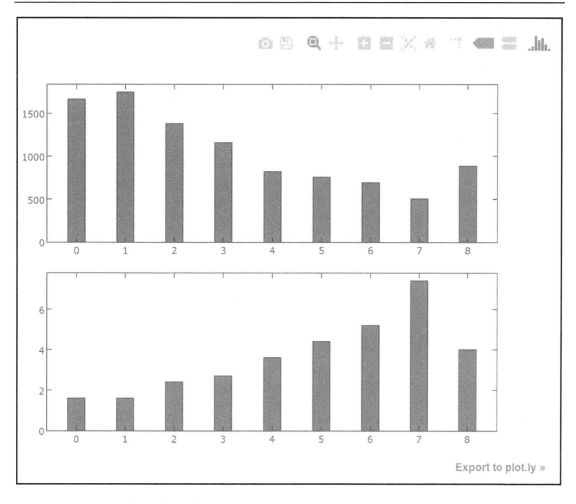

You may be greeted by the following error message when you run the preceding Plot.ly example:

```
IOPub data rate exceeded. The notebook server will temporarily stop sending
output to the client in order to avoid crashing it.
To change this limit, set the config variable
--NotebookApp.iopub_data_rate_limit.
```

To circumvent this error, you can relaunch Jupyter Notebook by setting a higher `iopub_data_rate_limit`:

```
jupyter notebook --NotebookApp.iopub_data_rate_limit=1.0e10
```

> You may also notice that the tick labels cannot be displayed properly, despite clear specifications in the code. This issue is also reported on the official GitHub page (`https://github.com/plotly/plotly.py/issues/735`). Unfortunately, there is no fix for this issue to date.

We admit that there are numerous materials online that describe the integration of Matplotlib plots in different GUI applications. Due to page limits, we are not going to go through each of these backends here. For readers who want to read more about these interactive backends, Alexandre Devert has written an excellent chapter (*Chapter 8, User Interface*) in *matplotlib Plotting Cookbook*. In *Chapter 8, User Interface* of that book, Alexandre has provided recipes for creating GUI applications using wxWidgets, GTK, and Pyglet as well.

Creating animated plots

As explained at the start of this chapter, Matplotlib was not originally designed for making animations, and there are GPU-accelerated Python animation packages that may be more suitable for such a task (such as PyGame). However, since we are already familiar with Matplotlib, it is quite easy to adapt existing plots to animations.

Installation of FFmpeg

Before we start making animations, we need to install either FFmpeg, avconv, MEncoder, or ImageMagick on our system. These additional dependencies are not bundled with Matplotlib, and so we need to install them separately. We are going to walk you through the steps of installing FFmpeg.

For Debian-based Linux users, FFmpeg can be installed by issuing the following command in the terminal:

```
sudo apt-get install ffmpeg
```

FFmpeg may not be available on Ubuntu 14.04 or earlier. To install FFmpeg on Ubuntu 14.04, please follow the steps below:

```
sudo add-apt-repository ppa:mc3man/trusty-media
```

Press *Enter* to confirm the addition of the repository.

```
Also note that with apt-get a sudo apt-get dist-upgrade
is needed for initial setup & with some package upgrades
More info:
https://launchpad.net/~mc3man/+archive/ubuntu/trusty-medi
a
Press [ENTER] to continue or ctrl-c to cancel adding it
```

Update and upgrade a few packages before installing FFmpeg.

```
sudo apt-get update
sudo apt-get dist-upgrade
```

Finally, proceed with the normal procedure of installing FFmpeg via `apt-get`:
```
sudo apt-get install ffmpeg
```

For Mac users, Homebrew (`https://brew.sh/`) is the simplest way to search and install the FFmpeg package. For those who don't have Homebrew, you can paste the following code in your terminal to install it:

```
/usr/bin/ruby -e "$(curl -fsSL
https://raw.githubusercontent.com/Homebrew/install/master/install)"
```

After that, we can install FFmpeg by issuing the following command in the terminal app:

```
brew install ffmpeg
```

Alternatively, you may install FFmpeg by copying the binaries (`https://evermeet.cx/ffmpeg/`) to the system path (for example, `/usr/local/bin`). Readers may visit the following page for more details: `http://www.renevolution.com/ffmpeg/2013/03/16/how-to-install-ffmpeg-on-mac-os-x.html`

The installation steps for Windows users are quite a bit more involved, as we need to download the executable ourselves, followed by adding the executable to the system path. Therefore, we have prepared a series of screen captures to guide you through the process.

First, we need to obtain a prebuilt binary from `http://ffmpeg.zeranoe.com/builds/`. Choose the CPU architecture that matches with your system, and select the latest release and static linked libraries.

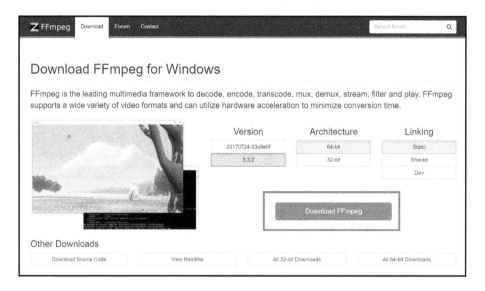

Next, we need to extract the downloaded ZIP file to the C drive as `c:\ffmpeg`, and add the folder `c:\ffmpeg\bin` to the `Path` variable. To do this, go to **Control Panel** and click on the **System and Security** link, followed by clicking on **System**. In the **System** window, click on the **Advanced system settings** link to the left:

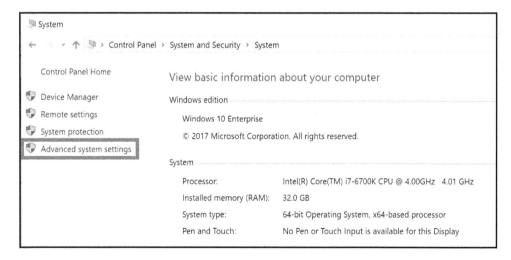

In the pop-up **System Properties** window, click on the **Environmental Variables...** button:

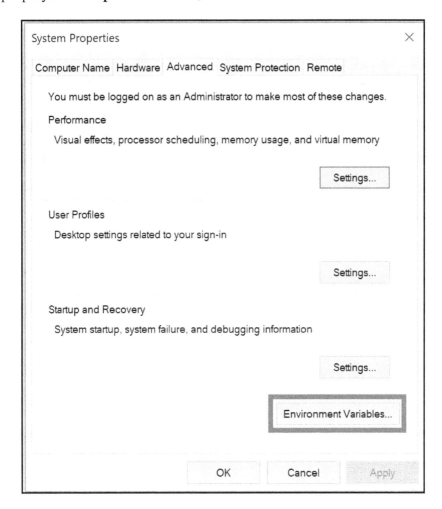

Select the **Path** entry, and click on the **Edit...** button:

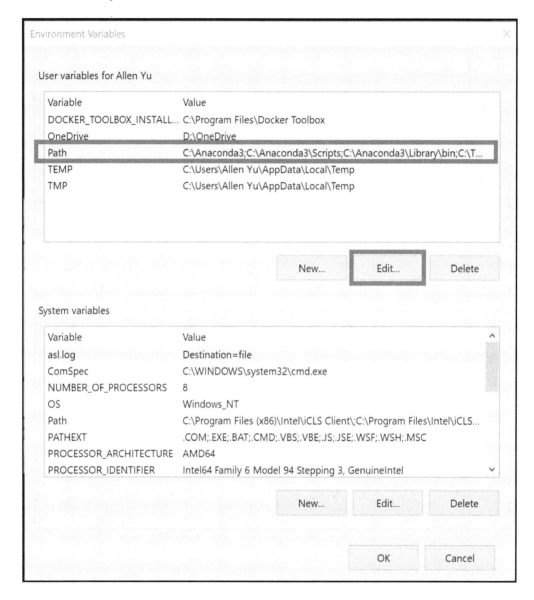

In the **Edit environmental variable** window, create a new entry that shows `c:\ffmpeg\bin`. Click on **OK** in all pop-up windows to save your changes. Restart Command Prompt and Jupyter Notebook and you are good to go.

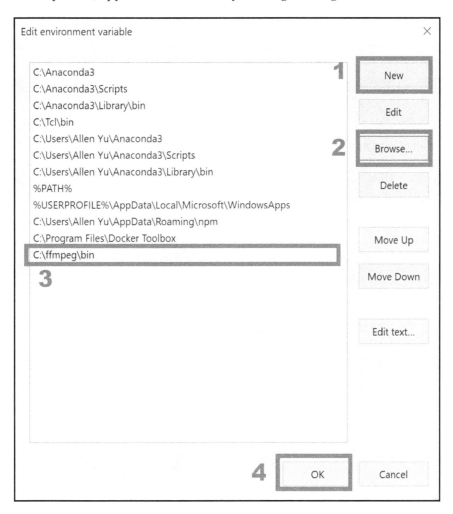

 Visit Wikihow (`http://www.wikihow.com/Install-FFmpeg-on-Windows`) for instructions on installing FFmpeg on Windows 7.

Creating animations

Matplotlib provides two main interfaces for creating animations: `TimedAnimation` and `FuncAnimation`. `TimedAnimation` is useful for creating time-based animations, while `FuncAnimation` can be used to create animations according to a custom-defined function. Given the much higher level of flexibility offered by `FuncAnimation`, we will only explore the use of `FuncAnimation` in this section. Readers can refer to the official documentation (`https://matplotlib.org/api/animation_api.html`) for more information about `TimedAnimation`.

`FuncAnimation` works by repeatedly calling a function that changes the properties of Matplotlib objects in each frame. In the following example, we've simulated the change in median weekly earnings by assuming a 5% annual increase. We are going to create a custom function--animate--which returns Matplotlib Artist objects that are changed in each frame. This function will be supplied to `animation.FuncAnimation()` together with a few more extra parameters:

```
import textwrap
import matplotlib.pyplot as plt
import random
# Matplotlib animation module
from matplotlib import animation
# Used for generating HTML video embed code
from IPython.display import HTML


# Adapted from previous example, codes that are modified are commented
fig, ax = plt.subplots(figsize=(6,7))
ind = range(df.shape[0])
rects = ax.barh(ind, df["Median usual weekly earnings ($)"], height=0.5)
ax.set_xlabel('Median weekly earnings (USD)')
ylabels=[textwrap.fill(label,15) for label in df["Educational attainment"]]
ax.set_yticks(ind)
ax.set_yticklabels(ylabels)
fig.subplots_adjust(left=0.3)

# Change the x-axis range
ax.set_xlim(0,7600)
```

```
# Add a text annotation to show the current year
title = ax.text(0.5,1.05, "Median weekly earnings (USD) in 2016",
                bbox={'facecolor':'w', 'alpha':0.5, 'pad':5},
                transform=ax.transAxes, ha="center")

# Animation related stuff
n=30 #Number of frames

# Function for animating Matplotlib objects
def animate(frame):
    # Simulate 5% annual pay rise
    data = df["Median usual weekly earnings ($)"] * (1.05 ** frame)

    # Update the bar heights
    for i, rect in enumerate(rects):
        rect.set_width(data[i])

    # Update the title
    title.set_text("Median weekly earnings (USD) in {}".format(2016+frame))

    return rects, title

# Call the animator. Re-draw only the changed parts when blit=True.
# Redraw all elements when blit=False
anim=animation.FuncAnimation(fig, animate, blit=False, frames=n)

# Save the animation in MPEG-4 format
anim.save('test.mp4')

# OR--Embed the video in Jupyter notebook
HTML(anim.to_html5_video())
```

Here is the screen capture of one of the video frames:

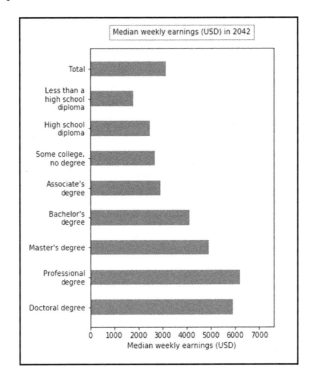

In this example, we output the animation in the form of MPEG-4-encoded videos. The video can also be embedded in Jupyter Notebook in the form of an H.264-encoded video. All you need to do is call the `Animation.to_html5_video()` method and supply the returned object to `IPython.display.HTML`. Video encoding and HTML5 code generation will happen automatically behind the scenes.

Summary

In this chapter, you further enriched your techniques for obtaining online data through the use of the BeautifulSoup web scraping library. You successfully learned the different ways of creating interactive figures and animations. These techniques will pave the way for you to create intuitive and engaging visualizations in more advanced applications.

10
Selecting Subsets of Data

Every dimension of data in a Series or DataFrame is labeled through an Index object. It is this Index that separates pandas data structures from NumPy's n-dimensional array. Indexes provide meaningful labels for each row and column of data, and pandas users have the ability to select data through the use of these labels. Additionally, pandas allow its users to select data by the integer location of the rows and columns. This dual selection capability, one using labels and the other using integer location, makes for powerful yet confusing syntax to select subsets of data.

Selecting data through the use of labels or integer location is not unique to pandas. Python dictionaries and lists are built-in data structures that select their data in exactly one of these ways. Both dictionaries and lists have precise instructions and limited use-cases for what may be passed to the indexing operator. A dictionary's key (its label) must be an immutable object, such as a string, integer, or tuple. Lists must either use integers or slice objects for selection. Dictionaries can only select one object at a time by passing the key to the indexing operator. In some sense, pandas is combining the ability to select data using integers, as with lists, and labels, as with dictionaries.

In this chapter, we will cover the following topics:

- Selecting Series data
- Selecting DataFrame rows
- Selecting DataFrame rows and columns simultaneously
- Selecting data with both integers and labels
- Speeding up scalar selection
- Slicing rows lazily
- Slicing lexicographically

Selecting Series data

Series and DataFrames are complex data containers that have multiple attributes that use the indexing operator to select data in different ways. In addition to the indexing operator itself, the .iloc and .loc attributes are available and use the indexing operator in their own unique ways. Collectively, these attributes are called the **indexers**.

The indexing terminology can get confusing. The term **indexing operator** is used here to distinguish it from the other indexers. It refers to the brackets, [] directly after a Series or DataFrame. For instance, given a Series s, you can select data in the following ways: s[item] and s.loc[item]. The first uses the indexing operator. The second uses the .loc indexer.

Series and DataFrame indexers allow selection by integer location (like Python lists) and by label (like Python dictionaries). The .iloc indexer selects only by integer location and works similarly to Python lists. The .loc indexer selects only by index label, which is similar to how Python dictionaries work.

Getting ready

Both .loc and .iloc work with Series and DataFrames. This recipe shows how to select Series data by integer location with .iloc and by label with .loc. These indexers not only take scalar values but also lists and slices.

How to do it...

1. Read in the college dataset with the institution name as the index, and select a single column as a Series with the indexing operator:

```
>>> college = pd.read_csv('data/college.csv', index_col='INSTNM')
>>> city = college['CITY']
>>> city.head()
INSTNM
Alabama A & M University                    Normal
University of Alabama at Birmingham     Birmingham
Amridge University                      Montgomery
University of Alabama in Huntsville      Huntsville
Alabama State University                Montgomery
Name: CITY, dtype: object
```

2. The `.iloc` indexer makes selections only by integer location. Passing an integer to it returns a scalar value:

```
>>> city.iloc[3]
Huntsville
```

3. To select several different integer locations, pass a list to `.iloc`. This returns a Series:

```
>>> city.iloc[[10,20,30]]
INSTNM
Birmingham Southern College                            Birmingham
George C Wallace State Community College-Hanceville    Hanceville
Judson College                                             Marion
Name: CITY, dtype: object
```

4. To select an equally spaced partition of data, use slice notation:

```
>>> city.iloc[4:50:10]
INSTNM
Alabama State University               Montgomery
Enterprise State Community College     Enterprise
Heritage Christian University            Florence
Marion Military Institute                  Marion
Reid State Technical College            Evergreen
Name: CITY, dtype: object
```

5. Now we turn to the `.loc` indexer, which selects only with index labels. Passing a single string returns a scalar value:

```
>>> city.loc['Heritage Christian University']
Florence
```

6. To select several disjoint labels, use a list:

```
>>> np.random.seed(1)
>>> labels = list(np.random.choice(city.index, 4))
>>> labels
['Northwest HVAC/R Training Center',
 'California State University-Dominguez Hills',
 'Lower Columbia College',
 'Southwest Acupuncture College-Boulder']

>>> city.loc[labels]
INSTNM
Northwest HVAC/R Training Center               Spokane
California State University-Dominguez Hills      Carson
Lower Columbia College                        Longview
```

```
          Southwest Acupuncture College-Boulder          Boulder
          Name: CITY, dtype: object
```

7. To select an equally spaced partition of data, use slice notation. Make sure that the start and stop values are strings. You can use an integer to specify the step size of the slice:

```
>>> city.loc['Alabama State University':
             'Reid State Technical College':10]
INSTNM
Alabama State University                   Montgomery
Enterprise State Community College         Enterprise
Heritage Christian University                Florence
Marion Military Institute                      Marion
Reid State Technical College                 Evergreen
Name: CITY, dtype: object
```

How it works...

The values in a Series are referenced by integers beginning from 0. Step 2 selects the fourth element of the Series with the .loc indexer. Step 3 passes a three-item integer list to the indexing operator, which returns a Series with those integer locations selected. This feature is an enhancement over a Python list, which is incapable of selecting multiple disjoint items in this manner.

In step 4, slice notation with start, stop, and step values specified is used to select an entire section of a Series.

Steps 5 through 7 replicate steps 2 through 4 with the label-based indexer, .loc. The labels must be exact matches of values in the index. To ensure our labels are exact, we choose four labels at random from the index in step 6 and store them to a list before selecting their values as a Series. Selections with the .loc indexer always include the last element, as seen in step 7.

There's more...

When passing a scalar value to the indexing operator, as with step 2 and step 5, a scalar value is returned. When passing a list or slice, as in the other steps, a Series is returned. This returned value might seem inconsistent, but if we think of a Series as a dictionary-like object that maps labels to values, then returning the value makes sense. To select a single item and retain the item in its Series, pass in as a single-item list rather than a scalar value:

```
>>> city.iloc[[3]]
INSTNM
University of Alabama in Huntsville    Huntsville
Name: CITY, dtype: object
```

Care needs to be taken when using slice notation with `.loc`. If the `start` index appears after the `stop` index, then an empty Series is returned without an exception raised:

```
>>> city.loc['Reid State Technical College':
              'Alabama State University':10]
Series([], Name: CITY, dtype: object)
```

See also

- Pandas official documentation on indexing (`http://bit.ly/2fdtZWu`)

Selecting DataFrame rows

The most explicit and preferred way to select DataFrame rows is with the `.iloc` and `.loc` indexers. They are capable of selecting rows or columns independently and simultaneously.

Getting ready

This recipe shows you how to select rows from a DataFrame using the `.iloc` and `.loc` indexers.

How to do it...

1. Read in the college dataset, and set the index as the institution name:

```
>>> college = pd.read_csv('data/college.csv', index_col='INSTNM')
>>> college.head()
```

	CITY	STABBR	HBCU	MENONLY	WOMENONLY	RELAFFIL	SATVRMID	SATMTMID	DISTANCEONLY	UGDS	...	UGDS_2MOR
INSTNM												
Alabama A & M University	Normal	AL	1.0	0.0	0.0	0	424.0	420.0	0.0	4206.0	...	0.0000
University of Alabama at Birmingham	Birmingham	AL	0.0	0.0	0.0	0	570.0	565.0	0.0	11383.0	...	0.0368
Amridge University	Montgomery	AL	0.0	0.0	0.0	1	NaN	NaN	1.0	291.0	...	0.0000
University of Alabama in Huntsville	Huntsville	AL	0.0	0.0	0.0	0	595.0	590.0	0.0	5451.0	...	0.0172
Alabama State University	Montgomery	AL	1.0	0.0	0.0	0	425.0	430.0	0.0	4811.0	...	0.0098

2. Pass an integer to the `.iloc` indexer to select an entire row at that position:

```
>>> college.iloc[60]
CITY                       Anchorage
STABBR                            AK
HBCU                               0
                          ...
UG25ABV                       0.4386
MD_EARN_WNE_P10                42500
GRAD_DEBT_MDN_SUPP           19449.5
Name: University of Alaska Anchorage, Length: 26, dtype: object
```

3. To get the same row as the preceding step, pass the index label to the `.loc` indexer:

```
>>> college.loc['University of Alaska Anchorage']
CITY                       Anchorage
STABBR                            AK
HBCU                               0
                          ...
UG25ABV                       0.4386
MD_EARN_WNE_P10                42500
GRAD_DEBT_MDN_SUPP           19449.5
Name: University of Alaska Anchorage, Length: 26, dtype: object
```

4. To select a disjointed set of rows as a DataFrame, pass a list of integers to the
`.iloc` indexer:

```
>>> college.iloc[[60, 99, 3]]
```

INSTNM	CITY	STABBR	HBCU	MENONLY	WOMENONLY	RELAFFIL	SATVRMID	SATMTMID	DISTANCEONLY	UGDS	...	UGDS_2MOR
University of Alaska Anchorage	Anchorage	AK	0.0	0.0	0.0	0	NaN	NaN	0.0	12865.0	...	0.0980
International Academy of Hair Design	Tempe	AZ	0.0	0.0	0.0	0	NaN	NaN	0.0	188.0	...	0.0160
University of Alabama in Huntsville	Huntsville	AL	0.0	0.0	0.0	0	595.0	590.0	0.0	5451.0	...	0.0172

5. The same DataFrame from step 4 may be reproduced using `.loc` by passing it a
list of the exact institution names:

```
>>> labels = ['University of Alaska Anchorage',
              'International Academy of Hair Design',
              'University of Alabama in Huntsville']
>>> college.loc[labels]
```

6. Use slice notation with `.iloc` to select an entire segment of the data:

```
>>> college.iloc[99:102]
```

INSTNM	CITY	STABBR	HBCU	MENONLY	WOMENONLY	RELAFFIL	SATVRMID	SATMTMID	DISTANCEONLY	UGDS	...	UGDS_2MOR
International Academy of Hair Design	Tempe	AZ	0.0	0.0	0.0	0	NaN	NaN	0.0	188.0	...	0.0160
GateWay Community College	Phoenix	AZ	0.0	0.0	0.0	0	NaN	NaN	0.0	5211.0	...	0.0127
Mesa Community College	Mesa	AZ	0.0	0.0	0.0	0	NaN	NaN	0.0	19055.0	...	0.0205

7. Slice notation also works with the `.loc` indexer and is inclusive of the last label:

```
>>> start = 'International Academy of Hair Design'
>>> stop = 'Mesa Community College'
>>> college.loc[start:stop]
```

How it works...

Passing a scalar value, a list of scalars, or a slice object to the `.iloc` or `.loc` indexers causes pandas to scan the index labels for the appropriate rows and return them. If a single scalar value is passed, a Series is returned. If a list or slice object is passed, then a DataFrame is returned.

There's more...

In step 5, the list of index labels can be selected directly from the DataFrame returned in step 4 without the need for copying and pasting:

```
>>> college.iloc[[60, 99, 3]].index.tolist()
['University of Alaska Anchorage',
 'International Academy of Hair Design',
 'University of Alabama in Huntsville']
```

See also

- Refer to the *Examining the Index object* recipe from `Chapter 12`, *Index Alignment*.

Selecting DataFrame rows and columns simultaneously

Directly using the indexing operator is the correct method to select one or more columns from a DataFrame. However, it does not allow you to select both rows and columns simultaneously. To select rows and columns simultaneously, you will need to pass both valid row and column selections separated by a comma to either the `.iloc` or `.loc` indexers.

Getting ready

The generic form to select rows and columns will look like the following code:

```
>>> df.iloc[rows, columns]
>>> df.loc[rows, columns]
```

The `rows` and `columns` variables may be scalar values, lists, slice objects, or boolean sequences.

Passing a boolean sequence to the indexers is covered in `Chapter 11,` *Boolean Indexing.*

In this recipe, each step shows a simultaneous row and column selection using `.iloc` and its exact replication using `.loc`.

How to do it...

1. Read in the college dataset, and set the index as the institution name. Select the first three rows and the first four columns with slice notation:

```
>>> college = pd.read_csv('data/college.csv', index_col='INSTNM')
>>> college.iloc[:3, :4]
>>> college.loc[:'Amridge University', :'MENONLY']
```

INSTNM	CITY	STABBR	HBCU	MENONLY
Alabama A & M University	Normal	AL	1.0	0.0
University of Alabama at Birmingham	Birmingham	AL	0.0	0.0
Amridge University	Montgomery	AL	0.0	0.0

2. Select all the rows of two different columns:

```
>>> college.iloc[:, [4,6]].head()
>>> college.loc[:, ['WOMENONLY', 'SATVRMID']].head()
```

	WOMENONLY	SATVRMID
INSTNM		
Alabama A & M University	0.0	424.0
University of Alabama at Birmingham	0.0	570.0
Amridge University	0.0	NaN
University of Alabama in Huntsville	0.0	595.0
Alabama State University	0.0	425.0

3. Select disjointed rows and columns:

```
>>> college.iloc[[100, 200], [7, 15]]
>>> rows = ['GateWay Community College',
            'American Baptist Seminary of the West']
>>> columns = ['SATMTMID', 'UGDS_NHPI']
>>> college.loc[rows, columns]
```

	SATMTMID	UGDS_NHPI
INSTNM		
GateWay Community College	NaN	0.0029
American Baptist Seminary of the West	NaN	NaN

4. Select a single scalar value:

```
>>> college.iloc[5, -4]
>>> college.loc['The University of Alabama', 'PCTFLOAN']
-.401
```

5. Slice the rows and select a single column:

```
>>> college.iloc[90:80:-2, 5]
>>> start = 'Empire Beauty School-Flagstaff'
>>> stop = 'Arizona State University-Tempe'
>>> college.loc[start:stop:-2, 'RELAFFIL']
INSTNM
Empire Beauty School-Flagstaff       0
```

```
Charles of Italy Beauty College    0
Central Arizona College             0
University of Arizona               0
Arizona State University-Tempe      0
Name: RELAFFIL, dtype: int64
```

How it works...

One of the keys to selecting rows and columns simultaneously is to understand the use of the comma in the brackets. The selection to the left of the comma always selects rows based on the row index. The selection to the right of the comma always selects columns based on the column index.

It is not necessary to make a selection for both rows and columns simultaneously. Step 2 shows how to select all the rows and a subset of columns. The colon represents a slice object that simply returns all the values for that dimension.

There's more...

When selecting a subset of rows, along with all the columns, it is not necessary to use a colon following a comma. The default behavior is to select all the columns if there is no comma present. The previous recipe selected rows in exactly this manner. You can, however, use a colon to represent a slice of all the columns. The following lines of code are equivalent:

```
>>> college.iloc[:10]
>>> college.iloc[:10, :]
```

Selecting data with both integers and labels

The .iloc and .loc indexers each select data by either integer or label location but are not able to handle a combination of both input types at the same time. In earlier versions of pandas, another indexer, .ix, was available to select data by both integer and label location. While this conveniently worked for those specific situations, it was ambiguous by nature and was a source of confusion for many pandas users. The .ix indexer has subsequently been deprecated and thus should be avoided.

Getting ready

Before the .ix deprecation, it was possible to select the first five rows and the columns of the college dataset from UGDS_WHITE through UGDS_UNKN using college.ix[:5, 'UGDS_WHITE':'UGDS_UNKN']. This is now impossible to do directly using .loc or .iloc. The following recipe shows how to find the integer location of the columns and then use .iloc to complete the selection.

How to do it...

1. Read in the college dataset and assign the institution name (INSTNM) as the index:

```
>>> college = pd.read_csv('data/college.csv', index_col='INSTNM')
```

2. Use the Index method get_loc to find the integer position of the desired columns:

```
>>> col_start = college.columns.get_loc('UGDS_WHITE')
>>> col_end = college.columns.get_loc('UGDS_UNKN') + 1
>>> col_start, col_end
```

3. Use col_start and col_end to select columns by integer location using .iloc:

```
>>> college.iloc[:5, col_start:col_end]
```

INSTNM	UGDS_WHITE	UGDS_BLACK	UGDS_HISP	UGDS_ASIAN	UGDS_AIAN	UGDS_NHPI	UGDS_2MOR	UGDS_NRA	UGDS_UNKN
Alabama A & M University	0.0333	0.9353	0.0055	0.0019	0.0024	0.0019	0.0000	0.0059	0.0138
University of Alabama at Birmingham	0.5922	0.2600	0.0283	0.0518	0.0022	0.0007	0.0368	0.0179	0.0100
Amridge University	0.2990	0.4192	0.0069	0.0034	0.0000	0.0000	0.0000	0.0000	0.2715
University of Alabama in Huntsville	0.6988	0.1255	0.0382	0.0376	0.0143	0.0002	0.0172	0.0332	0.0350
Alabama State University	0.0158	0.9208	0.0121	0.0019	0.0010	0.0006	0.0098	0.0243	0.0137

How it works...

Step 2 first retrieves the column index through the `columns` attribute. Indexes have a `get_loc` method, which accepts an index label and returns its integer location. We find both the start and end integer locations for the columns that we wish to slice. We add one because slicing with `.iloc` is exclusive of the last item. Step 3 uses slice notation with the rows and columns.

There's more...

We can do a very similar operation to make `.loc` work with a mixture of integers and positions. The following shows how to select the 10th through 15th (inclusive) rows, along with columns `UGDS_WHITE` through `UGDS_UNKN`:

```
>>> row_start = df_college.index[10]
>>> row_end = df_college.index[15]
>>> college.loc[row_start:row_end, 'UGDS_WHITE':'UGDS_UNKN']
```

Doing this same operation with `.ix` (which is deprecated, so don't do this) would look like this:

```
>>> college.ix[10:16, 'UGDS_WHITE':'UGDS_UNKN']
```

It is possible to achieve the same results by chaining `.loc` and `.iloc` together, but chaining indexers is typically a bad idea:

```
>>> college.iloc[10:16].loc[:, 'UGDS_WHITE':'UGDS_UNKN']
```

Speeding up scalar selection

Both the `.iloc` and `.loc` indexers are capable of selecting a single element, a scalar value, from a Series or DataFrame. However, there exist the indexers, `.iat` and `.at`, which respectively achieve the same thing at faster speeds. Like `.iloc`, the `.iat` indexer uses integer location to make its selection and must be passed two integers separated by a comma. Similar to `.loc`, the `.at` index uses labels to make its selection and must be passed an index and column label separated by a comma.

Getting ready

This recipe is valuable if computational time is of utmost importance. It shows the performance improvement of `.iat` and `.at` over `.iloc` and `.loc` when using scalar selection.

How to do it...

1. Read in the `college` scoreboard dataset with the institution name as the index. Pass a college name and column name to `.loc` in order to select a scalar value:

```
>>> college = pd.read_csv('data/college.csv', index_col='INSTNM')
>>> cn = 'Texas A & M University-College Station'
>>> college.loc[cn, 'UGDS_WHITE']
.661
```

2. Achieve the same result with `.at`:

```
>>> college.at[cn, 'UGDS_WHITE']
.661
```

3. Use the `%timeit` magic command to find the difference in speed:

```
>>> %timeit college.loc[cn, 'UGDS_WHITE']
8.97 µs ± 617 ns per loop (mean ± std. dev. of 7 runs, 100000 loops
each)

>>> %timeit college.at[cn, 'UGDS_WHITE']
6.28 µs ± 214 ns per loop (mean ± std. dev. of 7 runs, 100000 loops
each)
```

4. Find the integer locations of the preceding selections and then time the difference between `.iloc` and `.iat`:

```
>>> row_num = college.index.get_loc(cn)
>>> col_num = college.columns.get_loc('UGDS_WHITE')
>>> row_num, col_num
(3765, 10)

>>> %timeit college.iloc[row_num, col_num]
9.74 µs ± 153 ns per loop (mean ± std. dev. of 7 runs, 100000 loops
each)
```

```
>>> %timeit college.iat[row_num, col_num]
7.29 µs ± 431 ns per loop (mean ± std. dev. of 7 runs, 100000 loops
each)
```

How it works...

The scalar indexers, `.iat` and `.at`, only accept scalar values. They fail if anything else is passed to them. They are drop-in replacements for `.iloc` and `.loc` when doing scalar selection. The `timeit` magic command times entire blocks of code when preceded by two percentage signs and a single time when preceded by one percentage sign. It shows that about 2.5 microseconds are saved on average by switching to the scalar indexers. This might not be much but can add up quickly if scalar selection is repeatedly done in a program.

There's more...

Both `.iat` and `.at` work with Series as well. Pass them a single scalar value, and they will return a scalar:

```
>>> state = college['STABBR']    # Select a Series
>>> state.iat[1000]
'IL'

>>> state.at['Stanford University']
'CA'
```

Slicing rows lazily

The previous recipes in this chapter showed how the `.iloc` and `.loc` indexers were used to select subsets of both Series and DataFrames in either dimension. A shortcut to select the rows exists with just the indexing operator itself. This is just a shortcut to show additional features of pandas, but the primary function of the indexing operator is actually to select DataFrame columns. If you want to select rows, it is best to use `.iloc` or `.loc`, as they are unambiguous.

Getting ready

In this recipe, we pass a slice object to both the Series and DataFrame indexing operators.

How to do it...

1. Read in the college dataset with the institution name as the index and then select every other row from index 10 to 20:

```
>>> college = pd.read_csv('data/college.csv', index_col='INSTNM')
>>> college[10:20:2]
```

INSTNM	CITY	STABBR	HBCU	MENONLY	WOMENONLY	RELAFFIL	SATVRMID	SATMTMID	DISTANCEONLY	UGDS	...	UGDS_2MOR	UGDS_NR
Birmingham Southern College	Birmingham	AL	0.0	0.0	0.0	1	560.0	560.0	0.0	1180.0	...	0.0051	0.000
Concordia College Alabama	Selma	AL	1.0	0.0	0.0	1	420.0	400.0	0.0	322.0	...	0.0031	0.046
Enterprise State Community College	Enterprise	AL	0.0	0.0	0.0	0	NaN	NaN	0.0	1729.0	...	0.0254	0.001
Faulkner University	Montgomery	AL	0.0	0.0	0.0	1	NaN	NaN	0.0	2367.0	...	0.0173	0.018
New Beginning College of Cosmetology	Albertville	AL	0.0	0.0	0.0	0	NaN	NaN	0.0	115.0	...	0.0000	0.000

2. This same slicing exists with Series:

```
>>> city = college['CITY']
>>> city[10:20:2]
INSTNM
Birmingham Southern College                Birmingham
Concordia College Alabama                       Selma
Enterprise State Community College         Enterprise
Faulkner University                        Montgomery
New Beginning College of Cosmetology      Albertville
Name: CITY, dtype: object
```

3. Both Series and DataFrames can slice by label as well with just the indexing operator:

```
>>> start = 'Mesa Community College'
>>> stop = 'Spokane Community College'
>>> college[start:stop:1500]
```

INSTNM	CITY	STABBR	HBCU	MENONLY	WOMENONLY	RELAFFIL	SATVRMID	SATMTMID	DISTANCEONLY	UGDS	...	UGDS_2MOR	UGDS_NRA
Mesa Community College	Mesa	AZ	0.0	0.0	0.0	0	NaN	NaN	0.0	19055.0	...	0.0205	0.0257
Hair Academy Inc-New Carrollton	New Carrollton	MD	0.0	0.0	0.0	0	NaN	NaN	0.0	504.0	...	0.0000	0.0000
National College of Natural Medicine	Portland	OR	0.0	0.0	0.0	0	NaN	NaN	0.0	NaN	...	NaN	NaN

4. Here is the same slice by label with a Series:

```
>>> city[start:stop:1500]
INSTNM
Mesa Community College                              Mesa
Hair Academy Inc-New Carrollton           New Carrollton
National College of Natural Medicine            Portland
Name: CITY, dtype: object
```

How it works...

The indexing operator changes behavior based on what type of object is passed to it. The following pseudocode outlines how DataFrame indexing operator handles the object that it is passed:

```
>>> df[item]  # Where `df` is a DataFrame and item is some object

If item is a string then
    Find a column name that matches the item exactly
    Raise KeyError if there is no match
    Return the column as a Series

If item is a list of strings then
    Raise KeyError if one or more strings in item don't match columns
    Return a DataFrame with just the columns in the list
```

```
If item is a slice object then
    Works with either integer or string slices
    Raise KeyError if label from label slice is not in index
    Return all ROWS that are selected by the slice

If item is a list, Series or ndarray of booleans then
    Raise ValueError if length of item not equal to length of DataFrame
    Use the booleans to return only the rows with True in same location
```

The preceding logic covers all the most common cases but is not an exhaustive list. The logic for a Series is slightly different and actually more complex than it is for a DataFrame. Due to its complexity, it is probably a good idea to avoid using just the indexing operator itself on a Series and instead use the explicit .iloc and .loc indexers.

> One acceptable use case of the Series indexing operator is when doing boolean indexing. See Chapter 12, *Index Alignment* for more details.

I titled this type of row slicing in this section as *lazy*, as it does not use the more explicit .iloc or .loc. Personally, I always use these indexers whenever slicing rows, as there is never a question of exactly what I am doing.

There's more...

It is important to be aware that this lazy slicing does not work for columns, just for DataFrame rows and Series. It also cannot be used to select both rows and columns simultaneously. Take, for instance, the following code, which attempts to select the first ten rows and two columns:

```
>>> college[:10, ['CITY', 'STABBR']]
TypeError: unhashable type: 'slice'
```

To make a selection in this manner, you need to use .loc or .iloc. Here is one possible way that selects all the institution labels first and then uses the label-based indexer .loc:

```
>>> first_ten_instnm = college.index[:10]
>>> college.loc[first_ten_instnm, ['CITY', 'STABBR']]
```

Slicing lexicographically

The .loc indexer typically selects data based on the exact string label of the index. However, it also allows you to select data based on the lexicographic order of the values in the index. Specifically, .loc allows you to select all rows with an index lexicographically using slice notation. This works only if the index is sorted.

Getting ready

In this recipe, you will first sort the index and then use slice notation inside the .loc indexer to select all rows between two strings.

How to do it...

1. Read in the college dataset, and set the institution name as the index:

```
>>> college = pd.read_csv('data/college.csv', index_col='INSTNM')
```

2. Attempt to select all colleges with names lexicographically between 'Sp' and 'Su':

```
>>> college.loc['Sp':'Su']
KeyError: 'Sp'
```

3. As the index is not sorted, the preceding command fails. Let's go ahead and sort the index:

```
>>> college = college.sort_index()
```

INSTNM	CITY	STABBR	HBCU	MENONLY	WOMENONLY	RELAFFIL	SATVRMID	SATMTMID	DISTANCEONLY	UGDS	...	UGDS_2MOR
A & W Healthcare Educators	New Orleans	LA	0.0	0.0	0.0	0	NaN	NaN	0.0	40.0	...	0.0000
A T Still University of Health Sciences	Kirksville	MO	0.0	0.0	0.0	0	NaN	NaN	0.0	NaN	...	NaN
ABC Beauty Academy	Garland	TX	0.0	0.0	0.0	0	NaN	NaN	0.0	30.0	...	0.0000
ABC Beauty College Inc	Arkadelphia	AR	0.0	0.0	0.0	0	NaN	NaN	0.0	38.0	...	0.0000
AI Miami International University of Art and Design	Miami	FL	0.0	0.0	0.0	0	NaN	NaN	0.0	2778.0	...	0.0018

4. Now, let's rerun the same command from step 2:

```
>>> college.loc['Sp':'Su']
```

INSTNM	CITY	STABBR	HBCU	MENONLY	WOMENONLY	RELAFFIL	SATVRMID	SATMTMID	DISTANCEONLY	UGDS	...	UGDS_2MOR	UGDS_NRA
Spa Tech Institute-Ipswich	Ipswich	MA	0.0	0.0	0.0	0	NaN	NaN	0.0	37.0	...	0.000	0.0
Spa Tech Institute-Plymouth	Plymouth	MA	0.0	0.0	0.0	0	NaN	NaN	0.0	153.0	...	0.000	0.0
Spa Tech Institute-Westboro	Westboro	MA	0.0	0.0	0.0	0	NaN	NaN	0.0	90.0	...	0.000	0.0
...	...	...	...	...	...	...	...	...	...	...	...	...	...
Stylemaster College of Hair Design	Longview	WA	0.0	0.0	0.0	0	NaN	NaN	0.0	77.0	...	0.013	0.0
Styles and Profiles Beauty College	Selmer	TN	0.0	0.0	0.0	0	NaN	NaN	0.0	31.0	...	0.000	0.0
Styletrends Barber and Hairstyling Academy	Rock Hill	SC	0.0	0.0	0.0	0	NaN	NaN	0.0	45.0	...	0.000	0.0

201 rows × 26 columns

How it works...

The normal behavior of `.loc` is to make selections of data based on the exact labels passed to it. It raises a `KeyError` when these labels are not found in the index. However, one special exception to this behavior exists whenever the index is lexicographically sorted, and a slice is passed to it. Selection is now possible between the `start` and `stop` labels of the slice, even if they are not exact values of the index.

There's more...

With this recipe, it is easy to select colleges between two letters of the alphabet. For instance, to select all colleges that begin with the letter D through S, you would use `college.loc['D':'T']`. Slicing like this is still inclusive of the last index so this would technically return a college with the exact name T.

This type of slicing also works when the index is sorted in the opposite direction. You can determine which direction the index is sorted with the index attribute, `is_monotonic_increasing` or `is_monotonic_decreasing`. Either of these must be `True` in order for lexicographic slicing to work. For instance, the following code lexicographically sorts the index from Z to A:

```
>>> college = college.sort_index(ascending=False)
>>> college.index.is_monotonic_decreasing
True
>>> college.loc['E':'B']
```

INSTNM	CITY	STABBR	HBCU	MENONLY	WOMENONLY	RELAFFIL	SATVRMID	SATMTMID	DISTANCEONLY	UGDS	...	UGDS_2MOR
Dyersburg State Community College	Dyersburg	TN	0.0	0.0	0.0	0	NaN	NaN	0.0	2001.0	...	0.0185
Dutchess Community College	Poughkeepsie	NY	0.0	0.0	0.0	0	NaN	NaN	0.0	6885.0	...	0.0446
Dutchess BOCES-Practical Nursing Program	Poughkeepsie	NY	0.0	0.0	0.0	0	NaN	NaN	0.0	155.0	...	0.0581
...	...	...	...	...	...	...	...	...	...	...	...	...
BJ's Beauty & Barber College	Auburn	WA	0.0	0.0	0.0	0	NaN	NaN	0.0	28.0	...	0.0714
BIR Training Center	Chicago	IL	0.0	0.0	0.0	0	NaN	NaN	0.0	2132.0	...	0.0000
B M Spurr School of Practical Nursing	Glen Dale	WV	0.0	0.0	0.0	0	NaN	NaN	0.0	31.0	...	0.0000

1411 rows × 26 columns

Python sorts all capital letters before lowercase and all integers before capital letters.

11
Boolean Indexing

Filtering data from a dataset is one of the most common and basic operations. There are numerous ways to filter (or subset) data in pandas with **boolean indexing**. Boolean indexing (also known as **boolean selection**) can be a confusing term, but for the purposes of pandas, it refers to selecting rows by providing a boolean value (`True` or `False`) for each row. These boolean values are usually stored in a Series or NumPy `ndarray` and are usually created by applying a boolean condition to one or more columns in a DataFrame. We begin by creating boolean Series and calculating statistics on them and then move on to creating more complex conditionals before using boolean indexing in a wide variety of ways to filter data.

In this chapter, we will cover the following topics:

- Calculating boolean statistics
- Constructing multiple boolean conditions
- Filtering with boolean indexing
- Replicating boolean indexing with index selection
- Selecting with unique and sorted indexes
- Gaining perspective on stock prices
- Translating SQL WHERE clauses
- Determining the normality of stock market returns
- Improving readability of boolean indexing with the query method
- Preserving Series with the `where` method
- Masking DataFrame rows
- Selecting with booleans, integer location, and labels

Calculating boolean statistics

When first getting introduced to boolean Series, it can be informative to calculate basic summary statistics on them. Each value of a boolean series evaluates to 0 or 1 so all the Series methods that work with numerical values also work with booleans.

Getting ready

In this recipe, we create a boolean Series by applying a condition to a column of data and then calculate summary statistics from it.

How to do it...

1. Read in the `movie` dataset, set the index to the movie title, and inspect the first few rows:

```
>>> movie = pd.read_csv('data/movie.csv', index_col='movie_title')
>>> movie.head()
```

movie_title	color	director_name	num_critic_for_reviews	duration	director_facebook_likes	actor_3_facebook_likes	actor_2_name	actor_1_facebook_likes
Avatar	Color	James Cameron	723.0	178.0	0.0	855.0	Joel David Moore	1000.0
Pirates of the Caribbean: At World's End	Color	Gore Verbinski	302.0	169.0	563.0	1000.0	Orlando Bloom	40000.0
Spectre	Color	Sam Mendes	602.0	148.0	0.0	161.0	Rory Kinnear	11000.0
The Dark Knight Rises	Color	Christopher Nolan	813.0	164.0	22000.0	23000.0	Christian Bale	27000.0
Star Wars: Episode VII - The Force Awakens	NaN	Doug Walker	NaN	NaN	131.0	NaN	Rob Walker	131.0

2. Determine whether the duration of each movie is longer than two hours by using the greater than comparison operator with the duration Series:

```
>>> movie_2_hours = movie['duration'] > 120
>>> movie_2_hours.head(10)
movie_title
Avatar                                        True
Pirates of the Caribbean: At World's End      True
Spectre                                       True
The Dark Knight Rises                         True
Star Wars: Episode VII - The Force Awakens    False
John Carter                                   True
Spider-Man 3                                  True
Tangled                                       False
Avengers: Age of Ultron                       True
Harry Potter and the Half-Blood Prince        True
Name: duration, dtype: bool
```

3. We can now use this Series to determine the number of movies that are longer than two hours:

```
>>> movie_2_hours.sum()
1039
```

4. To find the percentage of movies in the dataset longer than two hours, use the mean method:

```
>>> movie_2_hours.mean()
0.2114
```

5. Unfortunately, the output from step 4 is misleading. The duration column has a few missing values. If you look back at the DataFrame output from step 1, you will see that the last row is missing a value for duration. The boolean condition in step 2 returns False for this. We need to drop the missing values first, then evaluate the condition and take the mean:

```
>>> movie['duration'].dropna().gt(120).mean()
.2112
```

6. Use the `describe` method to output a few summary statistics on the boolean Series:

```
>>> movie_2_hours.describe()
count         4916
unique           2
top          False
freq          3877
Name: duration, dtype: object
```

How it works...

Most DataFrames will not have columns of booleans like our movie dataset. The most straightforward method to produce a boolean Series is to apply a condition to one of the columns using one of the comparison operators. In step 2, we use the greater than operator to test whether or not the duration of each movie was more than two hours (120 minutes). Steps 3 and 4 calculate two important quantities from a boolean Series, its sum and mean. These methods are possible as Python evaluates `False`/`True` as 0/1.

You can prove to yourself that the mean of a boolean Series represents the percentage of `True` values. To do this, use the `value_counts` method to count with the `normalize` parameter set to `True` to get its distribution:

```
>>> movie_2_hours.value_counts(normalize=True)
False    0.788649
True     0.211351
Name: duration, dtype: float64
```

Step 5 alerts us to the incorrect result from step 4. Even though the `duration` column had missing values, the boolean condition evaluated all these comparisons against missing values as `False`. Dropping these missing values allows us to calculate the correct statistic. This is done in one step through method chaining.

Step 6 shows that pandas treats boolean columns similarly to how it treats object data types by displaying frequency information. This is a natural way to think about boolean Series, rather than display quantiles like it does with numeric data.

There's more...

It is possible to compare two columns from the same DataFrame to produce a boolean Series. For instance, we could determine the percentage of movies that have actor 1 with more Facebook likes than actor 2. To do this, we would select both of these columns and then drop any of the rows that had missing values for either movie. Then we would make the comparison and calculate the mean:

```
>>> actors = movie[['actor_1_facebook_likes',
                     'actor_2_facebook_likes']].dropna()
>>> (actors['actor_1_facebook_likes'] >
     actors['actor_2_facebook_likes']).mean()
.978
```

Constructing multiple boolean conditions

In Python, boolean expressions use the built-in logical operators `and`, `or`, and `not`. These keywords do not work with boolean indexing in pandas and are respectively replaced with `&`, `|`, and `~`. Additionally, each expression must be wrapped in parentheses or an error will be raised.

Getting ready

Constructing a precise filter for your dataset might have you combining multiple boolean expressions together to extract an exact subset. In this recipe, we construct multiple boolean expressions before combining them together to find all the movies that have an `imdb_score` greater than 8, a `content_rating` of PG-13, and a `title_year` either before 2000 or after 2009.

How to do it...

1. Load in the movie dataset and set the index as the title:

```
>>> movie = pd.read_csv('data/movie.csv', index_col='movie_title')
```

2. Create a variable to hold each set of criteria independently as a boolean Series:

```
>>> criteria1 = movie.imdb_score > 8
>>> criteria2 = movie.content_rating == 'PG-13'
>>> criteria3 = ((movie.title_year < 2000) |
                 (movie.title_year > 2009))

>>> criteria2.head()       # all criteria Series look similar
movie_title
Avatar                                       True
Pirates of the Caribbean: At World's End     True
Spectre                                      True
The Dark Knight Rises                        True
Star Wars: Episode VII - The Force Awakens   False
Name: content_rating, dtype: bool
```

3. Combine all the criteria together into a single boolean Series:

```
>>> criteria_final = criteria1 & criteria2 & criteria3
>>> criteria_final.head()
movie_title
Avatar                                       False
Pirates of the Caribbean: At World's End     False
Spectre                                      False
The Dark Knight Rises                        True
Star Wars: Episode VII - The Force Awakens   False
dtype: bool
```

How it works...

All values in a Series can be compared against a scalar value using the standard comparison operators(<, >, ==, !=, <=, >=). The expression `movie.imdb_score > 8` yields a Series of booleans where all `imdb_score` values prices exceeding 8 are `True` and those less than or equal to 8 are `False`. The index of this boolean Series retains the same index as the original and in this case, is the title of the movie.

The `criteria3` variable is created by two independent boolean expressions. Each expression must be enclosed in parentheses to function properly. The pipe character, `|`, is used to create a logical `or` condition between each of the values in both Series.

All three criteria need to be `True` to match the requirements of the recipe. They are each combined together with the ampersand character, `&`, which creates a logical `and` condition between each Series value.

There's more...

A consequence of pandas using different syntax for the logical operators is that operator precedence is no longer the same. The comparison operators have a higher precedence than `and`, `or`, and `not`. However, the new operators for pandas (the bitwise operators `&`, `|`, and `~`) have a higher precedence than the comparison operators, thus the need for parentheses. An example can help clear this up. Take the following expression:

```
>>> 5 < 10 and 3 > 4
False
```

In the preceding expression, `5 < 10` evaluates first, followed by `3 < 4`, and finally, the `and` evaluates. Python progresses through the expression as follows:

```
>>> 5 < 10 and 3 > 4
>>> True and 3 > 4
>>> True and False
>>> False
```

Let's take a look at what would happen if the expression in `criteria3` was written as follows:

```
>>> movie.title_year < 2000 | movie.title_year > 2009
TypeError: cannot compare a dtyped [float64] array with a scalar of type
[bool]
```

As the bitwise operators have higher precedence than the comparison operators, `2000 | movie.title_year` is evaluated first, which is nonsensical and raises an error. Therefore, parentheses are needed to have the operations evaluated in the correct order.

Why can't pandas use `and`, `or`, and `not`? When these keywords are evaluated, Python attempts to find the **truthiness** of the objects as a whole. As it does not make sense for a Series as a whole to be either True or False--only each element--pandas raises an error.

Many objects in Python have boolean representation. For instance, all integers except 0 are considered `True`. All strings except the empty string are `True`. All non-empty sets, tuples, dictionaries, and lists are `True`. An empty DataFrame or Series does not evaluate as True or False and instead an error is raised. In general, to retrieve the truthiness of a Python object, pass it to the `bool` function.

See also

- Python operator precedence (`http://bit.ly/2vxuqSn`)

Filtering with boolean indexing

Boolean selection for Series and DataFrame objects is virtually identical. Both work by passing a Series of booleans indexed identically to the object being filtered to the indexing operator.

Getting ready

This recipe constructs two complex and independent boolean criteria for different sets of movies. The first set of movies comes from the previous recipe and consists of those with an `imdb_score` greater than 8, a `content_rating` of PG-13, and a `title_year` either before 2000 or after 2009. The second set of movies consists of those with `imdb_score` less than 5, a `content_rating` of R, and a `title_year` between 2000 and 2010.

How to do it...

1. Read in the `movie` dataset, set the index to the `movie_title`, and create the first set of criteria:

```
>>> movie = pd.read_csv('data/movie.csv', index_col='movie_title')
>>> crit_a1 = movie.imdb_score > 8
>>> crit_a2 = movie.content_rating == 'PG-13'
>>> crit_a3 = (movie.title_year < 2000) | (movie.title_year > 2009)
>>> final_crit_a = crit_a1 & crit_a2 & crit_a3
```

2. Create criteria for the second set of movies:

```
>>> crit_b1 = movie.imdb_score < 5
>>> crit_b2 = movie.content_rating == 'R'
>>> crit_b3 = ((movie.title_year >= 2000) &
               (movie.title_year <= 2010))
>>> final_crit_b = crit_b1 & crit_b2 & crit_b3
```

3. Combine the two sets of criteria using the pandas or operator. This yields a boolean Series of all movies that are members of either set:

```
>>> final_crit_all = final_crit_a | final_crit_b
>>> final_crit_all.head()
movie_title
Avatar                                         False
Pirates of the Caribbean: At World's End       False
Spectre                                        False
The Dark Knight Rises                           True
Star Wars: Episode VII - The Force Awakens     False
dtype: bool
```

4. Once you have your boolean Series, you simply pass it to the indexing operator to filter the data:

```
>>> movie[final_crit_all].head()
```

movie_title	color	director_name	num_critic_for_reviews	duration	director_facebook_likes	actor_3_facebook_likes	actor_2_name	actor_1_facebook_likes
The Dark Knight Rises	Color	Christopher Nolan	813.0	164.0	22000.0	23000.0	Christian Bale	27000.0
The Avengers	Color	Joss Whedon	703.0	173.0	0.0	19000.0	Robert Downey Jr.	26000.0
Captain America: Civil War	Color	Anthony Russo	516.0	147.0	94.0	11000.0	Scarlett Johansson	21000.0
Guardians of the Galaxy	Color	James Gunn	653.0	121.0	571.0	3000.0	Vin Diesel	14000.0
Interstellar	Color	Christopher Nolan	712.0	169.0	22000.0	6000.0	Anne Hathaway	11000.0

5. We have successfully filtered the data and all the columns of the DataFrame. We can't easily perform a manual check to determine whether the filter worked correctly. Let's filter both rows and columns with the `.loc` indexer:

```
>>> cols = ['imdb_score', 'content_rating', 'title_year']
>>> movie_filtered = movie.loc[final_crit_all, cols]
>>> movie_filtered.head(10)
```

movie_title	imdb_score	content_rating	title_year
The Dark Knight Rises	8.5	PG-13	2012.0
The Avengers	8.1	PG-13	2012.0
Captain America: Civil War	8.2	PG-13	2016.0
Guardians of the Galaxy	8.1	PG-13	2014.0
Interstellar	8.6	PG-13	2014.0
Inception	8.8	PG-13	2010.0
The Martian	8.1	PG-13	2015.0
Town & Country	4.4	R	2001.0
Sex and the City 2	4.3	R	2010.0
Rollerball	3.0	R	2002.0

How it works...

In step 1 and step 2, each set of criteria is built from simpler boolean expressions. It is not necessary to create a different variable for each boolean expression as done here, but it does make it far easier to read and debug any logic mistakes. As we desire both sets of movies, step 3 uses the pandas logical `or` operator to combine them.

Step 4 shows the exact syntax of how boolean indexing works. You simply pass the Series of booleans created from step 3 directly to the indexing operator. Only the movies with `True` values from `final_crit_all` are selected.

Boolean indexing also works with the `.loc` indexer as seen in step 5 by simultaneously doing boolean indexing and individual column selection. This slimmed DataFrame is far easier to check manually whether the logic was implemented correctly.

Boolean indexing does not quite work with the `.iloc` indexing operator. If you pass in a boolean series to it, an exception will get raised. However, if you pass in a boolean ndarray it will the same as it does in this recipe with the other indexers.

There's more...

As was stated earlier, it is possible to use one long boolean expression in place of several other shorter ones. To replicate the `final_crit_a` variable from step 1 with one long line of code, we can do the following:

```
>>> final_crit_a2 = (movie.imdb_score > 8) & \
                    (movie.content_rating == 'PG-13') & \
                    ((movie.title_year < 2000) |
                     (movie.title_year > 2009))
>>> final_crit_a2.equals(final_crit_a)
True
```

See also

- Pandas official documentation on *boolean indexing* (http://bit.ly/2v1xK77)
- Checking the truth of a Python object (http://bit.ly/2vn8WXX)

Replicating boolean indexing with index selection

It is possible to replicate specific cases of boolean selection by taking advantage of the index. Selection through the index is more intuitive and makes for greater readability.

Getting ready

In this recipe, we use the `college` dataset to select all institutions from a particular state with both boolean indexing and index selection and then compare each of their performance against one another.

How to do it...

1. Read in the `college` dataset and use boolean indexing to select all institutions from the state of Texas (TX):

```
>>> college = pd.read_csv('data/college.csv')
>>> college[college['STABBR'] == 'TX'].head()
```

Pandas official documentation on

	INSTNM	CITY	STABBR	HBCU	MENONLY	WOMENONLY	RELAFFIL	SATVRMID	SATMTMID	DISTANCEONLY
3610	Abilene Christian University	Abilene	TX	0.0	0.0	0.0	1	530.0	545.0	0.0
3611	Alvin Community College	Alvin	TX	0.0	0.0	0.0	0	NaN	NaN	0.0
3612	Amarillo College	Amarillo	TX	0.0	0.0	0.0	0	NaN	NaN	0.0
3613	Angelina College	Lufkin	TX	0.0	0.0	0.0	0	NaN	NaN	0.0
3614	Angelo State University	San Angelo	TX	0.0	0.0	0.0	0	475.0	490.0	0.0

2. To replicate this using index selection, we need to move the `STABBR` column into the index. We can then use label-based selection with the `.loc` indexer:

```
>>> college2 = college.set_index('STABBR')
>>> college2.loc['TX'].head()
```

	INSTNM	CITY	HBCU	MENONLY	WOMENONLY	RELAFFIL	SATVRMID	SATMTMID	DISTANCEONLY	UGDS
STABBR										
TX	Abilene Christian University	Abilene	0.0	0.0	0.0	1	530.0	545.0	0.0	3572.0
TX	Alvin Community College	Alvin	0.0	0.0	0.0	0	NaN	NaN	0.0	4682.0
TX	Amarillo College	Amarillo	0.0	0.0	0.0	0	NaN	NaN	0.0	9346.0
TX	Angelina College	Lufkin	0.0	0.0	0.0	0	NaN	NaN	0.0	3825.0
TX	Angelo State University	San Angelo	0.0	0.0	0.0	0	475.0	490.0	0.0	5290.0

3. Let's compare the speed of both methods:

```
>>> %timeit college[college['STABBR'] == 'TX']
1.43 ms ± 53.5 µs per loop (mean ± std. dev. of 7 runs, 1000 loops
each)

>>> %timeit college2.loc['TX']
526 µs ± 6.67 µs per loop (mean ± std. dev. of 7 runs, 1000 loops
each)
```

4. Boolean indexing takes three times as long as index selection. As setting the index does not come for free, let's time that operation as well:

```
>>> %timeit college2 = college.set_index('STABBR')
1.04 ms ± 5.37 µs per loop (mean ± std. dev. of 7 runs, 1000 loops
each)
```

How it works...

Step 1 creates a boolean Series by determining which rows of data have STABBR equal to TX. This Series is passed to the indexing operator, which subsets the data. This process may be replicated by moving that same column to the index and simply using basic label-based index selection with .loc. Selection via the index is much faster than boolean selection.

There's more...

This recipe only selects a single state. It is possible to select multiple states with both boolean and index selection. Let's select **Texas (TX)**, **California (CA)**, and **New York (NY)**. With boolean selection, you can use the isin method but with indexing, just pass a list to .loc:

```
>>> states = ['TX', 'CA', 'NY']
>>> college[college['STABBR'].isin(states)]
>>> college2.loc[states]
```

There is quite a bit more to the story than what this recipe explains. Pandas implements the index differently based on whether the index is unique or sorted. See the following recipe for more details.

Selecting with unique and sorted indexes

Index selection performance drastically improves when the index is unique or sorted. The prior recipe used an unsorted index that contained duplicates, which makes for relatively slow selections.

Getting ready

In this recipe, we use the `college` dataset to form unique or sorted indexes to increase the performance of index selection. We will continue to compare the performance to boolean indexing as well.

How to do it...

1. Read in the college dataset, create a separate DataFrame with STABBR as the index, and check whether the index is sorted:

```
>>> college = pd.read_csv('data/college.csv')
>>> college2 = college.set_index('STABBR')
>>> college2.index.is_monotonic
False
```

2. Sort the index from `college2` and store it as another object:

```
>>> college3 = college2.sort_index()
>>> college3.index.is_monotonic
True
```

3. Time the selection of the state of Texas (TX) from all three DataFrames:

```
>>> %timeit college[college['STABBR'] == 'TX']
1.43 ms ± 53.5 µs per loop (mean ± std. dev. of 7 runs, 1000 loops
each)

>>> %timeit college2.loc['TX']
526 µs ± 6.67 µs per loop (mean ± std. dev. of 7 runs, 1000 loops
each)

>>> %timeit college3.loc['TX']
183 µs ± 3.67 µs per loop (mean ± std. dev. of 7 runs, 1000 loops
each)
```

4. The sorted index performs nearly an order of magnitude faster than boolean selection. Let's now turn towards unique indexes. For this, we use the institution name as the index:

```
>>> college_unique = college.set_index('INSTNM')
>>> college_unique.index.is_unique
True
```

5. Let's select Stanford University with boolean indexing:

```
>>> college[college['INSTNM'] == 'Stanford University']
```

	INSTNM	CITY	STABBR	HBCU	MENONLY	WOMENONLY	RELAFFIL	SATVRMID	SATMTMID	DISTANCEONLY	...	UGDS_2MOR	UGDS_NRA
4217	Stanford University	Stanford	CA	0.0	0.0	0.0	0	730.0	745.0	0.0	...	0.1067	0.0819

6. Let's select Stanford University with index selection:

```
>>> college_unique.loc['Stanford University']
CITY                    Stanford
STABBR                        CA
HBCU                           0
...
UG25ABV                   0.0401
MD_EARN_WNE_P10            86000
GRAD_DEBT_MDN_SUPP        12782
Name: Stanford University, dtype: object
```

7. They both produce the same data, just with different objects. Let's time each approach:

```
>>> %timeit college[college['INSTNM'] == 'Stanford University']
1.3 ms ± 56.8 µs per loop (mean ± std. dev. of 7 runs, 1000 loops each)

>>> %timeit college_unique.loc['Stanford University']
157 µs ± 682 ns per loop (mean ± std. dev. of 7 runs, 10000 loops each)
```

How it works...

When the index is not sorted and contains duplicates, as with `college2`, pandas will need to check every single value in the index in order to make the correct selection. When the index is sorted, as with `college3`, pandas takes advantage of an algorithm called **binary search** to greatly improve performance.

In the second half of the recipe, we use a unique column as the index. Pandas implements unique indexes with a hash table, which makes for even faster selection. Each index location can be looked up in nearly the same time regardless of its length.

There's more...

Boolean selection gives much more flexibility than index selection as it is possible to condition on any number of columns. In this recipe, we used a single column as the index. It is possible to concatenate multiple columns together to form an index. For instance, in the following code, we set the index equal to the concatenation of the city and state columns:

```
>>> college.index = college['CITY'] + ', ' + college['STABBR']
>>> college = college.sort_index()
>>> college.head()
```

	INSTNM	CITY	STABBR	HBCU	MENONLY	WOMENONLY	RELAFFIL	SATVRMID	SATMTMID	DISTANCEONLY	...	UGDS_2MOR
ARTESIA, CA	Angeles Institute	ARTESIA	CA	0.0	0.0	0.0	0	NaN	NaN	0.0	...	0.0175
Aberdeen, SD	Presentation College	Aberdeen	SD	0.0	0.0	0.0	1	440.0	480.0	0.0	...	0.0284
Aberdeen, SD	Northern State University	Aberdeen	SD	0.0	0.0	0.0	0	480.0	475.0	0.0	...	0.0219
Aberdeen, WA	Grays Harbor College	Aberdeen	WA	0.0	0.0	0.0	0	NaN	NaN	0.0	...	0.0937
Abilene, TX	Hardin-Simmons University	Abilene	TX	0.0	0.0	0.0	1	508.0	515.0	0.0	...	0.0298

From here, we can select all colleges from a particular city and state combination without boolean indexing. Let's select all colleges from `Miami, FL`:

```
>>> college.loc['Miami, FL'].head()
```

	INSTNM	CITY	STABBR	HBCU	MENONLY	WOMENONLY	RELAFFIL	SATVRMID	SATMTMID	DISTANCEONLY	...	UGDS_2MOR
Miami, FL	New Professions Technical Institute	Miami	FL	0.0	0.0	0.0	0	NaN	NaN	0.0	...	0.0000
Miami, FL	Management Resources College	Miami	FL	0.0	0.0	0.0	0	NaN	NaN	0.0	...	0.0000
Miami, FL	Strayer University-Doral	Miami	FL	NaN	NaN	NaN	1	NaN	NaN	NaN	...	NaN
Miami, FL	Keiser University-Miami	Miami	FL	NaN	NaN	NaN	1	NaN	NaN	NaN	...	NaN
Miami, FL	George T Baker Aviation Technical College	Miami	FL	0.0	0.0	0.0	0	NaN	NaN	0.0	...	0.0046

We can compare the speed of this compound index selection with boolean indexing. There is more than an order of magnitude difference:

```
>>> %%timeit
>>> crit1 = college['CITY'] == 'Miami'
>>> crit2 = college['STABBR'] == 'FL'
>>> college[crit1 & crit2]
2.43 ms ± 80.4 µs per loop (mean ± std. dev. of 7 runs, 100 loops each)

>>> %timeit college.loc['Miami, FL']
197 µs ± 8.69 µs per loop (mean ± std. dev. of 7 runs, 10000 loops each)
```

See also

- The *Binary search algorithm* (http://bit.ly/2wbMq20)

Gaining perspective on stock prices

Investors who have purchased long stock positions would obviously like to sell stocks at or near their all-time highs. This, of course, is very difficult to do in practice, especially if a stock price has only spent a small portion of its history above a certain threshold. We can use boolean indexing to find all points in time that a stock has spent above or below a certain value. This exercise may help us gain perspective as to what a common range for some stock to be trading within.

Getting ready

In this recipe, we examine Schlumberger stock from the start of 2010 until mid-2017. We use boolean indexing to extract a Series of the lowest and highest ten percent of closing prices during this time period. We then plot all points and highlight those that are in the upper and lower ten percent.

How to do it...

1. Read in the Schlumberger stock data, put the Date column into the index, and convert it to a DatetimeIndex:

```
>>> slb = pd.read_csv('data/slb_stock.csv', index_col='Date',
                      parse_dates=['Date'])
>>> slb.head()
```

	Open	High	Low	Close	Volume
Date					
2010-01-04	66.39	67.20	66.12	67.11	5771234
2010-01-05	66.99	67.62	66.73	67.30	7366270
2010-01-06	67.17	68.94	67.03	68.80	9949946
2010-01-07	68.49	69.81	68.21	69.51	7700297
2010-01-08	69.19	72.00	69.09	70.65	13487621

2. Select the closing price as a Series and use the describe method to return summary statistics as a Series:

```
>>> slb_close = slb['Close']
>>> slb_summary = slb_close.describe(percentiles=[.1, .9])
>>> slb_summary
count    1895.000000
mean       79.121905
std        11.767802
min        51.750000
10%        64.892000
50%        78.000000
90%        93.248000
max       117.950000
Name: Close, dtype: float64
```

3. Using boolean selection, select all closing prices in the upper or lower tenth percentile:

```
>>> upper_10 = slb_summary.loc['90%']
>>> lower_10 = slb_summary.loc['10%']
>>> criteria = (slb_close < lower_10) | (slb_close > upper_10)
>>> slb_top_bottom_10 = slb_close[criteria]
```

4. Plot the resulting filtered Series in light gray on top of all closing prices in black. Use the `matplotlib` library to draw horizontal lines at the tenth and ninetieth percentiles:

```
>>> slb_close.plot(color='black', figsize=(12,6))
>>> slb_top_bottom_10.plot(marker='o', style=' ',
                           ms=4, color='lightgray')

>>> xmin = criteria.index[0]
>>> xmax = criteria.index[-1]
>>> plt.hlines(y=[lower_10, upper_10], xmin=xmin,
               xmax=xmax, color='black')
```

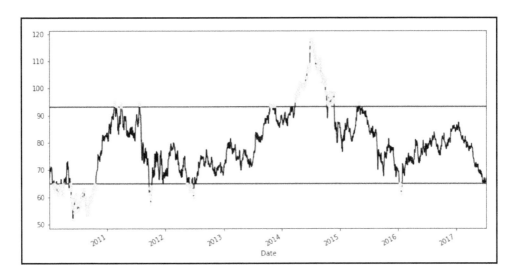

How it works...

The result of the `describe` method in step 2 is itself a Series with the identifying summary statistic as its index labels. This summary Series is used to store the tenth and ninetieth percentiles as their own variables. Step 3 uses boolean indexing to select only those values in the upper and lower tenth of the distribution.

Both Series and DataFrames have direct plotting capabilities through the `plot` method. This first call to the `plot` method comes from the `slb_close` Series, which contains all the SLB closing prices. This is the black line in the plot. The points from `slb_filtered` are plotted as gray markers directly on top of the closing prices. The `style` parameter is set to a single blank space so that no line is drawn. The `ms` parameter sets the marker size.

Matplotlib comes with a convenience function, `hlines`, that plots horizontal lines. It takes a list of `y` values and plots them from `xmin` to `xmax`.

Judging from our new perspective from the plots that we created, it's clear to see that although SLB's all-time high is close to $120 per share, only 10% of the trading days in the last seven years have been above $93 per share.

There's more...

Instead of plotting red points (black points) over the closing prices to indicate the upper and lower tenth percentiles, we can use matplotlib's `fill_between` function. This function fills in all the areas between two lines. It takes an optional `where` parameter that accepts a boolean Series, alerting it to exactly which locations to fill in:

```
>>> slb_close.plot(color='black', figsize=(12,6))
>>> plt.hlines(y=[lower_10, upper_10],
            xmin=xmin, xmax=xmax,color='lightgray')
>>> plt.fill_between(x=criteria.index, y1=lower_10,
                y2=slb_close.values, color='black')
>>> plt.fill_between(x=criteria.index,y1=lower_10,
                y2=slb_close.values, where=slb_close < lower_10,
                color='lightgray')
>>> plt.fill_between(x=criteria.index, y1=upper_10,
                y2=slb_close.values, where=slb_close > upper_10,
                color='lightgray')
```

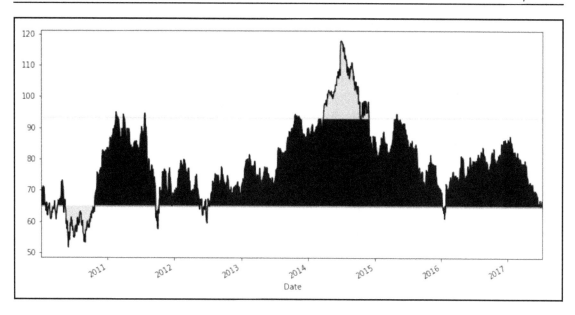

Translating SQL WHERE clauses

Many pandas users will have a background processing data directly from databases using the ubiquitous **Structured Query Language** (**SQL**). SQL is a standardized language to define, manipulate, and control data stored in a database. The SELECT statement is the most common way to use SQL to select, filter, aggregate, and order data. Pandas has the ability to connect to databases and send SQL statements to them.

SQL is a very important language to know for data scientists. Much of the world's data is stored in databases that necessitate SQL to retrieve, manipulate, and perform analyses on. SQL syntax is fairly simple and easy to learn. There are many different SQL implementations from companies such as Oracle, Microsoft, IBM, and more. Although the syntax is not compatible between the different implementations, the core of it will look very much the same.

Getting ready

Within a SQL SELECT statement, the WHERE clause is very common and filters data. This recipe will write pandas code that is equivalent to a SQL query that selects a certain subset of the employee dataset.

It is not necessary to understand any SQL syntax to make use of this recipe.

Suppose we are given a task to find all the female employees that work in the police or fire departments that have a base salary between 80 and 120 thousand dollars. The following SQL statement would answer this query for us:

```
SELECT
    UNIQUE_ID,
    DEPARTMENT,
    GENDER,
    BASE_SALARY
FROM
    EMPLOYEE
WHERE
    DEPARTMENT IN ('Houston Police Department-HPD',
                   'Houston Fire Department (HFD)') AND
    GENDER = 'Female' AND
    BASE_SALARY BETWEEN 80000 AND 120000;
```

How to do it...

1. Read in the `employee` dataset as a DataFrame:

   ```
   >>> employee = pd.read_csv('data/employee.csv')
   ```

2. Before filtering out the data, it is helpful to do some manual inspection of each of the filtered columns to know the exact values that will be used in the filter:

   ```
   >>> employee.DEPARTMENT.value_counts().head()
   Houston Police Department-HPD        638
   Houston Fire Department (HFD)        384
   Public Works & Engineering-PWE       343
   Health & Human Services              110
   Houston Airport System (HAS)         106
   Name: DEPARTMENT, dtype: int64

   >>> employee.GENDER.value_counts()
    Male 1397
    Female 603

   >>> employee.BASE_SALARY.describe().astype(int)
   count       1886
   mean        55767
   std         21693
   min         24960
   25%         40170
   50%         54461
   75%         66614
   max        275000
   Name: BASE_SALARY, dtype: int64
   ```

3. Write a single statement for each of the criteria. Use the `isin` method to test equality to one of many values:

   ```
   >>> depts = ['Houston Police Department-HPD',
                'Houston Fire Department (HFD)']
   >>> criteria_dept = employee.DEPARTMENT.isin(depts)
   >>> criteria_gender = employee.GENDER == 'Female'
   >>> criteria_sal = (employee.BASE_SALARY >= 80000) & \
                      (employee.BASE_SALARY <= 120000)
   ```

4. Combine all the boolean Series together:

```
>>> criteria_final = (criteria_dept &
                      criteria_gender &
                      criteria_sal)
```

5. Use boolean indexing to select only the rows that meet the final criteria:

```
>>> select_columns = ['UNIQUE_ID', 'DEPARTMENT',
                      'GENDER', 'BASE_SALARY']
>>> employee.loc[criteria_final, select_columns].head()
```

	UNIQUE_ID	DEPARTMENT	GENDER	BASE_SALARY
61	11087	Houston Fire Department (HFD)	Female	96668.0
136	6146	Houston Police Department-HPD	Female	81239.0
367	7589	Houston Police Department-HPD	Female	86534.0
474	5407	Houston Police Department-HPD	Female	91181.0
513	6252	Houston Police Department-HPD	Female	81239.0

How it works...

Before any filtering is actually done, you will obviously need to know the exact string names that will be used. The Series `value_counts` method is an excellent way to get both the exact string name and number of occurrences of that value.

The `isin` Series method is equivalent to the SQL IN operator and accepts a list of all possible values that you would like to keep. It is possible to use a series of OR conditions to replicate this expression but it would not be as efficient or idiomatic.

The criteria for salary, `criteria_sal`, is formed by combining two simple inequality expressions. All the criteria are finally combined together with the pandas and operator, &, to yield a single boolean Series as the filter.

There's more...

For many operations, pandas has multiple ways to do the same thing. In the preceding recipe, the criteria for salary uses two separate boolean expressions. Similarly to SQL, Series have a `between` method, with the salary criteria equivalently written as follows:

```
>>> criteria_sal = employee.BASE_SALARY.between(80000, 120000)
```

Another useful application of `isin` is to provide a sequence of values automatically generated by some other pandas statements. This would avoid any manual investigating to find the exact string names to store in a list. Conversely, let's try to exclude the rows from the top five most frequently occurring departments:

```
>>> top_5_depts = employee.DEPARTMENT.value_counts().index[:5]
>>> criteria = ~employee.DEPARTMENT.isin(top_5_depts)
>>> employee[criteria]
```

The SQL equivalent of this would be as follows:

```
SELECT
    *
FROM
    EMPLOYEE
WHERE
    DEPARTMENT not in
    (
      SELECT
          DEPARTMENT
     FROM (
          SELECT
              DEPARTMENT,
              COUNT(1) as CT
          FROM
              EMPLOYEE
          GROUP BY
              DEPARTMENT
          ORDER BY
              CT DESC
          LIMIT 5
          )
    );
```

Notice the use of the pandas not operator, ~, which negates all boolean values of a Series.

See also

- Pandas official documentation of the `isin` (`http://bit.ly/2v1GPfQ`) and `between` (`http://bit.ly/2wq9YPF`) Series methods
- Refer to the *Connecting to SQL databases recipe* in `Chapter 15`, *Combining Pandas Objects*
- A basic introduction to SQL from W3 schools (`http://bit.ly/2hsq8Wp`)
- The SQL IN operator (`http://bit.ly/2v3H7Bg`)
- The SQL BETWEEN operator (`http://bit.ly/2vn5UTP`)

Determining the normality of stock market returns

In elementary statistics textbooks, the normal distribution is heavily relied upon to describe many different populations of data. Although many random processes do appear to look like normal distributions most of the time, real-life tends to be more complex. Stock market returns are a prime example of a distribution that can look fairly normal but in actuality be quite far off.

Getting ready

This recipe describes how to find daily stock market returns of the internet retail giant Amazon and informally test whether they follow a normal distribution.

How to do it...

1. Load Amazon stock data and set the date as the index:

```
>>> amzn = pd.read_csv('data/amzn_stock.csv', index_col='Date',
                       parse_dates=['Date'])
>>> amzn.head()
```

	Open	High	Low	Close	Volume
Date					
2010-01-04	136.25	136.61	133.14	133.90	7600543
2010-01-05	133.43	135.48	131.81	134.69	8856456
2010-01-06	134.60	134.73	131.65	132.25	7180977
2010-01-07	132.01	132.32	128.80	130.00	11030124
2010-01-08	130.56	133.68	129.03	133.52	9833829

2. Create a Series by selecting only the closing price and then using the `pct_change` method to get the daily rate of return:

```
>>> amzn_daily_return = amzn.Close.pct_change()
>>> amzn_daily_return.head()
Date
2010-01-04         NaN
2010-01-05    0.005900
2010-01-06   -0.018116
2010-01-07   -0.017013
2010-01-08    0.027077
Name: Close, dtype: float64
```

3. Drop the missing value and plot a histogram of the returns to visually inspect the distribution:

```
>>> amzn_daily_return = amzn_daily_return.dropna()
>>> amzn_daily_return.hist(bins=20)
```

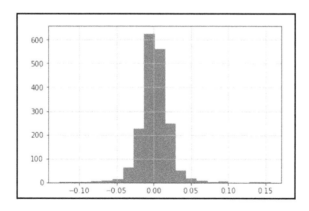

4. Normal distributions approximately follow the 68-95-99.7 rule--meaning that 68% of the data falls between 1 standard deviation of the mean, 95% between 2, and 99.7% between 3. We will now calculate the percentage of daily returns that fall between 1, 2, and 3 standard deviations from the mean. For this, we will need the mean and standard deviation:

```
>>> mean = amzn_daily_return.mean()
>>> std = amzn_daily_return.std()
```

5. Calculate the absolute value of the z-score for each observation. The z-score is the number of standard deviations away from the mean:

```
>>> abs_z_score = amzn_daily_return.sub(mean).abs().div(std)
```

6. Find the percentage of returns that are within 1, 2, and 3 standard deviations:

```
>>> pcts = [abs_z_score.lt(i).mean() for i in range(1,4)]
>>> print('{:.3f} fall within 1 standard deviation. '
          '{:.3f} within 2 and {:.3f} within 3'.format(*pcts))
0.787 fall within 1 standard deviation. 0.957 within 2 and 0.985
within 3
```

How it works...

By default, the `pct_change` Series method calculates the percentage change between the current element and the previous element. This transforms the raw stock closing prices into daily percentage returns. The first element of the returned Series is a missing value as there is no previous price.

Histograms are fantastic plots to summarize and visualize one-dimensional numeric data. It is clear from the plot that the distribution is symmetrical but it remains difficult to determine whether it is normal or not. There are formal statistical procedures to determine the normality of a distribution but we will simply find how close the data matches the 68-95-99.7 rule.

Step 5 calculates the number of standard deviations away from the mean for each observation which is referred to as the z-score. This step uses the methods and not the symbols (– and /) to do subtraction and division. The method for less than is also used in favor of the symbols in step 6.

It may seem odd that the mean is being taken in step 6. The result of the abs_z_score.lt(1) expression is a Series of booleans. As booleans evaluate to 0 or 1, taking the mean of this Series returns the percentage of elements that are True, which is what we desired.

We can now more easily determine the normality of the returns by comparing the resulting numbers (78.7-95.7-98.5) to the 68-95-99.7 rule. The percentages deviate greatly from the rule for 1 and 3 standard deviations, and we can conclude that Amazon daily stock returns do not follow a normal distribution.

There's more...

To automate this process, we can write a function that accepts stock data in the and outputs the histogram of daily returns along with the percentages that fall within 1, 2, and 3 standard deviations from the mean. The following function does this and replaces the methods with their symbol counterparts:

```
>>> def test_return_normality(stock_data):
        close = stock_data['Close']
        daily_return = close.pct_change().dropna()
        daily_return.hist(bins=20)
        mean = daily_return.mean()
        std = daily_return.std()

        abs_z_score = abs(daily_return - mean) / std
        pcts = [abs_z_score.lt(i).mean() for i in range(1,4)]

        print('{:.3f} fall within 1 standard deviation. '
              '{:.3f} within 2 and {:.3f} within 3'.format(*pcts))
```

```
>>> slb = pd.read_csv('data/slb_stock.csv', index_col='Date',
                      parse_dates=['Date'])
>>> test_return_normality(slb)
0.742 fall within 1 standard deviation. 0.946 within 2 and 0.986 within 3
```

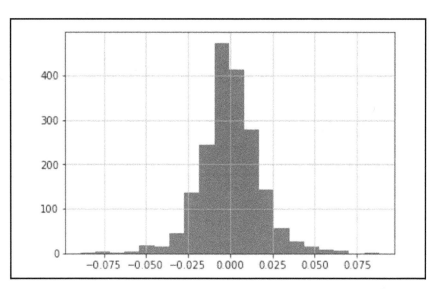

See also

- Pandas official documentation of the pct_change Series method (http://bit.ly/2wcjmqT)

Improving readability of boolean indexing with the query method

Boolean indexing is not necessarily the most pleasant syntax to read or write, especially when using a single line to write a complex filter. Pandas has an alternative string-based syntax through the DataFrame `query` method that can provide more clarity.

 The `query` DataFrame method is experimental and not as capable as boolean indexing and should not be used for production code.

Getting ready

This recipe replicates the earlier recipe in this chapter, *Translating SQL WHERE clauses*, but instead takes advantage of the `query` DataFrame method. The goal here is to filter the employee data for female employees from the police or fire departments that earn a salary between 80 and 120 thousand dollars.

How to do it...

1. Read in the employee data, assign the chosen departments, and import columns to variables:

```
>>> employee = pd.read_csv('data/employee.csv')
>>> depts = ['Houston Police Department-HPD',
             'Houston Fire Department (HFD)']
>>> select_columns = ['UNIQUE_ID', 'DEPARTMENT',
                      'GENDER', 'BASE_SALARY']
```

2. Build the query string and execute the method:

```
>>> qs = "DEPARTMENT in @depts " \
         "and GENDER == 'Female' " \
         "and 80000 <= BASE_SALARY <= 120000"
>>> emp_filtered = employee.query(qs)
>>> emp_filtered[select_columns].head()
```

	UNIQUE_ID	DEPARTMENT	GENDER	BASE_SALARY
61	11087	Houston Fire Department (HFD)	Female	96668.0
136	6146	Houston Police Department-HPD	Female	81239.0
367	7589	Houston Police Department-HPD	Female	86534.0
474	5407	Houston Police Department-HPD	Female	91181.0
513	6252	Houston Police Department-HPD	Female	81239.0

How it works...

Strings passed to the `query` method are going to look more like plain English than normal pandas code. It is possible to reference Python variables using the at symbol (@) as with `depts`. All DataFrame column names are available in the query namespace by simply referencing their name without inner quotes. If a string is needed, such as `Female`, inner quotes will need to wrap it.

Another nice feature of the `query` syntax is the ability to write a double inequality in a single expression and its ability to understand the verbose logical operators and, or, and not instead of their bitwise equivalents as with boolean indexing.

There's more...

Instead of manually typing in a list of department names, we could have programmatically created it. For instance, if we wanted to find all the female employees that were not a member of the top 10 departments by frequency, we can run the following code:

```
>>> top10_depts = employee.DEPARTMENT.value_counts() \
                                      .index[:10].tolist()
>>> qs = "DEPARTMENT not in @top10_depts and GENDER == 'Female'"
>>> employee_filtered2 = employee.query(qs)
>>> employee_filtered2.head()
```

	DEPARTMENT	GENDER
0	Municipal Courts Department	Female
73	Human Resources Dept.	Female
96	City Controller's Office	Female
117	Legal Department	Female
146	Houston Information Tech Svcs	Female

See also

- Pandas official documentation on the `query` method (`http://bit.ly/2vnlwXk`)

Preserving Series with the where method

Boolean indexing necessarily filters your dataset by removing all the rows that don't match the criteria. Instead of dropping all these values, it is possible to keep them using the `where` method. The `where` method preserves the size of your Series or DataFrame and either sets the values that don't meet the criteria for missing or replaces them with something else.

Getting ready

In this recipe, we pass the `where` method boolean conditions to put a floor and ceiling on the minimum and maximum number of Facebook likes for actor 1 in the `movie` dataset.

How to do it...

1. Read the `movie` dataset, set the movie title as the index, and select all the values in the `actor_1_facebook_likes` column that are not missing:

```
>>> movie = pd.read_csv('data/movie.csv', index_col='movie_title')
>>> fb_likes = movie['actor_1_facebook_likes'].dropna()
>>> fb_likes.head()
movie_title
Avatar                                    1000.0
Pirates of the Caribbean: At World's End  40000.0
```

```
Spectre                                           11000.0
The Dark Knight Rises                             27000.0
Star Wars: Episode VII - The Force Awakens          131.0
Name: actor_1_facebook_likes, dtype: float64
```

2. Let's use the `describe` method to get a sense of the distribution:

```
>>> fb_likes.describe(percentiles=[.1, .25, .5, .75, .9]) \
             .astype(int)
count      4909
mean       6494
std       15106
min           0
10%         240
25%         607
50%         982
75%       11000
90%       18000
max      640000
Name: actor_1_facebook_likes, dtype: int64
```

3. Additionally, we may plot a histogram of this Series to visually inspect the distribution:

```
>>> fb_likes.hist()
```

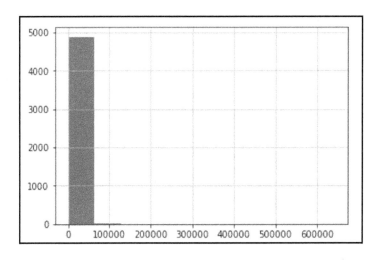

4. This is quite a bad visualization and very difficult to get a sense of the distribution. On the other hand, the summary statistics from step 2 appear to be telling us that it is highly skewed to the right with many observations more than an order of magnitude greater than the median. Let's create criteria to test whether the number of likes is less than 20,000:

```
>>> criteria_high = fb_likes < 20000
>>> criteria_high.mean().round(2)
.91
```

5. About 91% of the movies have an actor 1 with fewer than 20,000 likes. We will now use the `where` method, which accepts a boolean condition. The default behavior is to return a Series the same size as the original but which has all the `False` locations replaced with a missing value:

```
>>> fb_likes.where(criteria_high).head()
movie_title
Avatar                                          1000.0
Pirates of the Caribbean: At World's End           NaN
Spectre                                        11000.0
The Dark Knight Rises                              NaN
Star Wars: Episode VII - The Force Awakens       131.0
Name: actor_1_facebook_likes, dtype: float64
```

6. The second parameter to the `where` method, `other`, allows you to control the replacement value. Let's change all the missing values to 20,000:

```
>>> fb_likes.where(criteria_high, other=20000).head()
movie_title
Avatar                                          1000.0
Pirates of the Caribbean: At World's End       20000.0
Spectre                                        11000.0
The Dark Knight Rises                          20000.0
Star Wars: Episode VII - The Force Awakens       131.0
Name: actor_1_facebook_likes, dtype: float64
```

7. Similarly, we can create criteria to put a floor on the minimum number of likes. Here, we chain another `where` method and replace the values not meeting with the condition to `300`:

```
>>> criteria_low = fb_likes > 300
>>> fb_likes_cap = fb_likes.where(criteria_high, other=20000)\
                           .where(criteria_low, 300)
>>> fb_likes_cap.head()
movie_title
Avatar                                          1000.0
```

```
Pirates of the Caribbean: At World's End          20000.0
Spectre                                           11000.0
The Dark Knight Rises                             20000.0
Star Wars: Episode VII - The Force Awakens          300.0
Name: actor_1_facebook_likes, dtype: float64
```

8. The length of the original Series and modified Series is the same:

```
>>> len(fb_likes), len(fb_likes_cap)
(4909, 4909)
```

9. Let's make a histogram with the modified Series. With the data in a much tighter range, it should produce a better plot:

```
>>> fb_likes_cap.hist()
```

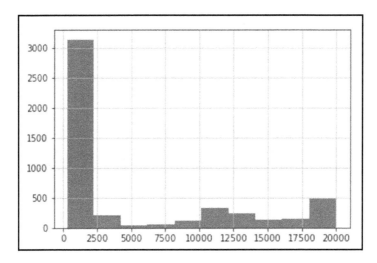

How it works...

The where method again preserves the size and shape of the calling object and does not modify the values where the passed boolean is True. It was important to drop the missing values in step 1 as the where method would have eventually replaced them with a valid number in future steps.

The summary statistics in step 2 give us some intuition where it would make sense to cap our data. The histogram from step 3, on the other hand, appears to clump all the data into one bin. The data has too many outliers for a plain histogram to make a good plot. The `where` method allows us to place a ceiling and floor on our data, which results in a histogram with many more visible bars.

There's more...

Pandas actually has built-in methods `clip`, `clip_lower`, and `clip_upper` that replicate this operation. The `clip` method can set a floor and ceiling at the same time. We also check whether this alternate method produces the exact same Series, which it does:

```
>>> fb_likes_cap2 = fb_likes.clip(lower=300, upper=20000)
>>> fb_likes_cap2.equals(fb_likes_cap)
True
```

See also

- Pandas official documentation on the `where` method (http://bit.ly/2vmW2cv)

Masking DataFrame rows

The `mask` method performs the exact opposite operation that the `where` method does. By default, it creates missing values wherever the boolean condition is `True`. In essence, it is literally masking, or covering up, values in your dataset.

Getting ready

In this recipe, we will mask all rows of the movie dataset that were made after 2010 and then filter all the rows with missing values.

How to do it...

1. Read the `movie` dataset, set the movie title as the index, and create the criteria:

```
>>> movie = pd.read_csv('data/movie.csv', index_col='movie_title')
>>> c1 = movie['title_year'] >= 2010
>>> c2 = movie['title_year'].isnull()
>>> criteria = c1 | c2
```

2. Use the `mask` method on a DataFrame to make all the values in rows with movies that were made from 2010 onward missing. Any movie that originally had a missing value for `title_year` is also masked:

```
>>> movie.mask(criteria).head()
```

movie_title	color	director_name	num_critic_for_reviews	duration	director_facebook_likes	actor_3_facebook_likes	actor_2_name	actor_1_facebook_likes
Avatar	Color	James Cameron	723.0	178.0	0.0	855.0	Joel David Moore	1000.0
Pirates of the Caribbean: At World's End	Color	Gore Verbinski	302.0	169.0	563.0	1000.0	Orlando Bloom	40000.0
Spectre	NaN	NaN	NaN	NaN	NaN	NaN	NaN	NaN
The Dark Knight Rises	NaN	NaN	NaN	NaN	NaN	NaN	NaN	NaN
Star Wars: Episode VII - The Force Awakens	NaN	NaN	NaN	NaN	NaN	NaN	NaN	NaN

3. Notice how all the values in the third, fourth, and fifth rows from the preceding DataFrame are missing. Chain the `dropna` method to remove rows that have all values missing:

```
>>> movie_mask = movie.mask(criteria).dropna(how='all')
>>> movie_mask.head()
```

	color	director_name	num_critic_for_reviews	duration	director_facebook_likes	actor_3_facebook_likes	actor_2_name	actor_1_facebook_likes
movie_title								
Avatar	Color	James Cameron	723.0	178.0	0.0	855.0	Joel David Moore	1000.0
Pirates of the Caribbean: At World's End	Color	Gore Verbinski	302.0	169.0	563.0	1000.0	Orlando Bloom	40000.0
Star Wars: Episode VII - The Force Awakens	NaN	Doug Walker	NaN	NaN	131.0	NaN	Rob Walker	131.0
Spider-Man 3	Color	Sam Raimi	392.0	156.0	0.0	4000.0	James Franco	24000.0
Harry Potter and the Half-Blood Prince	Color	David Yates	375.0	153.0	282.0	10000.0	Daniel Radcliffe	25000.0

4. The operation in step 3 is just a complex way of doing basic boolean indexing. We can check whether the two methods produce the same DataFrame:

```
>>> movie_boolean = movie[movie['title_year'] < 2010]
>>> movie_mask.equals(movie_boolean)
False
```

5. The `equals` method is telling us that they aren't equal. Something is wrong. Let's do some sanity checking and see if they are the same shape:

```
>>> movie_mask.shape == movie_boolean.shape
True
```

6. When we used the preceding `mask` method, it created many missing values. Missing values are `float` data types so any previous integer column is now a float. The `equals` method returns `False` if the data types of the columns are different, even if the values are the same. Let's check the equality of the data types to see whether this scenario happened:

```
>>> movie_mask.dtypes == movie_boolean.dtypes
color                     True
director_name             True
num_critic_for_reviews    True
duration                  True
director_facebook_likes   True
actor_3_facebook_likes    True
actor_2_name              True
actor_1_facebook_likes    True
gross                     True
```

```
genres                        True
actor_1_name                  True
num_voted_users               False
cast_total_facebook_likes     False
.....
dtype: bool
```

7. It turns out that a couple of columns don't have the same data type. Pandas has an alternative for these situations. In its testing module, which is primarily used by developers, there is a function, `assert_frame_equal`, that allows you to check the equality of Series and DataFrames without also checking the equality of the data types:

```
from pandas.testing import assert_frame_equal
>>> assert_frame_equal(movie_boolean, movie_mask,
check_dtype=False)
```

How it works...

By default, the `mask` method covers up data with missing values. The first parameter to the `mask` method is the condition which is often a boolean Series such as `criteria`. Because the `mask` method is called from a DataFrame, all the values in each row where the condition is `False` change to missing. Step 3 uses this masked DataFrame to drop the rows that contain all missing values. Step 4 shows how to do this same procedure with boolean indexing.

During a data analysis, it is very important to continually validate results. Checking the equality of Series and DataFrames is an extremely common approach to validation. Our first attempt, in step 4, yielded an unexpected result. Some basic sanity checking, such as ensuring that the number of rows and columns are the same or that the row and column names are the same, are good checks before going deeper.

Step 6 compares the two Series of data types together. It is here where we uncover the reason why the DataFrames were not equivalent. The `equals` method checks that both the values and data types are the same. The `assert_frame_equal` function from step 7 has many available parameters to test equality in a variety of ways. Notice that there is no output after calling `assert_frame_equal`. This method returns None when the two passed DataFrames are equal and raises an error when they are not.

There's more...

Let's compare the speed difference between masking and dropping missing rows and boolean indexing. Boolean indexing is about an order of magnitude faster in this case:

```
>>> %timeit movie.mask(criteria).dropna(how='all')
11.2 ms ± 144 µs per loop (mean ± std. dev. of 7 runs, 100 loops each)

>>> %timeit movie[movie['title_year'] < 2010]
1.07 ms ± 34.9 µs per loop (mean ± std. dev. of 7 runs, 1000 loops each)
```

See also

- Pandas official documentation on `assert_frame_equal` (http://bit.ly/2u5H5Yl)
- Python official documentation of the `assert` statement (http://bit.ly/2v1YKmY)

Selecting with booleans, integer location, and labels

`Chapter 10`, *Selecting Subsets of Data*, covered a wide range of recipes on selecting different subsets of data through the `.iloc` and `.loc` indexers. Both these indexers select rows and columns simultaneously by either integer location or label. Both these indexers can also do data selection through boolean indexing, even though booleans are not integers and not labels.

Getting ready

In this recipe, we will filter both rows and columns with boolean indexing for both the `.iloc` and `.loc` indexers.

How to do it...

1. Read in the movie dataset, set the index as the title, and then create a boolean Series matching all movies with a content rating of G and an IMDB score less than 4:

```
>>> movie = pd.read_csv('data/movie.csv', index_col='movie_title')
>>> c1 = movie['content_rating'] == 'G'
>>> c2 = movie['imdb_score'] < 4
>>> criteria = c1 & c2
```

2. Let's first pass these criteria to the .loc indexer to filter the rows:

```
>>> movie_loc = movie.loc[criteria]
>>> movie_loc.head()
```

movie_title	color	director_name	num_critic_for_reviews	duration	director_facebook_likes	actor_3_facebook_likes	actor_2_name	actor_1_facebook_likes
The True Story of Puss'N Boots	Color	Jérôme Deschamps	4.0	80.0	0.0	0.0	André Wilms	44.0
Doogal	Color	Dave Borthwick	31.0	77.0	3.0	593.0	Kylie Minogue	787.0
Thomas and the Magic Railroad	Color	Britt Allcroft	47.0	85.0	2.0	402.0	Colm Feore	1000.0
Barney's Great Adventure	Color	Steve Gomer	24.0	76.0	9.0	47.0	Kyla Pratt	595.0
Justin Bieber: Never Say Never	Color	Jon M. Chu	84.0	115.0	209.0	41.0	Sean Kingston	569.0

3. Let's check whether this DataFrame is exactly equal to the one generated directly from the indexing operator:

```
>>> movie_loc.equals(movie[criteria])
True
```

4. Now let's attempt the same boolean indexing with the `.iloc` indexer:

```
>>> movie_iloc = movie.iloc[criteria]
ValueError: iLocation based boolean indexing cannot use an
indexable as a mask
```

5. It turns out that we cannot directly use a Series of booleans because of the index. We can, however, use ndarray of booleans. To extract the array, use the `values` attribute:

```
>>> movie_iloc = movie.iloc[criteria.values]
>>> movie_iloc.equals(movie_loc)
True
```

6. Although not very common, it is possible to do boolean indexing to select particular columns. Here, we select all the columns that have a data type of 64-bit integers:

```
>>> criteria_col = movie.dtypes == np.int64
>>> criteria_col.head()
color                      False
director_name              False
num_critic_for_reviews     False
duration                   False
director_facebook_likes    False
dtype: bool

>>> movie.loc[:, criteria_col].head()
```

movie_title	num_voted_users	cast_total_facebook_likes	movie_facebook_likes
Avatar	886204	4834	33000
Pirates of the Caribbean: At World's End	471220	48350	0
Spectre	275868	11700	85000
The Dark Knight Rises	1144337	106759	164000
Star Wars: Episode VII - The Force Awakens	8	143	0

7. As `criteria_col` is a Series, which always has an index, you must use the underlying ndarray to make it work with `.iloc`. The following produces the same result as step 6.

```
>>> movie.iloc[:, criteria_col.values].head()
```

8. A boolean Series may be used to select rows and then simultaneously select columns with either integers or labels. Remember, you need to put a comma between the row and column selections. Let's keep the row criteria and select `content_rating`, `imdb_score`, `title_year`, and `gross`:

```
>>> cols = ['content_rating', 'imdb_score', 'title_year', 'gross']
>>> movie.loc[criteria, cols].sort_values('imdb_score')
```

movie_title	content_rating	imdb_score	title_year	gross
Justin Bieber: Never Say Never	G	1.6	2011.0	73000942.0
Sunday School Musical	G	2.5	2008.0	NaN
Doogal	G	2.8	2006.0	7382993.0
Barney's Great Adventure	G	2.8	1998.0	11144518.0
The True Story of Puss'N Boots	G	2.9	2009.0	NaN
Thomas and the Magic Railroad	G	3.6	2000.0	15911333.0

9. This same operation may be replicated with `.iloc`, but you need to get the integer location of all the columns:

```
>>> col_index = [movie.columns.get_loc(col) for col in cols]
>>> col_index
[20, 24, 22, 8]

>>> movie.iloc[criteria.values, col_index]
```

How it works...

Boolean indexing may be accomplished with both the `.iloc` and `.loc` indexers with the caveat that `.iloc` cannot be passed a Series but the underlying ndarray. Let's take a look at the one-dimensional ndarray underlying the criteria Series:

```
>>> a = criteria.values
>>> a[:5]
array([False, False, False, False, False], dtype=bool)

>>> len(a), len(criteria)
(4916, 4916)
```

The array is the same length as the Series, which is the same length as the movie DataFrame. The integer location for the boolean array aligns with the integer location of the DataFrame and the filter happens as expected. These arrays also work with the `.loc` operator as well but they are a necessity for `.iloc`.

Steps 6 and 7 show how to filter by columns instead of by rows. The colon, `:`, is needed to indicate the selection of all the rows. The comma following the colon separates the row and column selections. There is actually a much easier way to select columns with integer data types and that is through the `select_dtypes` method.

Steps 8 and 9 show a very common and useful way to do boolean indexing on the row and column selections simultaneously. You simply place a comma between the row and column selections. Step 9 uses a list comprehension to loop through all the desired column names to find their integer location with the index method `get_loc`.

There's more...

It is actually possible to pass arrays and lists of booleans to Series objects that are not the same length as the DataFrame you are doing the indexing on. Let's look at an example of this by selecting the first and third rows, and the first and fourth columns:

```
>>> movie.loc[[True, False, True], [True, False, False, True]]
```

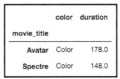

Both of the boolean lists are not the same length as the axis they are indexing. The rest of the rows and columns not explicitly given a boolean value in the lists are dropped.

See also

- Refer to the *Selecting data with both integers and labels* recipe from Chapter 10, *Selecting Subsets of Data*

12
Index Alignment

When multiple Series or DataFrames are combined in some way, each dimension of the data automatically aligns on each axis first before any computation happens. This silent and automatic alignment of axes can cause tremendous confusion for the uninitiated, but it gives great flexibility to the power user. This chapter explores the Index object in-depth before showcasing a variety of recipes that take advantage of its automatic alignment.

In this chapter, we will cover the following topics:

- Examining the Index object
- Producing Cartesian products
- Exploding indexes
- Filling values with unequal indexes
- Appending columns from different DataFrames
- Highlighting the maximum value from each column
- Replicating `idxmax` with method chaining
- Finding the most common maximum

Examining the Index object

Each axis of Series and DataFrames has an Index object that labels the values. There are many different types of Index objects, but they all share the same common behavior. All Index objects, except for the special MultiIndex, are single-dimensional data structures that combine the functionality and implementation of Python sets and NumPy ndarrays.

Getting ready

In this recipe, we will examine the column index of the college dataset and explore much of its functionality.

How to do it...

1. Read in the college dataset, assign for the column index to a variable, and output it:

```
>>> college = pd.read_csv('data/college.csv')
>>> columns = college.columns
>>> columns
Index(['INSTNM', 'CITY', 'STABBR', 'HBCU', ...], dtype='object')
```

2. Use the `values` attribute to access the underlying NumPy array:

```
>>> columns.values
array(['INSTNM', 'CITY', 'STABBR', 'HBCU', ...], dtype=object)
```

3. Select items from the index by integer location with scalars, lists, or slices:

```
>>> columns[5]
'WOMENONLY'

>>> columns[[1,8,10]]
Index(['CITY', 'SATMTMID', 'UGDS'], dtype='object')

>>> columns[-7:-4]
Index(['PPTUG_EF', 'CURROPER', 'PCTPELL'], dtype='object')
```

4. Indexes share many of the same methods as Series and DataFrames:

```
>>> columns.min(), columns.max(), columns.isnull().sum()
('CITY', 'WOMENONLY', 0)
```

5. Use basic arithmetic and comparison operators directly on `Index` objects:

```
>>> columns + '_A'
Index(['INSTNM_A', 'CITY_A', 'STABBR_A', 'HBCU_A', ...],
dtype='object')

>>> columns > 'G'
array([ True, False,  True,  True, ...], dtype=bool)
```

6. Trying to change an Index value directly after its creation fails. Indexes are immutable objects:

```
>>> columns[1] = 'city'
TypeError: Index does not support mutable operations
```

How it works...

As you can see from many of the Index object operations, it appears to have quite a bit in common with both Series and `ndarrays`. One of the biggest differences comes in step 6. Indexes are immutable and their values cannot be changed once created.

There's more...

Indexes support the set operations, union, intersection, difference, and symmetric difference:

```
>>> c1 = columns[:4]
>>> c1
Index(['INSTNM', 'CITY', 'STABBR', 'HBCU'], dtype='object')

>>> c2 = columns[2:6]
>>> c2
Index(['STABBR', 'HBCU', 'MENONLY'], dtype='object')

>>> c1.union(c2) # or `c1 | c2`
Index(['CITY', 'HBCU', 'INSTNM', 'MENONLY', 'RELAFFIL', 'STABBR'],
dtype='object')

>>> c1.symmetric_difference(c2) # or `c1 ^ c2`
Index(['CITY', 'INSTNM', 'MENONLY'], dtype='object')
```

Indexes share some of the same operations as Python sets. Indexes are similar to Python sets in another important way. They are (usually) implemented using hash tables, which make for extremely fast access when selecting rows or columns from a DataFrame. As they are implemented using hash tables, the values for the Index object need to be immutable such as a string, integer, or tuple just like the keys in a Python dictionary.

Indexes support duplicate values, and if there happens to be a duplicate in any Index, then a hash table can no longer be used for its implementation, and object access becomes much slower.

See also

- Pandas official documentation of Index (http://bit.ly/2upfgtr)

Producing Cartesian products

Whenever two Series or DataFrames operate with another Series or DataFrame, the indexes (both the row index and column index) of each object align first before any operation begins. This index alignment happens silently and can be very surprising for those new to pandas. This alignment always creates a Cartesian product between the indexes unless the indexes are identical.

A Cartesian product is a mathematical term that usually appears in set theory. A Cartesian product between two sets is all the combinations of pairs of both sets. For example, the 52 cards in a standard playing card deck represent a Cartesian product between the 13 ranks (A, 2, 3,..., Q, K) and the four suits.

Getting ready

Producing a Cartesian product isn't always the intended outcome, but it's extremely important to be aware of how and when it occurs to avoid unintended consequences. In this recipe, two Series with overlapping but non-identical indexes are added together, yielding a surprising result.

How to do it...

Follow these steps to create a Cartesian product:

1. Construct two Series that have indexes that are different but contain some of the same values:

```
>>> s1 = pd.Series(index=list('aaab'), data=np.arange(4))
>>> s1
a    0
a    1
a    2
b    3
dtype: int64

>>> s2 = pd.Series(index=list('cababb'), data=np.arange(6))
>>> s2
c    0
a    1
b    2
a    3
```

```
b    4
b    5
dtype: int64
```

2. Add the two Series together to produce a Cartesian product:

```
>>> s1 + s2
a    1.0
a    3.0
a    2.0
a    4.0
a    3.0
a    5.0
b    5.0
b    7.0
b    8.0
c    NaN
dtype: float64
```

How it works...

Each Series was created with the class constructor which accepts a wide variety of inputs with the simplest being a sequence of values for each of the parameters index and data.

Mathematical Cartesian products are slightly different from the outcome of operating on two pandas objects. Each a label in s1 pairs up with each a label in s2. This pairing produces six a labels, three b labels, and one c label in the resulting Series. A Cartesian product happens between all identical index labels.

As the element with label c is unique to Series s2, pandas defaults its value to missing, as there is no label for it to align to in s1. Pandas defaults to a missing value whenever an index label is unique to one object. This has the unfortunate consequence of changing the data type of the Series to a float, whereas each Series had only integers as values. This occurred because of NumPy's missing value object; np.nan only exists for floats but not for integers. Series and DataFrame columns must have homogeneous numeric data types; therefore, each value was converted to a float. This makes very little difference for this small dataset, but for larger datasets, this can have a significant memory impact.

There's more...

An exception to the preceding example takes place when the indexes contain the same exact elements in the same order. When this occurs, a Cartesian product does not take place, and the indexes instead align by their position. Notice here that each element aligned exactly by position and that the data type remained an integer:

```
>>> s1 = pd.Series(index=list('aaabb'), data=np.arange(5))
>>> s2 = pd.Series(index=list('aaabb'), data=np.arange(5))
>>> s1 + s2
a    0
a    2
a    4
b    6
b    8
dtype: int64
```

If the elements of the index are identical, but the order is different between the Series, a Cartesian product occurs. Let's change the order of the index in s2 and rerun the same operation:

```
>>> s1 = pd.Series(index=list('aaabb'), data=np.arange(5))
>>> s2 = pd.Series(index=list('bbaaa'), data=np.arange(5))
>>> s1 + s2
a    2
a    3
a    4
a    3
a    4
a    5
a    4
a    5
a    6
b    3
b    4
b    4
b    5
dtype: int64
```

It is quite interesting that pandas has two drastically different outcomes for this same operation. If a Cartesian product was the only choice for pandas, then something as simple as adding DataFrame columns together would explode the number of elements returned.

In this recipe, each Series had a different number of elements. Typically, array-like data structures in Python and other languages do not allow operations to take place when the operating dimensions do not contain the same number of elements. Pandas allows this to happen by aligning the indexes first before completing the operation.

Exploding indexes

The previous recipe walked through a trivial example of two small Series being added together with unequal indexes. This problem can produce comically incorrect results when dealing with larger data.

Getting ready

In this recipe, we add two larger Series that have indexes with only a few unique values but in different orders. The result will explode the number of values in the indexes.

How to do it...

1. Read in the employee data and set the index equal to the race column:

```
>>> employee = pd.read_csv('data/employee.csv', index_col='RACE')
>>> employee.head()
```

RACE	UNIQUE_ID	POSITION_TITLE	DEPARTMENT	BASE_SALARY	EMPLOYMENT_TYPE	GENDER	EMPLOYMENT_STATUS	HIRE_DATE
Hispanic/Latino	0	ASSISTANT DIRECTOR (EX LVL)	Municipal Courts Department	121862.0	Full Time	Female	Active	2006-06-12
Hispanic/Latino	1	LIBRARY ASSISTANT	Library	26125.0	Full Time	Female	Active	2000-07-19
White	2	POLICE OFFICER	Houston Police Department-HPD	45279.0	Full Time	Male	Active	2015-02-03
White	3	ENGINEER/OPERATOR	Houston Fire Department (HFD)	63166.0	Full Time	Male	Active	1982-02-08
White	4	ELECTRICIAN	General Services Department	56347.0	Full Time	Male	Active	1989-06-19

2. Select the BASE_SALARY column as two different Series. Check to see whether this operation actually did create two new objects:

```
>>> salary1 = employee['BASE_SALARY']
>>> salary2 = employee['BASE_SALARY']
>>> salary1 is salary2
True
```

3. The salary1 and salary2 variables are actually referring to the same object. This means that any change to one will change the other. To ensure that you receive a brand new copy of the data, use the copy method:

```
>>> salary1 = employee['BASE_SALARY'].copy()
>>> salary2 = employee['BASE_SALARY'].copy()
>>> salary1 is salary2
False
```

4. Let's change the order of the index for one of the Series by sorting it:

```
>>> salary1 = salary1.sort_index()
>>> salary1.head()
RACE
American Indian or Alaskan Native    78355.0
American Indian or Alaskan Native    81239.0
American Indian or Alaskan Native    60347.0
American Indian or Alaskan Native    68299.0
American Indian or Alaskan Native    26125.0
Name: BASE_SALARY, dtype: float64

>>> salary2.head()
RACE
Hispanic/Latino    121862.0
Hispanic/Latino     26125.0
```

```
White                   45279.0
White                   63166.0
White                   56347.0
Name: BASE_SALARY, dtype: float64
```

5. Let's add these `salary` Series together:

```
>>> salary_add = salary1 + salary2
>>> salary_add.head()
RACE
American Indian or Alaskan Native    138702.0
American Indian or Alaskan Native    156710.0
American Indian or Alaskan Native    176891.0
American Indian or Alaskan Native    159594.0
American Indian or Alaskan Native    127734.0
Name: BASE_SALARY, dtype: float64
```

6. The operation completed successfully. Let's create one more Series of `salary1` added to itself and then output the lengths of each Series. We just exploded the index from 2,000 values to more than 1 million:

```
>>> salary_add1 = salary1 + salary1
>>> len(salary1), len(salary2), len(salary_add), len(salary_add1)
(2000, 2000, 1175424, 2000)
```

How it works...

Step 2 appears at first to create two unique objects but in fact, it creates a single object that is referred to by two different variable names. The expression `employee['BASE_SALARY']`, technically creates a **view**, and not a brand new copy. This is verified with the `is` operator.

> In pandas, a view is not a new object but just a reference to another object, usually some subset of a DataFrame. This shared object can be a cause for many issues.

To ensure that both variables reference completely different objects, we use the `copy` Series method and again verify that they are different objects with the `is` operator. Step 4 uses the `sort_index` method to sort the Series by race. Step 5 adds these different Series together to produce some result. By just inspecting the head, it's still not clear what has been produced.

Step 6 adds `salary1` to itself to show a comparison between the two different Series additions. The length of all the Series in this recipe are output and we clearly see that `series_add` has now exploded to over one million values. A Cartesian product took place for each unique value in the index because the indexes were not exactly the same. This recipe dramatically shows how much of an impact the index can have when combining multiple Series or DataFrames.

There's more...

We can verify the number of values of `salary_add` by doing a little mathematics. As a Cartesian product takes place between all of the same index values, we can sum the square of their individual counts. Even missing values in the index produce Cartesian products with themselves:

```
>>> index_vc = salary1.index.value_counts(dropna=False)
>>> index_vc
Black or African American          700
White                              665
Hispanic/Latino                    480
Asian/Pacific Islander             107
NaN                                 35
American Indian or Alaskan Native   11
Others                               2
Name: RACE, dtype: int64

>>> index_vc.pow(2).sum()
1175424
```

Filling values with unequal indexes

When two Series are added together using the plus operator and one of the index labels does not appear in the other, the resulting value is always missing. Pandas offers the `add` method, which provides an option to fill the missing value.

Getting ready

In this recipe, we add together multiple Series from the `baseball` dataset with unequal indexes using the `fill_value` parameter of the `add` method to ensure that there are no missing values in the result.

How to do it...

1. Read in the three `baseball` datasets and set the index as `playerID`:

```
>>> baseball_14 = pd.read_csv('data/baseball14.csv',
                              index_col='playerID')
>>> baseball_15 = pd.read_csv('data/baseball15.csv',
                              index_col='playerID')
>>> baseball_16 = pd.read_csv('data/baseball16.csv',
                              index_col='playerID')
>>> baseball_14.head()
```

playerID	yearID	stint	teamID	lgID	G	AB	R	H	2B	3B	...	RBI	SB	CS	BB	SO	IBB	HBP	SH	SF	GIDP
altuvjo01	2014	1	HOU	AL	158	660	85	225	47	3	...	59.0	56.0	9.0	36	53.0	7.0	5.0	1.0	5.0	20.0
cartech02	2014	1	HOU	AL	145	507	68	115	21	1	...	88.0	5.0	2.0	56	182.0	6.0	5.0	0.0	4.0	12.0
castrja01	2014	1	HOU	AL	126	465	43	103	21	2	...	56.0	1.0	0.0	34	151.0	1.0	9.0	1.0	3.0	11.0
corpoca01	2014	1	HOU	AL	55	170	22	40	6	0	...	19.0	0.0	0.0	14	37.0	0.0	3.0	1.0	2.0	3.0
dominma01	2014	1	HOU	AL	157	564	51	121	17	0	...	57.0	0.0	1.0	29	125.0	2.0	5.0	2.0	7.0	23.0

2. Use the index method `difference` to discover which index labels are in `baseball_14` and not in `baseball_15`, and vice versa:

```
>>> baseball_14.index.difference(baseball_15.index)
Index(['corpoca01', 'dominma01', 'fowlede01', 'grossro01',
       'guzmaje01', 'hoeslj01', 'krausma01', 'preslal01',
       'singljo02'], dtype='object', name='playerID')

>>> baseball_14.index.difference(baseball_16.index)
Index(['congeha01', 'correca01', 'gattiev01', 'gomezca01',
       'lowrije01', 'rasmuco01', 'tuckepr01', 'valbulu01'],
       dtype='object', name='playerID')
```

3. There are quite a few players unique to each index. Let's find out how many hits each player has in total over the three-year period. The H column contains the number of hits:

```
>>> hits_14 = baseball_14['H']
>>> hits_15 = baseball_15['H']
>>> hits_16 = baseball_16['H']
>>> hits_14.head()
playerID
altuvjo01    225
cartech02    115
castrja01    103
corpoca01     40
dominma01    121
Name: H, dtype: int64
```

4. Let's first add together two Series using the plus operator:

```
>>> (hits_14 + hits_15).head()
playerID
altuvjo01    425.0
cartech02    193.0
castrja01    174.0
congeha01      NaN
corpoca01      NaN
Name: H, dtype: float64
```

5. Even though players `congeha01` and `corpoca01` have recorded hits for 2015, their result is missing. Let's use the `add` method and its parameter, `fill_value`, to avoid missing values:

```
>>> hits_14.add(hits_15, fill_value=0).head()
playerID
altuvjo01    425.0
cartech02    193.0
castrja01    174.0
congeha01     46.0
corpoca01     40.0
Name: H, dtype: float64
```

6. We add hits from 2016 by chaining the `add` method once more:

```
>>> hits_total = hits_14.add(hits_15, fill_value=0) \
                        .add(hits_16, fill_value=0)
>>> hits_total.head()
playerID
altuvjo01    641.0
bregmal01     53.0
cartech02    193.0
castrja01    243.0
congeha01     46.0
Name: H, dtype: float64
```

7. Check for missing values in the result:

```
>>> hits_total.hasnans
False
```

How it works...

The `add` method works similarly to the plus operator but allows for more flexibility by providing the `fill_value` parameter to take the place of a non-matching index. In this problem, it makes sense to default the non-matching index value to 0, but you could have used any other number.

There will be occasions when each Series contains index labels that correspond to missing values. In this specific instance, when the two Series are added, the index label will still correspond to a missing value regardless if the `fill_value` parameter is used. To clarify this, take a look at the following example where the index label `a` corresponds to a missing value in each Series:

```
>>> s = pd.Series(index=['a', 'b', 'c', 'd'],
                  data=[np.nan, 3, np.nan, 1])
>>> s
a    NaN
b    3.0
c    NaN
d    1.0
dtype: float64

>>> s1 = pd.Series(index=['a', 'b', 'c'], data=[np.nan, 6, 10])
>>> s1
a    NaN
b    6.0
c    10.0
```

```
dtype: float64

>>> s.add(s1, fill_value=5)
a      NaN
b      9.0
c     15.0
d      6.0
dtype: float64
```

There's more...

This recipe shows how to add Series with only a single index together. It is also entirely possible to add DataFrames together. Adding DataFrames together will align both the index and columns before computation and yield missing values for non-matching indexes. Let's start by selecting a few of the columns from the 2014 baseball dataset.

```
>>> df_14 = baseball_14[['G','AB', 'R', 'H']]
>>> df_14.head()
```

	G	AB	R	H
playerID				
altuvjo01	158	660	85	225
cartech02	145	507	68	115
castrja01	126	465	43	103
corpoca01	55	170	22	40
dominma01	157	564	51	121

Let's also select a few of the same and a few different columns from the 2015 baseball dataset:

```
>>> df_15 = baseball_15[['AB', 'R', 'H', 'HR']]
>>> df_15.head()
```

	AB	R	H	HR
playerID				
altuvjo01	638	86	200	15
cartech02	391	50	78	24
castrja01	337	38	71	11
congeha01	201	25	46	11
correca01	387	52	108	22

Adding the two DataFrames together create missing values wherever rows or column labels cannot align. Use the `style` attribute to access the `highlight_null` method to easily see where the missing values are:

```
>>> (df_14 + df_15).head(10).style.highlight_null('yellow')
```

	AB	G	H	HR	R
playerID					
altuvjo01	1298	nan	425	nan	171
cartech02	898	nan	193	nan	118
castrja01	802	nan	174	nan	81
congeha01	nan	nan	nan	nan	nan
corpoca01	nan	nan	nan	nan	nan
correca01	nan	nan	nan	nan	nan
dominma01	nan	nan	nan	nan	nan
fowlede01	nan	nan	nan	nan	nan
gattiev01	nan	nan	nan	nan	nan
gomezca01	nan	nan	nan	nan	nan

Only the rows with `playerID` appearing in both DataFrames will be non-missing. Similarly, the columns AB, H, and R are the only ones that appear in both DataFrames. Even if we use the `add` method with the `fill_value` parameter specified, we still have missing values. This is because some combinations of rows and columns never existed in our input data. For example, the intersection of `playerID` *congeha01* and column G. He only appeared in the 2015 dataset that did not have the G column. Therefore, no value was filled with it:

```
>>> df_14.add(df_15, fill_value=0).head(10) \
        .style.highlight_null('yellow')
```

	AB	G	H	HR	R
playerID					
altuvjo01	1298	158	425	15	171
cartech02	898	145	193	24	118
castrja01	802	126	174	11	81
congeha01	201	nan	46	11	25
corpoca01	170	55	40	nan	22
correca01	387	nan	108	22	52
dominma01	564	157	121	nan	51
fowlede01	434	116	120	nan	61
gattiev01	566	nan	139	27	66
gomezca01	149	nan	36	4	19

Appending columns from different DataFrames

All DataFrames can add new columns to themselves. However, as usual, whenever a DataFrame is adding a new column from another DataFrame or Series, the indexes align first before the new column is created.

Getting ready

This recipe uses the `employee` dataset to append a new column containing the maximum salary of that employee's department.

How to do it...

1. Import the `employee` data and select the `DEPARTMENT` and `BASE_SALARY` columns in a new DataFrame:

```
>>> employee = pd.read_csv('data/employee.csv')
>>> dept_sal = employee[['DEPARTMENT', 'BASE_SALARY']]
```

2. Sort this smaller DataFrame by salary within each department:

```
>>> dept_sal = dept_sal.sort_values(['DEPARTMENT', 'BASE_SALARY'],
                                    ascending=[True, False])
```

3. Use the `drop_duplicates` method to keep the first row of each `DEPARTMENT`:

```
>>> max_dept_sal = dept_sal.drop_duplicates(subset='DEPARTMENT')
>>> max_dept_sal.head()
```

	DEPARTMENT	BASE_SALARY
1494	Admn. & Regulatory Affairs	140416.0
149	City Controller's Office	64251.0
236	City Council	100000.0
647	Convention and Entertainment	38397.0
1500	Dept of Neighborhoods (DON)	89221.0

4. Put the `DEPARTMENT` column into the index for each DataFrames:

```
>>> max_dept_sal = max_dept_sal.set_index('DEPARTMENT')
>>> employee = employee.set_index('DEPARTMENT')
```

5. Now that the indexes contain matching values, we can append a new column to the `employee` DataFrame:

```
>>> employee['MAX_DEPT_SALARY'] = max_dept_sal['BASE_SALARY']
>>> employee.head()
```

	UNIQUE_ID	POSITION_TITLE	BASE_SALARY	...	HIRE_DATE	JOB_DATE	MAX_DEPT_SALARY
DEPARTMENT							
Municipal Courts Department	0	ASSISTANT DIRECTOR (EX LVL)	121862.0	...	2006-06-12	2012-10-13	121862.0
Library	1	LIBRARY ASSISTANT	26125.0	...	2000-07-19	2010-09-18	107763.0
Houston Police Department-HPD	2	POLICE OFFICER	45279.0	...	2015-02-03	2015-02-03	199596.0
Houston Fire Department (HFD)	3	ENGINEER/OPERATOR	63166.0	...	1982-02-08	1991-05-25	210588.0
General Services Department	4	ELECTRICIAN	56347.0	...	1989-06-19	1994-10-22	89194.0

6. We can validate our results with the `query` method to check whether there exist any rows where BASE_SALARY is greater than MAX_DEPT_SALARY:

```
>>> employee.query('BASE_SALARY > MAX_DEPT_SALARY')
```

	UNIQUE_ID	POSITION_TITLE	BASE_SALARY	...	HIRE_DATE	JOB_DATE	MAX_DEPT_SALARY
DEPARTMENT							

0 rows × 10 columns

How it works...

Steps 2 and 3 find the maximum salary for each department. For automatic index alignment to work properly, we set each DataFrame index as the department. Step 5 works because each row index from the left DataFrame; `employee` aligns with one and only one index from the right DataFrame, `max_dept_sal`. If `max_dept_sal` had repeats of any departments in its index, then the operation would fail.

For instance, let's see what happens when we use a DataFrame on the right-hand side of the equality that has repeated index values. We use the `sample` DataFrame method to randomly choose ten rows without replacement:

```
>>> np.random.seed(1234)
>>> random_salary = dept_sal.sample(n=10).set_index('DEPARTMENT')
>>> random_salary
```

	BASE_SALARY
DEPARTMENT	
Public Works & Engineering-PWE	50586.0
Houston Police Department-HPD	66614.0
Houston Police Department-HPD	66614.0
Housing and Community Devp.	78853.0
Houston Police Department-HPD	66614.0
Parks & Recreation	NaN
Public Works & Engineering-PWE	37211.0
Public Works & Engineering-PWE	54683.0
Human Resources Dept.	58474.0
Health & Human Services	47050.0

Notice how there are several repeated departments in the index. Now when we attempt to create a new column, an error is raised alerting us that there are duplicates. At least one index label in the `employee` DataFrame is joining with two or more index labels from `random_salary`:

```
>>> employee['RANDOM_SALARY'] = random_salary['BASE_SALARY']
ValueError: cannot reindex from a duplicate axis
```

There's more...

Not all indexes on the left-hand side of the equal sign need to have a match, but at most can have one. If there is nothing for the left DataFrame index to align to, the resulting value will be missing. Let's create an example where this happens. We will use only the first three rows of the `max_dept_sal` Series to create a new column:

```
>>> employee['MAX_SALARY2'] = max_dept_sal['BASE_SALARY'].head(3)
>>> employee.MAX_SALARY2.value_counts()
140416.0    29
100000.0    11
64251.0      5
Name: MAX_SALARY2, dtype: int64


>>> employee.MAX_SALARY2.isnull().mean()
```

```
.9775
```

The operation completed successfully but filled in salaries for only three of the departments. All the other departments that did not appear in the first three rows of the `max_dept_sal` Series resulted in a missing value.

Highlighting the maximum value from each column

The `college` dataset has many numeric columns describing different metrics about each school. Many people are interested in schools that perform the best for certain metrics.

Getting ready

This recipe discovers the school that has the maximum value for each numeric column and styles the DataFrame in order to highlight the information so that it is easily consumed by a user.

How to do it...

1. Read the college dataset with the institution name as the index:

```
>>> college = pd.read_csv('data/college.csv', index_col='INSTNM')
>>> college.dtypes
CITY                    object
STABBR                  object
HBCU                    float64
MENONLY                 float64
                         ...
PCTFLOAN                float64
UG25ABV                 float64
MD_EARN_WNE_P10         object
GRAD_DEBT_MDN_SUPP      object
Length: 26, dtype: object
```

2. All the other columns besides `CITY` and `STABBR` appear to be numeric. Examining the data types from the preceding step reveals unexpectedly that the `MD_EARN_WNE_P10` and `GRAD_DEBT_MDN_SUPP` columns are of type object and not numeric. To help get a better idea of what kind of values are in these columns, let's examine their first value:

```
>>> college.MD_EARN_WNE_P10.iloc[0]
'30300'

>>> college.GRAD_DEBT_MDN_SUPP.iloc[0]
'33888'
```

3. These values are strings but we would like them to be numeric. This means that there are likely to be non-numeric characters that appear elsewhere in the Series. One way to check for this is to sort these columns in descending order and examine the first few rows:

```
>>> college.MD_EARN_WNE_P10.sort_values(ascending=False).head()
INSTNM
Sharon Regional Health System School of Nursing
PrivacySuppressed
Northcoast Medical Training Academy
PrivacySuppressed
Success Schools
PrivacySuppressed
Louisiana Culinary Institute
PrivacySuppressed
Bais Medrash Toras Chesed
PrivacySuppressed
Name: MD_EARN_WNE_P10, dtype: object
```

4. The culprit appears to be that some schools have privacy concerns about these two columns of data. To force these columns to be numeric, use the pandas function `to_numeric`:

```
>>> cols = ['MD_EARN_WNE_P10', 'GRAD_DEBT_MDN_SUPP']
>>> for col in cols:
        college[col] = pd.to_numeric(college[col], errors='coerce')

>>> college.dtypes.loc[cols]
MD_EARN_WNE_P10        float64
GRAD_DEBT_MDN_SUPP     float64
dtype: object
```

---

5. Use the `select_dtypes` method to filter for only numeric columns. This will exclude `STABBR` and `CITY` columns, where a maximum value doesn't make sense with this problem:

```
>>> college_n = college.select_dtypes(include=[np.number])
>>> college_n.head()
```

INSTNM	HBCU	MENONLY	WOMENONLY	...	UG25ABV	MD_EARN_WNE_P10	GRAD_DEBT_MDN_SUPP
Alabama A & M University	1.0	0.0	0.0	...	0.1049	30300.0	33888.0
University of Alabama at Birmingham	0.0	0.0	0.0	...	0.2422	39700.0	21941.5
Amridge University	0.0	0.0	0.0	...	0.8540	40100.0	23370.0
University of Alabama in Huntsville	0.0	0.0	0.0	...	0.2640	45500.0	24097.0
Alabama State University	1.0	0.0	0.0	...	0.1270	26600.0	33118.5

6. By utilizing the data dictionary, there are several columns that have only binary (0/1) values that will not provide useful information. To programmatically find these columns, we can create boolean Series and find all the columns that have two unique values with the `nunique` method:

```
>>> criteria = college_n.nunique() == 2
>>> criteria.head()
HBCU          True
MENONLY       True
WOMENONLY     True
RELAFFIL      True
SATVRMID      False
dtype: bool
```

7. Pass this boolean Series to the indexing operator of the columns index object and create a list of the binary columns:

```
>>> binary_cols = college_n.columns[criteria].tolist()
>>> binary_cols
['HBCU', 'MENONLY', 'WOMENONLY', 'RELAFFIL', 'DISTANCEONLY',
'CURROPER']
```

8. Remove the binary columns with the `drop` method:

```
>>> college_n2 = college_n.drop(labels=binary_cols, axis='columns')
>>> college_n2.head()
```

	SATVRMID	SATMTMID	UGDS	...	UG25ABV	MD_EARN_WNE_P10	GRAD_DEBT_MDN_SUPP
INSTNM							
Alabama A & M University	424.0	420.0	4206.0	...	0.1049	30300.0	33888.0
University of Alabama at Birmingham	570.0	565.0	11383.0	...	0.2422	39700.0	21941.5
Amridge University	NaN	NaN	291.0	...	0.8540	40100.0	23370.0
University of Alabama in Huntsville	595.0	590.0	5451.0	...	0.2640	45500.0	24097.0
Alabama State University	425.0	430.0	4811.0	...	0.1270	26600.0	33118.5

9. Use the `idxmax` method to find the index label of the maximum value for each column:

```
>>> max_cols = college_n2.idxmax()
>>> max_cols
SATVRMID                        California Institute of Technology
SATMTMID                        California Institute of Technology
UGDS                                 University of Phoenix-Arizona
UGDS_WHITE                 Mr Leon's School of Hair Design-Moscow
                                          ...
PCTFLOAN                                    ABC Beauty College Inc
UG25ABV                          Dongguk University-Los Angeles
MD_EARN_WNE_P10                     Medical College of Wisconsin
GRAD_DEBT_MDN_SUPP     Southwest University of Visual Arts-Tucson
Length: 18, dtype: object
```

10. Call the `unique` method on the `max_cols` Series. This returns an `ndarray` of the unique column names:

```
>>> unique_max_cols = max_cols.unique()
>>> unique_max_cols[:5]
array(['California Institute of Technology',
       'University of Phoenix-Arizona',
       "Mr Leon's School of Hair Design-Moscow",
       'Velvatex College of Beauty Culture',
       'Thunderbird School of Global Management'], dtype=object)
```

11. Use the values of `max_cols` to select only the rows that have schools with a maximum value and then use the `style` attribute to highlight these values:

```
>>> college_n2.loc[unique_max_cols].style.highlight_max()
```

INSTNM	SATVRMID	SATMTMID	UGDS	UGDS_WHITE	UGDS_BLACK	UGDS_HISP	UGDS_ASIAN
California Institute of Technology	765	785	983	0.2787	0.0153	0.1221	0.4385
University of Phoenix-Arizona	nan	nan	151558	0.3098	0.1555	0.076	0.0082
Mr Leon's School of Hair Design-Moscow	nan	nan	16	1	0	0	0
Velvatex College of Beauty Culture	nan	nan	25	0	1	0	0
Thunderbird School of Global Management	nan	nan	1	0	0	1	0
Cosmopolitan Beauty and Tech School	nan	nan	110	0.0091	0	0.0182	0.9727

How it works...

The `idxmax` method is very powerful and becomes quite useful when the index is meaningfully labeled. It was unexpected that both `MD_EARN_WNE_P10` and `GRAD_DEBT_MDN_SUPP` were of `object` data type. When importing, pandas coerces all numeric values of columns to strings if the column contains at least one string.

By examining a specific column value in step 2, we were able to see clearly that we had strings in these columns. In step 3, we sort in descending order as numeric characters appear first. This elevates all alphabetical values to the top of the Series. We uncover the `PrivacySuppressed` string causing havoc. Pandas has the ability to force all strings that contain only numeric characters to actual numeric data types with the `to_numeric` function. To override the default behavior of raising an error when `to_numeric` encounters a string that cannot be converted, you must pass *coerce* to the `errors` parameter. This forces all non-numeric character strings to become missing values (`np.nan`).

Several columns don't have useful or meaningful maximum values. They were removed in step 4 through step 6. The `select_dtypes` can be extremely useful for very wide DataFrames with lots of columns.

In step 7, `idxmax` iterates through all the columns to find the index of the maximum value for each column. It outputs the results as a Series. The school with both the highest SAT math and verbal scores is California Institute of Technology. Dongguk University Los Angeles has the highest number of students older than 25.

Although the information provided by `idxmax` is nice, it does not yield the corresponding maximum value. To do this, we gather all the unique school names from the values of the `max_cols` Series.

Finally, in step 8, we use the `.loc` indexer to select rows based on the index label, which we made as school names in the first step. This filters for only schools that have a maximum value. DataFrames have an experimental `style` attribute that itself has some methods to alter the appearance of the displayed DataFrame. Highlighting the maximum value makes the result much clearer.

There's more...

By default, the `highlight_max` method highlights the maximum value of each column. We can use the `axis` parameter to highlight the maximum value of each row instead. Here, we select just the race percentage columns of the `college` dataset and highlight the race with the highest percentage for each school:

```
>>> college = pd.read_csv('data/college.csv', index_col='INSTNM')
>>> college_ugds = college.filter(like='UGDS_').head()
>>> college_ugds.style.highlight_max(axis='columns')
```

INSTNM	UGDS_WHITE	UGDS_BLACK	UGDS_HISP	UGDS_ASIAN	UGDS_AIAN	UGDS_NHPI	UGDS_2MOR	UGDS_NRA	UGDS_UNKN
Alabama A & M University	0.0333	0.9353	0.0055	0.0019	0.0024	0.0019	0	0.0059	0.0138
University of Alabama at Birmingham	0.5922	0.26	0.0283	0.0518	0.0022	0.0007	0.0368	0.0179	0.01
Amridge University	0.299	0.4192	0.0069	0.0034	0	0	0	0	0.2715
University of Alabama in Huntsville	0.6988	0.1255	0.0382	0.0376	0.0143	0.0002	0.0172	0.0332	0.035
Alabama State University	0.0158	0.9208	0.0121	0.0019	0.001	0.0006	0.0098	0.0243	0.0137

Attempting to apply a style on a large DataFrame can cause Jupyter to crash, which is why the style was only applied to the head of the DataFrame.

See also

- Pandas official documentation on Dataframe *Styling* (`http://bit.ly/2hsZkVK`)

Replicating idxmax with method chaining

It can be a good exercise to attempt an implementation of a built-in DataFrame method on your own. This type of replication can give you a deeper understanding of other pandas methods that you normally wouldn't have come across. `idxmax` is a challenging method to replicate using only the methods covered thus far in the book.

Getting ready

This recipe slowly chains together basic methods to eventually find all the row index values that contain a maximum column value.

How to do it...

1. Load in the college dataset and execute the same operations as the previous recipe to get only the numeric columns that are of interest:

```
>>> college = pd.read_csv('data/college.csv', index_col='INSTNM')
>>> cols = ['MD_EARN_WNE_P10', 'GRAD_DEBT_MDN_SUPP']

>>> for col in cols:
        college[col] = pd.to_numeric(college[col], errors='coerce')

>>> college_n = college.select_dtypes(include=[np.number])
>>> criteria = college_n.nunique() == 2
>>> binary_cols = college_n.columns[criteria].tolist()
>>> college_n = college_n.drop(labels=binary_cols, axis='columns')
```

2. Find the maximum of each column with the `max` method:

```
>>> college_n.max().head()
SATVRMID              765.0
SATMTMID              785.0
UGDS              151558.0
UGDS_WHITE             1.0
UGDS_BLACK             1.0
dtype: float64
```

3. Use the `eq` DataFrame method to test each value with its column `max`. By default, the `eq` method aligns the columns of the column DataFrame with the labels of the passed Series index:

```
>>> college_n.eq(college_n.max()).head()
```

INSTNM	SATVRMID	SATMTMID	UGDS	UGDS_WHITE	UGDS_BLACK	UGDS_HISP	UGDS_ASIAN	UGDS_AIAN	UGDS_NHPI	UGDS_2MOR
Alabama A & M University	False	False	False	False	False	False	False	False	False	False
University of Alabama at Birmingham	False	False	False	False	False	False	False	False	False	False
Amridge University	False	False	False	False	False	False	False	False	False	False
University of Alabama in Huntsville	False	False	False	False	False	False	False	False	False	False
Alabama State University	False	False	False	False	False	False	False	False	False	False

4. All the rows in this DataFrame that have at least one `True` value must contain a column maximum. Let's use the `any` method to find all such rows that have at least one `True` value:

```
>>> has_row_max = college_n.eq(college_n.max()).any(axis='columns')
>>> has_row_max.head()
INSTNM
Alabama A & M University                    False
University of Alabama at Birmingham         False
Amridge University                          False
University of Alabama in Huntsville         False
Alabama State University                    False
dtype: bool
```

5. There are only 18 columns, which means that there should only be at most 18 `True` values in `has_row_max`. Let's find out how many there actually are:

```
>>> college_n.shape
(7535, 18)

>>> has_row_max.sum()
401
```

6. This was a bit unexpected, but it turns out that there are columns with many rows that equal the maximum value. This is common with many of the percentage columns that have a maximum of 1. `idxmax` returns the first occurrence of the maximum value. Let's back up a bit, remove the `any` method, and look at the output from step 3. Let's run the `cumsum` method instead to accumulate all the `True` values. The first and last three rows are shown:

```
>>> college_n.eq(college_n.max()).cumsum()
```

INSTNM	SATVRMID	SATMTMID	UGDS	UGDS_WHITE	UGDS_BLACK	UGDS_HISP	UGDS_ASIAN	UGDS_AIAN	UGDS_NHPI	UGDS_2MOR
Alabama A & M University	0	0	0	0	0	0	0	0	0	0
University of Alabama at Birmingham	0	0	0	0	0	0	0	0	0	0
Amridge University	0	0	0	0	0	0	0	0	0	0
...	...	...	...	...	...	...	...	...	...	...
National Personal Training Institute of Cleveland	1	1	1	109	28	136	1	2	1	1
Bay Area Medical Academy - San Jose Satellite Location	1	1	1	109	28	136	1	2	1	1
Excel Learning Center-San Antonio South	1	1	1	109	28	136	1	2	1	1

7535 rows × 18 columns

7. Some columns have one unique maximum like `SATVRMID` and `SATMTMID`, while others like `UGDS_WHITE` have many. 109 schools have 100% of their undergraduates as white. If we chain the `cumsum` method one more time, the value 1 would only appear once in each column and it would be the first occurrence of the maximum:

```
>>> college_n.eq(college_n.max()).cumsum().cumsum()
```

INSTNM	SATVRMID	SATMTMID	UGDS	UGDS_WHITE	UGDS_BLACK	UGDS_HISP	UGDS_ASIAN	UGDS_AIAN	UGDS_NHPI	UGDS_2MOR	UGDS_NRA
Alabama A & M University	0	0	0	0	0	0	0	0	0	0	0
University of Alabama at Birmingham	0	0	0	0	0	0	0	0	0	0	0
Amridge University	0	0	0	0	0	0	0	0	0	0	0
...	...	...	...	...	...	...	...	...	...	...	...
National Personal Training Institute of Cleveland	7307	7307	417	379968	73163	341375	985	11386	3318	5058	1078
Bay Area Medical Academy - San Jose Satellite Location	7308	7308	418	380077	73191	341511	986	11388	3319	5059	1079
Excel Learning Center-San Antonio South	7309	7309	419	380186	73219	341647	987	11390	3320	5060	1080

8. We can now test the equality of each value against 1 with the `eq` method and then use the `any` method to find rows that have at least one `True` value:

```
>>> has_row_max2 = college_n.eq(college_n.max()) \
                            .cumsum() \
                            .cumsum() \
                            .eq(1) \
                            .any(axis='columns')
>>> has_row_max2.head()
INSTNM
Alabama A & M University                    False
University of Alabama at Birmingham         False
Amridge University                          False
University of Alabama in Huntsville         False
Alabama State University                    False
dtype: bool
```

9. Test that `has_row_max2` has no more `True` values than the number of columns:

```
>>> has_row_max2.sum()
16
```

10. We need all the institutions where `has_row_max2` is `True`. We can simply use boolean indexing on the Series itself:

```
>>> idxmax_cols = has_row_max2[has_row_max2].index
>>> idxmax_cols
Index(['Thunderbird School of Global Management',
       'Southwest University of Visual Arts-Tucson',
       'ABC Beauty College Inc',
       'Velvatex College of Beauty Culture',
       'California Institute of Technology',
       'Le Cordon Bleu College of Culinary Arts-San Francisco',
       'MTI Business College Inc', 'Dongguk University-Los
Angeles',
       'Mr Leon's School of Hair Design-Moscow',
       'Haskell Indian Nations University', 'LIU Brentwood',
       'Medical College of Wisconsin', 'Palau Community College',
       'California University of Management and Sciences',
       'Cosmopolitan Beauty and Tech School',
       'University of Phoenix-Arizona'], dtype='object',
name='INSTNM')
```

11. All 16 of these institutions are the index of the first maximum occurrence for at least one of the columns. We can check whether they are the same as the ones found with the `idxmax` method:

```
>>> set(college_n.idxmax().unique()) == set(idxmax_cols)
True
```

How it works...

The first step replicates work from the previous recipe by converting two columns to numeric and eliminating the binary columns. We find the maximum value of each column in step 2. Care needs to be taken here as pandas silently drops columns that it cannot produce a maximum. If this happens, then step 3 will still complete but produce all `False` values for each column without an available maximum.

Step 4 uses the `any` method to scan across each row in search of at least one `True` value. Any row with at least one `True` value contains a maximum value for a column. We sum up the resulting boolean Series in step 5 to determine how many rows contain a maximum. Somewhat unexpectedly, there are far more rows than columns. Step 6 gives insight on why this happens. We take a cumulative sum of the output from step 3 and detect the total number of rows that equal the maximum for each column.

Many colleges have 100% of their student population as only a single race. This is by far the largest contributor to the multiple rows with maximums. As you can see, there is only one row with a maximum value for both SAT score columns and undergraduate population, but several of the race columns have a tie for the maximum.

Our goal is to find the first row with the maximum value. We need to take the cumulative sum once more so that each column has only a single row equal to 1. Step 8 formats the code to have one method per line and runs the `any` method exactly as it was done in step 4. If this step is successful, then we should have no more `True` values than the number of columns. Step 9 asserts that this is true.

To validate that we have found the same columns as `idxmax` in the previous columns, we use boolean selection on `has_row_max2` with itself. The columns will be in a different order so we convert the sequence of column names to sets, which are inherently unordered to compare equality.

There's more...

It is possible to complete this recipe in one long line of code chaining the indexing operator with an anonymous function. This little trick removes the need for step 10. We can time the difference between the direct `idxmax` method and our manual effort in this recipe:

```
>>> %timeit college_n.idxmax().values
1.12 ms ± 28.4 µs per loop (mean ± std. dev. of 7 runs, 1000 loops each)

>>> %timeit college_n.eq(college_n.max()) \
                                 .cumsum() \
                                 .cumsum() \
                                 .eq(1) \
                                 .any(axis='columns') \
                                 [lambda x: x].index
5.35 ms ± 55.2 µs per loop (mean ± std. dev. of 7 runs, 100 loops each)
```

Our effort is, unfortunately, five times as slow as the built-in `idxmax` pandas method but regardless of its performance regression, many creative and practical solutions use the accumulation methods like `cumsum` with boolean Series to find streaks or specific patterns along an axis.

Finding the most common maximum

The college dataset contains the undergraduate population percentage of eight different races for over 7,500 colleges. It would be interesting to find the race with the highest undergrad population for each school and then find the distribution of this result for the entire dataset. We would be able to answer a question like, *What percentage of institutions have more white students than any other race?*

Getting ready

In this recipe, we find the race with the highest percentage of the undergraduate population for each school with the idxmax method and then find the distribution of these maximums.

How to do it...

1. Read in the college dataset and select just those columns with undergraduate race percentage information:

```
>>> college = pd.read_csv('data/college.csv', index_col='INSTNM')
>>> college_ugds = college.filter(like='UGDS_')
>>> college_ugds.head()
```

INSTNM	UGDS_WHITE	UGDS_BLACK	UGDS_HISP	UGDS_ASIAN	UGDS_AIAN	UGDS_NHPI	UGDS_2MOR	UGDS_NRA	UGDS_UNKN
Alabama A & M University	0.0333	0.9353	0.0055	0.0019	0.0024	0.0019	0.0000	0.0059	0.0138
University of Alabama at Birmingham	0.5922	0.2600	0.0283	0.0518	0.0022	0.0007	0.0368	0.0179	0.0100
Amridge University	0.2990	0.4192	0.0069	0.0034	0.0000	0.0000	0.0000	0.0000	0.2715
University of Alabama in Huntsville	0.6988	0.1255	0.0382	0.0376	0.0143	0.0002	0.0172	0.0332	0.0350
Alabama State University	0.0158	0.9208	0.0121	0.0019	0.0010	0.0006	0.0098	0.0243	0.0137

2. Use the `idxmax` method to get the column name with the highest race percentage for each row:

```
>>> highest_percentage_race = college_ugds.idxmax(axis='columns')
>>> highest_percentage_race.head()
INSTNM
Alabama A & M University                UGDS_BLACK
University of Alabama at Birmingham     UGDS_WHITE
Amridge University                      UGDS_BLACK
University of Alabama in Huntsville     UGDS_WHITE
Alabama State University                UGDS_BLACK
dtype: object
```

3. Use the `value_counts` method to return the distribution of maximum occurrences:

```
>>> highest_percentage_race.value_counts(normalize=True)
UGDS_WHITE    0.670352
UGDS_BLACK    0.151586
UGDS_HISP     0.129473
UGDS_UNKN     0.023422
UGDS_ASIAN    0.012074
UGDS_AIAN     0.006110
UGDS_NRA      0.004073
UGDS_NHPI     0.001746
UGDS_2MOR     0.001164
dtype: float64
```

How it works...

The key to this recipe is recognizing that the columns all represent the same unit of information. We can compare these columns with each other, which is usually not the case. For instance, it wouldn't make sense to directly compare SAT verbal scores with the undergraduate population. As the data is structured in this manner, we can apply the `idxmax` method to each row of data to find the column with the largest value. We need to alter its default behavior with the `axis` parameter.

Step 2 completes this operation and returns a Series, to which we can now simply apply the `value_counts` method to return the distribution. We pass `True` to the `normalize` parameter as we are interested in the distribution (relative frequency) and not the raw counts.

There's more...

We might want to explore more and answer the question: For the schools with more black students than any other race, what is the distribution of its second highest race percentage?

```
>>> college_black = college_ugds[highest_percentage_race == 'UGDS_BLACK']
>>> college_black = college_black.drop('UGDS_BLACK', axis='columns')
>>> college_black.idxmax(axis='columns').value_counts(normalize=True)
UGDS_WHITE     0.661228
UGDS_HISP      0.230326
UGDS_UNKN      0.071977
UGDS_NRA       0.018234
UGDS_ASIAN     0.009597
UGDS_2MOR      0.006718
UGDS_AIAN      0.000960
UGDS_NHPI      0.000960
dtype: float64
```

We needed to drop the UGDS_BLACK column before applying the same method from this recipe. Interestingly, it seems that these schools with higher black populations have a tendency to have higher Hispanic populations.

13

Grouping for Aggregation, Filtration, and Transformation

One of the most fundamental tasks during a data analysis involves splitting data into independent groups before performing a calculation on each group. This methodology has been around for quite some time but has more recently been referred to as **split-apply-combine**. This chapter covers the powerful `groupby` method, which allows you to group your data in any way imaginable and apply any type of function independently to each group before returning a single dataset.

 Hadley Wickham coined the term **split-apply-combine** to describe the common data analysis pattern of breaking up data into independent manageable chunks, independently applying functions to these chunks, and then combining the results back together. More details can be found in his paper (`http://bit.ly/2isFuL9`).

Before we get started with the recipes, we will need to know just a little terminology. All basic groupby operations have **grouping columns**, and each unique combination of values in these columns represents an independent grouping of the data. The syntax looks as follows:

```
>>> df.groupby(['list', 'of', 'grouping', 'columns'])
>>> df.groupby('single_column')  # when grouping by a single column
```

The result of this operation returns a groupby object. It is this groupby object that will be the engine that drives all the calculations for this entire chapter. Pandas actually does very little when creating this groupby object, merely validating that grouping is possible. You will have to chain methods on this groupby object in order to unleash its powers.

Technically, the result of the operation will either be a `DataFrameGroupBy` or `SeriesGroupBy` but for simplicity, it will be referred to as the groupby object for the entire chapter.

In this chapter, we will cover the following topics:

- Defining an aggregation
- Grouping and aggregating with multiple columns and functions
- Removing the MultiIndex after grouping
- Customizing an aggregation function
- Customizing aggregating functions with `*args` and `**kwargs`
- Examining the `groupby` object
- Filtering for states with a minority majority
- Transforming through a weight loss bet
- Calculating weighted mean SAT scores per state with apply
- Grouping by continuous variables
- Counting the total number of flights between cities
- Finding the longest streak of on-time flights

Defining an aggregation

The most common use of the `groupby` method is to perform an aggregation. What actually is an aggregation? In our data analysis world, an aggregation takes place when a sequence of many inputs get summarized or combined into a single value output. For example, summing up all the values of a column or finding its maximum are common aggregations applied on a single sequence of data. An aggregation simply takes many values and converts them down to a single value.

In addition to the grouping columns defined during the introduction, most aggregations have two other components, the **aggregating columns** and **aggregating functions**. The aggregating columns are those whose values will be aggregated. The aggregating functions define how the aggregation takes place. Major aggregation functions include `sum`, `min`, `max`, `mean`, `count`, `variance`, `std`, and so on.

Getting ready

In this recipe, we examine the flights dataset and perform the simplest possible aggregation involving only a single grouping column, a single aggregating column, and a single aggregating function. We will find the average arrival delay for each airline. Pandas has quite a few different syntaxes to produce an aggregation and this recipe covers them.

How to do it...

1. Read in the flights dataset, and define the grouping columns (`AIRLINE`), aggregating columns (`ARR_DELAY`), and aggregating functions (`mean`):

```
>>> flights = pd.read_csv('data/flights.csv')
>>> flights.head()
```

	MONTH	WEEKDAY	AIRLINE	ORG_AIR	DEST_AIR	SCHED_DEP	DEP_DELAY	AIR_TIME	DIST	SCHED_ARR	ARR_DELAY	DIVERTED	CANCELLED
0	1	4	WN	LAX	SLC	1625	58.0	94.0	590	1905	65.0	0	0
1	1	4	UA	DEN	IAD	823	7.0	154.0	1452	1333	-13.0	0	0
2	1	4	MQ	DFW	VPS	1305	36.0	85.0	641	1453	35.0	0	0
3	1	4	AA	DFW	DCA	1555	7.0	126.0	1192	1935	-7.0	0	0
4	1	4	WN	LAX	MCI	1720	48.0	166.0	1363	2225	39.0	0	0

2. Place the grouping column in the `groupby` method and then call the `agg` method with a dictionary pairing the aggregating column with its aggregating function:

```
>>> flights.groupby('AIRLINE').agg({'ARR_DELAY':'mean'}).head()
```

	ARR_DELAY
AIRLINE	
AA	5.542661
AS	-0.833333
B6	8.692593
DL	0.339691
EV	7.034580

3. Alternatively, you may place the aggregating column in the indexing operator and then pass the aggregating function as a string to `agg`:

```
>>> flights.groupby('AIRLINE')['ARR_DELAY'].agg('mean').head()
AIRLINE
AA     5.542661
AS    -0.833333
B6     8.692593
DL     0.339691
EV     7.034580
Name: ARR_DELAY, dtype: float64
```

4. The string names used in the previous step are a convenience pandas offers you to refer to a particular aggregation function. You can pass any aggregating function directly to the `agg` method such as the NumPy `mean` function. The output is the same as the previous step:

```
>>> flights.groupby('AIRLINE')['ARR_DELAY'].agg(np.mean).head()
```

5. It's possible to skip the `agg` method altogether in this case and use the `mean` method directly. This output is also the same as step 3:

```
>>> flights.groupby('AIRLINE')['ARR_DELAY'].mean().head()
```

How it works...

The syntax for the `groupby` method is not as straightforward as other methods. Let's intercept the chain of methods in step 2 by storing the result of the `groupby` method as its own variable

```
>>> grouped = flights.groupby('AIRLINE')
>>> type(grouped)
pandas.core.groupby.DataFrameGroupBy
```

A completely new intermediate object is first produced with its own distinct attributes and methods. No calculations take place at this stage. Pandas merely validates the grouping columns. This groupby object has an `agg` method to perform aggregations. One of the ways to use this method is to pass it a dictionary mapping the aggregating column to the aggregating function, as done in step 2.

There are several different flavors of syntax that produce a similar result, with step 3 showing an alternative. Instead of identifying the aggregating column in the dictionary, place it inside the indexing operator just as if you were selecting it as a column from a DataFrame. The function string name is then passed as a scalar to the `agg` method.

You may pass any aggregating function to the `agg` method. Pandas allows you to use the string names for simplicity but you may also explicitly call an aggregating function as done in step 4. NumPy provides many functions that aggregate values.

Step 5 shows one last syntax flavor. When you are only applying a single aggregating function as in this example, you can often call it directly as a method on the groupby object itself without `agg`. Not all aggregation functions have a method equivalent but many basic ones do. The following is a list of several aggregating functions that may be passed as a string to `agg` or chained directly as a method to the groupby object:

```
min      max      mean     median    sum      count     std      var
size     describe  nunique   idxmin    idxmax
```

There's more...

If you do not use an aggregating function with `agg`, pandas raises an exception. For instance, let's see what happens when we apply the square root function to each group:

```
>>> flights.groupby('AIRLINE')['ARR_DELAY'].agg(np.sqrt)
ValueError: function does not reduce
```

See also

- Pandas official documentation on *Aggregation* (http://bit.ly/2iuf1Nc)

Grouping and aggregating with multiple columns and functions

It is possible to do grouping and aggregating with multiple columns. The syntax is only slightly different than it is for grouping and aggregating with a single column. As usual with any kind of grouping operation, it helps to identify the three components: the grouping columns, aggregating columns, and aggregating functions.

Getting ready

In this recipe, we showcase the flexibility of the `groupby` DataFrame method by answering the following queries:

- Finding the number of cancelled flights for every airline per weekday
- Finding the number and percentage of cancelled and diverted flights for every airline per weekday
- For each origin and destination, finding the total number of flights, the number and percentage of cancelled flights, and the average and variance of the airtime

How to do it...

1. Read in the flights dataset, and answer the first query by defining the grouping columns (`AIRLINE`, `WEEKDAY`), the aggregating column (`CANCELLED`), and the aggregating function (`sum`):

```
>>> flights.groupby(['AIRLINE', 'WEEKDAY'])['CANCELLED'] \
        .agg('sum').head(7)
AIRLINE   WEEKDAY
AA        1              41
          2               9
          3              16
          4              20
          5              18
          6              21
```

```
        7              29
Name: CANCELLED, dtype: int64
```

2. Answer the second query by using a list for each pair of grouping and aggregating columns. Also, use a list for the aggregating functions:

```
>>> flights.groupby(['AIRLINE', 'WEEKDAY']) \
            ['CANCELLED', 'DIVERTED'].agg(['sum', 'mean']).head(7)
```

		CANCELLED		DIVERTED	
		sum	mean	sum	mean
AIRLINE	WEEKDAY				
AA	1	41	0.032106	6	0.004699
	2	9	0.007341	2	0.001631
	3	16	0.011949	2	0.001494
	4	20	0.015004	5	0.003751
	5	18	0.014151	1	0.000786
	6	21	0.018667	9	0.008000
	7	29	0.021837	1	0.000753

3. Answer the third query using a dictionary in the `agg` method to map specific aggregating columns to specific aggregating functions:

```
>>> group_cols = ['ORG_AIR', 'DEST_AIR']
>>> agg_dict = {'CANCELLED':['sum', 'mean', 'size'],
                'AIR_TIME':['mean', 'var']}
>>> flights.groupby(group_cols).agg(agg_dict).head()
```

		CANCELLED			AIR_TIME	
		sum	mean	size	mean	var
ORG_AIR	DEST_AIR					
ATL	ABE	0	0.0	31	96.387097	45.778495
	ABQ	0	0.0	16	170.500000	87.866667
	ABY	0	0.0	19	28.578947	6.590643
	ACY	0	0.0	6	91.333333	11.466667
	AEX	0	0.0	40	78.725000	47.332692

How it works...

To group by multiple columns as in step 1, we pass a list of the string names to the groupby method. Each unique combination of AIRLINE and WEEKDAY forms an independent group. Within each of these groups, the sum of the cancelled flights is found and then returned as a Series.

Step 2, again groups by both AIRLINE and WEEKDAY, but this time aggregates two columns. It applies each of the two aggregation functions, sum and mean, to each column resulting in four returned columns per group.

Step 3 goes even further, and uses a dictionary to map specific aggregating columns to different aggregating functions. Notice that the size aggregating function returns the total number of rows per group. This is different than the count aggregating function, which returns the number of non-missing values per group.

There's more...

There are a few main flavors of syntax that you will encounter when performing an aggregation. The following four blocks of pseudocode summarize the main ways you can perform an aggregation with the groupby method:

1. Using agg with a dictionary is the most flexible and allows you to specify the aggregating function for each column:

   ```
   >>> df.groupby(['grouping', 'columns']) \
          .agg({'agg_cols1':['list', 'of', 'functions'],
                'agg_cols2':['other', 'functions']})
   ```

2. Using agg with a list of aggregating functions applies each of the functions to each of the aggregating columns:

   ```
   >>> df.groupby(['grouping', 'columns'])['aggregating', 'columns'] \
          .agg([aggregating, functions])
   ```

3. Directly using a method following the aggregating columns instead of agg, applies just that method to each aggregating column. This way does not allow for multiple aggregating functions:

   ```
   >>> df.groupby(['grouping', 'columns'])['aggregating', 'columns'] \
          .aggregating_method()
   ```

4. If you do not specify the aggregating columns, then the aggregating method will be applied to all the non-grouping columns:

```
>>> df.groupby(['grouping', 'columns']).aggregating_method()
```

In the preceding four code blocks it is possible to substitute a string for any of the lists when grouping or aggregating by a single column.

Removing the MultiIndex after grouping

Inevitably, when using `groupby`, you will likely create a MultiIndex in the columns or rows or both. DataFrames with MultiIndexes are more difficult to navigate and occasionally have confusing column names as well.

Getting ready

In this recipe, we perform an aggregation with the `groupby` method to create a DataFrame with a MultiIndex for the rows and columns and then manipulate it so that the index is a single level and the column names are descriptive.

How to do it...

1. Read in the flights dataset; write a statement to find the total and average miles flown; and the maximum and minimum arrival delay for each airline for each weekday:

```
>>> flights = pd.read_csv('data/flights.csv')
>>> airline_info = flights.groupby(['AIRLINE', 'WEEKDAY'])\
                       .agg({'DIST':['sum', 'mean'],
                             'ARR_DELAY':['min', 'max']}) \
                       .astype(int)
>>> airline_info.head(7)
```

		DIST		ARR_DELAY	
		sum	mean	min	max
AIRLINE	WEEKDAY				
AA	1	1455386	1139	-60	551
	2	1358256	1107	-52	725
	3	1496665	1117	-45	473
	4	1452394	1089	-46	349
	5	1427749	1122	-41	732
	6	1265340	1124	-50	858
	7	1461906	1100	-49	626

2. Both the rows and columns are labeled by a MultiIndex with two levels. Let's squash it down to just a single level. To address the columns, we use the MultiIndex method, `get_level_values`. Let's display the output of each level and then concatenate both levels before setting it as the new column values:

```
>>> level0 = airline_info.columns.get_level_values(0)
Index(['DIST', 'DIST', 'ARR_DELAY', 'ARR_DELAY'], dtype='object')

>>> level1 = airline_info.columns.get_level_values(1)
Index(['sum', 'mean', 'min', 'max'], dtype='object')

>>> airline_info.columns = level0 + '_' + level1
>>> airline_info.head(7)
```

AIRLINE	WEEKDAY	DIST_sum	DIST_mean	ARR_DELAY_min	ARR_DELAY_max
AA	1	1455386	1139	-60	551
	2	1358256	1107	-52	725
	3	1496665	1117	-45	473
	4	1452394	1089	-46	349
	5	1427749	1122	-41	732
	6	1265340	1124	-50	858
	7	1461906	1100	-49	626

3. Return the row labels to a single level with `reset_index`:

```
>>> airline_info.reset_index().head(7)
```

	AIRLINE	WEEKDAY	DIST_sum	DIST_mean	ARR_DELAY_min	ARR_DELAY_max
0	AA	1	1455386	1139	-60	551
1	AA	2	1358256	1107	-52	725
2	AA	3	1496665	1117	-45	473
3	AA	4	1452394	1089	-46	349
4	AA	5	1427749	1122	-41	732
5	AA	6	1265340	1124	-50	858
6	AA	7	1461906	1100	-49	626

How it works...

When using the `agg` method to perform an aggregation on multiple columns, pandas creates an index object with two levels. The aggregating columns become the top level and the aggregating functions become the bottom level. Pandas displays MultiIndex levels differently than single-level columns. Except for the **innermost** levels, repeated index values do not get displayed on the screen. You can inspect the DataFrame from step 1 to verify this. For instance, the `DIST` column shows up only once but it refers to both of the first two columns.

 The innermost MultiIndex level is the one closest to the data. This would be the bottom-most column level and the right-most index level.

Step 2 defines new columns by first retrieving the underlying values of each of the levels with the MultiIndex method `get_level_values`. This method accepts an integer identifying the index level. They are numbered beginning with zero from the top/left. Indexes support vectorized operations, so we concatenate both levels together with a separating underscore. We assign these new values to the `columns` attribute.

In step 3, we make both index levels as columns with `reset_index`. We could have concatenated the levels together like we did in step 2, but it makes more sense to keep them as separate columns.

There's more...

By default, at the end of a groupby operation, pandas puts all of the grouping columns in the index. The `as_index` parameter in the `groupby` method can be set to `False` to avoid this behavior. You can chain the `reset_index` method after grouping to get the same effect as done in step 3. Let's see an example of this by finding the average distance traveled per flight from each airline:

```
>>> flights.groupby(['AIRLINE'], as_index=False)['DIST'].agg('mean') \
                                              .round(0)
```

	AIRLINE	DIST
0	AA	1114.0
1	AS	1066.0
2	B6	1772.0
3	DL	866.0
4	EV	460.0
5	F9	970.0
6	HA	2615.0
7	MQ	404.0
8	NK	1047.0
9	OO	511.0
10	UA	1231.0
11	US	1181.0
12	VX	1240.0
13	WN	810.0

Take a look at the order of the airlines in the previous result. By default, pandas sorts the grouping columns. The sort parameter exists within the groupby method and is defaulted to True. You may set it to False to keep the order of the grouping columns the same as how they are encountered in the dataset. You also get a small performance improvement by not sorting your data.

Customizing an aggregation function

Pandas provides a number of the most common aggregation functions for you to use with the groupby object. At some point, you will need to write your own customized user-defined functions that don't exist in pandas or NumPy.

Getting ready

In this recipe, we use the college dataset to calculate the mean and standard deviation of the undergraduate student population per state. We then use this information to find the maximum number of standard deviations from the mean that any single population value is per state.

How to do it...

1. Read in the college dataset, and find the mean and standard deviation of the undergraduate population by state:

```
>>> college = pd.read_csv('data/college.csv')
>>> college.groupby('STABBR')['UGDS'].agg(['mean', 'std']) \
                            .round(0).head()
```

STABBR	mean	std
AK	2493.0	4052.0
AL	2790.0	4658.0
AR	1644.0	3143.0
AS	1276.0	NaN
AZ	4130.0	14894.0

2. This output isn't quite what we desire. We are not looking for the mean and standard deviations of the entire group but the maximum number of standard deviations away from the mean for any one institution. In order to calculate this, we need to subtract the mean undergraduate population by state from each institution's undergraduate population and then divide by the standard deviation. This standardizes the undergraduate population for each group. We can then take the maximum of the absolute value of these scores to find the one that is farthest away from the mean. Pandas does not provide a function capable of doing this. Instead, we will need to create a custom function:

```
>>> def max_deviation(s):
        std_score = (s - s.mean()) / s.std()
        return std_score.abs().max()
```

3. After defining the function, pass it directly to the `agg` method to complete the aggregation:

```
>>> college.groupby('STABBR')['UGDS'].agg(max_deviation) \
                                     .round(1).head()
STABBR
AK    2.6
AL    5.8
AR    6.3
AS    NaN
AZ    9.9
Name: UGDS, dtype: float64
```

How it works...

There does not exist a predefined pandas function to calculate the maximum number of standard deviations away from the mean. We were forced to construct a customized function in step 2. Notice that this custom function `max_deviation` accepts a single parameter, s. Looking ahead at step 3, you will notice that the function name is placed inside the `agg` method without directly being called. Nowhere is the parameter s explicitly passed to `max_deviation`. Instead, pandas implicitly passes the UGDS column as a Series to `max_deviation`.

The `max_deviation` function is called once for each group. As s is a Series, all normal Series methods are available. It subtracts the mean of that particular grouping from each of the values in the group before dividing by the standard deviation in a process called **standardization**.

> Standardization is a common statistical procedure to understand how greatly individual values vary from the mean. For a normal distribution, 99.7% of the data lies within three standard deviations of the mean.

As we are interested in absolute deviation from the mean, we take the absolute value from all the standardized scores and return the maximum. The `agg` method necessitates that a single scalar value must be returned from our custom function, or else an exception will be raised. Pandas defaults to using the sample standard deviation which is undefined for any groups with just a single value. For instance, the state abbreviation *AS* (American Samoa) has a missing value returned as it has only a single institution in the dataset.

There's more...

It is possible to apply our customized function to multiple aggregating columns. We simply add more column names to the indexing operator. The `max_deviation` function only works with numeric columns:

```
>>> college.groupby('STABBR')['UGDS', 'SATVRMID', 'SATMTMID'] \
        .agg(max_deviation).round(1).head()
```

STABBR	UGDS	SATVRMID	SATMTMID
AK	2.6	NaN	NaN
AL	5.8	1.6	1.8
AR	6.3	2.2	2.3
AS	NaN	NaN	NaN
AZ	9.9	1.9	1.4

You can also use your customized aggregation function along with the prebuilt functions. The following does this and groups by state and religious affiliation:

```
>>> college.groupby(['STABBR', 'RELAFFIL']) \
        ['UGDS', 'SATVRMID', 'SATMTMID'] \
        .agg([max_deviation, 'mean', 'std']).round(1).head()
```

		UGDS			SATVRMID			SATMTMID		
		max_deviation	mean	std	max_deviation	mean	std	max_deviation	mean	std
STABBR	RELAFFIL									
AK	0	2.1	3508.9	4539.5	NaN	NaN	NaN	NaN	NaN	NaN
	1	1.1	123.3	132.9	NaN	555.0	NaN	NaN	503.0	NaN
AL	0	5.2	3248.8	5102.4	1.6	514.9	56.5	1.7	515.8	56.7
	1	2.4	979.7	870.8	1.5	498.0	53.0	1.4	485.6	61.4
AR	0	5.8	1793.7	3401.6	1.9	481.1	37.9	2.0	503.6	39.0

Notice that pandas uses the name of the function as the name for the returned column. You can change the column name directly with the rename method or you can modify the special function attribute __name__:

```
>>> max_deviation.__name__
'max_deviation'

>>> max_deviation.__name__ = 'Max Deviation'
>>> college.groupby(['STABBR', 'RELAFFIL']) \
            ['UGDS', 'SATVRMID', 'SATMTMID'] \
            .agg([max_deviation, 'mean', 'std']).round(1).head()
```

		UGDS			SATVRMID			SATMTMID		
		Max Deviation	mean	std	Max Deviation	mean	std	Max Deviation	mean	std
STABBR	RELAFFIL									
AK	0	2.1	3508.9	4539.5	NaN	NaN	NaN	NaN	NaN	NaN
	1	1.1	123.3	132.9	NaN	555.0	NaN	NaN	503.0	NaN
AL	0	5.2	3248.8	5102.4	1.6	514.9	56.5	1.7	515.8	56.7
	1	2.4	979.7	870.8	1.5	498.0	53.0	1.4	485.6	61.4
AR	0	5.8	1793.7	3401.6	1.9	481.1	37.9	2.0	503.6	39.0

Customizing aggregating functions with *args and **kwargs

When writing your own user-defined customized aggregation function, pandas implicitly passes it each of the aggregating columns one at a time as a Series. Occasionally, you will need to pass more arguments to your function than just the Series itself. To do so, you need to be aware of Python's ability to pass an arbitrary number of arguments to functions. Let's take a look at the signature of the groupby object's agg method with help from the inspect module:

```
>>> college = pd.read_csv('data/college.csv')
>>> grouped = college.groupby(['STABBR', 'RELAFFIL'])

>>> import inspect
>>> inspect.signature(grouped.agg)
<Signature (arg, *args, **kwargs)>
```

The argument *args allow you to pass an arbitrary number of non-keyword arguments to your customized aggregation function. Similarly, **kwargs allows you to pass an arbitrary number of keyword arguments.

Getting ready

In this recipe, we build a customized function for the college dataset that finds the percentage of schools by state and religious affiliation that have an undergraduate population between two values.

How to do it...

1. Define a function that returns the percentage of schools with an undergraduate population between 1,000 and 3,000:

```
>>> def pct_between_1_3k(s):
        return s.between(1000, 3000).mean()
```

2. Calculate this percentage grouping by state and religious affiliation:

```
>>> college.groupby(['STABBR', 'RELAFFIL'])['UGDS'] \
        .agg(pct_between_1_3k).head(9)
STABBR  RELAFFIL
AK      0              0.142857
        1              0.000000
AL      0              0.236111
        1              0.333333
AR      0              0.279412
        1              0.111111
AS      0              1.000000
AZ      0              0.096774
        1              0.000000
Name: UGDS, dtype: float64
```

3. This function works fine but it doesn't give the user any flexibility to choose the lower and upper bound. Let's create a new function that allows the user to define these bounds:

```
>>> def pct_between(s, low, high):
        return s.between(low, high).mean()
```

4. Pass this new function to the `agg` method along with lower and upper bounds:

```
>>> college.groupby(['STABBR', 'RELAFFIL'])['UGDS'] \
        .agg(pct_between, 1000, 10000).head(9)
STABBR  RELAFFIL
AK      0              0.428571
        1              0.000000
AL      0              0.458333
        1              0.375000
AR      0              0.397059
        1              0.166667
AS      0              1.000000
AZ      0              0.233871
        1              0.111111
Name: UGDS, dtype: float64
```

How it works...

Step 1 creates a function that doesn't accept any extra arguments. The upper and lower bounds must be hardcoded into the function itself, which isn't very flexible. Step 2 shows the results of this aggregation.

We create a more flexible function in step 3 that allows users to define both the lower and upper bounds dynamically. Step 4 is where the magic of `*args` and `**kwargs` come into play. In this particular example, we pass two non-keyword arguments, 1,000 and 10,000, to the `agg` method. Pandas passes these two arguments respectively to the `low` and `high` parameters of `pct_between`.

There are a few ways we could achieve the same result in step 4. We could have explicitly used the parameter names with the following command to produce the same result:

```
>>> college.groupby(['STABBR', 'RELAFFIL'])['UGDS'] \
        .agg(pct_between, high=10000, low=1000).head(9)
```

The order of the keyword arguments doesn't matter as long as they come after the function name. Further still, we can mix non-keyword and keyword arguments as long as the keyword arguments come last:

```
>>> college.groupby(['STABBR', 'RELAFFIL'])['UGDS'] \
        .agg(pct_between, 1000, high=10000).head(9)
```

For ease of understanding, it's probably best to include all the parameter names in the order that they are defined in the function signature.

Technically, when `agg` is called, all the non-keyword arguments get collected into a tuple named `args` and all the keyword arguments get collected into a dictionary named `kwargs`.

There's more...

Unfortunately, pandas does not have a direct way to use these additional arguments when using multiple aggregation functions together. For example, if you wish to aggregate using the `pct_between` and `mean` functions, you will get the following exception:

```
>>> college.groupby(['STABBR', 'RELAFFIL'])['UGDS'] \
        .agg(['mean', pct_between], low=100, high=1000)
TypeError: pct_between() missing 2 required positional arguments: 'low' and
'high'
```

Pandas is incapable of understanding that the extra arguments need to be passed to `pct_between`. In order to use our custom function with other built-in functions and even other custom functions, we can define a special type of nested function called a **closure**. We can use a generic closure to build all of our customized functions:

```
>>> def make_agg_func(func, name, *args, **kwargs):
        def wrapper(x):
            return func(x, *args, **kwargs)
        wrapper.__name__ = name
        return wrapper

>>> my_agg1 = make_agg_func(pct_between, 'pct_1_3k', low=1000, high=3000)
>>> my_agg2 = make_agg_func(pct_between, 'pct_10_30k', 10000, 30000)

>>> college.groupby(['STABBR', 'RELAFFIL'])['UGDS'] \
        .agg(['mean', my_agg1, my_agg2]).head()
```

		mean	pct_1_3k	pct_10_30k
STABBR	RELAFFIL			
AK	0	3508.857143	0.142857	0.142857
	1	123.333333	0.000000	0.000000
AL	0	3248.774648	0.236111	0.083333
	1	979.722222	0.333333	0.000000
AR	0	1793.691176	0.279412	0.014706

The make_agg_func function acts as a factory to create customized aggregation functions. It accepts the customized aggregation function that you already built (pct_between in this case), a name argument, and an arbitrary number of extra arguments. It returns a function with the extra arguments already set. For instance, my_agg1 is a specific customized aggregating function that finds the percentage of schools with an undergraduate population between one and three thousand. The extra arguments (*args and **kwargs) specify an exact set of parameters for your customized function (pct_between in this case). The name parameter is very important and must be unique each time make_agg_func is called. It will eventually be used to rename the aggregated column.

A closure is a function that contains a function inside of it (a nested function) and returns this nested function. This nested function must refer to variables in the scope of the outer function in order to be a closure. In this example, make_agg_func is the outer function and returns the nested function wrapper, which accesses the variables func, args, and kwargs from the outer function.

See also

- *Arbitrary Argument Lists* from the official Python documentation (http://bit.ly/2vumbTE)
- A tutorial on *Python Closures* (http://bit.ly/2xFdYga)

Examining the groupby object

The immediate result from using the `groupby` method on a DataFrame will be a groupby object. Usually, we continue operating on this object to do aggregations or transformations without ever saving it to a variable. One of the primary purposes of examining this groupby object is to inspect individual groups.

Getting ready

In this recipe, we examine the groupby object itself by directly calling methods on it as well as iterating through each of its groups.

How to do it...

1. Let's get started by grouping the state and religious affiliation columns from the college dataset, saving the result to a variable and confirming its type:

```
>>> college = pd.read_csv('data/college.csv')
>>> grouped = college.groupby(['STABBR', 'RELAFFIL'])
>>> type(grouped)
pandas.core.groupby.DataFrameGroupBy
```

2. Use the `dir` function to discover all its available functionality:

```
>>> print([attr for attr in dir(grouped) if not
attr.startswith('_')])
['CITY', 'CURROPER', 'DISTANCEONLY', 'GRAD_DEBT_MDN_SUPP', 'HBCU',
'INSTNM', 'MD_EARN_WNE_P10', 'MENONLY', 'PCTFLOAN', 'PCTPELL',
'PPTUG_EF', 'RELAFFIL', 'SATMTMID', 'SATVRMID', 'STABBR',
'UG25ABV', 'UGDS', 'UGDS_2MOR', 'UGDS_AIAN', 'UGDS_ASIAN',
'UGDS_BLACK', 'UGDS_HISP', 'UGDS_NHPI', 'UGDS_NRA', 'UGDS_UNKN',
'UGDS_WHITE', 'WOMENONLY', 'agg', 'aggregate', 'all', 'any',
'apply', 'backfill', 'bfill', 'boxplot', 'corr', 'corrwith',
'count', 'cov', 'cumcount', 'cummax', 'cummin', 'cumprod',
'cumsum', 'describe', 'diff', 'dtypes', 'expanding', 'ffill',
'fillna', 'filter', 'first', 'get_group', 'groups', 'head', 'hist',
'idxmax', 'idxmin', 'indices', 'last', 'mad', 'max', 'mean',
'median', 'min', 'ndim', 'ngroup', 'ngroups', 'nth', 'nunique',
'ohlc', 'pad', 'pct_change', 'plot', 'prod', 'quantile', 'rank',
'resample', 'rolling', 'sem', 'shift', 'size', 'skew', 'std',
'sum', 'tail', 'take', 'transform', 'tshift', 'var']
```

3. Find the number of groups with the `ngroups` attribute:

```
>>> grouped.ngroups
112
```

4. To find the uniquely identifying labels for each group, look in the `groups` attribute, which contains a dictionary of each unique group mapped to all the corresponding index labels of that group:

```
>>> groups = list(grouped.groups.keys())
>>> groups[:6]
[('AK', 0), ('AK', 1), ('AL', 0), ('AL', 1), ('AR', 0), ('AR', 1)]
```

5. Retrieve a single group with the `get_group` method by passing it a tuple of an exact group label. For example, to get all the religiously affiliated schools in the state of Florida, do the following:

```
>>> grouped.get_group(('FL', 1)).head()
```

	CITY	CURROPER	DISTANCEONLY	GRAD_DEBT_MDN_SUPP	HBCU	INSTNM	MD_EARN_WNE_P10	MENONLY	PCTFLOAN	PCTPELL
712	Graceville	1	0.0	20052	0.0	The Baptist College of Florida	30800	0.0	0.5602	0.5878
713	Miami	1	0.0	28250	0.0	Barry University	44100	0.0	0.6733	0.5045
714	Panama City	0	0.0	PrivacySuppressed	0.0	Gooding Institute of Nurse Anesthesia	NaN	0.0	NaN	NaN
715	Daytona Beach	1	0.0	36250	1.0	Bethune-Cookman University	29400	0.0	0.8867	0.7758
724	Kissimmee	1	0.0	20199	0.0	Johnson University Florida	26300	0.0	0.7384	0.6689

6. You may want to take a peek at each individual group. This is possible because groupby objects are iterable:

```
>>> from IPython.display import display
>>> for name, group in grouped:
        print(name)
        display(group.head(3))
```

('AK', 0)

	INSTNM	CITY	STABBR	HBCU	MENONLY	WOMENONLY	RELAFFIL	SATVRMID	SATMTMID	DISTANCEONLY
60	University of Alaska Anchorage	Anchorage	AK	0.0	0.0	0.0	0	NaN	NaN	0.0
62	University of Alaska Fairbanks	Fairbanks	AK	0.0	0.0	0.0	0	NaN	NaN	0.0

2 rows × 27 columns

('AK', 1)

	INSTNM	CITY	STABBR	HBCU	MENONLY	WOMENONLY	RELAFFIL	SATVRMID	SATMTMID	DISTANCEONLY	..
61	Alaska Bible College	Palmer	AK	0.0	0.0	0.0	1	NaN	NaN	0.0	..
64	Alaska Pacific University	Anchorage	AK	0.0	0.0	0.0	1	555.0	503.0	0.0	..

2 rows × 27 columns

('AL', 0)

	INSTNM	CITY	STABBR	HBCU	MENONLY	WOMENONLY	RELAFFIL	SATVRMID	SATMTMID	DISTANCEONLY
0	Alabama A & M University	Normal	AL	1.0	0.0	0.0	0	424.0	420.0	0.0
1	University of Alabama at Birmingham	Birmingham	AL	0.0	0.0	0.0	0	570.0	565.0	0.0

2 rows × 27 columns

7. You can also call the head method on your groupby object to get the first rows of each group together in a single DataFrame.

```
>>> grouped.head(2).head(6)
```

	INSTNM	CITY	STABBR	HBCU	MENONLY	WOMENONLY	RELAFFIL	SATVRMID	SATMTMID	DISTANCEONLY	...	UGDS_2MOR	UGDS_NRA
0	Alabama A & M University	Normal	AL	1.0	0.0	0.0	0	424.0	420.0	0.0	...	0.0000	0.0059
1	University of Alabama at Birmingham	Birmingham	AL	0.0	0.0	0.0	0	570.0	565.0	0.0	...	0.0368	0.0179
2	Amridge University	Montgomery	AL	0.0	0.0	0.0	1	NaN	NaN	1.0	...	0.0000	0.0000
10	Birmingham Southern College	Birmingham	AL	0.0	0.0	0.0	1	560.0	560.0	0.0	...	0.0051	0.0000
43	Prince Institute-Southeast	Elmhurst	IL	0.0	0.0	0.0	0	NaN	NaN	0.0	...	0.0000	0.0000
60	University of Alaska Anchorage	Anchorage	AK	0.0	0.0	0.0	0	NaN	NaN	0.0	...	0.0980	0.0181

How it works...

Step 1 formally creates our groupby object. It is useful to display all the public attributes and methods to reveal all the possible functionality as was done in step 2. Each group is uniquely identified by a tuple containing a unique combination of the values in the grouping columns. Pandas allows you to select a specific group as a DataFrame with the `get_group` method shown in step 5.

It is rare that you will need to iterate through your groups and in general, you should avoid doing so if necessary, as it can be quite slow. Occasionally, you will have no other choice. When iterating through a groupby object, you are given a tuple containing the group name and the DataFrame without the grouping columns. This tuple is unpacked into the variables `name` and `group` in the for-loop in step 6.

One interesting thing you can do while iterating through your groups is to display a few of the rows from each group directly in the notebook. To do this, you can either use the print function or the `display` function from the `IPython.display` module. Using the `print` function results in DataFrames that are in plain text without any nice HTML formatting. Using the `display` function will produce DataFrames in their normal easy-to-read format.

There's more...

There are several useful methods that were not explored from the list in step 2. Take for instance the nth method, which, when given a list of integers, selects those specific rows from each group. For example, the following operation selects the first and last rows from each group:

```
>>> grouped.nth([1, -1]).head(8)
```

STABBR	RELAFFIL	CITY	CURROPER	DISTANCEONLY	GRAD_DEBT_MDN_SUPP	HBCU	INSTNM	MD_EARN_WNE_P10	MENONLY	PCTFLOAN
AK	0	Fairbanks	1	0.0	19355	0.0	University of Alaska Fairbanks	36200	0.0	0.2550
	0	Barrow	1	0.0	PrivacySuppressed	0.0	Ilisagvik College	24900	0.0	0.0000
	1	Anchorage	1	0.0	23250	0.0	Alaska Pacific University	47000	0.0	0.5297
	1	Soldotna	1	0.0	PrivacySuppressed	0.0	Alaska Christian College	NaN	0.0	0.6792
AL	0	Birmingham	1	0.0	21941.5	0.0	University of Alabama at Birmingham	39700	0.0	0.5214
	0	Dothan	1	0.0	PrivacySuppressed	0.0	Alabama College of Osteopathic Medicine	NaN	0.0	NaN
	1	Birmingham	1	0.0	27000	0.0	Birmingham Southern College	44200	0.0	0.4809
	1	Huntsville	1	NaN	36173.5	NaN	Strayer University-Huntsville Campus	49200	NaN	NaN

See also

- Official documentation of the display function from IPython (http://bit.ly/2iAIogC)

Filtering for states with a minority majority

In Chapter 10, *Selecting Subsets of Data*, we marked every row as True or False before filtering out the False rows. In a similar fashion, it is possible to mark entire groups of data as either True or False before filtering out the False groups. To do this, we first form groups with the groupby method and then apply the filter method. The filter method accepts a function that must return either True or False to indicate whether a group is kept or not.

This `filter` method applied after a call to the `groupby` method is completely different than the DataFrame `filter` method.

Getting ready

In this recipe, we use the college dataset to find all the states that have more non-white undergraduate students than white. As this is a dataset from the US, whites form the majority and therefore, we are looking for states with a minority majority.

How to do it...

1. Read in the college dataset, group by state, and display the total number of groups. This should equal the number of unique states retrieved from the `nunique` Series method:

```
>>> college = pd.read_csv('data/college.csv', index_col='INSTNM')
>>> grouped = college.groupby('STABBR')
>>> grouped.ngroups
59

>>> college['STABBR'].nunique() # verifying the same number
59
```

2. The `grouped` variable has a `filter` method, which accepts a custom function that determines whether a group is kept or not. The custom function gets implicitly passed a DataFrame of the current group and is required to return a boolean. Let's define a function that calculates the total percentage of minority students and returns `True` if this percentage is greater than a user-defined threshold:

```
>>> def check_minority(df, threshold):
        minority_pct = 1 - df['UGDS_WHITE']
        total_minority = (df['UGDS'] * minority_pct).sum()
        total_ugds = df['UGDS'].sum()
        total_minority_pct = total_minority / total_ugds
        return total_minority_pct > threshold
```

3. Use the `filter` method passed with the `check_minority` function and a threshold of 50% to find all states that have a minority majority:

```
>>> college_filtered = grouped.filter(check_minority, threshold=.5)
>>> college_filtered.head()
```

INSTNM	CITY	STABBR	HBCU	MENONLY	WOMENONLY	RELAFFIL	SATVRMID	SATMTMID	DISTANCEONLY	UGDS
Everest College-Phoenix	Phoenix	AZ	0.0	0.0	0.0	1	NaN	NaN	0.0	4102.0
Collins College	Phoenix	AZ	0.0	0.0	0.0	0	NaN	NaN	0.0	83.0
Empire Beauty School-Paradise Valley	Phoenix	AZ	0.0	0.0	0.0	1	NaN	NaN	0.0	25.0
Empire Beauty School-Tucson	Tucson	AZ	0.0	0.0	0.0	0	NaN	NaN	0.0	126.0
Thunderbird School of Global Management	Glendale	AZ	0.0	0.0	0.0	0	NaN	NaN	0.0	1.0

4. Just looking at the output may not be indicative of what actually happened. The DataFrame starts with state Arizona (AZ) and not Alaska (AK) so we can visually confirm that something changed. Let's compare the `shape` of this filtered DataFrame with the original. Looking at the results, about 60% of the rows have been filtered, and only 20 states remain that have a minority majority:

```
>>> college.shape
(7535, 26)

>>> college_filtered.shape
(3028, 26)

>>> college_filtered['STABBR'].nunique()
20
```

How it works...

This recipe takes a look at the total population of all the institutions on a state-by-state basis. The goal is to keep all the rows from the states, as a whole, that have a minority majority. This requires us to group our data by state, which is done in step 1. We find that there are 59 independent groups.

The `filter` groupby method either keeps all the rows in a group or filters them out. It does not change the number of columns. The `filter` groupby method performs this gatekeeping through a user-defined function, for example, `check_minority` in this recipe. A very important aspect to filter is that it passes the entire DataFrame for that particular group to the user-defined function and returns a single boolean for each group.

Inside of the `check_minority` function, the percentage and the total number of non-white students for each institution are first calculated and then the total number of all students is found. Finally, the percentage of non-white students for the entire state is checked against the given threshold, which produces a boolean.

The final result is a DataFrame with the same columns as the original but with the rows from the states that don't meet the threshold filtered out. As it is possible that the head of the filtered DataFrame is the same as the original, you need to do some inspection to ensure that the operation completed successfully. We verify this by checking the number of rows and number of unique states.

There's more...

Our function, `check_minority`, is flexible and accepts a parameter to lower or raise the percentage of minority threshold. Let's check the shape and number of unique states for a couple of other thresholds:

```
>>> college_filtered_20 = grouped.filter(check_minority, threshold=.2)
>>> college_filtered_20.shape
(7461, 26)

>>> college_filtered_20['STABBR'].nunique()
57

>>> college_filtered_70 = grouped.filter(check_minority, threshold=.7)
>>> college_filtered_70.shape
(957, 26)

>>> college_filtered_70['STABBR'].nunique()
10
```

See also

- Pandas official documentation on *Filtration* (http://bit.ly/2xGUoA7)

Transforming through a weight loss bet

One method to increase motivation to lose weight is to make a bet with someone else. The scenario in this recipe will track weight loss from two individuals over the course of a four-month period and determine a winner.

Getting ready

In this recipe, we use simulated data from two individuals to track the percentage of weight loss over the course of four months. At the end of each month, a winner will be declared based on the individual who lost the highest percentage of body weight for that month. To track weight loss, we group our data by month and person, then call the `transform` method to find the percentage weight loss at each week from the start of the month.

How to do it...

1. Read in the raw weight_loss dataset, and examine the first month of data from the two people, Amy and Bob. There are a total of four weigh-ins per month:

```
>>> weight_loss = pd.read_csv('data/weight_loss.csv')
>>> weight_loss.query('Month == "Jan"')
```

	Name	Month	Week	Weight
0	Bob	Jan	Week 1	291
1	Amy	Jan	Week 1	197
2	Bob	Jan	Week 2	288
3	Amy	Jan	Week 2	189
4	Bob	Jan	Week 3	283
5	Amy	Jan	Week 3	189
6	Bob	Jan	Week 4	283
7	Amy	Jan	Week 4	190

2. To determine the winner for each month, we only need to compare weight loss from the first week to the last week of each month. But, if we wanted to have weekly updates, we can also calculate weight loss from the current week to the first week of each month. Let's create a function that is capable of providing weekly updates:

```
>>> def find_perc_loss(s):
        return (s - s.iloc[0]) / s.iloc[0]
```

3. Let's test out this function for Bob during the month of January.

```
>>> bob_jan = weight_loss.query('Name=="Bob" and Month=="Jan"')
>>> find_perc_loss(bob_jan['Weight'])
0     0.000000
2    -0.010309
4    -0.027491
6    -0.027491
Name: Weight, dtype: float64
```

You should ignore the index values in the last output. 0, 2, 4 and 6 simply refer to the original row labels of the DataFrame and have no relation to the week.

4. After the first week, Bob lost 1% of his body weight. He continued losing weight during the second week but made no progress during the last week. We can apply this function to every single combination of person and week to get the weight loss per week in relation to the first week of the month. To do this, we need to group our data by Name and Month , and then use the transform method to apply this custom function:

```
>>> pcnt_loss = weight_loss.groupby(['Name', 'Month'])['Weight'] \
                            .transform(find_perc_loss)
>>> pcnt_loss.head(8)
0     0.000000
1     0.000000
2    -0.010309
3    -0.040609
4    -0.027491
5    -0.040609
6    -0.027491
7    -0.035533
Name: Weight, dtype: float64
```

5. The `transform` method must return an object with the same number of rows as the calling DataFrame. Let's append this result to our original DataFrame as a new column. To help shorten the output, we will select Bob's first two months of data:

```
>>> weight_loss['Perc Weight Loss'] = pcnt_loss.round(3)
>>> weight_loss.query('Name=="Bob" and Month in ["Jan", "Feb"]')
```

	Name	Month	Week	Weight	Perc Weight Loss
0	Bob	Jan	Week 1	291	0.000
2	Bob	Jan	Week 2	288	-0.010
4	Bob	Jan	Week 3	283	-0.027
6	Bob	Jan	Week 4	283	-0.027
8	Bob	Feb	Week 1	283	0.000
10	Bob	Feb	Week 2	275	-0.028
12	Bob	Feb	Week 3	268	-0.053
14	Bob	Feb	Week 4	268	-0.053

6. Notice that the percentage weight loss resets after the new month. With this new column, we can manually determine a winner but let's see if we can find a way to do this automatically. As the only week that matters is the last week, let's select week 4:

```
>>> week4 = weight_loss.query('Week == "Week 4"')
>>> week4
```

	Name	Month	Week	Weight	Perc Weight Loss
6	Bob	Jan	Week 4	283	-0.027
7	Amy	Jan	Week 4	190	-0.036
14	Bob	Feb	Week 4	268	-0.053
15	Amy	Feb	Week 4	173	-0.089
22	Bob	Mar	Week 4	261	-0.026
23	Amy	Mar	Week 4	170	-0.017
30	Bob	Apr	Week 4	250	-0.042
31	Amy	Apr	Week 4	161	-0.053

7. This narrows down the weeks but still doesn't automatically find out the winner of each month. Let's reshape this data with the `pivot` method so that Bob's and Amy's percent weight loss is side-by-side for each month:

```
>>> winner = week4.pivot(index='Month', columns='Name',
                         values='Perc Weight Loss')
>>> winner
```

Name	Amy	Bob
Month		
Apr	-0.053	-0.042
Feb	-0.089	-0.053
Jan	-0.036	-0.027
Mar	-0.017	-0.026

8. This output makes it clearer who has won each month, but we can still go a couple steps farther. NumPy has a vectorized if-then-else function called `where`, which can map a Series or array of booleans to other values. Let's create a column for the name of the winner and highlight the winning percentage for each month:

```
>>> winner['Winner'] = np.where(winner['Amy'] < winner['Bob'],
                                'Amy', 'Bob')
>>> winner.style.highlight_min(axis=1)
```

Name	Amy	Bob	Winner
Month			
Apr	-0.053	-0.042	Amy
Feb	-0.089	-0.053	Amy
Jan	-0.036	-0.027	Amy
Mar	-0.017	-0.026	Bob

9. Use the `value_counts` method to return the final score as the number of months won:

```
>>> winner.Winner.value_counts()
Amy     3
Bob     1
Name: Winner, dtype: int64
```

How it works...

Throughout this recipe, the `query` method is used to filter data instead of boolean indexing. Refer to the *Improving readability of Boolean indexing with the query method* recipe from `Chapter 11`, *Boolean Indexing*, for more information.

Our goal is to find the percentage weight loss for each month for each person. One way to accomplish this task is to calculate each week's weight loss relative to the start of each month. This specific task is perfectly suited to the `transform` groupby method. The `transform` method accepts a function as its one required parameter. This function gets implicitly passed each non-grouping column (or only the columns specified in the indexing operator as was done in this recipe with `Weight`). It must return a sequence of values the same length as the passed group or else an exception will be raised. In essence, all values from the original DataFrame are transforming. No aggregation or filtration takes place.

Step 2 creates a function that subtracts the first value of the passed Series from all of its values and then divides this result by the first value. This calculates the percent loss (or gain) relative to the first value. In step 3 we test this function on one person during one month.

In step 4, we use this function in the same manner over every combination of person and week. In some literal sense, we are *transforming* the `Weight` column into the percentage of weight lost for the current week. The first month of data is outputted for each person. Pandas returns the new data as a Series. This Series isn't all that useful by itself and makes more sense appended to the original DataFrame as a new column. We complete this operation in step 5.

To determine the winner, only week 4 of each month is necessary. We could stop here and manually determine the winner but pandas supplies us functionality to automate this. The `pivot` function in step 7 reshapes our dataset by pivoting the unique values of one column into new column names. The `index` parameter is used for the column that you do not want to pivot. The column passed to the `values` parameter gets tiled over each unique combination of the columns in the `index` and `columns` parameters.

The `pivot` method only works if there is just a single occurrence of each unique combination of the columns in the `index` and `columns` parameters. If there is more than one unique combination, an exception will be raised. You can use the `pivot_table` method in that situation which allows you to aggregate multiple values together.

After pivoting, we utilize the highly effective and fast NumPy `where` function, whose first argument is a condition that produces a Series of booleans. `True` values get mapped to *Amy* and `False` values get mapped to *Bob*. We highlight the winner of each month and tally the final score with the `value_counts` method.

There's more...

Take a look at the DataFrame output from step 7. Did you notice that the months are in alphabetical and not chronological order? Pandas unfortunately, in this case at least, orders the months for us alphabetically. We can solve this issue by changing the data type of `Month` to a categorical variable. Categorical variables map all the values of each column to an integer. We can choose this mapping to be the normal chronological order for the months. Pandas uses this underlying integer mapping during the `pivot` method to order the months chronologically:

```
>>> week4a = week4.copy()
>>> month_chron = week4a['Month'].unique() # or use drop_duplicates
>>> month_chron
array(['Jan', 'Feb', 'Mar', 'Apr'], dtype=object)

>>> week4a['Month'] = pd.Categorical(week4a['Month'],
                                 categories=month_chron,
                                 ordered=True)
>>> week4a.pivot(index='Month', columns='Name',
              values='Perc Weight Loss')
```

Name	Amy	Bob
Month		
Jan	-0.036	-0.027
Feb	-0.089	-0.053
Mar	-0.017	-0.026
Apr	-0.053	-0.042

To convert the `Month` column, use the `Categorical` constructor. Pass it the original column as a Series and a unique sequence of all the categories in the desired order to the `categories` parameter. As the `Month` column is already in chronological order, we can simply use the `unique` method, which preserves order to get the array that we desire. In general, to sort columns of object data type by something other than alphabetical, convert them to categorical.

See also

- Pandas official documentation on `groupby` *Transformation* (http://bit.ly/2vBkpA7)
- NumPy official documentation on the `where` function (http://bit.ly/2weT211)

Calculating weighted mean SAT scores per state with apply

The groupby object has four methods that accept a function (or functions) to perform a calculation on each group. These four methods are `agg`, `filter`, `transform`, and `apply`. Each of the first three of these methods has a very specific output that the function must return. `agg` must return a scalar value, `filter` must return a boolean, and `transform` must return a Series with the same length as the passed group. The `apply` method, however, may return a scalar value, a Series, or even a DataFrame of any shape, therefore making it very flexible. It is also called only once per group, which contrasts with `transform` and `agg` that get called once for each non-grouping column. The `apply` method's ability to return a single object when operating on multiple columns at the same time makes the calculation in this recipe possible.

Getting ready

In this recipe, we calculate the weighted average of both the math and verbal SAT scores per state from the college dataset. We weight the scores by the population of undergraduate students per school.

How to do it...

1. Read in the college dataset, and drop any rows that have missing values in either the UGDS, SATMTMID, or SATVRMID columns. We must have non-missing values for each of these three columns:

```
>>> college = pd.read_csv('data/college.csv')
>>> subset = ['UGDS', 'SATMTMID', 'SATVRMID']
>>> college2 = college.dropna(subset=subset)
>>> college.shape
(7535, 27)

>>> college2.shape
(1184, 27)
```

2. The vast majority of institutions do not have data for our three required columns, but this is still more than enough data to continue. Next, create a user-defined function to calculate the weighted average of just the SAT math scores:

```
>>> def weighted_math_average(df):
        weighted_math = df['UGDS'] * df['SATMTMID']
        return int(weighted_math.sum() / df['UGDS'].sum())
```

3. Group by state and pass this function to the apply method:

```
>>> college2.groupby('STABBR').apply(weighted_math_average).head()
STABBR
AK     503
AL     536
AR     529
AZ     569
CA     564
dtype: int64
```

4. We successfully returned a scalar value for each group. Let's take a small detour and see what the outcome would have been by passing the same function to the agg method:

```
>>> college2.groupby('STABBR').agg(weighted_math_average).head()
```

STABBR	INSTNM	CITY	HBCU	MENONLY	WOMENONLY	RELAFFIL	SATVRMID	SATMTMID	DISTANCEONLY	UGDS
AK	503	503	503	503	503	503	503	503	503	503
AL	536	536	536	536	536	536	536	536	536	536
AR	529	529	529	529	529	529	529	529	529	529
AZ	569	569	569	569	569	569	569	569	569	569
CA	564	564	564	564	564	564	564	564	564	564

5. The `weighted_math_average` function gets applied to each non-aggregating column in the DataFrame. If you try and limit the columns to just `SATMTMID`, you will get an error as you won't have access to `UGDS`. So, the best way to complete operations that act on multiple columns is with `apply`:

```
>>> college2.groupby('STABBR')['SATMTMID'] \
            .agg(weighted_math_average)
KeyError: 'UGDS'
```

6. A nice feature of `apply` is that you can create multiple new columns by returning a Series. The index of this returned Series will be the new column names. Let's modify our function to calculate the weighted and arithmetic average for both SAT scores along with the count of the number of institutions from each group. We return these five values in a Series:

```
>>> from collections import OrderedDict
>>> def weighted_average(df):
        data = OrderedDict()
        weight_m = df['UGDS'] * df['SATMTMID']
        weight_v = df['UGDS'] * df['SATVRMID']
        wm_avg = weight_m.sum() / df['UGDS'].sum()
        wv_avg = weight_v.sum() / df['UGDS'].sum()

        data['weighted_math_avg'] = wm_avg
        data['weighted_verbal_avg'] = wv_avg
        data['math_avg'] = df['SATMTMID'].mean()
        data['verbal_avg'] = df['SATVRMID'].mean()
        data['count'] = len(df)
        return pd.Series(data, dtype='int')

>>> college2.groupby('STABBR').apply(weighted_average).head(10)
```

	weighted_math_avg	weighted_verbal_avg	math_avg	verbal_avg	count
STABBR					
AK	503	555	503	555	1
AL	536	533	504	508	21
AR	529	504	515	491	16
AZ	569	557	536	538	6
CA	564	539	562	549	72
CO	553	547	540	537	14
CT	545	533	522	517	14
DC	621	623	588	589	6
DE	569	553	495	486	3
FL	565	565	521	529	38

How it works...

In order for this recipe to complete properly, we need to first filter for institutions that do not have missing values for UGDS, SATMTMID, and SATVRMID. By default, the dropna method drops rows that have one or more missing values. We must use the subset parameter to limit the columns it looks at for missing values.

In step 2, we define a function that calculates the weighted average for just the SATMTMID column. The weighted average differs from an arithmetic mean in that each value is multiplied by some weight. This quantity is then summed and divided by the sum of the weights. In this case, our weight is the undergraduate student population.

In step 3, we pass this function to the apply method. Our function weighted_math_average gets passed a DataFrame of all the original columns for each group. It returns a single scalar value, the weighted average of SATMTMID. At this point, you might think that this calculation is possible using the agg method. Directly replacing apply with agg does not work as agg returns a value for each of its aggregating columns.

 It actually is possible to use agg indirectly by precomputing the multiplication of UGDS and SATMTMID.

Step 6 really shows the versatility of `apply`. We build a new function that calculates the weighted and arithmetic average of both SAT columns as well as the number of rows for each group. In order for `apply` to create multiple columns, you must return a Series. The index values are used as column names in the resulting DataFrame. You can return as many values as you want with this method.

Notice that the `OrderedDict` class was imported from the `collections` module, which is part of the standard library. This ordered dictionary is used to store the data. A normal Python dictionary could not have been used to store the data since it does not preserve insertion order.

 The constructor, `pd.Series`, does have an index parameter that you can use to specify order but using an `OrderedDict` is cleaner.

There's more...

In this recipe, we returned a single row as a Series for each group. It's possible to return any number of rows and columns for each group by returning a DataFrame. In addition to finding just the arithmetic and weighted means, let's also find the geometric and harmonic means of both SAT columns and return the results as a DataFrame with rows as the name of the type of mean and columns as the SAT type. To ease the burden on us, we use the NumPy function `average` to compute the weighted average and the SciPy functions `gmean` and `hmean` for geometric and harmonic means:

```
>>> from scipy.stats import gmean, hmean
>>> def calculate_means(df):
        df_means = pd.DataFrame(index=['Arithmetic', 'Weighted',
                                       'Geometric', 'Harmonic'])
        cols = ['SATMTMID', 'SATVRMID']
        for col in cols:
            arithmetic = df[col].mean()
            weighted = np.average(df[col], weights=df['UGDS'])
            geometric = gmean(df[col])
            harmonic = hmean(df[col])
            df_means[col] = [arithmetic, weighted,
                             geometric, harmonic]
        df_means['count'] = len(df)
        return df_means.astype(int)

>>> college2.groupby('STABBR').apply(calculate_means).head(12)
```

STABBR		SATMTMID	SATVRMID	count
AK	Arithmetic	503	555	1
	Weighted	503	555	1
	Geometric	503	555	1
	Harmonic	503	555	1
AL	Arithmetic	504	508	21
	Weighted	536	533	21
	Geometric	500	505	21
	Harmonic	497	502	21
AR	Arithmetic	515	491	16
	Weighted	529	504	16
	Geometric	514	489	16
	Harmonic	513	487	16

See also

- Pandas official documentation of the `apply` groupby method (http://bit.ly/2wmG9ki)
- Python official documentation of the `OrderedDict` class (http://bit.ly/2xwtUCa)
- SciPy official documentation of its stats module (http://bit.ly/2wHtQ4L)

Grouping by continuous variables

When grouping in pandas, you typically use columns with discrete repeating values. If there are no repeated values, then grouping would be pointless as there would only be one row per group. Continuous numeric columns typically have few repeated values and are generally not used to form groups. However, if we can transform columns with continuous values into a discrete column by placing each value into a bin, rounding them, or using some other mapping, then grouping with them makes sense.

Getting ready

In this recipe, we explore the flights dataset to discover the distribution of airlines for different travel distances. This allows us, for example, to find the airline that makes the most flights between 500 and 1,000 miles. To accomplish this, we use the pandas `cut` function to discretize the distance of each flight flown.

How to do it...

1. Read in the flights dataset, and output the first five rows:

```
>>> flights = pd.read_csv('data/flights.csv')
>>> flights.head()
```

	MONTH	DAY	WEEKDAY	AIRLINE	ORG_AIR	DEST_AIR	SCHED_DEP	DEP_DELAY	AIR_TIME	DIST	SCHED_ARR	ARR_DELAY	DIVERTED	CANCELLED
0	1	1	4	WN	LAX	SLC	1625	58.0	94.0	590	1905	65.0	0	0
1	1	1	4	UA	DEN	IAD	823	7.0	154.0	1452	1333	-13.0	0	0
2	1	1	4	MQ	DFW	VPS	1305	36.0	85.0	641	1453	35.0	0	0
3	1	1	4	AA	DFW	DCA	1555	7.0	126.0	1192	1935	-7.0	0	0
4	1	1	4	WN	LAX	MCI	1720	48.0	166.0	1363	2225	39.0	0	0

2. If we want to find the distribution of airlines over a range of distances, we need to place the values of the `DIST` column into discrete bins. Let's use the pandas `cut` function to split the data into five bins:

```
>>> bins = [-np.inf, 200, 500, 1000, 2000, np.inf]
>>> cuts = pd.cut(flights['DIST'], bins=bins)
>>> cuts.head()
0      (500.0, 1000.0]
1     (1000.0, 2000.0]
2      (500.0, 1000.0]
3     (1000.0, 2000.0]
4     (1000.0, 2000.0]
Name: DIST, dtype: category
Categories (5, interval[float64]): [(-inf, 200.0] < (200.0, 500.0]
< (500.0, 1000.0] < (1000.0, 2000.0] < (2000.0, inf]]
```

3. An ordered categorical Series is created. To help get an idea of what happened, let's count the values of each category:

```
>>> cuts.value_counts()
(500.0, 1000.0]     20659
(200.0, 500.0]      15874
(1000.0, 2000.0]    14186
(2000.0, inf]        4054
(-inf, 200.0]        3719
Name: DIST, dtype: int64
```

4. The `cuts` Series can now be used to form groups. Pandas allows you to form groups in any way you wish. Pass the `cuts` Series to the `groupby` method and then call the `value_counts` method on the `AIRLINE` column to find the distribution for each distance group. Notice that SkyWest (*OO*) makes up 33% of flights less than 200 miles but only 16% of those between 200 and 500 miles:

```
>>> flights.groupby(cuts)['AIRLINE'].value_counts(normalize=True) \
                                    .round(3).head(15)
DIST              AIRLINE
(-inf, 200.0]     OO          0.326
                  EV          0.289
                  MQ          0.211
                  DL          0.086
                  AA          0.052
                  UA          0.027
                  WN          0.009
(200.0, 500.0]    WN          0.194
                  DL          0.189
                  OO          0.159
                  EV          0.156
```

```
                    MQ          0.100
                    AA          0.071
                    UA          0.062
                    VX          0.028
          Name: AIRLINE, dtype: float64
```

How it works...

In step 2, the `cut` function places each value of the `DIST` column into one of five bins. The bins are created by a sequence of six numbers defining the edges. You always need one more edge than the number of bins. You can pass the `bins` parameter an integer, which automatically creates that number of equal-width bins. Negative infinity and positive infinity objects are available in NumPy and ensure that all values get placed in a bin. If you have values that are outside of the bin edges, they will be made missing and not be placed in a bin.

The `cuts` variable is now a Series of five ordered categories. It has all the normal Series methods and in step 3, the `value_counts` method is used to get a sense of its distribution.

Very interestingly, pandas allows you to pass the `groupby` method any object. This means that you are able to form groups from something completely unrelated to the current DataFrame. Here, we group by the values in the `cuts` variable. For each grouping, we find the percentage of flights per airline with `value_counts` by setting `normalize` to `True`.

Some interesting insights can be drawn from this result. Looking at the full result, SkyWest is the leading airline for under 200 miles but has no flights over 2,000 miles. In contrast, American Airlines has the fifth highest total for flights under 200 miles but has by far the most flights between 1,000 and 2,000 miles.

There's more...

We can find more results when grouping by the `cuts` variable. For instance, we can find the 25th, 50th, and 75th percentile airtime for each distance grouping. As airtime is in minutes, we can divide by 60 to get hours:

```
>>> flights.groupby(cuts)['AIR_TIME'].quantile(q=[.25, .5, .75]) \
                                     .div(60).round(2)
DIST
(-inf, 200.0]      0.25      0.43
                   0.50      0.50
                   0.75      0.57
(200.0, 500.0]     0.25      0.77
```

```
                       0.50      0.92
                       0.75      1.05
(500.0, 1000.0]        0.25      1.43
                       0.50      1.65
                       0.75      1.92
(1000.0, 2000.0]       0.25      2.50
                       0.50      2.93
                       0.75      3.40
(2000.0, inf]          0.25      4.30
                       0.50      4.70
                       0.75      5.03
Name: AIR_TIME, dtype: float64
```

We can use this information to create informative string labels when using the `cut` function. These labels replace the interval notation. We can also chain the `unstack` method which transposes the inner index level to column names:

```
>>> labels=['Under an Hour', '1 Hour', '1-2 Hours',
            '2-4 Hours', '4+ Hours']
>>> cuts2 = pd.cut(flights['DIST'], bins=bins, labels=labels)
>>> flights.groupby(cuts2)['AIRLINE'].value_counts(normalize=True) \
                               .round(3) \
                               .unstack() \
                               .style.highlight_max(axis=1)
```

AIRLINE	AA	AS	B6	DL	EV	F9	HA	MQ	NK	OO	UA	US	VX	WN
DIST														
Under an Hour	0.052	nan	nan	0.086	0.289	nan	nan	0.211	nan	0.326	0.027	nan	nan	0.009
1 Hour	0.071	0.001	0.007	0.189	0.156	0.005	nan	0.1	0.012	0.159	0.062	0.016	0.028	0.194
1-2 Hours	0.144	0.023	0.003	0.206	0.101	0.038	nan	0.051	0.03	0.106	0.131	0.025	0.004	0.138
2-4 Hours	0.264	0.016	0.003	0.165	0.016	0.031	nan	0.003	0.045	0.046	0.199	0.04	0.012	0.16
4+ Hours	0.212	0.012	0.08	0.171	nan	0.004	0.028	nan	0.019	nan	0.289	0.065	0.074	0.046

See also

- Pandas official documentation on the `cut` function (`http://bit.ly/2whcUkJ`)
- Refer to `Chapter 14`, *Restructuring Data into a Tidy Form*, for many more recipes with unstack

Counting the total number of flights between cities

In the flights dataset, we have data on the origin and destination airport. It is trivial to count the number of flights originating in Houston and landing in Atlanta, for instance. What is more difficult is counting the total number of flights between the two cities, regardless of which one is the origin or destination.

Getting ready

In this recipe, we count the total number of flights between two cities regardless of which one is the origin or destination. To accomplish this, we sort the origin and destination airports alphabetically so that each combination of airports always occurs in the same order. We can then use this new column arrangement to form groups and then to count.

How to do it...

1. Read in the flights dataset, and find the total number of flights between each origin and destination airport:

```
>>> flights = pd.read_csv('data/flights.csv')
>>> flights_ct = flights.groupby(['ORG_AIR', 'DEST_AIR']).size()
>>> flights_ct.head()
ORG_AIR   DEST_AIR
ATL       ABE          31
          ABQ          16
          ABY          19
          ACY           6
          AEX          40
dtype: int64
```

2. Select the total number of flights between Houston (*IAH*) and Atlanta (*ATL*) in both directions:

```
>>> flights_ct.loc[[('ATL', 'IAH'), ('IAH', 'ATL')]]
ORG_AIR   DEST_AIR
ATL       IAH            121
IAH       ATL            148
dtype: int64
```

3. We could simply sum these two numbers together to find the total flights between the cities but there is a more efficient and automated solution that can work for all flights. Let's independently sort the origin and destination cities for each row in alphabetical order:

```
>>> flights_sort = flights[['ORG_AIR', 'DEST_AIR']] \
                          .apply(sorted, axis=1)
>>> flights_sort.head()
```

	ORG_AIR	DEST_AIR
0	LAX	SLC
1	DEN	IAD
2	DFW	VPS
3	DCA	DFW
4	LAX	MCI

4. Now that each row has been independently sorted, the column names are not correct. Let's rename them to something more generic and then again find the total number of flights between all cities:

```
>>> rename_dict = {'ORG_AIR':'AIR1', 'DEST_AIR':'AIR2'}
>>> flights_sort = flights_sort.rename(columns=rename_dict)
>>> flights_ct2 = flights_sort.groupby(['AIR1', 'AIR2']).size()
>>> flights_ct2.head()
AIR1   AIR2
ABE    ATL      31
       ORD      24
ABI    DFW      74
ABQ    ATL      16
       DEN      46
dtype: int64
```

5. Let's select all the flights between Atlanta and Houston and verify that it matches the sum of the values in step 2:

```
>>> flights_ct2.loc[('ATL', 'IAH')]
269
```

6. If we try and select flights with Houston followed by Atlanta, we get an error:

```
>>> flights_ct2.loc[('IAH', 'ATL')]
IndexingError: Too many indexers
```

How it works...

In step 1, we form groups by the origin and destination airport columns and then apply the `size` method to the groupby object, which simply returns the total number of rows for each group. Notice that we could have passed the string `size` to the `agg` method to achieve the same result. In step 2, the total number of flights for each direction between Atlanta and Houston are selected. The Series `flights_count` has a MultiIndex with two levels. One way to select rows from a MultiIndex is to pass the `loc` indexing operator a tuple of exact level values. Here, we actually select two different rows, `('ATL', 'HOU')` and `('HOU', 'ATL')`. We use a list of tuples to do this correctly.

Step 3 is the most pertinent step in the recipe. We would like to have just one label for all flights between Atlanta and Houston and so far we have two. If we alphabetically sort each combination of origin and destination airports, we would then have a single label for flights between airports. To do this, we use the DataFrame `apply` method. This is different from the groupby `apply` method. No groups are formed in step 3.

The DataFrame `apply` method must be passed a function. In this case, it's the built-in `sorted` function. By default, this function gets applied to each column as a Series. We can change the direction of computation by using `axis=1` (or `axis='index'`). The `sorted` function has each row of data passed to it implicitly as a Series. It returns a list of sorted airport codes. Here is an example of passing the first row as a Series to the sorted function:

```
>>> sorted(flights.loc[0, ['ORG_AIR', 'DEST_AIR']])
['LAX', 'SLC']
```

The `apply` method iterates over all rows using `sorted` in this exact manner. After completion of this operation, each row is independently sorted. The column names are now meaningless. We rename the column names in the next step and then perform the same grouping and aggregating as was done in step 2. This time, all flights between Atlanta and Houston fall under the same label.

There's more...

You might be wondering why we can't use the simpler `sort_values` Series method. This method does not sort independently and instead, preserves the row or column as a single record as one would expect while doing a data analysis. Step 3 is a very expensive operation and takes several seconds to complete. There are only about 60,000 rows so this solution would not scale well to larger data. Calling the

Step 3 is a very expensive operation and takes several seconds to complete. There are only about 60,000 rows so this solution would not scale well to larger data. Calling the `apply` method with `axis=1` is one of the least performant operations in all of pandas. Internally, pandas loops over each row and does not provide any speed boosts from NumPy. If possible, avoid using `apply` with `axis=1`.

We can get a massive speed increase with the NumPy `sort` function. Let's go ahead and use this function and analyze its output. By default, it sorts each row independently:

```
>>> data_sorted = np.sort(flights[['ORG_AIR', 'DEST_AIR']])
>>> data_sorted[:10]
array([['LAX', 'SLC'],
       ['DEN', 'IAD'],
       ['DFW', 'VPS'],
       ['DCA', 'DFW'],
       ['LAX', 'MCI'],
       ['IAH', 'SAN'],
       ['DFW', 'MSY'],
       ['PHX', 'SFO'],
       ['ORD', 'STL'],
       ['IAH', 'SJC']], dtype=object)
```

A two-dimensional NumPy array is returned. NumPy does not easily do grouping operations so let's use the DataFrame constructor to create a new DataFrame and check whether it equals the `flights_sorted` DataFrame from step 3:

```
>>> flights_sort2 = pd.DataFrame(data_sorted, columns=['AIR1', 'AIR2'])
>>> fs_orig = flights_sort.rename(columns={'ORG_AIR':'AIR1',
                                           'DEST_AIR':'AIR2'})
>>> flights_sort2.equals(fs_orig)
True
```

As the DataFrames are the same, you can replace step 3 with the previous faster sorting routine. Let's time the difference between each of the different sorting methods:

```
>>> %%timeit
>>> flights_sort = flights[['ORG_AIR', 'DEST_AIR']] \
                         .apply(sorted, axis=1)
7.41 s ± 189 ms per loop (mean ± std. dev. of 7 runs, 1 loop each)

>>> %%timeit
>>> data_sorted = np.sort(flights[['ORG_AIR', 'DEST_AIR']])
>>> flights_sort2 = pd.DataFrame(data_sorted,
                              columns=['AIR1', 'AIR2'])
10.6 ms ± 453 µs per loop (mean ± std. dev. of 7 runs, 100 loops each)
```

The NumPy solution is an astounding 700 times faster than using `apply` with pandas.

See also

- NumPy official documentation on the `sort` function (http://bit.ly/2vtRt0M)

Finding the longest streak of on-time flights

One of the most important metrics for airlines is their on-time flight performance. The Federal Aviation Administration considers a flight delayed when it arrives at least 15 minutes later than its scheduled arrival time. Pandas has direct methods to calculate the total and percentage of on-time flights per airline. While these basic summary statistics are an important metric, there are other non-trivial calculations that are interesting, such as finding the length of consecutive on-time flights for each airline at each of its origin airports.

Getting ready

In this recipe, we find the longest consecutive streak of on-time flights for each airline at each origin airport. This requires each value in a column to be aware of the value immediately following it. We make clever use of the `diff` and `cumsum` methods in order to find streaks before applying this methodology to each of the groups.

How to do it...

1. Before we get started with the actual flights dataset, let's practice counting streaks of ones with a small sample Series:

```
>>> s = pd.Series([0, 1, 1, 0, 1, 1, 1, 0])
>>> s
0    0
1    1
2    1
3    0
4    1
5    1
6    1
7    0
dtype: int64
```

2. Our final representation of the streaks of ones will be a Series of the same length as the original with an independent count beginning from one for each streak. To get started, let's use the `cumsum` method:

```
>>> s1 = s.cumsum()
>>> s1
0    0
1    1
2    2
3    2
4    3
5    4
6    5
7    5
dtype: int64
```

3. We have now accumulated all the ones going down the Series. Let's multiply this Series by the original:

```
>>> s.mul(s1)
0    0
1    1
2    2
3    0
4    3
5    4
6    5
7    0
dtype: int64
```

4. We have only non-zero values where we originally had ones. This result is fairly close to what we desire. We just need to restart each streak at one instead of where the cumulative sum left off. Let's chain the `diff` method, which subtracts the previous value from the current:

```
>>> s.mul(s1).diff()
0     NaN
1     1.0
2     1.0
3    -2.0
4     3.0
5     1.0
6     1.0
7    -5.0
dtype: float64
```

5. A negative value represents the end of a streak. We need to propagate the negative values down the Series and use them to subtract away the excess accumulation from step 2. To do this, we will make all non-negative values missing with the `where` method:

```
>>> s.mul(s1).diff().where(lambda x: x < 0)
0     NaN
1     NaN
2     NaN
3    -2.0
4     NaN
5     NaN
6     NaN
7    -5.0
dtype: float64
```

6. We can now propagate these values down with the `ffill` method:

```
>>> s.mul(s1).diff().where(lambda x: x < 0).ffill()
0     NaN
1     NaN
2     NaN
3    -2.0
4    -2.0
5    -2.0
6    -2.0
7    -5.0
dtype: float64
```

7. Finally, we can add this Series back to `s1` to clear out the excess accumulation:

```
>>> s.mul(s1).diff().where(lambda x: x < 0).ffill() \
        .add(s1, fill_value=0)
0    0.0
1    1.0
2    2.0
3    0.0
4    1.0
5    2.0
6    3.0
7    0.0
dtype: float64
```

8. Now that we have a working consecutive streak finder, we can find the longest streak per airline and origin airport. Let's read in the flights dataset and create a column to represent on-time arrival:

```
>>> flights = pd.read_csv('data/flights.csv')
>>> flights['ON_TIME'] = flights['ARR_DELAY'].lt(15).astype(int)
>>> flights[['AIRLINE', 'ORG_AIR', 'ON_TIME']].head(10)
```

	AIRLINE	ORG_AIR	ON_TIME
0	WN	LAX	0
1	UA	DEN	1
2	MQ	DFW	0
3	AA	DFW	1
4	WN	LAX	0
5	UA	IAH	1
6	AA	DFW	0
7	F9	SFO	1
8	AA	ORD	1
9	UA	IAH	1

9. Use our logic from the first seven steps to define a function that returns the maximum streak of ones for a given Series:

```
>>> def max_streak(s):
        s1 = s.cumsum()
        return s.mul(s1).diff().where(lambda x: x < 0) \
            .ffill().add(s1, fill_value=0).max()
```

10. Find the maximum streak of on-time arrivals per airline and origin airport along with the total number of flights and percentage of on-time arrivals. First, sort the day of the year and scheduled departure time:

```
>>> flights.sort_values(['MONTH', 'DAY', 'SCHED_DEP']) \
        .groupby(['AIRLINE', 'ORG_AIR'])['ON_TIME'] \
        .agg(['mean', 'size', max_streak]).round(2).head()
```

AIRLINE	ORG_AIR	mean	size	max_streak
AA	ATL	0.82	233	15
	DEN	0.74	219	17
	DFW	0.78	4006	64
	IAH	0.80	196	24
	LAS	0.79	374	29

How it works...

Finding streaks in the data is not a straightforward operation in pandas and requires methods that look ahead or behind, such as `diff` or `shift`, or those that remember their current state, such as `cumsum`. The final result from the first seven steps is a Series the same length as the original that keeps track of all consecutive ones. Throughout these steps, we use the `mul` and `add` methods instead of their operator equivalents (*) and (+). In my opinion, this allows for a slightly cleaner progression of calculations from left to right. You, of course, can replace these with the actual operators.

Ideally, we would like to tell pandas to apply the `cumsum` method to the start of each streak and reset itself after the end of each one. It takes many steps to convey this message to pandas. Step 2 accumulates all the ones in the Series as a whole. The rest of the steps slowly remove any excess accumulation. In order to identify this excess accumulation, we need to find the end of each streak and subtract this value from the beginning of the next streak.

To find the end of each streak, we cleverly make all values not part of the streak zero by multiplying `s1` by the original Series of zeros and ones in step 3. The first zero following a non-zero, marks the end of a streak. That's good, but again, we need to eliminate the excess accumulation. Knowing where the streak ends doesn't exactly get us there.

In step 4, we use the `diff` method to find this excess. The `diff` method takes the difference between the current value and any value located at a set number of rows away from it. By default, the difference between the current and the immediately preceding value is returned.

Only negative values are meaningful in step 4. Those are the ones immediately following the end of a streak. These values need to be propagated down until the end of the following streak. To eliminate (make missing) all the values we don't care about, we use the `where` method, which takes a Series of conditionals of the same size as the calling Series. By default, all the `True` values remain the same, while the `False` values become missing. The `where` method allows you to use the calling Series as part of the conditional by taking a function as its first parameter. An anonymous function is used, which gets passed the calling Series implicitly and checks whether each value is less than zero. The result of step 5 is a Series where only the negative values are preserved with the rest changed to missing.

The `ffill` method in step 6 replaces missing values with the last non-missing value going forward/down a Series. As the first three values don't follow a non-missing value, they remain missing. We finally have our Series that removes the excess accumulation. We add our accumulation Series to the result of step 6 to get the streaks all beginning from zero. The `add` method allows us to replace the missing values with the `fill_value` parameter. This completes the process of finding streaks of ones in the dataset. When doing complex logic like this, it is a good idea to use a small dataset where you know what the final output will be. It would be quite a difficult task to start at step 8 and build this streak-finding logic while grouping.

In step 8, we create the ON_TIME column. One item of note is that the cancelled flights have missing values for ARR_DELAY, which do not pass the boolean condition and therefore result in a zero for the ON_TIME column. Canceled flights are treated the same as delayed.

Step 9 turns our logic from the first seven steps into a function and chains the max method to return the longest streak. As our function returns a single value, it is formally an aggregating function and can be passed to the agg method as done in step 10. To ensure that we are looking at actual consecutive flights, we use the sort_values method to sort by date and scheduled departure time.

There's more...

Now that we have found the longest streaks of on-time arrivals, we can easily find the opposite--the longest streak of delayed arrivals. The following function returns two rows for each group passed to it. The first row is the start of the streak, and the last row is the end of the streak. Each row contains the month and day that the streak started/ended, along with the total streak length:

```
>>> def max_delay_streak(df):
        df = df.reset_index(drop=True)
        s = 1 - df['ON_TIME']
        s1 = s.cumsum()
        streak = s.mul(s1).diff().where(lambda x: x < 0) \
                .ffill().add(s1, fill_value=0)
        last_idx = streak.idxmax()
        first_idx = last_idx - streak.max() + 1
        df_return = df.loc[[first_idx, last_idx], ['MONTH', 'DAY']]
        df_return['streak'] = streak.max()
        df_return.index = ['first', 'last']
        df_return.index.name='type'
        return df_return

>>> flights.sort_values(['MONTH', 'DAY', 'SCHED_DEP']) \
        .groupby(['AIRLINE', 'ORG_AIR']) \
        .apply(max_delay_streak) \
        .sort_values('streak', ascending=False).head(10)
```

			MONTH	DAY	streak
AIRLINE	**ORG_AIR**	**streak_row**			
AA	**DFW**	first	2.0	26.0	38.0
		last	3.0	1.0	38.0
MQ	**ORD**	first	1.0	6.0	28.0
		last	1.0	12.0	28.0
	DFW	first	2.0	21.0	25.0
		last	2.0	26.0	25.0
NK	**ORD**	first	6.0	7.0	15.0
		last	6.0	18.0	15.0
DL	**ATL**	first	12.0	23.0	14.0
		last	12.0	24.0	14.0

As we are using the `apply` groupby method, a DataFrame of each group is passed to the `max_delay_streak` function. Inside this function, the index of the DataFrame is dropped and replaced by a `RangeIndex` in order for us to easily find the first and last row of the streak. The `ON_TIME` column is inverted and then the same logic is used to find streaks of delayed flights. The index of the first and last rows of the streak are stored as variables. These indexes are then used to select the month and day when the streaks ended. We use a DataFrame to return our results. We label and name the index to make the final result clearer.

Our final results show the longest delayed streaks accompanied by the first and last date. Let's investigate to see if we can find out why these delays happened. Inclement weather is a common reason for delayed or canceled flights. Looking at the first row, American Airlines (AA) started a streak of 38 delayed flights in a row from the Dallas Fort-Worth (DFW) airport beginning February 26 until March 1 of 2015. Looking at historical weather data from February 27, 2015, two inches of snow fell, which was a record for that day (`http://bit.ly/2iLGsCg`). This was a major weather event for DFW and caused massive problems for the entire city (`http://bit.ly/2wmsHPj`). Notice that DFW makes another appearance as the third longest streak but this time a few days earlier and for a different airline.

See also

- Pandas official documentation of `ffill` (`http://bit.ly/2gn5zGU`

Restructuring Data into a Tidy Form

14

All the datasets used in the preceding chapters have not had much or any work done to change their structure. We immediately began processing the datasets in their original shape. Many datasets in the wild will need a significant amount of restructuring before commencing a more detailed analysis. In some cases, an entire project might only be concerned with formatting the data in such a way that it can be easily processed by someone else.

In this chapter, we will cover the following topics:

- Tidying variable values as column names with `stack`
- Tidying variable values as column names with `melt`
- Stacking multiple groups of variables simultaneously
- Inverting stacked data
- Unstacking after a `groupby` aggregation
- Replicating `pivot_table` with a `groupby` aggregation
- Renaming axis levels for easy reshaping
- Tidying when multiple variables are stored as column names
- Tidying when multiple variables are stored as column values
- Tidying when two or more values are stored in the same cell
- Tidying when variables are stored in column names and values
- Tidying when multiple observational units are stored in the same table

There are many terms that are used to describe the process of data restructuring, with **tidy data** being the most common to data scientists. Tidy data is a term coined by Hadley Wickham to describe a form of data that makes analysis easy to do. This chapter will cover many ideas formulated by Hadley and how to accomplish them with pandas. To learn a great deal more about tidy data, read Hadley's paper (`http://vita.had.co.nz/papers/tidy-data.pdf`).

What is tidy data? Hadley puts forth three simple guiding principles that determine whether a dataset is tidy or not:

- Each variable forms a column
- Each observation forms a row
- Each type of observational unit forms a table

Any dataset that does not meet these guidelines is considered messy. This definition will make more sense once we start restructuring our data into tidy form, but for now, we'll need to know what variables, observations, and observational units are.

To gain intuition about what a variable actually is, it is good to think about the distinction between a variable name and the variable value. The variable names are labels, such as gender, race, salary, and position. The variable values are those things liable to change for every observation, such as male/female for gender or white/black for race. A single observation is the collection of all variable values for a single observational unit. To help understand what an observational unit might be, consider a retail store, which has data for each transaction, employee, customer, item, and the store itself. Each of these can be considered an observational unit and would require its own table. Combining employee information (like the number of hours worked) with customer information (like amount spent) in the same table would break this tidy principle.

The first step to resolving messy data is to recognize it when it exists, and there are boundless possibilities. Hadley explicitly mentions five of the most common types of messy data:

- Column names are values, not variable names
- Multiple variables are stored in column names
- Variables are stored in both rows and columns
- Multiple types of observational units are stored in the same table
- A single observational unit is stored in multiple tables

It is important to understand that tidying data does not typically involve changing the values of your dataset, filling in missing values, or doing any sort of analysis. Tidying data involves changing the shape or structure of the data to meet the tidy principles. Tidy data is akin to having all your tools in the toolbox instead of scattered randomly throughout your house. Having the tools properly in the toolbox allows all other tasks to be completed easily. Once the data is in the correct form, it becomes much easier to perform further analysis.

Once you have spotted messy data, you will use the pandas tools to restructure the data, so that it is tidy. The main tidy tools that pandas has available for you are the DataFrame methods `stack`, `melt`, `unstack`, and `pivot`. More complex tidying involves ripping apart text, which necessitates the `str` accessor. Other helper methods, such as `rename`, `rename_axis`, `reset_index`, and `set_index` will help with applying the final touches to tidy data.

Tidying variable values as column names with stack

To help understand the differences between tidy and messy data, let's take a look at a simple table that may or may not be in tidy form:

```
>>> state_fruit = pd.read_csv('data/state_fruit.csv', index_col=0)
>>> state_fruit
```

	Apple	Orange	Banana
Texas	12	10	40
Arizona	9	7	12
Florida	0	14	190

There does not appear to be anything messy about this table, and the information is easily consumable. However, according to the tidy principles, it isn't actually tidy. Each column name is actually the value of a variable. In fact, none of the variable names are even present in the DataFrame. One of the first steps to transform a messy dataset into tidy data is to identify all of the variables. In this particular dataset, we have variables for **state** and **fruit**. There's also the numeric data that wasn't identified anywhere in the context of the problem. We can label this variable as **weight** or any other sensible name.

Getting ready

This particular messy dataset contains variable values as column names. We will need to transpose these column names into column values. In this recipe, we use the `stack` method to restructure our DataFrame into tidy form.

How to do it...

1. First, take note that the state names are in the index of the DataFrame. These states are correctly placed vertically and do not need to be restructured. It is the column names that are the problem. The `stack` method takes all of the column names and reshapes them to be vertical as a single index level:

```
>>> state_fruit.stack()
Texas      Apple       12
           Orange      10
           Banana      40
Arizona    Apple        9
           Orange       7
           Banana      12
Florida    Apple        0
           Orange      14
           Banana     190
dtype: int64
```

2. Notice that we now have a Series with a MultiIndex. There are now two levels in the index. The original index has been pushed to the left to make room for the old column names. With this one command, we now essentially have tidy data. Each variable, state, fruit, and weight is vertical. Let's use the `reset_index` method to turn the result into a DataFrame:

```
>>> state_fruit_tidy = state_fruit.stack().reset_index()
>>> state_fruit_tidy
```

	level_0	level_1	0
0	Texas	Apple	12
1	Texas	Orange	10
2	Texas	Banana	40
3	Arizona	Apple	9
4	Arizona	Orange	7
5	Arizona	Banana	12
6	Florida	Apple	0
7	Florida	Orange	14
8	Florida	Banana	190

3. Our structure is now correct, but the column names are meaningless. Let's replace them with proper identifiers:

```
>>> state_fruit_tidy.columns = ['state', 'fruit', 'weight']
>>> state_fruit_tidy
```

	state	fruit	weight
0	Texas	Apple	12
1	Texas	Orange	10
2	Texas	Banana	40
3	Arizona	Apple	9
4	Arizona	Orange	7
5	Arizona	Banana	12
6	Florida	Apple	0
7	Florida	Orange	14
8	Florida	Banana	190

4. Instead of directly changing the columns attribute, it's possible to use the lesser-known Series method `rename_axis` to set the names of the index levels before using `reset_index`:

```
>>> state_fruit.stack()\
            .rename_axis(['state', 'fruit'])

state    fruit
Texas    Apple      12
         Orange     10
         Banana     40
Arizona  Apple       9
         Orange      7
         Banana     12
Florida  Apple       0
         Orange     14
         Banana    190
dtype: int64
```

5. From here, we can simply chain the `reset_index` method with the `name` parameter to reproduce the output from step 3:

```
>>> state_fruit.stack()\
            .rename_axis(['state', 'fruit'])\
            .reset_index(name='weight')
```

How it works...

The `stack` method is powerful and it takes time to understand and appreciate fully. It takes all the column names and transposes them, so they become the new innermost index level. Notice how each old column name still labels its original value by being paired with each state. There were nine original values in a 3 x 3 DataFrame, which got transformed into a single Series with the same number of values. The original first row of data became the first three values in the resulting Series.

After resetting the index in step 2, pandas defaults our DataFrame columns to `level_0`, `level_1`, and `0`. This is because the Series calling this method has two index levels that were formally unnamed. Pandas also refers to indexes by integer beginning from zero from the outside.

Step 3 shows a simple and intuitive way to rename the columns. You can simply set new columns for the entire DataFrame by setting the columns attribute equal to a list.

Alternatively, it is possible to set the column names in a single step by chaining the
`rename_axis` method that, when passing a list as the first argument, uses those values as
the index level names. Pandas uses these index level names as the new column names
when the index is reset. Additionally, the `reset_index` method has a `name` parameter
corresponding to the new column name of the Series values.

> All Series have a `name` attribute that can be set directly or with the `rename`
> method. It is this attribute that becomes the column name when using
> `reset_index`.

There's more...

One of the keys to using `stack` is to place all of the columns that you do not wish to
transform in the index. The dataset in this recipe was initially read with the states in the
index. Let's take a look at what would have happened if we did not read the states into the
index:

```
>>> state_fruit2 = pd.read_csv('data/state_fruit2.csv')
>>> state_fruit2
```

	State	Apple	Orange	Banana
0	Texas	12	10	40
1	Arizona	9	7	12
2	Florida	0	14	190

As the state names are not in the index, using `stack` on this DataFrame reshapes all values
into one long Series of values:

```
>>> state_fruit2.stack()
0   State       Texas
    Apple          12
    Orange         10
    Banana         40
1   State     Arizona
    Apple           9
    Orange          7
    Banana         12
2   State     Florida
    Apple           0
    Orange         14
    Banana        190
```

```
dtype: object
```

This command reshapes all the columns, this time including the states, and is not at all what we need. In order to reshape this data correctly, you will need to put all the non-reshaped columns into the index first with the `set_index` method, and then use `stack`. The following code gives a similar result to step 1:

```
>>> state_fruit2.set_index('State').stack()
```

See also

- Pandas official documentation on *Reshaping and Pivot Tables* (http://bit.ly/2xbnNms)
- Pandas official documentation on the `stack` method (http://bit.ly/2vWZhH1)

Tidying variable values as column names with melt

Like most large Python libraries, pandas has many different ways to accomplish the same task--the differences usually being readability and performance. Pandas contains a DataFrame method named `melt` that works similarly to the `stack` method described in the previous recipe but gives a bit more flexibility.

Before pandas version 0.20, `melt` was only provided as a function that had to be accessed with `pd.melt`. Pandas is still an evolving library and you need to expect changes with each new version. Pandas has been making a push to move all functions that only operate on DataFrames to methods, such as they did with `melt`. This is the preferred way to use `melt` and the way this recipe uses it. Check the *What's New* part of the pandas documentation to stay up to date with all the changes (http://bit.ly/2xzXIhG).

Getting ready

In this recipe, we use the `melt` method to tidy a simple DataFrame with variable values as column names.

How to do it...

1. Read in the `state_fruit2` dataset and identify which columns need to be transformed and which ones do not:

```
>>> state_fruit2 = pd.read_csv('data/state_fruit2.csv')
>>> state_fruit2
```

	State	Apple	Orange	Banana
0	Texas	12	10	40
1	Arizona	9	7	12
2	Florida	0	14	190

2. Use the `melt` method by passing the appropriate columns to the `id_vars` and `value_vars` parameters:

```
>>> state_fruit2.melt(id_vars=['State'],
                      value_vars=['Apple', 'Orange', 'Banana'])
```

	State	variable	value
0	Texas	Apple	12
1	Arizona	Apple	9
2	Florida	Apple	0
3	Texas	Orange	10
4	Arizona	Orange	7
5	Florida	Orange	14
6	Texas	Banana	40
7	Arizona	Banana	12
8	Florida	Banana	190

3. This one step creates tidy data for us. By default, `melt` refers to the transformed former column names as *variable* and the corresponding values as *value*. Conveniently, `melt` has two additional parameters, `var_name` and `value_name`, that give you the ability to rename these two columns:

```
>>> state_fruit2.melt(id_vars=['State'],
                       value_vars=['Apple', 'Orange', 'Banana'],
                       var_name='Fruit',
                       value_name='Weight')
```

	State	Fruit	Weight
0	Texas	Apple	12
1	Arizona	Apple	9
2	Florida	Apple	0
3	Texas	Orange	10
4	Arizona	Orange	7
5	Florida	Orange	14
6	Texas	Banana	40
7	Arizona	Banana	12
8	Florida	Banana	190

How it works...

The `melt` method is powerful and dramatically reshapes your DataFrame. It takes up to five parameters, with two of them being crucial to understanding how to reshape your data correctly:

- `id_vars` is a list of column names that you want to preserve as columns and not reshape
- `value_vars` is a list of column names that you want to reshape into a single column

The `id_vars`, or the identification variables, remain in the same column but repeat for each of the columns passed to `value_vars`. One crucial aspect of `melt` is that it ignores values in the index, and, in fact, it silently drops your index and replaces it with a default `RangeIndex`. This means that if you do have values in your index that you would like to keep, you will need to reset the index first before using `melt`.

It is somewhat common terminology to refer to the transformation of horizontal column names into vertical column values as **melting, stacking,** or **unpivoting.**

There's more...

All the parameters for the `melt` method are optional, and if you desire all your values to be in a single column and their old column labels to be in the other, you may call `melt` with just its defaults:

```
>>> state_fruit2.melt()
```

	variable	value
0	State	Texas
1	State	Arizona
2	State	Florida
3	Apple	12
4	Apple	9
5	Apple	0
6	Orange	10
7	Orange	7
8	Orange	14
9	Banana	40
10	Banana	12
11	Banana	190

More realistically, you might have lots of variables that need melting and would like to specify only the identification variables. In that case, calling `melt` in the following manner will yield the same result as in step 2. You actually don't even need a list when melting a single column and can simply pass its string value:

```
>>> state_fruit2.melt(id_vars='State')
```

See also

- Pandas official documentation on the `melt` method (`http://bit.ly/2vcuZNJ`)
- Pandas developers discussion of `melt` and other similar functions being converted to methods (`http://bit.ly/2iqIQhI`)

Stacking multiple groups of variables simultaneously

Some datasets contain multiple groups of variables as column names that need to be stacked simultaneously into their own columns. An example of the `movie` dataset can help clarify this. Let's begin by selecting all columns containing the actor names and their corresponding Facebook likes:

```
>>> movie = pd.read_csv('data/movie.csv')
>>> actor = movie[['movie_title', 'actor_1_name',
                    'actor_2_name', 'actor_3_name',
                    'actor_1_facebook_likes',
                    'actor_2_facebook_likes',
                    'actor_3_facebook_likes']]
>>> actor.head()
```

	movie_title	actor_1_name	actor_2_name	actor_3_name	actor_1_facebook_likes	actor_2_facebook_likes	actor_3_facebook_likes
0	Avatar	CCH Pounder	Joel David Moore	Wes Studi	1000.0	936.0	855.0
1	Pirates of the Caribbean: At World's End	Johnny Depp	Orlando Bloom	Jack Davenport	40000.0	5000.0	1000.0
2	Spectre	Christoph Waltz	Rory Kinnear	Stephanie Sigman	11000.0	393.0	161.0
3	The Dark Knight Rises	Tom Hardy	Christian Bale	Joseph Gordon-Levitt	27000.0	23000.0	23000.0
4	Star Wars: Episode VII - The Force Awakens	Doug Walker	Rob Walker	NaN	131.0	12.0	NaN

If we define our variables as the title of the movie, the actor name, and the number of Facebook likes, then we will need to stack independently two sets of columns, which is not possible using a single call to `stack` or `melt`.

Getting ready

In this recipe, we will tidy our `actor` DataFrame by simultaneously stacking the actor names and their corresponding Facebook likes with the `wide_to_long` function.

How to do it...

1. We will be using the versatile `wide_to_long` function to reshape our data into tidy form. To use this function, we will need to change the column names that we are stacking, so that they end with a digit. We first create a user-defined function to change the column names:

```
>>> def change_col_name(col_name):
        col_name = col_name.replace('_name', '')
        if 'facebook' in col_name:
            fb_idx = col_name.find('facebook')
            col_name = col_name[:5] + col_name[fb_idx - 1:] \
                                + col_name[5:fb_idx-1]
        return col_name
```

2. Pass this function to the `rename` method to transform all the column names:

```
>>> actor2 = actor.rename(columns=change_col_name)
>>> actor2.head()
```

	movie_title	actor_1	actor_2	actor_3	actor_facebook_likes_1	actor_facebook_likes_2	actor_facebook_likes_3
0	Avatar	CCH Pounder	Joel David Moore	Wes Studi	1000.0	936.0	855.0
1	Pirates of the Caribbean: At World's End	Johnny Depp	Orlando Bloom	Jack Davenport	40000.0	5000.0	1000.0
2	Spectre	Christoph Waltz	Rory Kinnear	Stephanie Sigman	11000.0	393.0	161.0
3	The Dark Knight Rises	Tom Hardy	Christian Bale	Joseph Gordon-Levitt	27000.0	23000.0	23000.0
4	Star Wars: Episode VII - The Force Awakens	Doug Walker	Rob Walker	NaN	131.0	12.0	NaN

3. Use the `wide_to_long` function to stack the actor and Facebook sets of columns simultaneously:

```
>>> stubs = ['actor', 'actor_facebook_likes']
>>> actor2_tidy = pd.wide_to_long(actor2,
                                  stubnames=stubs,
                                  i=['movie_title'],
                                  j='actor_num',
                                  sep='_')
>>> actor2_tidy.head()
```

	movie_title	actor_num	actor	actor_facebook_likes
0	Avatar	1	CCH Pounder	1000.0
1	Pirates of the Caribbean: At World's End	1	Johnny Depp	40000.0
2	Spectre	1	Christoph Waltz	11000.0
3	The Dark Knight Rises	1	Tom Hardy	27000.0
4	Star Wars: Episode VII - The Force Awakens	1	Doug Walker	131.0

How it works...

The `wide_to_long` function works in a fairly specific manner. Its main parameter is `stubnames`, which is a list of strings. Each string represents a single column grouping. All columns that begin with this string will be stacked into a single column. In this recipe, there are two groups of columns: *actor*, and *actor_facebook_likes*. By default, each of these groups of columns will need to end in a digit. This digit will subsequently be used to label the reshaped data. Each of these column groups has an underscore character separating the `stubname` from the ending digit. To account for this, you must use the `sep` parameter.

The original column names do not match the pattern needed for `wide_to_long` to work. The column names could have been changed manually by exactly specifying their values with a list. This could quickly become a lot of typing so instead, we define a function that automatically converts our columns to a format that works. The `change_col_name` function removes **_name** from the actor columns and rearranges the Facebook columns so that now they both end in digits.

To actually accomplish the column renaming, we use the `rename` method in step 2. It accepts many different types of arguments, one of which is a function. When passing it to a function, every column name gets implicitly passed to it one at a time.

We have now correctly created two independent groups of columns, those beginning with **actor** and **actor_facebook_likes** that will be stacked. In addition to this, `wide_to_long` requires a unique column, parameter `i`, to act as an identification variable that will not be stacked. Also required is the parameter `j`, which simply renames the identifying digit stripped from the end of the original column names. By default, the prefix parameter contains the **regular expression**, **\d+** that searches for one more or more digits. The **\d** is a special token that matches the digits 0-9. The plus sign, **+**, makes the expression match for one or more of these digits.

To become a powerful user of the `str` methods, you will need to be familiar with regular expressions, which are a sequence of characters that match a particular pattern within some text. They consist of **metacharacters**, which have a special meaning, and **literal** characters. To make yourself useful with regular expressions check this short tutorial from *Regular-Expressions.info* (`http://bit.ly/2wiWPbz`).

There's more...

The function `wide_to_long` works when all groupings of variables have the same numeric ending as they did in this recipe. When your variables do not have the same ending or don't end in a digit, you can still use `wide_to_long` to do simultaneous column stacking. For instance, let's take a look at the following dataset:

```
>>> df = pd.read_csv('data/stackme.csv')
>>> df
```

	State	Country	a1	b2	Test	d	e
0	TX	US	0.45	0.3	Test1	2	6
1	MA	US	0.03	1.2	Test2	9	7
2	ON	CAN	0.70	4.2	Test3	4	2

Let's say we wanted columns `a1` and `b1` stacked together, as well as columns `d` and `e`. Additionally, we wanted to use `a1` and `b1` as labels for the rows. To accomplish this task, we would need to rename the columns so that they ended in the label we desired:

```
>>> df2 = df.rename(columns = {'a1':'group1_a1', 'b2':'group1_b2',
                               'd':'group2_a1', 'e':'group2_b2'})
>>> df2
```

	State	Country	group1_a1	group1_b2	Test	group2_a1	group2_b2
0	TX	US	0.45	0.3	Test1	2	6
1	MA	US	0.03	1.2	Test2	9	7
2	ON	CAN	0.70	4.2	Test3	4	2

We would then need to modify the suffix parameter, which normally defaults to a regular expression that selects digits. Here, we simply tell it to find any number of characters:

```
>>> pd.wide_to_long(df2,
                    stubnames=['group1', 'group2'],
                    i=['State', 'Country', 'Test'],
                    j='Label',
                    suffix='.+',
                    sep='_')
```

State	Country	Test	Label	group1	group2
TX	US	Test1	a1	0.45	2
			b2	0.30	6
MA	US	Test2	a1	0.03	9
			b2	1.20	7
ON	CAN	Test3	a1	0.70	4
			b2	4.20	2

See also

- Pandas official documentation for `wide_to_long` (http://bit.ly/2xb8NVP)

Inverting stacked data

DataFrames have two similar methods, `stack` and `melt`, to convert horizontal column names into vertical column values. DataFrames have the ability to invert these two operations directly with the `unstack` and `pivot` methods respectively. `stack`/`unstack` are simpler methods that allow control over only the column/row indexes, while `melt`/`pivot` gives more flexibility to choose which columns are reshaped.

Getting ready

In this recipe, we will `stack`/`melt` a dataset and promptly invert the operation with `unstack`/`pivot` back to its original form.

How to do it...

1. Read in the `college` dataset with the institution name as the index, and with only the undergraduate race columns:

```
>>> usecol_func = lambda x: 'UGDS_' in x or x == 'INSTNM'
>>> college = pd.read_csv('data/college.csv',
                          index_col='INSTNM',
                          usecols=usecol_func)
>>> college.head()
```

INSTNM	UGDS_WHITE	UGDS_BLACK	UGDS_HISP	UGDS_ASIAN	UGDS_AIAN	UGDS_NHPI	UGDS_2MOR	UGDS_NRA	UGDS_UNKN
Alabama A & M University	0.0333	0.9353	0.0055	0.0019	0.0024	0.0019	0.0000	0.0059	0.0138
University of Alabama at Birmingham	0.5922	0.2600	0.0283	0.0518	0.0022	0.0007	0.0368	0.0179	0.0100
Amridge University	0.2990	0.4192	0.0069	0.0034	0.0000	0.0000	0.0000	0.0000	0.2715
University of Alabama in Huntsville	0.6988	0.1255	0.0382	0.0376	0.0143	0.0002	0.0172	0.0332	0.0350
Alabama State University	0.0158	0.9208	0.0121	0.0019	0.0010	0.0006	0.0098	0.0243	0.0137

2. Use the `stack` method to convert each horizontal column name into a vertical index level:

```
>>> college_stacked = college.stack()
>>> college_stacked.head(18)
INSTNM
Alabama A & M University         UGDS_WHITE    0.0333
                                 UGDS_BLACK    0.9353
                                 UGDS_HISP     0.0055
                                 UGDS_ASIAN    0.0019
                                 UGDS_AIAN     0.0024
                                 UGDS_NHPI     0.0019
                                 UGDS_2MOR     0.0000
                                 UGDS_NRA      0.0059
                                 UGDS_UNKN     0.0138
University of Alabama at Birmingham  UGDS_WHITE    0.5922
                                 UGDS_BLACK    0.2600
                                 UGDS_HISP     0.0283
                                 UGDS_ASIAN    0.0518
                                 UGDS_AIAN     0.0022
                                 UGDS_NHPI     0.0007
                                 UGDS_2MOR     0.0368
                                 UGDS_NRA      0.0179
                                 UGDS_UNKN     0.0100
dtype: float64
```

3. Invert this stacked data back to its original form with the `unstack` Series method:

```
>>> college_stacked.unstack()
```

4. A similar sequence of operations can be done with `melt` followed by `pivot`. First, read in the data without putting the institution name in the index:

```
>>> college2 = pd.read_csv('data/college.csv',
                           usecols=usecol_func)
>>> college2.head()
```

	INSTNM	UGDS_WHITE	UGDS_BLACK	UGDS_HISP	UGDS_ASIAN	UGDS_AIAN	UGDS_NHPI	UGDS_2MOR	UGDS_NRA	UGDS_UNKN
0	Alabama A & M University	0.0333	0.9353	0.0055	0.0019	0.0024	0.0019	0.0000	0.0059	0.0138
1	University of Alabama at Birmingham	0.5922	0.2600	0.0283	0.0518	0.0022	0.0007	0.0368	0.0179	0.0100
2	Amridge University	0.2990	0.4192	0.0069	0.0034	0.0000	0.0000	0.0000	0.0000	0.2715
3	University of Alabama in Huntsville	0.6988	0.1255	0.0382	0.0376	0.0143	0.0002	0.0172	0.0332	0.0350
4	Alabama State University	0.0158	0.9208	0.0121	0.0019	0.0010	0.0006	0.0098	0.0243	0.0137

5. Use the `melt` method to transpose all the race columns into a single column:

```
>>> college_melted = college2.melt(id_vars='INSTNM',
                                   var_name='Race',
                                   value_name='Percentage')
>>> college_melted.head()
```

	INSTNM	Race	Percentage
0	Alabama A & M University	UGDS_WHITE	0.0333
1	University of Alabama at Birmingham	UGDS_WHITE	0.5922
2	Amridge University	UGDS_WHITE	0.2990
3	University of Alabama in Huntsville	UGDS_WHITE	0.6988
4	Alabama State University	UGDS_WHITE	0.0158

6. Use the `pivot` method to invert this previous result:

```
>>> melted_inv = college_melted.pivot(index='INSTNM',
                                        columns='Race',
                                        values='Percentage')
>>> melted_inv.head()
```

Race	UGDS_2MOR	UGDS_AIAN	UGDS_ASIAN	UGDS_BLACK	UGDS_HISP	UGDS_NHPI	UGDS_NRA	UGDS_UNKN	UGDS_WHITE
INSTNM									
A & W Healthcare Educators	0.0000	0.0	0.0000	0.9750	0.0250	0.0	0.0000	0.0000	0.0000
A T Still University of Health Sciences	NaN	NaN	NaN	NaN	NaN	NaN	NaN	NaN	NaN
ABC Beauty Academy	0.0000	0.0	0.9333	0.0333	0.0333	0.0	0.0000	0.0000	0.0000
ABC Beauty College Inc	0.0000	0.0	0.0000	0.6579	0.0526	0.0	0.0000	0.0000	0.2895
AI Miami International University of Art and Design	0.0018	0.0	0.0018	0.0198	0.4773	0.0	0.0025	0.4644	0.0324

7. Notice that the institution names are now shuttled over into the index and are not in their original order. The column names are not in their original order. To get an exact replication of our starting DataFrame from step 4, use the `.loc` indexing operator to select rows and columns simultaneously and then reset the index:

```
>>> college2_replication = melted_inv.loc[college2['INSTNM'],
                                           college2.columns[1:]]\
                           .reset_index()
>>> college2.equals(college2_replication)
True
```

How it works...

There are multiple ways to accomplish the same thing in step 1. Here, we show the versatility of the `read_csv` function. The `usecols` parameter accepts either a list of the columns that we would like to import or a function that dynamically determines them. We use an anonymous function that checks whether the column name contains `UGDS_` or is equal to `INSTNM`. The function is passed each column name as a string and must return a boolean. A huge amount of memory can be saved in this manner.

The `stack` method in step 2 puts all column names into the innermost index level and returns a Series. In step 3, the `unstack` method inverts this operation by taking all the values in the innermost index level converting them to column names.

 The result from step 3 isn't quite an exact replication of step 1. There are entire rows of missing values, and by default, the `stack` method drops these during step 2. To keep these missing values and create an exact replication, use `dropna=False` in the `stack` method.

Step 4 reads in the same dataset as in step 1 but does not put the institution name in the index because the `melt` method isn't able to access it. Step 5 uses the `melt` method to transpose all the **Race** columns. It does this by leaving the `value_vars` parameter as its default value `None`. When not specified, all the columns not present in the `id_vars` parameter get transposed.

Step 6 inverts the operation from step 5 with the `pivot` method, which accepts three parameters. Each parameter takes a single column as a string. The column referenced by the `index` parameter remains vertical and becomes the new index. The values of the column referenced by the `columns` parameter become the column names. The values referenced by the `values` parameter become tiled to correspond with the intersection of their former index and columns label.

To make an exact replication with `pivot`, we need to sort the rows and columns in the exact order from the original. As the institution name is in the index, we use the `.loc` indexing operator as a way to sort the DataFrame by its original index.

There's more...

To help further understand `stack`/`unstack`, let's use them to **transpose** the `college` DataFrame.

 In this context, we are using the precise mathematical definition of the transposing of a matrix, where the new rows are the old columns of the original data matrix.

If you take a look at the output from step 2, you'll notice that there are two index levels. By default, the `unstack` method uses the innermost index level as the new column values. Index levels are numbered beginning from zero from the outside. Pandas defaults the `level` parameter of the `unstack` method to -1, which refers to the innermost index. We can instead `unstack` the outermost column using `level=0`:

```
>>> college.stack().unstack(0)
```

INSTNM	Alabama A & M University	University of Alabama at Birmingham	Amridge University	University of Alabama in Huntsville	Alabama State University	The University of Alabama	Central Alabama Community College	Athens State University	Auburn University at Montgomery	Auburn University	...
UGDS_WHITE	0.0333	0.5922	0.2990	0.6988	0.0158	0.7825	0.7255	0.7823	0.5328	0.8507	...
UGDS_BLACK	0.9353	0.2600	0.4192	0.1255	0.9208	0.1119	0.2613	0.1200	0.3376	0.0704	...
UGDS_HISP	0.0055	0.0283	0.0069	0.0382	0.0121	0.0348	0.0044	0.0191	0.0074	0.0248	...
UGDS_ASIAN	0.0019	0.0518	0.0034	0.0376	0.0019	0.0106	0.0025	0.0053	0.0221	0.0227	...
UGDS_AIAN	0.0024	0.0022	0.0000	0.0143	0.0010	0.0038	0.0044	0.0157	0.0044	0.0074	...
UGDS_NHPI	0.0019	0.0007	0.0000	0.0002	0.0006	0.0009	0.0000	0.0010	0.0016	0.0000	...
UGDS_2MOR	0.0000	0.0368	0.0000	0.0172	0.0098	0.0261	0.0000	0.0174	0.0297	0.0000	...
UGDS_NRA	0.0059	0.0179	0.0000	0.0332	0.0243	0.0268	0.0000	0.0057	0.0397	0.0100	...
UGDS_UNKN	0.0138	0.0100	0.2715	0.0350	0.0137	0.0026	0.0019	0.0334	0.0246	0.0140	...

There is actually a very simple way to transpose a DataFrame that don't require `stack` or `unstack` by using the `transpose` method or the `T` attribute like this:

```
>>> college.T
>>> college.transpose()
```

See also

- Refer to the *Selecting DataFrame rows and columns simultaneously* recipe from `Chapter 10`, *Selecting Subsets of Data*
- Pandas official documentation of the `unstack` (`http://bit.ly/2xIyFvr`) and `pivot` (`http://bit.ly/2f3qAWP`) methods

Unstacking after a groupby aggregation

Grouping data by a single column and performing an aggregation on a single column returns a simple and straightforward result that is easy to consume. When grouping by more than one column, a resulting aggregation might not be structured in a manner that makes consumption easy. Since `groupby` operations by default put the unique grouping columns in the index, the `unstack` method can be extremely useful to rearrange the data so that it is presented in a manner that is more useful for interpretation.

Getting ready

In this recipe, we use the `employee` dataset to perform an aggregation, grouping by multiple columns. We then use the `unstack` method to reshape the result into a format that makes for easier comparisons of different groups.

How to do it...

1. Read in the employee dataset and find the mean salary by race:

```
>>> employee = pd.read_csv('data/employee.csv')
>>> employee.groupby('RACE')['BASE_SALARY'].mean().astype(int)
RACE
American Indian or Alaskan Native    60272
Asian/Pacific Islander               61660
Black or African American            50137
Hispanic/Latino                      52345
Others                               51278
White                                64419
Name: BASE_SALARY, dtype: int64
```

2. This is a very simple `groupby` operation that results in a Series that is easy to read and has no need to reshape. Let's now find the average salary for all races by gender:

```
>>> agg = employee.groupby(['RACE', 'GENDER'])['BASE_SALARY'] \
              .mean().astype(int)
>>> agg
RACE                             GENDER
American Indian or Alaskan Native Female      60238
                                 Male         60305
Asian/Pacific Islander           Female       63226
                                 Male         61033
Black or African American        Female       48915
                                 Male         51082
Hispanic/Latino                  Female       46503
                                 Male         54782
Others                           Female       63785
                                 Male         38771
White                            Female       66793
                                 Male         63940
Name: BASE_SALARY, dtype: int64
```

3. This aggregation is more complex and can be reshaped to make different comparisons easier. For instance, it would be easier to compare male versus female salaries for each race if they were side by side and not vertical as they are now. Let's unstack the gender index level:

```
>>> agg.unstack('GENDER')
```

GENDER	Female	Male
RACE		
American Indian or Alaskan Native	60238	60305
Asian/Pacific Islander	63226	61033
Black or African American	48915	51082
Hispanic/Latino	46503	54782
Others	63785	38771
White	66793	63940

4. Similarly, we can `unstack` the race index level:

```
>>> agg.unstack('RACE')
```

RACE	American Indian or Alaskan Native	Asian/Pacific Islander	Black or African American	Hispanic/Latino	Others	White
GENDER						
Female	60238	63226	48915	46503	63785	66793
Male	60305	61033	51082	54782	38771	63940

How it works...

Step 1 has the simplest possible aggregation with a single grouping column (`RACE`), a single aggregating column (`BASE_SALARY`), and a single aggregating function (`mean`). This result is easy to consume and doesn't require any more processing to evaluate. Step 2 slightly increases the complexity by grouping by both race and gender together. The resulting MultiIndex Series contains all the values in a single dimension, which makes comparisons more difficult. To make the information easier to consume, we use the `unstack` method to convert the values in one (or more) of the levels to columns.

By default, `unstack` uses the innermost index level as the new columns. You can specify the exact level you would like to unstack with the `level` parameter, which accepts either the level name as a string or the level integer location. It is preferable to use the level name over the integer location to avoid ambiguity. Steps 3 and 4 unstack each level, which results in a DataFrame with a single-level index. It is now much easier to compare salaries from each race by gender.

There's more...

If there are multiple grouping and aggregating columns, then the immediate result will be a DataFrame and not a Series. For instance, let's calculate more aggregations than just the mean, as was done in step 2:

```
>>> agg2 = employee.groupby(['RACE', 'GENDER'])['BASE_SALARY'] \
               .agg(['mean', 'max', 'min']).astype(int)
>>> agg2
```

RACE	GENDER	mean	max	min
American Indian or Alaskan Native	Female	60238	98536	26125
	Male	60305	81239	26125
Asian/Pacific Islander	Female	63226	130416	26125
	Male	61033	163228	27914
Black or African American	Female	48915	150416	24960
	Male	51082	275000	26125
Hispanic/Latino	Female	46503	126115	26125
	Male	54782	165216	26104
Others	Female	63785	63785	63785
	Male	38771	38771	38771
White	Female	66793	178331	27955
	Male	63940	210588	26125

Unstacking the **Gender** column will result in MultiIndex columns. From here, you can keep swapping row and column levels with both the `unstack` and `stack` methods until you achieve the structure of data you desire:

```
>>> agg2.unstack('GENDER')
```

GENDER	mean		max		min	
RACE	Female	Male	Female	Male	Female	Male
American Indian or Alaskan Native	60238	60305	98536	81239	26125	26125
Asian/Pacific Islander	63226	61033	130416	163228	26125	27914
Black or African American	48915	51082	150416	275000	24960	26125
Hispanic/Latino	46503	54782	126115	165216	26125	26104
Others	63785	38771	63785	38771	63785	38771
White	66793	63940	178331	210588	27955	26125

See also

- Refer to the *Grouping and aggregating with multiple columns* recipe and functions from Chapter 13, *Grouping for Aggregation, Filtration, and Transformation*

Replicating pivot_table with a groupby aggregation

At first glance, it may seem that the pivot_table method provides a unique way to analyze data. However, after a little massaging, it is possible to replicate its functionality exactly with a groupby aggregation. Knowing this equivalence can help shrink the universe of pandas functionality.

Getting ready

In this recipe, we use the flights dataset to create a pivot table and then recreate it using groupby operations.

How to do it...

1. Read in the flights dataset, and use the pivot_table method to find the total number of canceled flights per origin airport for each airline:

```
>>> flights = pd.read_csv('data/flights.csv')
>>> fp = flights.pivot_table(index='AIRLINE',
                             columns='ORG_AIR',
                             values='CANCELLED',
                             aggfunc='sum',
                             fill_value=0).round(2)
>>> fp.head()
```

ORG_AIR	ATL	DEN	DFW	IAH	LAS	LAX	MSP	ORD	PHX	SFO
AIRLINE										
AA	3	4	86	3	3	11	3	35	4	2
AS	0	0	0	0	0	0	0	0	0	0
B6	0	0	0	0	0	0	0	0	0	1
DL	28	1	0	0	1	1	4	0	1	2
EV	18	6	27	36	0	0	6	53	0	0

2. A `groupby` aggregation cannot directly replicate this table. The trick is to group by all the columns in the `index` and `columns` parameters first:

```
>>> fg = flights.groupby(['AIRLINE', 'ORG_AIR'])['CANCELLED'].sum()
>>> fg.head()
AIRLINE   ORG_AIR
AA        ATL         3
          DEN         4
          DFW        86
          IAH         3
          LAS         3
Name: CANCELLED, dtype: int64
```

3. Use the `unstack` method to pivot the `ORG_AIR` index level to column names:

```
>>> fg_unstack = fg.unstack('ORG_AIR', fill_value=0)
>>> fp.equals(fg_unstack)
True
```

How it works...

The `pivot_table` method is very versatile and flexible but performs a rather similar operation to a `groupby` aggregation with step 1 showing a simple example. The `index` parameter takes a column (or columns) that will not be pivoted and whose unique values will be placed in the index. The `columns` parameter takes a column (or columns) that will be pivoted and whose unique values will be made into column names. The `values` parameter takes a column (or columns) that will be aggregated.

There also exists an `aggfunc` parameter that takes an aggregating function (or functions) that determines how the columns in the `values` parameter get aggregated. It defaults to the mean, and, in this example, we change it to calculate the sum. Additionally, some unique combinations of `AIRLINE` and `ORG_AIR` do not exist. These missing combinations will default to missing values in the resulting DataFrame. Here, we use the `fill_value` parameter to change them to zero.

Step 2 begins the replication process using all the columns in the `index` and `columns` parameter as the grouping columns. This is the key to making this recipe work. A pivot table is simply an intersection of all the unique combinations of the grouping columns. Step 3 finishes the replication by pivoting the innermost index level into column names with the `unstack` method. Just like with `pivot_table`, not all combinations of `AIRLINE` and `ORG_AIR` exist; we again use the `fill_value` parameter to force these missing intersections to zero.

There's more...

It is possible to replicate much more complex pivot tables with `groupby` aggregations. For instance, take the following result from `pivot_table`:

```
>>> flights.pivot_table(index=['AIRLINE', 'MONTH'],
                        columns=['ORG_AIR', 'CANCELLED'],
                        values=['DEP_DELAY', 'DIST'],
                        aggfunc=[np.sum, np.mean],
                        fill_value=0)
```

		mean											...	sum									
		DEP_DELAY											...	DIST									
	ORG_AIR	ATL		DEN		DFW		IAH		LAS			...	LAX		MSP		ORD		PHX		SFO	
	CANCELLED	0	1	0	1	0	1	0	1	0	1	...	0	1	0	1	0	1	0	1	0	
AIRLINE	MONTH																						
AA	1	-3.250000	0	7.062500	0	11.977591	-3.0	9.750000	0	32.375000	0	...	135921	2475	7281	0	129334	0	21018	0	33483	
	2	-3.000000	0	5.461538	0	8.756579	0.0	1.000000	0	-3.055556	0	...	113483	5454	5040	0	120572	5398	17049	868	32110	
	3	-0.166667	0	7.666667	0	15.383784	0.0	10.900000	0	12.074074	0	...	131836	1744	14471	0	127072	802	25770	0	43580	
	4	0.071429	0	20.266667	0	10.501493	0.0	6.933333	0	27.241379	0	...	170285	0	4541	0	152154	4718	17727	0	51054	
	5	5.777778	0	23.466667	0	16.798780	0.0	3.055556	0	2.818182	0	...	167484	0	6298	0	110864	1999	11164	0	40233	

To replicate this with a `groupby` aggregation, simply follow the same pattern from the recipe and place all the columns from the `index` and `columns` parameters into the `groupby` method and then `unstack` the columns:

```
>>> flights.groupby(['AIRLINE', 'MONTH', 'ORG_AIR', 'CANCELLED']) \
        ['DEP_DELAY', 'DIST'] \
        .agg(['mean', 'sum']) \
        .unstack(['ORG_AIR', 'CANCELLED'], fill_value=0) \
        .swaplevel(0, 1, axis='columns')
```

There are a few differences. The `pivot_table` method does not accept aggregation functions as strings when passed as a list like the `agg` groupby method. Instead, you must use NumPy functions. The order of the column levels also differs, with `pivot_table` putting the aggregation functions at a level preceding the columns in the `values` parameter. This is equalized with the `swaplevel` method that, in this instance, switches the order of the top two levels.

As of the time of writing this book, there is a bug when unstacking more than one column. The `fill_value` parameter is ignored (http://bit.ly/2jCPnWZ). To work around this bug, chain `.fillna(0)` to the end of the code.

Renaming axis levels for easy reshaping

Reshaping with the `stack`/`unstack` methods is far easier when each axis (index/column) level has a name. Pandas allows users to reference each axis level by integer location or by name. Since integer location is implicit and not explicit, you should consider using level names whenever possible. This advice follows from *The Zen of Python* (http://bit.ly/2xE83uC), a short list of guiding principles for Python of which the second one is *Explicit is better than implicit*.

Getting ready

When grouping or aggregating with multiple columns, the resulting pandas object will have multiple levels in one or both of the axes. In this recipe, we will name each level of each axis and then use the methods `stack`/`unstack` to dramatically reshape the data to the desired form.

How to do it...

1. Read in the college dataset, and find a few basic summary statistics on the undergraduate population and SAT math scores by institution and religious affiliation:

```
>>> college = pd.read_csv('data/college.csv')
>>> cg = college.groupby(['STABBR', 'RELAFFIL']) \
               ['UGDS', 'SATMTMID'] \
               .agg(['size', 'min', 'max']).head(6)
```

		UGDS			SATMTMID		
		count	min	max	count	min	max
STABBR	RELAFFIL						
AK	0	7	109.0	12865.0	0	NaN	NaN
	1	3	27.0	275.0	1	503.0	503.0
AL	0	71	12.0	29851.0	13	420.0	590.0
	1	18	13.0	3033.0	8	400.0	560.0
AR	0	68	18.0	21405.0	9	427.0	565.0
	1	14	20.0	4485.0	7	495.0	600.0

2. Notice that both index levels have names and are the old column names. The column levels, on the other hand, do not have names. Use the `rename_axis` method to supply level names to them:

```
>>> cg = cg.rename_axis(['AGG_COLS', 'AGG_FUNCS'], axis='columns')
>>> cg
```

	AGG_COLS	UGDS			SATMTMID		
	AGG_FUNCS	count	min	max	count	min	max
STABBR	RELAFFIL						
AK	0	7	109.0	12865.0	0	NaN	NaN
	1	3	27.0	275.0	1	503.0	503.0
AL	0	71	12.0	29851.0	13	420.0	590.0
	1	18	13.0	3033.0	8	400.0	560.0
AR	0	68	18.0	21405.0	9	427.0	565.0
	1	14	20.0	4485.0	7	495.0	600.0

3. Now that each axis level has a name, reshaping is a breeze. Use the `stack` method to move the AGG_FUNCS column to an index level:

```
>>> cg.stack('AGG_FUNCS').head()
```

		AGG_COLS	UGDS	SATMTMID
STABBR	RELAFFIL	AGG_FUNCS		
AK	0	count	7.0	0.0
		min	109.0	NaN
		max	12865.0	NaN
	1	count	3.0	1.0
		min	27.0	503.0

4. By default, stacking places the new column level in the innermost position. Use the `swaplevel` method to switch the placement of the levels:

```
>>> cg.stack('AGG_FUNCS').swaplevel('AGG_FUNCS', 'STABBR',
                                    axis='index').head()
```

			AGG_COLS	UGDS	SATMTMID
AGG_FUNCS	**RELAFFIL**	**STABBR**			
count	0	AK	7.0	0.0
min	0	AK	109.0	NaN
max	0	AK	12865.0	NaN
count	1	AK	3.0	1.0
min	1	AK	27.0	503.0

5. We can continue to make use of the axis level names by sorting levels with the `sort_index` method:

```
>>> cg.stack('AGG_FUNCS') \
        .swaplevel('AGG_FUNCS', 'STABBR', axis='index') \
        .sort_index(level='RELAFFIL', axis='index') \
        .sort_index(level='AGG_COLS', axis='columns').head(6)
```

			AGG_COLS	SATMTMID	UGDS
AGG_FUNCS	**RELAFFIL**	**STABBR**			
count	0	AK	0.0	7.0
		AL	13.0	71.0
		AR	9.0	68.0
min	0	AK	NaN	109.0
		AL	420.0	12.0
		AR	427.0	18.0

6. To completely reshape your data, you might need to stack some columns while unstacking others. Chain the two methods together in a single command:

```
>>> cg.stack('AGG_FUNCS').unstack(['RELAFFIL', 'STABBR'])
```

AGG_COLS	UGDS						SATMTMID					
RELAFFIL	0	1	0	1	0	1	0	1	0	1	0	1
STABBR	AK	AK	AL	AL	AR	AR	AK	AK	AL	AL	AR	AR
AGG_FUNCS												
count	7.0	3.0	71.0	18.0	68.0	14.0	0.0	1.0	13.0	8.0	9.0	7.0
min	109.0	27.0	12.0	13.0	18.0	20.0	NaN	503.0	420.0	400.0	427.0	495.0
max	12865.0	275.0	29851.0	3033.0	21405.0	4485.0	NaN	503.0	590.0	560.0	565.0	600.0

7. Stack all the columns at once to return a Series:

```
>>> cg.stack(['AGG_FUNCS', 'AGG_COLS']).head(12)
STABBR  RELAFFIL  AGG_FUNCS  AGG_COLS
AK      0         count      UGDS          7.0
                             SATMTMID      0.0
                  min        UGDS        109.0
                  max        UGDS      12865.0
        1         count      UGDS          3.0
                             SATMTMID      1.0
                  min        UGDS         27.0
                             SATMTMID    503.0
                  max        UGDS        275.0
                             SATMTMID    503.0
AL      0         count      UGDS         71.0
                             SATMTMID     13.0
dtype: float64
```

How it works...

It is common for the result of a `groupby` aggregation to produce a DataFrame or Series with multiple axis levels. The resulting DataFrame from the `groupby` operation in step 1 has multiple levels for each axis. The column levels are not named, which would require us to reference them only by their integer location. To greatly ease our ability to reference the column levels, we rename them with the `rename_axis` method.

The `rename_axis` method is a bit strange in that it can modify both the level names and the level values based on the type of the first argument passed to it. Passing it a list (or a scalar if there is only one level) changes the names of the levels. Passing it a dictionary or a function changes the values of the levels. In step 2, we pass the `rename_axis` method a list and are returned a DataFrame with all axis levels named.

Once all the axis levels have names, we can easily and explicitly control the structure of data. Step 3 stacks the `AGG_FUNCS` column into the innermost index level. The `swaplevel` method in step 4 accepts the name or position of the levels that you want to swap as the first two arguments. The `sort_index` method is called twice and sorts the actual values of each level. Notice that the values of the column level are the column names `SATMTMID` and `UGDS`.

We can get vastly different output by both stacking and unstacking, as done in step 6. It is also possible to stack every single column level into the index to produce a Series.

There's more...

If you wish to dispose of the level values altogether, you may set them to `None`. A case for this can be made when there is a need to reduce clutter in the visual output of a DataFrame or when it is obvious what the column levels represent and no further processing will take place:

```
>>> cg.rename_axis([None, None], axis='index') \
        .rename_axis([None, None], axis='columns')
```

		UGDS			SATMTMID		
		count	min	max	count	min	max
AK	0	7	109.0	12865.0	0	NaN	NaN
	1	3	27.0	275.0	1	503.0	503.0
AL	0	71	12.0	29851.0	13	420.0	590.0
	1	18	13.0	3033.0	8	400.0	560.0
AR	0	68	18.0	21405.0	9	427.0	565.0
	1	14	20.0	4485.0	7	495.0	600.0

Tidying when multiple variables are stored as column names

One particular flavor of messy data appears whenever the column names contain multiple different variables themselves. A common example of this scenario occurs when age and sex are concatenated together. To tidy datasets like this, we must manipulate the columns with the pandas `str` accessor, an attribute that contains additional methods for string processing.

Getting ready...

In this recipe, we will first identify all the variables of which some will be concatenated together as column names. We then reshape the data and parse the text to extract the correct variable values.

How to do it...

1. Read in the men's `weightlifting` dataset, and identify the variables:

```
>>> weightlifting = pd.read_csv('data/weightlifting_men.csv')
>>> weightlifting
```

	Weight Category	M35 35-39	M40 40-44	M45 45-49	M50 50-54	M55 55-59	M60 60-64	M65 65-69	M70 70-74	M75 75-79	M80 80+
0	56	137	130	125	115	102	92	80	67	62	55
1	62	152	145	137	127	112	102	90	75	67	57
2	69	167	160	150	140	125	112	97	82	75	60
3	77	182	172	165	150	135	122	107	90	82	65
4	85	192	182	175	160	142	130	112	95	87	70
5	94	202	192	182	167	150	137	120	100	90	75
6	105	210	200	190	175	157	142	122	102	95	80
7	105+	217	207	197	182	165	150	127	107	100	85

2. The variables are the weight category, sex/age category, and the qualifying total. The age and sex variables have been concatenated together into a single cell. Before we can separate them, let's use the `melt` method to transpose the age and sex column names into a single vertical column:

```
>>> wl_melt = weightlifting.melt(id_vars='Weight Category',
                                  var_name='sex_age',
                                  value_name='Qual Total')
>>> wl_melt.head()
```

	Weight Category	sex_age	Qual Total
0	56	M35 35-39	137
1	62	M35 35-39	152
2	69	M35 35-39	167
3	77	M35 35-39	182
4	85	M35 35-39	192

3. Select the `sex_age` column, and use the `split` method available from the `str` accessor to split the column into two different columns:

```
>>> sex_age = wl_melt['sex_age'].str.split(expand=True)
>>> sex_age.head()
```

	0	1
0	M35	35-39
1	M35	35-39
2	M35	35-39
3	M35	35-39
4	M35	35-39

4. This operation returned a completely separate DataFrame with meaningless column names. Let's rename the columns so that we can explicitly access them:

```
>>> sex_age.columns = ['Sex', 'Age Group']
>>> sex_age.head()
```

	Sex	Age Group
0	M35	35-39
1	M35	35-39
2	M35	35-39
3	M35	35-39
4	M35	35-39

5. Use the indexing operator directly after the `str` accessor to select the first character from the `Sex` column:

```
>>> sex_age['Sex'] = sex_age['Sex'].str[0]
>>> sex_age.head()
```

	Sex	Age Group
0	M	35-39
1	M	35-39
2	M	35-39
3	M	35-39
4	M	35-39

6. Use the `pd.concat` function to concatenate this DataFrame with `wl_melt` to produce a tidy dataset:

```
>>> wl_cat_total = wl_melt[['Weight Category', 'Qual Total']]
>>> wl_tidy = pd.concat([sex_age, wl_cat_total], axis='columns')
>>> wl_tidy.head()
```

	Sex	Age Group	Weight Category	Qual Total
0	M	35-39	56	137
1	M	35-39	62	152
2	M	35-39	69	167
3	M	35-39	77	182
4	M	35-39	85	192

7. This same result could have been created with the following:

```
>>> cols = ['Weight Category', 'Qual Total']
>>> sex_age[cols] = wl_melt[cols]
```

How it works...

The `weightlifting` dataset, like many datasets, has easily digestible information in its raw form, but technically, it is messy, as all but one of the column names contain information for sex and age. Once the variables are identified, we can begin to tidy the dataset. Whenever column names contain variables, you will need to use the `melt` (or `stack`) method. The `Weight Category` variable is already in the correct position so we keep it as an identifying variable by passing it to the `id_vars` parameter. Note that we don't explicitly need to name all the columns that we are melting with `value_vars`. By default, all the columns not present in `id_vars` get melted.

The `sex_age` column needs to be parsed, and split into two variables. For this, we turn to the extra functionality provided by the `str` accessor, only available to Series (a single DataFrame column). The `split` method is one of the more common methods in this situation, as it can separate different parts of the string into their own column. By default, it splits on an empty space, but you may also specify a string or regular expression with the `pat` parameter. When the `expand` parameter is set to `True`, a new column forms for each independent split character segment. When `False`, a single column is returned, containing a list of all the segments.

After renaming the columns in step 4, we need to use the `str` accessor again. Interestingly enough, the indexing operator is available to select or slice segments of a string. Here, we select the first character, which is the variable for sex. We could go further and split the ages into two separate columns for minimum and maximum age, but it is common to refer to the entire age group in this manner, so we leave it as is.

Step 6 shows one of two different methods to join all the data together. The `concat` function accepts a collection of DataFrames and either concatenates them vertically (`axis='index'`) or horizontally (`axis='columns'`). Because the two DataFrames are indexed identically, it is possible to assign the values of one DataFrame to new columns in the other as done in step 7.

There's more...

Another way to complete this recipe, beginning after step 2, is by directly assigning new columns from the `sex_age` column without using the `split` method. The `assign` method may be used to add these new columns dynamically:

```
>>> age_group = wl_melt.sex_age.str.extract('(\d{2}[-+](?:\d{2})?)',
                                            expand=False)
>>> sex = wl_melt.sex_age.str[0]
>>> new_cols = {'Sex':sex,
                'Age Group': age_group}
>>> wl_tidy2 = wl_melt.assign(**new_cols) \
                   .drop('sex_age',axis='columns')

>>> wl_tidy2.sort_index(axis=1).equals(wl_tidy.sort_index(axis=1))
True
```

The `Sex` column is found in the exact same manner as done in step 5. Because we are not using `split`, the `Age Group` column must be extracted in a different manner. The `extract` method uses a complex regular expression to extract very specific portions of the string. To use `extract` correctly, your pattern must contain capture groups. A capture group is formed by enclosing parentheses around a portion of the pattern. In this example, the entire expression is one large capture group. It begins with `\d{2}`, which searches for exactly two digits, followed by either a literal plus or minus, optionally followed by two more digits. Although the last part of the expression, `(?:\d{2})?`, is surrounded by parentheses, the `?:` denotes that it is not actually a capture group. It is technically a non-capturing group used to express two digits together as optional. The `sex_age` column is no longer needed and is dropped. Finally, the two tidy DataFrames are compared against one another and are found to be equivalent.

See also

- Refer to the site *Regular-Expressions.info* for more on non-capturing groups (`http://bit.ly/2f60KSd`)

Tidying when multiple variables are stored as column values

Tidy datasets must have a single column for each variable. Occasionally, multiple variable names are placed in a single column with their corresponding value placed in another. The general format for this kind of messy data is as follows:

	attribute	value
0	variable_1	value_1
1	variable_2	value_2
2	variable_3	value_3
3	variable_1	value_1
4	variable_2	value_2
5	variable_3	value_3

In this example, the first and last three rows represent two distinct observations that should each be rows. The data needs to be pivoted such that it ends up like this:

	variable_1	variable_2	variable_3
0	value_1	value_2	value_3
1	value_1	value_2	value_3

Getting ready

In this recipe, we identify the column containing the improperly structured variables and pivot it to create tidy data.

How to do it...

1. Read in the restaurant `inspections` dataset, and convert the `Date` column data type to `datetime64`:

```
>>> inspections = pd.read_csv('data/restaurant_inspections.csv',
                              parse_dates=['Date'])
>>> inspections.head()
```

	Name	Date	Info	Value
0	E & E Grill House	2017-08-08	Borough	MANHATTAN
1	E & E Grill House	2017-08-08	Cuisine	American
2	E & E Grill House	2017-08-08	Description	Non-food contact surface improperly constructe...
3	E & E Grill House	2017-08-08	Grade	A
4	E & E Grill House	2017-08-08	Score	9.0
5	PIZZA WAGON	2017-04-12	Borough	BROOKLYN
6	PIZZA WAGON	2017-04-12	Cuisine	Pizza
7	PIZZA WAGON	2017-04-12	Description	Food contact surface not properly washed, rins...
8	PIZZA WAGON	2017-04-12	Grade	A
9	PIZZA WAGON	2017-04-12	Score	10.0

2. This dataset has two variables, `Name` and `Date`, that are each correctly contained in a single column. The `Info` column itself has five different variables: `Borough`, `Cuisine`, `Description`, `Grade`, and `Score`. Let's attempt to use the `pivot` method to keep the `Name` and `Date` columns vertical, create new columns out of all the values in the `Info` column, and use the `Value` column as their intersection:

```
>>> inspections.pivot(index=['Name', 'Date'],
                      columns='Info', values='Value')
NotImplementedError: > 1 ndim Categorical are not supported at this
time
```

3. Unfortunately, pandas developers have not implemented this functionality for us. There is a good chance that in the future, this line of code is going to work. Thankfully, for the most part, pandas has multiple ways of accomplishing the same task. Let's put `Name`, `Date`, and `Info` into the index:

```
>>> inspections.set_index(['Name','Date', 'Info']).head(10)
```

			Value
Name	**Date**	**Info**	
E & E Grill House	**2017-08-08**	**Borough**	MANHATTAN
		Cuisine	American
		Description	Non-food contact surface improperly constructe...
		Grade	A
		Score	9.0
PIZZA WAGON	**2017-04-12**	**Borough**	BROOKLYN
		Cuisine	Pizza
		Description	Food contact surface not properly washed, rins...
		Grade	A
		Score	10.0

4. Use the `unstack` method to pivot all the values in the `Info` column:

```
>>> inspections.set_index(['Name','Date', 'Info']) \
              .unstack('Info').head()
```

		Value				
	Info	**Borough**	**Cuisine**	**Description**	**Grade**	**Score**
Name	**Date**					
3 STAR JUICE CENTER	2017-05-10	BROOKLYN	Juice, Smoothies, Fruit Salads	Facility not vermin proof. Harborage or condit...	A	12.0
A & L PIZZA RESTAURANT	2017-08-22	BROOKLYN	Pizza	Facility not vermin proof. Harborage or condit...	A	9.0
AKSARAY TURKISH CAFE AND RESTAURANT	2017-07-25	BROOKLYN	Turkish	Plumbing not properly installed or maintained;...	A	13.0
ANTOJITOS DELI FOOD	2017-06-01	BROOKLYN	Latin (Cuban, Dominican, Puerto Rican, South &...	Live roaches present in facility's food and/or...	A	10.0
BANGIA	2017-06-16	MANHATTAN	Korean	Covered garbage receptacle not provided or ina...	A	9.0

5. Make the index levels into columns with the `reset_index` method:

```
>>> insp_tidy = inspections.set_index(['Name','Date', 'Info']) \
                           .unstack('Info') \
                           .reset_index(col_level=-1)
>>> insp_tidy.head()
```

Info	Name	Date	Borough	Cuisine	Description	Grade	Score
					Value		
0	3 STAR JUICE CENTER	2017-05-10	BROOKLYN	Juice, Smoothies, Fruit Salads	Facility not vermin proof. Harborage or condit...	A	12.0
1	A & L PIZZA RESTAURANT	2017-08-22	BROOKLYN	Pizza	Facility not vermin proof. Harborage or condit...	A	9.0
2	AKSARAY TURKISH CAFE AND RESTAURANT	2017-07-25	BROOKLYN	Turkish	Plumbing not properly installed or maintained;...	A	13.0
3	ANTOJITOS DELI FOOD	2017-06-01	BROOKLYN	Latin (Cuban, Dominican, Puerto Rican, South &...	Live roaches present in facility's food and/or...	A	10.0
4	BANGIA	2017-06-16	MANHATTAN	Korean	Covered garbage receptacle not provided or ina...	A	9.0

6. The dataset is tidy, but there is some annoying leftover pandas debris that needs to be removed. Let's use the MultiIndex method `droplevel` to remove the top column level and then rename the index level to `None`:

```
>>> insp_tidy.columns = insp_tidy.columns.droplevel(0) \
                                         .rename(None)
>>> insp_tidy.head()
```

	Name	Date	Borough	Cuisine	Description	Grade	Score
0	3 STAR JUICE CENTER	2017-05-10	BROOKLYN	Juice, Smoothies, Fruit Salads	Facility not vermin proof. Harborage or condit...	A	12.0
1	A & L PIZZA RESTAURANT	2017-08-22	BROOKLYN	Pizza	Facility not vermin proof. Harborage or condit...	A	9.0
2	AKSARAY TURKISH CAFE AND RESTAURANT	2017-07-25	BROOKLYN	Turkish	Plumbing not properly installed or maintained;...	A	13.0
3	ANTOJITOS DELI FOOD	2017-06-01	BROOKLYN	Latin (Cuban, Dominican, Puerto Rican, South &...	Live roaches present in facility's food and/or...	A	10.0
4	BANGIA	2017-06-16	MANHATTAN	Korean	Covered garbage receptacle not provided or ina...	A	9.0

7. The creation of the column MultiIndex in step 4 could have been avoided by converting that one column DataFrame into a Series with the `squeeze` method. The following code produces the same result as the previous step:

```
>>> inspections.set_index(['Name','Date', 'Info']) \
                .squeeze() \
                .unstack('Info') \
                .reset_index() \
                .rename_axis(None, axis='columns')
```

How it works...

In step 1, we notice that there are five variables placed vertically in the `Info` column with their corresponding value in the `Value` column. Because we need to pivot each of these five variables as horizontal column names, it would seem that the `pivot` method would work. Unfortunately, pandas developers have yet to implement this special case when there is more than one non-pivoted column. We are forced to use a different method.

The `unstack` method also pivots vertical data, but only for data in the index. Step 3 begins this process by moving both the columns that will and will not be pivoted into the index with the `set_index` method. Once these columns are in the index, `unstack` can be put to work as done in step 3.

Notice that as we are unstacking a DataFrame, pandas keeps the original column names (here, it is just a single column, `Value`) and creates a MultiIndex with the old column names as the upper level. The dataset is now essentially tidy but we go ahead and make our non-pivoted columns normal columns with the `reset_index` method. Because we have MultiIndex columns, we can choose which level the new column names will belong to with the `col_level` parameter. By default, the names are inserted into the uppermost level (level 0). We use -1 to indicate the bottommost level.

After all this, we have some excess DataFrame names and indexes that need to be discarded. Unfortunately, there isn't a DataFrame method that can remove levels, so we must drop down into the index and use its `droplevel` method. Here, we overwrite the old MultiIndex columns with single-level columns. These columns still have a useless name attribute, `Info`, which is renamed to `None`.

Cleaning up the MultiIndex columns could have been avoided by forcing the resulting DataFrame from step 3 to a Series. The `squeeze` method works only on single-column DataFrames and turns them into Series.

There's more...

It is actually possible to use the `pivot_table` method, which has no restrictions on how many non-pivoted columns are allowed. The `pivot_table` method differs from `pivot` by performing an aggregation for all the values that correspond to the intersection between the columns in the `index` and `columns` parameters. Because it is possible that there are multiple values in this intersection, `pivot_table` requires the user to pass it an aggregating function, in order to output a single value. We use the `first` aggregating function, which takes the first of the values of the group. In this particular example, there is exactly one value for each intersection, so there is nothing to be aggregated. The default aggregation function is the mean, which will produce an error here since some of the values are strings:

```
>>> inspections.pivot_table(index=['Name', 'Date'],
                            columns='Info',
                            values='Value',
                            aggfunc='first') \
            .reset_index() \
            .rename_axis(None, axis='columns')
```

See also

- Pandas official documentation of the `droplevel` (http://bit.ly/2yo5BXf) and `squeeze` (http://bit.ly/2yo5TgN) methods

Tidying when two or more values are stored in the same cell

Tabular data, by nature, is two-dimensional, and thus, there is a limited amount of information that can be presented in a single cell. As a workaround, you will occasionally see datasets with more than a single value stored in the same cell. Tidy data allows for exactly a single value for each cell. To rectify these situations, you will typically need to parse the string data into multiple columns with the methods from the `str` Series accessor.

Getting ready...

In this recipe, we examine a dataset that has a column containing multiple different variables in each cell. We use the `str` accessor to parse these strings into separate columns to tidy the data.

How to do it...

1. Read in the Texas `cities` dataset, and identify the variables:

```
>>> cities = pd.read_csv('data/texas_cities.csv')
>>> cities
```

	City	Geolocation
0	Houston	29.7604° N, 95.3698° W
1	Dallas	32.7767° N, 96.7970° W
2	Austin	30.2672° N, 97.7431° W

2. The `City` column looks good and contains exactly one value. The `Geolocation` column, on the other hand, contains four variables: `latitude`, `latitude direction`, `longitude`, and `longitude direction`. Let's split the `Geolocation` column into four separate columns:

```
>>> geolocations = cities.Geolocation.str.split(pat='. ',
                                                 expand=True)
>>> geolocations.columns = ['latitude', 'latitude direction',
                            'longitude', 'longitude direction']
>>> geolocations
```

	latitude	latitude direction	longitude	longitude direction
0	29.7604	N	95.3698	W
1	32.7767	N	96.7970	W
2	30.2672	N	97.7431	W

3. Because the original data type for the `Geolocation` was an object, all the new columns are also objects. Let's change `latitude` and `longitude` into floats:

```
>>> geolocations = geolocations.astype({'latitude':'float',
                                        'longitude':'float'})
>>> geolocations.dtypes
latitude              float64
latitude direction     object
longitude             float64
longitude direction    object
dtype: object
```

4. Concatenate these new columns with the `City` column from the original:

```
>>> cities_tidy = pd.concat([cities['City'], geolocations],
                            axis='columns')
>>> cities_tidy
```

	City	latitude	latitude direction	longitude	longitude direction
0	Houston	29.7604	N	95.3698	W
1	Dallas	32.7767	N	96.7970	W
2	Austin	30.2672	N	97.7431	W

How it works...

After reading the data, we decide how many variables there are in the dataset. Here, we chose to split the `Geolocation` column into four variables, but we could have just chosen two for latitude and longitude and used a negative sign to differentiate between west/east and south/north.

There are a few ways to parse the `Geolocation` column with the methods from the `str` accessor. The easiest way is to use the `split` method. We pass it a simple regular expression defined by any character (the period) and a space. When a space follows any character, a split is made, and a new column is formed. The first occurrence of this pattern takes place at the end of the latitude. A space follows the degree character, and a split is formed. The splitting characters are discarded and not kept in the resulting columns. The next split matches the comma and space following directly after the latitude direction.

A total of three splits are made, resulting in four columns. The second line in step 2 provides them with meaningful names. Even though the resulting `latitude` and `longitude` columns appear to be floats, they are not. They were originally parsed from an object column and therefore remain object data types. Step 3 uses a dictionary to map the column names to their new types.

Instead of using a dictionary, which would require a lot of typing if you had many column names, you can use the function `to_numeric` to attempt to convert each column to either integer or float. To apply this function iteratively over each column, use the `apply` method with the following:

```
>>> geolocations.apply(pd.to_numeric, errors='ignore')
```

Step 4 concatenates the city to the front of this new DataFrame to complete the process of making tidy data.

There's more...

The `split` method worked exceptionally well in this example with a simple regular expression. For other examples, some columns might require you to create splits on several different patterns. To search for multiple regular expressions, use the pipe character `|`. For instance, if we wanted to split only the degree symbol and comma, each followed by a space, we would do the following:

```
>>> cities.Geolocation.str.split(pat='° |, ', expand=True)
```

This returns the same DataFrame from step 2. Any number of additional split patterns may be appended to the preceding string pattern with the pipe character.

The `extract` method is another excellent method which allows you to extract specific groups within each cell. These capture groups must be enclosed in parentheses. Anything that matches outside the parentheses is not present in the result. The following line produces the same output as step 2:

```
>>> cities.Geolocation.str.extract('([0-9.]+). (N|S), ([0-9.]+). (E|W)',
                                   expand=True)
```

This regular expression has four capture groups. The first and third groups search for at least one or more consecutive digits with decimals. The second and fourth groups search for a single character (the direction). The first and third capture groups are separated by any character followed by a space. The second capture group is separated by a comma and then a space.

Tidying when variables are stored in column names and values

One particularly difficult form of messy data to diagnose appears whenever variables are stored both horizontally across the column names and vertically down column values. You will typically encounter this type of dataset, not in a database, but from a summarized report that someone else has already generated.

Getting ready

In this recipe, variables are identified both vertically and horizontally and reshaped into tidy data with the `melt` and `pivot_table` methods.

How to do it...

1. Read in the `sensors` dataset and identify the variables:

   ```
   >>> sensors = pd.read_csv('data/sensors.csv')
   >>> sensors
   ```

	Group	Property	2012	2013	2014	2015	2016
0	A	Pressure	928	873	814	973	870
1	A	Temperature	1026	1038	1009	1036	1042
2	A	Flow	819	806	861	882	856
3	B	Pressure	817	877	914	806	942
4	B	Temperature	1008	1041	1009	1002	1013
5	B	Flow	887	899	837	824	873

2. The only variable placed correctly in a vertical column is `Group`. The `Property` column appears to have three unique variables, `Pressure`, `Temperature`, and `Flow`. The rest of the columns `2012` to `2016` are themselves a single variable, which we can sensibly name `Year`. It isn't possible to restructure this kind of messy data with a single DataFrame method. Let's begin with the `melt` method to pivot the years into their own column:

```
>>> sensors.melt(id_vars=['Group', 'Property'], var_name='Year') \
        .head(6)
```

	Group	Property	Year	value
0	A	Pressure	2012	928
1	A	Temperature	2012	1026
2	A	Flow	2012	819
3	B	Pressure	2012	817
4	B	Temperature	2012	1008
5	B	Flow	2012	887

3. This takes care of one of our issues. Let's use the `pivot_table` method to pivot the `Property` column into new column names:

```
>>> sensors.melt(id_vars=['Group', 'Property'], var_name='Year') \
        .pivot_table(index=['Group', 'Year'],
                     columns='Property', values='value') \
        .reset_index() \
        .rename_axis(None, axis='columns')
```

	Group	Year	Flow	Pressure	Temperature
0	A	2012	819	928	1026
1	A	2013	806	873	1038
2	A	2014	861	814	1009
3	A	2015	882	973	1036
4	A	2016	856	870	1042
5	B	2012	887	817	1008
6	B	2013	899	877	1041
7	B	2014	837	914	1009
8	B	2015	824	806	1002
9	B	2016	873	942	1013

How it works...

Once we have identified the variables in step 1, we can begin our restructuring. Pandas does not have a method to pivot columns simultaneously, so we must take on this task one step at a time. We correct the years by keeping the `Property` column vertical by passing it to the `id_vars` parameter in the `melt` method.

The result is now precisely the pattern of messy data found in the preceding recipe, *Tidying when multiple variables are stored as column values.* As explained in the *There's more* section of that recipe, we must use `pivot_table` to pivot a DataFrame when using more than one column in the `index` parameter. After pivoting, the `Group` and `Year` variables are stuck in the index. We push them back out as columns. The `pivot_table` method preserves the column name used in the `columns` parameter as the name of the column index. After resetting the index, this name is meaningless, and we remove it with `rename_axis`.

There's more...

Whenever a solution involves `melt`, `pivot_table`, or `pivot`, you can be sure that there is an alternative method using `stack` and `unstack`. The trick is first to move the columns that are not currently being pivoted into the index:

```
>>> sensors.set_index(['Group', 'Property']) \
        .stack() \
        .unstack('Property') \
        .rename_axis(['Group', 'Year'], axis='index') \
        .rename_axis(None, axis='columns') \
        .reset_index()
```

Tidying when multiple observational units are stored in the same table

It is generally easier to maintain data when each table contains information from a single observational unit. On the other hand, it can be easier to find insights when all data is in a single table, and in the case of machine learning, all data must be in a single table. The focus of tidy data is not on directly performing analysis. Rather, it is structuring the data so that analysis is easier further down the line, and when there are multiple observational units in one table, they may need to get separated into their own tables.

Getting ready

In this recipe, we use the `movie` dataset to identify the three observational units (movies, actors, and directors) and create separate tables for each. One of the keys to this recipe is understanding that the actor and director Facebook likes are independent of the movie. Each actor and director is mapped to a single value representing their number of Facebook likes. Due to this independence, we can separate the data for the movies, directors, and actors into their own tables. Database folks call this process normalization, which increases data integrity and reduces redundancy.

How to do it...

1. Read in the altered `movie` dataset, and output the first five rows:

```
>>> movie = pd.read_csv('data/movie_altered.csv')
>>> movie.head()
```

	title	rating	year	duration	director_1	director_fb_likes_1	actor_1	actor_2	actor_3	actor_fb_likes_1	actor_fb_likes_2	actor_fb_likes_3
0	Avatar	PG-13	2009.0	178.0	James Cameron	0.0	CCH Pounder	Joel David Moore	Wes Studi	1000.0	936.0	855.0
1	Pirates of the Caribbean: At World's End	PG-13	2007.0	169.0	Gore Verbinski	563.0	Johnny Depp	Orlando Bloom	Jack Davenport	40000.0	5000.0	1000.0
2	Spectre	PG-13	2015.0	148.0	Sam Mendes	0.0	Christoph Waltz	Rory Kinnear	Stephanie Sigman	11000.0	393.0	161.0
3	The Dark Knight Rises	PG-13	2012.0	164.0	Christopher Nolan	22000.0	Tom Hardy	Christian Bale	Joseph Gordon-Levitt	27000.0	23000.0	23000.0
4	Star Wars: Episode VII - The Force Awakens	NaN	NaN	NaN	Doug Walker	131.0	Doug Walker	Rob Walker	NaN	131.0	12.0	NaN

2. This dataset contains information on the movie itself, the director, and actors. These three entities can be considered observational units. Before we start, let's use the `insert` method to create a column to uniquely identify each movie:

```
>>> movie.insert(0, 'id', np.arange(len(movie)))
>>> movie.head()
```

	id	title	rating	year	duration	director_1	director_fb_likes_1	actor_1	actor_2	actor_3	actor_fb_likes_1	actor_fb_likes_2	actor_fb_likes_3
0	0	Avatar	PG-13	2009.0	178.0	James Cameron	0.0	CCH Pounder	Joel David Moore	Wes Studi	1000.0	936.0	855.0
1	1	Pirates of the Caribbean: At World's End	PG-13	2007.0	169.0	Gore Verbinski	563.0	Johnny Depp	Orlando Bloom	Jack Davenport	40000.0	5000.0	1000.0
2	2	Spectre	PG-13	2015.0	148.0	Sam Mendes	0.0	Christoph Waltz	Rory Kinnear	Stephanie Sigman	11000.0	393.0	161.0
3	3	The Dark Knight Rises	PG-13	2012.0	164.0	Christopher Nolan	22000.0	Tom Hardy	Christian Bale	Joseph Gordon-Levitt	27000.0	23000.0	23000.0
4	4	Star Wars: Episode VII - The Force Awakens	NaN	NaN	NaN	Doug Walker	131.0	Doug Walker	Rob Walker	NaN	131.0	12.0	NaN

3. Let's attempt to tidy this dataset with the `wide_to_long` function to put all the actors in one column and their corresponding Facebook likes in another, and do the same for the director, even though there is only one per movie:

```
>>> stubnames = ['director', 'director_fb_likes',
                 'actor', 'actor_fb_likes']
>>> movie_long = pd.wide_to_long(movie,
                        stubnames=stubnames,
                        i='id',
                        j='num',
                        sep='_').reset_index()

>>> movie_long['num'] = movie_long['num'].astype(int)
>>> movie_long.head(9)
```

	id	num	year	duration	rating	title	director	director_fb_likes	actor	actor_fb_likes
0	0	1	2009.0	178.0	PG-13	Avatar	James Cameron	0.0	CCH Pounder	1000.0
1	0	2	2009.0	178.0	PG-13	Avatar	NaN	NaN	Joel David Moore	936.0
2	0	3	2009.0	178.0	PG-13	Avatar	NaN	NaN	Wes Studi	855.0
3	1	1	2007.0	169.0	PG-13	Pirates of the Caribbean: At World's End	Gore Verbinski	563.0	Johnny Depp	40000.0
4	1	2	2007.0	169.0	PG-13	Pirates of the Caribbean: At World's End	NaN	NaN	Orlando Bloom	5000.0
5	1	3	2007.0	169.0	PG-13	Pirates of the Caribbean: At World's End	NaN	NaN	Jack Davenport	1000.0
6	2	1	2015.0	148.0	PG-13	Spectre	Sam Mendes	0.0	Christoph Waltz	11000.0
7	2	2	2015.0	148.0	PG-13	Spectre	NaN	NaN	Rory Kinnear	393.0
8	2	3	2015.0	148.0	PG-13	Spectre	NaN	NaN	Stephanie Sigman	161.0

4. The dataset is now ready to be split into multiple smaller tables:

```
>>> movie_table = movie_long[['id', 'title', 'year', 'duration',
'rating']]
>>> director_table = movie_long[['id', 'num',
                        'director', 'director_fb_likes']]
>>> actor_table = movie_long[['id', 'num',
                        'actor', 'actor_fb_likes']]
```

	id	title	year	duration	rating
0	0	Avatar	2009.0	178.0	PG-13
1	0	Avatar	2009.0	178.0	PG-13
2	0	Avatar	2009.0	178.0	PG-13
3	1	Pirates of the Caribbean: At World's End	2007.0	169.0	PG-13
4	1	Pirates of the Caribbean: At World's End	2007.0	169.0	PG-13
5	1	Pirates of the Caribbean: At World's End	2007.0	169.0	PG-13
6	2	Spectre	2015.0	148.0	PG-13
7	2	Spectre	2015.0	148.0	PG-13
8	2	Spectre	2015.0	148.0	PG-13

	id	director	num	director_fb_likes
0	0	James Cameron	1	0.0
1	0	NaN	2	NaN
2	0	NaN	3	NaN
3	1	Gore Verbinski	1	563.0
4	1	NaN	2	NaN
5	1	NaN	3	NaN
6	2	Sam Mendes	1	0.0
7	2	NaN	2	NaN
8	2	NaN	3	NaN

	id	actor	num	actor_fb_likes
0	0	CCH Pounder	1	1000.0
1	0	Joel David Moore	2	936.0
2	0	Wes Studi	3	855.0
3	1	Johnny Depp	1	40000.0
4	1	Orlando Bloom	2	5000.0
5	1	Jack Davenport	3	1000.0
6	2	Christoph Waltz	1	11000.0
7	2	Rory Kinnear	2	393.0
8	2	Stephanie Sigman	3	161.0

5. There are still several issues with these tables. The `movie` table duplicates each movie three times, the director table has two missing rows for each ID, and a few movies have missing values for some of the actors. Let's take care of these issues:

```
>>> movie_table = movie_table.drop_duplicates() \
                             .reset_index(drop=True)
>>> director_table = director_table.dropna() \
                             .reset_index(drop=True)
>>> actor_table = actor_table.dropna() \
                             .reset_index(drop=True)
```

	id	title	year	duration	rating
0	0	Avatar	2009.0	178.0	PG-13
1	1	Pirates of the Caribbean: At World's End	2007.0	169.0	PG-13
2	2	Spectre	2015.0	148.0	PG-13
3	3	The Dark Knight Rises	2012.0	164.0	PG-13
4	4	Star Wars: Episode VII - The Force Awakens	NaN	NaN	NaN

	id	director	num	director_fb_likes
0	0	James Cameron	1	0.0
1	1	Gore Verbinski	1	563.0
2	2	Sam Mendes	1	0.0
3	3	Christopher Nolan	1	22000.0
4	4	Doug Walker	1	131.0

6. Now that we have separated the observational units into their own tables, let's compare the memory of the original dataset with these three tables:

```
>>> movie.memory_usage(deep=True).sum()
2318234

>>> movie_table.memory_usage(deep=True).sum() + \
    director_table.memory_usage(deep=True).sum() + \
    actor_table.memory_usage(deep=True).sum()
2627306
```

7. Our new tidier data actually takes up a little more memory. This is to be expected, as all the data in the original columns are simply spread out into the new tables. The new tables also each have an index, and two of them have an extra num column, which accounts for the extra memory. We can, however, take advantage of the fact that the count of Facebook likes is independent of the movie, meaning that each actor and director has exactly one count of Facebook likes for all movies. Before we can do this, we need to create another table mapping each movie to each actor/director. Let's first create id columns specific to the actor and director tables, uniquely identifying each actor/director:

```
>>> director_cat = pd.Categorical(director_table['director'])
>>> director_table.insert(1, 'director_id', director_cat.codes)

>>> actor_cat = pd.Categorical(actor_table['actor'])
>>> actor_table.insert(1, 'actor_id', actor_cat.codes)
```

	id	actor_id	actor	num	actor_fb_likes
0	0	824	CCH Pounder	1	1000.0
1	0	2867	Joel David Moore	2	936.0
2	0	6099	Wes Studi	3	855.0
3	1	2971	Johnny Depp	1	40000.0
4	1	4536	Orlando Bloom	2	5000.0

	id	director_id	director	num	director_fb_likes
0	0	922	James Cameron	1	0.0
1	1	794	Gore Verbinski	1	563.0
2	2	2020	Sam Mendes	1	0.0
3	3	373	Christopher Nolan	1	22000.0
4	4	600	Doug Walker	1	131.0

8. We can use these tables to form our intermediate tables and unique actor/director tables. Let's first do this with the director tables:

```
>>> director_associative = director_table[['id', 'director_id',
                                            'num']]
>>> dcols = ['director_id', 'director', 'director_fb_likes']
>>> director_unique = director_table[dcols].drop_duplicates() \
                                           .reset_index(drop=True)
```

	id	director_id	num
0	0	922	1
1	1	794	1
2	2	2020	1
3	3	373	1
4	4	600	1

	director_id	director	director_fb_likes
0	922	James Cameron	0.0
1	794	Gore Verbinski	563.0
2	2020	Sam Mendes	0.0
3	373	Christopher Nolan	22000.0
4	600	Doug Walker	131.0

9. Let's do the same thing with the `actor` table:

```
>>> actor_associative = actor_table[['id', 'actor_id', 'num']]
>>> acols = ['actor_id', 'actor', 'actor_fb_likes']
>>> actor_unique = actor_table[acols].drop_duplicates() \
                                     .reset_index(drop=True)
```

	id	actor_id	num
0	0	824	1
1	0	2867	2
2	0	6099	3
3	1	2971	1
4	1	4536	2

	actor_id	actor	actor_fb_likes
0	824	CCH Pounder	1000.0
1	2867	Joel David Moore	936.0
2	6099	Wes Studi	855.0
3	2971	Johnny Depp	40000.0
4	4536	Orlando Bloom	5000.0

10. Let's find out how much memory our new tables consume:

```
>>> movie_table.memory_usage(deep=True).sum() + \
    director_associative.memory_usage(deep=True).sum() + \
    director_unique.memory_usage(deep=True).sum() + \
    actor_associative.memory_usage(deep=True).sum() + \
    actor_unique.memory_usage(deep=True).sum()
1833402
```

11. Now that we have normalized our tables, we can build an entity-relationship diagram showing all the tables (entities), columns, and relationships. This diagram was created with the easy to use ERDPlus (https://erdplus.com):

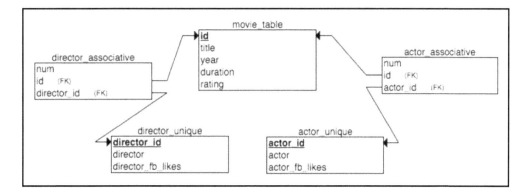

How it works...

After importing the data and identifying the three entities, we must create a unique identifier for each observation so that we can link to the movies, actors and directors together once they have been separated into different tables. In step 2, we simply set the ID column as the row number beginning from zero. In step 3, we use the `wide_to_long` function to simultaneously `melt` the `actor` and `director` columns. It uses the integer suffix of the columns to align the data vertically and places this integer suffix in the index. The parameter `j` is used to control its name. The values in the columns not in the `stubnames` list repeat to align with the columns that were melted.

In step 4, we create our three new tables, keeping the `id` column in each. We also keep the `num` column to identify the exact `director/actor` column from which it was derived. Step 5 condenses each table by removing duplicates and missing values.

After step 5, the three observational units are in their own tables, but they still contain the same amount of data as the original (and a bit more), as seen in step 6. To return the correct number of bytes from the `memory_usage` method for `object` data type columns, you must set the `deep` parameter to `True`.

Each actor/director needs only one entry in his or her respective tables. We can't simply make a table of just actor name and Facebook likes, as there would be no way to link the actors back to the original movie. The relationship between movies and actors is called a **many-to-many relationship**. Each movie is associated with multiple actors, and each actor can appear in multiple movies. To resolve this relationship, an intermediate or associative table is created, which contains the unique identifiers (**primary keys**) of both the movie and actor.

To create associative tables, we must uniquely identify each actor/director. One trick is to create a categorical data type out of each actor/director name with `pd.Categorical`. Categorical data types have an internal map from each value to an integer. This integer is found in the `codes` attribute, which is used as the unique ID. To set up the creation of the associative table, we add this unique ID to the `actor/director` tables.

Step 8 and step 9 create the associative tables by selecting both of the unique identifiers. Now, we can reduce the `actor` and `director` tables to just the unique names and Facebook likes. This new arrangement of tables uses 20% less memory than the original. Formal relational databases have entity-relationship diagrams to visualize the tables. In step 10, we use the simple ERDPlus tool to make the visualization, which greatly eases the understanding of the relationships between the tables.

There's more...

It is possible to recreate the original `movie` table by joining all the tables back together. First, join the associative tables to the `actor`/`director` tables. Then pivot the num column, and add the column prefixes back:

```
>>> actors = actor_associative.merge(actor_unique, on='actor_id') \
                               .drop('actor_id', 1) \
                               .pivot_table(index='id',
                                            columns='num',
                                            aggfunc='first')

>>> actors.columns = actors.columns.get_level_values(0) + '_' + \
                     actors.columns.get_level_values(1).astype(str)

>>> directors = director_associative.merge(director_unique,
                                           on='director_id') \
                                    .drop('director_id', 1) \
                                    .pivot_table(index='id',
                                                 columns='num',
                                                 aggfunc='first')

>>> directors.columns = directors.columns.get_level_values(0) + '_' + \
                        directors.columns.get_level_values(1) \
                                        .astype(str)
```

id	actor_1	actor_2	actor_3	actor_fb_likes_1	actor_fb_likes_2	actor_fb_likes_3
0	CCH Pounder	Joel David Moore	Wes Studi	1000.0	936.0	855.0
1	Johnny Depp	Orlando Bloom	Jack Davenport	40000.0	5000.0	1000.0
2	Christoph Waltz	Rory Kinnear	Stephanie Sigman	11000.0	393.0	161.0
3	Tom Hardy	Christian Bale	Joseph Gordon-Levitt	27000.0	23000.0	23000.0
4	Doug Walker	Rob Walker	None	131.0	12.0	NaN

id	director_1	director_fb_likes_1
0	James Cameron	0.0
1	Gore Verbinski	563.0
2	Sam Mendes	0.0
3	Christopher Nolan	22000.0
4	Doug Walker	131.0

These tables can now be joined together with `movie_table`:

```
>>> movie2 = movie_table.merge(directors.reset_index(),
                               on='id', how='left') \
                        .merge(actors.reset_index(),
                               on='id', how='left')
>>> movie.equals(movie2[movie.columns])
True
```

See also

- More on database normalization (http://bit.ly/2w8wahQ), associative tables (http://bit.ly/2yqE4oh), and primary and foreign keys (http://bit.ly/2xgIvEb)
- Refer to the *Stacking multiple groups of variables simultaneously* recipe in this chapter for more information on the `wide_to_long` function

15
Combining Pandas Objects

A wide variety of options are available to combine two or more DataFrames or Series together. The `append` method is the least flexible and only allows for new rows to be appended to a DataFrame. The `concat` method is very versatile and can combine any number of DataFrames or Series on either axis. The `join` method provides fast lookups by aligning a column of one DataFrame to the index of others. The `merge` method provides SQL-like capabilities to join two DataFrames together.

In this chapter, we will cover the following topics:

- Appending new rows to DataFrames
- Concatenating multiple DataFrames together
- Comparing President Trump's and Obama's approval ratings
- Understanding the differences between `concat`, `join`, and `merge`
- Connecting to SQL databases

Appending new rows to DataFrames

When performing a data analysis, it is far more common to create new columns than new rows. This is because a new row of data usually represents a new observation and, as an analyst, it is typically not your job to continually capture new data. Data capture is usually left to other platforms like relational database management systems. Nevertheless, it is a necessary feature to know as it will crop up from time to time.

Getting ready

In this recipe, we will begin by appending rows to a small dataset with the `.loc` indexer and then transition to using the `append` method.

How to do it...

1. Read in the names dataset, and output it:

```
>>> names = pd.read_csv('data/names.csv')
>>> names
```

	Name	Age
0	Cornelia	70
1	Abbas	69
2	Penelope	4
3	Niko	2

2. Let's create a list that contains some new data and use the `.loc` indexer to set a single row label equal to this new data:

```
>>> new_data_list = ['Aria', 1]
>>> names.loc[4] = new_data_list
>>> names
```

	Name	Age
0	Cornelia	70
1	Abbas	69
2	Penelope	4
3	Niko	2
4	Aria	1

3. The `.loc` indexer uses labels to refer to the rows. In this case, the row labels exactly match the integer location. It is possible to append more rows with non-integer labels:

```
>>> names.loc['five'] = ['Zach', 3]
>>> names
```

	Name	Age
0	Cornelia	70
1	Abbas	69
2	Penelope	4
3	Niko	2
4	Aria	1
five	Zach	3

4. To be more explicit in associating variables to values, you may use a dictionary. Also, in this step, we can dynamically choose the new index label to be the length of the DataFrame:

```
>>> names.loc[len(names)] = {'Name':'Zayd', 'Age':2}
>>> names
```

	Name	Age
0	Cornelia	70
1	Abbas	69
2	Penelope	4
3	Niko	2
4	Aria	1
five	Zach	3
6	Zayd	2

5. A Series can hold the new data as well and works exactly the same as a dictionary:

```
>>> names.loc[len(names)] = pd.Series({'Age':32,
                                        'Name':'Dean'})
>>> names
```

	Name	Age
0	Cornelia	70
1	Abbas	69
2	Penelope	4
3	Niko	2
4	Aria	1
five	Zach	3
6	Zayd	2
7	Dean	32

6. The preceding operations all use the `.loc` indexing operator to make changes to the `names` DataFrame in-place. There is no separate copy of the DataFrame that is returned. In the next few steps, we will look at the `append` method, which does not modify the calling DataFrame. Instead, it returns a new copy of the DataFrame with the appended row(s). Let's begin with the original `names` DataFrame and attempt to append a row. The first argument to `append` must be either another DataFrame, Series, dictionary, or a list of these, but not a list like the one in step 2. Let's see what happens when we attempt to use a dictionary with `append`:

```
>>> names = pd.read_csv('data/names.csv')
>>> names.append({'Name':'Aria', 'Age':1})
TypeError: Can only append a Series if ignore_index=True or if the
Series has a name
```

7. This error message appears to be slightly incorrect. We are passing a DataFrame and not a Series but nevertheless, it gives us instructions on how to correct it:

```
>>> names.append({'Name':'Aria', 'Age':1}, ignore_index=True)
```

	Name	Age
0	Cornelia	70
1	Abbas	69
2	Penelope	4
3	Niko	2
4	Aria	1

8. This works but `ignore_index` is a sneaky parameter. When set to `True`, the old index will be removed completely and replaced with a `RangeIndex` from 0 to n-1. For instance, let's specify an index for the `names` DataFrame:

```
>>> names.index = ['Canada', 'Canada', 'USA', 'USA']
>>> names
```

	Name	Age
Canada	Cornelia	70
Canada	Abbas	69
USA	Penelope	4
USA	Niko	2

9. Rerun the code from step 7 and you will get the same result. The original index is completely ignored.

10. Let's continue with this `names` dataset with these country strings in the index and use a Series that has a `name` attribute with the `append` method:

```
>>> s = pd.Series({'Name': 'Zach', 'Age': 3}, name=len(names))
>>> s
Age          3
Name      Zach
Name: 4, dtype: object

>>> names.append(s)
```

	Name	Age
Canada	Cornelia	70
Canada	Abbas	69
USA	Penelope	4
USA	Niko	2
4	Zach	3

11. The `append` method is more flexible than the `.loc` indexer. It supports appending multiple rows at the same time. One way to accomplish this is with a list of Series:

```
>>> s1 = pd.Series({'Name': 'Zach', 'Age': 3}, name=len(names))
>>> s2 = pd.Series({'Name': 'Zayd', 'Age': 2}, name='USA')
>>> names.append([s1, s2])
```

	Name	Age
Canada	Cornelia	70
Canada	Abbas	69
USA	Penelope	4
USA	Niko	2
4	Zach	3
USA	Zayd	2

12. Small DataFrames with only two columns are simple enough to manually write out all the column names and values. When they get larger, this process will be quite painful. For instance, let's take a look at the 2016 baseball dataset:

```
>>> bball_16 = pd.read_csv('data/baseball16.csv')
>>> bball_16.head()
```

	playerID	yearID	stint	teamID	lgID	G	AB	R	H	2B	...	RBI	SB	CS	BB	SO	IBB	HBP	SH	SF	GIDP
0	altuvjo01	2016	1	HOU	AL	161	640	108	216	42	...	96.0	30.0	10.0	60	70.0	11.0	7.0	3.0	7.0	15.0
1	bregmal01	2016	1	HOU	AL	49	201	31	53	13	...	34.0	2.0	0.0	15	52.0	0.0	0.0	0.0	1.0	1.0
2	castrja01	2016	1	HOU	AL	113	329	41	69	16	...	32.0	2.0	1.0	45	123.0	0.0	1.0	1.0	0.0	9.0
3	correca01	2016	1	HOU	AL	153	577	76	158	36	...	96.0	13.0	3.0	75	139.0	5.0	5.0	0.0	3.0	12.0
4	gattiev01	2016	1	HOU	AL	128	447	58	112	19	...	72.0	2.0	1.0	43	127.0	6.0	4.0	0.0	5.0	12.0

13. This dataset contains 22 columns and it would be easy to mistype a column name or forget one altogether if you were manually entering new rows of data. To help protect against these mistakes, let's select a single row as a Series and chain the `to_dict` method to it to get an example row as a dictionary:

```
>>> data_dict = bball_16.iloc[0].to_dict()
>>> print(data_dict)
{'playerID': 'altuvjo01', 'yearID': 2016, 'stint': 1, 'teamID':
'HOU', 'lgID': 'AL', 'G': 161, 'AB': 640, 'R': 108, 'H': 216, '2B':
42, '3B': 5, 'HR': 24, 'RBI': 96.0, 'SB': 30.0, 'CS': 10.0, 'BB':
60, 'SO': 70.0, 'IBB': 11.0, 'HBP': 7.0, 'SH': 3.0, 'SF': 7.0,
'GIDP': 15.0}
```

14. Clear the old values with a dictionary comprehension assigning any previous string value as an empty string and all others, missing values. This dictionary can now serve as a template for any new data you would like to enter:

```
>>> new_data_dict = {k: '' if isinstance(v, str) else
                        np.nan for k, v in data_dict.items()}
>>> print(new_data_dict)
{'playerID': '', 'yearID': nan, 'stint': nan, 'teamID': '', 'lgID':
'', 'G': nan, 'AB': nan, 'R': nan, 'H': nan, '2B': nan, '3B': nan,
'HR': nan, 'RBI': nan, 'SB': nan, 'CS': nan, 'BB': nan, 'SO': nan,
'IBB': nan, 'HBP': nan, 'SH': nan, 'SF': nan, 'GIDP': nan}
```

How it works...

The .loc indexing operator is used to select and assign data based on the row and column labels. The first value passed to it represents the row label. In step 2, names.loc[4] refers to the row with a label equal to the integer 4. This label does not currently exist in the DataFrame. The assignment statement creates a new row with data provided by the list. As was mentioned in the recipe, this operation modifies the names DataFrame itself. If there was a previously existing row with a label equal to the integer 4, this command would have written over it. This modification in-place makes this indexing operator riskier to use than the append method, which never modifies the original calling DataFrame.

Any valid label may be used with the .loc indexing operator, as seen in step 3. Regardless of what the new label value actually is, the new row will always be appended at the end. Even though assigning with a list works, for clarity it's best to use a dictionary so that we know exactly which columns are associated with each value, as done in step 4.

Step 5 shows a little trick to dynamically set the new label to be the current number of rows in the DataFrame. Data stored in a Series will also get assigned correctly as long as the index labels match the column names.

The rest of the steps use the append method, which is a simple method that only appends new rows to DataFrames. Most DataFrame methods allow both row and column manipulation through an axis parameter. One exception is with append, which can only append rows to DataFrames.

Using a dictionary of column names mapped to values isn't enough information for append to work, as seen by the error message in step 6. To correctly append a dictionary without a row name, you will have to set the ignore_index parameter to True. Step 10 shows you how to keep the old index by simply converting your dictionary to a Series. Make sure to use the name parameter, which is then used as the new index label. Any number of rows may be added with append in this manner by passing a list of Series as the first argument.

When wanting to append rows in this manner with a much larger DataFrame, you can avoid lots of typing and mistakes by converting a single row to a dictionary with the to_dict method and then using a dictionary comprehension to clear out all the old values replacing them with some defaults.

There's more...

Appending a single row to a DataFrame is a fairly expensive operation and if you find yourself writing a loop to append single rows of data to a DataFrame, then you are doing it wrong. Let's first create 1,000 rows of new data as a list of Series:

```
>>> random_data = []
>>> for i in range(1000):
        d = dict()
        for k, v in data_dict.items():
            if isinstance(v, str):
                d[k] = np.random.choice(list('abcde'))
            else:
                d[k] = np.random.randint(10)
        random_data.append(pd.Series(d, name=i + len(bball_16)))

>>> random_data[0].head()
2B    3
3B    9
AB    3
BB    9
CS    4
Name: 16, dtype: object
```

Let's time how long it takes to loop through each item making one append at a time:

```
>>> %%timeit
>>> bball_16_copy = bball_16.copy()
>>> for row in random_data:
        bball_16_copy = bball_16_copy.append(row)
4.88 s ± 190 ms per loop (mean ± std. dev. of 7 runs, 1 loop each)
```

That took nearly five seconds for only 1,000 rows. If we instead pass in the entire list of Series, we get an enormous speed increase:

```
>>> %%timeit
>>> bball_16_copy = bball_16.copy()
>>> bball_16_copy = bball_16_copy.append(random_data)
78.4 ms ± 6.2 ms per loop (mean ± std. dev. of 7 runs, 10 loops each)
```

By passing in the list of Series, the time has been reduced to under one-tenth of a second. Internally, pandas converts the list of Series to a single DataFrame and then makes the append.

Concatenating multiple DataFrames together

The versatile `concat` function enables concatenating two or more DataFrames (or Series) together, both vertically and horizontally. As per usual, when dealing with multiple pandas objects simultaneously, concatenation doesn't happen haphazardly but aligns each object by their index.

Getting ready

In this recipe, we combine DataFrames both horizontally and vertically with the `concat` function and then change the parameter values to yield different results.

How to do it...

1. Read in the 2016 and 2017 stock datasets, and make their ticker symbol the index:

```
>>> stocks_2016 = pd.read_csv('data/stocks_2016.csv',
                              index_col='Symbol')
>>> stocks_2017 = pd.read_csv('data/stocks_2017.csv',
                              index_col='Symbol')
```

Symbol	Shares	Low	High
AAPL	80	95	110
TSLA	50	80	130
WMT	40	55	70

Symbol	Shares	Low	High
AAPL	50	120	140
GE	100	30	40
IBM	87	75	95
SLB	20	55	85
TXN	500	15	23
TSLA	100	100	300

2. Place all the `stock` datasets into a single list, and then call the `concat` function to concatenate them together:

```
>>> s_list = [stocks_2016, stocks_2017]
>>> pd.concat(s_list)
```

Symbol	Shares	Low	High
AAPL	80	95	110
TSLA	50	80	130
WMT	40	55	70
AAPL	50	120	140
GE	100	30	40
IBM	87	75	95
SLB	20	55	85
TXN	500	15	23
TSLA	100	100	300

3. By default, the `concat` function concatenates DataFrames vertically, one on top of the other. One issue with the preceding DataFrame is that there is no way to identify the year of each row. The `concat` function allows each piece of the resulting DataFrame to be labeled with the `keys` parameter. This label will appear in the outermost index level of the concatenated frame and force the creation of a MultiIndex. Also, the `names` parameter has the ability to rename each index level for clarity:

```
>>> pd.concat(s_list, keys=['2016', '2017'],
              names=['Year', 'Symbol'])
```

		Shares	Low	High
Year	Symbol			
2016	AAPL	80	95	110
	TSLA	50	80	130
	WMT	40	55	70
2017	AAPL	50	120	140
	GE	100	30	40
	IBM	87	75	95
	SLB	20	55	85
	TXN	500	15	23
	TSLA	100	100	300

4. It is also possible to concatenate horizontally by changing the `axis` parameter to *columns* or *1*:

```
>>> pd.concat(s_list, keys=['2016', '2017'],
              axis='columns', names=['Year', None])
```

Year	2016			2017		
	Shares	Low	High	Shares	Low	High
AAPL	80.0	95.0	110.0	50.0	120.0	140.0
GE	NaN	NaN	NaN	100.0	30.0	40.0
IBM	NaN	NaN	NaN	87.0	75.0	95.0
SLB	NaN	NaN	NaN	20.0	55.0	85.0
TSLA	50.0	80.0	130.0	100.0	100.0	300.0
TXN	NaN	NaN	NaN	500.0	15.0	23.0
WMT	40.0	55.0	70.0	NaN	NaN	NaN

5. Notice that missing values appear whenever a stock symbol is present in one year but not the other. The `concat` function, by default, uses an outer join, keeping all rows from each DataFrame in the list. However, it gives us options to only keep rows that have the same index values in both DataFrames. This is referred to as an inner join. We set the `join` parameter to *inner* to change the behavior:

```
>>> pd.concat(s_list, join='inner', keys=['2016', '2017'],
              axis='columns', names=['Year', None])
```

Year	2016			2017		
	Shares	Low	High	Shares	Low	High
Symbol						
AAPL	80	95	110	50	120	140
TSLA	50	80	130	100	100	300

How it works...

The first argument is the only argument required for the `concat` function and it must be a sequence of pandas objects, typically a list or dictionary of DataFrames or Series. By default, all these objects will be stacked vertically one on top of the other. In this recipe, only two DataFrames are concatenated, but any number of pandas objects work. When we were concatenating vertically, the DataFrames align by their column names.

In this dataset, all the column names were the same so each column in the 2017 data lined up precisely under the same column name in the 2016 data. However, when they were concatenated horizontally, as in step 4, only two of the index labels matched from both years--*AAPL* and *TSLA*. Therefore, these ticker symbols had no missing values for either year. There are two types of alignment possible using `concat`, *outer* (the default) and *inner* referred to by the `join` parameter.

There's more...

The `append` method is a heavily watered down version of `concat` that can only append new rows to a DataFrame. Internally, `append` just calls the `concat` function. For instance, step 2 from this recipe may be duplicated with the following:

```
>>> stocks_2016.append(stocks_2017)
```

Comparing President Trump's and Obama's approval ratings

Public support of the current President of the United States is a topic that frequently makes it into news headlines and is formally measured through opinion polls. In recent years, there has been a rapid increase in the frequency of these polls and lots of new data rolls in each week. There are many different pollsters that each have their own questions and methodology to capture their data, and thus there exists quite a bit of variability among the data. The American Presidency Project from the University of California, Santa Barbara, provides an aggregate approval rating down to a single data point each day.

Unlike most of the recipes in this book, the data is not readily available in a CSV file. Often, as a data analyst, you will need to find data on the web, and use a tool that can scrape it into a format that you can then parse through your local workstation.

Getting ready

In this recipe, we will use the `read_html` function, which comes heavily equipped to scrape data from tables online and turn them into DataFrames. You will also learn how to inspect web pages to find the underlying HTML for certain elements. I used Google Chrome as my browser and suggest you use it, or Firefox, for the web-based steps.

How to do it...

1. Navigate to *The American Presidency Project* approval page for President Donald Trump (`http://www.presidency.ucsb.edu/data/popularity.php?pres=45`). You should get a page that contains a time series plot with the data in a table directly following it:

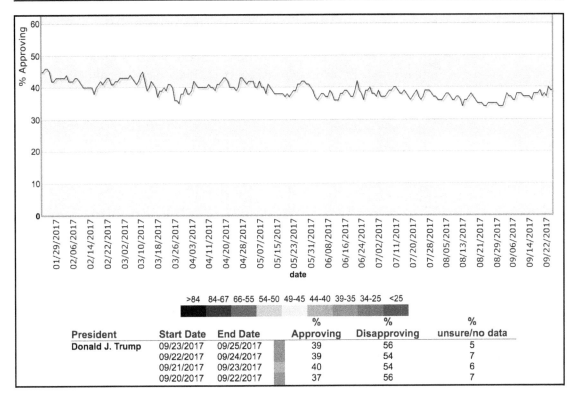

President	Start Date	End Date		% Approving	% Disapproving	% unsure/no data
Donald J. Trump	09/23/2017	09/25/2017		39	56	5
	09/22/2017	09/24/2017		39	54	7
	09/21/2017	09/23/2017		40	54	6
	09/20/2017	09/22/2017		37	56	7

2. The `read_html` function is able to scrape tables off web pages and place their data into DataFrames. It works best with simple HTML tables and provides some useful parameters to select the exact table you desire in case there happen to be multiple tables on the same page. Let's go ahead and use `read_html` with its default values, which will return all the tables as DataFrames in a list:

```
>>> base_url =
'http://www.presidency.ucsb.edu/data/popularity.php?pres={}'
>>> trump_url = base_url.format(45)
>>> df_list = pd.read_html(trump_url)
>>> len(df_list)
14
```

3. The function has returned 14 tables, which seems preposterous at first, as the web page appears to show only a single element that most people would recognize as a table. The `read_html` function formally searches for HTML table elements that begin with *<table*. Let's inspect the HTML page by right-clicking on the approval data table and selecting **inspect** or **inspect element**:

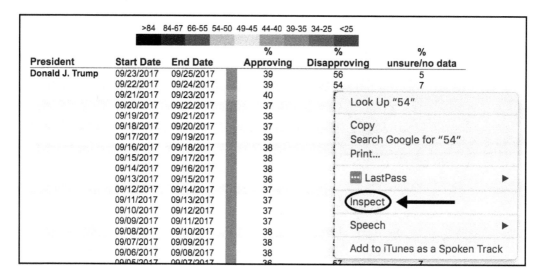

4. This opens up the console, which is a very powerful tool for web development. For this recipe, we will only need it for a few tasks. All consoles allow you to search the HTML for a specific word. Let's search for the word `table`. My browser found 15 different HTML tables, very close to the number returned by `read_html`:

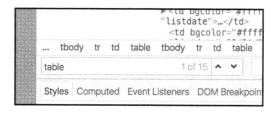

5. Let's begin inspecting the DataFrames in `df_list`:

```
>>> df0 = df_list[0]
>>> df0.shape
(308, 1794)

>>> df0.head(7)
```

	0	1	2	3	4	5	6	7
0	NaN	NaN	NaN	NaN	NaN	NaN	NaN	NaN
1	NaN	NaN	NaN	NaN	NaN	NaN	NaN	NaN
2	NaN	NaN	NaN	NaN	NaN	NaN	NaN	NaN
3	NaN	NaN	NaN	NaN	NaN	NaN	NaN	NaN
4	NaN	NaN	NaN	NaN	NaN	NaN	NaN	NaN
5	NaN	NaN	NaN	NaN	NaN	NaN	NaN	NaN
6	Document Archive • Public Papers of the Presi...	Document Archive • Public Papers of the Presi...	Document Archive • Public Papers of the Presi...	NaN	NaN	Document Archive	• Public Papers of the Presidents	• State of the Union Addresses & Messages

6. Looking back at the web page, there is a row in the approval table for nearly each day beginning January 22, 2017, until the day the data was scraped--September 25, 2017. This is a little more than eight months or 250 rows of data, which is somewhat close to the 308 lines in that first table. Scanning through the rest of the tables, you can see that lots of empty meaningless tables were discovered, as well as tables for different parts of the web page that don't actually resemble tables. Let's use some of the parameters of the `read_html` function to help us select the table we desire. We can use the `match` parameter to search for a specific string in the table. Let's search for a table with the word *Start Date* in it:

```
>>> df_list = pd.read_html(trump_url, match='Start Date')
>>> len(df_list)
3
```

7. By searching for a specific string in the table, we have reduced the number of tables down to just three. Another useful parameter is `attrs`, which accepts a dictionary of HTML attributes paired with their value. We would like to find some unique attributes for our particular table. To do this, let's right-click again in our data table. This time, make sure to click at the very top in one of the table headers. For example, right click on *President,* and select **inspect** or **inspect element** again:

8. The element that you selected should be highlighted. This is actually not the element we are interested in. Keep looking until you come across an HTML tag beginning with *<table*. All the words to the left of the equal signs are the attributes or `attrs` and to the right are the values. Let's use the *align* attribute with its value *center* in our search:

```
>>> df_list = pd.read_html(trump_url, match='Start Date',
                           attrs={'align':'center'})
>>> len(df_list)
1

>>> trump = df_list[0]
>>> trump.shape
(249, 19)

>>> trump.head(8)
```

	0	1	2	3	4	5	6
0	>84 84-67 66-55 54-50 49-45 44-40 39-35 ...	>84	84-67	66-55	54-50	49-45	44-40
1		>84	84-67	66-55	54-50	49-45	44-40	39-35
2	NaN	NaN	NaN	NaN	NaN	NaN	NaN
3	NaN	NaN	NaN	NaN	%	%	%
4	President	Start Date	End Date	NaN	Approving	Disapproving	unsure/no data
5	NaN	NaN	NaN	NaN	NaN	NaN	NaN
6	Donald J. Trump	09/23/2017	09/25/2017	NaN	39	56	5
7	NaN	09/22/2017	09/24/2017	NaN	39	54	7

9. We only matched with one table and the number of rows is very close to the total days between the first and last dates. Looking at the data, it appears that we have indeed found the table we are looking for. The six column names appear to be on line 4. We can go even further and precisely select the rows we want to skip and which row we would like to use for the column names with the `skiprows` and `header` parameters. We can also make sure that the start and end dates are coerced correctly to the right data type with the `parse_dates` parameter:

```
>>> df_list = pd.read_html(trump_url, match='Start Date',
                           attrs={'align':'center'},
                           header=0, skiprows=[0,1,2,3,5],
                           parse_dates=['Start Date',
                                        'End Date'])
>>> trump = df_list[0]
>>> trump.head()
```

	President	Start Date	End Date	Unnamed: 3	Approving	Disapproving	unsure/no data	Unnamed: 7	Unnamed: 8	Unnamed: 9	Unnamed: 10	Unnamed: 11	Unnamed: 12
0	Donald J. Trump	09/23/2017	09/25/2017	NaN	39	56	5	NaN	NaN	NaN	NaN	NaN	NaN
1	NaN	09/22/2017	09/24/2017	NaN	39	54	7	NaN	NaN	NaN	NaN	NaN	NaN
2	NaN	09/21/2017	09/23/2017	NaN	40	54	6	NaN	NaN	NaN	NaN	NaN	NaN
3	NaN	09/20/2017	09/22/2017	NaN	37	56	7	NaN	NaN	NaN	NaN	NaN	NaN
4	NaN	09/19/2017	09/21/2017	NaN	38	56	6	NaN	NaN	NaN	NaN	NaN	NaN

10. This is almost exactly what we want, except for the columns with missing values. Let's use the `dropna` method to drop columns with all values missing:

```
>>> trump = trump.dropna(axis=1, how='all')
>>> trump.head()
```

	President	Start Date	End Date	Approving	Disapproving	unsure/no data
0	Donald J. Trump	2017-09-23	2017-09-25	39	56	5
1	NaN	2017-09-22	2017-09-24	39	54	7
2	NaN	2017-09-21	2017-09-23	40	54	6
3	NaN	2017-09-20	2017-09-22	37	56	7
4	NaN	2017-09-19	2017-09-21	38	56	6

11. Let's fill the missing values in the `President` column in a forward direction with the `ffill` method. Let's first check whether there are any missing values in the other columns:

```
>>> trump.isnull().sum()
President        242
Start Date         0
End Date           0
Approving          0
Disapproving       0
unsure/no data     0
dtype: int64

>>> trump = trump.ffill()
trump.head()
```

	President	Start Date	End Date	Approving	Disapproving	unsure/no data
0	Donald J. Trump	2017-09-23	2017-09-25	39	56	5
1	Donald J. Trump	2017-09-22	2017-09-24	39	54	7
2	Donald J. Trump	2017-09-21	2017-09-23	40	54	6
3	Donald J. Trump	2017-09-20	2017-09-22	37	56	7
4	Donald J. Trump	2017-09-19	2017-09-21	38	56	6

12. Finally, it is important to check the data types to ensure they are correct:

```
>>> trump.dtypes
President                    object
Start Date          datetime64[ns]
End Date            datetime64[ns]
Approving                     int64
Disapproving                  int64
unsure/no data                int64
dtype: object
```

13. Let's build a function with all the steps combined into one to automate the process of retrieving approval data for any President:

```
>>> def get_pres_appr(pres_num):
        base_url =\
'http://www.presidency.ucsb.edu/data/popularity.php?pres={}'
        pres_url = base_url.format(pres_num)
        df_list = pd.read_html(pres_url, match='Start Date',
                               attrs={'align':'center'},
                               header=0, skiprows=[0,1,2,3,5],
                               parse_dates=['Start Date',
                                            'End Date'])
        pres = df_list[0].copy()
        pres = pres.dropna(axis=1, how='all')
        pres['President'] = pres['President'].ffill()
        return pres.sort_values('End Date') \
                   .reset_index(drop=True)
```

14. The only parameter, pres_num, denotes the order number of each president. Barack Obama was the 44th President of the United States; pass 44 to the get_pres_appr function to retrieve his approval numbers:

```
>>> obama = get_pres_appr(44)
>>> obama.head()
```

	President	Start Date	End Date	Approving	Disapproving	unsure/no data
0	Barack Obama	2009-01-21	2009-01-23	68	12	21
1	Barack Obama	2009-01-22	2009-01-24	69	13	18
2	Barack Obama	2009-01-23	2009-01-25	67	14	19
3	Barack Obama	2009-01-24	2009-01-26	65	15	20
4	Barack Obama	2009-01-25	2009-01-27	64	16	20

15. There is Presidential approval rating data dating back to 1941 during President Franklin Roosevelt's third term. With our custom function along with the `concat` function, it is possible to grab all the presidential approval rating data from this site. For now, let's just grab the approval rating data for the last five presidents and output the first three rows for each President:

```
>>> pres_41_45 = pd.concat([get_pres_appr(x) for x in
range(41,46)],
                                ignore_index=True)
>>> pres_41_45.groupby('President').head(3)
```

	President	Start Date	End Date	Approving	Disapproving	unsure/no data
0	George Bush	1989-01-24	1989-01-26	51	6	43
1	George Bush	1989-02-24	1989-02-27	60	11	27
2	George Bush	1989-02-28	1989-03-02	62	13	24
158	William J. Clinton	1993-01-24	1993-01-26	58	20	22
159	William J. Clinton	1993-01-29	1993-01-31	53	30	16
160	William J. Clinton	1993-02-12	1993-02-14	51	33	15
386	George W. Bush	2001-02-01	2001-02-04	57	25	18
387	George W. Bush	2001-02-09	2001-02-11	57	24	17
388	George W. Bush	2001-02-19	2001-02-21	61	21	16
656	Barack Obama	2009-01-21	2009-01-23	68	12	21
657	Barack Obama	2009-01-22	2009-01-24	69	13	18
658	Barack Obama	2009-01-23	2009-01-25	67	14	19
3443	Donald J. Trump	2017-01-20	2017-01-22	45	45	10
3444	Donald J. Trump	2017-01-21	2017-01-23	45	46	9
3445	Donald J. Trump	2017-01-22	2017-01-24	46	45	9

16. Before continuing, let's determine if there are any dates with multiple approval ratings:

```
>>> pres_41_45['End Date'].value_counts().head(8)
1990-08-26    2
1990-03-11    2
1999-02-09    2
2013-10-10    2
1990-08-12    2
1992-11-22    2
1990-05-22    2
1991-09-30    1
Name: End Date, dtype: int64
```

17. Only a few of the days have duplicate values. To help simplify our analysis, let's keep only the first row where the duplicate date exists:

```
>>> pres_41_45 = pres_41_45.drop_duplicates(subset='End Date')
```

18. Let's get a few summary statistics on the data:

```
>>> pres_41_45.shape
(3679, 6)

>>> pres_41_45['President'].value_counts()
Barack Obama         2786
George W. Bush        270
Donald J. Trump       243
William J. Clinton    227
George Bush           153
Name: President, dtype: int64

>>> pres_41_45.groupby('President', sort=False) \
              .median().round(1)
```

President	Approving	Disapproving	unsure/no data
George Bush	63.0	22.0	9.0
William J. Clinton	57.0	36.0	6.0
George W. Bush	50.5	45.5	4.0
Barack Obama	47.0	47.0	7.0
Donald J. Trump	39.0	56.0	6.0

19. Let's plot each President's approval rating on the same chart. To do this, we will group by each President, iterate through each group, and individually plot the approval rating for each date:

```
>>> from matplotlib import cm
>>> fig, ax = plt.subplots(figsize=(16,6))

>>> styles = ['-.', '-', ':', '-', ':']
>>> colors = [.9, .3, .7, .3, .9]
>>> groups = pres_41_45.groupby('President', sort=False)

>>> for style, color, (pres, df) in zip(styles, colors, groups):
        df.plot('End Date', 'Approving', ax=ax,
```

```
                        label=pres, style=style, color=cm.Greys(color),
                        title='Presedential Approval Rating')
```

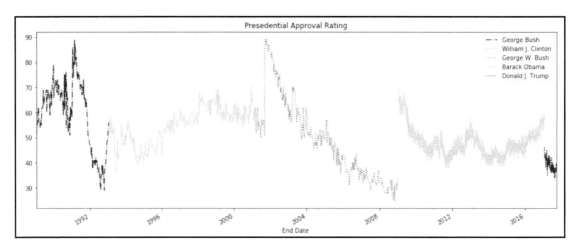

20. This chart places all the Presidents sequentially one after the other. We can compare them on a simpler scale by plotting their approval rating against the number of days in office. Let's create a new variable to represent the number of days in office:

```
>>> days_func = lambda x: x - x.iloc[0]
>>> pres_41_45['Days in Office'] = pres_41_45.groupby('President') \
                                        ['End Date'] \
                                        .transform(days_func)
>>> pres_41_45.groupby('President').head(3)
```

	President	Start Date	End Date	Approving	Disapproving	unsure/no data	Days in Office
0	George Bush	1989-01-24	1989-01-26	51	6	43	0 days
1	George Bush	1989-02-24	1989-02-27	60	11	27	32 days
2	George Bush	1989-02-28	1989-03-02	62	13	24	35 days
158	William J. Clinton	1993-01-24	1993-01-26	58	20	22	0 days
159	William J. Clinton	1993-01-29	1993-01-31	53	30	16	5 days
160	William J. Clinton	1993-02-12	1993-02-14	51	33	15	19 days
386	George W. Bush	2001-02-01	2001-02-04	57	25	18	0 days
387	George W. Bush	2001-02-09	2001-02-11	57	24	17	7 days
388	George W. Bush	2001-02-19	2001-02-21	61	21	16	17 days
656	Barack Obama	2009-01-21	2009-01-23	68	12	21	0 days
657	Barack Obama	2009-01-22	2009-01-24	69	13	18	1 days
658	Barack Obama	2009-01-23	2009-01-25	67	14	19	2 days
3443	Donald J. Trump	2017-01-20	2017-01-22	45	45	10	0 days
3444	Donald J. Trump	2017-01-21	2017-01-23	45	46	9	1 days
3445	Donald J. Trump	2017-01-22	2017-01-24	46	45	9	2 days

21. We have successfully given each row a relative number of days since the start of the presidency. It's interesting that the new column, Days in Office, has a string representation of its value. Let's check its data type:

```
>>> pres_41_45.dtypes
...
Days in Office     timedelta64[ns]
dtype: object
```

22. The Days in Office column is a timedelta64 object with nanosecond precision. This is far more precision than is needed. Let's change the data type to integer by getting just the days:

```
>>> pres_41_45['Days in Office'] = pres_41_45['Days in Office'] \
                                        .dt.days
>>> pres_41_45['Days in Office'].head()
0     0
1     32
2     35
3     43
4     46
Name: Days in Office, dtype: int64
```

23. We could plot this data in a similar fashion to what we did in step 19, but there is a completely different method that doesn't involve any looping. By default, when calling the `plot` method on a DataFrame, pandas attempts to plot each column of data as a line plot and uses the index as the x-axis. Knowing this, let's pivot our data so that each President has his own column for approval rating:

```
>>> pres_pivot = pres_41_45.pivot(index='Days in Office',
                                  columns='President',
                                  values='Approving')
>>> pres_pivot.head()
```

President	Barack Obama	Donald J. Trump	George Bush	George W. Bush	William J. Clinton
Days in Office					
0	68.0	45.0	51.0	57.0	58.0
1	69.0	45.0	NaN	NaN	NaN
2	67.0	46.0	NaN	NaN	NaN
3	65.0	46.0	NaN	NaN	NaN
4	64.0	45.0	NaN	NaN	NaN

24. Now that each President has his own column of approval ratings, we can plot each column directly without grouping. To reduce the clutter in the plot, we will only plot Barack Obama and Donald J. Trump:

```
>>> plot_kwargs = dict(figsize=(16,6), color=cm.gray([.3, .7]),
                       style=['-', '--'], title='Approval Rating')
>>> pres_pivot.loc[:250, ['Donald J. Trump', 'Barack Obama']] \
              .ffill().plot(**plot_kwargs)
```

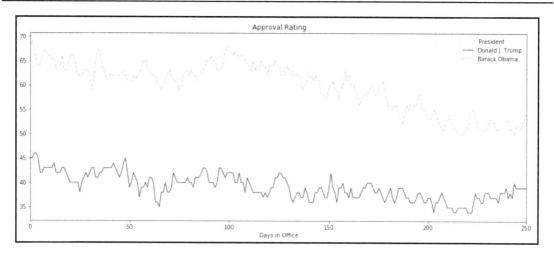

How it works...

It is typical to call `read_html` multiple times before arriving at the table (or tables) that you desire. There are two primary parameters at your disposal to specify a table, `match` and `attrs`. The string provided to `match` is used to find an exact match for the actual text in the table. This is text that will show up on the web page itself. The `attrs` parameter, on the other hand, searches for HTML table attributes found directly after the start of the table tag, `<table`. To see more of the table attributes, visit this page from W3 Schools (`http://bit.ly/2hzUzdD`).

Once we find our table in step 8, we can still take advantage of some other parameters to simplify things. HTML tables don't typically translate directly to nice DataFrames. There are often missing column names, extra rows, and misaligned data. In this recipe, `skiprows` is passed a list of row numbers to skip over when reading the file. They correspond to the rows of missing values in the DataFrame output from step 8. The `header` parameter is also used to specify the location of the column names. Notice that `header` is equal to zero, which may seem wrong at first. Whenever the header parameter is used in conjunction with `skiprows`, the rows are skipped first resulting in a new integer label for each row. The correct column names are in row 4 but as we skipped rows 0 through 3, the new integer label for it is 0.

In step 11, the `ffill` method fills any missing values vertically, going down with the last non-missing value. This method is just a shortcut for `fillna(method='ffill')`.

Step 13 builds a function composed of all the previous steps to automatically get approval ratings from any President, provided you have the order number. There are a few differences in the function. Instead of applying the `ffill` method to the entire DataFrame, we only apply it to the `President` column. In Trump's DataFrame, the other columns had no missing data but this does not guarantee that all the scraped tables will have no missing data in their other columns. The last line of the function sorts the dates in a more natural way for data analysis from the oldest to newest. This changes the order of the index too, so we discard it with `reset_index` to have it begin from zero again.

Step 16 shows a common pandas idiom for collecting multiple, similarly indexed DataFrames into a list before combining them together with the `concat` function. After concatenation into a single DataFrame, we should visually inspect it to ensure its accuracy. One way to do this is to take a glance at the first few rows from each President's section by grouping the data and then using the `head` method on each group.

The summary statistics in step 18 are interesting as each successive President has had lower median approval than the last. Extrapolating the data would lead to naively predicting a negative approval rating within the next several Presidents.

The plotting code in step 19 is fairly complex. You might be wondering why we need to iterate through a `groupby` object, to begin with. In the DataFrame's current structure, it has no ability to plot different groups based on values in a single column. However, step 23 shows you how to set up your DataFrame so that pandas can directly plot each President's data without a loop like this.

To understand the plotting code in step 19, you must first be aware that a `groupby` object is iterable and, when iterating through, yields a tuple containing the current group (here it's just the name of the President) and the sub-DataFrame for just that group. This `groupby` object is zipped together with values controlling the color and linestyle of the plot. We import the colormap module, `cm`, from matplotlib which contains dozens of different colormaps. Passing a float between 0 and 1 chooses a specific color from that colormap and we use it in our `plot` method with the `color` parameter. It is also important to note that we had to create the figure, `fig`, along with a plotting surface, `ax`, to ensure that each approval line was placed on the same plot. At each iteration in the loop, we use the same plotting surface with the identically named parameter, `ax`.

To make a better comparison between Presidents, we create a new column equal to the number of days in office. We subtract the first date from the rest of the dates per President group. When two `datetime64` columns are subtracted, the result is a `timedelta64` object, which represents some length of time, days in this case. If we leave the column with nanosecond precision, the x-axis will similarly display too much precision by using the special `dt` accessor to return the number of days.

A crucial step comes in step 23. We structure the data such that each President has a unique column for their approval rating. Pandas makes a separate line for each column. Finally, in step 24, we use the `.loc` indexer to simultaneously select the first 250 days (rows) along with only the columns for just Trump and Obama. The `ffill` method is used in the rare instances that one of the Presidents has a missing value for a particular day. In Python, it is possible to pass dictionaries that contain the parameter names and their values to functions by preceding them with `**` in a process called **dictionary unpacking**.

There's more...

The plot from step 19 shows quite a lot of noise and the data might be easier to interpret if it were smoothed. One common smoothing method is called the **rolling average**. Pandas offers the `rolling` method for DataFrames and `groupby` objects. It works analogously to the `groupby` method by returning an object waiting for an additional action to be performed on it. When creating it, you must pass the size of the window as the first argument, which can either be an integer or a date offset string.

In this example, we take a 90-day moving average with the date offset string *90D*. The `on` parameter specifies the column from which the rolling window is calculated:

```
>>> pres_rm = pres_41_45.groupby('President', sort=False) \
                  .rolling('90D', on='End Date')['Approving'] \
                  .mean()
>>> pres_rm.head()
President     End Date
George Bush   1989-01-26    51.000000
              1989-02-27    55.500000
              1989-03-02    57.666667
              1989-03-10    58.750000
              1989-03-13    58.200000
Name: Approving, dtype: float64
```

From here, we can restructure the data so that it looks similar to the output from step 23 with the `unstack` method, and then make our plot:

```
>>> styles = ['-.', '-', ':', '-', ':']
>>> colors = [.9, .3, .7, .3, .9]
>>> color = cm.Greys(colors)
>>> title='90 Day Approval Rating Rolling Average'
>>> plot_kwargs = dict(figsize=(16,6), style=styles,
                       color = color, title=title)
>>> correct_col_order = pres_41_45.President.unique()

>>> pres_rm.unstack('President')[correct_col_order].plot(**plot_kwargs)
```

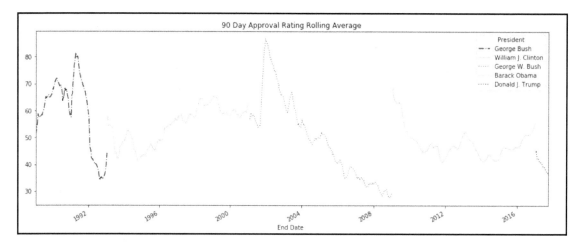

See also

- Colormap references for matplotlib (http://bit.ly/2yJZOvt)
- A list of all the date offsets and their aliases (http://bit.ly/2xO5Yg0)

Understanding the differences between concat, join, and merge

The `merge` and `join` DataFrame (and not Series) methods and the `concat` function all provide very similar functionality to combine multiple pandas objects together. As they are so similar and they can replicate each other in certain situations, it can get very confusing when and how to use them correctly. To help clarify their differences, take a look at the following outline:

- `concat`:
  - Pandas function
  - Combines two or more pandas objects vertically or horizontally
  - Aligns only on the index
  - Errors whenever a duplicate appears in the index
  - Defaults to outer join with option for inner

- `join`:
  - DataFrame method
  - Combines two or more pandas objects horizontally
  - Aligns the calling DataFrame's column(s) or index with the other objects' index (and not the columns)
  - Handles duplicate values on the joining columns/index by performing a cartesian product
  - Defaults to left join with options for inner, outer, and right

- `merge`:
  - DataFrame method
  - Combines exactly two DataFrames horizontally
  - Aligns the calling DataFrame's column(s)/index with the other DataFrame's column(s)/index
  - Handles duplicate values on the joining columns/index by performing a cartesian product
  - Defaults to inner join with options for left, outer, and right

The first parameter to the join method is `other` which can either be a single DataFrame/Series or a list of any number of DataFrames/Series.

Getting ready

In this recipe, we will do what is required to combine DataFrames. The first situation is simpler with `concat` while the second is simpler with `merge`.

How to do it...

1. Let's read in stock data for 2016, 2017, and 2018 into a list of DataFrames using a loop instead of three different calls to the `read_csv` function. Jupyter notebooks currently only allow a single DataFrame to be displayed on one line. However, there is a way to customize the HTML output with help from the `IPython` library. The user-defined `display_frames` function accepts a list of DataFrames and outputs them all in a single row:

```
>>> from IPython.display import display_html

>>> years = 2016, 2017, 2018
>>> stock_tables = [pd.read_csv('data/stocks_{}.csv'.format(year),
                                index_col='Symbol')
                    for year in years]

>>> def display_frames(frames, num_spaces=0):
        t_style = '<table style="display: inline;"'
        tables_html = [df.to_html().replace('<table', t_style)
                       for df in frames]

        space = ' ' * num_spaces
        display_html(space.join(tables_html), raw=True)

>>> display_frames(stock_tables, 30)
>>> stocks_2016, stocks_2017, stocks_2018 = stock_tables
```

	Shares	Low	High
Symbol			
AAPL	80	95	110
TSLA	50	80	130
WMT	40	55	70

	Shares	Low	High
Symbol			
AAPL	50	120	140
GE	100	30	40
IBM	87	75	95
SLB	20	55	85
TXN	500	15	23
TSLA	100	100	300

	Shares	Low	High
Symbol			
AAPL	40	135	170
AMZN	8	900	1125
TSLA	50	220	400

2. The `concat` function is the only one able to combine DataFrames vertically. Let's do this by passing it the list `stock_tables`:

```
>>> pd.concat(stock_tables, keys=[2016, 2017, 2018])
```

		Shares	Low	High
	Symbol			
2016	**AAPL**	80	95	110
	TSLA	50	80	130
	WMT	40	55	70
2017	**AAPL**	50	120	140
	GE	100	30	40
	IBM	87	75	95
	SLB	20	55	85
	TXN	500	15	23
	TSLA	100	100	300
2018	**AAPL**	40	135	170
	AMZN	8	900	1125
	TSLA	50	220	400

3. It can also combine DataFrames horizontally by changing the `axis` parameter to `columns`:

```
>>> pd.concat(dict(zip(years,stock_tables)), axis='columns')
```

	2016			2017			2018		
	Shares	Low	High	Shares	Low	High	Shares	Low	High
AAPL	80.0	95.0	110.0	50.0	120.0	140.0	40.0	135.0	170.0
AMZN	NaN	NaN	NaN	NaN	NaN	NaN	8.0	900.0	1125.0
GE	NaN	NaN	NaN	100.0	30.0	40.0	NaN	NaN	NaN
IBM	NaN	NaN	NaN	87.0	75.0	95.0	NaN	NaN	NaN
SLB	NaN	NaN	NaN	20.0	55.0	85.0	NaN	NaN	NaN
TSLA	50.0	80.0	130.0	100.0	100.0	300.0	50.0	220.0	400.0
TXN	NaN	NaN	NaN	500.0	15.0	23.0	NaN	NaN	NaN
WMT	40.0	55.0	70.0	NaN	NaN	NaN	NaN	NaN	NaN

4. Now that we have started combining DataFrames horizontally, we can use the `join` and `merge` methods to replicate this functionality of `concat`. Here, we use the `join` method to combine the `stock_2016` and `stock_2017` DataFrames. By default, the DataFrames align on their index. If any of the columns have the same names, then you must supply a value to the `lsuffix` or `rsuffix` parameters to distinguish them in the result:

```
>>> stocks_2016.join(stocks_2017, lsuffix='_2016',
                     rsuffix='_2017', how='outer')
```

Symbol	Shares_2016	Low_2016	High_2016	Shares_2017	Low_2017	High_2017
AAPL	80.0	95.0	110.0	50.0	120.0	140.0
GE	NaN	NaN	NaN	100.0	30.0	40.0
IBM	NaN	NaN	NaN	87.0	75.0	95.0
SLB	NaN	NaN	NaN	20.0	55.0	85.0
TSLA	50.0	80.0	130.0	100.0	100.0	300.0
TXN	NaN	NaN	NaN	500.0	15.0	23.0
WMT	40.0	55.0	70.0	NaN	NaN	NaN

5. To exactly replicate the output of the `concat` function from step 3, we can pass a list of DataFrames to the `join` method:

```
>>> other = [stocks_2017.add_suffix('_2017'),
             stocks_2018.add_suffix('_2018')]
>>> stocks_2016.add_suffix('_2016').join(other, how='outer')
```

	Shares_2016	Low_2016	High_2016	Shares_2017	Low_2017	High_2017	Shares_2018	Low_2018	High_2018
AAPL	80.0	95.0	110.0	50.0	120.0	140.0	40.0	135.0	170.0
AMZN	NaN	NaN	NaN	NaN	NaN	NaN	8.0	900.0	1125.0
GE	NaN	NaN	NaN	100.0	30.0	40.0	NaN	NaN	NaN
IBM	NaN	NaN	NaN	87.0	75.0	95.0	NaN	NaN	NaN
SLB	NaN	NaN	NaN	20.0	55.0	85.0	NaN	NaN	NaN
TSLA	50.0	80.0	130.0	100.0	100.0	300.0	50.0	220.0	400.0
TXN	NaN	NaN	NaN	500.0	15.0	23.0	NaN	NaN	NaN
WMT	40.0	55.0	70.0	NaN	NaN	NaN	NaN	NaN	NaN

6. Let's check whether they actually are exactly equal:

```
>>> stock_join = stocks_2016.add_suffix('_2016').join(other,
                                                 how='outer')
>>> stock_concat = pd.concat(dict(zip(years, stock_tables)),
                             axis='columns')
>>> level_1 = stock_concat.columns.get_level_values(1)
>>> level_0 = stock_concat.columns.get_level_values(0).astype(str)
>>> stock_concat.columns = level_1 + '_' + level_0
>>> stock_join.equals(stock_concat)
True
```

7. Now, let's turn to `merge` that, unlike `concat` and `join`, can combine exactly two DataFrames together. By default, `merge` attempts to align the values in the columns that have the same name for each of the DataFrames. However, you can choose to have it align on the index by setting the boolean parameters `left_index` and `right_index` to `True`. Let's merge the 2016 and 2017 stock data together:

```
>>> stocks_2016.merge(stocks_2017, left_index=True,
                      right_index=True)
```

Symbol	Shares_x	Low_x	High_x	Shares_y	Low_y	High_y
AAPL	80	95	110	50	120	140
TSLA	50	80	130	100	100	300

8. By default, merge uses an inner join and automatically supplies suffixes for identically named columns. Let's change to an outer join and then perform another outer join of the 2018 data to exactly replicate `concat`:

```
>>> step1 = stocks_2016.merge(stocks_2017, left_index=True,
                              right_index=True, how='outer',
                              suffixes=('_2016', '_2017'))

>>> stock_merge = step1.merge(stocks_2018.add_suffix('_2018'),
                              left_index=True, right_index=True,
                              how='outer')

>>> stock_concat.equals(stock_merge)
True
```

9. Now let's turn our comparison to datasets where we are interested in aligning together the values of columns and not the index or column labels themselves. The `merge` method is built exactly for this situation. Let's take a look at two new small datasets, `food_prices` and `food_transactions`:

```
>>> names = ['prices', 'transactions']
>>> food_tables = [pd.read_csv('data/food_{}.csv'.format(name))
                   for name in names]
>>> food_prices, food_transactions = food_tables
>>> display_frames(food_tables, 30)
```

	item	store	price	Date
0	pear	A	0.99	2017
1	pear	B	1.99	2017
2	peach	A	2.99	2017
3	peach	B	3.49	2017
4	banana	A	0.39	2017
5	banana	B	0.49	2017
6	steak	A	5.99	2017
7	steak	B	6.99	2017
8	steak	B	4.99	2015

	custid	item	store	quantity
0	1	pear	A	5
1	1	banana	A	10
2	2	steak	B	3
3	2	pear	B	1
4	2	peach	B	2
5	2	steak	B	1
6	2	coconut	B	4

10. If we wanted to find the total amount of each transaction, we would need to join these tables on the `item` and `store` columns:

```
>>> food_transactions.merge(food_prices, on=['item', 'store'])
```

	custid	item	store	quantity	price	Date
0	1	pear	A	5	0.99	2017
1	1	banana	A	10	0.39	2017
2	2	steak	B	3	6.99	2017
3	2	steak	B	3	4.99	2015
4	2	steak	B	1	6.99	2017
5	2	steak	B	1	4.99	2015
6	2	pear	B	1	1.99	2017
7	2	peach	B	2	3.49	2017

11. The price is now aligned correctly with its corresponding item and store, but there is a problem. Customer 2 has a total of four `steak` items. As the `steak` item appears twice in each table for store B, a Cartesian product takes place between them, resulting in four rows. Also, notice that the item, `coconut`, is missing because there was no corresponding price for it. Let's fix both of these issues:

```
>>> food_transactions.merge(food_prices.query('Date == 2017'),
                            how='left')
```

	custid	item	store	quantity	price	Date
0	1	pear	A	5	0.99	2017.0
1	1	banana	A	10	0.39	2017.0
2	2	steak	B	3	6.99	2017.0
3	2	pear	B	1	1.99	2017.0
4	2	peach	B	2	3.49	2017.0
5	2	steak	B	1	6.99	2017.0
6	2	coconut	B	4	NaN	NaN

12. We can replicate this with the `join` method but we must first put the joining columns of the `food_prices` DataFrame into the index:

```
>>> food_prices_join = food_prices.query('Date == 2017') \
                                  .set_index(['item', 'store'])
>>> food_prices_join
```

		price	Date
item	**store**		
pear	**A**	0.99	2017
	B	1.99	2017
peach	**A**	2.99	2017
	B	3.49	2017
banana	**A**	0.39	2017
	B	0.49	2017
steak	**A**	5.99	2017
	B	6.99	2017

13. The `join` method only aligns with the index of the passed DataFrame but can use the index or the columns of the calling DataFrame. To use columns for alignment on the calling DataFrame, you will need to pass them to the `on` parameter:

```
>>> food_transactions.join(food_prices_join, on=['item', 'store'])
```

14. The output matches the result from step 11 exactly. To replicate this with the `concat` method, you would need to put the item and store columns into the index of both DataFrames. However, in this particular case, an error would be produced as a duplicate index value occurs in at least one of the DataFrames (with item `steak` and store `B`):

```
>>> pd.concat([food_transactions.set_index(['item', 'store']),
               food_prices.set_index(['item', 'store'])],
           axis='columns')
Exception: cannot handle a non-unique multi-index!
```

How it works...

It can get tedious to repeatedly write the `read_csv` function when importing many DataFrames at the same time. One way to automate this process is to put all the file names in a list and iterate through them with a for loop. This was done in step 1 with a list comprehension.

The rest of this step builds a function to display multiple DataFrames on the same line of output in a Jupyter notebook. All DataFrames have a `to_html` method, which returns a raw HTML string representation of the table. The CSS (cascading style sheet) of each table is changed by altering the `display` attribute to *inline* so that elements get displayed horizontally next to one another rather than vertically. To properly render the table in the notebook, you must use the helper function `read_html` provided by the IPython library.

At the end of step 1, we unpack the list of DataFrames into their own appropriately named variables so that each individual table may be easily and clearly referenced. The nice thing about having a list of DataFrames is that, it is the exact requirement for the `concat` function, as seen in step 2. Notice how step 2 uses the `keys` parameter to name each chunk of data. This can be also be accomplished by passing a dictionary to `concat`, as done in step 3.

In step 4, we must change the type of `join` to `outer` to include all of the rows in the passed DataFrame that do not have an index present in the calling DataFrame. In step 5, the passed list of DataFrames cannot have any columns in common. Although there is an `rsuffix` parameter, it only works when passing a single DataFrame and not a list of them. To work around this limitation, we change the names of the columns beforehand with the `add_suffix` method, and then call the `join` method.

In step 7, we use `merge`, which defaults to aligning on all column names that are the same in both DataFrames. To change this default behavior, and align on the index of either one or both, set the `left_index` or `right_index` parameters to `True`. Step 8 finishes the replication with two calls to merge. As you can see, when you are aligning multiple DataFrames on their index, `concat` is usually going to be a far better choice than merge.

In step 9, we switch gears to focus on a situation where `merge` has the advantage. The `merge` method is the only one capable of aligning both the calling and passed DataFrame by column values. Step 10 shows you how easy it is to merge two DataFrames. The `on` parameter is not necessary but provided for clarity.

Unfortunately, it is very easy to duplicate or drop data when combining DataFrames, as shown in step 10. It is vital to take some time to do some sanity checks after combining data. In this instance, the `food_prices` dataset had a duplicate price for `steak` in store `B` so we eliminated this row by querying for only the current year in step 11. We also change to a left join to ensure that each transaction is kept regardless if a price is present or not.

It is possible to use join in these instances but all the columns in the passed DataFrame must be moved into the index first. Finally, `concat` is going to be a poor choice whenever you intend to align data by values in their columns.

There's more...

It is possible to read all files from a particular directory into DataFrames without knowing their names. Python provides a few ways to iterate through directories, with the `glob` module being a popular choice. The gas prices directory contains five different CSV files, each having weekly prices of a particular grade of gas beginning from 2007. Each file has just two columns--the date for the week and the price. This is a perfect situation to iterate through all the files, read them into DataFrames, and combine them all together with the `concat` function. The `glob` module has the `glob` function, which takes a single parameter--the location of the directory you would like to iterate through as a string. To get all the files in the directory, use the string *. In this example, *.*csv* returns only files that end in *.csv*. The result from the `glob` function is a list of string filenames, which can be directly passed to the `read_csv` function:

```
>>> import glob

>>> df_list = []
>>> for filename in glob.glob('data/gas prices/*.csv'):
        df_list.append(pd.read_csv(filename, index_col='Week',
                        parse_dates=['Week']))

>>> gas = pd.concat(df_list, axis='columns')
>>> gas.head()
```

Week	All Grades	Diesel	Midgrade	Premium	Regular
2017-09-25	2.701	2.788	2.859	3.105	2.583
2017-09-18	2.750	2.791	2.906	3.151	2.634
2017-09-11	2.800	2.802	2.953	3.197	2.685
2017-09-04	2.794	2.758	2.946	3.191	2.679
2017-08-28	2.513	2.605	2.668	2.901	2.399

See also

- IPython official documentation of the `read_html` function (`http://bit.ly/2fzFRzd`)
- Refer to the *Exploding indexes* recipe from `Chapter 12`, *Index Alignment*

Connecting to SQL databases

To become a serious data analyst, you will almost certainly have to learn some amount of SQL. Much of the world's data is stored in databases that accept SQL statements. There are many dozens of relational database management systems, with SQLite being one of the most popular and easy to use.

Getting ready

We will be exploring the Chinook sample database provided by SQLite that contains 11 tables of data for a music store. One of the best things to do when first diving into a proper relational database is to study a database diagram (sometimes called an entity relationship diagram) to better understand how tables are related. The following diagram will be immensely helpful when navigating through this recipe:

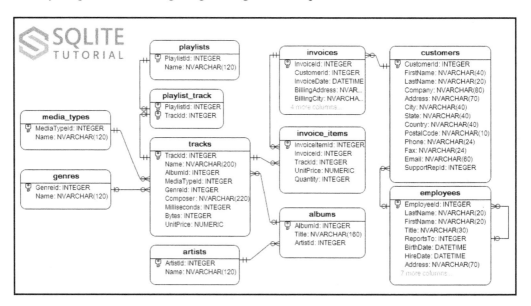

In order for this recipe to work, you will need to have the `sqlalchemy` Python package installed. If you installed the Anaconda distribution, then it should already be available to you. SQLAlchemy is the preferred pandas tool when making connections to databases. In this recipe, you will learn how to connect to a SQLite database. You will then ask two different queries, and answer them by joining together tables with the `merge` method.

How to do it...

1. Before we can begin reading tables from the `chinook` database, we need to set up our SQLAlchemy engine:

```
>>> from sqlalchemy import create_engine
>>> engine = create_engine('sqlite:///data/chinook.db')
```

2. We can now step back into the world of pandas and remain there for the rest of the recipe. Let's complete a simple command and read in the `tracks` table with the `read_sql_table` function. The name of the table is the first argument and the SQLAlchemy engine is the second:

```
>>> tracks = pd.read_sql_table('tracks', engine)
>>> tracks.head()
>>> genres = pd.read_sql_table('genres', engine)
```

	TrackId	Name	AlbumId	MediaTypeId	GenreId	Composer	Milliseconds	Bytes	UnitPrice
0	1	For Those About To Rock (We Salute You)	1	1	1	Angus Young, Malcolm Young, Brian Johnson	343719	11170334	0.99
1	2	Balls to the Wall	2	2	1	None	342562	5510424	0.99
2	3	Fast As a Shark	3	2	1	F. Baltes, S. Kaufman, U. Dirkscneider & W. Ho...	230619	3990994	0.99
3	4	Restless and Wild	3	2	1	F. Baltes, R.A. Smith-Diesel, S. Kaufman, U. D...	252051	4331779	0.99
4	5	Princess of the Dawn	3	2	1	Deaffy & R.A. Smith-Diesel	375418	6290521	0.99

3. For the rest of the recipe, we will answer a couple of different specific queries with help from the database diagram. To begin, let's find the average length of song per genre:

```
>>> genre_track = genres.merge(tracks[['GenreId', 'Milliseconds']],
                               on='GenreId', how='left') \
                        .drop('GenreId', axis='columns')

>>> genre_track.head()
```

	Name	Milliseconds
0	Rock	343719
1	Rock	342562
2	Rock	230619
3	Rock	252051
4	Rock	375418

4. Now we can easily find the average length of each song per genre. To help ease interpretation, we convert the `Milliseconds` column to the `timedelta` data type:

```
>>> genre_time = genre_track.groupby('Name')['Milliseconds'].mean()
>>> pd.to_timedelta(genre_time, unit='ms').dt.floor('s')
                                                    .sort_values()
Name
Rock And Roll          00:02:14
Opera                  00:02:54
Hip Hop/Rap            00:02:58
...
Drama                  00:42:55
Science Fiction        00:43:45
Sci Fi & Fantasy       00:48:31
Name: Milliseconds, dtype: timedelta64[ns]
```

5. Now let's find the total amount spent per customer. We will need the `customers`, `invoices`, and `invoice_items` tables all connected to each other:

```
>>> cust = pd.read_sql_table('customers', engine,
                             columns=['CustomerId','FirstName',
                                      'LastName'])
>>> invoice = pd.read_sql_table('invoices', engine,
columns=['InvoiceId','CustomerId'])
>>> ii = pd.read_sql_table('invoice_items', engine,
                           columns=['InvoiceId', 'UnitPrice',
                                    'Quantity'])

>>> cust_inv = cust.merge(invoice, on='CustomerId') \
                   .merge(ii, on='InvoiceId')
>>> cust_inv.head()
```

	CustomerId	FirstName	LastName	InvoiceId	UnitPrice	Quantity
0	1	Luís	Gonçalves	98	1.99	1
1	1	Luís	Gonçalves	98	1.99	1
2	1	Luís	Gonçalves	121	0.99	1
3	1	Luís	Gonçalves	121	0.99	1
4	1	Luís	Gonçalves	121	0.99	1

6. We can now multiply the quantity by the unit price and then find the total amount spent per customer:

```
>>> total = cust_inv['Quantity'] * cust_inv['UnitPrice']
>>> cols = ['CustomerId', 'FirstName', 'LastName']
>>> cust_inv.assign(Total = total).groupby(cols)['Total'] \
                                  .sum() \
                                  .sort_values(ascending=False) \
                                  .head()
CustomerId  FirstName  LastName
6           Helena     Holý          49.62
26          Richard    Cunningham    47.62
57          Luis       Rojas         46.62
46          Hugh       O'Reilly      45.62
45          Ladislav   Kovács        45.62
Name: Total, dtype: float64
```

How it works...

The `create_engine` function requires a connection string in order to work properly. The connection string for SQLite is very simple, and is just the location of the database, which is located in the data directory. Other relational database management systems have more complex connection strings. You will need to provide a username, password, hostname, port, and optionally, a database. You will also need to supply the SQL dialect and the driver. The general form for the connection string is as follows:
`dialect+driver://username:password@host:port/database`. The driver for your particular relational database might need to be installed separately.

Once we have created the engine, selecting entire tables into DataFrames is very easy with the `read_sql_table` function in step 2. Each of the tables in the database has a primary key uniquely identifying each row. It is identified graphically with a key symbol in the diagram. In step 3, we link genres to tracks through `GenreId`. As we only care about the track length, we trim the tracks DataFrame down to just the columns we need before performing the merge. Once the tables have merged, we can answer the query with a basic `groupby` operation.

We go one step further and convert the integer milliseconds into a Timedelta object that is far easier to read. The key is passing in the correct unit of measurement as a string. Now that we have a Timedelta Series, we can use the `dt` attribute to access the `floor` method, which rounds the time down to the nearest second.

The query required to answer step 5 involves three tables. We can trim the tables down significantly to only the columns we need by passing them to the `columns` parameter. When using `merge`, the joining columns are not kept when they have the same name. In step 6, we could have assigned a column for the price times quantity with the following:

```
cust_inv['Total'] = cust_inv['Quantity'] * cust_inv['UnitPrice']
```

There is nothing wrong with assigning columns in this manner. We chose to dynamically create a new column with the assign method to allow a continuous chain of methods.

There's more...

If you are adept with SQL, you can write a SQL query as a string and pass it to the `read_sql_query` function. For example, the following will reproduce the output from step 4:

```
>>> sql_string1 = '''
    select
        Name,
        time(avg(Milliseconds) / 1000, 'unixepoch') as avg_time
    from (
            select
                g.Name,
                t.Milliseconds
            from
                genres as g
            join
                tracks as t
                on
                    g.genreid == t.genreid
        )
```

```
    group by
        Name
    order by
        avg_time
'''
>>> pd.read_sql_query(sql_string1, engine)
```

	Name	avg_time
0	Rock And Roll	00:02:14
1	Opera	00:02:54
2	Hip Hop/Rap	00:02:58

To reproduce the answer from step 6, use the following SQL query:

```
>>> sql_string2 = '''
    select
        c.customerid,
        c.FirstName,
        c.LastName,
        sum(ii.quantity * ii.unitprice) as Total
    from
        customers as c
    join
        invoices as i
            on c.customerid = i.customerid
    join
        invoice_items as ii
            on i.invoiceid = ii.invoiceid
    group by
        c.customerid, c.FirstName, c.LastName
    order by
        Total desc
'''
>>> pd.read_sql_query(sql_string2, engine)
```

	CustomerId	FirstName	LastName	Total
0	6	Helena	Holý	49.62
1	26	Richard	Cunningham	47.62
2	57	Luis	Rojas	46.62

See also

- All engine configurations for *SQLAlchemy* (http://bit.ly/2kb07vV)
- Pandas official documentation on *SQL Queries* (http://bit.ly/2fFsOQ8

Other Books You May Enjoy

If you enjoyed this book, you may be interested in these other books by Packt:

Machine Learning Fundamentals
Hyatt Saleh

ISBN: 978-1-78980-355-6

- Understand the importance of data representation
- Gain insights into the differences between supervised and unsupervised models
- Explore data using the Matplotlib library
- Study popular algorithms, such as k-means, Mean-Shift, and DBSCAN
- Measure model performance through different metrics
- Implement a confusion matrix using scikit-learn
- Study popular algorithms, such as Naïve-Bayes, Decision Tree, and SVM
- Perform error analysis to improve the performance of the model
- Learn to build a comprehensive machine learning program

Python Machine Learning By Example
Yuxi (Hayden) Liu

ISBN: 978-1-78355-311-2

- Exploit the power of Python to handle data extraction, manipulation, and exploration techniques
- Use Python to visualize data spread across multiple dimensions and extract useful features
- Dive deep into the world of analytics to predict situations correctly
- Implement machine learning classification and regression algorithms from scratch in Python
- Be amazed to see the algorithms in action
- Evaluate the performance of a machine learning model and optimize it
- Solve interesting real-world problems using machine learning and Python as the journey unfolds

Leave a review - let other readers know what you think

Please share your thoughts on this book with others by leaving a review on the site that you bought it from. If you purchased the book from Amazon, please leave us an honest review on this book's Amazon page. This is vital so that other potential readers can see and use your unbiased opinion to make purchasing decisions, we can understand what our customers think about our products, and our authors can see your feedback on the title that they have worked with Packt to create. It will only take a few minutes of your time, but is valuable to other potential customers, our authors, and Packt. Thank you!

Index

state 186
state-value, versus state-action function 188
terminal state 186
value function 187
BeautifulSoup
about 350
reference 350
Bellman equations
example, with grid world problem 201
for Markov decision process (MDP) 195
bias
versus variance trade-off 30
Big Mac index 263
binary search 414
Binary search algorithm
reference 415
bivariate distribution
visualizing 277
blackjack example, of Monte Carlo methods
modelling, Python used 215, 216, 218, 220
Boolean indexing
about 399
filtering with 406, 407, 408
readability, improving with query method 429, 430
reference 409
replicating, with index selection 409, 411
Boolean selection 399
boolean statistics
calculating 400, 401, 402
booleans
data, selecting with 439, 440, 443
boosting 68
box plot 292

C

candlestick plot
in matplotlib.finance 331
stock market indicators, visualizing 333
Cartesian products
producing 449, 450
Cascading Style Sheets (CSS) selectors
about 353
reference 353
categorical data

visualizing 286
categorical scatter plot 287, 288, 290
categories, RL agent taxonomy
about 189
Actor-Critic 191
model-based 192
model-free 192
policy-based 191
value-based 190
changed settings, Matplotlib 2.0
change, in Axes property keywords 245
new configuration parameters (rcParams) 245
style parameter blacklist 245
chi-square 20, 22
class weights
tuning, in DecisionTreeClassifier 53, 55
cliff walking grid-world example
of off-policy (Q-learning) 232
of on-policy (SARSA) 232
clustering
about 132
examples 132
color cycle
about 241
color palettes
diverging 304
example 305
qualitative 304
sequential 304
color schemes
modifying, of Seaborn plot 307, 308
colormap 241
colors, in visualization
reference 304
colors
about 304
columns
appending, from DataFrames 461, 463
maximum value, highlighting from 465, 466, 470
comma-separated values (CSV) 249
Commodity Channel Index (CCI) 333
concat method 629
conditional probability
about 116
Naive Bayes, theorem 116

figure, viewing 251
  importing 249
Matplotlib
  about 240
  reference 345
maximum likelihood estimate (MLE) 27
maximum value
  highlighting, from column 465, 466, 470
mean 11
measure of variation 13
median 11
melt
  used, for tidying variable values as column
    names 546, 548
merge method 629
method chaining
  idxmax, replicating with 471, 473, 474, 476,
    477
mode 11
model stacking 84
model, pushing towards ideal region
  remedial actions 46, 47
Monte Carlo prediction
  about 213
  on grid-world problems 214
Monte-Carlo methods
  about 212
most common maximum
  finding 478, 479
Moving Average Convergence Divergence
  (MACD) 333
MultiIndex
  removing, after grouping 489, 490, 492
multiple boolean conditions
  constructing 403, 404, 405
multiple columns
  grouping with 486
multiple DataFrames
  concatenating 608, 609, 610, 611
multiple groups of variables
  stacking, simultaneously 550, 551, 552
multiple observational units, stored in same table
  tidying scenario 590, 591, 596
multiple values, stored in same cell
  tidying scenario 583, 584, 585, 586

multiple variables, stored as column names
  tidying scenario 573, 577
multiple variables, stored as column values
  tidying scenario 578, 581, 582

N

Naive Bayes
  about 114
  classification 118
  SMS spam classification example, used 120
  theorem, with conditional probability 116
natural language processing (NLP) 97
new changes, Matplotlib 2.0
  default style 240
  reference 240
NLP techniques
  lemmatization of words 122
  Part-of-speech (POS) tagging 122
  removal of punctuations 121
  stop word removal 122
  word tokenization 121
  words of length, keeping at least three 122
  words, converting into lower case 122
non-interactive backends 356
normal distribution 19
normality
  determining, of stock market returns 424, 425,
    426
Numpy array 246

O

object-oriented (OO) interface 249
observation 26
online population data
  importing, in CSV format 258
Open-High-Low-Close (OHLC) 342
out-of-time validation 26
outlier 11
output formats
  PDF (Portable Document Format) 252
  PNG (Portable Network Graphics) 252
  Post (Postscript) 253
  setting 252
  SVG (Scalable Vector Graphics) 253

www.ingramcontent.com/pod-product-compliance
Lightning Source LLC
La Vergne TN
LVHW081505050326
832903LV00025B/1393

* 9 7 8 1 7 8 9 9 5 3 6 3 3 *